Database Design and Programming

with Access, SQL, Visual Basic and ASP

Second Edition

John Carter
Sligo Institute of Technology

McGraw Hill Education

London · Boston · Burr Ridge, IL · Dubuque, IA · Madison, WI
New York · San Francisco · St. Louis · Bangkok · Bogotá · Caracas
Kuala Lumpur · Lisbon · Madrid · Mexico City · Milan · Montreal
New Delhi · Santiago · Seoul · Singapore · Sydney · Taipei · Toronto

Database Design and Programming with Access, SQL, Visual Basic and ASP, Second Edition
John Carter
ISBN 0–07–709974–5

Published by McGraw-Hill Education
Shoppenhangers Road
Maidenhead
Berkshire
SL6 2QL
Telephone: 44 (0) 1628 502 500
Fax: 44 (0) 1628 770 224
Website: www.mcgraw-hill.co.uk

British Library Cataloguing in Publication Data
A catalogue record for this book is available from the British Library

Library of Congress Cataloging in Publication Data
The Library of Congress data for this book has been applied for from the Library of Congress

Acquisitions Editor: Conor Graham
Associate Development Editor: Catriona Watson
Editorial Assistant: Paul von Kesmark
Senior Marketing Manager: Jacqueline Harbor
Production Editor: Eleanor Hayes
New Media Developer: Doug Greenwood

Text design by Claire Brodmann
Cover design by Fielding Design Ltd.
Typeset by RefineCatch Ltd., Bungay, Suffolk
Printed and bound in United Kingdom by Bell and Bain Ltd., Glasgow

The McGraw·Hill Companies

Contents – overview

Contents – Detailed

7 Access query design using SQL – the SELECT statement – further features 215

8 Access forms, macros and reports 297

9   Visual Basic database programming using the Data Control   345

10   Visual Basic database programming using Data Access Objects (DAO)   377

11   Visual Basic database programming using ActiveX Data Objects (ADO)   417

Preface to second edition

This book takes you through all the stages of developing a database application, from initial database design, through SQL query design, Access form, report, macro and module design, and on to Visual Basic database programming. We also show how to develop ASP web pages using HTML and VBScript.

We have placed an emphasis on a number of aspects of the subject that are rarely found together in a single publication. These include the fundamentals of database design, namely, entity modelling and normalization; a comprehensive treatment of SQL; a thoroughgoing treatment of software implementation using all aspects of Visual Basic; and ASP web page development for database-driven websites using HTML and server-side VBScript. Treatment of the features and variations of functionality encountered in various versions of Access, SQL and Visual Basic is also provided.

Many practical examples are included to illustrate the design and programming techniques involved, and these examples should prove useful in developing your own database designs and applications, both on and off the internet.

These practical examples should also enable students to learn the techniques required when dealing with assignments, and the types of problems encountered in employment.

Each chapter provides the student with several exercises taken from examination papers and these represent the sorts of problems likely to be encountered during assessment.

The book has its own author website at:

http://www.databasedesign.co.uk/book

and a publisher website at:

http://www.mcgraw-hill.co.uk/textbooks/carter

The author website contains:

- a chatline where you can discuss your database questions with the author and other students and practitioners;
- downloadable versions of all the databases used in this book;
- further exercises;
- solutions to exercises for lecturers and practitioners;
- updates on Access, SQL and Visual Basic;
- related items of interest to programmers and database developers.

General information about database design can be found at:

http://www.databasedesign.co.uk

The chatline is at:

http://www.databasedesign.co.uk/chatline

Another useful resource for users of the second edition of this book is a free ASP server:

http://www.itsjc.biz

This allows you to:

- try out all the ASP/HTML/VBScript examples used in this book as you read about them – they're on this server;
- upload and run your own experimental ASP scripts on the server.

You can also send email about anything related to this book to:

John.Carter@databasedesign.co.uk

I would like to thank Conor Graham and Catriona Watson for their help in completing the second edition of this book.

I would also like to thank readers of the first edition, including students, lecturers and practitioners from around the world, for their many hundreds of email and chatline contributions.

Finally, let me wish you good fortune with your studies; I hope that this book will prove helpful in their pursuit.

John Carter
Co. Sligo, 2002

Acknowledgements

Our thanks go to the following reviewers for their comments at various stages in the text's development:

Dr Dhiya Al-Jumeily, *Liverpool John Moores University*

Jeremy Brown, *National University of Ireland, Galway*

Dr Keeley Crockett, *Manchester Metropolitan University*

Hongbo Du, *University of Buckingham*

John Harpur, *National University of Ireland, Maynooth*

Stuart Roberts, *University of Leeds*

Con Sheahan, *University of Limerick*

Ken Thomas, *University of Southampton*

To Sylvia

1

How to develop a database application

In this chapter you will learn:

- what the chapters in this book contain
- the steps involved in developing a database application
- how to choose compatible versions of Visual Basic and Access.

 ## 1.1 How to develop a database application – what this book contains

This short introductory chapter describes the steps involved in database application development and points to where they are discussed in the book.

In developing any relational database application there are always the same basic steps to follow. (Microsoft Access is a *relational* database management system because all data is stored in an Access database in the form of simple *tables*. Another name for a table is a *relation*.) This book is divided up into the following way to reflect these steps:

- Entity modelling and normalization   Chapter 2
- Database design   Chapter 3
- Query design   Chapters 4 to 7
- Form and report design   Chapter 8
- Database programming   Chapters 9 to 12
- Internet database programming   Chapters 13 to 15

1.1.1 The database application system life cycle

All database applications are different. You might be modifying an existing application or starting from a vague idea that something needs to be done.

It might be a small application for a local business involving just one or two database tables or a large project involving twenty or thirty tables. In Fig. 1.1, we

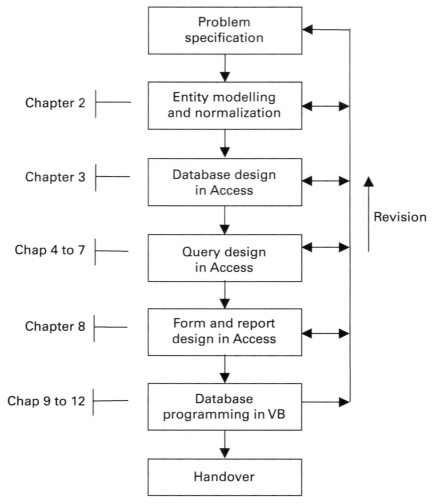

Fig.1.1 The database system development life cycle of a typical non-internet database application.

show the basic stages we recommend in development of a typical non-internet database system. We call this the database system development life cycle.

Some of these stages might be omitted in particular circumstances although they'll usually all occur to some extent. In simpler applications, for example, you may be able to avoid any programming at all by using the Wizards in Access to generate all the forms and reports. This won't always be the case, and experience shows that time spent learning to program in VB and getting to know the database manipulation facilities VB offers will give you, the developer, more flexibility and control so that you can tailor the application to work the way you want. Experience also shows that the areas novice developers are weakest on are database design, SQL and then programming. We place the emphasis in this book on those three areas. Notice that in the life cycle shown in Fig. 1.1 there is a line going backwards from virtually every stage to previous stages. This is in recognition of the fact that you won't (if you are anything like us) get everything right first time. For example, you might be testing a VB database program and discover that one of the SQL queries it uses is not quite right, so you go back and change the query and try again. We call this process of looping back and repeating steps *iteration*.

Some of the steps shown in the life cycle can themselves be broken down into a set of smaller steps. For example in Chapter 3, you will see that the process of developing a viable *entity model* (part of the database design process) itself consists of an iterative set of steps.

If the application is to be web-based, i.e. located on the internet, there are two additional stages:

- uploading the database onto a web server;
- developing ASP web pages and uploading those onto the web server.

Chapters 13 to 15 cover these additional stages.
We now give an overview of each of the steps in the life cycle.

1.1.2 Entity modelling and normalization

In **Chapter 2** we describe some techniques from systems analysis theory that can be usefully employed in putting the database-system-to-be in context. There are really three things you will want to do at this stage. You will want to be clear on the objectives of the new system, how the current system works and its problems, and how the new database system will work and its likely costs and benefits. We describe two techniques: entity modelling and normalization. These techniques are useful in understanding both the existing system (if there is one) and the proposed database system. Other systems analysis techniques that can be used in this analysis phase are dataflow diagramming, structured English and decision tables.

Although we often distinguish between analysis and design by saying analysis is study of the old system and design is development of the new system, the two may overlap. If you are working in a team, you may decide to divide the work and some of you may still be analysing parts of the existing system in greater detail while others are designing parts of the new system.

All of these 'analysis' techniques can also be used in the design of the new system.

We pay particular attention to entity modelling and normalization because they are most useful in the analysis and design of modern database systems. These techniques are fully described in Chapter 2.

Entity modelling and normalization can be used in the design and development of *any* database application, whether it's going to be implemented in Access, SQL*Server, Oracle, Sybase, Informix, FoxPro or any other relational database management system (DBMS), and whether or not the database will ultimately reside on the internet. However, the steps you take in actually creating the database are different in each DBMS. Here we concentrate on Access.

Entity modelling involves drawing boxes for the entity types you want to store data about and lines for the relationships between these entity types. Normalization is a technique for checking your entity model. Once mastered, these standard techniques will ensure minimum redundancy and maximum understandability for your database. They are well worth learning, because as we have said, they can be used on any relational database project, no matter which DBMS is to be the implementation platform.

Most professional database developers spend (or *should* spend) much of their time discussing entity models. Some more abbreviations for you: ERM entity relationship model/modelling; ERD entity relationship diagram/diagramming; RDA relational data analysis. These are all virtual equivalents to what we call an entity model/entity modelling, although RDA is usually taken to mean entity modelling *with* normalization.

1.1.3 Database design in Access

In **Chapter 3** we describe the next step, which is implementing your paper database design in Access. In this step you create a database table for each entity type, identify *primary keys* and create *relationships*. The tables contain *attributes*, which are the facts you want to store about each entity type.

Each table has a *primary key* to identify each of its records, making each record different from all the others. (Records are sometimes called *rows* or *tuples*.) A primary key is one or more of the attributes in the table. For a Customer table you might have Customer Number as a primary key. Each customer record will have a unique value of Customer Number.

To show the orders that each customer has sent in, you might want to create a *relationship* between the Customer table and the Order table. Once you've designed your database, Access makes the process of implementing the database relatively easy, although it's best to know entity modelling and normalization to avoid a poor database design containing redundancy (the duplication of data in different parts of the database) and which may be unnecessarily complex. Access can't do entity modelling and normalization for you; you have to do that part yourself, because it involves knowing what the data *means*.

The design of the database, which is performed only once, is a crucial and entirely separate step from query design and database program development. Many applications may share the data on your database, and any weaknesses in its design will be felt by all those applications. It *is* sometimes possible to patch up a database that has design errors, but it may then be necessary to find all the programs that access the changed part and modify them too.

1.1.4 Query design in Access

In **Chapters 4 to 7** we move to *query design*. A query is a question you 'ask' the database. Another way of looking at it is that a query is a short description – a few simple words – that describes what you want to retrieve from the database. Another way to look at it is that a query is code you write to extract data from the database and put it in a *recordset* which you could then display or further process using a VB program. We use two techniques in Access to implement our queries: Query Design view and SQL.

Query Design view is a very simple graphical method of showing on a form what you want to have in your query output and is good for simple queries.

SQL (Structured Query Language) is better for queries that are more complex. It is worthwhile getting to know SQL (it's not too hard!) because it's used by virtually *all* modern relational DBMSs (Database Management Systems). It's the universal way of writing database queries.

SQL can also be used to update the database, even to create new tables at runtime.

When we go on to database programming we will show how to embed SQL commands in Visual Basic code so that the VB program can process the recordsets retrieved from the database by the SQL queries. In many cases the SQL can be made to do all the hard work of retrieving the data your VB (Visual Basic) program needs from the Access database. A bonus is that you can develop and test your SQL queries interactively in Access before you embed them in VB program code, so you'll *know* they're right!

1.1.5   *Access forms, macros and reports*

There's no point in doing things the hard way, and once the database has been created, simple applications can be developed entirely using the facilities of Access. In **Chapter 8** we show how to use Access forms and reports and how to develop macros.

A *form* is a rectangular screen object used to input and display database data. You might want to display a customer and all of his/her orders on a form, for example, maybe adding a new order or altering one or more of the existing orders and perhaps deleting an order. You might use another Access form to input, update and delete customer details.

Forms are used as the input/output medium for nearly all windows-based applications, including Visual Basic. Unfortunately, Access Forms can't easily be reused in VB applications.

A *report* shows formatted data that has been extracted from the database and that is intended to be printed. You might want to produce a report for a salesman showing the top ten products sold in the month or for a manager showing the expenditure on various categories for each department.

Access can be used in various ways to develop forms and reports. The quickest way is to use Form Wizards and Report Wizards. The wizards ask you what data you want to access and how you want the form or report to look, and then generates the form or report for you. This is an excellent way of producing simple forms and reports.

Access *macros* are simple sequences of commands that can be run together at one time. You might want to show a customer form and then print a report if the customer's balance exceeds his or her credit limit. You can branch (do conditional executions of commands) in a macro but you can't iterate (loop). You can also automate menu commands using macros.

Access also allows database program code to be written in Visual Basic and stored with the database in *modules*. Writing custom VB code gives you, the developer, more control over what the application will do and how it does it, at the expense of a greater development time.

The program development environment in Visual Basic is in many ways more powerful and flexible than it is in Access. Whether to stick to Access or to branch out into VB is a decision you must make. Both approaches are described in this book. The VB code used now in many Microsoft applications, such as Word, Excel, Access and VB, is called VBA – Visual Basic for Applications. VBA is the common core of programming language statements that you can use in any of these environments. This is useful, because learning VB in one of these situations will help you program in the others. However, each environment has its own special commands. Excel VBA has commands for accessing spreadsheet cells, for example.

1.1.6 Database programming in Visual Basic

In **Chapter 9** we start database programming in VB. The version of VB we use here is Version 6, but any changes you will need to make for previous versions (3, 4 and 5) – and there are very few – are described where necessary. Although this book is not intended to be an introduction to programming or an introduction to VB programming, all the VB programming statements used in these database programs are fully described. In this chapter we use the first method of linking VB forms to Access databases, called the *data control*.

The data control is a simple VB control that you drag onto a VB form to link it to your chosen database. Using the data control you can get simple database applications up and running with minimal code. The data can be displayed and updated using tied text boxes, list boxes, combo boxes and grids. We give examples using both the traditional DAO data control and the new ADO data control.

In **Chapter 10** we note some of the limitations of the data control approach and move over to an alternative – DAO – *Data Access Objects*. The DAO approach to database programming often requires more code, but like SQL compared to the Query Design view, offers greater control to the database programmer over what's going on in his or her application.

The data control is a powerful tool but it imposes its own methods of working and for more complex applications, if you use a data control you may find yourself having to 'code round' these methods. For these applications the DAO approach is recommended.

Data access objects are things like databases, recordsets, table and query definitions, and fields. Rather than tying a recordset to a data control, when we use DAO we shall allow our programs to create and manipulate recordsets as and when required, and close them as soon as they are no longer required.

In this chapter we develop some simple and typical VB database programming examples to illustrate DAO programming techniques. We make full use of embedded SQL commands (SQL commands contained in VB program code) and investigate some of the database programming alternatives available to the database programmer. How to navigate around the database, retrieving and updating data from various linked tables, is shown.

In **Chapter 11** we introduce ADO (ActiveX Data Objects) programming. ADO programming is in principle very similar to DAO programming but contains some new commands. ADO is Microsoft's new approach to database programming, which aims to give the programmer a more consistent way of connecting to a broad range of different types of data source. In this second edition, we have expanded this chapter to include more examples, including a description of a database being shared on a LAN. The other reason for expanding this chapter is that ADO commands are used in ASP applications – the subject of Chapter 15.

In **Chapter 12** we give examples of programming in Access modules. Using modules you can develop database programs in VB which are kept inside the database itself. We give an example of *transaction processing* in this chapter.

Transaction processing gives the programmer a way to define a *transaction* in his or her program. All database updates within the bounds of a transaction must either all go ahead or all be negated ('rolled back'). This prevents partial updates caused by interruptions (brought about by user action or a crash, for example) leaving the database in an inconsistent state.

For example, you wouldn't want to store details of the despatch of a customer order without also storing an invoice record; these two record insertions should be part of a transaction.

Chapters 13, 14 and 15 are new to the second edition, and concern the question of how you can put your database application on the internet so that it can be accessed globally.

Chapter 13 discusses internet terminology. It discusses in some detail the components you use when developing internet applications, and the alternatives available. It argues in favour of the approach used in this book, namely the HTML/ASP/Server-side VBScript approach.

Chapter 14 contains a primer on HTML. It's comprehensive enough, we think, for most or all of the web database applications you'll want to implement. A knowledge of HTML is essential for developing web-based database applications. HTML is the language of the internet in the same way that SQL is the language of relational databases.

Chapter 15 contains examples of ASP web applications. The ADO database commands used in Chapter 11 are also used here. As with other chapters, new concepts are described using examples. All of these applications can be tried as you read on one of the book's websites:

http://www.itsjc.biz

As readers of this book, you are also able to upload your own ASP applications to this website. Instructions are given in Chapters 14 and 15 and on the website itself.

Appendix 1 contains the database schemas for the databases used in the examples in this book. Understanding the schema of a database is essential for its users and application developers. You can download these databases from:

http://www.databasedesign.co.uk/book

Appendix 2 lists the main differences between the database commands in the various versions of Visual Basic and between the various versions of Access. All the popular versions are covered.

Appendix 3 is a summary of the HTML language version 4.

Appendix 4 is a summary of the SQL language.

The **glossary** gives definitions of the various database, programming and internet terms used throughout the book.

In **references** we list other sources of related information, including other books, websites, web pages and news groups.

The **index** has been made as comprehensive as possible. If you are anything like us, this is where you often start reading a technical book. You don't want to have to search; you want to go straight there.

1.2 Visual Basic and Access

Microsoft Access is the DBMS (Database Management System) we shall use in this book. It's a very popular DBMS and every user of Microsoft Office will have a copy. It is used for creating databases and provides facilities for inputting data via forms, performing queries using Query Design view and SQL, and producing nice-looking reports. Macros give the ability to store simple sequences of commands that manipulate forms and reports. It is also possible to write programs in Visual Basic within Access and these are stored in modules. Access databases can be uploaded onto ASP web servers and accessed using HTML/VBScript pages containing ADO commands.

Microsoft Visual Basic (VB) is not included in Microsoft Office and has to be purchased separately. It is a general-purpose programming environment, and its HCI (Human–Computer Interface) is via forms, as with Access. The reason we recommend using both VB and Access in developing database applications is that for non-trivial database applications, VB offers more flexibility to the developer than the VB that comes with Access.

It is relatively easy to link VB forms to an Access database and in this book we show how to do this. Another reason for learning Visual Basic is that the VBScript you use in ASP pages has an almost identical syntax.

As we described above, the method of database application development we recommend in this book consists of three basic steps:

- Database design
- Query design
- Database programming.

We shall recommend developing the *database design* first on paper and then using Access to create the tables, fields, keys and relationships. The design of the main *queries* we shall also do in Access. The *database programming* we shall do in VB, linking it to the Access database using VB program code and setting properties. Forming these links is quite simple and intuitive once you get the hang of it.

As we mentioned, Access has forms, and our VB projects (all VB applications are called *projects*) also have forms. It would be nice to be able to develop some of the application – the simple parts – in Access forms and then import them into a VB project, as we do with the SQL queries. Unfortunately this is not possible. The method we recommend is to use the forms of Access to design the simple data entry and lookup functions so that you can get some functionality up and running quickly, and then treat these as prototypes for VB forms which you can develop later to replace the Access ones. For any forms with more complex functionality, start straight away in VB.

1.3 Versions of Visual Basic and Access

In this book, all versions of VB and Access are covered. The primary examples and diagrams are in Access 97/2000 and VB version 6, but variations in the code for other versions are given where this is different (surprisingly rarely). The following versions of VB and Access are therefore covered:

Visual Basic	Access
Version 3	Version 2
Version 4	Version 7 – also known as Access 95
Version 5	Version 8 – also known as Access 97
Version 6	Access 97 and Access 2000

1.4 Compatibility between versions of Access and Visual Basic

There are some incompatibilities between the different versions of Access and Visual Basic. This is because both Access and VB link up to databases using something called the *Jet Engine*. The Jet Engine is a piece of Microsoft software that comes with both Visual Basic and Access. It is the software that contains the code for retrieving and updating records in the database. There are different versions of the Jet Engine. The versions of VB and Access you use must be compatible with the same Jet Engine. You can't store data using the Jet Engine from the old Access 2 DBMS (now very rare) and expect it to work with another version of Access or a recent version of VB, say Version 6.

The following table shows some safe combinations of Access and VB:

Access	Visual Basic
Version 2	Version 3
Version 7 (Access 95)	Version 4 Version 5
Access 97	Version 5 Version 6
Access 2000	Version 6

If you are trying to work with two different versions of Access the later version will offer to upgrade your database to its version, but you won't then be able to use that database again on the old version of Access. For example, if you started designing your database at home or at college in Access 97 and took it to work to develop it further in Access 2000, then Access 2000 would offer to upgrade your database to

Access 2000 but then you wouldn't be able to take it home and develop it some more in Access 97. It *is* possible to keep both versions, but the development you did at work in Access 2000 would have to be repeated back at home in Access 97. The safest thing is to stick to one version of Access and one (compatible) version of Visual Basic. At this writing (April 2002), the most likely combinations are VB6 with Access 2000 or Access 97.

1.5 Exercises

Note: You might need to consult the index, the glossary and other chapters to obtain full answers to these questions.

1. Define the following terms:

    (a) Data control
    (b) Data redundancy
    (c) Database design iteration
    (d) Embedded SQL
    (e) Entity modelling
    (f) Forms
    (g) Macro
    (h) Module
    (i) Query Design view
    (j) Records
    (k) Relationships
    (l) Reports
    (m) Rows
    (n) SQL
    (o) Transaction processing
    (p) Tuples
    (q) Wizards

2. Discuss the advantages and disadvantages of having a precise methodology for developing database applications.

3. Discuss the advantages and disadvantages of using Access modules compared to developing database applications in Visual Basic.

4. Discuss the advantages and disadvantages of putting database applications on the internet.

2

Entity modelling and normalization

In this chapter you will learn:

- how to produce an entity model
- how to convert your entity model to a relational model
- how to check your database design using normalization.

2.1 Introduction

In the next chapter we show how to create a database in Access. However, before that, we describe the methods known as entity modelling and normalization. It is essential for you to know these techniques so that you can design a database that contains no redundancy, and which, provided you name things thoughtfully, will be easy for you, other database developers and end users to understand. A well-designed fully normalized database should also result in easier-to-write SQL queries and VB database programs.

Just as it would be difficult for you to get answers to problems from a book if you didn't know what the book was about, it's difficult to obtain answers to queries and to produce reports from a database whose 'meaning' is not clear.

The aims of entity modelling and normalization, then, include:

- the production of a database which can be understood by everyone who uses it;
- the minimization of the duplication of data on the database;
- the production of a document, the entity model, which shows clearly the tables and relationships that the database contains;
- the production of a document that shows the fields in the tables.

We employ entity modelling to produce an initial design and then check it using normalization, repeating the process where necessary. A fully normalized database schema results. The documentation set consisting of the entity model and attribute lists is called the *database schema* or just the *schema*. Figure 2.1 shows the steps in producing the schema. These steps are fully described below.

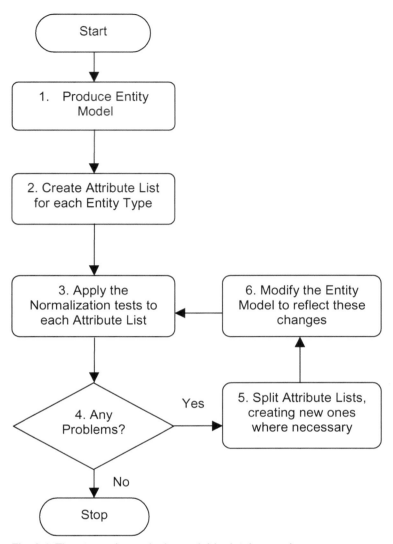

Fig. 2.1 The stages in producing a viable database schema.

Step 1 After having gathered sufficient information about the problem situation and understood it reasonably well, you draw an entity model. We show how to do this later in this chapter. The entity model consists of boxes for entity types and lines for relationships. You will see various examples in this chapter. Entity models are sometimes called entity-relationship diagrams. The entity types are objects that you will want to store data about on the database. A typical entity type in an accounting system would be a customer entity type because we would want to store data facts about each customer. The whole set of customers is an entity *type*, and each customer is an *entity*.

Step 2 For each entity type in the entity model, produce a list of attributes. Attributes are the properties (qualities or data facts) you want to store about each entity type. For example, you might want to store the following facts about the customer entity type: account number, name, address, telephone number, balance. Those are the attributes.

Step 3 There are five normalization tests. You apply these tests to each of the attribute sets. We describe these normalization tests later. Normalization is a way of checking that you've done your analysis well; that is, that you've categorized the data correctly into separate entity types. Without normalization, for example, you might have decided to create an entity type called customer order and given it the following set of attributes: order number, order date, account number, product number, product description, number required, and order total. As we shall see, this design would result in data duplication. The five normalization steps are called first normal form (1NF) through to fifth normal form (5NF). Many database designers just use the first three.

Step 4 You might have found in Step 3 that some of the groups of attributes for each entity type broke one or more of the normalization tests. They did not obey the rules of normalization. That means you will have to split (regroup) the sets of attributes, creating (I like to think of it as 'discovering') new entity types to put them in. It's good to have normalization as a tool in our database design toolbox of techniques that we know, because it offers a mechanical method of getting the design correct. This will pay off in removing duplication and possible inconsistency in your database. Duplicating the same fact in different parts of the database because of poor design will also make the design of the programs that update the database harder because the programmer will have to remember to update each fact, rather than just once with a fully normalized database. If you're lucky though, the attribute lists associated with each of the entity types in the original entity model will all be in 5NF and your entity model and attribute lists are complete.

Step 5 As mentioned in Step 4, any attribute sets that break one or more normalization rules will have to be recast into new entity types. This analysis will result in new attribute groups that you will have to associate with a new, previously undiscovered and un-named entity type. You have to give each new entity type a name. You will ask a question like 'What is it in the real world that has these attributes?'.

Step 6 As a result of the discovery of new entity types, the entity model will have to be redrawn, adding the new entity types and probably new relationship lines linking the new entity types to other entity types. Naturally you might still have some errors, so go round the loop as many times as it takes to get it right.

At the end of this process, your entity model and your groups of attributes, one for each entity type, should be consistent with each other. In the following sections, we describe how to do entity modelling and normalization.

It is important to note that the database schema design process is an entirely separate activity from database program design. In general, the database schema (the design of the tables, their fields, primary keys and relationships) will be designed only once. Many different SQL queries and VB programs will subsequently be written, probably by different programmers, to access and update the

data in the database, but they will not alter its basic design; they will not alter its schema.

2.2 Entity modelling

Entity modelling is a simple graphical technique, which is used to decide which database tables, fields and relationships will be needed in the Access (or any other) database. The technique we show here can be used as the first step in database design no matter what DBMS you are going to use to implement your database application. Entity modelling is sometimes called *entity relationship* modelling. The diagram is called an entity model, an entity-relationship model, or an E-R diagram.

2.2.1 Entity types and relationships

There are only two components in entity modelling: entity types and relationships. An entity type is represented as a box with a name in it. Relationships are represented by lines. An entity type represents a set of entities all of the same type. Relationship lines represent relationships between entities either in the same relationship (*unary* relationships) or between entities in two different entity types (*binary* relationships).

An entity type is a set of entities ('things') that you want to store data about on your database. Each entity in the set is of the same type. For example, a customer entity type would be a set of customers. An order entity type would be a set of orders etc.

In this example, you would probably want to have a way of showing which customers sent in which orders. In entity modelling we do this by creating a relationship between the customer entity type and the order entity type. To make it clear what the relationship is all about, we would give it a name – 'sent in' would be a good name because it would make the meaning of the relationship clear.

In Fig. 2.2 we show this relationship between the customer and order entity types. This is a binary relationship, because it relates entities in the two different entity types customer and order. We also show the *inverse* of the 'sent in' relationship. We've called it 'was sent in by'. If a customer sent in an order, that order was sent in by that customer. Simple, isn't it?

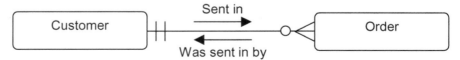

Fig. 2.2 A simple entity model.

There are some other symbols on the relationship line. At the right-hand end, you can see a circle and a crow's foot. The circle means *zero* and the crow's foot means *many*. Together they are read as *zero or more*. That means that a customer (there are lots of them, remember) may have sent in zero or more orders. The minimum number is zero and the maximum is many. This is a very simple counting system but it's all we need for entity modelling.

For the inverse relationship 'was sent in by', the minimum number of customers an order can have been sent in by is one. And the maximum number of customers an order can have been sent in by is also one. The little lines mean one. Some people say 'one and only one' for this situation.

The maximum in a relationship is called its *cardinality* (as in cardinal, cardinal number – counting numbers) and the minimum is called its *optionality* (whether it's optional or not). You can see these terms used in Fig. 2.3. The cardinality of the 'sent in' relationship is 'many' and its optionality is 'optional'. It's optional because some customers might not have sent in any orders yet. The cardinality of the inverse relationship is 'one' and its optionality is 'one', that is, *mandatory*. The optionality of 'was sent in by' is mandatory because it must exist; an order must be sent in by a customer (where else could it come from?).

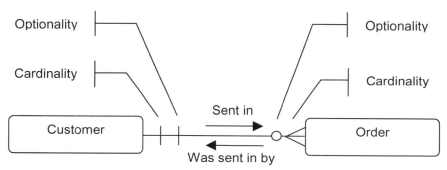

Fig. 2.3 Cardinality and optionality.

Just considering the cardinalities for a moment, we introduce another piece of terminology for relationships – the *degree* of the relationship. The degree of 'sent in' in Figs 2.2 and 2.3 is said to be *one-to-many*. The degree of its inverse is, naturally, *many-to-one*.

We shall also meet *one-to-one* and *many-to-many* relationships. The degree is what database designers and programmers most often refer to when describing a relationship. They will say with respect to Figs 2.2 and 2.3 for example that "Customer-Order is one-to-many" or "The degree of the 'sent in' relationship between the customer and order entity types is one-to-many", or similar.

Sometimes the following abbreviations for relationship degree are used:

One-to-one	1 : 1
One-to-many	1 : N
Many-to-one	N : 1
Many-to-many	M : N

Fig. 2.4 Abbreviations for relationship degree.

So we might say when describing the relationship in Figs 2.2 and 2.3 that the 'Sent in' relationship is of degree 1:N. Its inverse relationship 'Was sent in by' has degree N:1.

Notice that when we mention the degree of a relationship, we are just talking about its cardinalities at each end; we are not saying anything about the optionalities. To give a complete description of the 'Sent in' relationship we could say it's a 1:N optional relationship.

It's important to get the cardinalities and optionalities of all relationships in an entity model right, because these have an impact on the eventual database design and this is a common source of error.

One safe method of ensuring you get the right cardinalities, optionalities and degree for each relationship is to describe it and its inverse using two separate sentences.

For the example of Figs 2.2 and 2.3, you should say:

> "Each customer sent in zero or more orders."
> *and*
> "Each order was sent in by one customer."

Note that there have to be two sentences and both sentences must start with the word 'each'.

In Fig. 2.5 we show a summary of the terms we have used to describe the nature of relationships.

Unary	The relationship relates entities in one entity type.
Binary	The relationship relates entities in two different entity types.
Degree	Whether the relationship is 1:1, 1:N, N:1 or M:N.
Cardinality	The maximum number of entities that can be involved in the relationship. Either one or many. (You can't have a maximum of zero or the relationship would never exist!)
Optionality	The minimum number of entities that can be involved in the relationship. Either zero or one. If it's zero, we say the relationship is 'optional'. If it's one, we say the relationship is 'mandatory'.

Fig. 2.5 A summary of the terminology used with respect to relationships.

We've seen an example of a one-to-many relationship (Figs 2.2 and 2.3). Let's look now at a one-to-one relationship.

Suppose it's true that each employee in a company has one birth certificate and each birth certificate is owned by one employee. That would be a *one-to-one* relationship. See Fig. 2.6.

Note also that in this example, the relationship is mandatory in both directions; an employee has to have a birth certificate, and a birth certificate must be owned by an employee.

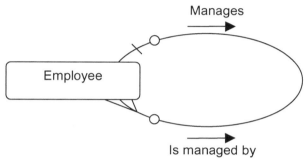

Fig. 2.6 An example of a one-to-one relationship.

Next we consider an example of a *unary* relationship (Fig. 2.7). Only one entity type is involved in a unary relationship and the relationship relates entities in this single entity type. Unary relationships occur quite frequently in practice.

Suppose we have an Employee entity type, which contains all employees whether or not they are managers.

We want to show which employees manage which other employees. See Fig. 2.7.

Fig. 2.7 An example of a unary relationship.

The two sentences which describe the situation in Fig. 2.7 are:

> "Each employee manages zero or more other employees."
>   *and*
> "Each employee is managed by zero or one other employee."

This is true in a hierarchical management structure. The person at the top of the hierarchy will not be managed by anyone (which explains the upper optionality circle in Fig. 2.7) and some employees will not manage anyone (which explains the lower optionality circle).

2.2.2 Replacing M:N relationships with new entity types

You will notice that in the previous section we did not discuss M:N relationships. This is because they can always be replaced by a set of one or more (usually one) entity types and some 1:N relationships (usually two). This is important for two reasons. Firstly, M:N relationships cannot be represented on a relational database (but see the note at the end of this section). Secondly, replacing an M:N relationship will sometimes reveal a whole set of entity types that would otherwise have remained hidden.

In Fig. 2.8 we show an example of an M:N relationship prior to its replacement with a new entity type.

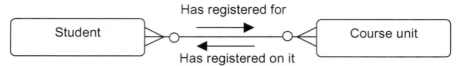

Fig. 2.8 An M:N relationship prior to its replacement with a new entity type.

The sentences for Fig. 2.8 (before replacing the M:N) are:

"Each student has registered for zero or more course units."
 and
"Each course unit has registered on it zero or more students."

Figure 2.9 shows the M:N relationship replaced by the new entity type Registration.

Fig. 2.9 The M:N has been replaced by a new entity type and two 1:N's.

The sentences now (after replacing the M:N) are:

"Each student is involved in zero or more registrations."
 and
"Each registration involves one student."
 and
"Each registration is for one course unit."
 and
"Each course unit is involved in zero or more registrations."

One benefit in this example of replacing the M:N relationship with a new entity type is that now we are likely to ask whether the new Registration entity type is related to any other entity types. In this example it is. Now we have the Registration entity type, we can link it to the Staff Member entity type to show which staff member registered a given student on a given course. The resulting entity model is shown in Fig. 2.10. This would have been impossible if we had not followed the rule of replacing M:N relationships with a set of relationships of degree 1:N. Following the rule has allowed us to enrich the entity model and show a relationship that might not have otherwise occurred to us. The database is now capable of answering additional queries, such as:

ENTITY MODELLING AND NORMALIZATION 19

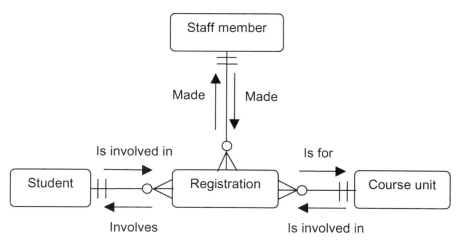

Fig. 2.10 The Registration entity type can now be linked to another entity type.

- *"Which staff member registered this student on this course unit and on what day?"*
- *"Which staff member was involved in registering students for this course?"*
- *"Which courses was this staff member involved in registering students on?"*

We now give another example in which replacing an M:N relationship pays off in terms of enriching the entity model. Suppose an initial analysis for a database design for the Sales Ledger part of an accounting system resulted in the entity model shown in Fig. 2.11.

Fig. 2.11 An initial analysis for part of a sales ledger system.

This contains an M:N relationship, which our method tells us we should replace with a new entity type.

After some thought and discussion with workers on the existing sales ledger system it emerges that the information about who purchased what is contained in an Order. The next step then is to insert an order entity type where the M:N 'purchased' relationship currently is. This results in the entity model shown in Fig. 2.12.

Fig. 2.12 After the 'purchased' relationship is replaced.

Note that in Fig. 2.12 there is now *another* M:N relationship. The next question for the database designer to ask then is: 'What is the medium in the current system that tells us which products have been ordered in which orders?'. When a customer sends in an order, he or she will often want to order more then one item. Each of these items on an order may be called an order line. Each order line appears in one order and mentions one product. An order contains one or more order lines. The resulting entity model is shown in Fig. 2.13.

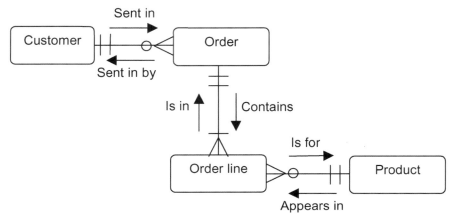

Fig. 2.13 The final entity model, in which the second M:N has been replaced.

This example again shows the benefit of replacing M:N relationships by considering what real-world entity types are 'hidden' by the M:N. Here, *two* new entity types emerged.

Note: Some database designers will say that a relational database *can* represent an M:N relationship using a 'linker' and two 1:N relationships.

We prefer to say that an M:N relationship is *hiding* one or more entity types and two or more relationships that will be revealed by a deeper analysis.

It amounts to the same thing, except that the analysts who use the 'linker' concept won't try to identify the real-world entity type(s) that the linker is hiding.

As we have seen, there can be more than one hidden entity type. Moreover, these new entity types can be involved in other relationships. This would probably have remained obscured in the example above if a 'linker' analysis were used.

In summary, always replace many-to-many relationships with one or more new entity types and associated one-to-many relationships. It may reveal new entity types and relationships.

2.2.3 Replacing relationships involving more than two entity types with a new entity type

Figure 2.14 shows an example where an early analysis produced a relationship involving three entity types. This is called a *ternary* relationship.

There are several problems with this diagram.

1. It's not clear who is doing what to whom.

2. You can't represent ternary relationships on a relational database.

3. It's difficult to name the relationship lines.

4. It's difficult to show all the cardinalities and optionalities.

The English sentence corresponding to the diagram is "This worker performed this operation on this part."

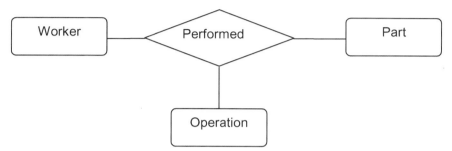

Fig. 2.14 An initial analysis produced this ternary relationship.

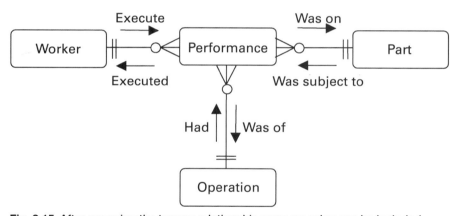

Fig. 2.15 After removing the ternary relationship more meaning can be included.

It is necessary to know all of the cardinalities and optionalities in order to implement the entity model on a relational database. Having replaced the ternary relationship (Figure 2.15), we have to ask quite a few more questions about this situation too. For example, the question of whether a worker might exist who had never performed an operation on a part would probably not have been asked otherwise.

Not every ternary relationship will be replaced by a single entity type; it depends on the individual situation. In some cases it might be replaced by two or more relationships and zero or more new entity types. What we can say, however, is that there is never a necessity for relationships involving more than two entity types.

In summary, always replace ternary relationships with one or more new entity types and associated one-to-many relationships.

2.2.4 *Parallel relationships*

It is possible that there can be not just one but two or even more relationships between the same two entity types. Figure 2.16 gives an example.

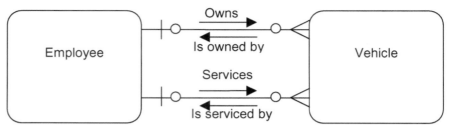

Fig. 2.16 An example of parallel relationships.

2.2.5 *Mutually exclusive relationships*

Sometimes the existence of a relationship between two entities excludes the possibility of another relationship. This can be shown using an arc. In Fig. 2.17, an invoice line can be for either a product or a service.

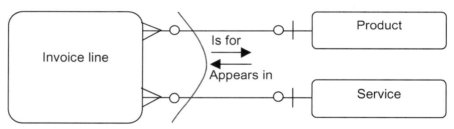

Fig. 2.17 An example of a mutually exclusive relationship.

2.2.6 *Unnecessary relationships*

Sometimes the existence of a set of relationships can imply another relationship. It is not necessary to represent the implied relationship on the entity model. In the E-R diagram shown in Fig. 2.18, the direct relationship 'Sent/Was sent by' is redundant and should be removed. If a customer received an invoice and an

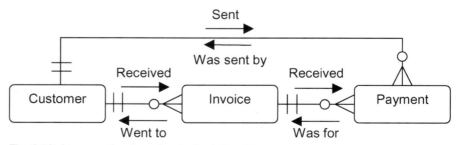

Fig. 2.18 An example of a redundant relationship.

invoice received a payment, it is clear that the customer who received the invoice sent the payment.

2.3 The relational model

Having produced a satisfactory entity model that nobody among you, your colleagues, and your clients/lecturers can see as faulty, the next step is to start thinking about the *attributes* that you will want to store about each entity type.

The attributes are the basic properties or facts about the entity types that you are setting the database up for. You can view the database as just a collection of attributes carefully grouped into entity types. Normalization (the next step – Section 2.4) will help you check that you have done this grouping correctly. If you haven't, you will have to re-allocate some of the attributes to different entity types.

2.3.1 Selecting an initial set of attributes

Suppose that part of your entity model looks like Fig. 2.19. The next step is to select an initial set of attributes you want to store about each entity type.

Fig. 2.19 An example entity model.

The initial set of attributes you and your clients choose for each of these entity types may be as shown in Fig. 2.20. Each attribute and its value is a basic fact about the entity. These facts can be used in answering database queries and in producing reports.

Note that the attributes shown here are fairly typical, but the attributes you choose depend on the content of queries and reports you want to produce.

It's a good idea to record for each attribute what its *meaning* is, as we have done in Fig. 2.20. This will help you and other developers and users understand your database. Without this understanding, they won't be able to write queries and applications, and won't be able to interpret output from the database correctly.

2.3.2 Terminology

Since we are going to implement our entity model eventually as a *relational database* we'd better just say a few words about that word 'relational'. A *relation* is the name given by mathematicians to 'a subset of a cartesian product of domains'.

A *domain* is the set of values that an attribute can take.

To a relational database designer, a *domain* is the set of values that an attribute can take.

Customer	Invoice	Payment
C_no: Customer number	Inv_no: Invoice number. Each invoice (bill) we send to a customer will have a unique invoice number.	Inv_no: The invoice number the payment was 'posted' (allocated) to.
Title: Mr, Mrs etc.		
Sname: Surname		
Inits: Initials, e.g. G.R.	C_no: Customer number. We need this to show which customer we sent the invoice to.	Pmt_no: Payment sequence number, e.g. 1, 2, 3. Used for instalment payments.
Street: Street name and number, e.g. 10 Downing St.		
City: e.g. London	Inv_date: Invoice date – the date on which we sent the invoice to the customer.	Pmt_date: The date we received the payment from the customer.
Postcode: e.g. W1		
Cred_lim: Credit limit – the maximum the customer is allowed to owe.	Amount: The invoice amount.	Amount: The amount the customer paid against the invoice.
Balance: The amount the customer actually owes.		

Fig. 2.20 Attributes of the entity types in Fig. 2.19.

For example, the domain associated with our credit limit attribute in Fig. 2.20 is all nonzero positive currency values up to £10,000.00. The domain associated with our surname attribute is all alphabetic strings of length between 1 and 30.

> A *cartesian product* of a set of domains is all the combinations of those possible domain values.

A *cartesian product* of a set of domains is all the combinations of those possible domain values. For example, the cartesian product of the (very small) domains {1,2} and {A,B} is the set {(1,A), (1,B), (2,A), (2,B)}.

> A *relation* is any subset of a cartesian product of domains.

A *relation* is any subset of a cartesian product of domains. In practical databases, the *tables* in which the *records* are stored are also sometimes called 'relations'. That is where relational databases get their name. A relation then is a subset of all the possible value combinations the domains can take.

The person credited with being first to use the mathematical theory of relations and set theory as a basis for database table and query design was E.F. Codd, who subsequently (1985) specified a set of rules that relational databases should conform to. These are discussed in [References, Books, 1].

The terminology used in entity modelling and relational databases differs; they give different names to what are often very similar concepts. Figure 2.21(a) shows some equivalences or near-equivalences.

File-based systems	Entity-modelling	Relational theory	Access databases
File	Entity type	Relation	Table
Record	Entity	Tuple or n-tuple or Row	Record
Field	Attribute or Domain	Domain or Column	Field

Fig. 2.21(a) Some terminological near-equivalences.

Note that every *entity type* in our finished entity model will be represented as a *table* in the Access database. From now on in this discussion, we shall often refer to *tables* as well as entity types, since we are now considering the relational representation of the entity type, and this is tabular.

Two important aspects of the relational model are *primary keys* and *foreign keys*.

2.3.3 *Primary keys*

After deciding on the initial set of attributes for each entity type (table), the next step in relational database design is to select for each table a *primary key*.

A primary key is an attribute or group of attributes that will uniquely identify each entity in the entity type, that is, each record in the database table.

You can think of a primary key as a unique ID for each entity.

> A *primary key* is an attribute or group of attributes that uniquely identifies each entity in the entity type, and each record in the corresponding database table.

No two records in a relational database table are allowed to contain the same value of the primary key.

We need to select a primary key for each entity type. Ideally, we will be able to find a single attribute whose values are 'unique' for each entity – a field for which no two entities in the entity type will ever have the same value.

If the primary key consists of just a single field, we call it an *atomic* primary key.

Sometimes this is not possible and we have to use a combination of several attributes to uniquely identify each entity. This we call a *composite key*, or *composite primary key*. If each of these attributes is a primary key in some other entity type, it's called a *compound key*.

In selecting a primary key, you are obliged to select one that is of the minimum length possible, that is, of the fewest number of attributes. It should not be possible to remove any attribute and still have the primary key 'unique'.

Sometimes there are several attributes or groups of attributes that will fit the bill – that will have different values for each entity. When this happens, we have a choice to make from these possible keys.

Each of these choices is called a *candidate key* or *candidate primary key*. The database designer will select one of the candidate keys to become the primary key.

Figure 2.21(b) summarizes these primary key definitions.

Term	Definition
Primary key	An attribute or group of attributes in an entity type whose value(s) uniquely identify each entity. No two entities have the same value for the primary key. The primary key should contain no more attributes than necessary.
Atomic primary key	A primary key consisting of just one attribute.
Composite primary key	A primary key consisting of more than one attribute.
Candidate primary key	Each of the potential primary keys, where there is a choice.

Fig. 2.21(b) Definitions relating to primary keys.

2.3.4 Foreign keys

To represent the relationships between entities in a relational database, foreign keys are used. In a one–many relationship, the primary key of the entity type at the '1' side of the relationship also appears in the entity type at the 'many' side of the relationship. A similar method is used in representing one–one relationships.

> Foreign keys are the method used in relational databases to show relationships. In a 1:N relationship between two entity types A and B, the primary key in A will also appear as a foreign key in B. That's how the link between entities in A and B is made.

Suppose the primary key of table A is A_no. (Fig. 2.22). Then there will have to be an A_no field in table B. The A_no in table B is called the *foreign key* from table A. By sharing a common value, the primary key and foreign key show the link between records in the A table and records in the B table.

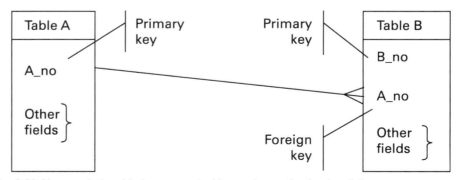

Fig. 2.22 How a relationship is represented by a primary–foreign key link.

Let's give an example. Figures 2.19 and 2.20 show details of the entity types and attributes for a simple customer–invoice–payment scenario. We reproduce this scenario in slightly modified form here in Figs 2.23 and 2.24.

Fig. 2.23 An example entity model.

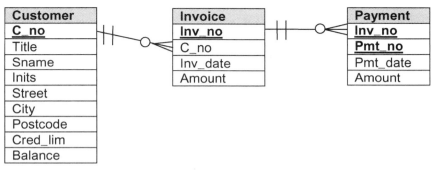

Fig. 2.24 The entity model showing attributes, including primary and foreign keys.

In Fig. 2.24, the 1:N relationship between the Customer entity type and the Invoice entity type is represented in the tables by `Customer.C_no`, which is the primary key in the Customer table, appearing also as `Invoice.C_no`, which is the foreign key in the Invoice table. Primary keys are shown here in bold and underlined. We use a dot notation (e.g. `Customer.C_no`) as a way of specifying the table name and the field name.

You can see where the foreign keys are; they are at the 'many' end of 1:N relationships. The primary key of the Payment table is a *composite key* made up from `Inv_no` with `Pmt_no`. Part of this composite key (namely `Payment.Inv_no`) is the foreign key.

So you can see that if you want to create a 1:N (one-to-many) relationship between two tables, you take a copy of the primary key field of the table at the 'one' side and make it also one of the fields in the table at the 'many' side of the relationship. That's how it's done in relational databases.

To see how this works out in practice, look at Figs A1.2 and A1.3 in Appendix 1.

These show records from the `Customer` and `Invoice` tables. Some typical records are shown for this database. In practice there would be many more records in the database than this!

Get to know this database because it is used in many of the examples that follow.

You can see that customer Sallaway, customer number 1, has two invoices, invoice numbers 940 and 1003.

The relationship between the customer record and the two invoice records is shown by the fact that the primary key value 1 for `Cus.C_no` appears in the invoice records in the field `Invoice.C_no`.

For 1:1 relationships, you generally have a choice of either combining the attributes of both tables, resulting in a single table, or placing the foreign key from either table into the other table as a foreign key. However, if one end of the relationship is optional it's better to have the foreign key at that end. You might not want to combine the tables if both ends are optional. This is discussed in greater detail in [References, Books, 1, pages 83 to 86].

In Access, this process of creating relationships is made quite easy because of Access's graphical facilities. You just click and drag from the primary key to the foreign key. We shall see how to do this in Chapter 3.

> To summarize, in relational modelling, entity types become tables, entities are records, attributes are fields, each table has a primary key, and relationships are represented using foreign keys.

2.4 Normalization

Having produced on paper a provisional set of table designs for the new database, the next step is to check for any anomalies in the design by using the rules of normalization. Some database designers leave this step out, but if you normalized your database design, you can be more confident that there will be no redundancy (duplication of data) in the final database. As a consequence, the database 'makes sense', that is, it will be a better model of the part of the real world your database is about.

There are three basic checks that most relational database designers carry out. These are called *first normal form* (1NF), *second normal form* (2NF), and *third normal form* (3NF). There are two further normal forms (4NF and 5NF), which are also described here.

2.4.1 First normal form

This check says to *remove all repeating groups*. A repeating group is a group of attributes in a record that occurs a variable number of times in each record. For example, if we had in error at an earlier stage of analysis combined the attributes of the customer and invoice entity types, we might have produced the design for Customer that is shown in Fig. 2.25.

The repeating group of attributes in this case is (`Inv_no`, `Inv_date`, `Amount`). As the customer receives more invoices and then pays them, his/her Customer record will grow and shrink. Different customer records will have different lengths.

There are several problems with this non-1NF design:

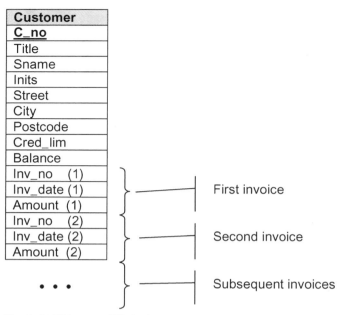

Fig. 2.25 This non-1NF design combines the attributes of the Customer and Invoice tables

1. Relational databases cannot accommodate variable length records – records with different numbers of fields in the same table.

2. The data in the Invoice part of the record cannot be processed independently from the Customer data.

3. If there had been an M:N relationship between the two entity types and they had been combined in this way, data duplication would have resulted.

4. Searching the database for a given invoice could be a lengthy process on a large database unless an extra index were maintained to show which customer record each invoice was in.

One of the major selling points for normalized 'relational' databases is that tables are simple and allow a standardized approach to data retrieval. Records with complex data structures (such as non-1NF files) might allow faster processing for particular processes, but are incompatible with the idea of a database as a repository of data in a simple form that can be accessed (using SQL) in a variety of ways, depending on immediate demand.

First normal form says that we should remove this repeating group. We put it into its own Invoice table, remembering to retain the link to the Customer table by including C_no as a foreign key. This would result in the situation shown in Fig. 2.26.

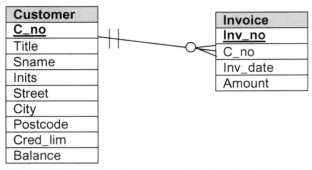

Fig. 2.26 The 1NF test has removed the invoice data into a separate Invoice table.

Summary of 1NF: remove repeating groups.

2.4.2 Second normal form

Second normal form says that where there is a composite primary key, *all non-key attributes must be dependent on the* whole *of the primary key*.

This check needs to be done only where there is a composite primary key. What can go wrong is that a non-key attribute is dependent on just a *part* of the composite key. This is called a *partial dependency*. We explain what we mean by 'dependent' shortly.

Consider this example. We are planning to store data about which customers have purchased which products. The table design we have in front of us is as shown in Fig. 2.27. There is a partial dependency of the five fields containing customer data on C_no and of the two fields containing product data on Prod_no. It is only Qty_required that truly depends on both C_no and Prod_no.

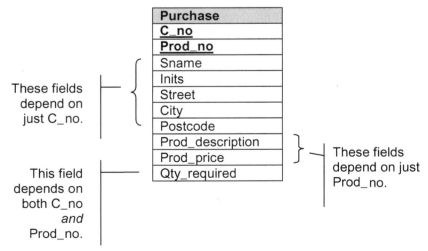

Fig. 2.27 A non-2NF table design.

'Dependency' here means that, for example, given a customer number, say C_no = 1, then there will be only one corresponding value of surname Sname. Sname is *dependent* on C_no.

Sname is said to be *partially dependent* on C_no because C_no is not the whole primary key.

This design would result in duplication of data, because every time a given customer purchased something, his or her Sname, Inits, Street, City and Postcode would be stored again in the Purchase record.

Similarly, every time a given product was purchased, its Prod_description and Prod_price would be stored again in the Purchase record.

Looking at it from an entity-modelling point of view, we could say that Sname, Inits, Street, City and Postcode are not really attributes of a Purchase, but of a Customer, and similarly that Prod_description and Prod_price are really attributes of a Product, not of a Purchase.

Removing these partial dependencies in accordance with 2NF results in Fig. 2.28.

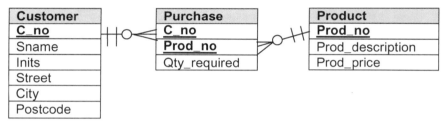

Fig. 2.28 The 2NF test has split the table into three.

This design will remove the redundancy mentioned. It also frees the Customer, Product and Purchase entity types to take part in other relationships.

In the non-2NF design of Fig. 2.27, the normalization jargon would say that Sname, Inits, Street, City and Postcode took part in a *partial dependency*. Let's explain the technical meaning of 'dependency' again.

In this example, to say that Sname is 'dependent' on C_no means that given one value of C_no there is only one corresponding value of Sname.

To be a little more technical, the mapping from the C_no attribute to the Sname attribute is a function, that is, 1:1 or N:1. It is said that C_no 'functionally determines' Sname. Again, C_no 'determines' or 'functionally determines' Sname. What makes this dependency of Sname on C_no a 'partial dependency' is that C_no is only a part of the primary key.

Summary of 2NF: remove partial dependencies.

2.4.3 Third normal form

Third normal form covers the case where there are dependencies between attributes that are not primary keys. To be in third normal form, *there should be no functional dependencies between non-key attributes*.

Here's an example where there *are* dependencies between non-key attributes. See Fig. 2.29. This table shows details of our products and the supplier we use for each one.

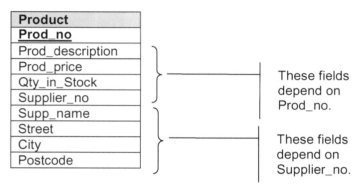

Fig. 2.29 A non-3NF table design.

This table is not in 3NF because the attributes `Supp_name`, `Street`, `City` and `Postcode` depend on `Supplier_no`, which is not the primary key for the table. These non-key dependencies can result in data duplication. It's quite likely that a supplier will supply more than one product to us. Where that's true, the supplier's `Supp_name`, `Street`, `City` and `Postcode` will be repeated. Applying 3NF splits the table into two, as shown in Fig. 2.30.

If a supplier were to change his or her address, then on the database that change would have to be made for each occurrence in an un-normalized Product table. This is known as an *update anomaly*. Also, there would be nowhere to store details of suppliers who didn't yet supply us anything (*insertion anomaly*) and deleting a product could delete the last copy of a supplier's address (*deletion anomaly*). Normalization solves these problems.

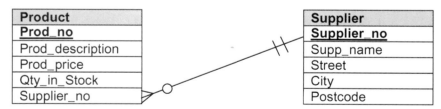

Fig. 2.30 The 3NF test has split the table into two.

Another formulation of third normal form is called Boyce–Codd normal form (BCNF). This amounts to the same thing as the definition above for 3NF but it clears up an anomaly in the old definition where there is more than one candidate key. BCNF states that *every determinant must be a candidate key*. A 'determinant' is a field or group of fields that determine (functionally determine) one or more other fields. In Fig. 2.29, BCNF would say that the problem is that the field `Supplier_no` is a determinant (it determines `Supp_name`, `Street`, `City` and `Postcode`) but it is not a candidate key for Product.

> **Summary of 3NF: remove non-key dependencies.**

If entity modelling and normalization up to third normal form has been carried out carefully, fourth and fifth normal form are not often likely to reveal further errors. However, it is useful to have them as further checks.

2.4.4 Fourth normal form

Like the other normal forms, anomalies related to 4NF are brought about by putting the attributes of more than one entity type into the same table. This of course should not be done.

Fourth normal form is generally applicable to the situation in which there are dependencies, called multi-valued dependencies, existing within a compound key. To ensure a table is in 4NF, *all multi-valued dependencies must be functional dependencies*.

A multi-valued dependency is like a functional dependency except that the co-domain (the item at the finishing end of the dependency – the 'object' or 'target' of the dependency), is an attribute not with a single value for each value of the domain, but a set of values.

Take the following case as an example. Each employee works in a number of departments and is qualified to do a number of jobs. They do all these jobs in all of the departments they work in. Suppose the database designer has come up with the design shown in Fig. 2.31.

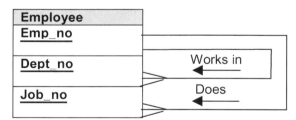

Fig. 2.31 A non-4NF table design.

To make the primary key unique, all three of the attributes have to be included. For a given employee, every combination of department he/she works in and job he/she does has to be shown.

The table is in 3NF. However, there are clearly redundancies.

If a given employee worked in four departments and did three jobs, for each department, we would be told the three jobs – and we would be told four times that he/she did these three jobs. The solution is to split the table to remove these 'multi-valued dependencies'. The solution is shown in Fig. 2.32.

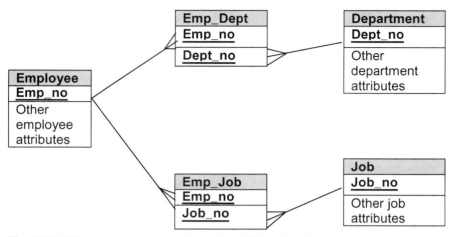

Fig. 2.32 4NF has removed redundancy by splitting the table.

Even though Fig. 2.32 looks more complicated, it's actually simpler because the assignment of employees to departments has now been separated from the jobs they are qualified to do. The quantity of data on the database will be less because redundancy has been removed.

> **Summary of 4NF: remove multi-valued dependencies**

2.4.5 Fifth normal form

A table is in fifth normal form if and only if *the only non-loss decompositions all have a candidate key of the table as their candidate key*.

This definition is not as difficult as it sounds. A non-loss decomposition is the result of splitting a table in the way we have shown before. For example, the Employee table in Fig. 2.31 was non-loss decomposed into the tables Emp_dept and Emp_job of Fig. 2.32. It was a non-loss decomposition because no data would have been lost by splitting it in this way.

All the other splits of tables we have performed in the preceding examples were non-loss decompositions too.

The largest part of the definition, the clause '*all have a candidate key of the table as their candidate key*' is really a minor point. It's clear that any fully-normalized table could be non-loss decomposed by splitting it up into several tables, each with the original primary key (or any other candidate key) as its primary key.

For example, a Customer table with fields (**c_no**, sname, address, balance) *could* be non-loss decomposed into (**c_no**, sname), (**c_no**, address) and (**c_no**, balance). There would be no point in doing this though.

What 5NF is saying is that if this is the only kind of non-loss decomposition possible, then the table is in 5NF. If we ignore this minor point, the definition can be simplified to: *A table in 5NF can't be split without losing data*. There is no easy method of testing whether a table is in 5NF other than trying every possible split (apart from the simple decomposition mentioned above) and showing that data would be lost in each case.

> **Summary of 5NF:** If, even after 4NF, you can still find a way (apart from the trivial case mentioned above) of splitting the table without losing data, then do it.

Figure 2.33 summarizes all five normal forms.

Normal form	Short Definition / Action
First	Remove repeating groups
Second	Remove partial dependencies
Third	Remove non-key dependencies
Fourth	Remove multi-valued dependencies
Fifth	No nontrivial non-loss decompositions exist

Fig. 2.33 Simplified summary of all five normal forms.

2.5 Exercises

1. In the context of entity modelling, explain the following terms:

Entity type	Entity
Attribute	Relationship
Entity model	Entity-relationship diagram
Degree	Cardinality
Optionality	Binary relationship
Unary relationship	One:Many relationship
One:One relationship	Many:Many relationship
Parallel relationship	Mutually exclusive relationships
Unnecessary relationship	

2. State the entity types you would expect to find in the following systems:

   (a) A database to store details of your CD collection

   (b) An estate agent

   (c) A travel agent

   (d) A student records system for a college or university

   (e) A doctors' surgery

   (f) A dating agency

3. Draw up a list of attributes you would expect to find for each of the entity types in any one of the situations in exercise 2.

4. List the relationships you would expect to find between entity types in any one of the situations in exercise 2.

5. Draw the entity model for any of the situations in exercise 2.

6. Give examples of binary relationships of the following type:

   (a) One:Many

   (b) One:One

   (c) Many:Many

7. Give examples of unary relationships of the following type:

   (a) One:Many

   (b) One:One

   (c) Many:Many

8. Give examples of relationships of the following type:

   (a) Mandatory in both directions

   (b) Mandatory in one direction, optional in the other

   (c) Optional in both directions

9. State giving reasons whether or not you think it's possible to have a unary One:Many relationship which is:

   (a) Mandatory in both directions

   (b) Mandatory in one direction, optional in the other

   (c) Optional in both directions

10. Give examples of relationships of the following type:

    (a) Parallel

    (b) Mutually exclusive

    (c) Unnecessary

11. Give examples of One:One relationships for which:

    (a) the entity types can *be merged*

    (b) the entity types *should not* be merged

12. Give an example entity model which contains a Many:Many relationship which can be replaced by a new entity type and two new One:Many relationships. Draw the new entity model.

13. Give an example entity model which contains a Many:Many relationship which when replaced results in more than one new entity type. Draw the new entity model.

14. A university consists of several faculties. Within each faculty there are several departments. Each department may run a number of courses. All teaching staff are attached to departments, each staff member belonging to one department. Every course is composed of sub-courses. Some sub-courses are part of more than one course. Staff may teach on many sub-courses and each sub-course may be taught by a number of staff.

    Draw an entity model for this example.

15. ABC Ltd plans to computerize its sales ordering and stock control system. A feasibility study has indicated that a relational database should be installed. The details of ABC's sales and stock control are as follows:

Customers send in orders for goods. Each order may contain requests for variable quantities of one or more products from ABC's range. ABC keeps a stock file showing for each product the product number, the product details, including product description, quantity in stock, reorder level and reorder quantity, and the preferred supplier.

ABC delivers those goods that it has in stock in response to the customer order and an invoice is produced for the despatched items. Any items that were not in stock are placed on a back order list and these items are usually reordered from the preferred supplier. Occasionally items are ordered from alternative sources.

In response to the invoices that are sent out to ABC's customers, the customers send in payments. Sometimes a payment will be for one invoice, sometimes for part of an invoice and sometimes for several invoices and part-invoices.

Draw an entity model, stating any assumptions made. Remove any M:N relationships, replacing them with new entity types and relationships.

16. The sociology department of a university is embarking on a research project in which the religious beliefs of the university's students are to be studied. The core results of the study are to be held on a relational database. An initial investigation has revealed the following.

There are several major religions (Tao, Jewish, Hindu, Christian, Buddhist, Muslim, Sikh etc.) and some smaller ones (Theosophists, Scientologists, Sun Worshippers etc.). Some religions (also known as faiths) are divided up into sects (Christadelphians, Jehovah's Witnesses, Coptic Christians, Shakers, Quakers, Sunni, Shia etc).

Each sect has a number of places of worship (synagogue, temple, mosque, church etc), and a number of doctrines, each of which involves a belief (reincarnation, angels, eternal life, omnipotent God, sin, redemption, hell etc.).

A belief may be part of one or more doctrines, but occasionally falls out of favour with all doctrines. In this case the department wishes to keep a record of the belief since (a) it may be restored to the doctrine at a later date, and (b) some students still hold the belief, not realizing it is no longer part of the doctrine of the sect to which they belong. Each doctrine is linked to just one sect. Occasionally, disagreement over a doctrine may result in the emergence of a new sect.

In general, students adhere to just one sect, and profess adherence to all of its doctrines, but some students hold no religious beliefs, and others belong to several sects, some of which are from different religions. Some profess beliefs that are not part of any of the sects to which they belong. Some attend places of worship of sects to which they do not belong.

Draw an entity-relationship diagram for the religious beliefs database. Show all cardinalities and optionalities where known. Name both directions of each relationship. Resolve any M:N relationships.

17. It is proposed to set up a genealogy database showing all family relationships such as parentage, descendants, siblings, cousins, grandparents, nephews, nieces etc.

Draw an entity model and show the attributes required, including primary and foreign keys.

18. In the context of relational modelling, explain the following terms:

Cartesian product	Relation
Tuple	Domain
Attribute	File
Record	Field
Table	Primary key
Candidate key	Composite key
Compound key	Foreign key

19. An organization makes many models of cars, where a model is characterized by a name and a suffix (such as GL or XL), which indicates the degree of luxury, and an engine size.

Each model is made up from many parts and each part type may be used in the manufacture of more than one model. Each part has a description and an ID code.

Each model of car is produced at just one of the firm's factories, which are located in London, Birmingham, Bristol, Wolverhampton and Manchester – one in each city.

A factory produces many models of car and many types of part although each type of part is produced at one factory only.

(a) Identify all entity types and relationships in this example and draw an entity model.

(b) List the attributes for each entity type and indicate all primary and foreign keys.

20. It is proposed to set up a database on students, courses and sub-courses.

Each student has a name, identification number, home address, term address, and a number of qualifications for which the subject (e.g. Applied Maths), level (e.g. Advanced level) and grade (e.g. C) are recorded.

Each student is registered for one course. Each course has a name (e.g. BSc Computing) and an identification number. A record is kept of the number of students registered for each course.

Each course is divided into sub-courses and a sub-course may be part of more than one course. Information on sub-courses includes the name, identification number and the number of students taking the sub-course.

(a) Identify all entity types and relationships in this example and draw an entity model.

(b) List the attributes for each entity type and indicate all primary and foreign keys.

21. A local library holds stocks of books, some of which it lends to its members. Reference books cannot be borrowed. The library maintains a catalogue of books that it holds. In this catalogue, each book title is allocated a reference number, a Dewey category, and where there is more than one copy held, a copy number. The author or authors are also listed.

When a reader becomes a member of the library, his or her name, address and telephone number are taken, and a unique member number assigned. Readers may have up to five books on loan at a time.

A fine of £1 per book per week is levied on books that have been out on loan to a member for over a month. A reminder is sent each week for ten weeks. Details of any loan extending over two months are passed to the legal department. Readers who consistently fail to return borrowed books are blacklisted and are not lent books again. Books in the catalogue all of whose copies are out on loan can be reserved at the request of a library member. Blacklisted members cannot reserve books.

(a) Draw an entity model for the library system. Show all cardinalities and optionalities where known. Name both directions of each relationship. Resolve any M:N relationships.

(b) Draw up a list of attributes for each entity type and identify all primary keys and foreign keys.

22. In the context of normalization, explain the following terms:

Normalization	Repeating group
First normal form	Functional dependency
Partial dependency	Second normal form
Non-key dependency	Third normal form
Determinant	Boyce–Codd normal form
Multi-valued dependency	Fourth normal form
Non-loss decomposition	Fifth normal form

23. An un-normalized computer staff file has the following structure:

COMPUTING_STAFF (Staff_number, Staff_name, Department_number, Department_name, Manager_number, Manager_name, (Project_code, Project_name, Time_spent))

The table below shows some of the records in the file:

Staff No	Staff Name	Dept No	Dept Name	Mgr No	Mgr Name	Proj Code	Proj Name	Time Spent
CS1	V. Good	D1	Systems	M1	A. Smith	P1	Payroll	3
						P2	Stock Control	2
						P3	Invoicing	7
CS2	N. Jones	D1	Systems	M1	A. Smith	P2	Stock Control	3
						P3	Invoicing	5
CS3	M. Patel	D3	Design	M5	U. Li	P1	Payroll	2
						P2	Stock Control	10
						P3	Research	2
CS4	S. Olody	D3	Design	M5	U. Li	P2	Stock Control	3
						P4	Research	5

Normalize the data, showing clearly the stages involved.

24. An order file in a computerized accounting system has the following structure. Three typical records in the file are shown.

Ord No	Order Date	Cus Acct No	Cus Name	Cus Addr	Cus Balance	Prod No	Descr	Qty Reqd	Price Each	Row Total	Order Total
1	1/1/90	10	ABC Ltd	10 Boundary Rd	1499.26	43	Table	1	100	100	230
						51	Chair	4	20	80	
						22	Dinner Service	1	50	50	
2	1/1/90	20	DX Ltd	5 The Links	230.00	51	Chair	2	20	40	40
3	4/1/90	10	ABC Ltd	10 Boundary Rd	1729.26	51	Chair	2	20	40	140
						80	Cutlery Set	1	100	100	

(a) Show where data duplication results from this file design.

(b) Normalize the file to third normal form, showing the normalization steps.

3

Access database design

In this chapter you will learn:

- how to organize an application
- how to create a database in Access
- how to create tables in Access
- how to create relationships in Access.

3.1 Introduction

In this chapter we describe how to implement the tables we designed on paper in the previous chapter in Access. We create a table for each entity type, put in the attributes for each table and then create the relationships.

3.2 Organizing an application

Make sure you know where the database is going to be held and where the programs that access it are going to be held. Each Access database you create is stored in an *.mdb* (Microsoft database) file. We are going to create a database called **accts.mdb**. It's going to contain just three tables: Customer, Invoice and Payment. In the next two chapters we shall create some SQL queries and forms and reports. These all go into the same .mdb file. That's convenient, since you can copy all the data, all the queries, all the forms and reports from one place to another with a single copy. However, in subsequent chapters we shall develop separate VB (Visual Basic) programs to do more complex processing of the data in the .mdb database and these will be stored separately. To allow you to keep the database and its associated VB programs together and to allow you to copy them all from one place to another in one go, use the folders and subfolders provided by Microsoft Windows. The general tips then for organizing your applications are:

1. Every application (database plus programs) should go in one suitably named folder.

2. This folder has a subfolder for the database.

3. There is also a separate subfolder for each VB project.

The main things to avoid are:

1. Putting all your database and program files in the root (c:\ or a:\) of a disk.

2. Putting all your database and program files in the same folder. The forms, modules and database files will get mixed up.

It is also a good idea to back up your database and program files regularly. Small databases and programs may fit on a single floppy disk. If they don't then compressing the files using WinZip is a useful backup method.

One tip we have found very useful is this. Whenever you're about to create a new database or a new VB project, before you go into Access or VB, go into Windows Explorer and create a new folder for it to go into. Then go into Access or VB and save the database or project immediately in that new folder.

However, you may have your own tried and tested methods of organizing your applications. Figures 3.1 and 3.2 are examples of how you might want to organize your applications.

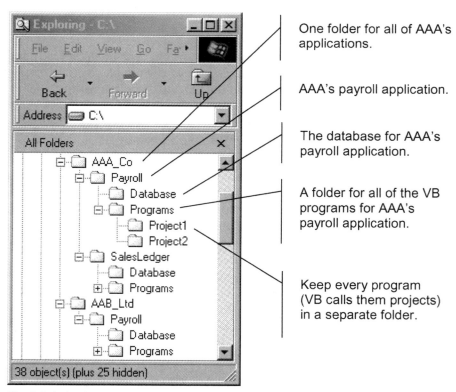

Fig. 3.1 A database consultant might organize his or her applications like this.

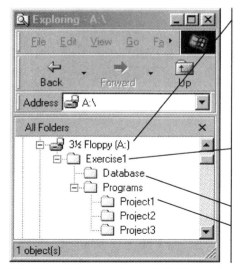

Keep a copy of your application on a floppy disk so you can move between computers. For speed, copy Exercise1 to the computer's hard disk, work on it, then copy it back to the floppy when you're finished. The floppy copy acts as a backup too.

If you can, put the database and all related programs on one floppy under one folder. Then they can all be copied in one go.
The database gets its own folder.

Keep each VB project in its own folder.

Fig. 3.2 A database student might organize an application like this.

An Access application lumps the database and all of the processes, such as queries, macros, forms, reports and modules, into one .mdb file.

With Visual Basic, it's different. A typical VB project will consist of several related files: one project file (e.g. Project1.vbp – Project1.mak in VB3), one or more forms (e.g. Form1.frm) and one or more code modules (e.g. Module1.bas). These should all be kept in the same folder where possible. The exception is where a form or a module is used in several applications and a single copy is held at a central location. This is rare.

A VB project should be contained in one folder and a folder should hold just one project, to avoid the files of different projects becoming mixed up. A typical Visual Basic project will contain the following files.

- Project1.vbp   the project file
- Form1.frm, Form2.frm, . . .   form files
- Module1.bas, Module2.bas, . . .   code module files

Most projects contain a .vbp file and at least one .frm file. Modules contain code that is called from other forms and modules. An .exe file is a compiled version of the project.

3.3 The facilities of Access

Microsoft Access is a relational DBMS (Database Management System) with all the features necessary to develop and use a database application. The facilities it offers can be found on most modern relational DBMSs and all versions of Access. Figure 3.3 shows the opening database window of Access 97 and Access 2000 and this serves to illustrate what those facilities are.

Fig. 3.3 The facilities of Access.

- Tables are where all the data is stored. They are usually linked by relationships.
- Queries are the way you extract data from the database.
- Forms are the method used for input and display of database data.
- Reports are used to display nicely formatted data on paper.
- Macros are sets of simple commands that execute sequences of database operations.
- Modules are used to store general-purpose VB database program code.

3.4 Creating a database

The first step is to create the database file in which all the data and the queries, forms, reports, macros and modules will be stored. With Access, they are all stored in a single .mdb (Microsoft Database) file (Fig. 3.4).

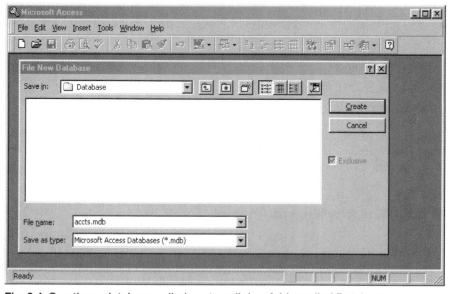

Fig. 3.4 Creating a database called accts.mdb in a folder called Database.

We now show from the beginning how to create the database and the tables and relationships.

3.5 Creating tables

For a new database, after having specified the database name and path as above, you will be confronted with the following window (Fig. 3.5).

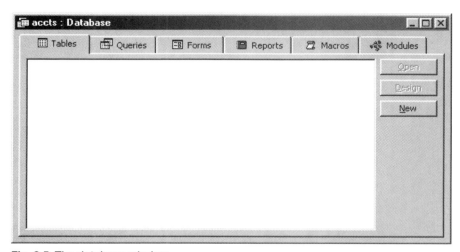

Fig. 3.5 The database window.

This window shows that there are no tables in the database yet.
Click the New button.

Fig. 3.6 Select the Design View.

Select the Design View (Fig. 3.6) by clicking on the list box and then the OK button. Design view gives us more control over the design of our database than either the Table Wizard or the Datasheet view. Import Table is used to bring in data from an existing database and Link Table is used to link this database to an external table.

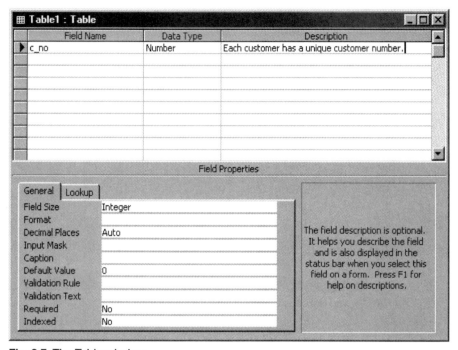

Fig. 3.7 The Table window.

The next window you see is the Table window. This is where we define the fields that are going to go into the table, their data types, and which field (or fields – it's usually one field though) will be the primary key. In Fig. 3.7 we are about to create the CUSTOMER table, and have already put in the first field c_no. The Data Type column lets us specify whether the field is to be a number, text, date-time, currency etc. With some data types the length also can be defined. For example, our c_no field has been specified as an Integer. This is a 16-bit field and its possible range of values is from −32 768 to 32 767. If you wanted to use a numeric field for c_no and you wanted customer numbers greater than 32 767, you should consider using a Long Integer. Long integers are 32-bit fields. The range of values you are allowed for a Long Integer is −2 147 483 648 to 2 147 483 647. For a 16-bit field, the range of values is $-(2 \wedge 15)$ to $(2 \wedge 15) - 1$. For a 32-bit field it's $-(2 \wedge 31)$ to $(2 \wedge 31) - 1$. This range is a consequence of two's complement notation, which is a scheme for representing negative and positive numbers in computer memory. You can find the range of field values for all data types in Help.

The table below gives a simple summary of the data types available in Access and their normal usage.

Data Type	Usage	Size
Text	Any characters. Not numbers that require calculations.	Up to 255 characters.
Memo	Any characters. Not numbers that require calculations. You can't sort or index on a Memo field.	Up to 65 535 characters.
Number – Byte	Numeric data used in mathematical calculations. No decimals.	1 byte. Range −128 to +127.
Number – Integer	Numeric data used in mathematical calculations. No decimals.	2 bytes. Range −32 768 to +32 767.
Number – Long	Numeric data used in mathematical calculations. No decimals.	4 bytes. Range −2 147 483 648 to +2 147 483 647.
Number – Single	Numeric data (floating point 7 significant figures) used in mathematical calculations. Includes decimals.	4 bytes. Range −3.402823E38 to +3.402823E38
Number – Double	Numeric data (floating point 15 significant figures) used in mathematical calculations. Includes decimals.	8 bytes. Range −1.79769313486231E308 to +1.79769313486231E308
Currency	Numeric data including currency (15 digits on left of decimal point and 4 digits on the right) used in mathematical calculations.	8 bytes. Range −922 337 203 685 477.5808 to 922 337 203 685 477.5807.
Date/Time	Date and time	8 bytes. Range 00/01/00 00:00:00 to 31/12/9999 23:59:59
Auto-number	A machine-generated number: either sequential or random, depending on whether New Values property is set to Increment or Random.	4 bytes if Field Size set to Long Integer in which case Range is −3.402823E38 to +3.402823E38; or 8 bytes if Field Size set to Replication ID
Yes/No	(Yes/No, True/False, or On/Off)	1 bit.
OLE Object	Link to another application	Up to 1 Gigabyte. Limited by available disk space.
Hyperlink	An internet URL, e.g. **http://www.databasedesign.co.uk/**	Each of the three parts (see below) can contain up to 2048 characters.
Lookup Wizard	The wizard helps you create a list box containing values that you type in, or that are derived from the values of a field in a database table.	If derived from a set of values you type in, you specify the size using the Field Size property. If derived from a table, the size of the primary key of the table from which the values are derived.

Notes:

1. Both Text and Memo data types store only the characters entered in a field; space characters for unused positions in the field aren't stored.

2. A LIKE clause in an SQL statement (see SQL chapters) *will* match text in a Memo field.

3. Storing numeric data in a Number field is more *compact* than storing it in a Text field. A text field needs one byte for each digit. A number field stores the number in binary. Example: storing the integer 1 234 567 890 in a Text field takes 10 bytes; storing it in a Long Integer takes 4 bytes.

4. Storing numeric data in a Number field results in *faster calculations* than storing it in a Text field. If numeric data is stored as text, it has to be converted to numeric format before the CPU (Central Processor Unit) can do the arithmetic. This may be significant when finding the sum or average of a field in a large table.

5. In exponential notation, xEy means x * 10^y, where ^ means 'to the power of'. x is called the mantissa and y is called the exponent.

6. The number of decimal places on a Currency field can be set from 0 to 15 using the Decimal Places property, but the decimal part is accurate to only four decimal places. The data is rounded to four decimal places.

7. If you add a record with an Autonumber field with its New Values property set to Increment, then you delete it and add it again, you won't be able to get the original number back again.

8. A Yes/No field is displayed as a checkbox. Its positive value tests positive against True, Yes and On (without quotes). For example in SQL:

```
SELECT *
FROM test1
where g = On
```

will retrieve all records where the value of field g is either Yes or True or On. The negations of these names for the values are No, False and Off. Note that quotes are not used around these values.

9. When the user clicks on a Hyperlink field, he or she is taken to that website, ftp site, newsgroup, file or email address.

10. Hyperlink fields contain these parts:

- *displaytext*: (optional) the text that appears in the hyperlink field of the record. It's underlined to make it look like a hyperlink, but the URL is replaced with this more 'user-friendly' text.

- *address*: (not optional), which is either:

  a path to a file – a UNC: Universal Naming Convention – e.g.

  \\server\share\path\filename or

  a path to a web page – a URL: a Uniform Resource Locator, which can be an FTP or HTTP or an email – e.g.

  ftp://ftp.server.somewhere/ftp.file

  http://www.19Pelham.freeserve.co.uk

  news:alt.hypertext

  john14@uel.ac.uk

- *subaddress*: (optional) a location within the file or page. In HTML terms, the NAME property of an Anchor tag.

  An example of an Access hyperlink field content is:

11. Lookup Wizard fields are potentially useful where you want the value of the field that the user enters to be made available through a drop-down list rather than by having to type in the value. This can enhance database integrity by allowing only valid values for a field.

To continue with our example of creating a small database, look at the Fig. 3.8 below to see the fields we created when we were designing the CUSTOMER table of the accts.mdb database.

Field Name	Data Type	Description
c_no	Number	Each customer has a unique customer number.
title	Text	Mr., Mrs., Miss., Ms., Prof., Dr., etc.
sname	Text	Surname
inits	Text	Initials. Limited to 4 characters. e.g. J.R.
street	Text	Street number and name.
city	Text	City name.
postc	Text	Post code. Zip codes can also be typed here.
cred_lim	Currency	The maximum amount the customer can owe us.
balance	Currency	The amount the customer actually owes us.

Field Properties

General | Lookup

Field Size	Integer
Format	
Decimal Places	Auto
Input Mask	
Caption	
Default Value	0
Validation Rule	
Validation Text	
Required	No
Indexed	Yes (No Duplicates)

A field name can be up to 64 characters long, including spaces. Press F1 for help on field names.

Fig. 3.8 The complete design of the CUSTOMER table.

After all the fields have been created, a primary key must be chosen for the table. This is a field (or if necessary a set of fields where no single field will do) that uniquely identifies each record in the table. You have to select a primary key such that no two records in the table could ever have the same value of this primary key. Occasionally, you will have a choice. In this case, each of the choices is called a *candidate key*. Choose one to be the primary key. Choose the shortest one. Remember this primary key value may be repeated many times as a foreign key in related records.

You specify the primary key by selecting it and then clicking the key button in the toolbar at the top of the window, just under the menu, see next page.

In Access, creating a primary key creates an index called *PrimaryKey*. You can see all the indexes for a table by using the following menu sequence: View/Indexes. In the case of the CUSTOMER table, this gives the result shown in Fig. 3.9.

It is always necessary, in a truly relational database, to have a primary key (and in Access, an index called PrimaryKey). However, we might want to have indexes on other fields. At the bottom of the table design window, there is a property we can set for any field and this property is called 'Indexed'. The reason for creating these extra indexes is just to do with performance. Suppose we had a *large* CUSTOMER table and we had a set of database programs that frequently accessed our customer table via the postcode field `postc`.

Rather than searching sequentially through all of the customer records for records with a given postcode, we would like, for the sake of speed, to be able to access them more directly. Indexing on the `postc` field will do this. The new index will show immediately which customers are in that postcode.

An index is a two-column table that the system keeps. On the left-hand side of the table is (in this case) the postcode value, and on the right-hand side of the table is the set of customer numbers who live in that postcode. In this way, a process that wanted to retrieve from the database all customers in a given postcode will use this index.

Whether an index is used or not in, say, an SQL query, is usually left up to the database engine (Jet) itself. For a truly relational database, the programmer (VB and/or SQL) does not need to be concerned about whether a particular process would be faster using the index or not.

Indexes: Customer			
Index Name	Field Name	Sort Order	
PrimaryKey	c_no	Ascending	

Index Properties

Primary	Yes	
Unique	Yes	The name for this index. Each
Ignore Nulls	No	index can use up to 10 fields.

Fig. 3.9 The Indexes window for the CUSTOMER table.

The programmer in fact has no way to see the contents of the index in most database management systems. Access is no exception.

One of the consequences of this 'index independence' (see the reference to Codd's database laws) is that if all the non-primary keys on the database are deleted, all the SQL queries and VB programs *will still work*.

The purpose to which indexes are put in databases are thus:

- speeding up access to certain records on the indexed field(s);
- in Jet databases, defining the primary key.

It should also be noted that every time a record is added or deleted from the table, all of the indexes must all be updated. This can lead to slower inserts and deletes than you would get *without* the indexes.

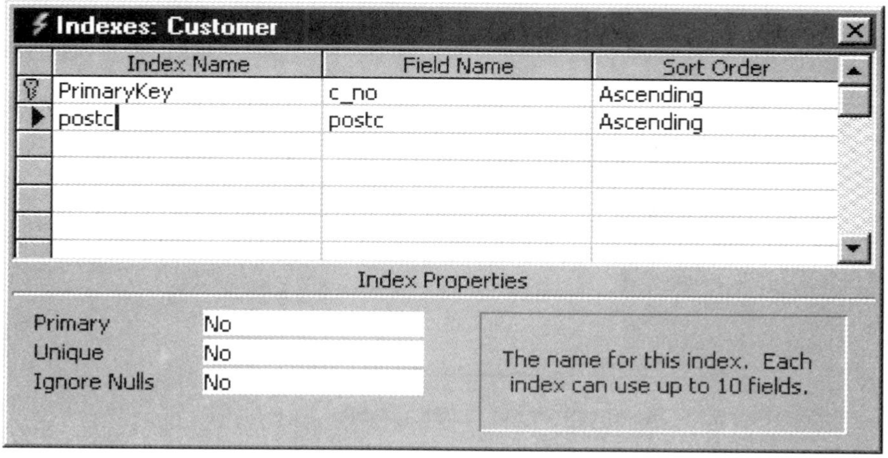

Fig. 3.10 The Indexes window after the postc index has been added.

Figure 3.10 shows the indexes window after we added an index on the `postc` field. As you can see, there are now two indexes. The lower part of the Indexes window shows that we have specified non-uniqueness for the `postc` index. This is necessary because of course many customers can live in the same postcode area.

You are asked when you close the design window for the table what name you want to give it. We called it CUSTOMER and you can see this in the title bar. The table design can easily be changed by going into the Design window for the table. The only problems you are likely to have when you change the design of a table are:

1. Deleting the primary key field. Every table must have a primary key. Also, if there is a 1: N relationship from this table to another table, this primary key will be the foreign key there. That will cause a problem. Links between related records will be lost. If you really need to do this, you will have to delete the relationship between the two tables temporarily (see later in this chapter for a description of Access relationships) and re-create it later.

2. Changing the data type of a primary or a related foreign key. They must be the *same* data type.

3. Deleting a foreign key field. Links between records will again be lost. You have to delete the relationship first and re-create it again after the change.

In our example, the INVOICE and PAYMENT tables are created in a similar way. The table designs are shown below in Figs 3.11 and 3.12.

Notice that in the case of the PAYMENT table, there is a composite primary key. This is necessary because neither the `inv_no` field nor the `pmt_no` field is 'unique' in itself. That is, duplicates can occur in each column. However, the *combination* is always unique. You create a composite key by holding down the Ctrl key on the keyboard and clicking *both fields* to highlight them, before finally clicking the key button at the top in the toolbar.

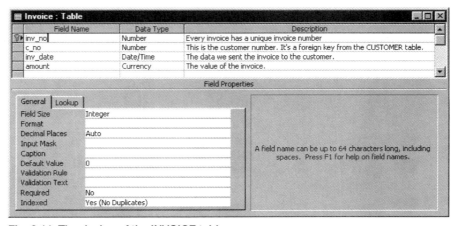

Fig. 3.11 The design of the INVOICE table.

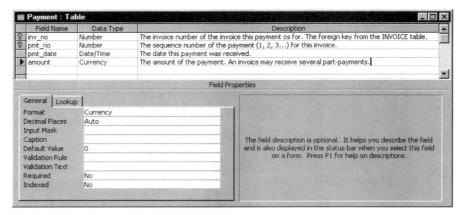

Fig. 3.12 The design of the PAYMENT table.

Note that we have attempted to give a concise description of the meaning of each field in the 'Description' column of the table design window. While it does not affect database performance (being merely documentation), using this Description column aids understanding of the database and can reduce errors due to misunderstanding. Choose your words carefully – there's very limited space available. Many errors occur in database work not because of incorrect database design, but because of inadequate or misleading documentation. Poor English, including unwitting ambiguity and other forms of muddle are prime culprits. (We hope we have used clear English in this book!). Documentation is an important part of any system. Some organizations use a separate *data dictionary* to put this documentation into.

Your database window should now look like Fig. 3.13. There are three tables. None of them yet contains any data. The next step is to create relationships between pairs of tables.

Fig. 3.13 The three tables we have created in database accts.mdb.

 ## 3.6 Creating relationships

The relationships you create between Access database tables correspond to the relationships discussed in the sections on entity modelling in Chapter 2. They show the links between records in tables. For example, we shall create a relationship in a moment between the CUSTOMER table and the INVOICE table. It will link the primary key `customer.c_no` in the CUSTOMER table to the corresponding foreign key `invoice.c_no` in the INVOICE table. It will show which invoices belong to which customers. Note: 'customer.c_no' means 'the c_no field in the customer table'.

Creating relationships in Access not only helps out programmers who design their queries using the query grid (it gives a default *join* type – see Chapter 4); it also helps to maintain *database integrity* (the correctness and completeness of the data on the database) by disallowing some invalid updates, as we explain below.

To create relationships between the tables, you first have to open the Relationships window in Access. You do this by clicking the Relationships button as shown below.

Clicking this button will open up the Relationships window. Click the Add button to add all three tables to the window and you should end up with a Relationship window like the one shown in Fig. 3.14. Adding or removing a table can be achieved at any time by right-clicking the Relationships window. (In Access 2 and earlier versions of Access you have to use the menu to do this.) The primary key fields in each table are highlighted. We now want to add the relationships. First we shall add the relationship between the CUSTOMER and INVOICE tables. This is performed by dragging `Customer.c_no` (the primary key of the Customer table) to `Invoice.c_no` (the corresponding foreign key in the Invoice table).

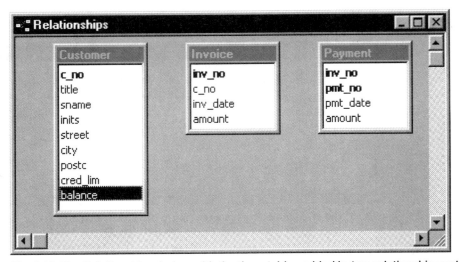

Fig. 3.14 The Relationship window with the three tables added but no relationships yet.

Doing this will result in another window opening up. This window is shown in Fig. 3.15.

Fig. 3.15 This window opens up when you create a relationship.

At the top of the window/form you can see the two tables (CUSTOMER and INVOICE) that are being related by the new relationship, and the two fields (`Customer.c_no` and `Invoice.c_no`) that are involved. The drop-down lists let you change your mind on which fields you use. There is really no choice, however. You must link the primary key of the 'one' side of the one-to-many relationship to the foreign key on the 'many' side.

Look at the other decisions you have to make on this form regarding the new relationship you are creating:

- Enforce Referential Integrity. You tick this if you want every record on the 'many' side of the relationship to have a 'corresponding' record on the 'one' side of the relationship.

- Cascade Update Related Fields. You tick this if you want a change of value in the primary key field on the 'one' side of the relationship to be reflected in the foreign key of all related records on the 'many' side of the relationship.

- Cascade Delete Related Records. You tick this if you want the user to be able to delete a record on the 'one' side of the relationship and have the database automatically delete all the related records on the 'many' side of the relationship without telling the user. You leave it un-ticked if you want such an event to cause a trappable error. (Errors can be 'trapped' by Visual Basic code and you can create code to 'handle' the error using On Error Goto – see Chapters 9 to 12.)

- Join Type. Clicking this opens up another window allowing you to choose among three default join types (inner, left and right joins). This is the default join type that appears in the query design grid for people who design queries that way (see Chapter 4). SQL programmers don't need this because they define the join type they need in their SQL SELECT statements (see Chapters 6 and 7).

We now describe these options in further detail by continuing with our CUSTOMER–INVOICE–PAYMENT example.

Referential Integrity

When creating the relationship between CUSTOMER and INVOICE, we now have to decide whether to tick the checkbox marked 'Enforce Referential Integrity'. We decide in this case that we *shall* tick it because we want to ensure that every invoice is for a customer who has a record on the database. It should be impossible to create an INVOICE record with a customer number that does not exist in the CUSTOMER table. If an attempt is made to do this, the database should cause an error condition to occur. This error can be trapped by VB code and the user encouraged to think again using suitable error messages, prompts and advice.

Cascade Update

We shall also opt for this by checking the check box. This means that if the user changes the value of a customer number (`c_no`) field in a CUSTOMER record, all of the corresponding `c_no` fields in INVOICE records will change to that value too.

Cascade Delete

We shall not opt for this because if the user attempts to delete a CUSTOMER record for a customer who has outstanding INVOICE records then that user should be informed of this. If we *did* have Cascade Delete, the system would delete the customer record *and* all of its invoices with 'no questions asked' (assuming the INVOICE–PAYMENT relationship *also* had Cascade Delete, in which case linked payments would also be deleted).

Join Type

Clicking the Join Type button opens up the form shown in Fig. 3.16.

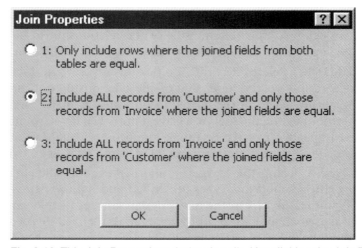

Fig. 3.16 This Join Properties window is called by clicking the Join Type button on the Relationships window.

You have a choice of three join types. These are default join types, used only for query building using the Query Design grid (see Chapter 4 for a description of building queries this way – queries are the way you retrieve data from the database to provide answers to questions people in the organization ask). The join types can be changed for individual queries in the Query Design grid anyway, and if you program your own queries using SQL, you specify the join type explicitly in each SQL query anyway, so this default join type is not very important. What *is* important is that you understand what each join type means. These are explained in detail in Chapter 6, but we give an overview here.

- **Join type 1** is an *inner join*. When you create a query with an inner join, only those records in the two tables that match on the join criteria are passed to the output. In the present case, where we are joining records from the CUSTOMER and INVOICE tables, if we used the inner join, only customers who have at least one invoice would be output. Any customers with no invoices would not be output.

- **Join type 2** is a *left join*. When you create a query with a left join, all matching records in the two tables are passed to the output, but in addition, any record in the *first* table that *doesn't have a match* in the *second* table is output too. You get all the output you get with an inner join *plus* any unmatched records from the first table. In the present example, CUSTOMER left join INVOICE joins all records from the two tables that match on c_no and passes them to the output, and *in addition*, passes all CUSTOMER records with no matching INVOICE records to the output too. This would be useful if you wanted to list customer and invoice data for *all* customers, whether or not they had any invoices. For a customer with no invoices, blanks ('NULLs') appear in the joined record where the invoice fields would be.

- **Join type 3** is a *right join*. When you create a query with a right join, all matching records in the two tables are passed to the output, but in addition, any record in the *second* table that *doesn't have a match* in the *first* table is output too. Clearly, TableA *left join* TableB is the same as TableB *right join* TableA.

In our example, we choose Join type 2, because it is the safest, most 'permissive' default. We repeat, however, that the query designer should, rather than just use the default when writing a query, use the join type that the logic of the particular query requires.

Clicking the OK button on the Join Properties window (Fig. 3.16) returns us to the Relationships window, which should now appear as in Fig. 3.17.

Clicking the Create button on the Relationships window returns us to the original Relationships window as shown in Fig. 3.18. Note the new relationship.

The '1' and the infinity symbol together show that this is a one-to-many relationship, the solid bar at each end shows that referential integrity has been enforced, and the right-pointing arrow shows that the default join type is a left join. However, rather than remember this, the properties of the relationship can be seen at any time by double-clicking the relationship line. The relationship can be deleted at any time by clicking it and then hitting the Delete key on the keyboard.

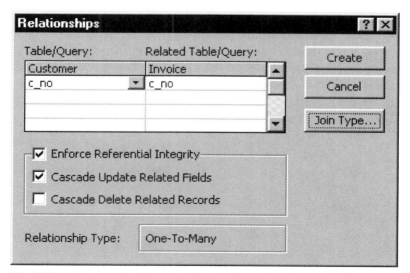

Fig. 3.17 The completed Relationships window, showing our choices.

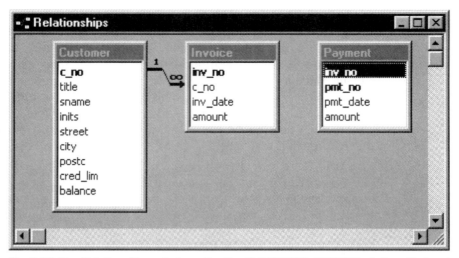

Fig. 3.18 The Relationships window after the CUSTOMER–INVOICE relationship has been created.

Just to make the above concepts clearer, we now illustrate the effects of referential integrity, cascade update, and cascade delete. We illustrate these using the relationship we have just created. If you just want to continue constructing the database schema, you can skip these sections.

Illustrating the effects of enforcing Referential Integrity
The foreign key value of every record on the 'many' side of a relationship with referential integrity must have a corresponding value in the primary key of a record on the 'one' side of the relationship.

In our example, every invoice must correspond to a customer record that has the same value of customer number.

Let's test this. We shall attempt to insert into the INVOICE table an invoice record with a value of the field c_no which doesn't exist for any record in the CUSTOMER table; put simply: an invoice without a customer.

Because we have opted for referential integrity on this relationship, the Jet Engine should reject the new invoice record.

Suppose the CUSTOMER and INVOICE tables are as shown in Figs 3.19 and 3.20.

Fig. 3.19 The CUSTOMER table.

Fig. 3.20 The INVOICE table.

Notice that every c_no in the INVOICE table exists in the CUSTOMER table.

Now let's attempt to insert an invoice number 2000 with a customer number 7. In Fig. 3.21 we have typed the new record into the INVOICE table and are just about to save it by clicking the grid somewhere out of the record. (That is when updates occur in Jet: when you move to another record.)

Fig. 3.21 Inserting the new invoice.

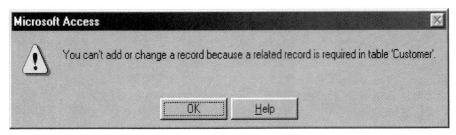

Fig. 3.22 The error message that occurs when you try to save the new invoice.

Figure 3.22 shows the error message. The 'related' record it requires in table 'Customer' is one with a customer number 7. The referential integrity rule has been broken, so the insertion of the new invoice record has had to be abandoned.

Note that there will be some relationships where referential integrity is *not* appropriate. For example, in a theatre booking system, there may be a one-to-many relationship between customer and ticket.

However, there may be some (unsold) tickets, which have no customer. In that case, the foreign key from the 'customer' table into the 'ticket' table would be null.

Note also that referential integrity is, in entity modelling terms, simply the optionality of the relationship from the entity on the 'many' side of the relationship to the entity on the 'one' side.

Illustrating the effects of Cascade Update
If we opt for Cascade Update in a relationship, it means that a change to the value of a primary key field value on the 'one' side of a relationship is immediately reflected in a change to the values of the foreign key of all related records on the 'many' side. Given the CUSTOMER tables of Figs 3.19 and 3.20, let's change the value of Sallaway's customer number from 1 to 100. See Fig. 3.23.

c_no	title	sname	inits	street	city	postc	cred_lim	balance
100	Mr	Sallaway	G.R.	12 Fax Rd	London	WC1	£1,000.00	£42.56
2	Miss	Lauri	P.	5 Dux St	London	N1	£500.00	£200.00
3	Mr	Jackson	R.	2 Lux Ave	Leeds	LE1 2AB	£500.00	£510.00
4	Mr	Dziduch	M.	31 Low St	Dover	DO2 9CD	£100.00	£149.23
5	Ms	Woods	S.Q.	17 Nax Rd	London	E18 4WW	£1,000.00	£350.10
6	Mrs	Williams	C.	41 Cax St	Dover	DO2 8WD		£412.21
0							£0.00	£0.00

Record: ⏮ ◀ | 1 | ▶ ⏭ ▶* of 6

Fig. 3.23 Changing Sallaway's customer number.

▦ Invoice : Table			_ ☐ ✕
inv_no	**c_no**	**inv_date**	**amount**
▶ 940	100	05/12/99	£26.20
1002	4	12/01/00	£149.23
1003	100	12/01/00	£16.26
1004	2	14/01/00	£200.00
1005	3	20/01/00	£510.00
1006	5	21/01/00	£250.10
1017	6	22/01/00	£412.21
✱ 0	0		£0.00

Record: ⏮ ◀ | 1 | ▶ ⏭ ▶✱ of 7

Fig. 3.24 The customer number in Sallaway's two invoices have changed too.

When we save the change to the CUSTOMER record, and then open the INVOICE table, we notice that the foreign key values have changed as well (Fig. 3.24). That demonstrates Cascade Update.

Now let's experimentally remove the Cascade Update facility from the relationship (by going into the Relationships window, double-clicking the relationship, and un-checking the appropriate checkbox). If we now attempt to change Sallaway's customer number, we get the error shown in Fig. 3.25.

If we had not opted for referential integrity, the database would have allowed us to change Sallaway's customer number without changing it on his invoices. Those invoices would then not be traceable back to him. Clearly, referential integrity is desirable in this example.

Note that Jet insists that if you opt for Cascade Update then you must also have Referential Integrity.

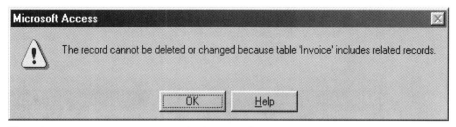

Microsoft Access

⚠ The record cannot be deleted or changed because table 'Invoice' includes related records.

[OK]   [Help]

Fig. 3.25 The error message you obtain when Cascade Update is not in force and you attempt to change the value of a customer number where that customer has invoices.

Illustrating the effects of Cascade Delete

If we opt for Cascade Delete in a relationship, then deleting a record in a table on the 'one' side of a relationship will automatically delete related records in the table on the 'many' side of the relationship.

We shall demonstrate the effect of a cascade delete on the CUSTOMER, INVOICE and PAYMENT tables shown in Figs 3.26, 3.27 and 3.28.

c_no	title	sname	inits	street	city	postc	cred_lim	balance
1	Mr	Sallaway	G.R.	12 Fax Rd	London	WC1	£1,000.00	£42.56
2	Miss	Lauri	P.	5 Dux St	London	N1	£500.00	£200.00
3	Mr	Jackson	R.	2 Lux Ave	Leeds	LE1 2AB	£500.00	£510.00
4	Mr	Dziduch	M.	31 Low St	Dover	DO2 9CD	£100.00	£149.23
5	Ms	Woods	S.Q.	17 Nax Rd	London	E18 4WW	£1,000.00	£350.10
6	Mrs	Williams	C.	41 Cax St	Dover	DO2 8WD		£412.21
0							£0.00	£0.00

Fig. 3.26 The CUSTOMER table *before* deleting customer 1.

Note that customer 1 has invoices, and some of these invoices have payments.

The effect of Cascade Delete being opted for will be that deleting this customer will delete all his invoices and all the related payments.

inv_no	c_no	inv_date	amount
940	1	05/12/99	£26.20
1002	4	12/01/00	£149.23
1003	1	12/01/00	£16.26
1004	2	14/01/00	£200.00
1005	3	20/01/00	£510.00
1006	5	21/01/00	£250.10
1017	6	22/01/00	£412.21
0	0		£0.00

Fig. 3.27 The INVOICE table *before* deleting customer 1.

inv_no	pmt_no	pmt_date	amount
940	2	12/12/99	£13.00
940	3	19/01/00	£10.00
1005	1	14/01/00	£510.00
1017	1	30/01/00	£100.00
0	0		£0.00

Fig. 3.28 The PAYMENT table *before* deleting customer 1.

Remembering that we have *not* specified Cascade Delete for the relationship between these tables, we now proceed to attempt to delete the customer record for customer 1.

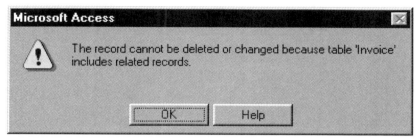

Fig. 3.29 The error message that results from trying to delete customer 1's CUSTOMER record (Cascade Delete *not* specified).

The deletion of the customer record is rejected (Fig. 3.29) because customer 1 has two invoices: invoices 940 and 1003 (see Fig. 3.27). We now opt for Cascade Delete by opening the Relationship window, double-clicking the relationship line on the diagram and ticking the Cascade Delete checkbox (Fig. 3.30).

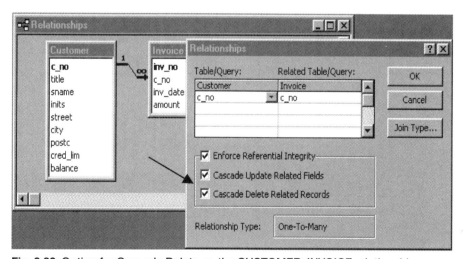

Fig. 3.30 Opting for Cascade Delete on the CUSTOMER–INVOICE relationship.

In our accts.mdb database, there is also a relationship between the INVOICE and PAYMENT tables.

So, if this relationship does not have Cascade Delete, then this will also prevent the deletion of the customer record and the related invoices and payments.

Assuming we have specified Cascade Delete for this relationship too, the deletion of customer 1 goes ahead.

The results are shown in Figs 3.31, 3.32 and 3.33.

	c_no	title	sname	inits	street	city	postc	cred_lim	balance
▶	2	Miss	Lauri	P.	5 Dux St	London	N1	£500.00	£200.00
	3	Mr	Jackson	R.	2 Lux Ave	Leeds	LE1 2AB	£500.00	£510.00
	4	Mr	Dziduch	M.	31 Low St	Dover	DO2 9CD	£100.00	£149.23
	5	Ms	Woods	S.Q.	17 Nax Rd	London	E18 4WW	£1,000.00	£350.10
	6	Mrs	Williams	C.	41 Cax St	Dover	DO2 8WD		£412.21
*	0							£0.00	£0.00

Record: I◀ ◀ | 1 | ▶ ▶I ▶* of 5

Fig. 3.31 The CUSTOMER table *after* deleting the customer 1 record.

In Fig. 3.31, note that the database record in the CUSTOMER table has been deleted.

	inv_no	c_no	inv_date	amount
	#Deleted	#Deleted	#Deleted	#Deleted
	1002	4	12/01/00	£149.23
	#Deleted	#Deleted	#Deleted	#Deleted
	1004	2	14/01/00	£200.00
	1005	3	20/01/00	£510.00
	1006	5	21/01/00	£250.10
▶	1017	6	22/01/00	£412.21
*	0	0		£0.00

Record: I◀ ◀ | 7 | ▶ ▶I ▶* of 7

Fig. 3.32 The INVOICE table *after* deleting the customer 1 record.

In Fig. 3.32, note that two records, the INVOICE records for customer number 1, have been deleted.

In Fig. 3.33, note that two PAYMENT records have also been deleted.

The effect of deleting one customer record has been to also delete his two invoices and the two payments that one of the invoices had. That is the nature of Cascade Delete.

In our database, we do not want this to occur. Instead, we want the user to be prompted when an attempt is made to delete a customer with outstanding

inv_no	pmt_no	pmt_date	amount
#Deleted	#Deleted	#Deleted	#Deleted
#Deleted	#Deleted	#Deleted	#Deleted
1017	1	30/01/00	£100.00
1005	1	14/01/00	£510.00
0	0		£0.00

Record: 1 of 4

Fig. 3.33 The PAYMENT table *after* deleting the customer 1 record.

invoices, so we have not opted for Cascade Delete in the final version of the database accts.mdb.

In our update programs we shall trap such error conditions and then ask the user to delete the relevant invoices and payments first (should he/she so desire).

We now continue the description of the creation of the accts.mdb CUSTOMER–INVOICE–PAYMENT database. We reproduce in Fig. 3.34 the state of the database as we left it in Fig. 3.18.

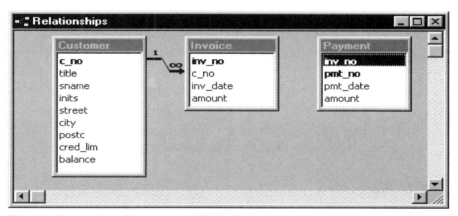

Fig. 3.34 The accts.mdb database with the first relationship created.

We now create the INVOICE–PAYMENT relationship by dragging from `Invoice.inv_no` (the invoice number in the Invoice table) to `Payment.inv_no` (the invoice number in the Payment table). Note that:

- `Invoice.inv_no` is the primary key in the Invoice table
- the Payment table has a composite key consisting of `Payment.inv_no` with `Payment.pmt_no`
- `Payment.inv_no` is the foreign key from the Invoice table.

Dragging and dropping from `Invoice.inv_no` to Payment.inv_no brings up the Relationships form and we choose the options shown in Fig. 3.35.

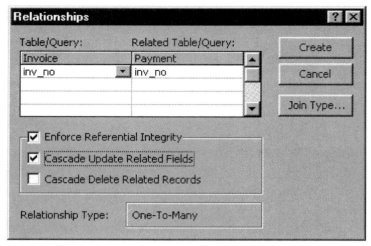

Fig. 3.35 Setting the properties of the INVOICE–PAYMENT relationship.

The reasons for choosing these options are:

- *Enforce Referential Integrity*: we want to prevent the insertion of PAYMENT records that have no related INVOICE record.

- *Cascade Update Related Fields*: if any invoice has its invoice number changed, we want the invoice number on corresponding payments to change accordingly.

- *Cascade Delete Related Records*: if any attempt is made to delete an INVOICE record that has associated PAYMENT records, we want the user to be notified. We have therefore not opted for this.

- *Join Type*: we opted for Join type 2 – the 'left join' – as the default join type. This default can be overridden for individual queries.

All of these items were discussed in greater detail earlier in this chapter in the section dealing with the creation of the first relationship.

3.7 Exercises

1. Create the database accts.mdb according to the instructions given above.

2. Modify the CUSTOMER table so that it includes fields for the customers' email addresses. Clicking on the field should open up the email package ready to send a message. Use a hyperlink field.

3. Alter the INVOICE–PAYMENT relationship to include the Cascade Delete facility.

4. Consider the implications of having Cascade Delete on the CUSTOMER–INVOICE relationship but not on the INVOICE–PAYMENT relationship.

5. In this chapter we have created tables and relationships using the graphical design facilities of Access. In Chapter 5 we describe how to create and alter table designs using SQL commands. Give examples where each of these methods would be suitable.

6. Suppose that it is discovered that a frequent requirement of your accts.mdb database is to search through the INVOICE table on the customer number field **c_no**. Give illustrative examples of the circumstances where you would advise adding an index on this field. Create such an index.

7. Change the data type of **customer.c_no** to AutoNumber. This means that each new customer will automatically be allocated a customer number. (You will have to change **invoice.c_no** data type too. Why?) Explain the circumstances in which you would use an AutoNumber field.

Chapter **4**

Access query design using Query Design view

In this chapter you will learn:

- how to design queries using the Access Query Design view.

4.1 Introduction

Database queries allow you to retrieve data from the database and to update it.

There are two basic ways that queries can be made in all versions of Access: graphically, using the Design View (also known as the Design Grid), and by using SQL. In most databases, including Access, SQL (Structured Query Language) is the main method used to query and update databases.

If you use the Access design grid, you don't have to know SQL. You just drag and drop, specify criteria, and run the query. We use the design grid in this chapter. SQL is covered in Chapters 5, 6 and 7.

While the query design grid is suitable for simple queries, it's a good idea for a database programmer also to know SQL, because SQL is used on other databases, such as SQL*Server and ORACLE, while those other databases don't have the same design grid as Access does. Understanding SQL gives you a better idea of what the database operations actually mean. You may also find that some of the more complex queries you will need to write will actually be easier to develop in 'raw' SQL than in the design grid. All the queries we discuss in this and following chapters are based on the databases shown in Appendix 1.

4.2 Developing queries using the Access Query Design view

The design grid queries shown in this section were all produced in Access 97 and 2000, but the procedure is identical in all versions. We shall now show how to develop various Access queries using the design grid.

To use the design grid in the following examples, go into Access, select the database **accts.mdb** and click the Queries tab.

> *Query 1: List all customer records.*

Select the Design View from the list and Add the Customer table to the design grid. Drag the asterisk symbol into the first column of the grid. The grid should now appear as in Fig. 4.1.

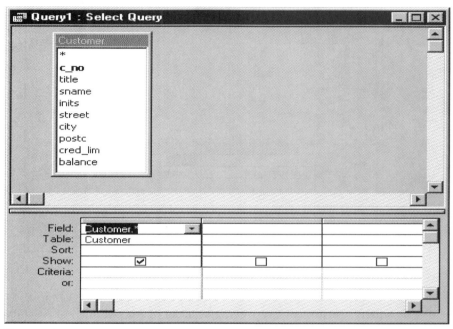

Fig. 4.1 Query 1 after dragging the asterisk into column 1.

The asterisk means 'all columns', i.e. *all fields* of the Customer table are to be displayed. And because we have not specified any selection criteria ('Criteria') for the query, *all records* will be displayed too. Click the Datasheet View or the exclamation mark to run the query. The output is the whole table, as shown in Fig. 4.2.

	c_no	title	sname	inits	street	city	postc	cred_lim	balance
▶	1	Mr	Sallaway	G.R.	12 Fax Rd	London	WC1	£1,000.00	£42.56
	2	Miss	Lauri	P.	5 Dux St	London	N1	£500.00	£200.00
	3	Mr	Jackson	R.	2 Lux Ave	Leeds	LE1 2AB	£500.00	£510.00
	4	Mr	Dziduch	M.	31 Low St	Dover	DO2 9CD	£100.00	£149.23
	5	Ms	Woods	S.Q.	17 Nax Rd	London	E18 4WW	£1,000.00	£250.10
	6	Mrs	Williams	C.	41 Cax St	Dover	DO2 8WD		£412.21
✻	0							£0.00	£0.00

Record: ◄◄ ◄ 1 ► ►► ►✻ of 6

Fig. 4.2 Outputting the whole Customer table using Query 1.

> *Query 2*: List the customer numbers and surnames of all customers.

This time we drag just the c_no and sname fields from the picture of the table in the top panel into the first two columns of the second panel of the grid. The grid then appears as in Fig. 4.3 and the output as in Fig. 4.4.

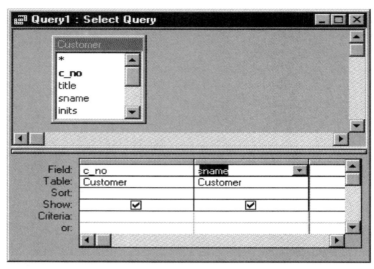

Fig. 4.3 The design grid for Query 2.

Note that only the c_no and sname columns appear in the output from this query. Technically, retrieving a subset of the columns of a database table is called *projection*. We saved all of the queries in this section using names such as DGQuery1 (Data Grid Query 1), DGQuery2 etc. The diagrams show Query 1 in the title bar because that's the default name for a new query before you save it.

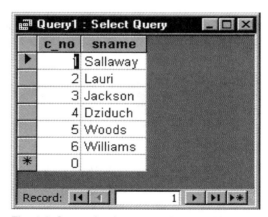

Fig. 4.4 Outputting just two columns of **Customer** using Query 2.

Notice that there is a record selector bar at the bottom of the output window, which includes a button with an asterisk. There is also a blank row at the bottom of the output. This allows you to insert records into the query. The effect of inserting into this particular query would be to insert just two fields c_no and sname into the new record. The rest would be NULL. That would be all right provided we had not specified any of the other fields as Required when we designed the table (see Chapter 3).

> _Query 3_: Same as Query 2 but sorted on surname.

To sort on a field, click the Sort: cell in the appropriate field of the grid. Here, we shall sort on sname ascending (A to Z) rather than descending (Z to A). See Figs 4.5 and 4.6.

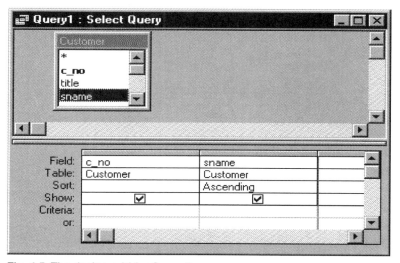

Fig. 4.5 The design grid for Query 3.

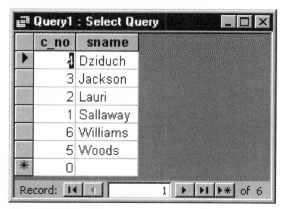

Fig. 4.6 Sorting the output on ascending order of **sname** using Query 3.

> *Query 4: List all the cities from the Customer table.*

Here, only one field, `city`, is dragged into the query design grid. See Figs 4.7 and 4.8.

Notice that the city names are duplicated. This is because several customers have addresses in the same city.

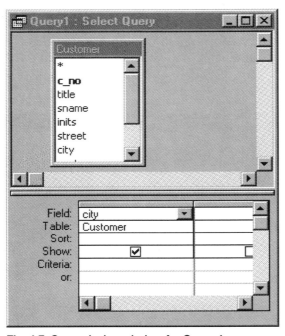

Fig. 4.7 Query design window for Query 4.

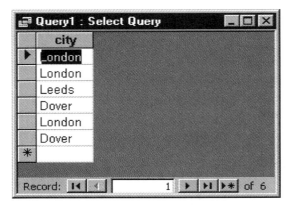

Fig. 4.8 The output of Query 4 showing duplicates.

In the next query, we remove these duplicates.

> *Query 5: Same as Query 4 but with duplicate cities removed.*

To remove duplicates using the query design grid, you have to change one of the query's properties. To do this, open the query in Design view, select the query by clicking anywhere in query Design view outside the design grid and the field lists, and click Properties on the toolbar to display the query's property sheet. Then set the UniqueValues property to Yes. See Figs 4.9 and 4.10.

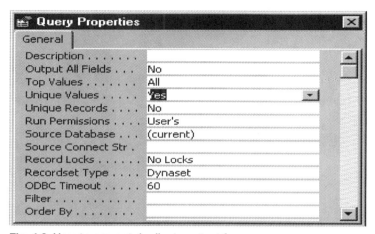

Fig. 4.9 How to prevent duplicate output from a query.

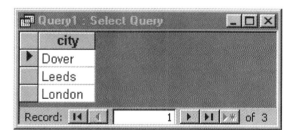

Fig. 4.10 Duplicate output removed.

For every query you develop in Design view, Access generates its own SQL version of the query. Figure 4.11 shows the SQL generated by Query 4. Provided you know SQL, it may sometimes be simpler to type in the SQL yourself.

Fig. 4.11 The SQL statement generated by Access for Query 5.

> *Query 6:* List the customer number, surname and city for all London customers. Show the city.

Here we must set a value in the Criteria: cell of the `City` column of the query grid. The value is "London". Only London customers will then be selected. See Figs 4.12 and 4.13. Note that Access puts quotes around London because it's textual data.

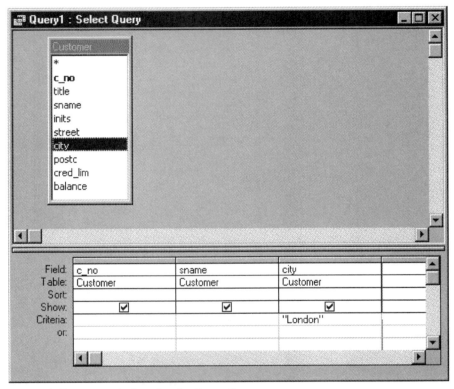

Fig. 4.12 The query design view for Query 6.

Fig. 4.13 The output from Query 6, showing just London customers.

The fields you want to see at the output are specified by a tick in the corresponding checkbox in Show.

Query 7: List the customer number and surname of all London customers without listing the city.

This query is the same as Query 6 but we uncheck the Show: cell in the `City` column. This illustrates the fact that you can use one or more fields in selection criteria without necessarily listing them. See Figs 4.14 and 4.15.

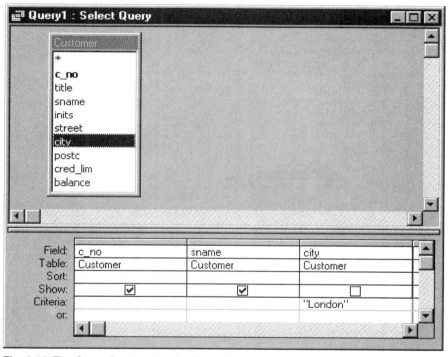

Fig. 4.14 The Query Design view for Query 7.

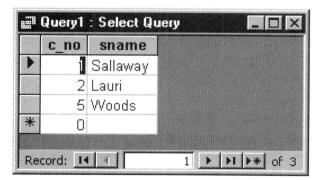

Fig. 4.15 The query output for Query 7.

> *Query 8*: List all details of all London customers whose balance is not less than £200.

In relational database theory, retrieving just some of the fields is called a *projection* operation, as we have seen. In the previous two queries we retrieved a subset of the records too. This is called a *selection* operation. The rule we use for determining which records are selected is called the *selection criterion*. In the previous two queries the selection criterion was that `City` should be London.

In this query we have two selection criteria: city is London, and Balance is over £200. The Query Design view for this query is shown in Fig. 4.16 and its output in Fig. 4.17.

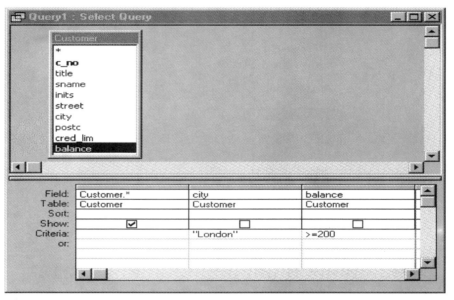

Fig. 4.16 The Query Design view for Query 8.

Fig. 4.17 The output from Query 8.

In SQL, selection criteria for records are implemented in the WHERE clause. This is covered in greater detail in the SQL chapters.

The ">=" sign in Query 8 means "greater than or equal to". It's an example of a *relational operator*. If you've done any maths or programming before you've probably come across relational operators. Figure 4.18 summarizes the relational operator symbols and their meanings.

Relational operator	Meaning	Alternative phrasing	Example
=	Equals		A = B: A equals B
<	Less than		A < B: A is less than B
<=	Less than or equal to	Not greater than	A <= B: A is less than or equal to B
>	Greater than		A > B: A is greater than B
>=	Greater than or equal to	Not less than	A >= B: A is greater than or equal to B
<>	Not equal to	Less than or greater than	A <> B: A is not equal to B

Fig. 4.18 The relational operators.

In Access, these relational operators work just as well with text as with numbers. So for example "Dziduch" < "Jackson", meaning that Dziduch is less than (i.e. before) Jackson in alphabetical order. There is also a 'Between' operator which allows selection on a range of values of a field. This is actually a little bit of SQL, which we describe in the SQL chapters.

Query 9: List all customers whose surnames start from J onwards.

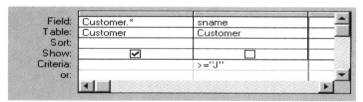

Fig. 4.19 The design grid for Query 9.

Query 10: List all customers whose balance is between £200 and £300.

Fig. 4.20 The design grid for Query 10.

> _Query 11_: List all customers who live in London or have a balance of not less than £200.

In this query there are two ways to qualify for being output:

1. live in London;

2. balance > = £200.

Note that you might interpret this English query in two different ways. You might think it means condition 1 or condition 2 _or both_ (inclusive or), or you might think it means condition 1 or condition 2 _but not both_ (exclusive or). Go back to the client and ask them what they mean. Let's assume it's the inclusive or they want.

In these situations, we use the or: rows of the query design grid. The query Design view and the resulting output are shown in Figs 4.21 and 4.22.

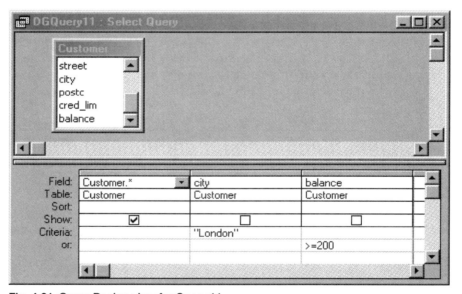

Fig. 4.21 Query Design view for Query 11.

	c_no	title	sname	inits	street	city	postc	cred_lim	balance
▶	1	Mr	Sallaway	G.R.	12 Fax Rd	London	WC1	£1,000.00	£42.56
	2	Miss	Lauri	P.	5 Dux St	London	N1	£500.00	£200.00
	3	Mr	Jackson	R.	2 Lux Ave	Leeds	LE1 2AB	£500.00	£510.00
	5	Ms	Woods	S.Q.	17 Nax Rd	London	E18 4WW	£1,000.00	£250.10
	6	Mrs	Williams	C.	41 Cax St	Dover	DO2 8WD		£412.21
*	0							£0.00	£0.00

Record: ◄ ◄ 1 ► ►I ►* of 5

Fig. 4.22 Query output for Query 11.

There are actually nine rows in the or: section of the query design grid allowing various combinations of conditions. A slightly more complex example is shown in the next query.

> *Query 12:* List all customers who either live outside London or have a credit limit of £1000 and a balance of over £500.

There are three conditions here:

A. live outside London;
B. have a credit limit of £1000;
C. have a balance of over £200.

The logic the query requires is:

A or (B and C).

The query grid corresponding to this is shown in Fig. 4.23.

Field:	Customer.*	city	cred_lim	balance	
Table:	Customer	Customer	Customer	Customer	
Sort:					
Show:	✓	☐	☐	☐	☐
Criteria:		<>"London"			
or:			1000	>200	

Fig. 4.23 Query grid for Query 12.

> *Query 13:* List all customers who either live outside London and have a credit limit of £1000 or do not have a credit limit of £1000 and have a balance of over £200.

The logic of this query is:

(A and B) or (not B and C).

The query corresponding to this is shown in Fig. 4.24.

Field:	Customer.*	city	cred_lim	cred_lim	balance	
Table:	Customer	Customer	Customer	Customer	Customer	
Sort:						
Show:	✓	☐	☐	☐	☐	☐
Criteria:		<>"London"	1000			
or:				<>1000	>200	

Fig. 4.24 Query grid for Query 13.

In general, any logical expression can be put into *disjunctive normal form (DNF)*, that is, a string of and-ed terms connected by or's. (Disjunction is another name for logical *or* and conjunction is another name for logical *and*.) Using the Access query grid, you put each of the conjunctions on a separate line in the Criteria section.

It might take a bit of logical manipulation to get the logic for your query into DNF. A knowledge of logic is clearly an advantage here. However, just considering each combination of conditions is the key idea.

Query 14: List the total balance outstanding for each city.

In this query we want to list a single value – the sum of all the customer balances for each city. For this we need to *group by* city, and *sum* the balances for each city. We discuss GROUP BY in more detail in Section 6.28. SUM is an example of an SQL *aggregate function*.

To get the Total: row in the grid, you have to click View/Totals in the Access menu. See Figs 4.25(a) and (b).

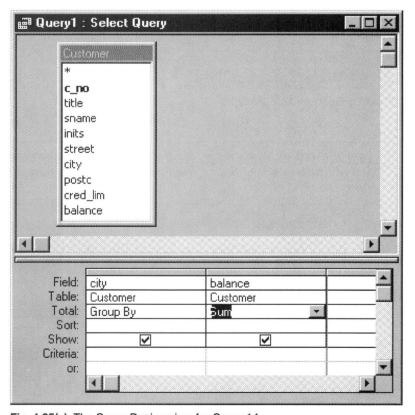

Fig. 4.25(a) The Query Design view for Query 14.

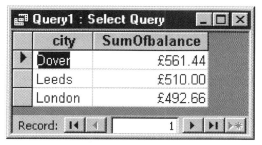

Fig. 4.25(b) The output from Query 14.

Query 15: List the highest outstanding balance for each city.

In the previous example we saw the SUM aggregate function. In this query we use another one: MAX. Aggregate functions are discussed in more detail in Chapter 6. See Figs 4.26 and 4.27.

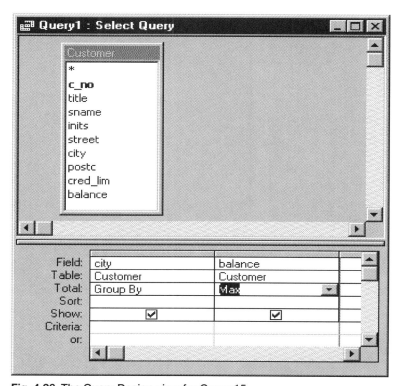

Fig. 4.26 The Query Design view for Query 15.

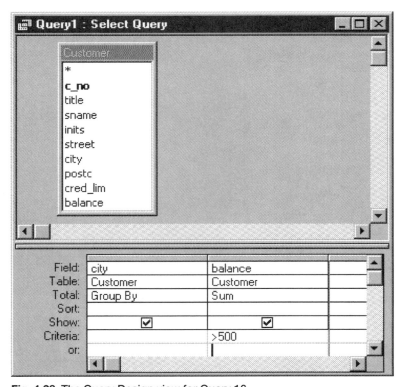

Fig. 4.27 The output from Query 15.

As can be seen in the output, the maximum balance for each city is shown. However, showing the customer or customers who *had* that balance would be more difficult and would be better done in SQL. It requires a *subquery*. We cover the subject of subqueries in section 7.2.

> *Query 16*: List the total outstanding balance for each city but only where that total exceeds £500.

Here we wish to apply selection criteria, as in a previous query, but not on individual customers; rather on the sum of balances. In the Query Design grid, we simply put an entry in the Criteria: cell under the aggregate function. See Figs 4.28 and 4.29.

Fig. 4.28 The Query Design view for Query 16.

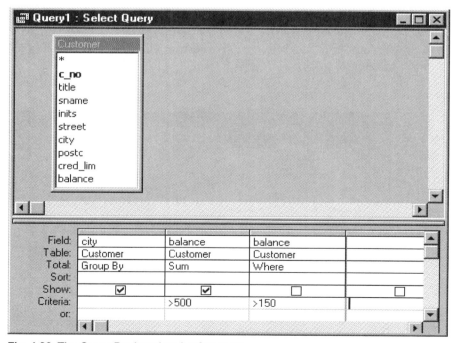

Fig. 4.29 The output from Query 16.

Selecting on the value of aggregated data is covered in more detail in section 6.2.9 on the HAVING clause.

Note that the selection criterion applies to the sum of the balances for a city rather than the balance field itself.

> *Query 17*: List the total outstanding balance for each city but only where that total exceeds £500. In this calculation only include customers whose balance exceeds £150.

In this query, there are selection criteria on both the individual Customer records and on the aggregated sum of balances. This means, in SQL terms (see later), that we need to use both a WHERE clause *and* a HAVING clause. In the Query Design view, this means having separate columns for 'Sum(balance)' and 'balance'. See Figs 4.30 and 4.31.

Fig. 4.30 The Query Design view for Query 17.

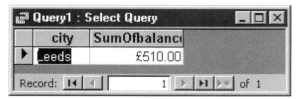

Fig. 4.31 The output from Query 17.

Note that since Dziduch's balance of £149.23 was not taken into account because of the WHERE clause (in the third column of the Query Design grid), the total balance for Dover was pushed below £500 and it didn't appear at the output.

Query 18: For each customer, list the customer number, the surname, and details of all invoices.

All the previous queries have entailed extracting data from just one table. However in this query, the surname is in the `Customer` table and the invoice details are in the `Invoice` table. This requires us to create a query that *joins* records from the two tables. When creating the query using the Query Design view, add both tables. See Figs 4.32 and 4.33.

If you check with the content of the `Customer` and `Invoice` tables shown in Appendix 1, you will see that the correct records have been joined up, using matching values of the `Customer` primary key `Customer.c_no` and the `Invoice` foreign key `Invoice.c_no`. Note that Sallaway has two invoices so he appears twice.

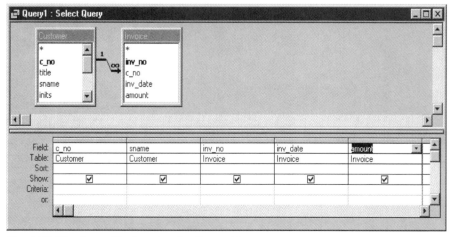

Fig. 4.32 The Query Design view for Query 18.

	c_no	sname	inv_no	inv_date	amount
►	1	Sallaway	940	05/12/99	£26.20
	1	Sallaway	1003	12/01/00	£16.26
	2	Lauri	1004	14/01/00	£200.00
	3	Jackson	1005	20/01/00	£510.00
	4	Dziduch	1002	12/01/00	£149.23
	5	Woods	1006	21/01/00	£250.10
	6	Williams	1017	22/01/00	£412.21

Record: 1 of 7

Fig. 4.33 The output from Query 18.

The default join type (LEFT JOIN) created at database design time is used. Join type is discussed in Chapters 3 and 6.

Query 19: List all invoices and any payments the invoices have received.

In the previous query, *every* customer happened to have at least one invoice in the database as it stands. In this case, a LEFT JOIN and an INNER JOIN (q.v.) would give identical results. In this query, where we have to join `Invoice` and `Payment` records, it happens to be the case that some invoices have no payments. It is clear from the English version of the query that we want to see all invoices *whether or not* they have any payments. In this case, the LEFT JOIN is called for. See Figs 4.34 and 4.35.

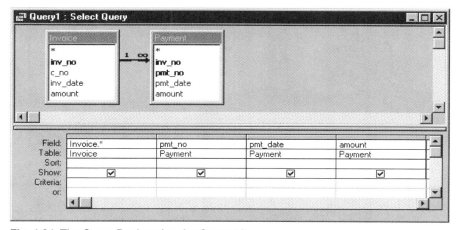

Fig. 4.34 The Query Design view for Query 19.

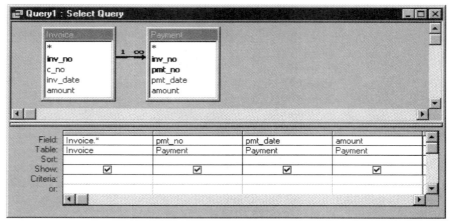

Fig. 4.35 The output from Query 19.

Notice that in this left join:

● invoice number 940 has two payments so it appears twice;

● invoice numbers 1002, 1003, 1004 and 1006 have no payments, so NULLs appear in the payment fields.

If we had specified an INNER JOIN, invoice numbers 1002, 1003, 1004 and 1006 would not have appeared at the output.

Note that in later versions of Access, you can change the *join type* by right-clicking on the join line.

> *Query 20*: List all payments and the invoices they were posted to.

Here we have the 'opposite' situation to the previous query: we want to list invoices and payments but only where the invoices *have* payments. An INNER JOIN between Invoice and Payment will give the desired result. See Figs 4.36 and 4.37.

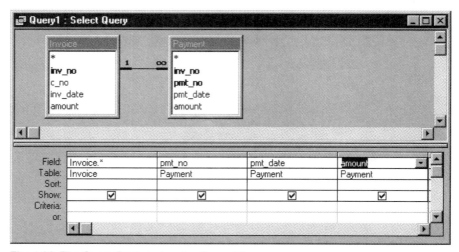

Fig. 4.36 The Query Design view for Query 20.

	inv_no	c_no	inv_date	Invoice.amou	pmt_no	pmt_date	Payment.amo
▶	940	1	05/12/99	£26.20	2	12/12/99	£13.00
	940	1	05/12/99	£26.20	3	19/01/00	£10.00
	1005	3	20/01/00	£510.00	1	14/01/00	£510.00
	1017	6	22/01/00	£412.21	1	30/01/00	£100.00
*							

Record: ⏮ ◀ 1 ▶ ⏭ ▶* of 4

Fig. 4.37 The output from Query 20.

Notes:

- A *left join* between Payment and Invoice (meaning all payments whether or not they have invoices) would yield the same result here, since all payments *do* have invoices and in our database they have to because we specified *referential integrity* for this relationship at design time (see discussions in Chapters 2 and 3 on referential integrity).

- A *right join* between Invoice and Payment would have the same result too, because A LEFT JOIN B is the same thing as B RIGHT JOIN A for all tables A and B.

> *Query 21*: List all customers, their invoices and their payments.

Here we require a three-way join. See Figs 4.38 and 4.39.

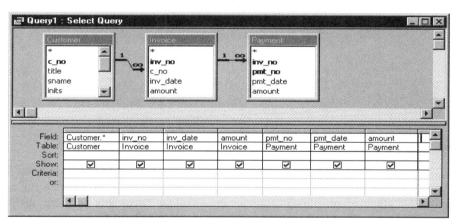

Fig. 4.38 The Query Design view for Query 21.

c_no	title	sname	inits	street	city	postc	cred_lim	balance	inv_no	inv_date	Invoice.amou	pmt_no	pmt_date	Payment.amount
1	Mr	Sallaway	G.R.	12 Fax Rd	London	WC1	£1,000.00	£42.56	940	05/12/99	£26.20	2	12/12/99	£13.00
1	Mr	Sallaway	G.R.	12 Fax Rd	London	WC1	£1,000.00	£42.56	940	05/12/99	£26.20	3	19/01/00	£10.00
1	Mr	Sallaway	G.R.	12 Fax Rd	London	WC1	£1,000.00	£42.56	1003	12/01/00	£16.26			
2	Miss	Lauri	P.	5 Dux St	London	N1	£500.00	£200.00	1004	14/01/00	£200.00			
3	Mr	Jackson	R.	2 Lux Ave	Leeds	LE1 2AB	£500.00	£510.00	1005	20/01/00	£510.00	1	14/01/00	£510.00
4	Mr	Dziduch	M.	31 Low St	Dover	DO2 9CD	£100.00	£149.23	1002	12/01/00	£149.23			
5	Ms	Woods	S.Q.	17 Nax Rd	London	E18 4WW	£1,000.00	£250.10	1006	21/01/00	£250.10			
6	Mrs	Williams	C.	41 Cax St	Dover	DO2 8WD		£412.21	1017	22/01/00	£412.21	1	30/01/00	£100.00

Record: ⏮ ◀ 1 ▶ ⏭ ▶* of 8

Fig. 4.39 The output from Query 21.

Suppose we had only required details of customers and their payments. It would still be necessary to include the `Invoice` table in the query because there is no direct link between `Customer` and `Payment`. This can be achieved by including only the required fields in the Data Design grid as shown in Fig. 4.40.

Field:	Customer.*	inv_no	pmt_no	pmt_date	amount	
Table:	Customer	Payment	Payment	Payment	Payment	
Sort:						
Show:	☑	☑	☑	☑	☑	
Criteria:						
or:						

Fig. 4.40 Eliminating **Invoice** fields from the output.

The linking `Invoice` table must still be included in this query though.

> *Query 22*: List the customer number, surname, invoice number, invoice date and payment date for any case where the payment was received before the invoice was sent.

Here we have again a three-way join with an extra condition involving two fields. In SQL terms, the WHERE condition is:

WHERE PAYMENT.PMT–DATE < INVOICE.INV–DATE

In the Query Design grid, you just type the condition in the Criteria: cell as shown in Fig. 4.41. The output is shown in Fig. 4.42.

4.3 Exercises

Using the Access Query Design grid, and the test databases **accts.mdb** and **prod-_del.mdb** given in Appendix 1, develop and test queries to do the following. Copies of these databases can be downloaded via the Website **http://www.databasedesign.co.uk/book** if required.

Exercises 1 to 30 relate to the **accts.mdb** database.

1. List the customer number and balance of all customers.
2. List the customer number, city and balance of all London customers.
3. List all details of all customers, sorted in ascending order of city.
4. List all details of all customers not living in Leeds.
5. List all details of all customers living in neither London nor Leeds.
6. List all details of customers who either (a) live in London or (b) live outside London and have a balance exceeding £500.

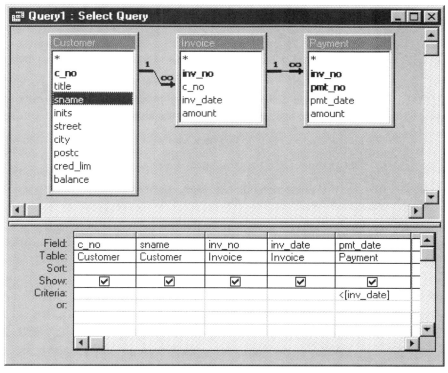

Fig. 4.41 The Query Design view for Query 22.

Fig. 4.42 The output from Query 22.

7. List all details of customers who either (a) live in London or (b) live outside London and have a balance exceeding £500, but not both (a) and (b).

8. List all details of all customers with a null credit limit.

9. List the customer number, surname, balance and credit limit of all customers whose balance exceeds their credit limit.

10. List the customer number, surname, balance and credit limit of all customers whose balance does not exceed their credit limit.

11. Explain why Mrs Williams does not appear in the output of either Query 7 or Query 8.

12. List the total balance of all customers.

13. List the total balance of all London customers.

14. List the total balance of customers in each city.

15. List the total balance of customers in each city, but only where that total is over £500.

16. List the total balance of customers in each city, but only where that total is over £500. List in descending order of total balance, i.e. highest total balance first.

17. List all customers who live near Mrs Williams. Use fuzzy matching on postcode.

18. List all details of all customers and all their invoices.

19. List the customer number, surname, city, invoice numbers and amounts of all customers.

20. List the customer number, surname, city, invoice numbers and amounts of all London customers but only list the invoice details where the invoice amount is greater than or equal to £20.

21. List all details of all customers and all their invoices (as in Query 18). Use an inner join.

22. List all details of all customers and all their invoices (as in Query 18). Use a left join.

23. Comment on the output from Query 21 and Query 22.

24. List all details of all customers and their invoices. Sort the output on descending order of invoice amount within ascending order of customer surname.

25. List all customer, invoice and payment details for each customer.

26. List all invoices and their payments. If an invoice has no payments, still list it.

27. List all invoices and their payments. If an invoice has no payments, don't list it.

28. List all payments and the invoices they're related to. Compare this query with Query 26.

29. List all invoices that have at least one payment.

30. List all invoices that have no payments.

Exercises 31 to 40 relate to the **prod_del.mdb** database.

31. List the product number and description of all products that need reordering, and show how many of each to reorder.

32. List all details of products that have been delivered.

33. List all details of products that have been delivered to customer 3.

34. List the product number and description of all products that have not been delivered.

35. List all details of products that have not been delivered.

36. List all details of products that have been delivered since 10 November 1999.

37. List all details of products that have been delivered in the last three days. Hint: Use the Now function.

38. For each product, list the product number, the product description, and the total delivery quantity.

39. For each product, list the percentage margin of quantity in stock over the minimum quantity.

40. List the total value of all the products in stock.

Late extra: modify Query 11 so that it uses the exclusive or and then modify the English version of the query so it's clear that it's the exclusive or that's being asked for. [Thanks to Hongbo Du from University of Buckingham].

Chapter **5**

Access query design using SQL – DDL and DML statements

In this chapter you will learn:

- how to design queries using the Access SQL view

- how Access SQL is divided into DDL and DML statements

- how to use all Access DDL statements

- how to use all Access DML statements except SELECT.

5.1 Introduction to SQL

In the previous chapter, we saw how to develop simple queries using a graphical method – the Access Query Design view. In this chapter and the next two, we describe in detail SQL – Structured Query Language. SQL allows you to retrieve data from the database and to update it. It also allows you to create and modify the design of database tables and create indexes to speed up certain database accesses. In most databases, including Access, SQL is the main method used to do this.

Although the Access Query Design view is a fast way of developing simple queries, and it is *possible* to develop very useful queries that way, there are definite advantages in learning SQL.

It is always useful to have an agreed language for communication of ideas in particular domains and for database queries, SQL is the agreed language. As a database application developer, you will often come across examples of SQL in Help and in textbooks and in other programmers' code.

Because SQL is the standard database language, you will find it not just in Access but also in other database management systems, such as SQL*Server, ORACLE, Sybase, INGRES etc. We present here a pretty comprehensive description of SQL. If you understand all the examples here, you will be justified in calling yourself something of an expert in SQL, not just in Access, but in most relational databases.

SQL can be used *interactively*, meaning that you type an SQL statement directly into Access and you get the results immediately, or it can be *embedded* in a Visual

Basic program. In this chapter and the next two, we concentrate on the interactive use of SQL. In later chapters, you will see SQL commands embedded in VB code wherever it is necessary to retrieve or update data from the database and then process it in code.

Interactive use of SQL is the easiest way to learn the language because you get the results back immediately on the screen. It is also a good idea to interactively develop SQL statements that are later going to become embedded in a Visual Basic program. That way you can test them thoroughly.

Why would we ever want to embed SQL statements in Visual Basic when we can use it interactively? Your clients, the users of the database, will not know SQL. The output from interactive SQL is also in a rather primitive form – just columns of data. They may want to perform a query as part of a more extensive process involving other queries, programs, inputs and reports. The VB code will tie all these processes together and relate them logically, probably in a menu system.

The SQL commands we cover here and in the next two chapters are:

● CREATE TABLE
● ALTER TABLE
● DROP TABLE
● CREATE INDEX
● DROP INDEX
● INSERT INTO
● UPDATE
● DELETE
● SELECT

All but SELECT are covered in this chapter. SELECT is covered in the next two chapters. It gets two chapters to itself because of its rich syntax and the fact that it's the most-used SQL command.

5.2 Versions of SQL: Jet and ANSI

SQL has evolved slightly and thus it exists in several versions. However, the variations are minor.

As we go through the examples in these three chapters, we note any differences between versions, paying particular attention to the variations within Access, but also noting where Access differs in its syntax from other SQL versions. Fortunately, these differences are rare.

The Microsoft Jet database engine is the core of Access and Visual Basic's data retrieval and storage features.

We shall speak of Jet databases and Access databases and mean the same thing. ANSI-89 is an agreed syntax standard for contemporary relational databases. ANSI stands for American National Standards Institute.

The following is an extract from the Access Help item *SQL, ANSI vs. Jet*:

> *The Microsoft Jet database engine SQL is generally ANSI-89 Level 1 compliant. However, certain ANSI SQL features aren't implemented in Microsoft Jet SQL. Conversely, Microsoft Jet SQL includes reserved words and features not supported in ANSI SQL.*

We recommend you read that Help page at some time. Also useful in Help is *Microsoft Jet database engine, reserved words*. That gives you a complete language definition of Jet SQL. Appendix 4 also gives a useful summary of SQL syntax.

5.3 Categories of SQL statement

Some database developers and references categorize SQL statements into three classes:

- DDL – Data Definition Language
- DCL – Data Control Language
- DML – Data Manipulation Language

DDL is used for defining the structure of the database and includes the SQL statements:

- CREATE TABLE is used to create database tables, defining their structure in terms of fields.
- ALTER TABLE is used to change the structure of a table, adding, removing or changing the length or type of fields.
- DROP TABLE is used for removing tables.
- CREATE INDEX is used to create indexes on one or more specified fields in a table.
- DROP INDEX is used for removing an index.

We saw in Chapter 3 how to create, amend and delete database tables and indexes using the GUI (Graphical User Interface) facilities of Access. This is the recommended way. However, some databases do not have these facilities and to comply closely with the ANSI standard, Jet includes DDL statements (commands) like CREATE TABLE, CREATE INDEX, DROP TABLE, DROP INDEX and ALTER TABLE.

Apart from standardization, the advantage of having these DDL SQL statements available is that they can be included in Visual Basic code. You could create a temporary table in the middle of an application run, process the data in it, and drop the table later.

DCL is used for controlling access to the database and covers SQL statements such as the following:

- GRANT and REVOKE concern security issues involving the granting and revoking of 'privileges' such as who can have access to which parts of the database and what type of access they can have.

- COMMIT and ROLLBACK are used in *transaction processing*, a style of database programming in which the program holds off the actual database update until a number of related and interdependent updates and queries (a transaction) have all been accepted. COMMIT means save the updates in the transaction; ROLLBACK means don't.

- LOCK is used in *concurrency control*, which allows a program to lock certain parts of the database until a transaction is committed.

In Jet databases (those Microsoft databases used in Access and VB) none of these SQL DCL commands exists. Security issues are dealt with not by SQL but in a similar way to networks, using workgroups, passwords and permissions, allowing both database and user-level security. Transaction processing, including commit, rollback and locking, is dealt with using the idea of a workspace and BeginTrans, CommitTrans and Rollback methods. Locking is dealt with by locking pages of the database using the LockEdits property.

DML is used for retrieving and updating the database records and includes the SQL statements:

- INSERT
- UPDATE
- DELETE
- SELECT

As mentioned above, we devote two separate chapters to the SELECT statement, because it has the richest syntax and the database application developer will spend more time on SELECT than on the other SQL commands.

We now consider the syntax of each of the SQL statements. For each statement, we give its syntax (the rules governing the grammar of the statement – what you can and can't put into it). We then discuss the meaning of the statement definition, and then go into examples of its use.

5.4 How we describe the syntax of SQL statements

First a word about how we shall describe the syntax of the various SQL statements used in this book. We use the same way of describing the syntax as is used in Access Help. The syntax of an SQL statement is the way the statements can be constructed.

Let's use the syntax of the CREATE TABLE command as an example.

The CREATE TABLE definition given in Section 5.5 is:

```
CREATE TABLE table
( field1 type [(size)] [NOT NULL] [index1]
[, field2 type [(size)] [NOT NULL] [index2]
[, . . . ]]
[, CONSTRAINT multifieldindex [, . . . ]])
```

In this definition:

`[ ]`
means 'optional'. For example `[index1]` means `index1` is optional.

`[ , . . . ]`
means 'and so on'. In this CREATE TABLE example, it means 'zero or more fields like the above'.

`[ , field2 type [(size)] [NOT NULL] [index2]`
`[ , . . . ]]`
means that this whole item – this whole set of fields in this case – is optional (because of the outer square brackets).

Anything in *italics* is something that you, the developer, have to put in – to give a value for.

In short, the definition of the CREATE TABLE statement given above is saying that all CREATE TABLE statements start with the words CREATE TABLE, followed by the table name. This is followed by one or more field definitions, each of which consists of a field name, a field type, an optional size, an optional NOT NULL clause, and an optional index. This is followed by an optional constraint clause which consists of the word CONSTRAINT followed by one or more multifield indexes. There is also a set of symbols used in defining *alternatives* in an SQL statement. In a later section in this chapter, the following definition appears:

```
CONSTRAINT name
{PRIMARY KEY | UNIQUE | NOT NULL |
   REFERENCES foreigntable [(foreignfield1, foreignfield2)]}
```

In this definition, the curly brackets and bars indicate *alternatives*. Just one should be picked from the list.

In general, the meaning of:

`{ A | B | C | D }`

is A *or* B *or* C *or* D.

5.5 CREATE TABLE

```
CREATE TABLE table
( field1 type [(size)] [NOT NULL] [index1]
[, field2 type [(size)] [NOT NULL] [index2]
[, . . . ]]
[, CONSTRAINT multifieldindex [, . . . ]])
```

Fig. 5.1 The syntax of the SQL CREATE TABLE statement.

Example1: Use a CREATE TABLE statement to create a Customer table.

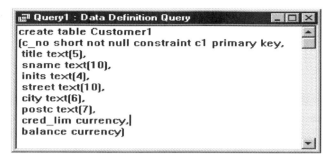

Query1 : Data Definition Query

```
create table Customer1
(c_no short not null constraint c1 primary key,
 title text[5],
 sname text[10],
 inits text[4],
 street text[10],
 city text[6],
 postc text[7],
 cred_lim currency,
 balance currency)
```

Fig. 5.2 CREATE TABLE statement for Example 1.

This CREATE TABLE statement was typed into the SQL view of the Queries tab of Access. This is one way to use the DDL commands – interactively using the SQL view. Just type them in and have them executed immediately. Figure 5.3 shows the Design view of the table created by this statement.

Customer1 : Table

Field Name	Data Type	Description
c_no	Number	
title	Text	
sname	Text	
inits	Text	
street	Text	
city	Text	
postc	Text	
cred_lim	Currency	
balance	Currency	

Field Properties

General | Lookup

Field Size	Integer
Format	
Decimal Places	Auto
Input Mask	
Caption	
Default Value	
Validation Rule	
Validation Text	
Required	Yes
Indexed	Yes (No Duplicates)

Fig. 5.3 The table created by the CREATE TABLE of Example 1.

The index created by the CREATE TABLE statement as shown in the Table Design view – View Indexes option is illustrated in Fig. 5.4.

If you want to produce a field of type Integer, you have to use SHORT in the CREATE TABLE statement. See Access Help *Equivalent ANSI SQL Data Types* for a full list of data type equivalences.

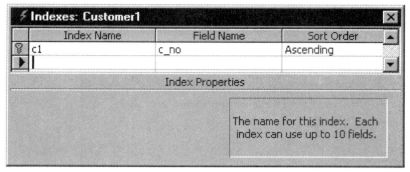

Fig. 5.4 The index created by the CREATE TABLE of Example 1.

If you want to embed your CREATE TABLE command into a Visual Basic program, you could use a program similar to that shown in Fig. 5.5.

```
Form_Form1 : Class Module

Command0                              Click

  Private Sub Command0_Click()
    Dim dbs As Database
    Set dbs = OpenDatabase("c:\My Documents\NewBook\Databases\Access97Jet3_5\accts.mdb")
    'Create a table containing customer data.
    x$ = "create table Customer1"
    x$ = x$ & "(c_no short not null constraint c1 primary key,"
    x$ = x$ & "title text(5),"
    x$ = x$ & "sname text(10),"
    x$ = x$ & "inits text(4),"
    x$ = x$ & "street text(10),"
    x$ = x$ & "city text(6),"
    x$ = x$ & "postc text(7),"
    x$ = x$ & "cred_lim currency,"
    x$ = x$ & "balance currency)"
    dbs.Execute x$
    dbs.Close
  End Sub
```

Fig. 5.5 Using a CREATE TABLE statement embedded in Visual Basic.

In later chapters, we discuss the embedding of SQL DDL and DML statements in VB code, in both Visual Basic and Access modules. As you can see, the SQL code to create the table is identical.

We just have to open the database, put the SQL into the string variable x$, and then execute the embedded SQL using the VB Execute method.

We now have to discuss in a little more detail the syntax of the CREATE TABLE statement given in Fig. 5.1, in particular *index1* and *index2*.

In the CREATE TABLE and ALTER TABLE statements, an index is a type of CONSTRAINT. There are two types of constraint: a single-field constraint and a multiple-field constraint. Example 1 uses a single-field constraint to establish field c_no as the primary key. The syntax of single-field constraints is given in Fig. 5.6.

```
CONSTRAINT name
{PRIMARY KEY | UNIQUE | NOT NULL |
  REFERENCES foreigntable [(foreignfield1, foreignfield2)]}
```

Fig. 5.6 Syntax of the single-field constraint used with CREATE TABLE and ALTER TABLE statements.

In Fig. 5.6, the curly brackets and bars indicate alternatives. In Example 1 we used a single-field constraint to specify field c_no as a primary key. This implies that it must be unique and not null, as with all primary keys. We could have specified one or more other fields UNIQUE or NOT NULL if required, by specifying an appropriate single-field constraint for each of them.

> *Example 2:* Use a CREATE TABLE statement to create an INVOICE table linked to the CUSTOMER table.

In Fig. 5.6, *foreigntable* is the table on the 'one' side of a 1:N relationship. So if we want, in SQL code, to create a relationship between two tables at runtime (instead of at table design time, which is when it would normally be done) we use the REFERENCES clause. Consider the example in Fig. 5.7.

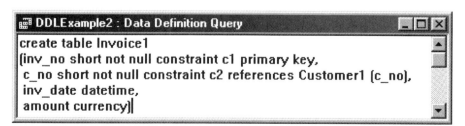

Fig. 5.7 Creating the INVOICE1 table which 'references' the CUSTOMER1 table.

INVOICE1.C_NO is the foreign key in INVOICE1 which *references* CUSTOMER1.C_NO, which is the primary key in the *foreigntable* CUSTOMER1.

The resulting relationship diagram is shown in Fig. 5.8. Note the new table INVOICE1 and the relationship to CUSTOMER1.

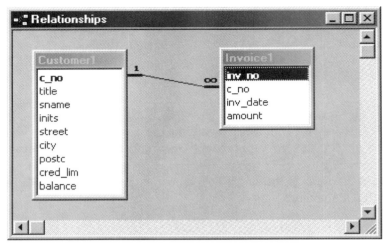

Fig. 5.8 INVOICE1 and the relationship to CUSTOMER1 were created by the CREATE TABLE SQL statement of Fig. 5.7.

Note that the relationship created is, by default, one in which referential integrity is enforced, no cascading update or delete is specified, and join type 1 is specified, as shown in Fig. 5.9, which was produced by left-clicking on the relationship shown in Fig. 5.8.

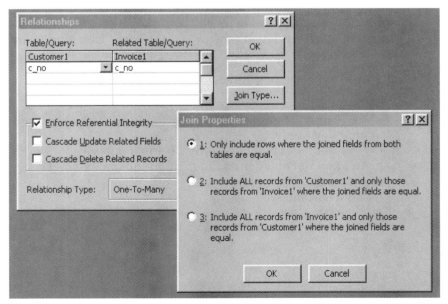

Fig. 5.9 The default properties of the relationship produced by the SQL CREATE TABLE statement of Fig. 5.7.

> *Example 3:* Create a PAYMENT table linked to INVOICE.

Here we are going to create a new table PAYMENT1 and link it to INVOICE1, using another SQL CREATE TABLE statement. However, since the PAYMENT1 table has a compound primary key consisting of INV_NO *with* PMT_NO, the second form of the CONSTRAINT clause for a CREATE TABLE or ALTER statement (shown in Fig. 5.10) has to be used.

```
    CONSTRAINT name
    {PRIMARY KEY (primary1[, primary2 [, ... ]]) |
    UNIQUE (unique1[, unique2 [, ... ]]) |
    NOT NULL (notnull1[, notnull2 [, ... ]]) |
    FOREIGN KEY (ref1[, ref2 [, ... ]]) REFERENCES
 foreigntable [(foreignfield1 [, foreignfield2 [, ... ]])]}
```

Fig. 5.10 The 'multiple-field constraint' version of the CONSTRAINT clause.

Note that with the multiple-field version of the CONSTRAINT clause, all the constraints go at the end of the CREATE TABLE (or ALTER TABLE) statement. See Fig. 5.11.

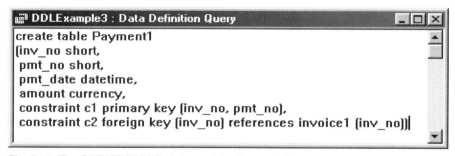

Fig. 5.11 The CREATE TABLE statement for Example 3.

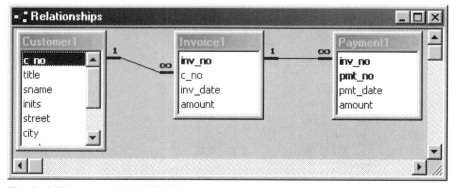

Fig. 5.12 The new table PAYMENT1 and relationship to INVOICE1.

5.6 ALTER TABLE

The SQL DDL (Data Definition Language) statement ALTER TABLE is used for altering the structure of a database table in any of the following ways:

- ADD COLUMN and DROP COLUMN
- ADD CONSTRAINT: Add a single or multiple-field index
- DROP CONSTRAINT: Delete a multiple-field index.

The syntax of the ALTER TABLE statement is shown in Fig. 5.13.

```
ALTER TABLE table {ADD {COLUMN field type[(size)]
[NOT NULL] [CONSTRAINT index] |
CONSTRAINT multifieldindex} |
DROP {COLUMN field I CONSTRAINT indexname} }
```

Fig. 5.13 The syntax of the SQL ALTER TABLE statement.

Example 4: Add a 'phone' field to the CUSTOMER1 table.

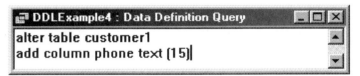

Fig. 5.14 Adding a new field to the CUSTOMER1 table.

Field Name	Data Type	Description
c_no	Number	
title	Text	
sname	Text	
inits	Text	
street	Text	
city	Text	
postc	Text	
cred_lim	Currency	
balance	Currency	
phone	Text	

Field Properties

General | Lookup

Field Size	Integer
Format	
Decimal Places	Auto
Input Mask	
Caption	
Default Value	
Validation Rule	
Validation Text	
Required	Yes
Indexed	Yes (No Duplicates)

The data type determines the kind of values that users can store in the field. Press F1 for help on data types.

Fig. 5.15 Note the new field CUSTOMER1.PHONE.

> *Example 5:* Remove the 'phone' field from table CUSTOMER1.

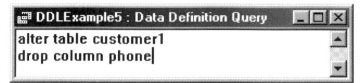

Fig. 5.16 Deleting the CUSTOMER1.PHONE field.

> *Example 6:* Remove a relationship between CUSTOMER1 and INVOICE1.

The only types of index you can add and remove using ALTER TABLE are primary keys and foreign keys. See the CREATE INDEX statement below for indexing on *any* field or fields.

In this example, we are going to create and then remove a relationship c3 between CUSTOMER1 and INVOICE1. The way to do this in an SQL ALTER TABLE statement is to use the DROP CONSTRAINT clause.

First, we show the Access Relationship window with all relationships between CUSTOMER1 and INVOICE1 removed (Fig. 5.17).

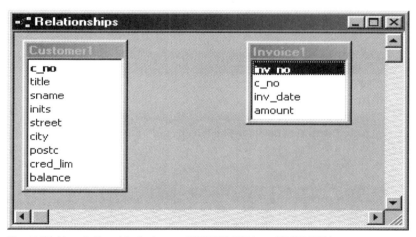

Fig. 5.17 No relationship between CUSTOMER1 and INVOICE1.

In the following sequence, we first add and then drop a 'foreign key references' constraint between these tables. Note that this could be done much more easily in the Relationship window itself at design time. Using SQL commands to do these DDL (Data Definition Language) tasks is appropriate only on those rare occasions when tables and constraints need to be modified at runtime.

We then add a relationship using the ALTER table statement shown in Fig. 5.18. In Fig. 5.20, we remove the relationship using ALTER TABLE with a DROP CON-STRAINT clause.

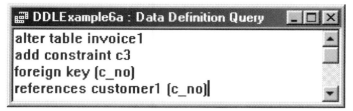

Fig. 5.18 The SQL to create the relationship between CUSTOMER1 and INVOICE1.

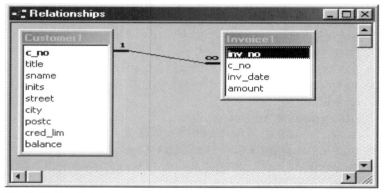

Fig. 5.19 The Relationship window shows that the relationship has been created.

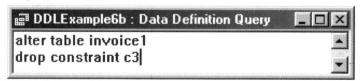

Fig. 5.20 The SQL to delete the relationship.

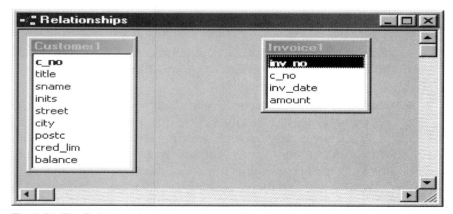

Fig. 5.21 The Relationship window showing that the relationship has been deleted.

```
Form_frmCreateAndDropRelationship1 : Class Module                          _ □ ×
Command0                              ▼   Click                            ▼
    Private Sub Command0_Click()
        'Open the database
        Dim dbs As Database
        Set dbs = OpenDatabase("c:\My Documents\NewBook\Databases\Access97Jet3_5\accts.mdb")
        'Create the relationship:
        x$ = "alter table invoice1 "
        x$ = x$ & "add constraint c3 "
        x$ = x$ & "foreign key (c_no) "
        x$ = x$ & "references customer1 (c_no)"
        dbs.Execute x$
        'Coding using this temporary relationship would go here.
        '
        '
        '
        'Drop the relationship:
        dbs.Execute "alter table invoice1 drop constraint c3"
        'Close the database:
        dbs.Close
    End Sub
```

Fig. 5.22 How the ALTER table commands would appear as embedded SQL in Visual Basic code.

Figure 5.22 is a reminder that DDL and other SQL commands can be embedded in a VB or other 'host' program. One of the advantages of embedding your SQL is that various validation tasks, such as identifying the user and checking the current state of the database, can be performed before and between the SQL commands.

5.7 DROP TABLE

Dropping a table means removing it from the database.

```
DROP TABLE table
```

Fig. 5.23 The syntax of the DROP TABLE SQL statement.

Example 7: Remove the INVOICE1 table.

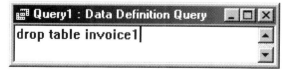

Fig. 5.24 Dropping table INVOICE1.

Note that if a table is involved in a one–many relationship with another table, you will have to delete the relationship first, otherwise you will get the error message shown in Fig. 5.25. One way round this is to use an ALTER TABLE statement as discussed above.

The problem in this example is that there is a relationship between INVOICE1 and PAYMENT1 which specifies a referential integrity constraint.

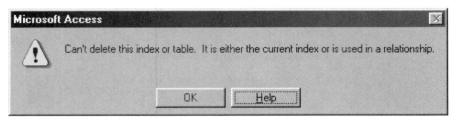

Fig. 5.25 The error you get if you break a referential integrity constraint.

We illustrate this in the following sequence.
Suppose we have the familiar database schema as shown in Fig. 5.26.

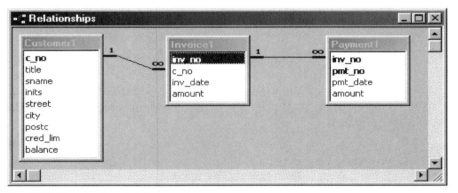

Fig. 5.26 The starting database schema.

Both relationships have a referential integrity constraint specified. Figure 5.27 shows this for the relationship between INVOICE1 and PAYMENT1.

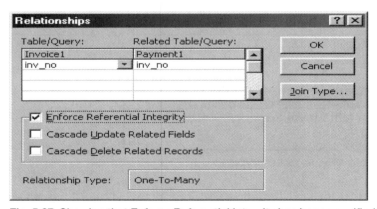

Fig. 5.27 Showing that Enforce Referential Integrity has been specified.

We now attempt to drop the INVOICE1 table using the DROP TABLE statement shown in Fig. 5.24 and get the error mentioned above (Fig. 5.25).

The referential integrity constraint shown in Fig. 5.27 means that every record in the PAYMENT1 table must have an 'owning' record in INVOICE1. (See Chapter 4.) This would be impossible if the INVOICE1 table was deleted, so the Jet Engine of Access prevents it happening.

If we first delete the relationship (Fig. 5.28), then it is possible to delete the INVOICE1 table.

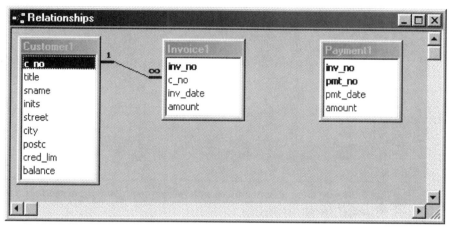

Fig. 5.28 The INVOICE1–PAYMENT1 relationship has been removed.

This relationship can be removed either by using the ALTER TABLE statement (see above) or by just clicking it in the Relationship window and pressing the Delete key. Running the DROP TABLE statement (Fig. 5.24) now works and INVOICE1 is removed (Fig. 5.29).

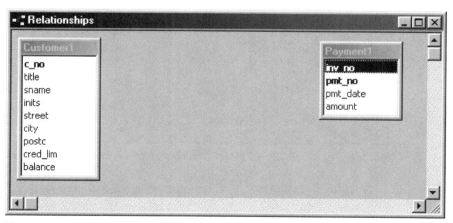

Fig. 5.29 The INVOICE1 table has been successfully dropped.

Notice that the relationship between CUSTOMER1 and INVOICE1 was not preventing INVOICE1 being dropped. When INVOICE1 *was* dropped, the relationship between CUSTOMER1 and INVOICE1 went with it. A referential integrity constraint only prevents the table in the 'one' side the relationship being dropped.

If there had been no referential integrity constraint specified in the INVOICE1–PAYMENT1 relationship, there would have been no error, as Figs 5.30 and 5.31 confirm.

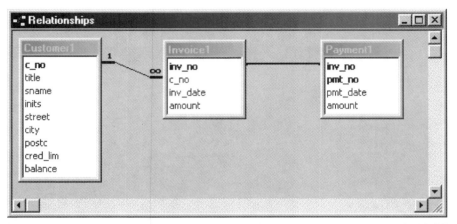

Fig. 5.30 The original schema but with referential integrity removed from the INVOICE1–PAYMENT1 relationship.

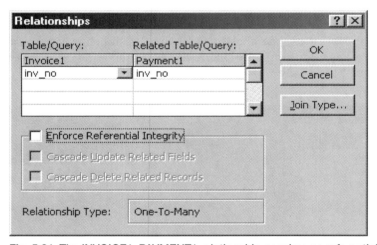

Fig. 5.31 The INVOICE1–PAYMENT1 relationship now has no referential integrity set.

Running the DROP TABLE statement (Fig. 5.24) for the INVOICE1 table successfully drops the table, now that the referential integrity constraint has been removed.

5.8 CREATE INDEX

While it is possible to create indexes using CREATE TABLE and ALTER TABLE, these indexes are only of the type concerned with primary and foreign keys. In many circumstances, particularly where you will often want to search a large database table (one containing several hundred records or more, typically) on a non-primary-key field or collection of fields, specifying an index on that field or those fields will be likely to speed up the search. The larger the table, the more likely it is that an extra index is desirable.

You should use extra indexes sparingly, though. Indexes themselves take up space on the database, and whenever a record is inserted or deleted from the table, an entry in the index has to be inserted or deleted too, which may actually *slow down* insertions and deletions.

In a truly relational database all SQL queries will work with or without indexes, according to rule 2 and rule 8 of *E.F. Codd's rules for relational databases* [See, for example, References, Books, 1]. It is worth noting that indexes are just about speed and nothing else. This is true of Jet databases, except that specifying a field or group of fields as a primary key will automatically create an index called, by default, 'PrimaryKey'.

You can think of an index as a lookup table in which the left column contains the value of the 'key', i.e. the indexed field or set of fields, and the right column shows where on the disk records with this value of the field are to be found. The index will help find those records quickly. The syntax of the SQL DDL CREATE INDEX statement is given in Fig. 5.32.

```
CREATE [ UNIQUE ] INDEX index
ON table (field [ASC|DESC][, field [ASC|DESC], ... ])
[WITH { PRIMARY | DISALLOW NULL | IGNORE NULL }]
```

Fig. 5.32 The syntax of the CREATE INDEX statement.

- field is the name of the field or fields which are going to form the index 'key'.
- UNIQUE specifies that no two records in the table should have the same value of the key.
- PRIMARY specifies that this index will form a primary key for the table. If you specify PRIMARY, then UNIQUE is unnecessary.
- DISALLOW NULL specifies that no record in the table can have a NULL value of the key.
- IGNORE NULL specifies that records in the table *can* have a NULL value of the key; such records won't be included in the index.
- ASC|DESC specifies whether the key is held in ascending or descending order in the index.

> *Example 8*: Create an index on the surname field of the CUSTOMER1 table.

One reason for wanting to create this index may be that there is a frequent requirement to search the CUSTOMER1 table on the surname field SNAME. As a customer I may have forgotten my customer number and the computer operator will want to quickly locate all the 'Carter' records, display them on the screen, and pick the right one out on the basis of, say, initials or address. If CUSTOMER1 is a large table, the SELECT query (see the SELECT chapter) that finds the records will perform considerably faster if there is an index on CUSTOMER1, because rather than having to scan the *entire table* to pick up all the 'Carter' records, it can look in the index and locate them all 'immediately'. More precisely, the index will show where on the disk they all are without having to sequentially inspect every record on the database table to see if its SNAME field has the value 'Carter'.

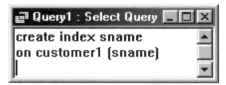

Fig. 5.33 CREATE INDEX statement for Example 8.

There is no UNIQUE clause, since there could be several customers with the same surname. There is no PRIMARY clause because CUSTOMER1 already has a primary key and anyway that would also require uniqueness. We haven't specified DISALLOW NULL because we want it to be possible for records to temporarily have a null value in the surname field (for some reason). Figure 5.34 shows that the only index on the CUSTOMER1 table before the CREATE INDEX command above was run was the primary key index. (You can view indexes by clicking View/Indexes on the Access menu.)

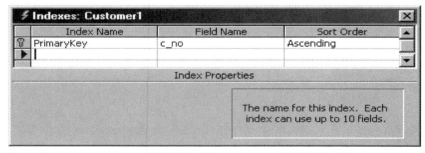

Fig. 5.34 No index on CUSTOMER1.SNAME *before* CREATE INDEX.

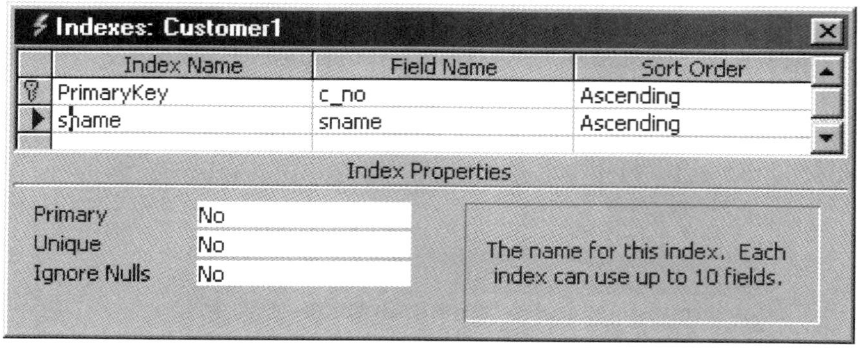

Fig. 5.35 The new index created by the CREATE INDEX command.

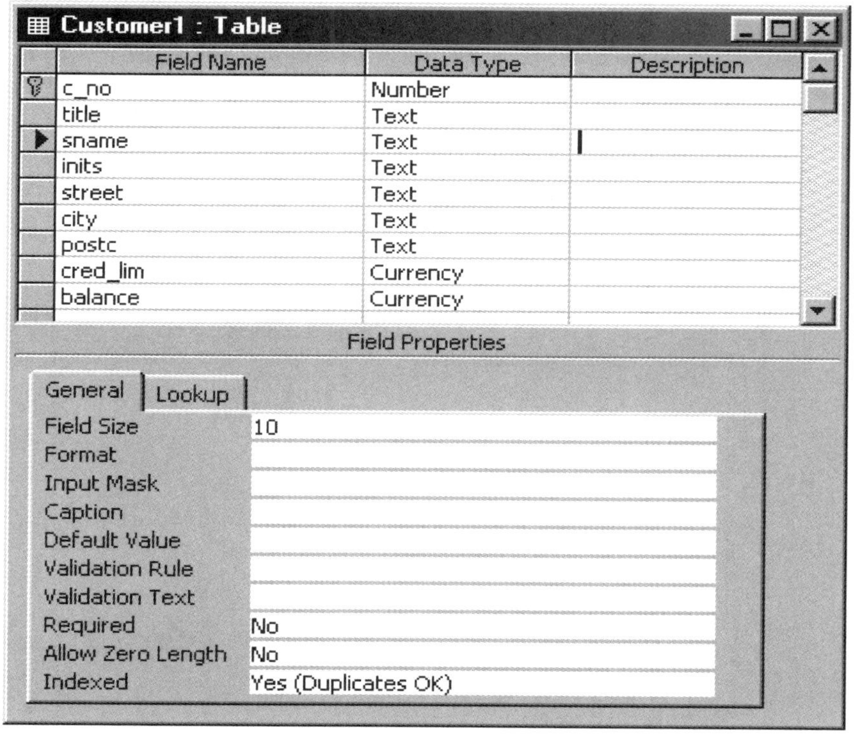

Fig. 5.36 The Table design view for CUSTOMER1 confirms the existence of the new index.

Given the fact that there are only six records in the test database for the CUS-TOMER table, there is of course no need for such an index. (With six customers there is probably no need for a database!)

However, at what point should you create an index on a search field? There is no simple answer, because there are so many variables, including frequency of search on the indexed field, acceptable delay, overhead of slower updates etc. One author-ity says that as a rough rule of thumb, you shouldn't use an index on any table containing fewer than 500 records.

> *Example 9:* Create an index on the surname and initials fields of the CUSTOMER1 table. Specify that neither field should be null.

This index (Fig. 5.37) would be used to speed up searches on the *combination* of the surname and initials fields.

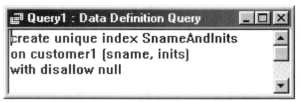

Fig. 5.37 The CREATE INDEX statement.

We have specified UNIQUE so that no two customers can be entered with the same surname and initials combination. Some way of distinguishing similarly named customers would have to be employed, such as adding extra initials.

We have also specified WITH DISALLOW NULL, which will ensure that both fields are required to have a non-null value.

Field Name	Data Type	Description
c_no	Number	
title	Text	
sname	Text	
inits	Text	
street	Text	
city	Text	
postc	Text	
cred_lim	Currency	
balance	Currency	

Field Properties

General | Lookup

Field Size	10
Format	
Input Mask	
Caption	
Default Value	
Validation Rule	
Validation Text	
Required	No
Allow Zero Length	No
Indexed	Yes (Duplicates OK)

Fig. 5.38 The CUSTOMER1 table design *before* the CREATE INDEX command was executed.

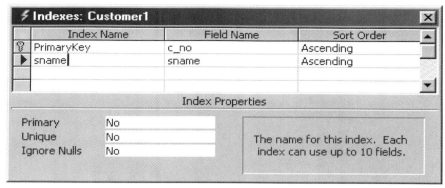

Fig. 5.39 The indexes on CUSTOMER1 *before* the CREATE INDEX command was executed.

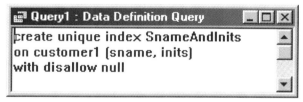

Fig. 5.40 The CREATE INDEX command.

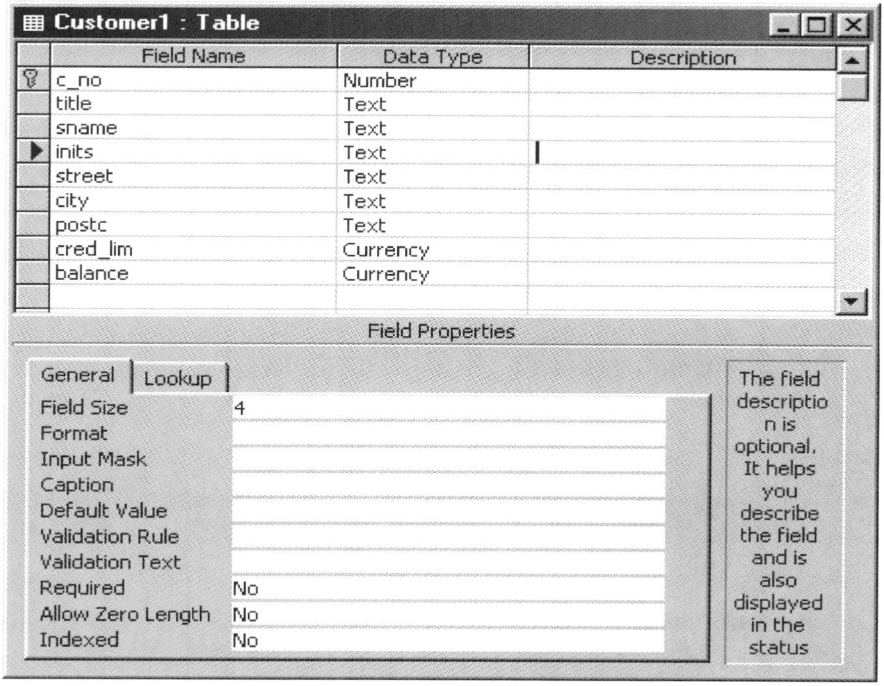

Fig. 5.41 The CUSTOMER1 table design *after* the CREATE INDEX command was executed.

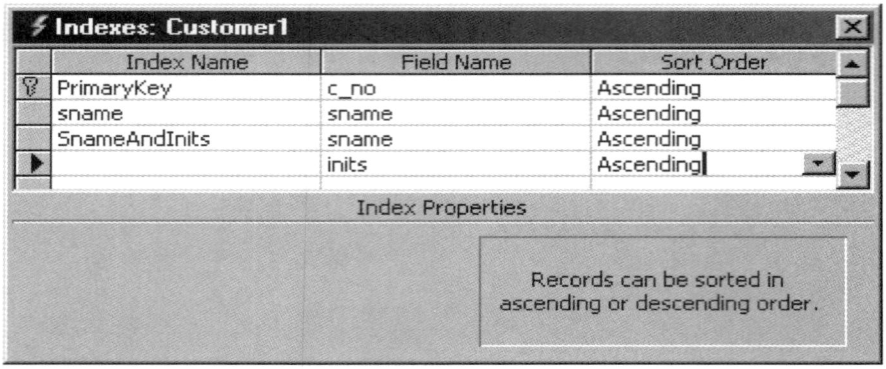

Fig. 5.42 The new index has been added.

Note that although the new index 'SnameAndInits' has been added, the CUS-TOMER1 table design window shows no index on the INITS field or the SNAME field *individually* (Fig. 5.41). The index is on the *combination* of fields.

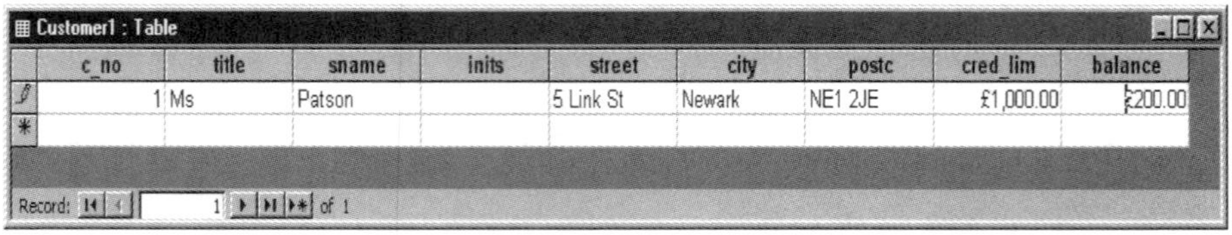

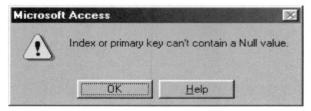

Fig. 5.43 An attempt at adding a new record with null INITS to CUSTOMER1.

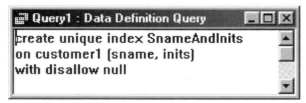

Fig. 5.44 The Access error message that results.

Attempting to add a new CUSTOMER1 record (Fig. 5.43) results in an error message (Fig. 5.44). This is because of the DISALLOW NULL clause (Fig. 5.45). The index mustn't contain a Null value.

```
Query1 : Data Definition Query
create unique index SnameAndInits
on customer1 (sname, inits)
with disallow null
```

Fig. 5.45 The CREATE INDEX command.

Example 10: Create an index on INVOICE1.C_NO to speed up the joining of CUSTOMER1 and INVOICE1 records.

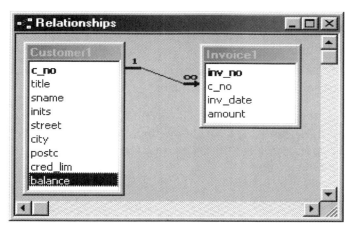

Fig. 5.46 The relationship between CUSTOMER1 and INVOICE1.

To speed up joins between records in the CUSTOMER1 and INVOICE1 tables based on the relationship shown (Fig. 5.46), where CUSTOMER1.C_NO = INVOICE1.C_NO, it may be advisable to add an index on INVOICE1.C_NO.

A join of a CUSTOMER1 record to all of its associated INVOICE1 records involves searching the entire INVOICE1 table for records with a matching value of C_NO.

If there is an index on INVOICE1.C_NO, the search will be quicker because the index will show immediately where in the INVOICE1 table all of the records with the matching value of C_NO are. The read/write heads of the disk drive will be sent immediately to the correct places on the disk to get the matching INVOICE1 records, skipping over all those non-matching records in between. If INVOICE1 contains a large number of records, the index will thus speed up the join procedure.

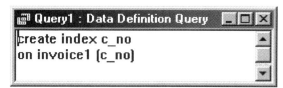

Fig. 5.47 The CREATE INDEX statement for Example 10.

The new index created by this CREATE INDEX command is shown in Fig. 5.48. Note that the primary key index c1 would not have been of any use in speeding up the join because it retrieves records in order of INV_NO.

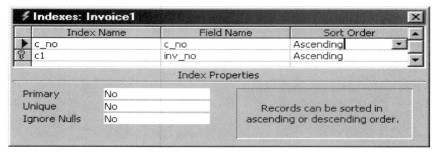

Fig. 5.48 The new index 'c–no' has been added.

Note that you can call the indexes anything you want. The primary key index, created in an earlier ALTER TABLE command, was called there 'c1' in a CONSTRAINT clause. We called the index on C–NO 'c–no', but any other meaningful name would have done.

5.9 DROP INDEX

In attempts to speed up database processing, many indexes may have been added to tables. It is worthwhile periodically to try *removing* various indexes and measuring the effects on various procedures that use the tables. You might even notice speed *improvements* for some update procedures, because the removed indexes won't have to be updated for each table update. Removing an index in SQL is performed by the DROP INDEX command.

```
DROP INDEX index ON table
```

Fig. 5.49 The syntax of the SQL DROP INDEX statement.

> *Example 11*: Remove the 'c–no' index from the INVOICE1 table.

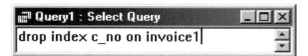

Fig. 5.50 The DROP INDEX command for Example 11.

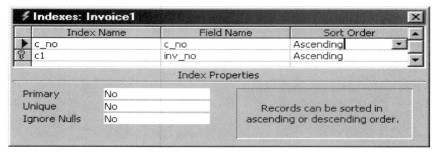

Fig. 5.51 The 'c–no' index has been removed.

5.10 INSERT INTO

The previous SQL commands (CREATE TABLE, ALTER TABLE, DROP TABLE, CRE-ATE INDEX and DROP INDEX) were all DDL (Data Definition Language) commands, so called because they define the *structure* of the database. The rest of the SQL commands in this chapter are DML (Data Manipulation Language) commands, so called because they determine the *content* of the database, the field values in the records. INSERT INTO is a DML command. It is used to insert new records into a database table (or even into a query – see later).

There are two forms of INSERT INTO. The first is shown in Fig. 5.52 and the second in Fig. 5.53.

```
INSERT INTO target [(field1[, field2[, . . . ]])]
VALUES (value1[, value2[, . . . ])
```

Fig. 5.52 The 'Single-record append' form of the SQL INSERT INTO command.

```
INSERT INTO target [IN externaldatabase]
[(field1[, field2[, . . . ]])]
SELECT [source.]field1[, field2[, . . . ]
FROM tableexpression
```

Fig. 5.53 The 'Multiple-record append' form of the SQL INSERT INTO command.

The first form of the INSERT INTO command is called by Microsoft the 'Single-record append' form. The effect of such a statement being executed is to add a single record into `target`.

The second form of the INSERT INTO command is called by Microsoft the 'Multiple-record append' form. The effect of such a statement being executed is to add several records into `target`. First the SELECT query is run to retrieve some records from `tableexpression`. These records are then appended to `target`. Here, 'append' means to add to the end of a table (or query).

An INSERT INTO may fail if it breaks any of the database integrity rules, such as trying to duplicate a primary key value, or breaking referential integrity, or putting a NULL into a mandatory field.

Let's consider the first form of the INSERT INTO statement first (the Single-record append form). In this form of INSERT INTO:

● `target` is the table or query that the record will be appended to;
● `field1`, `field2` etc. are the names of the fields to append data to;
● `value1`, `value2` etc. are the values to be placed into the fields.

As you can see, the field list is optional. If you leave it out, make sure you add the right number of values.

It is worth reminding ourselves here that there are various alternatives to the SQL INSERT INTO in Access and Visual Basic. You could use the Access Datasheet view and just type the record in there. Or you could use an Access Form (see Chapter 8). Or you could use a VB Data Control (see Chapter 9) or a VB DAO (Data Access Object – see Chapter 10) or ADO (ActiveX Data Object – see Chapter 11) with an AddNew method.

But it's worth getting to know the INSERT INTO approach, because it's standard SQL and can be used with DBMSs other than Jet.

Example 12: Add a new record to the CUSTOMER1 table.

We shall use the first form of the INSERT INTO command here.

```
Query1 : Append Query                              _ □ ×
insert into customer1
values
(2,'Ms','Cryle','E.L.','3 Low St','Dover','DO2 9CE',1000,51.22)
```

Fig. 5.54 The INSERT INTO command for Example 12.

c_no	title	sname	inits	street	city	postc	cred_lim	balance
1	Ms	Patson	M.	5 Link St	Newark	NE1 2JE	£1,000.00	£200.00

Record: 2 of 2

Fig. 5.55 The CUSTOMER1 table *before* the INSERT INTO.

c_no	title	sname	inits	street	city	postc	cred_lim	balance
1	Ms	Patson	M.	5 Link St	Newark	NE1 2JE	£1,000.00	£200.00
2	Ms	Cryle	E.L.	3 Low St	Dover	DO2 9CE	£1,000.00	£51.22

Record: 1 of 2

Fig. 5.56 The CUSTOMER1 table *after* the INSERT INTO.

Example 13: Add a new record to the CUSTOMER1 table. Show all the field named in the INSERT INTO command.

```
Query1 : Append Query                              _ □ ×
insert into customer1
(c_no, title, sname, inits, street, city, postc, cred_lim, balance)
values
(3, 'Mrs','Carter','S.Q.','1 High Rd','London','E18 3RJ',1500,780.11)
```

Fig. 5.57 The INSERT INTO command for Example 13.

The CUSTOMER1 table has had the new record appended, as is shown in Fig. 5.58.

c_no	title	sname	inits	street	city	postc	cred_lim	balance
1 Ms		Patson	M.	5 Link St	Newark	NE1 2JE	£1,000.00	£200.00
2 Ms		Cryle	E.L.	3 Low St	Dover	DO2 9CE	£1,000.00	£51.22
3 Mrs		Carter	S.Q.	1 High Rd	London	E18 3RJ	£1,500.00	£780.11

Record: 1 of 3

Fig. 5.58 The CUSTOMER1 table after executing the INSERT INTO command of Example 13.

Example 14: *Add a new record to the CUSTOMER1 table. Leave the CRED_LIM field null.*

You can leave a field null by simply not mentioning it in the field list, as in Fig. 5.59. Make sure the field list and the values match up.

Query1 : Append Query
```
insert into customer1
(c_no, title, sname, inits, street, city, postc, balance)
values
(4, 'Mr','Carter','J.R.','1 High Rd','London','E18 3RJ',14.96)
```

Fig. 5.59 Adding a CUSTOMER1 record with a null value for CRED_LIM.

c_no	title	sname	inits	street	city	postc	cred_lim	balance
1 Ms		Patson	M.	5 Link St	Newark	NE1 2JE	£1,000.00	£200.00
2 Ms		Cryle	E.L.	3 Low St	Dover	DO2 9CE	£1,000.00	£51.22
3 Mrs		Carter	S.Q.	1 High Rd	London	E18 3RJ	£1,500.00	£780.11
4 Mr		Carter	J.R.	1 High Rd	London	E18 3RJ		£14.96

Record: 1 of 4

Fig. 5.60 The record with the null CRED_LIM has been added.

You can expect to get an error if you attempt to insert a record with a duplicate primary key value.

Example 15: *Attempt to add a CUSTOMER1 record with a duplicate primary key value.*

DMLExample15 : Append Query
```
insert into customer1
(c_no, title, sname, inits, street, city, postc, cred_lim, balance )
values
(4,'Mr','Gulson','J','5 West St','Leeds','LE8 4RZ',1000,500)
```

Fig. 5.61 An attempt to add a record with a duplicate c_no value.

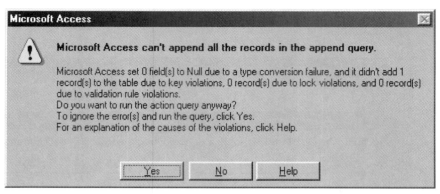

Fig. 5.62 The error message resulting from attempting to add a record with a duplicate key value.

As we can see from Fig. 5.60, a CUSTOMER1 record with a c_no value of 4 already exists, and c_no is the primary key. Duplicate values of the primary key are not allowed in any table, and Fig. 5.62 shows the error message that results. If the 'Yes' command button on the message box is clicked, no record is added anyway.

Example 16: Add an INVOICE and PAYMENT record using a single INSERT INTO command.

As we saw in the syntax statement for the INSERT INTO command (Figs 5.52, 5.53), `target`, the place you are going to insert the record data into, can be not just a table, but a query too, meaning really a view of one or more tables, in effect a virtual table that contains 'bits' of one or more 'real' tables.

In some DBMSs, these virtual tables are called VIEWs, and there is an associated SQL command called CREATE VIEW to create them. Jet SQL dispenses with the VIEW but does the equivalent thing by calling such stored views *queries* and equivalently *query definitions*. Such queries are created using the SQL SELECT statement. So for the Microsoft Jet database and all its documentation across all the products that use it, we have the idea of storing data into a query. It just means storing data into a virtual data structure defined by the SELECT statement that defined the query. The SQL SELECT statement is designed to retrieve (i.e. query) a database and display what it has retrieved. This set of data is also known as a *recordset* in Jet and a *cursor* in some other databases.

We cover the SELECT statement in detail in the next chapter, but to illustrate the insertion of data into a virtual table defined by a query, we shall jump ahead a little and use a SELECT statement to define a query here and then use the INSERT INTO command to store data into it. (We could have used a stored query defined using the Access Query design view instead.)

Let's start with a reminder of the database schema we are working with (Fig. 5.63).

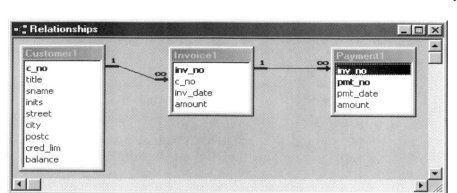

Fig. 5.63 The familiar Customer–Invoice–Payment schema.

We want to insert a new invoice and payment into INVOICE1 and PAYMENT1 in one operation – as if they were a single table. We could do it separately, inserting the invoice first then the payment, in two separate INSERT INTO statements. But we want to illustrate INSERT INTO into a query.

Suppose we already have a query called DMLExample16a (in the real world it would probably be called something more meaningful, such as 'InvoicePayment'), and that this query is defined as in Fig. 5.64.

Fig. 5.64 The stored query.

See the SELECT section in this chapter for details of the meaning of this query. This query is not only a way of *retrieving* related data from both the INVOICE1 and PAYMENT1 tables together; it also presents a view of a virtual record containing both sets of fields. See Fig. 5.65.

Invoice1.inv_no	c_no	inv_date	Invoice1.amount	Payment1.inv_no	pmt_no	pmt_date	Payment1.amount

Record: [buttons] 1 of 1

Fig. 5.65 The result of running the SQL query of Fig. 5.64.

In this particular case, we note that there are not yet any records in the INVOICE1 and PAYMENT1 tables. We can insert a pair of related records into these two tables in one INSERT INTO command.

Fig. 5.66 gives the INSERT INTO command to create such a pair of INVOICE1 and PAYMENT1 records in one go.

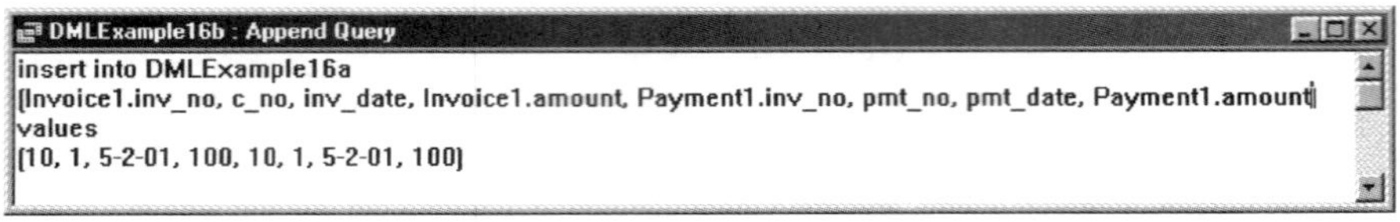

Fig. 5.66 The INSERT INTO command of Example 16.

When it is run, this INSERT INTO command inserts these two records. This can be shown by re-running the query and looking at the output again, as in Fig. 5.67.

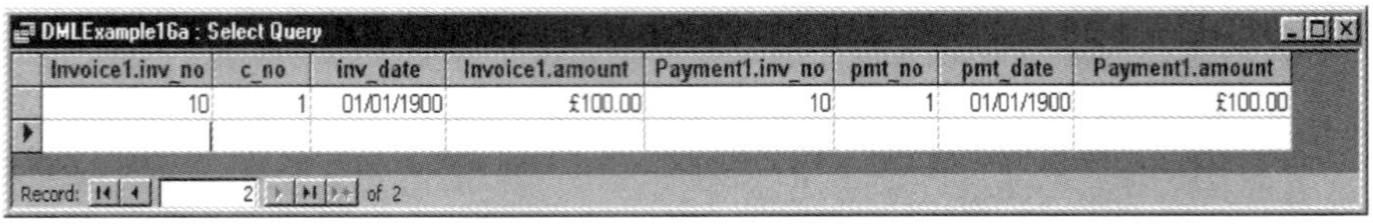

Fig. 5.67 The result of running the INSERT INTO command of Fig. 5.66 and then inspecting the result using the SELECT query of Fig. 5.64.

The two separate records can be seen (separately) in Figs 5.68 and 5.69.

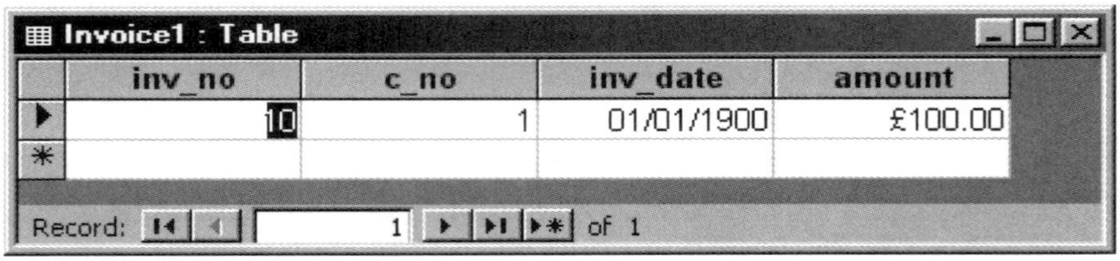

Fig. 5.68 The INVOICE1 table after the INSERT INTO command of Fig. 5.66 has been run.

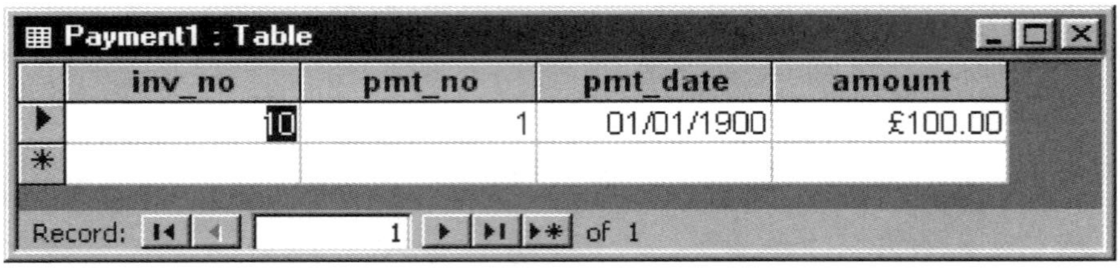

Fig. 5.69 The PAYMENT1 table after the INSERT INTO command of Fig. 5.66 has been run.

We can see that the two records have been inserted using the INSERT INTO command where the `target`, i.e. the place to put the data, is a join query previously defined. This stored query presents a convenient 'view' of the database, suitable for such updates.

We now consider the second form of the SQL INSERT INTO command, which is reproduced in Fig. 5.70.

```
INSERT INTO target [IN externaldatabase]
[(field1[, field2[, ... ]])]
SELECT [source.]field3[, field4[, ... ]
FROM tableexpression
```

Fig. 5.70 The 'Multiple-record append' form of the SQL INSERT INTO command.

In this second form of the INSERT INTO statement (the 'Multiple-records append') form:

- `target` is the table or query that the record will be appended to;
- `externaldatabase` can be either an ODBC database, or a Paradox, Foxpro, Excel, Access, Lotus 1–2–3, HTML external database, or text (see Chapter 11);
- `field1`, `field2` etc. are the names of the fields in `target` to append data to;
- `source` is the name of the table or query to copy records from;
- `field3`, `field4` etc. are the names of the fields in `source` to copy data from;
- `tableexpression` is the name of the table or query to copy records from. Unlike `source`, it may contain further navigational SQL clauses.

This 'Multiple-record append' form of the INSERT INTO command differs from the first form ('Single-record append') of the command in that there is a SELECT statement in it.

The SELECT clause within the INSERT INTO is used to retrieve a set of records from some other part of the current database, defined in `tableexpression`, which can then be inserted into target, which is a table or query to put the data into.

You might wonder why we would want to copy the same data from one part of the database to another. Surely this would result in data duplication! Well, one reason is that a program may want to create a temporary table, combining data from several different tables, which presents a simpler 'view' of the data – a view that makes the program easier to write, simplifying the processing required. The same effect could be obtained, however, by creating a stored SELECT query (a 'view', as above) and updating that.

Another reason is that you might be in the process of redesigning parts of your database, which may already contain data. You want to copy data from the old tables into the new ones.

Another reason for using this second form of the INSERT INTO command, with its SELECT clause, is that you might want to 'upload' (i.e. copy) data from your database to some external database (`externaldatabase` in Fig. 5.70).

> *Example 17*: Copy all of the records for customers from table CUSTOMER to table CUSTOMER1.

You might have noticed that the tables CUSTOMER and CUSTOMER1 have the same structure (as do INVOICE and INVOICE1 and PAYMENT and PAYMENT1).

Rather than continually adding and deleting and modifying the original tables, we have created three 'clones' to experiment with, as in this example.

Before we design and run this INSERT INTO command, let's inspect the current contents of the CUSTOMER and CUSTOMER1 tables. See Figs 5.71 and 5.72.

c_no	title	sname	inits	street	city	postc	cred_lim	balance
1	Mr	Sallaway	G.R.	12 Fax Rd	London	WC1	£1,000.00	£42.56
2	Miss	Lauri	P.	5 Dux St	London	N1	£500.00	£200.00
3	Mr	Jackson	R.	2 Lux Ave	Leeds	LE1 2AB	£500.00	£510.00
4	Mr	Dziduch	M.	31 Low St	Dover	DO2 9CD	£100.00	£149.23
5	Ms	Woods	S.Q.	17 Nax Rd	London	E18 4WW	£1,000.00	£250.10
6	Mrs	Williams	C.	41 Cax St	Dover	DO2 8WD		£412.21
0							£0.00	£0.00

Record: 1 of 6

Fig. 5.71 The CUSTOMER table.

c_no	title	sname	inits	street	city	postc	cred_lim	balance

Record: 1 of 1

Fig. 5.72 The CUSTOMER1 table *before* the INSERT INTO.

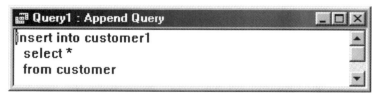

Query1 : Append Query

insert into customer1
  select *
  from customer

Fig. 5.73 The INSERT INTO command for Example 17.

As can be seen from Fig. 5.74, the records from CUSTOMER have been appended to CUSTOMER1.

c_no	title	sname	inits	street	city	postc	cred_lim	balance
1	Mr	Sallaway	G.R.	12 Fax Rd	London	WC1	£1,000.00	£42.56
2	Miss	Lauri	P.	5 Dux St	London	N1	£500.00	£200.00
3	Mr	Jackson	R.	2 Lux Ave	Leeds	LE1 2AB	£500.00	£510.00
4	Mr	Dziduch	M.	31 Low St	Dover	DO2 9CD	£100.00	£149.23
5	Ms	Woods	S.Q.	17 Nax Rd	London	E18 4WW	£1,000.00	£250.10
6	Mrs	Williams	C.	41 Cax St	Dover	DO2 8WD		£412.21

Record: 1 of 6

Fig. 5.74 The CUSTOMER1 table *after* the INSERT INTO.

We didn't specify the optional field1, field2 ... in this INSERT INTO because the structure of CUSTOMER and CUSTOMER1 are identical and we wanted all of every record copied across. The '*' in the SELECT clause means 'all fields'.

> *Example 18: Copy the C_NO, SNAME, INITS and CITY fields from the CUS-TOMER table to the CUSTOMER1 table. Do this for just the London customers.*

To demonstrate this example, we shall start by deleting all of the records from CUSTOMER1.

The SQL INSERT INTO statement is shown in Fig. 5.75.

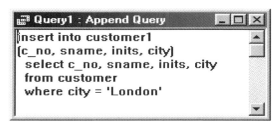

Fig. 5.75 The SQL INSERT INTO command for Example 18.

c_no	title	sname	inits	street	city	postc	cred_lim	balance
1		Sallaway	G.R.		London			
2		Lauri	P.		London			
5		Woods	S.Q.		London			

Record: 1 of 3

Fig. 5.76 The CUSTOMER1 table after executing the INSERT INTO command of Fig. 5.75.

Notice that only the fields and records specified in the SELECT clause have been copied into the CUSTOMER1 table.

> *Example 19: Copy the London customer numbers, surnames and invoice details from the CUSTOMER and INVOICE tables of the Jet accts.mdb database into the CUSDETAILS table of the Jet accts1.mdb database.*

Here we are going to demonstrate the IN externaldatabase clause of the Multiple-record INSERT INTO statement (Fig. 5.70). To do this we have created another database *accts1.mdb* to copy the data from the CUSTOMER and INVOICE tables of our database *accts.mdb*.

The schema design of the relevant parts of accts.mdb and accts1.mdb are shown in Figs 5.77 and 5.78. Notice that the source and target schema are different.

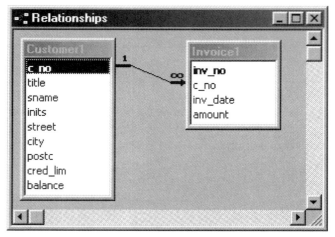

Fig. 5.77 The relevant part of the accts.mdb schema.

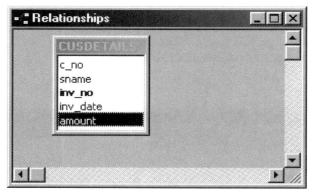

Fig. 5.78 The relevant part of the accts1.mdb database.

There are considerable differences between the source and destination database schema. The field names are the same but are in different tables in different databases. The primary key in CUSDETAILS is INV_NO.

The data in the CUSTOMER1 and INVOICE1 tables of accts.mdb and the CUS-DETAILS table of accts1.mdb are shown in Figs 5.79, 5.80 and 5.81 respectively.

c_no	title	sname	inits	street	city	postc	cred_lim	balance
1	Mr	Sallaway	G.R.	12 Fax Rd	London	WC1	£1,000.00	£42.56
2	Miss	Lauri	P.	5 Dux St	London	N1	£500.00	£200.00
3	Mr	Jackson	R.	2 Lux Ave	Leeds	LE1 2AB	£500.00	£510.00
4	Mr	Dziduch	M.	31 Low St	Dover	DO2 9CD	£100.00	£149.23
5	Ms	Woods	S.Q.	17 Nax Rd	London	E18 4WW	£1,000.00	£250.10
6	Mrs	Williams	C.	41 Cax St	Dover	DO2 8WD		£412.21
0							£0.00	£0.00

Fig. 5.79 The data in the CUSTOMER table of accts.mdb.

Invoice : Table

	inv_no	c_no	inv_date	amount
▶	940	1	05/12/99	£26.20
	1002	4	12/01/00	£149.23
	1003	1	12/01/00	£16.26
	1004	2	14/01/00	£200.00
	1005	3	20/01/00	£510.00
	1006	5	21/01/00	£250.10
	1017	6	22/01/00	£412.21
*	0	0		£0.00

Record: |◀| ◀ | 1 | ▶ | ▶| | ▶* | of 7

Fig. 5.80 The data in the INVOICE table of accts.mdb.

cusdetails : Table

	c_no	sname	inv_no	inv_date	amount
▶	0		0		£0.00

Record: |◀| ◀ | 1 | ▶ | ▶| | ▶* | of 1

Fig. 5.81 The data in the CUSDETAILS table of accts1.mdb *before* running the INSERT INTO command of Fig. 5.82.

Query1 : Append Query

```
Insert into cusdetails
in accts1.mdb
  select customer.c_no, sname, inv_no, inv_date, amount
  from customer, invoice
  where customer.c_no = invoice.c_no
  and city = 'London'
```

Fig. 5.82 The INSERT INTO command of Example 19.

Figures 5.82 and 5.83 show the INSERT INTO command and the resulting data in the CUSDETAILS table in the external database accts1.mdb.

cusdetails : Table

	c_no	sname	inv_no	inv_date	amount
▶	1	Sallaway	940	05/12/99	£26.20
	1	Sallaway	1003	12/01/00	£16.26
	2	Lauri	1004	14/01/00	£200.00
	5	Woods	1006	21/01/00	£250.10
*	0		0		£0.00

Record: |◀| ◀ | 1 | ▶ | ▶| | ▶* | of 4

Fig. 5.83 Data has been copied from the accts.mdb database to the accts1.mdb database.

> *Example 20:* Show how to implement an INSERT INTO to insert a record into the CUSTOMER1 table using embedded SQL.

We now show how a simple SQL INSERT INTO can be implemented when it's embedded in Visual Basic code. The details of embedded SQL and all the VB statements that go with it are given in Chapter 8 onwards, but we show a simple example here for reference purposes. The VB environment we have chosen in this example is VBA in Access, but the code would be identical in the Visual Basic development environment.

Suppose we have the table and input form shown in Figs 5.84 and 5.85.

c_no	title	sname	inits	street	city	postc	cred_lim	balance
1		Sallaway	G.R.		London			
2		Lauri	P.		London			
5		Woods	S.Q.		London			

Record: 14 ◄ | 4 | ► | ►I | ►* | of 4

Fig. 5.84 The data in CUSTOMER1 before embedded INSERT INTO.

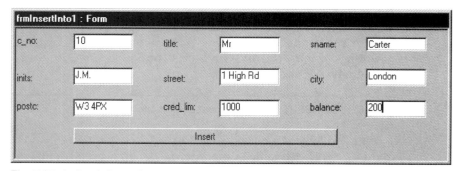

Fig. 5.85 A simple input form for inputting CUSTOMER1 records.

The form is a very simple input form designed in Access. We are not using here Access's ability to automatically link a form to a recordset and generate its own code. (Access forms are covered in Chapter 7.) The form we are using here and its controls are 'Unbound', that is, it is just a simple form with nine text boxes, nine labels and a command button. We 'run' the form and type into it the data shown in Fig. 5.85. After hitting the 'Insert' command button, the CUSTOMER1 table now contains the new record, as shown in Fig. 5.86.

Fig. 5.86 The new record has been added to the CUSTOMER1 table.

Fig. 5.87 The SQL INSERT INTO statement embedded in VBA code.

The Visual Basic code containing the INSERT INTO statement is shown in Fig. 5.87. Note that the INSERT INTO statement is built up into the string variable x$, and it is then executed using the Execute method. (Visual Basic code in Access or Excel or Word is called VBA – Visual Basic for Applications.) This type of code is explained in Chapters 9 to 12.

5.11 UPDATE

The purpose of the SQL DML UPDATE statement is to change the values in fields of existing records.

The syntax of the UPDATE statement is shown in Fig. 5.88.

```
UPDATE table
SET newvalue
WHERE criteria
```

Fig. 5.88 Syntax of the SQL UPDATE statement.

In the UPDATE command:

- `table` is the database table whose records' field values you want to change;
- `newvalue` is the new value you want the field to take;
- `criteria` are the tests to be applied to decide which records will have their fields' values modified.

Example 21: Increase the credit limit of all London customers by 5 per cent.

The CUSTOMER table before the update is shown in Fig. 5.89.

c_no	title	sname	inits	street	city	postc	cred_lim	balance
1	Mr	Sallaway	G.R.	12 Fax Rd	London	WC1	£1,000.00	£42.56
2	Miss	Lauri	P.	5 Dux St	London	N1	£500.00	£200.00
3	Mr	Jackson	R.	2 Lux Ave	Leeds	LE1 2AB	£500.00	£510.00
4	Mr	Dziduch	M.	31 Low St	Dover	DO2 9CD	£100.00	£149.23
5	Ms	Woods	S.Q.	17 Nax Rd	London	E18 4WW	£1,000.00	£250.10
6	Mrs	Williams	C.	41 Cax St	Dover	DO2 8WD		£412.21
0							£0.00	£0.00

Record: |◄ | ◄ | 1 | ► | ►| | ►* | of 6

Fig. 5.89 The CUSTOMER table before the UPDATE.

The UPDATE statement is shown in Fig. 5.90.

```
UPDATE customer
SET cred_lim = cred_lim * 1.05
WHERE city = 'London';
```

Fig. 5.90 The SQL UPDATE command.

Figure 5.91 shows the CUSTOMER table after the update command has been executed. Note that all of the London customers' credit limits have been increased by 5 per cent.

c_no	title	sname	inits	street	city	postc	cred_lim	balance
1	Mr	Sallaway	G.R.	12 Fax Rd	London	WC1	£1,050.00	£42.56
2	Miss	Lauri	P.	5 Dux St	London	N1	£525.00	£200.00
3	Mr	Jackson	R.	2 Lux Ave	Leeds	LE1 2AB	£500.00	£510.00
4	Mr	Dziduch	M.	31 Low St	Dover	DO2 9CD	£100.00	£149.23
5	Ms	Woods	S.Q.	17 Nax Rd	London	E18 4WW	£1,050.00	£250.10
6	Mrs	Williams	C.	41 Cax St	Dover	DO2 8WD		£412.21
0							£0.00	£0.00

Record: 1 of 6

Fig. 5.91 The CUSTOMER table after running the SQL UPDATE statement of Example 21.

Example 22: Increase the credit limit of customers 2, 3 and 6 by £1000.

Suppose the CUSTOMER table is still as shown in Fig. 5.89, and that we apply to it the SQL UPDATE statement shown in Fig. 5.92.

```
DMLExample22 : Update Query
UPDATE customer
SET cred_lim = cred_lim + 1000
WHERE c_no in (2, 3, 6);
```

Fig. 5.92 The UPDATE statement for Example 22.

The result on the CUSTOMER table is shown in Fig. 5.93.

Note that the credit limit for customers 2 and 3 has been updated, but for customer 6 it is still NULL. This is because null values can't be involved in arithmetic or logical operations.

c_no	title	sname	inits	street	city	postc	cred_lim	balance
1	Mr	Sallaway	G.R.	12 Fax Rd	London	WC1	£1,000.00	£42.56
2	Miss	Lauri	P.	5 Dux St	London	N1	£1,500.00	£200.00
3	Mr	Jackson	R.	2 Lux Ave	Leeds	LE1 2AB	£1,500.00	£510.00
4	Mr	Dziduch	M.	31 Low St	Dover	DO2 9CD	£100.00	£149.23
5	Ms	Woods	S.Q.	17 Nax Rd	London	E18 4WW	£1,000.00	£250.10
6	Mrs	Williams	C.	41 Cax St	Dover	DO2 8WD		£412.21
0							£0.00	£0.00

Record: 1 of 6

Fig. 5.93 The CUSTOMER table after executing the UPDATE command.

> *Example 23*: Set the credit limit of all customers who made a payment in January 2000 to £2100.

This update to the CUSTOMER table involves accessing the PAYMENT table to see whether the given customer has made a payment in the period specified. The only link from CUSTOMER to PAYMENT is via the INVOICE table. PAYMENT records don't contain C_NO (see Fig. 5.94). This UPDATE statement will use subqueries (covered in detail in Chapter 7) to make the link. Note that we are updating only the CUSTOMER table, but it's necessary to access INVOICE and PAYMENT to determine which CUSTOMER records to update.

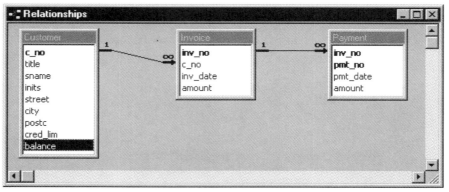

Fig. 5.94 The schema diagram of the part of the accts.mdb database relevant to Example 23.

```
UPDATE customer
SET cred_lim = 2100
WHERE c_no in
 (select c_no
  from invoice
  where inv_no in
   (select inv_no
    from payment
    where pmt_date
    between
    #1-1-00#
    and
    #31-1-00#));
```

Fig. 5.95 The SQL UPDATE statement for Example 23.

The *before* and *after* shots of the CUSTOMER table are shown in Figs 5.96 and 5.97.

Fig. 5.96 The CUSTOMER table *before* the update of Fig. 5.95.

Fig. 5.97 The CUSTOMER table *after* the update of Fig. 5.95.

It can be seen from Figs 5.98 and 5.99 that the correct CUSTOMER records have been updated.

Fig. 5.98 The INVOICE table.

Fig. 5.99 The PAYMENT table.

> *Example 24*: *Change customer number 5's name to 'Mrs Carter'.*

This example shows two fields being updated in a single SQL UPDATE command. See Fig. 5.100.

```
DMLExample24 : Update Query        _ □ ×
UPDATE customer
SET title = 'Mrs',
sname = 'Carter'
WHERE c_no = 5;
```

Fig. 5.100 Updating two fields in a single UPDATE command.

> *Example 25*: *Decrease every invoice amount of London customers by 5 per cent.*

This example shows that a stored query can be updated. We are going to update a query based on a join of the CUSTOMER table and the INVOICE table. The state of the CUSTOMER and INVOICE tables *before* the update is shown in Figs 5.101 and 5.102.

	c_no	title	sname	inits	street	city	postc	cred_lim	balance
▶	1	Mr	Sallaway	G.R.	12 Fax Rd	London	WC1	£1,000.00	£42.56
	2	Miss	Lauri	P.	5 Dux St	London	N1	£500.00	£200.00
	3	Mr	Jackson	R.	2 Lux Ave	Leeds	LE1 2AB	£500.00	£510.00
	4	Mr	Dziduch	M.	31 Low St	Dover	DO2 9CD	£100.00	£149.23
	5	Ms	Woods	S.Q.	17 Nax Rd	London	E18 4WW	£1,000.00	£250.10
	6	Mrs	Williams	C.	41 Cax St	Dover	DO2 8WD		£412.21
*	0							£0.00	£0.00

Record: ◄◄ ◄ 1 ► ►◄ ►* of 6

Fig. 5.101 The original contents of the CUSTOMER table.

First, we create a stored SQL query (DMLExample25a), which is an inner join of CUSTOMER and INVOICE for just London customers. The SQL for the creation of this stored query is shown in Fig. 5.103. Joins are covered in the chapter on the SQL SELECT statement. Running this query before the update shows what data is involved. See Fig. 5.104.

Next, we create the UPDATE statement itself, as in Fig. 5.105. Notice that in the top line, DMLExample25a is the name we gave to the stored query of Figs 5.103 and 5.104.

Running this UPDATE command has the effect of updating all the London invoice amounts in the desired way. This can be seen both by re-running the SELECT query (Fig. 5.106) and by listing out the INVOICE 'base' table (Fig. 5.107). Notice that only the invoice amounts of invoices of London customers have been affected.

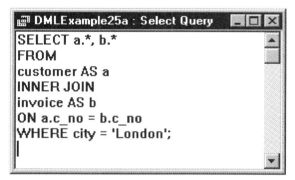

Fig. 5.102 The original contents of the INVOICE table.

```
DMLExample25a : Select Query
SELECT a.*, b.*
FROM
customer AS a
INNER JOIN
invoice AS b
ON a.c_no = b.c_no
WHERE city = 'London';
```

Fig. 5.103 The SQL SELECT statement that creates (is) the stored query.

a.c_no	title	sname	inits	street	city	postc	cred_lim	balance	inv_no	b.c_no	inv_date	amount
1	Mr	Sallaway	G.R.	12 Fax Rd	London	WC1	£1,000.00	£42.56	940	1	05/12/99	£26.20
1	Mr	Sallaway	G.R.	12 Fax Rd	London	WC1	£1,000.00	£42.56	1003	1	12/01/00	£16.26
2	Miss	Lauri	P.	5 Dux St	London	N1	£500.00	£200.00	1004	2	14/01/00	£200.00
5	Ms	Woods	S.Q.	17 Nax Rd	London	E18 4WW	£1,000.00	£250.10	1006	5	21/01/00	£250.10

Record: 1 of 4

Fig. 5.104 The data retrieved from the database by the query of Fig. 5.103.

```
DMLExample25b : Update Query
UPDATE DMLExample25a
SET amount = amount * 0.95;
```

Fig. 5.105 The SQL UPDATE statement that updates the query.

Fig. 5.106 The effect of running the SQL UPDATE on the stored query data.

Fig. 5.107 The effect of running the SQL UPDATE on the INVOICE base table.

This example demonstrates that it is possible to update a base table or tables by updating a relevant query. The point of doing it in this example is that the query defined which invoices we wanted to update. The relevant invoices were updated in the INVOICE table. CUSTOMER records were unaffected.

It is worth making a few notes about this process of updating base tables (tables that are actually stored on the database), via a stored query. Some DBMSs use the term *view* to represent the view of parts of a database observed or revealed through a stored query.

The terminology used with Jet databases, the kind native to Access and Visual Basic, calls these views *queries* or *stored queries*. The data represented by these stored queries (Figs 5.103 and 5.104) is thought of as a virtual table. 'View' is a good word for it, as you are viewing the data as if it were an actual table, oriented to the task you have in mind for it.

In most DBMSs there are restrictions on the extent to which you are allowed to update base tables via views. Some are more restrictive than others. In one DBMS, for example, there is a restriction that you can only update views that are based on a single table.

This is not so in Jet, as this example shows.

Example 26: *Demonstrate cascade update.*

'Cascade update' means the process of updating matching foreign key values when the value of a primary key changes.

Consider the relationship between CUSTOMER and INVOICE (Fig. 5.108).

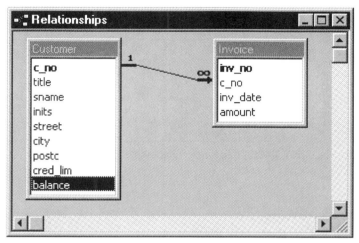

Fig. 5.108 The relationship between CUSTOMER and INVOICE.

By right-clicking on the relationship line we can show the properties of the relationship (Fig. 5.109).

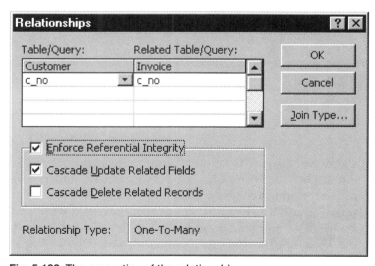

Fig. 5.109 The properties of the relationship.

In Fig. 5.109 we can see that Cascade Update has been opted for at database design time. (See the second checkbox.)

This means that if we change the value of the primary key field CUS in the CUSTOMER table, then the corresponding C_NO in the INVOICE table should change correspondingly.

c_no	title	sname	inits	street	city	postc	cred_lim	balance
1	Mr	Sallaway	G.R.	12 Fax Rd	London	WC1	£1,000.00	£42.56
2	Miss	Lauri	P.	5 Dux St	London	N1	£500.00	£200.00
3	Mr	Jackson	R.	2 Lux Ave	Leeds	LE1 2AB	£500.00	£510.00
4	Mr	Dziduch	M.	31 Low St	Dover	DO2 9CD	£100.00	£149.23
5	Ms	Woods	S.Q.	17 Nax Rd	London	E18 4WW	£1,000.00	£250.10
6	Mrs	Williams	C.	41 Cax St	Dover	DO2 8WD		£412.21
0							£0.00	£0.00

Record: 1 of 6

Fig. 5.110 The CUSTOMER table before changing Sallaway's C_NO.

inv_no	c_no	inv_date	amount
940	1	05/12/99	£26.20
1002	4	12/01/00	£149.23
1003	1	12/01/00	£16.26
1004	2	14/01/00	£200.00
1005	3	20/01/00	£510.00
1006	5	21/01/00	£250.10
1017	6	22/01/00	£412.21
0	0		£0.00

Record: 1 of 7

Fig. 5.111 The INVOICE table before changing Sallaway's C_NO.

Let's change Sallaway's customer number from 1 to 100. If Cascade Update works, we should see both of his invoices, invoice numbers 940 and 1003, have their customer number change to 100 too.

In Figs 5.110 and 5.111 we see the states of the CUSTOMER and INVOICE tables before the update command is executed.

Fig. 5.112 shows the UPDATE command. Note that the line following the 1 is just the cursor and can be ignored.

When the UPDATE command is run, CUSTOMER.C_NO changes to 100 as expected, and the Cascade Update constraint has automatically updated the two corresponding INVOICE.C_NO values, i.e. for invoices 940 and 1003. See Figs 5.113 and Fig. 5.114.

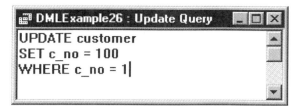

Fig. 5.112 The UPDATE command.

	c_no	title	sname	inits	street	city	postc	cred_lim	balance
▶	2	Miss	Lauri	P.	5 Dux St	London	N1	£500.00	£200.00
	3	Mr	Jackson	R.	2 Lux Ave	Leeds	LE1 2AB	£500.00	£510.00
	4	Mr	Dziduch	M.	31 Low St	Dover	DO2 9CD	£100.00	£149.23
	5	Ms	Woods	S.Q.	17 Nax Rd	London	E18 4WW	£1,000.00	£250.10
	6	Mrs	Williams	C.	41 Cax St	Dover	DO2 8WD		£412.21
	100	Mr	Sallaway	G.R.	12 Fax Rd	London	WC1	£1,000.00	£42.56
*	0							£0.00	£0.00

Record: ◄◄ ◄ [1   ] ► ►◄ ►* of 6

Fig. 5.113 The UPDATE has changed Sallaway's C_NO to 100.

	inv_no	c_no	inv_date	amount
▶	940	100	05/12/99	£26.20
	1002	4	12/01/00	£149.23
	1003	100	12/01/00	£16.26
	1004	2	14/01/00	£200.00
	1005	3	20/01/00	£510.00
	1006	5	21/01/00	£250.10
	1017	6	22/01/00	£412.21
*	0	0		£0.00

Record: ◄◄ ◄ [1   ] ► ►◄ ►* of 7

Fig. 5.114 The UPDATE has changed Sallaway's invoices' C_NOs to 100 too.

5.12 DELETE

The SQL DML command DELETE is used for deleting one or more rows (records) from a database table. The syntax of the DELETE command is shown in Fig. 5.115.

```
DELETE
FROM table
WHERE criteria
```

Fig. 5.115 The syntax of the SQL DML DELETE statement.

- `table` is the database table from which the records are to be removed.
- `criteria` are the tests performed to decide which records in the table will be removed.

The WHERE clause is the same as that used in the SQL SELECT statement, as covered in the next chapter.

Note that it is not necessary to mention any field names in the DELETE statement, since entire records are removed. Note also that when a record is 'deleted', it is still physically present on the disk storage medium; it is just *marked* as deleted. The surrounding records are not reorganized to take up the space until the database is *compacted*. But having deleted a record you won't be able to undelete that record and see it again.

Example 27: Delete invoice 1002.

Before the delete, table INVOICE1 contains the records shown in Fig. 5.116.

Invoice1 : Table

inv_no	c_no	inv_date	amount
940	1	05/12/99	£26.20
1002	4	12/01/00	£149.23
1003	1	12/01/00	£16.26
1004	2	14/01/00	£200.00
1005	3	20/01/00	£510.00
1006	5	21/01/00	£250.10
1017	6	22/01/00	412.21

Record: 7 of 7

Fig. 5.116 The INVOICE1 table *before* the delete of Example 27.

The SQL for this delete query is shown in Fig. 5.117.

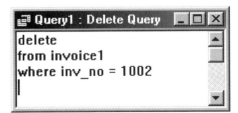

```
Query1 : Delete Query
delete
from invoice1
where inv_no = 1002
```

Fig. 5.117 The DELETE statement for Example 27.

The INVOICE1 table *after* the delete query of Fig. 5.117 is shown in Fig. 5.118. Note that the record for invoice number 1002 has been deleted.

Note that although it is being called a query, the DELETE command, along with all of the other DDL and DML commands in this chapter, is not really a query in the pure sense. The only real query is the SELECT.

Still on a terminological note, SQL 'statements' are really commands. However, this is the terminology in use.

inv_no	c_no	inv_date	amount
940	1	05/12/99	£26.20
1003	1	12/01/00	£16.26
1004	2	14/01/00	£200.00
1005	3	20/01/00	£510.00
1006	5	21/01/00	£250.10
1017	6	22/01/00	412.21

Invoice1 : Table — Record: 6 of 6

Fig. 5.118 The INVOICE1 table *after* the delete of Example 27.

Example 28: Delete all invoices for the first two weeks of January 2000.

This query demonstrates the use of a BETWEEN in the WHERE clause of a DELETE command.

Suppose the INVOICE1 table *before* the delete is as in Fig. 5.116. The SQL for this deletion is as shown in Fig. 5.119.

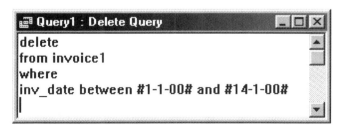

Query1 : Delete Query

```
delete
from invoice1
where
inv_date between #1-1-00# and #14-1-00#
```

Fig. 5.119 The DELETE statement for Example 28.

The INVOICE1 table is as shown in Fig. 5.120 *after* the deletion of Fig. 5.119 has occurred.

inv_no	c_no	inv_date	amount
940	1	05/12/99	£26.20
1005	3	20/01/00	£510.00
1006	5	21/01/00	£250.10
1017	6	22/01/00	412.21

Invoice1 : Table — Record: 4 of 4

Fig. 5.120 The INVOICE1 table *after* the DELETE of Fig. 5.119.

Example 29: Demonstrate Cascade Delete by deleting the customer record for customer number 1.

In this delete query, we are going to demonstrate the cascade delete effect. Customer number 1 has two invoices, invoice number 940 and invoice number 1003. Invoice number 940 has two payments, payment number 2 and payment number 3. We shall modify the relationship between CUSTOMER1 and INVOICE1, and the relationship between INVOICE1 and PAYMENT1, so that cascade delete is specified in each. We shall then delete the record for customer number 1 and both invoices and both payments will be automatically deleted.

In Fig. 5.121 we show the relationship diagram involving the CUSTOMER1, INVOICE1 and PAYMENT1 tables. Figures 5.122 and 5.123 show that Cascade Delete is in force for both of the relationships between these three tables.

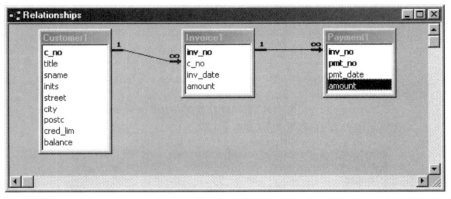

Fig. 5.121 The Relationship diagram for the CUSTOMER1, INVOICE1 and PAYMENT1 tables.

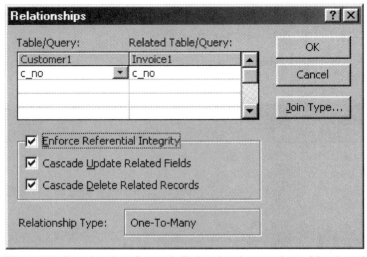

Fig. 5.122 Showing that Cascade Delete has been selected for the relationship between the CUSTOMER1 and INVOICE1 tables.

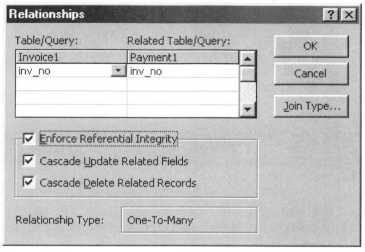

Fig. 5.123 Showing that Cascade Delete has been selected for the relationship between the INVOICE1 and PAYMENT1 tables.

Customer1 : Table

	c_no	title	sname	inits	street	city	postc	cred_lim	balance
▶	1	Mr	Sallaway	G.R.	12 Fax Rd	London	WC1	£1,000.00	£16.26
	2	Miss	Lauri	P.	5 Dux St	London	N1	£500.00	£200.00
	3	Mr	Jackson	R.	2 Lux Ave	Leeds	LE1 2AB	£500.00	£510.00
	4	Mr	Dziduch	M.	31 Low St	Dover	DO2 9CD	£100.00	£149.23
	5	Ms	Woods	S.Q.	17 Nax Rd	London	E18 4WW	£1,000.00	£250.10
	6	Mrs	Williams	C.	41 Cax St	Dover	DO2 8WD		£412.21
*									

Record: ◄◄ ◄ 1 ► ►► ►* of 6

Fig. 5.124 The CUSTOMER1 table *before* the deletion of customer 1.

Invoice1 : Table

	inv_no	c_no	inv_date	amount
▶	940	1	05/12/99	£26.20
	1002	4	12/01/00	£149.23
	1003	1	12/01/00	£16.26
	1004	2	14/01/00	£200.00
	1005	3	20/01/00	£510.00
	1006	5	21/01/00	£250.10
	1017	6	22/01/00	£412.21
*				

Record: ◄◄ ◄ 1 ► ►► ►* of 7

Fig. 5.125 The INVOICE1 table *before* the deletion of customer 1.

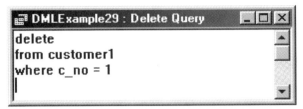

Fig. 5.126 The PAYMENT1 table *before* the deletion of customer1.

Figs 5.124, 5.125 and 5.126 show the data in the CUSTOMER1, INVOICE1 and PAYMENT1 tables before the deletion of the customer 1 record. Figure 5.127 shows the DELETE statement.

```
delete
from customer1
where c_no = 1
```

Fig. 5.127 The SQL DELETE statement.

Note that after the DELETE statement has been executed:

● in Fig. 5.128, the customer 1 record has been deleted;
● in Fig. 5.129, the two invoices for customer 1, namely invoice number 940 and invoice number 1003, have been automatically deleted by the cascade delete;
● in Fig. 5.130, the two payments for invoice number 940 have been deleted.

This illustrates the effect of a cascade delete. The deletion of one record has 'cascaded' down to records in two 'lower' levels.

If the DELETE statement of Fig. 5.127 were executed the user would get no warning and all the records 'under' the customer 1 record would be deleted automatically if cascade delete were in force. In practice, cascade delete would probably not be specified on these relationships. In that case, attempting to delete the record for a customer who had outstanding invoices on the database, such as customer 1, would result in an error. The user would then have to consciously delete the payments and then the invoices before finally deleting the customer record. If the DELETE statement were embedded in a Visual Basic program, the error could be trapped, a record kept of the invoices and payments involved, and should the user give his or her assent after being warned of this, the records could be deleted. Error trapping of this sort is displayed in many of the examples of embedded SQL in later chapters.

Customer1 : Table

c_no	title	sname	inits	street	city	postc	cred_lim	balance
2	Miss	Lauri	P.	5 Dux St	London	N1	£500.00	£200.00
3	Mr	Jackson	R.	2 Lux Ave	Leeds	LE1 2AB	£500.00	£510.00
4	Mr	Dziduch	M.	31 Low St	Dover	DO2 9CD	£100.00	£149.23
5	Ms	Woods	S.Q.	17 Nax Rd	London	E18 4WW	£1,000.00	£250.10
6	Mrs	Williams	C.	41 Cax St	Dover	DO2 8WD		£412.21

Record: 1 of 5

Fig. 5.128 The CUSTOMER1 table *after* the deletion of customer 1.

Invoice1 : Table

inv_no	c_no	inv_date	amount
1002	4	12/01/00	£149.23
1004	2	14/01/00	£200.00
1005	3	20/01/00	£510.00
1006	5	21/01/00	£250.10
1017	6	22/01/00	£412.21

Record: 1 of 5

Fig. 5.129 The INVOICE1 table *after* the deletion of customer 1.

Payment1 : Table

inv_no	pmt_no	pmt_date	amount
1005	1	14/01/00	£510.00
1017	1	30/01/00	£100.00

Record: 1 of 2

Fig. 5.130 The PAYMENT1 table *after* the deletion of customer 1.

> *Example 30: Demonstrate a deletion being prevented by violation of a Referential Integrity constraint.*

We shall now restore the CUSTOMER1, INVOICE1 and PAYMENT1 tables so that they contain their original records, and to demonstrate referential integrity being broken by a deletion, we shall remove cascade delete from the relationship between CUSTOMER1 and INVOICE1.

In practice of course, these integrity constraints would not be casually changed as we are doing here. We do it for demonstration purposes only.

Assume the data in CUSTOMER1, INVOICE1 and PAYMENT1 are as shown in Figs 5.124, 5.125 and 5.126, i.e. that customer 1 and his invoice and payment records are still there.

We now uncheck the Cascade Delete checkbox for the CUSTOMER1–INVOICE1 relationship (see Fig. 5.121) so that the dialogue box appears as in Fig. 5.131.

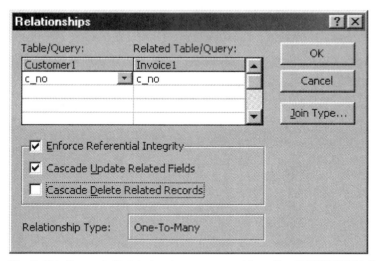

Fig. 5.131 Cascade Delete has been removed from the CUSTOMER1–INVOICE1 relationship.

An attempt to re-run the SQL DELETE statement (Fig. 5.127) now results in the error message of Fig. 5.132.

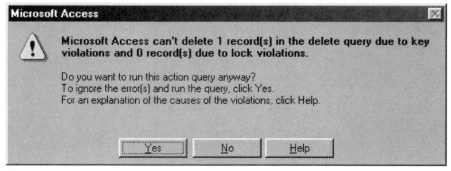

Fig. 5.132 The error message resulting when attempting to violate the referential integrity constraint shown in Fig. 5.131.

It can be seen that opting for Cascade Delete *seems* to override the referential integrity constraint. However, this isn't the case. Referential integrity is not broken by allowing cascade delete; in fact it is maintained by deleting invoices and payments that would otherwise violate the constraint. Refer to Chapter 3 for a description of referential integrity.

> *Example 31:* Delete any payment received before the invoice was sent out.

This fairly contrived example illustrates the use of a subquery in a DELETE statement. The subquery inspects another table to decide which records to delete.

Suppose the data in the INVOICE1 and PAYMENT1 tables is as shown in Figs 5.133 and 5.134.

inv_no	c_no	inv_date	amount
940	1	05/12/99	£26.20
1002	4	12/01/00	£149.23
1003	1	12/01/00	£16.26
1004	2	14/01/00	£200.00
1005	3	20/01/00	£510.00
1006	5	21/01/00	£250.10
1017	6	22/01/00	£412.21

Record: 1 of 7

Fig. 5.133 The records in the INVOICE1 table *before* the DELETE.

inv_no	pmt_no	pmt_date	amount
940	2	12/12/99	£13.00
1005	1	14/01/00	£510.00
940	3	19/01/00	£10.00
1017	1	30/01/00	£100.00

Record: 5 of 5

Fig. 5.134 The records in the PAYMENT1 table *before* the DELETE.

Notice that a payment for invoice 1005 was received before the invoice was sent out.

If we now implement the SQL DELETE command shown in Fig. 5.135, the payment for invoice 1005 is deleted.

This subquery is a little unusual in that the matching invoice number criteria between the two tables is actually specified twice. However, it demonstrates how a subquery can be used in a DELETE statement.

```
Query1 : Delete Query                        _ □ ×
delete
from payment1 as a
where inv_no =
  (select inv_no
   from invoice1 as b
   where
   a.inv_no = b.inv_no
   and
   a.pmt_date < b.inv_date)
```

Fig. 5.135 The DELETE statement for Example 31.

Payment1 : Table			_ □ ×
inv_no	**pmt_no**	**pmt_date**	**amount**
940	2	12/12/99	£13.00
940	3	19/01/00	£10.00
1017	1	30/01/00	£100.00

Record: |◀ ◀ [1] ▶ ▶| ▶* of 3

Fig. 5.136 The PAYMENT1 table *after* the DELETE statement is executed.

Subqueries are covered in detail in the chapter on the SELECT statement.

Note that it is not possible to delete, using an SQL DELETE command, from any Access stored query.

5.13 Exercises

Using SQL statements, and the test database **accts.mdb** given in Appendix 1, develop and test DDL and DML queries to do the following. Copies of this database can be downloaded from the Website **http://www.databasedesign.co.uk/book** if required.

Create a database of your own called **MyAccts.mdb** and in this database:

1. Create the CUSTOMER table as in accts.mdb. Make C_NO the primary key field. Specify the data type of C_NO to allow for over 100,000 customers. Specify realistic lengths for all text fields.

2. Create the INVOICE table as in accts.mdb, including the primary key INV_NO which should be long enough to accommodate at least 10,000,000 invoices. Don't link it to the CUSTOMER table at this stage.

3. Alter your CUSTOMER table by dropping columns STREET, CITY and POSTC and replacing them with the four address lines ADDR1, ADDR2, ADDR3, ADDR4. Make the first two address lines non-nullable. Add the following fields: PHONE, FAX, EMAIL, all of appropriate lengths and data types.

4. Using an ALTER TABLE command, add a constraint to the INVOICE table to link it to the CUSTOMER table. The relationship you create should specify CUSTOMER.C_NO as the field on the 'one' side of the relationship, and INVOICE.C_NO as the field on the 'many' side.

5. By adding test records to the CUSTOMER and INVOICE tables, demonstrate referential integrity in the relationship created in 4.

6. In MyAccts.mdb, create the PAYMENT table as in accts.mdb, but ensure the data type of INV_NO is compatible with INVOICE.INV_NO. Leave out the primary key constraint at this point.

7. In your PAYMENT table, use a CREATE INDEX command to create the compound primary key consisting of INV_NO with PMT_NO.

8. Create the primary key to foreign key link between INVOICE and PAYMENT.

9. Use the INSERT INTO command to manually insert five customer records, three invoices and two payments.

10. Develop a simple Visual Basic program which embeds the INSERT INTO command in VB code so that the user can enter CUSTOMER field values into text boxes and on clicking a Command button, the record is entered into the table.

6

Access query design using SQL – the SELECT statement – single tables and joins

In this chapter you will learn:

- how to design single-table queries using the SQL SELECT statement
- how to design multiple-table queries using the SQL SELECT statement with joins.

6.1 Introduction

The purpose of the SQL SELECT statement is to retrieve and display data gathered from one or more database tables. SELECT is the most frequently used SQL command and can be used *interactively* to obtain immediate answers to queries, and *embedded* in a host program written in a language such as Visual Basic for more complex data retrieval and reporting.

Interactive use of SELECT is where the power of SQL is most readily demonstrated, with many complex data retrieval operations often requiring just a few well-chosen lines of SQL. A good way to develop Visual Basic database programs with embedded SQL is to develop and test the SQL statements interactively in Access first and then when they're proved correct, embed them in the host VB program.

In this chapter we use SQL interactively. We show an English version of the query, then an SQL version and finally the results. The results are of course sections of the database that answer the query. For test data, we use the **accts.mdb**, **prod_del.mdb**, **emp_sales.mdb** and **musicians.mdb** test databases. The description and contents of these databases are shown in Appendix 1. The databases themselves only contain a few records each, but they can be downloaded from **http://www.databasedesign.co.uk/book** if required.

We divide the SELECT statement into two parts. This chapter deals with single tables and joins, and Chapter 7 deals with all the other features of the SELECT statement. We also show how to build one query on another to simplify some of the more complex queries you may want to write.

6.2 SELECT with a single table

The basic syntax of the SELECT statement for a single table is shown in Fig. 6.1.

```
SELECT       [DISTINCT] {*|col_exp [,col_exp, . . . ]}
FROM         table_name [as table_alias]
[WHERE       condition
[AND/OR      condition, [AND/OR condition, . . . ]]]
[GROUP BY    col_name [,col_name, . . . ]
[HAVING      condition]]
[ORDER BY    {col, [,col, . . . ]}]
```

Fig. 6.1 SELECT syntax for a single table.

Square brackets show nonmandatory items. Braces { } and bars | show alternative items, and three dots . . . mean the preceding item may be repeated. Additional clauses in the SELECT statement are covered in subsequent sections. The syntax may vary slightly from one implementation of SQL to another but all versions should contain at least this minimum set.

The sequence of processing in a SELECT command is:

FROM	Specifies the table(s) to be accessed
WHERE	Filters the rows on some condition
GROUP BY	Forms a single row from a group of rows
HAVING	Filters the groups on some condition
SELECT	Specifies which results will be output
ORDER BY	Determines the order of the output rows

The following examples illustrate the usage of each of these clauses.

6.2.1 Selecting columns

The simplest SELECT statement it is possible to enter will retrieve all columns from every row of a table. Remember that 'column' is SQL's name for a field or attribute and 'row' is the term used in SQL for a record. The SQL 'row–column' terminology will be used here. For example, to list the entire CUSTOMER table the following SQL command would be entered:

> *Query 1: List all details stored on every customer.*

Fig. 6.2 List all data from the CUSTOMER table.

Following the word SELECT is the list of columns that are to be retrieved. Here, the asterisk means that *all* columns are required. The FROM clause states the database tables the retrieved columns are to come from. In this SELECT, the table is the CUSTOMER table. So the command means 'Select all columns from the CUSTOMER table and since no WHERE clause is specified, do this for every row, i.e. list all rows'. The command could alternatively have been typed in a single line or in capitals:

Fig. 6.3 The same query typed in a single line.

Fig. 6.4 The same query typed in capitals.

Note that in Access it doesn't matter whether you use capitals or lower case when you name and refer to table or field names. For example, you could name a table CUSTOMER when creating it and refer to it as customer when writing an SQL query or referring to it in a VB program. However, if you imbed spaces in table or field names, Access will want you to enclose the name in square brackets. For example, if we'd named the customer credit limit field as Credit Limit, we'd always have to refer to it in SQL and VB as [Credit Limit]. We never put spaces in table or field names.

Assuming the CUSTOMER table is as shown in Appendix 1, the output resulting from this SELECT command is:

c_no	title	sname	inits	street	city	postc	cred_lim	balance
1	Mr	Sallaway	G.R.	12 Fax Rd	London	WC1	£1,000.00	£16.26
2	Miss	Lauri	P.	5 Dux St	London	N1	£500.00	£200.00
3	Mr	Jackson	R.	2 Lux Ave	Leeds	LE1 2AB	£500.00	£510.00
4	Mr	Dziduch	M.	31 Low St	Dover	DO2 9CD	£100.00	£149.23
5	Ms	Woods	S.Q.	17 Nax Rd	London	E18 4WW	£1,000.00	£250.10
6	Mrs	Williams	C.	41 Cax St	Dover	DO2 8WD		£412.21
0							£0.00	£0.00

Record: |◀ ◀ | 1 | ▶ ▶| ▶* | of 6

Fig. 6.5 The output from Query 1.

You can see that every column in every row has been retrieved and displayed. In the SELECT line, the '*' means 'all columns'.

The use of NULL

Notice that there is no value shown for CRED-LIM for C-NO 6. This field value is as yet unknown and contains NULL.

NULL is a special value provided by SQL. You can use it in a variety of ways, to mean a variety of things. Be clear on what it is going to mean in your own application. In the present example, we have used NULL to mean 'as yet unknown'.

You might want to use a NULL to mean 'not applicable' (this customer doesn't have a credit limit) or to have some other meaning.

SQL treats NULL in a special way. For example, you can retrieve all rows containing a column with the value NULL. The other properties of NULL are indicated in context in later examples.

One useful property of NULL is that it takes no part in *aggregate functions* (see below).

Project

If only a subset of the columns is wanted, then a list of the required column names is placed after the SELECT. Retrieving a subset of the columns in the table is called *projection*.

Query 2 contains a projection because only two of the columns in the table are required to be output.

> *Query 2: List the customer account numbers and the invoice amounts of all customers who have outstanding invoices.*

Here it is assumed that the database table INVOICE contains only outstanding invoices, i.e. those that have not been paid in full. All fully paid invoices from previous months have been removed to an archive file. The SQL query is:

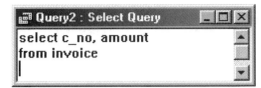

Fig. 6.6 Retrieve just two columns from the INVOICE table.

Instead of listing *all* columns from INVOICE, only columns C_NO and AMOUNT are required. These column names are the usual form of the 'col_exp' (column expression) shown in Fig. 6.1. Column expressions can also contain arithmetic and various functions. In this query, the column expressions are simply column names.

The output from this command is:

c_no	amount
1	£26.20
4	£149.23
1	£16.26
2	£200.00
3	£510.00
5	£250.10
6	£412.21
0	£0.00

Record: 1

Fig. 6.7 The output from Query 2.

Notice that the only output is from the two columns specified.

There is no standard way of specifying the required columns negatively, for example 'All columns except the third and the fifth'; all columns required must be explicitly stated. So if you wanted to list all columns except *one* from a table with many columns, you would have a fair amount of typing to do.

6.2.2 *DISTINCT*

Duplicate output rows may arise because rows that are in other ways different may hold similar values of the projected columns. An relational algebraic project operation removes those duplicates. In SQL you can choose to have the duplicates removed or leave them in.

> *Query 3*: List the customer numbers of all customers with outstanding invoices.

If we try:

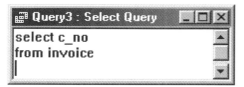

Fig. 6.8 First attempt at listing all C–NOs in the INVOICE table.

the output is:

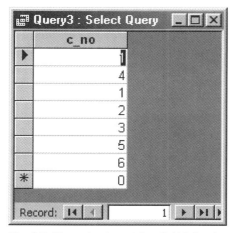

Fig. 6.9 The output contains C–NO 1 twice.

The C–NO 1 has appeared twice in the output because it appeared twice on the INVOICE table.

Duplicate output rows can be removed using the DISTINCT option in the SELECT statement:

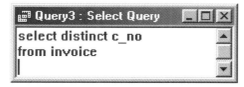

Fig. 6.10 Using the DISTINCT clause to remove duplicate rows.

This gives the output:

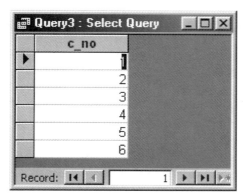

Fig. 6.11 Duplicates have been removed.

It is important to note that DISTINCT does not refer to individual columns, but to the complete column list that appears after the SELECT. Its only effect is to prevent duplicate *rows* appearing in the output as a result of a projection.

There should of course be no duplicate rows in the original table since that would contravene one of the fundamental integrity constraints of relational databases, which should contain no duplicate rows.

Column expressions

Column expressions may be more than simply column names, as in the following query:

> *Query 4*: For each product, list the percentage by which the current stock level exceeds minimum stock level.

This query uses test database **prod_del.mdb**. The SQL is:

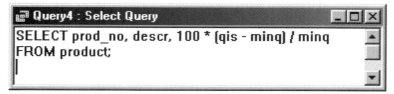

Fig. 6.12 The SQL SELECT statement for Query 4.

The third column expression is an arithmetic expression involving two column names QIS and MINQ (quantity in stock and minimum stock level) and the constant 100. The output is:

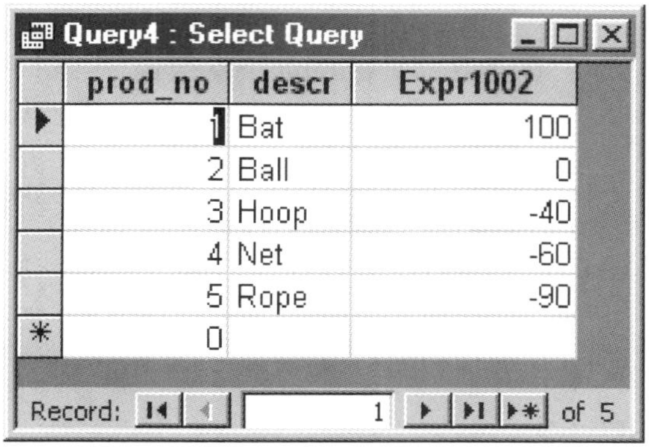

Fig. 6.13 The output from Query 4.

Column aliases

Columns may be given aliases. In this query we could use the command:

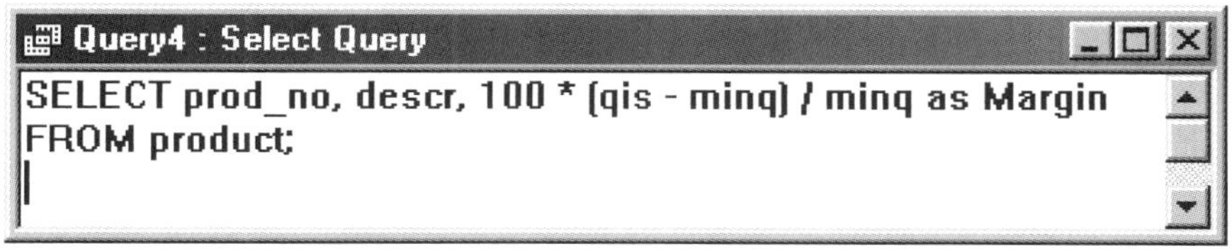

Fig. 6.14 Using a column alias.

This command uses the *column alias* 'Margin' for the arithmetic expression preceding it. An SQL column alias is an alternative name for a column expression. In this example a column alias is being used to make the output more presentable. The output is now:

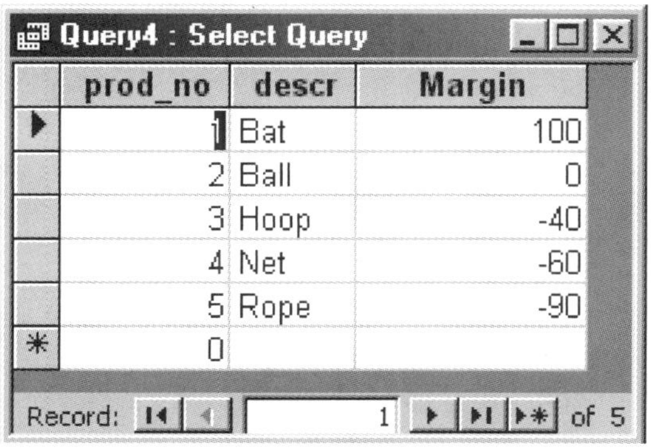

Fig. 6.15 Using the column alias Margin for the arithmetic expression.

6.2.3 *WHERE*

The WHERE clause in the SQL SELECT statement syntax is used to specify a subset of rows that will be delivered to the output. The test is applied to each row of the table in turn and if the condition in the WHERE clause is true for a row, then the row will be output. This operation is sometimes known as a *select* or *restrict*. In practice select and project operations are often used together so that in SQL, after the WHERE clause has decided which rows pass the test, the list of column expressions decides which column data will be output.

Simple WHERE conditions

Here we show queries using just one WHERE condition.

Query 5: List the products whose price is greater than five pounds.

We are again using the **prod_del.mdb** database.
The SQL SELECT statement for this query is:

```
Query5 : Select Query

SELECT prod_no, descr, price
FROM product
WHERE price > 5
```

Fig. 6.16 This query uses a simple WHERE clause.

The WHERE clause in Fig. 6.16 contains the simple condition 'PRICE > 5' which says that the only rows in the table PRODUCT that will be output are those where the value of the PRICE column in the row is greater than 5.

The SELECT line 'projects out' (displays only) the columns PROD_NO, DESCR and PRICE.

SQL uses the following simple comparison ('relational') operators:

= equals
< is less than
> is greater than
<= is less than or equal to (i.e. not greater than)
>= is greater than or equal to (i.e. not less than)
<> is not equal to

All operators work with character and date as well as numeric data types. With inequality tests involving character data, the alphanumerical order (i.e. the collating sequence) of the data is used, and for dates, chronological sequence is used.

The following example uses a comparison involving a date.

> *Query 6:* List details of all invoices sent out before January 2000.

Here we are using the **accts.mdb** database. The SQL SELECT statement is:

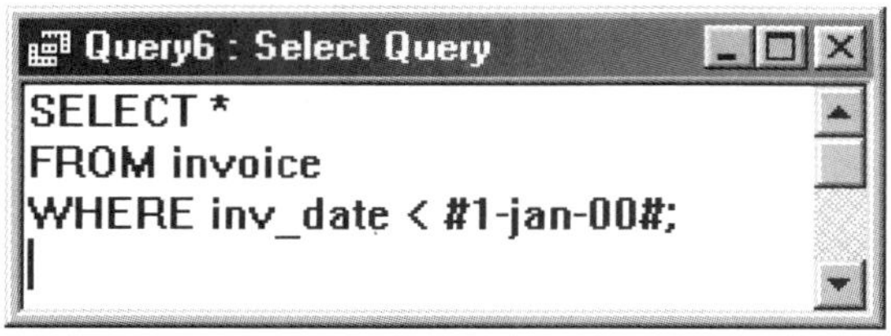

```
Query6 : Select Query
SELECT *
FROM invoice
WHERE inv_date < #1-jan-00#;
```

Fig. 6.17 A comparison involving a date.

The WHERE clause selects out all rows where the invoice date is before the third millennium.

The output from this Query is:

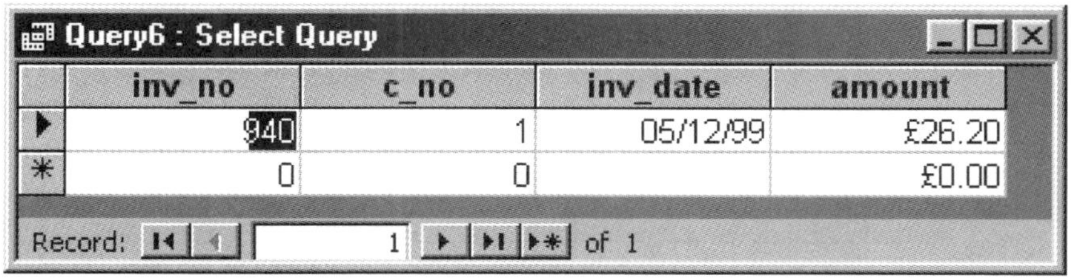

inv_no	c_no	inv_date	amount
940	1	05/12/99	£26.20
0	0		£0.00

Record: ◄◄ ◄ 1 ► ►► ►* of 1

Fig. 6.18 The output from query 6.

Comparisons with NULL

Note that any of the comparison operators used to compare a value with a field containing the value NULL *will fail*. So if you used the WHERE clause:

WHERE CRED_LIM = 1000

and the customer had a NULL value for CRED_LIM (Mrs Williams, for example), the row would not be output.

Similarly, the tests

WHERE CRED_LIM < 1000
WHERE CRED_LIM < = 1000
WHERE CRED_LIM > 1000
WHERE CRED_LIM > = 1000
WHERE CRED_LIM <> 1000

would all fail for such a customer.

The only test that will succeed with NULL is 'IS NULL'. This is illustrated in the next examples.

Query 7: *List details of all customers who have a NULL credit limit.*

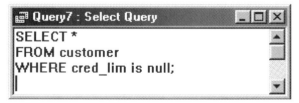

Fig. 6.19 The use of IS NULL.

	c_no	title	sname	inits	street	city	postc	cred_lim	balance
▶	6	Mrs	Williams	C.	41 Cax St	Dover	DO2 8WD		£412.21
*	0							£0.00	£0.00

Record: I◄ ◄ | 1 | ► | ►I | ►* | of 1

Fig. 6.20 The output of Query 7.

Note that the only customer whose CUSTOMER record is output is Mrs Williams' record since she is the only one with a NULL credit limit.

Query 8: *List details of all customers who don't have a NULL credit limit.*

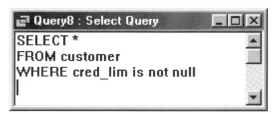

Fig. 6.21 The use of IS NOT NULL.

	c_no	title	sname	inits	street	city	postc	cred_lim	balance
▶	1	Mr	Sallaway	G.R.	12 Fax Rd	London	WC1	£1,000.00	£16.26
	2	Miss	Lauri	P.	5 Dux St	London	N1	£500.00	£200.00
	3	Mr	Jackson	R.	2 Lux Ave	Leeds	LE1 2AB	£500.00	£510.00
	4	Mr	Dziduch	M.	31 Low St	Dover	DO2 9CD	£100.00	£149.23
	5	Ms	Woods	S.Q.	17 Nax Rd	London	E18 4WW	£1,000.00	£250.10
*	0							£0.00	£0.00

Record: I◄ ◄ | 1 | ► | ►I | ►* | of 5

Fig. 6.22 The output of Query 8.

Note that this time the only customer whose CUSTOMER record is *not* output is Mrs Williams' record since she is the only one with a NULL credit limit.

6.2.4   *LIKE*

The LIKE operator works with character fields and allows 'fuzzy matching'. The query contains an approximation to the spelling of the required column contents and all rows where the corresponding characters match up are retrieved.

The general form of an SQL command containing LIKE is:

SELECT . . .
FROM . . .
WHERE A LIKE B

. . .

A will generally be a column name and *B* is a 'mask' containing a combination of known characters and one or more of:

* *   which matches with zero or more characters
* ?   which matches with just one character.

In other SQLs,

* %   matches with zero or more characters
* _   (underscore) matches with just one character.

> *Query 9*: List all customers whose surnames begin with 'Dz'.

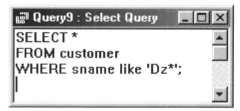

```
Query9 : Select Query
SELECT *
FROM customer
WHERE sname like 'Dz*';
```

Fig. 6.23 Using the LIKE operator for fuzzy matching.

	c_no	title	sname	inits	street	city	postc	cred_lim	balance
▶	4	Mr	Dziduch	M.	31 Low St	Dover	DO2 9CD	£100.00	£149.23
*	0							£0.00	£0.00

Record: |◄ ◄ 1 ► ►| ►* of 1

Fig. 6.24 The output from Query 9.

Note that the only customer whose SNAME field value begins with 'Dz' is Mr Dziduch. It is also possible to use NOT LIKE, as in:

WHERE sname NOT LIKE 'Dz*'

> *Query 10*: List all customers whose TITLE field value ends in 's'.

The SQL SELECT statement is:

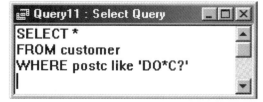

Fig. 6.25 The SQL SELECT statement for Query 10.

```
Query10 : Select Query

SELECT *
FROM customer
WHERE title like '*s';
```

	c_no	title	sname	inits	street	city	postc	cred_lim	balance
▶	2	Miss	Lauri	P.	5 Dux St	London	N1	£500.00	£200.00
	5	Ms	Woods	S.Q.	17 Nax Rd	London	E18 4WW	£1,000.00	£250.10
	6	Mrs	Williams	C.	41 Cax St	Dover	DO2 8WD		£412.21
*	0							£0.00	£0.00

Record: 1 of 3

Fig. 6.26 The output of Query 10.

This query is an attempt to retrieve all female customers but since the TITLE field may contain values Prof., Rt. Hon., etc., a GENDER field would have to be included in the CUSTOMER table to make this work.

> *Query 11*: List all customers, the first two characters of whose postcode are 'DO' and the second-last character of whose postcode is 'C'.

The SQL for this is:

```
Query11 : Select Query

SELECT *
FROM customer
WHERE postc like 'DO*C?'
```

Fig. 6.27 Fuzzy matching using both '*' and '?'.

'?' represents one character. The output is:

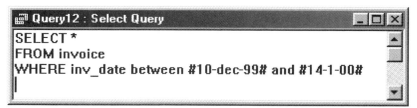

Fig. 6.28 Output of Query 11.

6.2.5 BETWEEN

The BETWEEN operator can be used in a WHERE clause to select rows where the value of a column is within a given range.

> *Query 12*: List details of all invoices with an invoice date between 10 December 1999 and 14 January 2000.

Query12 : Select Query

```
SELECT *
FROM invoice
WHERE inv_date between #10-dec-99# and #14-1-00#
```

Fig. 6.29 Using BETWEEN in the WHERE clause.

Query12 : Select Query

inv_no	c_no	inv_date	amount
1002	4	12/01/00	£149.23
1003	1	12/01/00	£16.26
1004	2	14/01/00	£200.00
0	0		£0.00

Record: 1 of 3

Fig. 6.30 The output from Query 12.

BETWEEN is *inclusive*. In the current query invoice number 1004, with an invoice date of 14/01/00 is output. Note the various formats that can be used for dates in Jet. Numeric months and text months are accepted. In Jet databases, dates have to be surrounded by '#' ('hash') symbols.

> _Query 13_: List all customers whose surnames go from 'D' to 'J'.

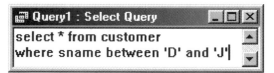

```
select * from customer
where sname between 'D' and 'J'
```

Fig. 6.31 The SQL for Query 13.

	c_no	title	sname	inits	street	city	postc	cred_lim	balance
▶	1	Mr	Dziduch	M.	31 Low St	Dover	DO2 9CD	£100.00	£149.23
*	0							£0.00	£0.00

Record: ◄◄ ◄ 1 ► ►◄ ►* of 1

Fig. 6.32 Output from Query 13. (Jackson is not shown, coming after 'J'.)

6.2.6 IN

In situations where it is required to test the value of some column against a given _set_ of values, the IN operator can be used. NOT IN can also be used, in which case the row passes the test if the value is _not_ in the list.

> _Query 14_: List details of all deliveries of product numbers 1, 3 and 5.

This query uses the **prod_del.mdb** database.

	c_no	prod_no	qty	del_date
▶	3	1	3	03/11/99
	3	2	2	03/11/99
	1	4	6	07/11/99
	3	3	1	12/11/99
	5	3	4	12/11/99
*	0	0	0	

Record: ◄◄ ◄ 1 ► ►◄ ►* of 5

Fig. 6.33 The DELIVERY table in the **prod_del.mdb** database.

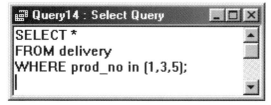

```
SELECT *
FROM delivery
WHERE prod_no in (1,3,5);
```

Fig. 6.34 The SQL SELECT statement for Query 14.

Each row in the DELIVERY table (see Fig. 6.33) is checked to see if its PROD–NO value is in the list (1,3,5). If it is, the row is output, resulting in:

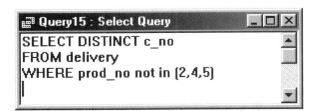

Fig. 6.35 The output from Query 14.

For each of these records, PROD–NO is either 1, 3 or 5.

> *Query 15:* List the customer numbers of customers who have purchased products other than product numbers 2, 4 and 5.

```
Query15 : Select Query
SELECT DISTINCT c_no
FROM delivery
WHERE prod_no not in (2,4,5)
```

Fig. 6.36 Using NOT IN.

This query assumes that DELIVERY shows all the purchases that have occurred. The WHERE clause tests each row and if the product number is not 2 and not 4 and not 5 (i.e. it is not a member of the set (2,4,5)) then the row passes the test and its C–NO is output.

The DISTINCT option is used here to prevent the repeated output of customer account numbers for customers who have purchased more than one product that is not in the list.

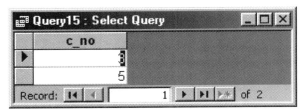

Fig. 6.37 The output from Query 15.

Note that the query

'Customers who have purchased products not in the list (2,4,5)'

is quite different from the query

'Customers who have not purchased products in the list (2,4,5)'.

Despite the superficial resemblance between them, the second query has a different meaning, a different result (usually) and an entirely different SQL SELECT command. In the second query two tables have to be consulted – CUS is consulted to access each customer, and DELIVERY is consulted for each customer to check whether he or she has purchased the listed products. The reason that consulting DELIVERY alone is not satisfactory for the second query is that the table shows what *has* been purchased; it cannot show what has *not* been purchased.

So make sure you understand the English version of the query first!

6.2.7 AND, OR and NOT

Here we describe *compound conditions*, i.e conditions in a WHERE clause of an SQL SELECT statement that use AND, OR and NOT.

So far in this chapter, all the WHERE clauses used simple conditions, that is, the conditions involved only one test per row. To perform two or more tests in a single WHERE clause, the AND and OR operators, together with round brackets () and NOT, can be used to string several conditions together to form a *compound condition*.

Query 16: List details of all overdrawn London customers.

To be output, customers must (Condition 1) have a debt greater than their credit limit AND (Condition 2) be based in London.

```
Query16 : Select Query          _ □ ✕
SELECT *
FROM customer
WHERE balance > cred_lim
and city = 'London'
```

Fig. 6.38 A compound WHERE condition using AND.

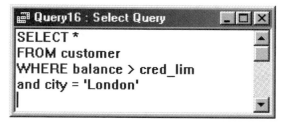

c_no	title	sname	inits	street	city	postc	cred_lim	balance
0							£0.00	£0.00

Record: ◄ ◄ 1 ► ►► ►* of 1

Fig. 6.39 There are no overdrawn customers in London in **accts.mdb**.

It is possible to string several ANDs into a logical expression in an SQL WHERE clause. Every extra condition you add linked by an AND requires that extra condition to be fulfilled for the row to be output.

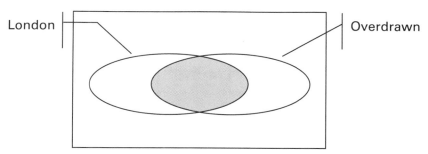

Fig. 6.40 The shaded section corresponds to London AND Overdrawn.

The rectangle in this *Venn diagram* is the set of *all* customers.

Query 17: List the customers who are overdrawn or live in London.

To be output, customers must (Condition 1) have a debt greater than their credit limit OR (Condition 2) be based in London, or both.

The SQL SELECT command is:

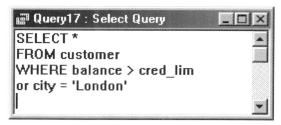

```
SELECT *
FROM customer
WHERE balance > cred_lim
or city = 'London'
```

Fig. 6.41 The SELECT statement for Query 17.

The output for this query is:

	c_no	title	sname	inits	street	city	postc	cred_lim	balance
▶	1	Mr	Sallaway	G.R.	12 Fax Rd	London	WC1	£1,000.00	£16.26
	2	Miss	Lauri	P.	5 Dux St	London	N1	£500.00	£200.00
	3	Mr	Jackson	R.	2 Lux Ave	Leeds	LE1 2AB	£500.00	£510.00
	4	Mr	Dziduch	M.	31 Low St	Dover	DO2 9CD	£100.00	£149.23
	5	Ms	Woods	S.Q.	17 Nax Rd	London	E18 4WW	£1,000.00	£250.10
*	0							£0.00	£0.00

Record: ◀◀ ◀ 1 ▶ ▶I ▶* of 5

Fig. 6.42 The output from Query 17.

This query uses an OR to link the two conditions. There are now *two* ways for a row to pass the test of the WHERE clause. Naturally, you would expect more records to be output when you use an OR than when you use an AND. Roughly speaking, you could say 'With OR you get more'.

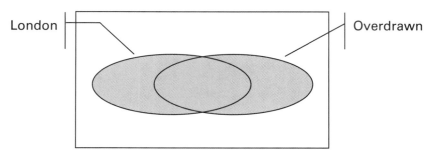

Fig. 6.43 The shaded section corresponds to London OR Overdrawn.

Notice that OR is *inclusive*, meaning that it includes customers that are both London and Overdrawn *as well as* just London or just Overdrawn.

Query 18: List details of London customers who are not overdrawn.

To be output, a customer must be in London but not overdrawn.
The SQL is:

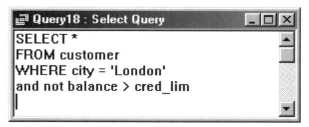

Fig. 6.44 The SQL for Query 18.

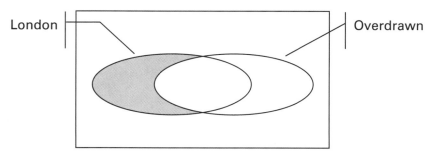

Fig. 6.45 The Venn diagram corresponding to London AND NOT Overdrawn.

An alternative way of saying the same thing in this SQL query would be to replace the phrase 'and not balance > cred_lim' with 'and balance < = cred_lim', as in Fig. 6.46.

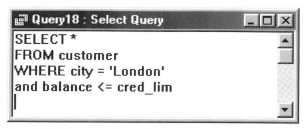

```
Query18 : Select Query                    _ □ ×
SELECT *
FROM customer
WHERE city = 'London'
and balance <= cred_lim
```

Fig. 6.46 This query is equivalent to that in Fig. 6.44.

There are many (16) ways of combining these two conditions using ANDs, ORs and NOTs. Here are two others:

- Not London and Not Overdrawn
- Not London or Not Overdrawn

> *Query 19*: List the details of all customers who are overdrawn or living in London but not both.

This is another of the possible combinations of the two conditions on the CUSTOMER table involving whether or not the customer is a London customer (Condition 1) and whether or not they are overdrawn (Condition 2). This particular combination has the name *Exclusive OR*, and is also called *Non-equivalence*.

The Venn diagram we require is shown in Fig. 6.47.

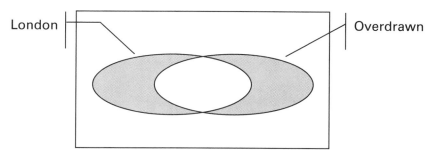

Fig. 6.47 The Venn diagram for the Exclusive OR of the two conditions.

We have seen the *Inclusive OR* in Query 17. If you compare the Venn diagrams for this query and Query 17, you will see that this query *excludes* those customers who fulfil both conditions.

Looking at the Venn diagram of Fig. 6.47 we can see that two possible WHERE clauses would be:

- WHERE (city = 'London' AND NOT balance > cred_lim)
  OR   (NOT city = 'London' AND balance > cred_lim)
- WHERE city = ('London' OR balance > cred_lim)
  AND NOT (city = 'London' AND balance > cred_lim)

The full SQL SELECT statement for the former is shown in Fig. 6.48.

```
Query19 : Select Query                     _ □ ✕
SELECT *
FROM customer
WHERE (city = 'London' AND NOT balance > cred_lim)
OR       (NOT city = 'London' AND balance > cred_lim)
```

Fig. 6.48 One of the ways to implement the SQL for Query 19.

Compound conditions and NULL

The table below shows the result of compound conditions involving two conditions X and Y, where one or both evaluate to NULL.

X	Y	NOT Y	X AND Y	X OR Y
NULL	NULL	NULL	NULL	NULL
NULL	TRUE	FALSE	NULL	TRUE
NULL	FALSE	TRUE	FALSE	NULL

Fig. 6.49 How NULL combines with AND, OR and NOT.

Query 20: List customers who have a balance over £400 or a credit limit over £500.

```
Query20 : Select Query     _ □ ✕
SELECT *
FROM customer
WHERE balance > 400
or cred_lim > 500;
```

Fig. 6.50 The SQL for Query 20.

The output from this query is:

c_no	title	sname	inits	street	city	postc	cred_lim	balance
1	Mr	Sallaway	G.R.	12 Fax Rd	London	WC1	£1,000.00	£42.56
3	Mr	Jackson	R.	2 Lux Ave	Leeds	LE1 2AB	£500.00	£510.00
5	Ms	Woods	S.Q.	17 Nax Rd	London	E18 4WW	£1,000.00	£250.10
6	Mrs	Williams	C.	41 Cax St	Dover	DO2 8WD		£412.21
0							£0.00	£0.00

Record: 5 of 5

Fig. 6.51 The output from Query 20.

For C_NO 6, the test

- balance > 400

evaluates to TRUE and the test

- cred_lim > 500

evaluates to NULL, since CRED_LIM is NULL.

By line 2 of Fig. 6.49, the result is TRUE, so the row is output.

Aggregating data and groups

It is often necessary to obtain summary or aggregate results from database tables. With this idea goes the idea of a *group*. A number of rows in a table are considered as a group and some summary data extracted, such as the number of rows in the group or the maximum, minimum or average value of a column in the group. For example, a manager may want to know the number of employees in each department or the average salary of a particular grade. The group will be a group of rows that have a common value of some attribute, for example the same value in the 'department' column of an employee table in which case there will be one result for each department group.

The following *aggregate functions* in SQL are used to produce summary results from groups of rows in database tables:

AVG(X)	Average value of numeric column X in the group of rows
COUNT(X)	Number of rows where X is non-null in the group of rows
MAX(X)	Maximum value in numeric column X in the group of rows
MIN(X)	Minimum value in numeric column X in the group of rows
SUM(X)	Sum of values in numeric column X in the group of rows
VAR(X)	The variance (measure of spread) of numeric column X in the group of rows
STDDEV(X)	The standard deviation (another measure of spread) of numeric column X in the group of rows

Fig. 6.52 SQL aggregate functions.

The statistic *Mode* (most popular value of X) can be performed using a *subquery*. Mode may or not be numeric. The statistic *Median* is also sometimes required. There is no in-built SQL function for Mode and Median in Access. Note that in calculating the value of an aggregate function, all rows with a NULL value of X are ignored, so that for example the AVG of the set of numbers (2,4,null,6,8) is 5 since there are considered to be four numbers in the set, not five. We repeat here the sequence of execution of the clauses in the SELECT command.

FROM	Specifies the table(s) to be accessed
WHERE	Filters rows on some condition
GROUP BY	Forms groups of rows with same value of some column(s)
HAVING	Filters groups on some condition
SELECT	Specifies what columns will be output
ORDER BY	Determines the order of the output results

Fig. 6.53 The order of execution of the clauses in a SELECT statement.

We now consider the GROUP BY clause.

6.2.8 *GROUP BY*

Groups are specified in the SQL SELECT command by the GROUP BY clause. After the groups have been formed there is the possibility of further filtering the results with the HAVING clause which acts on the group results in a similar way to the action of the WHERE clause on the table itself so that only data from selected groups will be output. Our first example uses an aggregate function but doesn't actually need a GROUP BY clause.

Query 21: What is the total amount owed by our customers?

We don't need a GROUP BY here because we don't want to put our customers into groups, one group for each city for example. We want a single statistic for the whole set of customers. The SQL is:

```
Query21 : Select Query          _ □ ✕
SELECT sum(balance)
FROM customer
```

Fig. 6.54 An aggregate function SUM being used *without* a GROUP BY.

Fig. 6.55 The output from Query 21.

We can use a column alias to give the output a meaningful name. Embedded spaces in a column alias require square brackets.

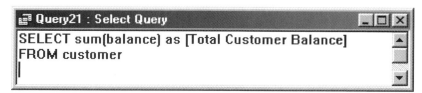

Fig. 6.56 Using a column alias to explicitly name the output column.

Fig. 6.57 The output with the column alias.

Query 22: *What is the total amount owed by customers in each city?*

In the previous query, the 'group' on which the aggregate function SUM operated to obtain its numeric results was the whole table.

In many queries the result of an aggregate function will be required on each of several groups, where groups are identified or obtain their group identity by sharing some common attribute values, that is, by sharing common values of some columns. If the SELECT command contains the code ' . . . GROUP BY CITY' then there will be just one row output for each city.

c_no	title	sname	inits	street	city	postc	cred_lim	balance
1	Mr	Sallaway	G.R.	12 Fax Rd	London	WC1	£1,000.00	£42.56
2	Miss	Lauri	P.	5 Dux St	London	N1	£500.00	£200.00
3	Mr	Jackson	R.	2 Lux Ave	Leeds	LE1 2AB	£500.00	£510.00
4	Mr	Dziduch	M.	31 Low St	Dover	DO2 9CD	£100.00	£149.23
5	Ms	Woods	S.Q.	17 Nax Rd	London	E18 4WW	£1,000.00	£250.10
6	Mrs	Williams	C.	41 Cax St	Dover	DO2 8WD		£412.21
0							£0.00	£0.00

Record: 1 of 6

Fig. 6.58 The CUSTOMER table in the **accts.mdb** database.

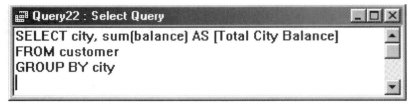

Fig. 6.59 The SQL SELECT statement using a GROUP BY for Query 22.

city	Total City Balance
Dover	£561.44
Leeds	£510.00
London	£492.66

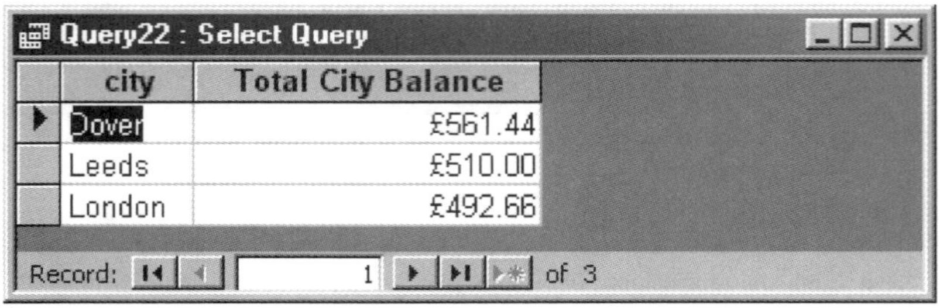

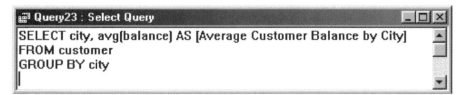

Fig. 6.60 The output from Query 22.

As can be seen from Fig. 6.60, the output includes a single row for each city. CITY was the field the query first grouped the data on, one record per group, before it calculated the sum of the balances for the group.

This is how GROUP BY works. If you group by a field, SQL delivers one row for each different value of that field, here, city.

> *Query 23: What is the average amount owed by customers in each city?*

This query is similar to the previous one. We still want to group the records by the CITY field, but we require the AVG aggregate function instead.

Fig. 6.61 The SQL SELECT command for Query 23.

city	Average Customer Balance by City
Dover	£280.72
Leeds	£510.00
London	£164.22

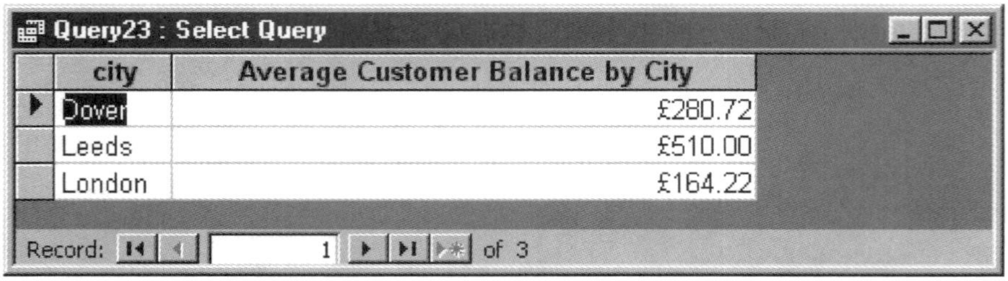

Fig. 6.62 The output of Query 23.

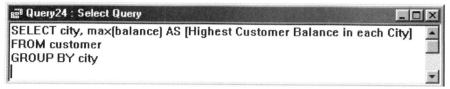

Query 24: *What is the maximum amount owed by any customer in each city?*

Fig. 6.63 The SQL SELECT command for Query 24.

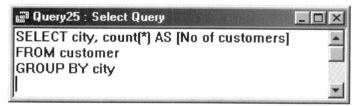

Fig. 6.64 The output of Query 24.

Note that it's not possible to show *which customer* has this highest balance. For that, we need a subquery (see Section 6.3).

Query 25: *How many customers are there in each city?*

Fig. 6.65 SQL for Query 25.

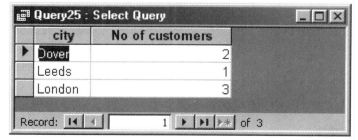

Fig. 6.66 The output of Query 25.

Note that the argument of the COUNT aggregate function is always (*). COUNT only ever counts whole records. In this query we are, for each city, counting the number of records in that city group.

Query 26: List the number of customers, and the minimum and the maximum balance in each city.

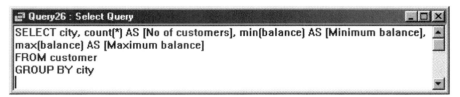

Fig. 6.67 Using multiple aggregate functions in the same GROUP BY.

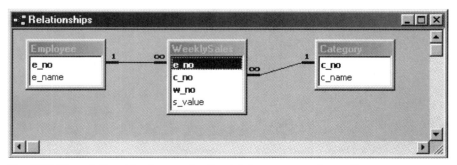

Fig. 6.68 The output of Query 26.

This query outputs several aggregate results for each city group.

Grouping on more than one column

Sometimes it is necessary to group on more than one column. For this example we use the database **emp_sales.mdb**, the schema for which is shown in Appendix 1, and reproduced here in Fig. 6.69.

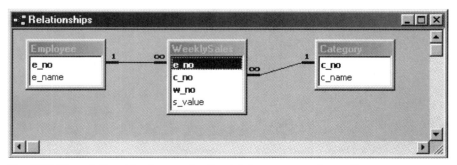

Fig. 6.69 The relationship diagram for the database **emp_sales.mdb**.

In this database, the fields in the WEEKLYSALES table have the following meanings:

e_no	employee number
c_no	category number of item sold
w_no	week number (1 to 52)
s_value	value of sales of that category of item sold by that employee in that week.

The data in the WEEKLYSALES table of the test database is shown in Fig. 6.70.

WeeklySales : Table

e_no	c_no	w_no	s_value
1	10	1	£100.00
1	10	2	£150.00
1	20	1	£20.00
1	30	2	£30.00
2	20	2	£60.00
3	10	1	£70.00
3	10	2	£85.00
3	20	1	£160.00
3	30	1	£90.00
3	30	2	£40.00
0	0	0	£0.00

Record: 1 of 10

Fig. 6.70 The data in the WEEKLYSALES table.

Query 27: List the total sales value across all the weeks for each employee and category.

Here we are required to group on the combination of fields e_no and c_no, since we wish to know what the total sales figure is for each employee–category combination.

The SQL for this query is shown in Fig. 6.71.

Query27 : Select Query

```
SELECT e_no, c_no, sum(s_value) as [Total Sales Value]
FROM WeeklySales
GROUP BY e_no, c_no
```

Fig. 6.71 Grouping on the field combination E_NO with C_NO.

Query27 : Select Query

e_no	c_no	Total Sales Value
1	10	£250.00
1	20	£20.00
1	30	£30.00
2	20	£60.00
3	10	£155.00
3	20	£160.00
3	30	£130.00

Record: 1 of 7

Fig. 6.72 The output from Query 27.

Grouping by just E_NO alone would give the total sales for each employee across *all* sales categories and weeks.

Grouping by just C_NO alone would give the total sales for each category across *all* employees and weeks.

Grouping by just W_NO would give the total sales for each week across *all* employees and categories.

Grouping by E_NO and C_NO together would give the total sales for each employee for each category.

Grouping by E_NO and W_NO together would give the total sales for each employee for each week.

Grouping by C_NO and W_NO together would give the total sales for each category for each week.

There is no point in grouping by all three fields E_NO, C_NO and W_NO together, because the data output would be the complete WEEKLYSALES table.

6.2.9 *HAVING*

After the groups have been formed using GROUP BY, the group data that would be output can itself be filtered using the HAVING clause of SQL. HAVING thus acts towards groups in the same way that WHERE acts towards table rows. Instead of a result being output for every group, only selected groups pass through the filtering effect of HAVING.

Query 28: List all the cities whose total outstanding customer balance exceeds £500.

Here we clearly need to group the CUSTOMER records by city and find each city's total customer balance. However, we only want to output that city and its balance if the balance is greater than £500. This test can only be done *after* the grouping has occurred, so a WHERE clause would be no good; a HAVING clause must be used.

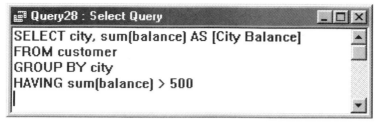

Fig. 6.73 The SQL for Query 28 showing a HAVING clause.

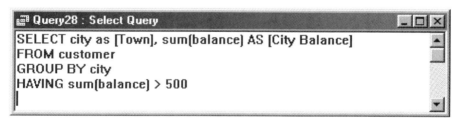

Fig. 6.74 The output from Query 28.

Incidentally, it is possible to put an alias on the field that is being grouped by too, as in Fig. 6.75.

SELECT city as [Town], sum(balance) AS [City Balance]
FROM customer
GROUP BY city
HAVING sum(balance) > 500

Fig. 6.75 Using an alias on both output columns.

If it is not required to output the results of the aggregate functions, they can be calculated in the HAVING clause itself. For example:

Query 29: List all cities with a total outstanding balance of over £500.

This query is virtually identical with Query 29. The only difference is that we don't want to output the city balance, just use it in a calculation. The SQL for this is:

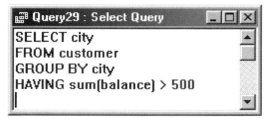

Fig. 6.76 SQL for Query 29.

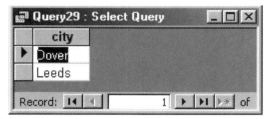

Fig. 6.77 Output of Query 29.

> *Query 30:* List the total balance of cities other than London with more than one customer and an average balance over £200.

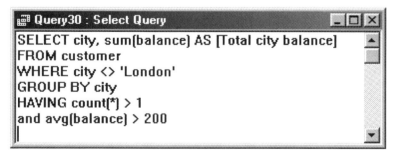

Fig. 6.78 A mixture of WHERE and HAVINGs.

This query shows that you can use AND in the HAVING clause and that the aggregate functions in the HAVING clause don't have to be the same as those displayed by the SELECT line of the query.

The query also has a WHERE clause. The WHERE clause filters the records *before* grouping by GROUP BY.

The output from Query 30 is shown in Fig. 6.79.

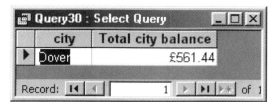

Fig. 6.79 The output from Query 30.

How to avoid a common mistake when using GROUP BY

Although the idea of GROUP BY is fairly straightforward once the notion of a group is understood, its misuse is a common source of error. Thus, the following query would be incorrect because the field in the SELECT line could have more than one value per group:

```
select c_no, max(balance)
from customer
group by city
```

C_NO could have more than one value per CITY. Since GROUP BY outputs only one row per group, which customer number is it going to output? No, this query will cause an error. The simple way to avoid this error is to remember that any field in the SELECT line that is not an aggregate function must also appear in the GROUP BY. Look back in all of our GROUP BY examples and you will see that this is true.

Two limitations of Access GROUP BY

Here are two things that some other SQLs can do that Access SQL can't. You have to use different methods to achieve them in Access.

> *Query 31: How many different cities are there in the CUSTOMER table?*

```
select count(distinct city)
from customer
```

Access doesn't allow count(distinct x).

> *Query 32: Which city has the highest total outstanding balance?*

```
select city, max(sum(balance))
from customer
group by city
```

Access doesn't allow nested aggregate functions.

6.2.10   ORDER BY

The purpose of the SQL ORDER BY clause is to sort the output and present it in either ascending or descending order of an expression involving one or more columns of the table. The order of the rows in the table in the database is not altered; ORDER BY simply changes the order in which the results of a query are displayed.

The syntax of the ORDER BY clause is:

```
SELECT . . .
ORDER BY expr [ASC|DESC], . . .
```

where

expr	is the expression, usually a field, that the output will be sorted on;
[ASC|DESC]	is optional. It means either ascending or descending;
, . . .	means that there can be more than one expression on which to sort and each of them can be in either ascending or descending order.

Query 33: List the CUSTOMER table in alphabetical order of surname.

```
SELECT *
FROM customer
ORDER BY sname
```

Fig. 6.80 ORDER BY on a single field.

	c_no	title	sname	inits	street	city	postc	cred_lim	balance
▶	4	Mr	Dziduch	M.	31 Low St	Dover	DO2 9CD	£100.00	£149.23
	3	Mr	Jackson	R.	2 Lux Ave	Leeds	LE1 2AB	£500.00	£510.00
	2	Miss	Lauri	P.	5 Dux St	London	N1	£500.00	£200.00
	1	Mr	Sallaway	G.R.	12 Fax Rd	London	WC1	£1,000.00	£42.56
	6	Mrs	Williams	C.	41 Cax St	Dover	DO2 8WD		£412.21
	5	Ms	Woods	S.Q.	17 Nax Rd	London	E18 4WW	£1,000.00	£250.10
*	0							£0.00	£0.00

Record: ⏮ ◀ | 1 | ▶ ⏭ ▶* of 6

Fig. 6.81 The CUSTOMER table sorted on SNAME.

> Query 34: List the customer surname and balance, in descending order of balance.

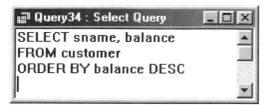

Fig. 6.82 Sorting the CUSTOMER table on descending order of the BALANCE field.

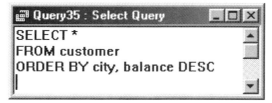

Fig. 6.83 The output of Query 34.

Since ASCending is the default, you actually have to put in DESC for descending order.

> Query 35: List the CUSTOMER table in descending order of balance, i.e. highest first, within ascending order of city.

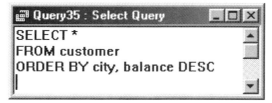

Fig. 6.84 The SQL SELECT statement for Query 35.

Here we are sorting on one field 'within' another: BALANCE 'within' CITY. Another way of putting this is that we want to have the output in alphabetical order of the field CITY and within each city, the BALANCEs should be ordered too, in this case in descending order. CITY can be called the *major* sort key and BALANCE the *minor* sort key.

The output from Query 35 is shown in Fig. 6.85.

Query35 : Select Query

c_no	title	sname	inits	street	city	postc	cred_lim	balance
6	Mrs	Williams	C.	41 Cax St	Dover	DO2 8WD		£412.21
4	Mr	Dziduch	M.	31 Low St	Dover	DO2 9CD	£100.00	£149.23
3	Mr	Jackson	R.	2 Lux Ave	Leeds	LE1 2AB	£500.00	£510.00
5	Ms	Woods	S.Q.	17 Nax Rd	London	E18 4WW	£1,000.00	£250.10
2	Miss	Lauri	P.	5 Dux St	London	N1	£500.00	£200.00
1	Mr	Sallaway	G.R.	12 Fax Rd	London	WC1	£1,000.00	£42.56
0							£0.00	£0.00

Record: 1 of 6

Fig. 6.85 The output from Query 35.

Note that the output records have been sorted in ascending order of city: Dover, Leeds, London, and that within each city's records the records are in descending order of balance. For example, within Dover, the balances go £412.21, £149.23 – descending order.

> *Query 36: In the **emp_sales** database, sort the WeeklySales table to show, for each week, each employee and the categories he or she sold and the sales figure for each. Sort on category within employee number within week, all ascending.*

The original WEEKLYSALES table, as it is stored on the database, is shown in Fig. 6.86.

WeeklySales : Table

e_no	c_no	w_no	s_value
1	10	1	£100.00
1	10	2	£150.00
1	20	1	£20.00
1	30	2	£30.00
2	20	2	£60.00
3	10	1	£70.00
3	10	2	£85.00
3	20	1	£160.00
3	30	1	£90.00
3	30	2	£40.00
0	0	0	£0.00

Record: 1 of 10

Fig. 6.86 The WEEKLYSALES table.

The sequence of the records output (week number within category number within employee number) is a consequence of the primary key index we created at table design time. See Fig. 6.87.

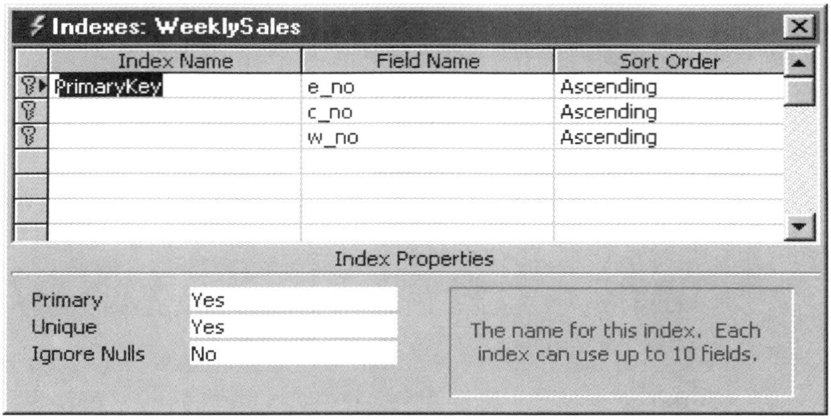

Fig. 6.87 The primary key index of the WEEKLYSALES table.

However, this query requires the output in a different order. As well as sorting on the required sequence, we might as well present the output fields with the required major sort key on the left through to the minor key on the right. This will be more meaningful to the user and easier to read.

The SQL is shown in Fig. 6.88.

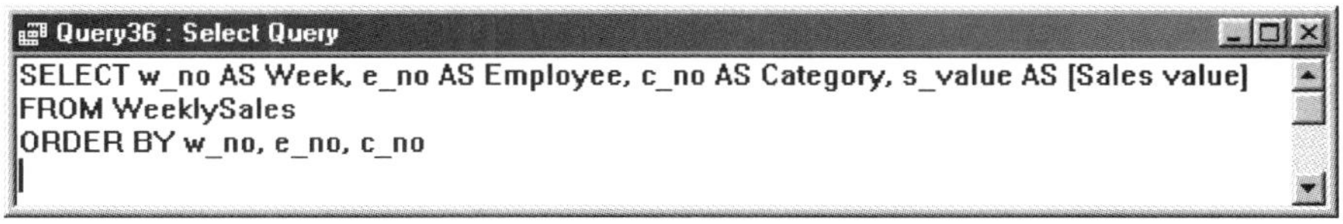

```
Query36 : Select Query
SELECT w_no AS Week, e_no AS Employee, c_no AS Category, s_value AS [Sales value]
FROM WeeklySales
ORDER BY w_no, e_no, c_no
```

Fig. 6.88 The SQL SELECT statement for Query 36.

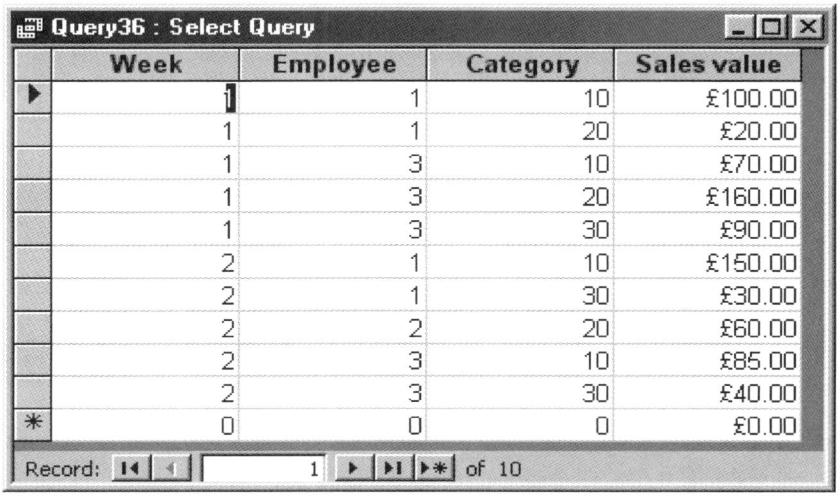

Week	Employee	Category	Sales value
1	1	10	£100.00
1	1	20	£20.00
1	3	10	£70.00
1	3	20	£160.00
1	3	30	£90.00
2	1	10	£150.00
2	1	30	£30.00
2	2	20	£60.00
2	3	10	£85.00
2	3	30	£40.00
0	0	0	£0.00

Record: 1 of 10

Fig. 6.89 The sorted output from Query 36.

6.2.11 TOP

TOP *n* returns the first *n* records that satisfy the WHERE clause.

The syntax of the TOP option is:

```
SELECT TOP n [PERCENT]
FROM table
WHERE ...
ORDER BY ...
```

[PERCENT]   returns n percent of the rows, rather than n rows.

If there is no ORDER BY clause in the SELECT statement, TOP *n* returns the first *n* records that satisfy the WHERE clause. If fewer than *n* records satisfy the where clause, just those will be returned.

If an ORDER BY clause is included, TOP *n* returns the first *n* rows that satisfy the query, but without breaking up a group of duplicates. This may result in more than *n* records being output. If it's used with ORDER BY, TOP *n* returns the first *n* records, except that if the *n*th record has records after it with the same value of the field you're sorting on, they will be output too. For example, if there are another two records with that value then instead of having *n* records returned, you'll get *n* + 2.

> *Query 37*: List details of the customers with the highest two customer balances.

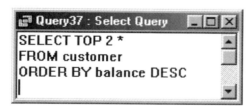

Query37 : Select Query
```
SELECT TOP 2 *
FROM customer
ORDER BY balance DESC
```

Fig. 6.90 Selecting the customers with the highest two balances.

Query37 : Select Query

c_no	title	sname	inits	street	city	postc	cred_lim	balance
3	Mr	Jackson	R.	2 Lux Ave	Leeds	LE1 2AB	£500.00	£510.00
6	Mrs	Williams	C.	41 Cax St	Dover	DO2 8WD		£412.21
* 0							£0.00	£0.00

Record: |◄| ◄| 1 |►|►I|►*| of 2

Fig. 6.91 The output of Query 37.

By sorting in descending order of balance and then picking off the top two using TOP 2, we display the customers with the highest two balances.

> *Query 38:* List the customer number and surname of the customer with the lowest balance.

Query38 : Select Query

```
SELECT TOP 1 c_no, sname, balance
FROM customer
ORDER BY balance
```

Fig. 6.92 Selecting the customer with the lowest balance.

Query38 : Select Query

	c_no	sname	balance
▶	1	Sallaway	£42.56
*	0		£0.00

Record: 1 of o

Fig. 6.93 The output of Query 38.

Here, we've sorted in ascending order of balance and just looked at the first row. If there had been two customers with this lowest balance then they would both have been shown, because TOP when used with ORDER BY doesn't break up a group of duplicates.

> *Query 39:* List the customers with the highest credit limit.

Query39 : Select Query

```
SELECT TOP 1 *
FROM customer
ORDER BY cred_lim DESC
```

Fig. 6.94 Selecting the customers with the highest credit limit.

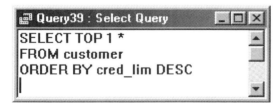

Query39 : Select Query

	c_no	title	sname	inits	street	city	postc	cred_lim	balance
▶	5	Ms	Woods	S.Q.	17 Nax Rd	London	E18 4WW	£1,000.00	£250.10
	1	Mr	Sallaway	G.R.	12 Fax Rd	London	WC1	£1,000.00	£42.56
*	0							£0.00	£0.00

Record: 1 of 2

Fig. 6.95 *Two* customers have this highest credit limit of £1000.

Even though we've specified TOP 1, we get two rows output. This is because TOP n when used with ORDER BY doesn't break up a group of duplicates on the ORDER BY field(s).

We can return now to Query 32, which could not be performed in Access SQL using just a GROUP BY because Access doesn't allow nested aggregate functions. TOP provides the method we require.

Query 40 (Query 32 revisited): Which city has the highest total outstanding balance?

Query40 : Select Query

```
SELECT TOP 1 city, sum(balance) AS [City total balance]
FROM customer
GROUP BY city
ORDER BY sum(balance) DESC;
```

Fig. 6.96 The SQL SELECT statement for Query 40.

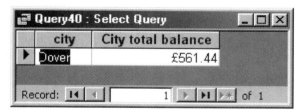

Fig. 6.97 The output of Query 40.

This query performs the following steps:

- GROUP BY groups the CUSTOMER records by CITY;
- sum(balance) calculates the total balance for each city;
- ORDER BY . . . DESC sorts the resulting groups in reverse order of sum(balance);
- SELECT TOP 1 lists the row(s) – 1 in this case – with the highest sum(balance).

Query 41: List the customers with the top 20% of balances.

Query41 : Select Query

```
SELECT TOP 20 PERCENT *
FROM customer
ORDER BY balance DESC
```

Fig. 6.98 Listing the customers in the highest 20% category on balance.

	c_no	title	sname	inits	street	city	postc	cred_lim	balance
▶	3	Mr	Jackson	R.	2 Lux Ave	Leeds	LE1 2AB	£500.00	£510.00
	6	Mrs	Williams	C.	41 Cax St	Dover	DO2 8WD		£412.21
*	0							£0.00	£0.00

Query41 : Select Query
Record: 1 of 2

Fig. 6.99 The customers in the highest 20% band of balances.

Notice that we have expressed the English version of the query three different ways. We hope you will agree that they are equivalent. The steps involved in this query were:

- sort the CUSTOMER records in descending order of balance;
- output the first 20 per cent of the records.

There are six records in the test CUSTOMER table. Twenty per cent of this is 1.2 records. SQL rounds this up to two records. If we'd asked for the top 15 per cent (just under a sixth), we would have got just one record.

> _Query 42_: List the employees with the top 25 per cent of sales in the first two weeks of the year.

Query42 : Select Query
```
SELECT TOP 25 PERCENT e_no, sum(s_value) AS [Total sales]
FROM WeeklySales
WHERE w_no in (1,2)
GROUP BY e_no
ORDER BY sum(s_value) DESC;
```

Fig. 6.100 The SQL for Query 42.

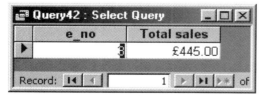

e_no	Total sales
3	£445.00

Query42 : Select Query
Record: 1 of

Fig. 6.101 The output from Query 42.

The sequence of events in this query is:

- retrieve only week 1 and 2 sales figures;
- group the WEEKLYSALES records by E_NO and total each group's sales;
- sort the records in descending order of sales and take the first 25 per cent.

WeeklySales : Table

	e_no	c_no	w_no	s_value
▶	1	10	1	£100.00
	1	10	2	£150.00
	1	20	1	£20.00
	1	30	2	£30.00
	2	20	2	£60.00
	3	10	1	£70.00
	3	10	2	£85.00
	3	20	1	£160.00
	3	30	1	£90.00
	3	30	2	£40.00
*	0	0	0	£0.00

Record: ◀ ◀ 1 ▶ ▶ ▶* of 10

Fig. 6.102 The WEEKLYSALES table from the **emp_sales.mdb** database.

The WEEKLYSALES table is shown in Fig. 6.102. All of these records relate to week 1 and week 2. After grouping by E_NO (employee number), and summing on S_VALUE (sales value) there are three records – one for each employee. Finally, the TOP 25 per cent operation takes a quarter of these three records and rounds up, giving one record.

> _Query 43_: List the first three records in the WEEKLYSALES table.

This query shows that you can use TOP without ORDER BY.

Query43 : Select Query

```
SELECT TOP 3 *
FROM WEEKLY SALES
```

Fig. 6.103 Just get the first three records.

Query43 : Select Query

	e_no	c_no	w_no	s_value
▶	1	10	1	£100.00
	1	10	2	£150.00
	1	20	1	£20.00
*	0	0	0	£0.00

Record: ◀ ◀ 1 ▶ ▶ ▶* of 3

Fig. 6.104 The output of Query 43.

6.3   SELECT with multiple tables

All the SELECT queries so far described involve the use of only one table. In many practical situations it will be necessary to access information from two or more tables in order to find the answer to database queries. There are essentially three ways of accessing data in multiple tables in Access (Jet) SQL:

- Joins
- Subqueries
- Union queries.

Although these methods can be mixed in queries, we treat each separately here. However, many of the examples that follow *do* show queries which combine these features. Also note that all of the clauses used in the previous section (single-table queries) can also be used with joins, subqueries and union queries.

6.3.1   *SELECT with joined tables*

The idea of joining tables in SQL is that rows in one table are 'attached' to some 'corresponding' rows in another table. This creates a set of rows that contain columns from both tables. The rows are joined horizontally, the fields from the two joined rows being combined into a single row. The original tables are not altered and the joined rows exist only for the duration of the query. It is possible to save the joined rows in a new table but this is usually not necessary, the purpose of the join being only to answer the immediate query.

The criteria for joining rows are decided by the SQL user. In many cases the 'join criteria' are the identical values of columns which are foreign keys in one of the tables and primary keys in the other. This is not necessarily the case and there are several examples below where columns other than primary and foreign keys are involved as join criteria.

The main differences between selecting data from one table and selecting data from two (or more) tables are:

- The FROM clause contains reference to the *two* (or more) tables to be joined.
- The WHERE (or ON) clause must contain one or more additional conditions ('join criteria') stating the test for deciding which rows from the tables are to be joined.

When you create relationships in the Access relationship window, you are asked to specify a default join type. We discussed these in Chapter 3, and used them in Chapter 4 when designing queries using the grid. In SQL, you explicitly specify the join type you want, ignoring the default.

6.3.2   *INNER JOIN*

With an inner join, records from two tables are joined only where the join criteria are fulfilled. If there is a record in the first table that does not match a record in the second table, then that record will not be output.

Query 44: List the names, addresses and invoice details of all customers who have invoices.

Here the output will contain information from the two tables CUSTOMER and INVOICE. Names and addresses will come from CUSTOMER and 'invoice details' will come from INVOICE.

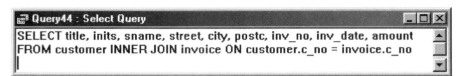

Fig. 6.105 An INNER JOIN joins matching records from the CUSTOMER and INVOICE tables.

In the SELECT line, the list of column names required in the output is given. Note that this is a combination of column names from the two tables CUSTOMER and INVOICE; the first six columns come from CUSTOMER and the other three from INVOICE. The FROM clause shows the two tables from which data values are to be drawn, and the ON clause gives the join criterion, i.e. that the customer account numbers on the CUSTOMER and INVOICE tables should be equal. Notice that the identically named customer account numbers: C–NO in both tables, have to be qualified by prefixing them with their respective table names in order to avoid ambiguity.

The output from this query is as follows:

title	inits	sname	street	city	postc	inv_no	inv_date	amount
Mr	G.R.	Sallaway	12 Fax Rd	London	WC1	940	05/12/99	£26.20
Mr	G.R.	Sallaway	12 Fax Rd	London	WC1	1003	12/01/00	£16.26
Miss	P.	Lauri	5 Dux St	London	N1	1004	14/01/00	£200.00
Mr	R.	Jackson	2 Lux Ave	Leeds	LE1 2AB	1005	20/01/00	£510.00
Mr	M.	Dziduch	31 Low St	Dover	DO2 9CD	1002	12/01/00	£149.23
Ms	S.Q.	Woods	17 Nax Rd	London	E18 4WW	1006	21/01/00	£250.10
Mrs	C.	Williams	41 Cax St	Dover	DO2 8WD	1017	22/01/00	£412.21

Record: 8 of 8

Fig. 6.106 The output from the INNER JOIN of Query 44.

Note that data for Mr G.R. Sallaway appears twice because he has two outstanding invoices.

The Jet DBMS of Access uses the ANSI-89 standard for SQL and in this standard, the syntax of INNER JOIN is as shown above.

However, Jet will also accept the ANSI-86 syntax for INNER JOIN. In the ANSI-86 standard, there were no outer joins; they either had to be simulated by other means or individual vendors' DBMSs had their own means of implementing outer joins.

The ANSI-86 syntax for the above query is shown below. It has the same output result as in Fig. 6.106.

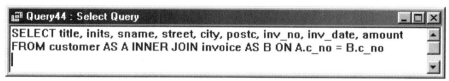

Fig. 6.107 The INNER JOIN implemented using the old ANSI-86 syntax.

The difference is that the tables to be joined are just listed separated by commas. A conventional WHERE clause is used for the join criteria.

Table aliases

Instead of using the full table name to qualify identically named column names in the two tables, it is possible to use *table aliases*, that is, alternative names for the tables. The output from the current query would have been the same if the following form of the SQL SELECT command had been used:

Fig. 6.108 'A' and 'B' are table aliases for CUSTOMER and INVOICE.

The table alias follows the table name in the FROM clause to establish, for example, that 'A' is an alias for CUS for the duration of the query. Similarly, 'B' is an alias for the INVOICE table. In ANSI-89, these aliases are preceded by the word 'AS'; in ANSI-86 they are not. These aliases are used in this query in the WHERE clause to qualify the identically named C_NO columns from both tables. Any name could be used as an alias, although it is usual to use a short alias name. The use of aliases in this example simply reduces the amount of typing necessary. Instead of typing:

ON customer.c_no = invoice.c_no

you type:

ON A.c_no = B.c_no.

When a table appears more than once in a query, as for example in a *self-join*, the aliases are mandatory, as a later example will illustrate.

> *Query 45*: List the account numbers, names, addresses and invoice details of all customers who have invoices.

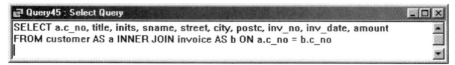

Fig. 6.109 Using a table alias to avoid ambiguity on field C_NO.

Since C_NO appears in both tables, ambiguity must be avoided in the SELECT line by qualifying the column name with the table name, in this case the alias 'a', otherwise SQL would have reported an error of the form 'Ambiguous column name'. Using 'b' or 'CUSTOMER' or 'INVOICE' as the qualifier would have worked just as well.

It is not necessary to list columns from both tables. Take the following query for example:

> *Query 46*: List the account numbers, names and addresses of all customers who have outstanding invoices.

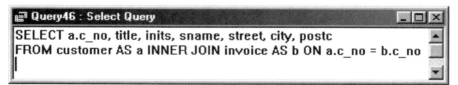

Fig. 6.110 Output from only one of the tables in a join.

	c_no	title	inits	sname	street	city	postc
▶	1	Mr	G.R.	Sallaway	12 Fax Rd	London	WC1
	1	Mr	G.R.	Sallaway	12 Fax Rd	London	WC1
	2	Miss	P.	Lauri	5 Dux St	London	N1
	3	Mr	R.	Jackson	2 Lux Ave	Leeds	LE1 2AB
	4	Mr	M.	Dziduch	31 Low St	Dover	DO2 9CD
	5	Ms	S.Q.	Woods	17 Nax Rd	London	E18 4WW
	6	Mrs	C.	Williams	41 Cax St	Dover	DO2 8WD
*							

Record: I◄ ◄ [1] ► ►I ►* of 7

Fig. 6.111 The output from Query 46.

All of these columns are from the CUS table, but the second table was necessary in order to eliminate the output of details of any customers who did not have outstanding invoices (in this case every customer had at least one outstanding invoice so that every customer appeared).

Note that G.R. Sallaway has again appeared twice, this time with entirely identical data values. This duplication of output can be eliminated using DISTINCT as follows:

```
Query46 : Select Query                                    _ □ ×
SELECT DISTINCT a.c_no, title, inits, sname, street, city, postc
FROM customer AS a INNER JOIN invoice AS b ON a.c_no = b.c_no
```

Fig. 6.112 Using DISTINCT to remove a duplicate output row.

c_no	title	inits	sname	street	city	postc
1	Mr	G.R.	Sallaway	12 Fax Rd	London	WC1
2	Miss	P.	Lauri	5 Dux St	London	N1
3	Mr	R.	Jackson	2 Lux Ave	Leeds	LE1 2AB
4	Mr	M.	Dziduch	31 Low St	Dover	DO2 9CD
5	Ms	S.Q.	Woods	17 Nax Rd	London	E18 4WW
6	Mrs	C.	Williams	41 Cax St	Dover	DO2 8WD

Record: 14 ◄ 1 ► ►I ►* of 6

Fig. 6.113 The duplicate row has been removed.

6.3.3 Greater-than join

The queries so far have had a single join criterion involving equality. In the following example a 'greater-than' join is performed. Suppose we have EMPLOYEE and JOB tables as in Figs 6.114 and 6.115.

> *Query 47: For each employee, list the jobs that will give him or her a standard salary higher than his or her current salary.*

The SQL for this query (Fig. 6.116), will give every combination of employee and job details where the STD_SALARY is greater than the current salary for that employee.

This may be of some use to a personnel department in discussions with employees about their possible career paths. The output is as shown in Fig. 6.117.

Note that no column name qualifiers or aliases are required since there are no common column names in the two tables. The output indicates that Alan has two choices of jobs with higher salaries than his, Bill has just one, and for Carol there is no job with a higher standard salary than her own.

Employee : Table

e_no	name	salary
1	Alan	£10,000.00
2	Bill	£20,000.00
3	Carol	£30,000.00
0		£0.00

Record: 1 of 3

Fig. 6.114 EMPLOYEE table from **emp_job.mdb** database.

Job : Table

Descr	Std_salary
Accountant	£18,000.00
Clerk	£9,000.00
Manager	£25,000.00
	£0.00

Record: 1

Fig. 6.115 JOB table.

Query47 : Select Query

```
SELECT *
FROM employee, job
WHERE std_salary > salary
```

Fig. 6.116 The SQL for the 'greater-than' join.

Query47 : Select Query

e_no	name	salary	Descr	Std_salary
1	Alan	£10,000.00	Accountant	£18,000.00
1	Alan	£10,000.00	Manager	£25,000.00
2	Bill	£20,000.00	Manager	£25,000.00

Record: 1 of 3

Fig. 6.117 The output of Query 47.

In this query, we can't use the INNER JOIN syntax. This is not an inner join. Inner joins are looking for *equality* between fields in the two tables.

If you try to use an inner join with inequality, as in the current query, the Jet engine will give you an error message: 'Join not supported'.

In addition to the greater-than join we have just seen, we can also define joins such as less than, less than or equal etc.

6.3.4 Self-join

A self-join is a join in which rows of a table are joined to other rows in the same table.

> *Query 48: For each employee show all employees who are earning a higher salary.*

Assuming the same database as for the previous query, only one table, EMPLOYEE, needs to be accessed since that is the source of all current salary data. For each employee it is required to inspect the salary of every other employee in the table to see if any of those employees receives a higher salary. The table is being used in two different ways and one way the SQL user can deal with this is to use a *self-join*. In this case the table is notionally joined to itself – every row to every other row – in the fashion of a Cartesian product on a single table, and then only those rows where the second salary is higher than the first are selected for output.

Another way to view what is going on in the SQL self-join, as with all joins, is to imagine a pointer pointing to rows in each table. The pointer to the first table starts by pointing to the first row and while it is there, the pointer to rows in the second table 'scans' the second table row by row, checking to see if the join and all other criteria on the second table have been satisfied. If so, it puts a copy of the first table's row together with a copy of the second table's matching row and passes the result to the output.

With the self-join, the 'first' and 'second' tables can be imagined as separate but identical tables although of course there is only one table. The query SQL is as follows:

```
Query48 : Select Query

SELECT *
FROM employee AS a, employee AS b
WHERE b.salary > a.salary
```

Fig. 6.118 The SQL for the 'greater-than self-join' of Query 48.

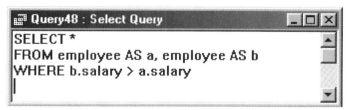

a.e_no	a.name	a.salary	b.e_no	b.name	b.salary
1	Alan	£10,000.00	2	Bill	£20,000.00
1	Alan	£10,000.00	3	Carol	£30,000.00
2	Bill	£20,000.00	3	Carol	£30,000.00

Record: 14 ◀ 1 ▶ ▶l ▶* of 3

Fig. 6.119 The output of Query 48.

This is a self-join because a table is being joined to itself. It is also a greater-than join because in the join criteria we are not looking for equality but are matching on the inequality b.salary > a.salary.

6.3.5 *Joining more than two tables*

It is sometimes necessary to access data from three or more database tables. The rules are similar to the two-table situation. Every table used is mentioned in the FROM clause of the SELECT command, and join criteria for matching rows from the tables to be joined must appear in the ON clause in the ANSI-89 syntax that Jet SQL uses, or in the WHERE clause for the ANSI-86 syntax that Jet also allows.

> *Query 49: From the accts.mdb database, list the customer number, surname, invoice number, invoice amount, payment number, payment date and payment amount for all customers.*

We give the SQL for the ANSI-89 syntax first. See Fig. 6.120.

```
Query49 : Select Query
SELECT a.c_no, sname, b.inv_no, b.amount, pmt_no, pmt_date, c.amount
FROM [customer AS a INNER JOIN invoice AS b ON a.c_no = b.c_no]
INNER JOIN payment AS c ON b.inv_no = c.inv_no
```

Fig. 6.120 A double inner join for Query 49.

The output obtained from this query is shown in Fig. 6.121.

c_no	sname	inv_no	b.amount	pmt_no	pmt_date	c.amount
1	Sallaway	940	£26.20	2	12/12/99	£13.00
1	Sallaway	940	£26.20	3	19/01/00	£10.00
3	Jackson	1005	£510.00	1	14/01/00	£510.00
6	Williams	1017	£412.21	1	30/01/00	£100.00

Record: 1 of 4

Fig. 6.121 The output from Query 49.

Firstly, consider the query itself.

In the SELECT line, the table alias qualifiers in A.C_NO and B.INV_NO are necessary because these column names appear in two tables and without them SQL would give an 'ambiguity' error. In the CUSTOMER table C_NO is the primary key and in the INVOICE table C_NO is a foreign key indicating the one-to-many relationship between the CUSTOMER entity type and the INVOICE entity type. (See Appendix 1 for the schema design of **accts.mdb**.)

There is also a 1:N relationship between INVOICE and PAYMENT, because in the company using this database, one invoice can have many payments (instalments) but one payment is allowed to cover (i.e. is allocated to) only one invoice.

Hence this relationship between INVOICE and PAYMENT can be shown by the primary key INV_NO in the INVOICE table appearing as a foreign key in PAYMENT.

The reason for the table alias qualifier 'B.' in B.AMOUNT in the SELECT line of the query is slightly different. There are two identically named AMOUNT columns in the INVOICE and PAYMENT tables. The meanings of the two AMOUNT columns are, however, different. In the INVOICE table, AMOUNT means the invoice amount, i.e. the value of the bill sent to the customer, whereas AMOUNT in the PAYMENT table is the value of the payment made by the customer in response to the invoice.

This double meaning for a column name causes no problems in practice since the column name can always be qualified by the table name to remove any ambiguity and this is achieved by the 'B.' and 'C.' qualifiers in this query. The table alias names A, B and C are established in the FROM clause (yes, *after* their use in the SELECT line) and the join criteria are also established in the FROM clause.

Now referring to the output obtained from this query, notice that customer Sallaway appears twice because he has made two payments (both against invoice number 940) in this accounting period. The other two customers Jackson and Williams appear once because they both have a single invoice with a single payment associated with each.

What is interesting about the output is the data that does NOT appear. Firstly, only three of the six customers appear. Secondly, only three of the seven invoices appear. Why? The answer is clear when the mechanism of the INNER JOIN is considered.

In the WHERE clause (customer AS a INNER JOIN invoice AS b ON a.c_no = b.c_no) which is used for joining rows from the CUSTOMER and INVOICE tables, it is possible to imagine the temporary result before the matching PAYMENT rows are joined on in the second INNER JOIN. This intermediate result would be:

c_no	sname	inv_no	amount
1	Sallaway	940	£26.20
1	Sallaway	1003	£16.26
2	Lauri	1004	£200.00
3	Jackson	1005	£510.00
4	Dziduch	1002	£149.23
5	Woods	1006	£250.10
6	Williams	1017	£412.21

Fig. 6.122 The intermediate result of CUSTOMER INNER JOIN INVOICE.

Every customer account appears in this intermediate result because every customer happens to have at least one outstanding invoice. If any customer did not have an outstanding invoice, that customer's details would be eliminated at this stage because the join criterion of the first INNER JOIN would not have been satisfied. Customer Sallaway appears twice because he has two outstanding invoices.

The next step in the SQL query is to join the payment details onto this intermediate result and this is performed in the second INNER JOIN. The join criterion 'ON b.inv_no = c.inv_no' says that in order for a row from this intermediate result to be passed to the output, B.INV_NO, which is column 3 in the intermediate result, should match with a C.INV_NO in the PAYMENT table. The INV_NO of the first row of the intermediate result matches with the INV_NO of the first row of the PAYMENT table (both equal to 940) so a joined row consisting of the columns mentioned in the SELECT line of the query is passed to the output. The second row of PAYMENT also matches the first row of the intermediate result so the projected columns of these rows are also joined, forming the second row of the output. There are no further payments for invoice 940 so the 'pointer' to the intermediate result table is incremented to point to its second row (INV_NO = 1003). There are *no* matches in the PAYMENT table for this intermediate table row so the row is abandoned and produces no output. Thus the invoice details of Sallaway's invoice number 1003 are lost and are eliminated from the output. Similarly, the intermediate data for Lauri, Dziduch and Woods is eliminated from the output because none of them has a payment to his or her credit. It is not certain whether this was what was wanted when the English query was formulated since it is rather vague. If the query had been put in the form: 'List all current invoice and payment details for all of our customers', then this SQL form of the query would definitely *not* be correct since:

- any customer with no current invoices would not be output, and more importantly
- invoice details for any customer with current invoices having no payments would not be output.

LEFT JOINs (see Section 6.3.6) would have resulted in all of the invoices being shown, whether or not they had payments. For the sake of completeness, we show the ANSI-86 version of this INNER JOIN query in Fig. 6.123. The output results are the same as before (Fig. 6.121).

```
Query1 : Select Query
select a.c_no, sname, b.inv_no, b.amount, pmt_no, pmt_date, c.amount
from customer as a, invoice as b, payment as c
where a.c_no = b.c_no
and b.inv_no = c.inv_no
```

Fig. 6.123 The ANSI-86 version of Query 49.

How do I know if my SQL query is correct?

A few comments about query testing seem appropriate here. It is easy to see the shortcomings of the SQL query above by inspecting the small amount of data in the tables, but spotting errors this way cannot be relied upon when large tables are being queried. The remedy is found by a combination of:

- making sure you understand what the client wants with regard to the query,
- making sure the English version of the query accurately reflects this – spend some time with the client getting a clear, unambiguous and succinct English statement of their requirements,
- a thorough understanding of the operation of SQL, and
- thorough desk checking of the query output using carefully chosen test data.

Inspection of important queries by a programming colleague can also prove helpful.

One of the disadvantages of a powerful programming language like SQL is that more mistakes can be made more quickly. On the positive side, it is usually considerably easier to comprehend the logic of an SQL query than that of a program written entirely in a procedural language such as COBOL, FORTRAN, PASCAL, C or even VB, and a good SQL programmer will generally get results faster than a good 3GL programmer.

The same comments apply to embedded SQL. In this case, it is worthwhile thoroughly testing the SQL statement separately in Access before embedding it in procedural code.

6.3.6   *LEFT JOIN and RIGHT JOIN*

We have seen the INNER JOIN (Section 6.3.2). In contrast to this, there are two types of Outer Join. Although they are not named as such in SQL, the LEFT JOIN and the RIGHT JOIN are collectively known as Outer Joins.

We deal first with the LEFT JOIN. It is used far more frequently than the RIGHT JOIN.

Given two tables TableA and TableB, then TableA LEFT JOIN TableB gives all of the records in TableA joined to any records in TableB that match. Where a record in TableA has no matching record in TableB, it is output with NULLs where the TableB fields would be.

Given two tables TableA and TableB, then TableB RIGHT JOIN TableA gives all of the records in TableA joined to any records in TableB that match. Where a record in TableA has no matching record in TableB, it is output with NULLs where the TableB fields would be.

So TableA LEFT JOIN TableB is equivalent to TableB RIGHT JOIN Table A.

To demonstrate this, we set up two tables, TableA and TableB, as shown in Figs 6.124 and 6.125, overleaf.

The primary key for TableA is a_no and the primary key for TableB is b_no. A consequence of primary keys being 'unique' is that any relationship between TableA and TableB based on a link between a_no and b_no would be 1:1, optional both directions. We have not created any relationship between these tables.

The tables have one key value (1) in common and a key value in each that is not in the other (2 and 3).

Fig. 6.124 TableA.

Fig. 6.125 TableB.

*Query 50: TableA LEFT JOIN TableB in the **tablea_tableb** database.*

Fig. 6.126 TableA LEFT JOIN TableB.

The result of this join is shown in Fig. 6.127.

Note that there are NULLs in the second output row where a record exists in TableA with no corresponding join criteria value in TableB. That characterizes the LEFT JOIN.

Fig. 6.127 TableA LEFT JOIN TableB output.

Query 51: *TableB RIGHT JOIN TableA.*

Query51 : Select Query

```
SELECT TableA.*, TableB.*
FROM TableB RIGHT JOIN TableA ON TableB.b_no = TableA.a_no
```

Fig. 6.128 TableB RIGHT JOIN TableA.

Query51 : Select Query

a_no	a_field1	a_field2	b_no	b_field1	b_field2
1	a11	a12	1	b11	b12
2	a21	a22			

Record: 1 of 2

Fig. 6.129 TableB RIGHT JOIN TableA output.

As you can see, the output for TableA LEFT JOIN TableB is equivalent to the output for TableB RIGHT JOIN TableA. Similarly, TableA RIGHT JOIN TableB is equivalent to TableB LEFT JOIN TableA.

We now consider LEFT JOIN and RIGHT JOIN in two tables that have a one–many relationship between them.

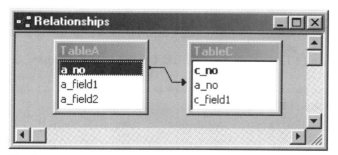

Fig. 6.130 There's a one–many relationship from TableA to TableB.

We have opted for no referential integrity in the relationship between TableA and TableB. That allows us to have records in TableC whose a_no matches no a_no in TableA.

The data in the two tables, TableA and TableC, are shown in Figs 6.131 and 6.132.

TableA : Table

a_no	a_field1	a_field2
1	a11	a12
2	a21	a22
0		

Record: 3 of 3

Fig. 6.131 TableA.

TableC : Table

c_no	a_no	c_field1
1	1	c11
2	1	c21
3		c31
0	0	

Record: 4 of 4

Fig. 6.132 TableC.

We now perform TableA LEFT JOIN TableC and TableC RIGHT JOIN TableA and compare the output.

Query 52: TableA LEFT JOIN TableC.

Query52 : Select Query

```
SELECT *
FROM TableA LEFT JOIN TableC ON TableA.a_no = TableC.a_no
```

Fig. 6.133 TableA LEFT JOIN TableC.

Query52 : Select Query

TableA.a_no	a_field1	a_field2	c_no	TableC.a_no	c_field1
1	a11	a12	2	1	c21
1	a11	a12	1	1	c11
2	a21	a22			

Record: 1 of 3

Fig. 6.134 TableA LEFT JOIN TableC output.

As you would expect, this LEFT JOIN has output the record for TableA with no corresponding record in TableC.

Query 53: *TableC RIGHT JOIN TableA.*

Query53 : Select Query

```
SELECT TableA.*, TableC.*
FROM TableC RIGHT JOIN TableA ON TableC.a_no = TableA.a_no
```

Fig. 6.135 TableC RIGHT JOIN TableA.

Query53 : Select Query

TableA.a_no	a_field1	a_field2	c_no	TableC.a_no	c_field1
1	a11	a12	2	1	c21
1	a11	a12	1	1	c11
2	a21	a22			

Record: 1 of 3

Fig. 6.136 TableC RIGHT JOIN TableA output.

As can be seen from these queries, and from the definition of LEFT JOIN and RIGHT JOIN, it is in general true that A LEFT JOIN B is equivalent to B RIGHT JOIN A for any two tables A and B.

As a consequence of this, we omit any further discussion of RIGHT JOIN.

We now demonstrate the difference between INNER JOIN and LEFT JOIN using the **accts.mdb** database tables INVOICE and PAYMENT. Note that whatever default Join Type is specified when creating a relationship in the Relationship View of Access is ignored when writing SQL joins because you explicitly say what type of join you want in the SQL statement.

Query 54: *INVOICE INNER JOIN PAYMENT.*

Query54 : Select Query

```
SELECT a.inv_no, c_no, inv_date, a.amount AS [Invoice amount],
pmt_no, pmt_date, b.amount AS [Payment amount]
FROM invoice AS a INNER JOIN payment AS b ON a.inv_no = b.inv_no
```

Fig. 6.137 INVOICE INNER JOIN PAYMENT.

We have seen this query before.

The output, being the result of an INNER JOIN, only contains rows where the INV_NO of INVOICE and the INV_NO of PAYMENT match up. Invoices with no payments don't appear at the output.

inv_no	c_no	inv_date	Invoice amout	pmt_no	pmt_date	Payment amo
940	1	05/12/99	£26.20	2	12/12/99	£13.00
940	1	05/12/99	£26.20	3	19/01/00	£10.00
1005	3	20/01/00	£510.00	1	14/01/00	£510.00
1017	6	22/01/00	£412.21	1	30/01/00	£100.00

Record: 1 of 4

Fig. 6.138 INVOICE INNER JOIN PAYMENT output.

Invoices 1002, 1003, 1004 and 1006 consequently don't appear at the output of this join (Fig. 6.138).

Query 55: INVOICE LEFT JOIN PAYMENT.

```
SELECT a.inv_no, c_no, inv_date, a.amount AS [Invoice amount], pmt_no, pmt_date,
b.amount AS [Payment amount]
FROM invoice AS a LEFT JOIN payment AS b ON a.inv_no = b.inv_no
```

Fig. 6.139 INVOICE LEFT JOIN PAYMENT.

inv_no	c_no	inv_date	Invoice amount	pmt_no	pmt_date	Payment amount
940	1	05/12/99	£26.20	2	12/12/99	£13.00
940	1	05/12/99	£26.20	3	19/01/00	£10.00
1002	4	12/01/00	£149.23			
1003	1	12/01/00	£16.26			
1004	2	14/01/00	£200.00			
1005	3	20/01/00	£510.00	1	14/01/00	£510.00
1006	5	21/01/00	£250.10			
1017	6	22/01/00	£412.21	1	30/01/00	£100.00

Record: 1 of 8

Fig. 6.140 INVOICE LEFT JOIN PAYMENT output.

Comparing Figs 6.138 and 6.140, the difference between the INNER JOIN and the LEFT JOIN is immediately apparent. With the LEFT JOIN, *all* invoices appear at the output, whether or not they have any payments. Where they have no payments, they appear with NULLs where the payment field values would otherwise be.

This query illustrates one of the improvements of ANSI-89 SQL over ANSI-86.

ANSI-86 SQL only had the inner join. If you wanted to get the effect of a left join, you had to either depend on the custom, non-standard outer join facilities of the particular DBMS you were working with (if they existed), or perform a UNION query with a NOT EXISTS or NOT IN to append all the non-matching records separately.

We cover UNION queries and compare IN and NOT IN with EXISTS and NOT EXISTS in Chapter 7.

6.3.7 Combining INNER JOINs and LEFT JOINs

In Query 49 we found that when joining three tables, the CUSTOMER, INVOICE and PAYMENT tables, the output was not as we wanted. Inner joining CUSTOMER to INVOICE listed all the customers who had invoices. This result was then inner joined to the PAYMENT table, and any invoices with no payments were eliminated – that is what INNER JOIN does. Further, any customers who only had invoices which had been eliminated in this way were eliminated too. In this section we show how to solve this and similar problems by correctly combining INNER JOINs and LEFT JOINs. (Remember in the previous section, section 6.3.6, we showed that RIGHT JOIN is never needed.) Let's return to query 49. We'll take the opportunity to remove some ambiguity in the English version of the query too and to keep in sequence call it Query 56.

> *Query 56: List customers and their invoices and associated payments from the* **accts.mdb** *database. Only list customers who have invoices, but list all invoices, whether or not they have payments.*

The basic strategy is to use an INNER JOIN to join CUSTOMER to INVOICE. That will eliminate any customers without invoices. We shall then combine that record-set with the PAYMENT table using a LEFT JOIN. All the records in the first recordset will remain; they will just have PAYMENT records joined on where appropriate,

```
SELECT a.c_no, sname, street, city, postc, b.inv_no, inv_date,
b.amount, pmt_no, pmt_date, c.amount
FROM (customer AS a INNER JOIN invoice AS b ON a.c_no = b.c_no)
LEFT JOIN payment AS c ON b.inv_no = c.inv_no;
```

Fig. 6.141 Combination of an INNER JOIN and a LEFT JOIN.

c_no	sname	street	city	postc	inv_no	inv_date	b.amount	pmt_no	pmt_date	c.amount
1	Sallaway	12 Fax Rd	London	WC1	940	05/12/99	£26.20	2	12/12/99	£13.00
1	Sallaway	12 Fax Rd	London	WC1	940	05/12/99	£26.20	3	19/01/00	£10.00
4	Dziduch	31 Low St	Dover	DO2 9CD	1002	12/01/00	£149.23			
1	Sallaway	12 Fax Rd	London	WC1	1003	12/01/00	£16.26			
2	Lauri	5 Dux St	London	N1	1004	14/01/00	£200.00			
3	Jackson	2 Lux Ave	Leeds	LE1 2AB	1005	20/01/00	£510.00	1	14/01/00	£510.00
5	Woods	17 Nax Rd	London	E18 4WW	1006	21/01/00	£250.10			
6	Williams	41 Cax St	Dover	DO2 8WD	1017	22/01/00	£412.21	1	30/01/00	£100.00

Record: 1 of 8

Fig. 6.142 The output from Query 56.

and where there is more than one payment for an invoice, the records in the original recordset will be repeated, which is in the nature of *all* joins.

The output now contains what the query requires. Since all of the customers on our test database have at least one invoice, they all appear at the output. All invoices appear, whether or not they have payments. Even customers who only have invoices with no payments appear.

Note that the position of the brackets in Fig. 6.141 ensured the CUSTOMER INNER JOIN INVOICE join occurred first. If we rearrange the brackets in an attempt to force the INVOICE LEFT JOIN PAYMENT to occur first, as in Fig. 6.143, we get the same output. The LEFT JOIN is said to be 'nested' inside the INNER JOIN.

```
Query56b : Select Query
SELECT a.c_no, sname, street, city, postc, b.inv_no, inv_date, b.amount,
pmt_no, pmt_date, c.amount
FROM customer AS a INNER JOIN (invoice AS b LEFT JOIN payment AS c
ON b.inv_no = c.inv_no) ON a.c_no = b.c_no;
```

Fig. 6.143 Forcing the INVOICE LEFT JOIN PAYMENT to occur first.

In both cases, the order of the output records is the same. This can easily be put into the sequence of PMT_NO within INV_NO within C_NO using an appropriate ORDER BY clause. See Fig. 6.144.

```
Query56c : Select Query
SELECT a.c_no, sname, street, city, postc, b.inv_no, inv_date,
b.amount, pmt_no, pmt_date, c.amount
FROM (customer AS a INNER JOIN invoice AS b ON a.c_no = b.c_no)
LEFT JOIN payment AS c ON b.inv_no = c.inv_no
ORDER BY a.c_no, b.inv_no, pmt_no
```

Fig. 6.144 Adding an ORDER BY clause.

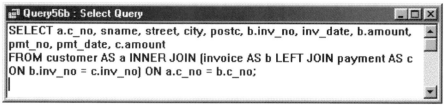

c_no	sname	street	city	postc	inv_no	inv_date	b.amount	pmt_no	pmt_date	c.amount
1	Sallaway	12 Fax Rd	London	WC1	940	05/12/99	£26.20	2	12/12/99	£13.00
1	Sallaway	12 Fax Rd	London	WC1	940	05/12/99	£26.20	3	19/01/00	£10.00
1	Sallaway	12 Fax Rd	London	WC1	1003	12/01/00	£16.26			
2	Lauri	5 Dux St	London	N1	1004	14/01/00	£200.00			
3	Jackson	2 Lux Ave	Leeds	LE1 2AB	1005	20/01/00	£510.00	1	14/01/00	£510.00
4	Dziduch	31 Low St	Dover	DO2 9CD	1002	12/01/00	£149.23			
5	Woods	17 Nax Rd	London	E18 4WW	1006	21/01/00	£250.10			
6	Williams	41 Cax St	Dover	DO2 8WD	1017	22/01/00	£412.21	1	30/01/00	£100.00

Record: 1 of 8

Fig. 6.145 The output after sorting with the ORDER BY clause.

The ORDER BY clause is discussed in Section 6.2.10. To further 'tidy up' the output, appropriate column aliases can be used.

This query could form the basis for an end-of-month customer Statement of Account report run. The INNER JOIN in the query would ensure that any customer with no current invoices would not be sent a statement.

Suppose, however, that we wanted to send a statement to all customers, whether or not they have any current invoices, as in the next query.

> *Query 57*: List customers and their invoices and associated payments from the **accts.mdb** database. List all customers, whether or not they have invoices, and list all invoices, whether or not they have payments.

In our test database **accts.mdb** we shall add a customer, customer 10, who has no invoices. The new CUSTOMER table is shown in Fig. 6.146.

	c_no	title	sname	inits	street	city	postc	cred_lim	balance
	1	Mr	Sallaway	G.R.	12 Fax Rd	London	WC1	£1,000.00	£42.56
	2	Miss	Lauri	P.	5 Dux St	London	N1	£500.00	£200.00
	3	Mr	Jackson	R.	2 Lux Ave	Leeds	LE1 2AB	£500.00	£510.00
	4	Mr	Dziduch	M.	31 Low St	Dover	DO2 9CD	£100.00	£149.23
	5	Ms	Woods	S.Q.	17 Nax Rd	London	E18 4WW	£1,000.00	£250.10
	6	Mrs	Williams	C.	41 Cax St	Dover	DO2 8WD		£412.21
	10	Mr	Jones	T.	3 Side St	Leeds	LE2 4NN	£1,000.00	£0.00
▶	0							£0.00	£0.00

Record: 8 of 8

Fig. 6.146 A new customer Jones has been added. He has no invoices.

If we re-run Query 56, we still get the output shown in Fig. 6.145. The INNER JOIN prevents customer 10 being output because he has no invoices. To see him in the output we must change this INNER JOIN to a LEFT JOIN, as in Fig. 6.147.

```
SELECT a.c_no, sname, street, city, postc, b.inv_no, inv_date,
b.amount, pmt_no, pmt_date, c.amount
FROM (customer AS a LEFT JOIN invoice AS b ON a.c_no = b.c_no)
LEFT JOIN payment AS c ON b.inv_no = c.inv_no
ORDER BY a.c_no, b.inv_no, pmt_no;
```

Fig. 6.147 Converting the first join to a LEFT JOIN.

The output from the query is shown in Fig. 6.148. Note that the new customer – customer number 10 – is now shown at the output of the query.

The LEFT JOIN between CUSTOMER and INVOICE has ensured that customers are output even if they have no invoices.

The LEFT JOIN between this result (CUSTOMER LEFT JOIN INVOICE) and PAYMENT ensures that customer–invoice joined records are output even if there is no payment for the invoice.

c_no	sname	street	city	postc	inv_no	inv_date	b.amount	pmt_no	pmt_date	c.amount
1	Sallaway	12 Fax Rd	London	WC1	940	05/12/99	£26.20	2	12/12/99	£13.00
1	Sallaway	12 Fax Rd	London	WC1	940	05/12/99	£26.20	3	19/01/00	£10.00
1	Sallaway	12 Fax Rd	London	WC1	1003	12/01/00	£16.26			
2	Lauri	5 Dux St	London	N1	1004	14/01/00	£200.00			
3	Jackson	2 Lux Ave	Leeds	LE1 2AB	1005	20/01/00	£510.00	1	14/01/00	£510.00
4	Dziduch	31 Low St	Dover	DO2 9CD	1002	12/01/00	£149.23			
5	Woods	17 Nax Rd	London	E18 4WW	1006	21/01/00	£250.10			
6	Williams	41 Cax St	Dover	DO2 8WD	1017	22/01/00	£412.21	1	30/01/00	£100.00
10	Jones	3 Side St	Leeds	LE2 4NN						

Record: |◀ ◀ 1 ▶ ▶| ▶* of 9

Fig. 6.148 The LEFT JOIN between CUSTOMER and INVOICE allows customer Jones (no invoices) to be output.

6.3.8 Jet's join nesting rule

It is not permissible to follow a LEFT JOIN by an INNER JOIN in the Jet database. To quote Access 97 Help for INNER JOIN:

> *A LEFT JOIN or a RIGHT JOIN may be nested inside an INNER JOIN, but an INNER JOIN may not be nested inside a LEFT JOIN or a RIGHT JOIN.*

We give below an example of a query which breaks this rule.

> *Query 58: (CUSTOMER LEFT JOIN INVOICE) INNER JOIN PAYMENT.*

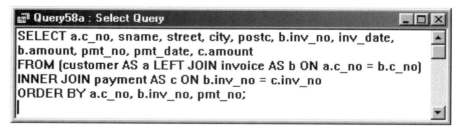

```
SELECT a.c_no, sname, street, city, postc, b.inv_no, inv_date,
b.amount, pmt_no, pmt_date, c.amount
FROM (customer AS a LEFT JOIN invoice AS b ON a.c_no = b.c_no)
INNER JOIN payment AS c ON b.inv_no = c.inv_no
ORDER BY a.c_no, b.inv_no, pmt_no;
```

Fig. 6.149 This query (Query58a) breaks Jet's nested INNER JOIN rule.

Microsoft Access

⚠ Join expression not supported.

OK   Help

Fig. 6.150 The error resulting from trying to run Query58a.

The error is caused by trying to follow a LEFT JOIN by an INNER JOIN. Jet does not permit this.

To investigate this restriction a little further, let's separate the two joins. Figure 6.151 shows Query58b, which is the LEFT JOIN between CUSTOMER and INVOICE, and Fig. 6.152 shows its output.

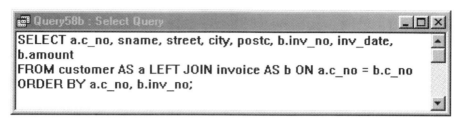

```
Query58b : Select Query                              _ |□| x
SELECT a.c_no, sname, street, city, postc, b.inv_no, inv_date,
b.amount
FROM customer AS a LEFT JOIN invoice AS b ON a.c_no = b.c_no
ORDER BY a.c_no, b.inv_no;
```

Fig. 6.151 Query58b: The LEFT JOIN taken on its own.

c_no	sname	street	city	postc	inv_no	inv_date	amount
1	Sallaway	12 Fax Rd	London	WC1	940	05/12/99	£26.20
1	Sallaway	12 Fax Rd	London	WC1	1003	12/01/00	£16.26
2	Lauri	5 Dux St	London	N1	1004	14/01/00	£200.00
3	Jackson	2 Lux Ave	Leeds	LE1 2AB	1005	20/01/00	£510.00
4	Dziduch	31 Low St	Dover	DO2 9CD	1002	12/01/00	£149.23
5	Woods	17 Nax Rd	London	E18 4WW	1006	21/01/00	£250.10
6	Williams	41 Cax St	Dover	DO2 8WD	1017	22/01/00	£412.21
10	Jones	3 Side St	Leeds	LE2 4NN			

Record: 1 of 8

Fig. 6.152 The output of the Query58b.

We now want to INNER JOIN this to the PAYMENT table, which is shown in Fig. 6.153.

inv_no	pmt_no	pmt_date	amount
940	2	12/12/99	£13.00
940	3	19/01/00	£10.00
1005	1	14/01/00	£510.00
1017	1	30/01/00	£100.00
0	0		£0.00

Record: 1 of 4

Fig. 6.153 The PAYMENT table.

Looking at these recordsets, we would expect an INNER JOIN between them to succeed. It does, as is shown in Figs 6.154 and 6.155.

```
Query58c : Select Query
SELECT c_no, sname, street, city, postc, b.inv_no, inv_date,
b.amount, pmt_no, pmt_date, c.amount
FROM query58b AS b INNER JOIN payment AS c ON b.inv_no =
c.inv_no
ORDER BY c_no, b.inv_no, pmt_no;
```

Fig. 6.154 Inner Joining the results of Query58b to PAYMENT.

c_no	sname	street	city	postc	inv_no	inv_date	b.amount	pmt_no	pmt_date	c.amount
1	Sallaway	12 Fax Rd	London	WC1	940	05/12/99	£26.20	2	12/12/99	£13.00
1	Sallaway	12 Fax Rd	London	WC1	940	05/12/99	£26.20	3	19/01/00	£10.00
3	Jackson	2 Lux Ave	Leeds	LE1 2AB	1005	20/01/00	£510.00	1	14/01/00	£510.00
6	Williams	41 Cax St	Dover	DO2 8WD	1017	22/01/00	£412.21	1	30/01/00	£100.00

Record: 1 of 4

Fig. 6.155 The output of Query58c.

The output from Query58c is as expected.

This sequence (Query58a to Query58c) has demonstrated that Jet's rule concerning the 'nesting' of an INNER JOIN inside a LEFT JOIN is unnecessarily restrictive. The solution, however, is simply to perform the queries separately, as shown with Query58b and Query58c.

Using NULLs from a join

The NULLs that are returned from a left join can be used.

Query 59: List customers with no invoices.

```
Query59 : Select Query
SELECT a.*
FROM customer AS a LEFT JOIN invoice AS b ON a.c_no = b.c_no
WHERE b.c_no is null
```

Fig. 6.156 Customers without invoices have NULLs where the INVOICE would be.

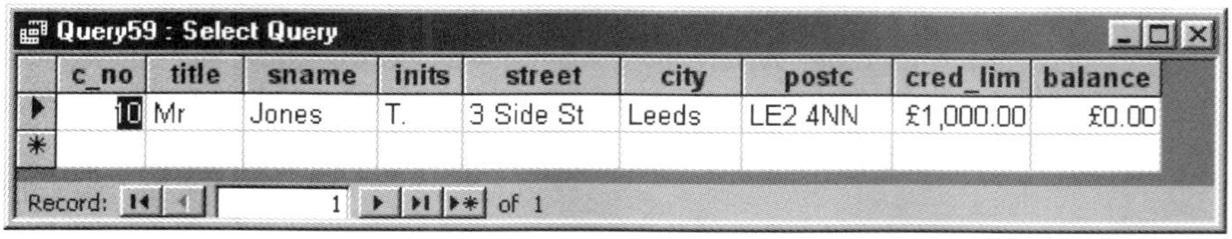
Query59 : Select Query

c_no	title	sname	inits	street	city	postc	cred_lim	balance
10	Mr	Jones	T.	3 Side St	Leeds	LE2 4NN	£1,000.00	£0.00

Record: 1 of 1

Fig. 6.157 The customer without an invoice.

C_NO (and all other INVOICE fields) are NULL for customer 10.

6.4 Exercises

Using SQL statements, and the tables of the test databases given in Appendix 1, develop and test SQL queries to do the following. Copies of these databases can be downloaded from the Website **http://www.databasedesign.co.uk/book** if required.

Exercises 1 to 12 are single-table queries and involve only the CUSTOMER and INVOICE tables of the **accts.mdb** database.

1. List details of all customers based in Leeds or Dover.
2. List details of all customers not based in Leeds.
3. List details of all non-overdrawn customers not based in Bradford, Leeds or London. Take 'non-overdrawn' to mean that the customer's balance does not exceed his or her credit limit.
4. List the customer numbers of all customers with outstanding invoices. Assume that all the invoices in the INVOICE table are 'outstanding'. Each customer number should appear only once, and the list should be in descending order.
5. List the number of different cities there are in the CUSTOMER file. Use two queries, the second based on the first.
6. List the total balance for each city.
7. List the cities that have a total balance exceeding £500.
8. List the number of cities that have a total balance exceeding £500.
9. List the outstanding balance in each city having more than one customer.
10. List the customer(s) with the highest balance.
11. List the customer(s) with the highest available credit.
12. List the city or cities with the highest balance.

Exercises 13 to 22 involve joins and several of the test databases.

13. List the customer numbers, names, addresses and invoice details of all non-London customers who have outstanding invoices with invoice amounts over £10. Use an inner join.
14. For each customer, show all customers who have a higher balance. Use a self-join.
15. List details of all payments and the corresponding invoices. Use a left join.

16. List the customer details, the invoice details, and the details of any payments for each invoice. Where a customer has no invoices, do not list him or her out. List invoices whether or not they have payments. Use an inner join and a left join.

17. List all customers in the same city as Sallaway. Use a join.

18. List details of all customers who have invoices. Use a join. Ensure no customer details appear more than once.

19. List the names of all customers who have made a payment before the invoice was sent. Use joins.

20. List details of all customers who have an invoice equal in value to their current balance. Use joins.

21. List details of all customers who have sent a payment over £400. Use joins.

22. List the city or cities with the highest total outstanding balance. See how many different ways you can do this.

Chapter 7

Access query design using SQL – the SELECT statement – further features

In this chapter you will learn:

- further features of the SQL SELECT statement
- how to use subqueries, including the use of IN, ANY and ALL
- how to use EXISTS and NOT EXISTS
- how to combine joins and subqueries to best effect
- how to use UNION queries
- how to simulate INTERSECT and MINUS set operations
- how stored queries can be used as views
- how to use SELECT INTO
- how to use CROSSTAB queries.

7.1 Introduction

To complete our study of the SQL SELECT statement, we continue in this chapter with the topics shown above. Subqueries add powerful selection and navigational features to SELECT statements. UNION queries combine the results of two or more SELECTs. SELECT INTO allows you to save the data from a query into a table. Crosstab queries can be used to present data from certain queries in a grid format.

7.2 SELECT with subqueries

SQL contains the facility for nesting one SELECT command within another. The nested SELECT is called a *subquery* and it is always surrounded by parentheses. The SELECT statement that contains the subquery is called the *outer query*.

The purpose of a subquery is to help to specify the set of values to be returned by the outer query. The subquery runs first, and returns a set of values or a condition that can be used to define the output from the outer query. It is not possible to output any data returned by a subquery.

The outer query and the subquery can be linked in one of three ways. These are shown in Fig. 7.1.

```
comparison [ANY | ALL | SOME] (subquery)
expression [NOT] IN (subquery)
[NOT] EXISTS (subquery)
```

in which

comparison   is an expression and a comparison operator that compares the expression with the results of the subquery.

expression   is an expression for which the result set of the subquery is searched.

subquery   is a SELECT statement, following the same format and rules as any other SELECT statement. It must be enclosed in parentheses.

Fig. 7.1 How the subquery may be linked to the outer query.

Figure 7.2 shows a subquery in the WHERE clause of the outer query.

```
SELECT ...                    ⎫
FROM    ...                    ⎬  Outer Query
WHERE X IN                     ⎭
    (SELECT   ...              ⎫
     FROM     ...              ⎬  Subquery
     WHERE    ... )            ⎭
```

Fig. 7.2 A subquery being used in a WHERE clause.

Figure 7.3 shows a subquery returning a set of values that are checked against field X in the current record in the outer recordset.

In the query of Fig. 7.3, the subquery has its own compound WHERE condition, and its own GROUP BY and compound HAVING condition. The outer query also has these and an ORDER BY clause too.

The only restriction on a subquery is that it can't have its own ORDER BY clause.

This makes sense since ORDER BY is only used to sequence the output, and nothing from the subquery *can* be output; it's just there to help restrict the output of the outer query.

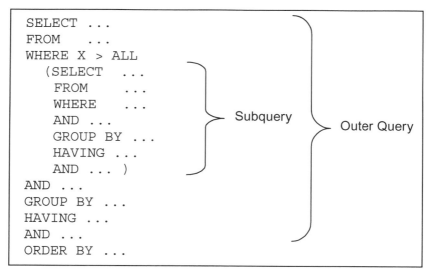

```
SELECT ...
FROM    ...
WHERE X > ALL
   (SELECT   ...
     FROM    ...
     WHERE   ...
     AND ...
     GROUP BY ...
     HAVING ...
     AND ... )
AND ...
GROUP BY ...
HAVING ...
AND ...
ORDER BY ...
```

Fig. 7.3 A subquery being used in a WHERE clause.

Figure 7.4 shows subqueries in various positions.

```
SELECT ...
FROM    ...
WHERE X <= ANY
   (SELECT   ...
     FROM    ...
     WHERE NOT EXISTS
        (SELECT *
         FROM ...
         WHERE ...)
     AND ...
     AND ...)
AND ...
GROUP BY ...
HAVING SUM(Y) IN
   (SELECT Z
     FROM ...
     WHERE ...)
```

Fig. 7.4 Subqueries in various positions.

In Fig. 7.4 we have a subquery nested inside another subquery and a subquery in a HAVING clause.

The subquery consists of a SELECT statement, which will retrieve a set of values from one or more tables in the database. It is *these* values which are then used in the selection criteria of the outer SELECT's WHERE or HAVING clause to determine which rows from the tables in the outer select (or from the intermediate grouped values in the case of HAVING) will appear at the output. Subqueries are in practice, for many programmers, a more 'natural' alternative to the join and there are some situations in which there is no alternative to using a subquery. There are also some situations in which there is no alternative to using a join.

As stated above, one important restriction in the use of subqueries is that the values selected by the subquery do not themselves appear at the output; they are simply used as part of the selection criteria of the outer SELECT.

We continue with a few general points about subqueries.

- The subquery is considered as part of the WHERE (or HAVING) clause of the outer SELECT and the outer SELECT may continue after the subquery's closing parenthesis with the usual GROUP BY, HAVING and ORDER BY clauses. This is shown in both Figs 7.3 and 7.4.

- An ORDER BY must not be included in the subquery itself.

- The 'comparison' in Fig. 7.2 is '=' or '<' or '>' or '>=' or '<=' or '<>'.

- If ALL, ANY, IN or NOT IN are included, then the subquery is expected to return a *set* of one or more values from a single column in the subquery. If none of these terms (ALL, ANY, IN or NOT IN) appears, then the subquery must return a *single* value.

- Some SQLs, such as ORACLE SQL*PLUS, have a useful additional feature which allows more than one column to be returned from the subquery and compared to corresponding columns in the outer query. This is not possible in the Jet DBMS of Access and VB.

- The WHERE and HAVING clauses in the subquery may themselves contain further subqueries. It is usual in most queries for the nesting of subqueries to go no further than four or five deep.

- Subqueries can be used as an alternative to joins in navigating around a database where the query is required to span several entity types in the logical schema. In such cases it is essential to have the entity-relationship diagram (in addition to the table definitions) available.

- When navigating between tables in this way, whether using joins or subqueries, the normal procedure is to join adjacent tables in the navigation path by equating the primary key on the 'one' side of a one-to-many relationship with the corresponding foreign key on the 'many' side. This is the procedure we adopted in the section on joins. However, not all joins relate primary and foreign key values, and the same is true of subquery links.

- As a matter of interest, the SQL query interpreter, in its attempt to optimize the sequence of database search operations required, may convert SQL subqueries into joins as one of its early translation steps.

All of the above points on subqueries are demonstrated in the following examples.

7.2.1 Simple subqueries and their join equivalents

> *Query 60*: List all the customers in the CUSTOMER table who are in the same city as Sallaway.

The answer to this query *could* be obtained in two steps, by first querying the CUSTOMER table to establish which city Sallaway is in (Figs 7.5 and 7.6).

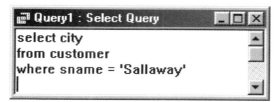

```
select city
from customer
where sname = 'Sallaway'
```

Fig. 7.5 Finding which city Sallaway is in.

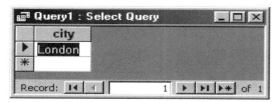

Fig. 7.6 Sallaway is in London.

To find out who else lives in London, query the CUSTOMER table again, having 'remembered' 'London', as in Figs 7.7 and 7.8.

```
select *
from customer
where city = 'London'
```

Fig. 7.7 Finding who lives in London.

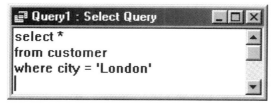

	c_no	title	sname	inits	street	city	postc	cred_lim	balance
►	1	Mr	Sallaway	G.R.	12 Fax Rd	London	WC1	£1,000.00	£42.56
	2	Miss	Lauri	P.	5 Dux St	London	N1	£500.00	£200.00
	5	Ms	Woods	S.Q.	17 Nax Rd	London	E18 4WW	£1,000.00	£250.10
*	0							£0.00	£0.00

Record: ◄◄ ◄ 1 ► ►► ►* of 3

Fig. 7.8 The customers who live in London.

Using a subquery, we can achieve these two steps in one. We make a subquery to find Sallaway's city.

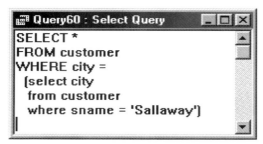

Fig. 7.9 The SELECT statement, containing a subquery, for Query 60.

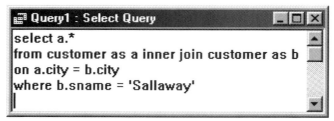

Fig. 7.10 The output from the query of Fig. 7.9.

Lines 4 to 6 in Fig. 7.9 are the subquery. The subquery must be enclosed in parentheses as shown. The subquery must be executed before the outer query so that it can deliver the value 'London' to the outer query's WHERE clause.

This simple example illustrates the basic flavour and functionality of SQL subqueries.

Note that Sallaway is output since he obviously lives in the same city as himself!

The same result can be achieved, less elegantly perhaps, using the self-join shown in Fig. 7.11. The comparison with the subquery version is interesting.

```
select a.*
from customer as a inner join customer as b
on a.city = b.city
where b.sname = 'Sallaway'
```

Fig. 7.11 A self-join version of Query 60.

This does a self-join on CUSTOMER on CITY and then selects out rows where the second SNAME is 'Sallaway'. The form of the query that is used – either subquery or join – is a matter of programming style. Most SQL programmers seem to prefer the subquery form, probably because the question of what is to be output (outer SELECT) is separated from the question of the selection criteria (inner SELECT). Notice also the absence of table aliases in the subquery version, whereas they are necessary in the self-join version to distinguish between the two 'copies' of the CUSTOMER table.

Query 61: List details of all products that have had deliveries.

This query uses the **prod_del.mdb** database, shown in Figs 7.12, 7.13 and 7.14.

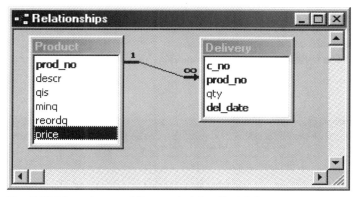

Fig. 7.12 The schema of the **prod_del.mdb** database.

Product : Table

prod_no	descr	qis	minq	reordq	price
1	Bat	10	5	10	£12.00
2	Ball	5	5	20	£2.00
3	Hoop	3	5	10	£3.00
4	Net	2	5	10	£20.00
5	Rope	1	10	10	£6.00
*	0		0	0	0	£0.00

Record: 1 of 5

Fig. 7.13 The PRODUCT table.

Delivery : Table

c_no	prod_no	qty	del_date
3	1	3	03/11/99
3	2	2	03/11/99
1	4	6	07/11/99
3	3	1	12/11/99
5	3	4	12/11/99
*	0	0	0	

Record: 1 of 5

Fig. 7.14 The DELIVERY table.

Notice that PROD_NO in the DELIVERY table is a foreign key from PRODUCT. The subquery version of the query is shown in Fig. 7.15.

Query61 : Select Query

```
SELECT *
FROM product
WHERE prod_no in
  (select prod_no
   from delivery)
```

Fig. 7.15 The subquery version of Query 61.

Query61 : Select Query

prod_no	descr	qis	minq	reordq	price
1	Bat	10	5	10	£12.00
2	Ball	5	5	20	£2.00
3	Hoop	3	5	10	£3.00
4	Net	2	5	10	£20.00
0		0	0	0	£0.00

Record: 1 of 4

Fig. 7.16 The output from the query of Fig. 7.15.

The subquery is executed first and delivers the list of values (2,1,4,3,3) from the DELIVERY table because this is the set of products that have been delivered. The value of PROD_NO in each row of the PRODUCT table is checked to see if it is contained in this set of values and if it is, the PRODUCT row is output.

(2,1,4,3,3) is not, strictly speaking, a set since it contains a duplicate. This does little harm in practice and will not affect the output from the query, since if any number is IN (2,1,4,3) then it is also IN (2,1,4,3,3). This duplication within the set can easily be removed using a DISTINCT in the subquery:

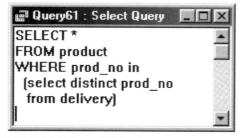

Query61 : Select Query

```
SELECT *
FROM product
WHERE prod_no in
  (select distinct prod_no
   from delivery)
```

Fig. 7.17 Using a DISTINCT in the subquery.

Note that this query could also have been implemented relatively simply as a join:

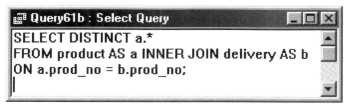

Fig. 7.18 A join version of Query 61.

The INNER JOIN ensures that only products that have had deliveries are output.

Note that if any data from the DELIVERY table had been required in the output the subquery version could not have been used.

Query 62: List details of all products which have had no deliveries.

The only change required compared with the previous query is to replace IN with NOT IN since what the query will now need to output is all products in the PRODUCTS table whose product numbers do *not* appear in the list of product numbers in DELIVERY:

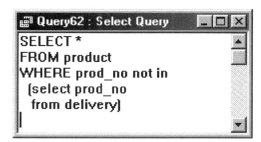

Fig. 7.19 The SQL SELECT statement for Query 62.

The output from this query is of course:

	prod_no	descr	qis	minq	reordq	price
▶	5	Rope	1	10	10	£6.00
＊	0		0	0	0	£0.00

Record: |◀| ◀ | 1 | ▶ |▶I|▶＊| of 1

Fig. 7.20 The output of Query 62.

Rope is the only product that has not been delivered.

The join version of Query 62 has to be a LEFT JOIN of the two tables.

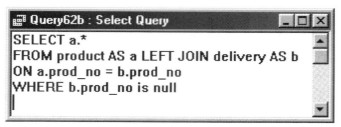

Fig. 7.21 The join version is less obvious.

In the join version, we perform a LEFT JOIN between PRODUCT and DELIVERY, which ensures that any product with no delivery will appear at the output, with NULLs in the DELIVERY field positions. This is taken advantage of in the WHERE clause.

You will probably agree that the subquery version is more 'direct'.

7.2.2 Subquery with join in the outer SELECT

> *Query 63*: List the customer number and name and invoice details for invoices which have had payments in the first two weeks of January 2000.

Clearly, the CUSTOMER and INVOICE tables must be consulted for output data, and PAYMENT must also be consulted to decide which invoices to output.

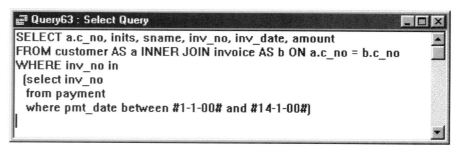

Fig. 7.22 The SQL SELECT with subquery for Query 63.

c_no	inits	sname	inv_no	inv_date	amount
3	R.	Jackson	1005	20/01/00	£510.00

Record: 2 of 2

Fig. 7.23 Invoice 1005 is the only one that received a payment in the first two weeks of January 2000.

7.2.3 Where a join must be used instead of a subquery

In a subquery, the only data that can appear at the output of the query comes from the table or tables contained in the *outer query*. The two tables CUSTOMER and INVOICE are joined in the outer SELECT in Query 63 *since outputs are required from both tables*.

If any PAYMENT details, such as the payment amount for example, had been required to be output then *all* the tables would have had to be joined (and a subquery would not have been possible) since no data from a subquery can be output, as already mentioned. We met a similar situation in Query 61.

While subqueries may seem less complex than joins in some cases, sometimes joins are the only possibility.

7.2.4 Joins in the subquery

> *Query 64*: List the names of all customers who have made a payment before the invoice was sent.

The general strategy in this query is to join the INVOICE and PAYMENT tables in the subquery so that the invoice and payment dates can be compared.

The selected customer numbers are then fed to the outer query so the customer names can be output from the CUSTOMER table. The resulting SQL query is thus:

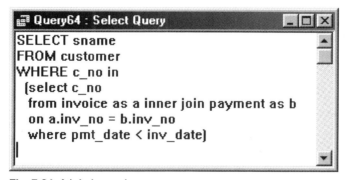

```
SELECT sname
FROM customer
WHERE c_no in
  (select c_no
   from invoice as a inner join payment as b
   on a.inv_no = b.inv_no
   where pmt_date < inv_date)
```

Fig. 7.24 A join in a subquery.

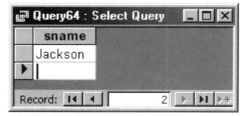

Fig. 7.25 The output of Query 64.

The subquery joins tables INVOICE and PAYMENT where the INV_NOs are equal and the PMT_DATE is less than (*before*) the INV_DATE, and it delivers to the outer query the set of customer numbers (3) since this is the only customer who has paid before he was asked. The output is as shown in Fig. 7.25 because the payment date of payment number 1 of invoice number 1005 is earlier than its invoice date, and customer Jackson was the one the invoice was sent to. (Check Appendix 1 for the data in the CUSTOMER, INVOICE and PAYMENT tables.)

Since output data is only required from the CUSTOMER table, a doubly nested subquery can be used.

```
Query64b : Select Query

SELECT sname
FROM customer
WHERE c_no in
  (select c_no
   from invoice as a
   where inv_no in
     (select inv_no
      from payment as b
      where b.pmt_date < a.inv_date])
```

Fig. 7.26 A subquery within a subquery.

In the double-subquery version of this query (Fig. 7.26), we have one subquery within another.

The outer query says:

"Output the sname of this customer record if the customer number is in the set of . . .

the first subquery continues the sentence with:

". . . customer numbers in the invoice table whose invoice numbers are in the set of . . .

and the inner subquery completes the sentence with:

". . . invoice numbers in the payment table whose payment date is less than the current invoice record's invoice date."

The inner subquery is in fact an example of a *correlated subquery*. The current payment has to refer back to the current invoice not only via the IN clause to equal its INV_NO, but also to check its own payment date with the invoice's invoice date. This is done using the table aliases 'a' and 'b'. It's the second check referring back to a higher-levelled query via aliases that makes it a correlated subquery.

We shall meet correlated subqueries again in a later section.

Not all doubly nested subqueries are correlated subqueries. If the English version of this query had been: "List the names of all customers who have made payments in the first two weeks of the year 2000", then no correlation back to the INVOICE record, other than via INV_NO, would be necessary.

7.2.5 *Returning more than one column from a subquery*

This cannot be done in Jet. In some DBMSs it can, though. On the basis that it's just as useful to know what *can't* be done as what *can*, we proceed with the following query, which *does* work in ORACLE SQL*PLUS. We then proceed to consider a join solution in Jet.

> *Query 65*: List all customers who live in the same city and have the same credit limit as Sallaway.

This query uses the **accts.mdb** database, whose schema and table content are shown in Appendix 1.

The SQL*PLUS solution is quite simply:

```
select *
from customer
where (city, cred_lim) =
  (selest (city, cred_lim)
  from customer
  where sname = 'Sallaway'.
```

Here, *two* fields from the outer query's current record are being compared with two corresponding fields in the subquery.

This isn't possible in Jet, and the following error results if you try:

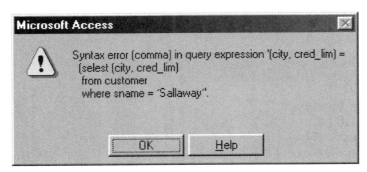

However, the self-join shown in Fig. 7.27 is a satisfactory workaround in Jet.

In this version, all CUSTOMER records that have the same credit limit and city as Sallaway are joined to his CUSTOMER record. The joined records (signified by the 'b' table alias) are then output.

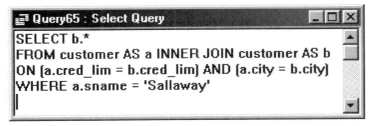

Fig. 7.27 Jet's INNER JOIN solution to Query 65.

7.2.6 ANY and ALL

These subquery options are best demonstrated by examples.

ANY (Also known as SOME)

> Query 66: From the **employee.mdb** database, list the details of all employees who are not receiving the maximum salary.

emp_no	name	salary	mgr_no
1	Audrey	£10,000.00	3
2	Betty	£20,000.00	4
3	Carol	£15,000.00	2
4	Denise	£15,000.00	7
5	Erica	£20,000.00	
0		£0.00	0

Record: 6 of 6

Fig. 7.28 The EMPLOYEE table in the **employee.mdb** database.

The idea is that a given employee's details will be output if it is possible to find ANY employee who receives a higher salary. One way of writing the SQL version of this query is:

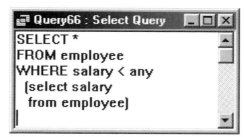

```
SELECT *
FROM employee
WHERE salary < any
  (select salary
   from employee)
```

Fig. 7.29 Using ANY for Query 66.

emp_no	name	salary	mgr_no
1	Audrey	£10,000.00	3
3	Carol	£15,000.00	2
4	Denise	£15,000.00	7
0		£0.00	0

Record: 1 of 3

Fig. 7.30 The output of Query 66.

In this query, Betty and Erica are removed from the output because there are no employees who receive a lower salary than they do. The operation of the ANY is to output a row from the outer query wherever there is *at least one* row in the subquery which makes the selection criterion TRUE. Here, for Audrey, for example, there is at least one employee (e.g. Betty but also Carol, Denise and Erica) who receives a higher salary.

Possible ambiguities with ANY and ALL

In spoken language the phrase 'less than any' may be given a similar meaning to 'less than all'. Care must be taken in formulating SQL queries using ANY and ALL that their precise meaning in SQL is understood. One of the responsibilities of an analyst-programmer is to clarify this type of imprecision in normal language.

The difference between the functioning of the SQL versions of ANY and ALL is often misunderstood (probably, as stated, because of fuzziness of their usage in spoken language).

One way round this potential source of error is to remember that in SQL 'ANY' means 'one or more'.

A clearer SQL formulation of Query 66 uses an aggregate function in the subquery. It's given in Fig. 7.31.

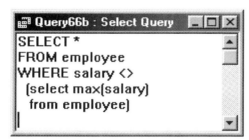

Fig. 7.31 Using an aggregate function in the subquery.

ALL

ALL is quite different in its operation from ANY and is more intuitively obvious in its function. Staying with the EMPLOYEE table, consider the following query.

> *Query 67: List details of all employees in table EMPLOYEE3 who earn the maximum salary.*

The SQL is shown in Fig. 7.32 and the output is shown in Fig. 7.33.

Betty and Erica earn the maximum salary. For each of them, her salary is greater than or equal to ALL employees in the table. If the '>=' had been replaced by a '>', no rows would have been selected because in order to have a salary higher than ALL employees in the table, they would have had to earn a higher salary than themselves!

```
Query67 : Select Query    _ □ ×
SELECT *
FROM employee
WHERE salary >= all
  (select salary
   from employee)
```

Fig. 7.32 Using >= ALL to get maxima.

	emp_no	name	salary	mgr_no
▶	2	Betty	£20,000.00	4
	5	Erica	£20,000.00	
*	0		£0.00	0

Record: |◀ ◀ 1 ▶ ▶| ▶* of 2

Fig. 7.33 The output from the query in Fig. 7.32.

Alternative SQL formulations, which don't use ALL, are:

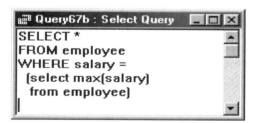

```
Query67b : Select Query    _ □ ×
SELECT *
FROM employee
WHERE salary =
  (select max(salary)
   from employee)
```

Fig. 7.34 Using an aggregate function in the subquery instead.

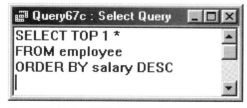

```
Query67c : Select Query    _ □ ×
SELECT TOP 1 *
FROM employee
ORDER BY salary DESC
```

Fig. 7.35 Using TOP 1 instead.

7.2.7 Replacing ANY and ALL

Note that the following SQL ANY/ALL – English mappings apply.

```
 1. X = any Y      X equal to one of Y.
                   Equivalent to: X IN Y.
 2. X < any Y      X less than one or more of Y. Equivalent to:
                   less than the maximum of Y.
 3. X <= any Y     X less than or equal to one or more of Y.
                   Equivalent to: less than or equal to the maximum
                   of Y.
 4. X > any Y      X greater than one or more of Y.
                   Equivalent to: greater than the minimum of Y.
 5. X >= any Y     X greater than or equal to one or more of Y.
                   Equivalent to: greater than or equal to the
                   minimum of Y.
 6. X <> any Y     X different from one of Y.
                   Always true except where Y contains only X.
                   Y doesn't consist of just X.
 7. X = all Y      X equal to all of Y.
                   Never true except where Y contains only X.
                   Y consists of just X.
 8. X < all Y      X less than all Y.
                   Equivalent to: less than the minimum of Y.
 9. X <= all Y     X less than or equal to all Y.
                   Equivalent to: less than or equal to the minimum
                   of Y.
10. X > all Y      X greater than all Y.
                   Equivalent to: greater than the maximum of Y.
11. X >= all Y     X greater than or equal to all Y.
                   Equivalent to: greater than or equal to the
                   maximum of Y.
12. X <> all Y     X different from all elements of the set Y.
                   Equivalent to: X NOT IN Y.
```

Fig. 7.36 How to replace ANY and ALL. X is a single value and Y is a set of values returned from a subquery.

As we said above, we think there are problems with ANY and ALL. We believe their use is likely to lead to error.

Suppose your client were to ask you to list employees who earned more than anyone else.

If you used

```
where salary > any ...
```

you would get all but the lowest earners, which is incorrect.

If you used

```
where salary > all . . .
```

you would get no one, which is also incorrect.

In fact, as our list above (Fig. 7.36) shows, you wouldn't be able to use ANY or ALL with *any* of the relational operators (= , <, < = , >, >=, <>) to achieve the desired effect.

It is fortunate that these 12 equivalences exist, because it means that, except for cases 6 and 7 above, you won't ever have to use ANY or ALL; you can use MAX, MIN, IN and NOT IN instead.

Cases 6 and 7 above are very similar to <> and = . However, <> and = can't be used to replace them because <> and = with a subquery that can return more than one value will cause an error.

7.2.8 *Where a subquery seems essential*

It is difficult to see how Query 66 (or Query 68) could be implemented using a join instead of a subquery. The SQL for Query 66 is reproduced here:

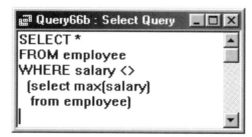

```
Query66b : Select Query
SELECT *
FROM employee
WHERE salary <>
  (select max(salary)
   from employee)
```

Fig. 7.37 All employees not receiving the maximum salary.

The reason it seems unlikely that a join could be used here is that there seems to be a need for two distinct steps.

● Find the maximum salary.
● List everyone who doesn't get it.

Can you think of a way of using TOP to do it?

7.2.9 *Correlated subqueries*

In a correlated subquery, the subquery is executed repeatedly, once for each row considered for selection by the outer query and its WHERE clause.

Consider this query:

> *Query 68: List details of the employee in table EMPLOYEE of the **employee.mdb** database who earns more than anyone else.*

Now clearly, if more than one employee has the highest salary, nobody should be output; if there really is one employee who has a higher salary than anyone else, then that employee's record should be output.

For that reason, the following SQL is inadequate:

```
select *
from employee
where salary =
  (select max(salary)
  from employee)
```

In this query, if more than one employee is on the highest salary, then *all* those employees will be output.

What is needed is a correlated subquery. If, for *each* employee, we scan the whole table (using the subquery) to see if anyone *else* gets a higher salary and output that employee only if it isn't true, we will get the desired effect. That is an identifying characteristic of a correlated subquery – the subquery is run for each record in the outer query. (This naturally implies that correlated subqueries are inclined to be slow for large tables.)

Just as a further note on speed, before we go on to describe the SQL for this query, we note that having established the 'winner', i.e. an employee who *does* have a higher salary than anyone else, the search is finished; processing does not need to continue. With SQL, we have to leave it up to the query interpreter/ optimizer to decide on the algorithm used. If we write our own lower-level procedural code, we can control this type of thing. Let's proceed now to the correct SQL for this query. First we use a query with a '> ALL' and then, by the table in Fig. 7.36, use a '> MAX' query.

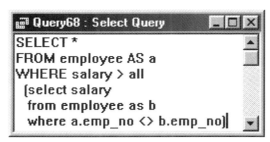

Fig. 7.38 A correlated subquery for Query 68.

emp_no	name	salary	mgr_no
0		£0.00	0

Record: 1 of 1

Fig. 7.39 The output of Query 68 when there is no clear leader in salary.

In Fig. 7.39, we see that the query has correctly returned no rows, because there are two employees who both receive the highest salary.

If we now add a new employee Fabi to the EMPLOYEE table, who receives a salary higher than anyone else (Fig. 7.40), and run the SQL correlated subquery of Fig. 7.38 again, we again obtain the correct output, which is shown in Fig. 7.41.

	emp_no	name	salary	mgr_no
	1	Audrey	£10,000.00	3
	2	Betty	£20,000.00	4
	3	Carol	£15,000.00	2
	4	Denise	£15,000.00	7
	5	Erica	£20,000.00	
	6	Fabi	£22,000.00	5
*	0		£0.00	0

Record: 6 of 6

Fig. 7.40 A new highest-salary earner, Fabi, has been added to the EMPLOYEE table.

	emp_no	name	salary	mgr_no
▶	6	Fabi	£22,000.00	5
*	0		£0.00	0

Record: 1 of 1

Fig. 7.41 The output of Query 68 when there is a clear leader in salary.

One way to recognize a correlated subquery is that the subquery refers back to the current outer query record for comparison using table aliases.

For each employee in the 'b' copy of the EMPLOYEE table, the subquery in Query 68 has to check back with the employee in the 'a' copy to see whether it's the same employee. If it is the same employee, reject this 'b' employee record, otherwise compare their salaries.

We now look at the equivalent '> MAX' version of this query.

The SQL for this version of the query is shown in Fig. 7.42.

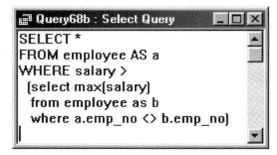

```
Query68b : Select Query
SELECT *
FROM employee AS a
WHERE salary >
 (select max(salary)
  from employee as b
  where a.emp_no <> b.emp_no)
```

Fig. 7.42 Avoiding ALL in the correlated subquery of Query 68.

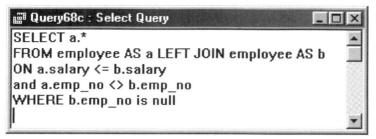

Fig. 7.43 A Join equivalent of Query 68.

A left self-join equivalent of this query is shown in Fig. 7.43.

This version of the query joins all rows of the employee table where the employee on the left has less than or equal salary than the employee on the right, and it's not the same employee. It then looks for a null on the right. Nulls on the right mean that an employee with a higher or equal salary can't be found. The output is the same as for the correlated subquery versions for both situations, i.e. whether or not there is a clear leader in salary.

We now briefly revisit Query 64, because one of its SQL versions was a correlated subquery. The English version of the query is:

"List the names of all customers who have made payments before the invoice was sent."

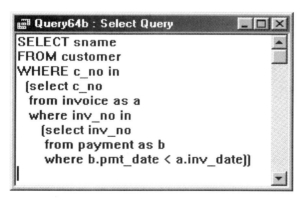

Fig. 7.44 The correlated subquery for Query 64.

This is a correlated subquery because for each invoice, *all* of the payments have to be inspected to see whether those with the same invoice number have a preceding date.

We close this section with the following summary:

> The way to recognize the *need* for a correlated subquery is:
> *For each row in the outer query, all rows in the subquery must be inspected.*
>
> The way to recognize the *existence* of a correlated subquery is to look for:
> *A table alias that appears in both the outer query and the subquery.*

Fig. 7.45 Summary regarding correlated subqueries.

Before going on to EXISTS and NOT EXISTS, we present two miscellaneous subquery examples.

> *Query 69*: *Which customers have made payments on all their invoices?*

Here it is advisable to break the query down into two parts. Firstly, it can be established which customers have invoices that have had *no* payments, with the query:

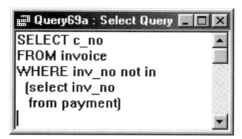

```
SELECT c_no
FROM invoice
WHERE inv_no not in
  (select inv_no
   from payment)
```

Fig. 7.46 Customers who have invoices with no payments – query.

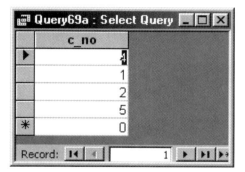

Fig. 7.47 Customers who have invoices with no payments – output.

The next step is to retrieve details of all customers who do *not* appear in this list. The above SQL can be used as a subquery to 'feed' these C_NOs to an outer query, which will provide the required data:

```
SELECT *
FROM customer
WHERE c_no not in
  (select c_no
   from invoice
   where inv_no not in
     (select inv_no
      from payment))
```

Fig. 7.48 The completed double NOT IN query.

Query69b : Select Query

c_no	title	sname	inits	street	city	postc	cred_lim	balance
3	Mr	Jackson	R.	2 Lux Ave	Leeds	LE1 2AB	£500.00	£510.00
6	Mrs	Williams	C.	41 Cax St	Dover	DO2 8WD		£412.21
0							£0.00	£0.00

Record: 1 of 2

Fig. 7.49 The output from the SQL query of Fig. 7.48.

The query specifies (in line 3) that a customer's details will only be output if his or her customer number is not in the list delivered by the first subquery.

This query contains a double NOT IN.

Tip: When the English version of a query contains the word 'all', consider using a double NOT IN or a double NOT EXISTS.

We now revisit Query 32 and Query 40. The English version of the query is re-presented here as Query 70.

> *Query 70: Which is the city in the CUSTOMER table with the highest total outstanding balance?*

The CUSTOMER table is reproduced in Fig. 7.50 for convenience.

In Query 32 we noted that this query could be performed very simply if the SQL you use had nested aggregate functions (Jet doesn't). In Query 40 we found a solution using TOP.

We now consider a solution using subqueries. Some versions of SQL don't have TOP, so this exercise is worth while. It also leads to greater insight into the use of aggregate functions in subqueries.

Customer : Table

c_no	title	sname	inits	street	city	postc	cred_lim	balance
1	Mr	Sallaway	G.R.	12 Fax Rd	London	WC1	£1,000.00	£42.56
2	Miss	Lauri	P.	5 Dux St	London	N1	£500.00	£200.00
3	Mr	Jackson	R.	2 Lux Ave	Leeds	LE1 2AB	£500.00	£510.00
4	Mr	Dziduch	M.	31 Low St	Dover	DO2 9CD	£100.00	£149.23
5	Ms	Woods	S.Q.	17 Nax Rd	London	E18 4WW	£1,000.00	£250.10
6	Mrs	Williams	C.	41 Cax St	Dover	DO2 8WD		£412.21
0							£0.00	£0.00

Record: 7 of 7

Fig. 7.50 The CUSTOMER table.

We wish to know which city has the highest total outstanding balance. Looking at the CUSTOMER table, it is clear that there are two basic steps in achieving this:

1. Find out what the total balance for each city is.

2. Find the city whose total balance is the greatest of those.

Step 1

To find the total balance for each city, we must use a GROUP BY:

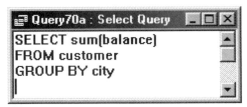

Fig. 7.51 Step 1: Total balance for each city – query.

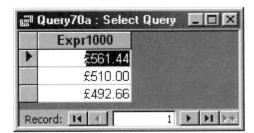

Fig. 7.52 Step 1: Total balance for each city – output.

Step 2

To find which city has the highest of these, without using TOP, and without using nested aggregate functions, we must use '>=ALL'.

Fig. 7.53 shows the SQL for this and Fig. 7.54 shows the output.

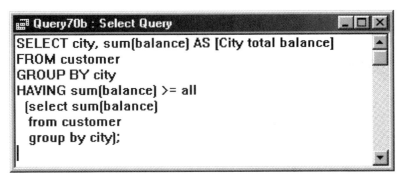

Fig. 7.53 Step 2: City or cities having the highest total balance in the set – query.

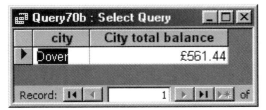

Fig. 7.54 Step 2: City or cities having the highest total balance in the set – output.

The query in Fig. 7.53 executes with the following steps:

1. The subquery runs first (subqueries always run first) to produce a list of outstanding balances for each city using GROUP BY.

2. The outer query runs its own GROUP BY, *again* summing the balances for each city.

3. The HAVING clause in the outer query, together with its >=ALL, filters the outer query's groups, outputting only the group with the highest total balance.

In SQLs with nested aggregate functions, we could have used this SELECT statement instead:

```
select city, sum(balance) as [City total balance] from customer
group by city
having sum(balance) =
  (select max(sum(balance))
   from customer
   group by city)
```

Jet SQL, as used in Access and VB, does not allow nested aggregate functions.

7.2.10 EXISTS and NOT EXISTS

EXISTS and NOT EXISTS are used in SQL SELECT statements to test, as their names suggest, for the existence or nonexistence of rows in a database table. The general structure of a query containing an EXISTS is shown in Fig. 7.55 below:

```
SELECT ...
FROM . . .
WHERE EXISTS
  (SELECT *
   FROM ...
   WHERE ...
       ... )
```

Fig. 7.55 Positioning of EXISTS in an SQL query.

A NOT EXISTS takes the same position. Data from a row in the outer query is delivered to the output provided the WHERE selection criteria are all true, including the EXISTS or NOT EXISTS condition. Each row of the table in the outer query is tested. The EXISTS condition becomes true if the subquery can locate a row in its table(s) which satisfies the subquery's WHERE conditions and the NOT EXISTS condition becomes true if such a row cannot be located.

Where EXISTS and NOT EXISTS cannot be replaced by IN and NOT IN

EXISTS and NOT EXISTS are often replaceable by IN and NOT IN, but there are several situations in which they are not. EXISTS and NOT EXISTS are more flexible than IN and NOT IN in the following ways.

1. IN and NOT IN require some value to be passed from the outer query to the subquery for comparison; EXISTS and NOT EXISTS do not.

2. IN and NOT IN usually allow only *one* column to be passed to the subquery for comparison (this is true in Jet databases; there is an exception in the case of ORACLE SQL*PLUS which allows values of more than one column to be passed). In the case of EXISTS and NOT EXISTS, the values are passed directly into the WHERE conditions of the subquery and so the number of columns whose values are compared is not limited.

3. Where doubly nested subqueries are involved, EXISTS and NOT EXISTS allow values to be passed from the outer query to the second subquery, whereas IN and NOT IN do not.

Examples illustrating these differences appear in the following text.

EXISTS

Consider the following small three-table database concerning the purchases of products that customers have made. This database is **cus_purchase_prod.mdb**. It is described in Appendix 1. Its schema and tables are shown below.

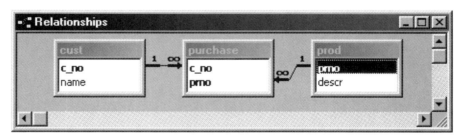

Fig. 7.56 The schema of the **cus_purchase_prod.mdb** database.

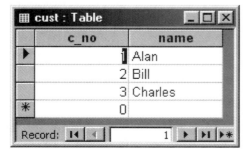

Fig. 7.57 The CUST table.

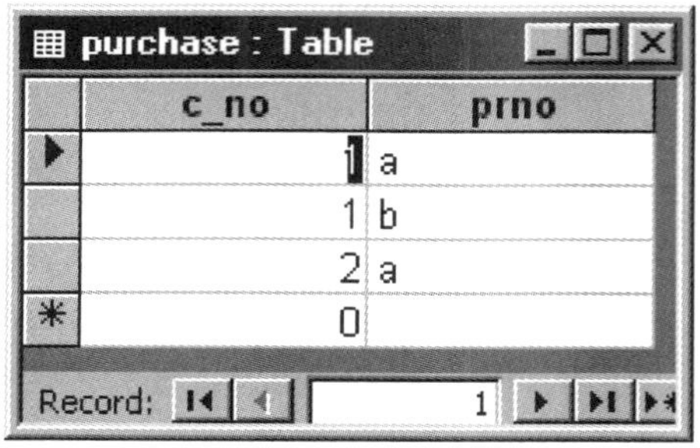

Fig. 7.58 The PURCHASE table.

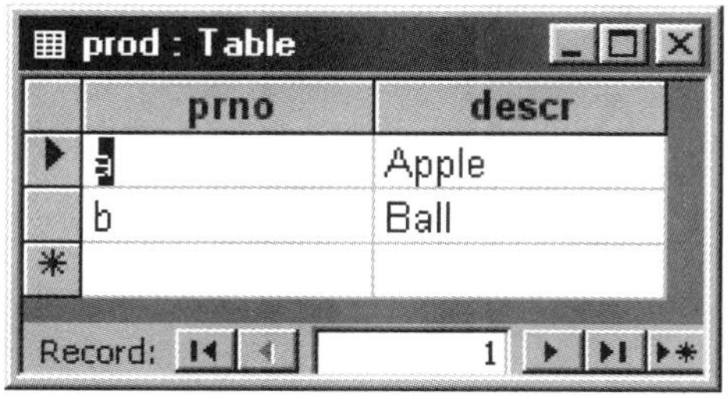

Fig. 7.59 The PROD table.

The tables show who has purchased what; for example the first rows of each table show that Alan has purchased an apple.

> *Query 71:* List all customers who have purchased any product.

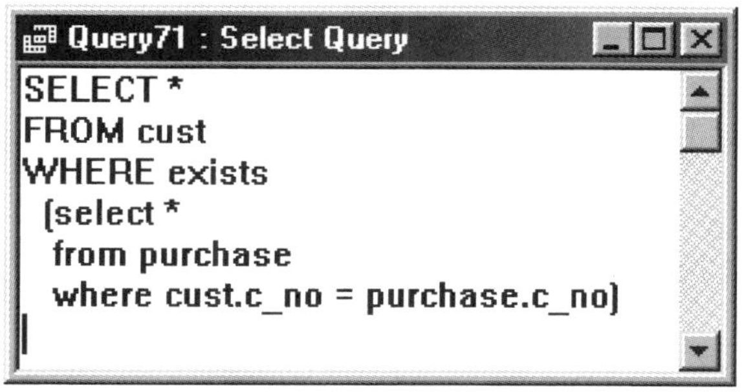

Fig. 7.60 EXISTS query for Query 71.

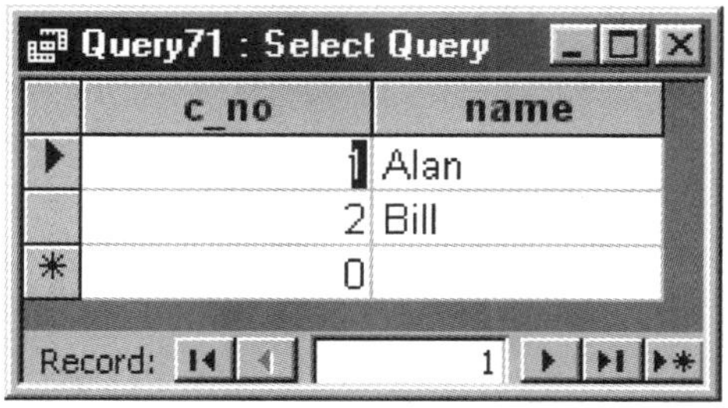

Fig. 7.61 The output from Query 71.

Rows from CUST are selected in lines 1 to 3 only where there exists a row in PURCHASE with a matching CNO. Each row in the outer query is tested in turn to see if there is a corresponding row generated by the subquery, that is, that there is a matching customer number in the PURCHASE table. This simple example shows how EXISTS works in general and what it is intended for.

Note that it will only ever be necessary to include a '*' in the subquery SELECT (rather than column names) since it is the existence or nonexistence of a matching *row* that is being tested for. The same result could of course have been obtained using IN:

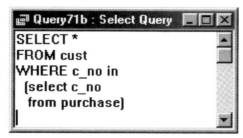

Fig. 7.62 The IN version of Query 71.

In the EXISTS version the value passing is via the WHERE clause of the subquery whereas in the IN version, the value is passed via IN and the SELECT clause in the subquery.

There is also a join version of the query yielding the same results:

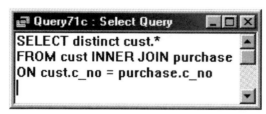

Fig. 7.63 The INNER JOIN version.

The DISTINCT is necessary because Alan has made two purchases and would otherwise be output twice. It is not necessary in the EXISTS or IN versions because EXISTence and set membership take no account of the number of occurrences. This need for DISTINCT is an example of the slightly more machine-oriented nature of the join method as compared to the subquery methods.

EXISTS query does not have a join or IN equivalent

> *Query 72*: If there are any current purchases, produce a list of customers.

This is a somewhat contrived example to show that unlike IN, EXISTS does not *require* a value to be passed to the subquery, even via the WHERE clause, although

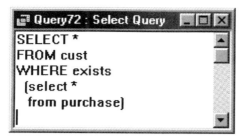

Fig. 7.64 The SQL EXISTS query for Query 72.

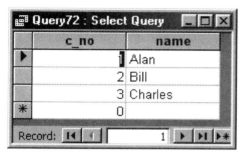

Fig. 7.65 The output of Query 72.

in most queries a value or values will be passed. Thus, this query could not be programmed in either IN or 'join' formats.

Notice that each row appears only once. This points up a characteristic of EXISTS (shared by other subquery forms), that each row in the outer query table is tested only once.

NOT EXISTS

Query 73: List details of all customers who have not purchased any product.

Any trace of ambiguity in the English version of this query could be removed by adopting the descriptive style of the *Predicate Calculus* and rewording it:

List details of all customers for whom there does not exist a purchase.

SQL EXISTS is closely analogous to the existential quantifier ∃ of the Predicate Calculus. As will be seen in a later example, there is not a direct SQL equivalent of the universal quantifier 'for all' ∀; this has to be *simulated* using a double NOT EXISTS. A *Set Theory* oriented form of the query would be:

List details of all customers whose customer number is not a member of the set of customer numbers in the PURCHASE table.

A *numerical* alternative is:

List details of all customers for whom the number of purchases is zero.

The query can also be performed using a join (a left join), but the English equivalent of the join version is not very natural:

Perform a left join on the CUST and PURCHASE tables on CNO and select out only the rows with a null PURCHASE.CNO.

(This rather mechanical join formulation seems to go against SQL's aim of being a declarative rather than procedural language.)

Each of these English formulations, biased towards a different approach, has its own SQL equivalent.

These differing versions are now shown. In each case the output is:

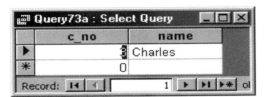

Fig. 7.66 The output of Query 73.

NOT EXISTS

```
Query73a : Select Query
SELECT *
FROM cust
WHERE not exists
  (select *
  from purchase
  where cust.c_no = purchase.c_no)
```

Fig. 7.67 The NOT EXISTS version of Query 73.

NOT IN

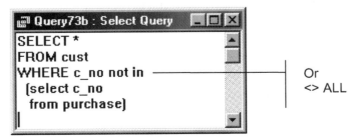

Fig. 7.68 The NOT IN version of Query 73.

COUNT

```
Query73c : Select Query    _ □ ×
SELECT *
FROM cust
WHERE 0 =
 (select count(*)
  from purchase
  where cust.c_no = purchase.c_no)
```

Fig. 7.69 The COUNT version of Query 73.

LEFT JOIN

```
Query73d : Select Query    _ □ ×
SELECT cust.*
FROM cust LEFT JOIN purchase
ON cust.c_no = purchase.c_no
WHERE purchase.c_no is null
```

Fig. 7.70 The LEFT JOIN version of Query 73.

> *Query 74:* List all customers who have purchased a ball.

Here all three tables must be accessed. PROD is needed to convert the product description 'Ball' into a product number for searching the PURCHASE table.

```
Query74a : Select Query    _ □ ×
SELECT *
FROM cust
WHERE exists
 (select *
  from purchase
  where cust.c_no = purchase.c_no
  and prno =
   (select prno
    from prod
    where descr = 'Ball'))
```

Fig. 7.71 EXISTS with two subqueries for Query 74.

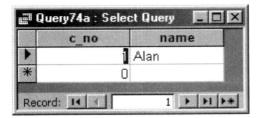

Fig. 7.72 The output of Query 74.

With our test data (shown in Figs 7.57–7.59), Alan is the only ball-purchaser.

There are equivalent, and similar-looking, queries using IN. Two join versions are given below:

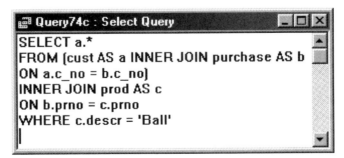

Fig. 7.73 Using a Join in the subquery for Query 74.

This version (Fig. 7.73) joins PURCHASE to PROD to obtain the PRNO for 'Ball' instead of using a separate subquery.

```
Query74c : Select Query
SELECT a.*
FROM (cust AS a INNER JOIN purchase AS b
ON a.c_no = b.c_no)
INNER JOIN prod AS c
ON b.prno = c.prno
WHERE c.descr = 'Ball'
```

Fig. 7.74 An all-join version of Query 74.

> *Query 75*: List customers who have purchased all products.

As can be seen by inspecting the data, Alan is the only such customer. The way this can be seen (and this is of course only practicable with small amounts of data) is:

1. Inspect the PROD table and keep in mind the set of product numbers (a and b).

2. Inspect the PURCHASE table to see which customer number has purchased all product numbers a and b (1).

3. Inspect the CUST table to find the names corresponding to those customer numbers (Alan).

There *is* an 'ALL' operator in SQL, as we have seen, but its operation is limited to arithmetical and string comparisons; it cannot easily be made to perform in the way that is required by this query (the universal quantifier 'for all' $\forall$). In fact what is required is a double NOT EXISTS or a double NOT IN.

In its NOT EXISTS form the query can be written in English as:

List customers for whom there does not exist a product that they have not purchased.

or

List customers for whom there does not exist a product for which there does not exist a purchase by that customer.

This NOT EXISTS format can easily be translated into SQL as:

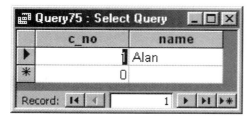

Query75 : Select Query

```
SELECT *
FROM cust
WHERE not exists
  (select *
  from prod
  where not exists
    (select *
    from purchase
    where cust.c_no = purchase.c_no
    and prod.prno = purchase.prno))
```

Fig. 7.75 The SQL double NOT EXISTS query for Query 75.

Query75 : Select Query

c_no	name
1	Alan
0	

Record: 14 | 4 | 1 | ▶ | ▶I | ▶*

Fig. 7.76 The output of Query 75.

The query can be read as 'Select all columns from CUST rows where there does not exist (lines 1 to 3) any row from PROD where there does not exist (lines 4 to 6) a PURCHASE row for that customer and product (lines 7 to 10)'.

In general, when the English version of the query contains the word 'all', there is a strong possibility that the double NOT EXISTS form will be required.

This double NOT EXISTS version is the most feasible solution in Jet.

Query 76: List details of customers who have not purchased all products.

As with the above query, there are many different approaches. The EXISTS/NOT EXISTS version only is given here. It is the most direct method.

Query76 : Select Query

```
SELECT *
FROM cust
WHERE exists
 (select *
  from prod
  where not exists
   (select *
    from purchase
    where cust.c_no = purchase.c_no
    and prod.prno = purchase.prno))
```

Fig. 7.77 The EXISTS/NOT EXISTS solution for Query 76.

Query76 : Select Query

c_no	name
2	Bill
3	Charles
0	

Record: 1

Fig. 7.78 The output from Query 76.

Neither Bill nor Charles has purchased both products. Bill has purchased only one and Charles has purchased neither.

The SQL query is interpreted back into English as:

List customers for whom there exists a product they have not purchased.

This is very similar in principle to the previous query. Note that customers who have purchased no products are included in the output.

If line 3 is changed to a NOT EXISTS and line 6 to an EXISTS, all that results is a rather lengthy version of Query 73. The English would read:

List customers for whom there does not exist a product they have purchased.

i.e. customers who have purchased nothing.

7.3 UNION queries

UNION is used to combine the results of two or more queries or tables. The data from the recordsets are appended below each other. The number of fields in each recordset has to be the same, but they don't have to have the same names. UNION is a set-oriented SQL command. Some other SQLs have INTERSECT and MINUS operations too, but the Jet DBMS of VB and Access does not. However, as with other omissions from Jet SQL, they can be simulated. We show how.

Jet calls any query with a UNION in it a union query.

The syntax of the Jet UNION statement is:

```
{[TABLE] | query} UNION [ALL] {[TABLE] | query} ...
```

where `query` can be a stored query name or an SQL SELECT statement.

In its simplest form, a UNION of two or more tables simply *appends* the rows from one table to those of another to produce a set of rows for output. That is, it adds rows from the second table under the rows from the first table. The individual tables remain unchanged; the appending just occurs in the output from the query.

There are other issues to consider, such as attempting to find the UNION of tables which have a different number of columns, differently named columns, differently typed columns, identical columns in a different order, or duplicated rows. Various WHERE conditions, joins and subqueries can also be 'mixed in'.

7.3.1 Simple UNION examples

Query 77: Produce a list of students who play either violin or piano.

The data for this query comes from the **musicians.mdb** database. The schema for this database is shown in Appendix 1.

The two tables involved are shown in Figs 7.79 and 7.80.

In practice the tables would probably be different in a shared database:

STUDENT(STUD_NO,NAME,AGE),
SUBJECT(SUBJ_NO, SUBJ_NAME)
CLASS(STUD_NO, SUBJ_NO)

which would eliminate the type of redundancy inherent in the separate tables shown. However, for the sake of the example, assume the given structure. The SQL for the query would be as shown in Fig. 7.81. Note that, consistent with the definition of set union, SQL has eliminated the duplicate row (4,'David',10). It has to do this since the output is considered to be a set and by definition, sets contain no duplicates.

violin : Table

stud_no	name	age
1	Fred	10
3	Sally	11
4	David	10
0		0

Record: 4 of 4

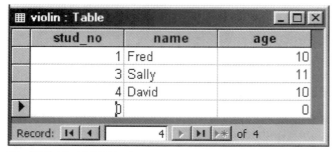

Fig. 7.79 The VIOLIN table.

piano : Table

stud_no	name	age
2	Jane	12
4	David	10
5	Zena	11
0		0

Record: 1 of 3

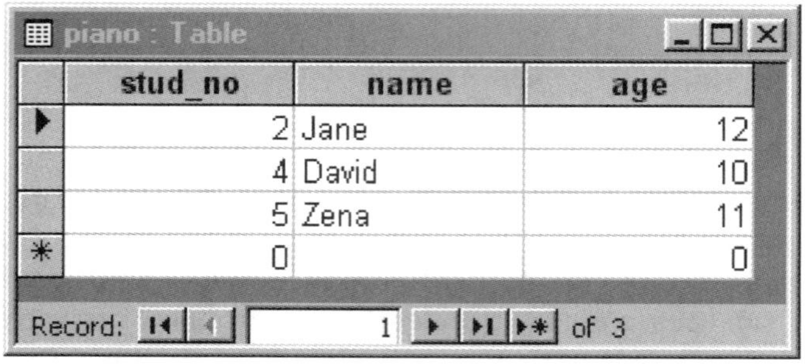

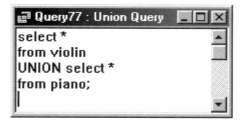

Fig. 7.80 The PIANO table.

Query77 : Union Query

```
select *
from violin
UNION select *
from piano;
```

Fig. 7.81 The SQL UNION query for Query 77.

Query77 : Union Query

stud_no	name	age
1	Fred	10
2	Jane	12
3	Sally	11
4	David	10
5	Zena	11

Record: 1 of 5

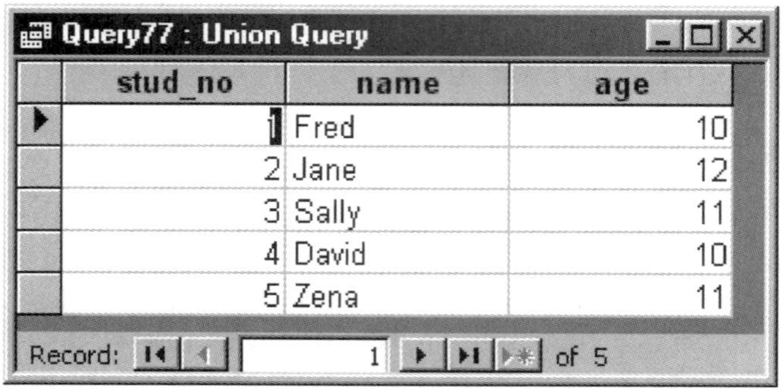

Fig. 7.82 The output of the UNION query of Fig. 7.81.

In effect, the PIANO table has been 'appended' to the bottom of the VIOLIN table although a better description might be 'merged', since the output has clearly been sorted and duplicates eliminated.

This example illustrates the basic operation of UNION. Two or more SELECTs, no matter how complex, are separated by the word UNION.

Where you are retrieving *all* of the data from a table, as we are from both tables here, Jet allows you just to say the name of the table instead of 'SELECT * FROM'. So we could have used the SQL in Fig. 7.83 for this query. The output is identical with Fig. 7.82.

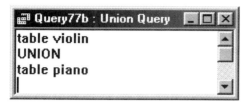

Fig. 7.83 Alternative syntax for forming the union of two complete tables.

The SQL UNION query in Fig. 7.81 eliminated the duplicate row. If for any reason you want all duplicates to stay in the output, use the ALL option.

Fig. 7.84 shows the query with the ALL option of the UNION operation included.

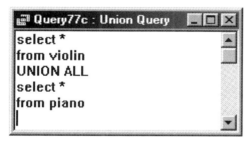

Fig. 7.84 UNION ALL.

stud_no	name	age
1	Fred	10
3	Sally	11
4	David	10
2	Jane	12
4	David	10
5	Zena	11

Record: 6 of 6

Fig. 7.85 UNION ALL includes the duplicates.

Note that David now appears twice. The PIANO table has literally been appended to the VIOLIN table.

Access Help says that UNION ALL runs faster than UNION. This is clearly because in order to eliminate duplicates in a 'pure' UNION operation, both recordsets have to be sorted before they are merged so the duplicates appear together. With UNION ALL this is not necessary.

Suppose we wished to UNION the data from the VIOLIN and PIANO tables as above, but wanted to say which instrument the children played in the output. The SQL to do this is shown in Fig. 7.86, with the output in Fig. 7.87.

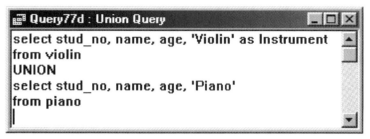

```
select stud_no, name, age, 'Violin' as Instrument
from violin
UNION
select stud_no, name, age, 'Piano'
from piano
```

Fig. 7.86 The SQL UNION query to display instruments too.

stud_no	name	age	Instrument
1	Fred	10	Violin
2	Jane	12	Piano
3	Sally	11	Violin
4	David	10	Piano
4	David	10	Violin
5	Zena	11	Piano

Record: I◄ ◄ [1] ► ►I ►* of 6

Fig. 7.87 The output of the query of Fig. 7.86.

The instrument a musician plays is not contained in the table itself, so in Fig. 7.87, we have added a virtual column of our own – the literal string 'Violin' next to the data from the VIOLIN table, and the literal string 'Piano' next to the PIANO rows.

To give the column a meaningful name, we have used a column alias 'Instrument'. Note that this column alias only has to appear in the top SELECT.

Notice that David has been output twice, once for each instrument, even though we didn't use UNION ALL, just UNION.

This is because UNION acts on *complete rows*. It only removes completely duplicated rows.

Because the sort-merge had to go ahead (due to not using ALL), the rows appear in primary key order. To get the violinists together and the pianists together again, simply use an ORDER BY. This is shown in Fig. 7.88.

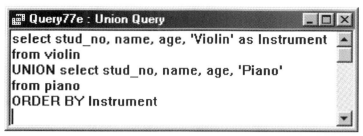

Fig. 7.88 Sorting the output on Instrument.

stud_no	name	age	Instrument
2	Jane	12	Piano
4	David	10	Piano
5	Zena	11	Piano
1	Fred	10	Violin
3	Sally	11	Violin
4	David	10	Violin

Record: 1 of 6

Fig. 7.89 The sorted output.

Note that just as only one set of column aliases (if you use them) are required (they appear in the *top* SELECT), only one ORDER BY clause (if you use one) is required. It appears at the end, after the last query or table. The ORDER BY is the last item in an SQL query to be executed. It orders the recordset resulting from all the other operations.

Notice also that the pianists came before the violinists. This is simply because 'Piano' comes before 'Violin' alphabetically. Using ORDER BY Instrument DESC (descending) would have put the violinists first.

7.3.2 Column homogeneity

The two tables VIOLIN and PIANO are said to be 'column homogeneous' since they contain the same field names, types and lengths.

It is possible, however, to UNION tables of different field names, different field sequences and, with certain restrictions, different data types.

In Figs 7.90 and Fig. 7.91 we list the fields of VIOLIN and CELLO.

violin : Table

Field Name	Data Type	Description
stud_no	Number	Integer
name	Text	Length 20
age	Number	Integer

Fig. 7.90 The fields of the VIOLIN table.

cello : Table

Field Name	Data Type	Description
stud_no	Number	Long Integer
age	Text	Length 10
name	Text	Length 10

Fig. 7.91 The fields of the CELLO table.

Note that the field names are the same in these two tables, but that the corresponding fields are in a different sequence and they have different data types.

For STUD_NO we have Integer corresponding to Long Integer.

For NAME we have Text(20) corresponding to Text(10).

For AGE we have Integer corresponding to Text(10).

The data in the two tables is shown in Figs 7.92 and 7.93.

violin : Table

stud_no	name	age
1	Fred	10
3	Sally	11
4	David	10
0		0

Record: 1 of 3

Fig. 7.92 The rows of the VIOLIN table.

cello : Table

stud_no	age	name
4	10	David
6	11	Josey
0		

Record: 3 of 3

Fig. 7.93 The rows of the CELLO table.

In the following query we find the union of these two tables.

> *Query 78*: List all the violinists with all the cellists.

As noted above, the format of the CELLO table is different from that of the VIOLIN table; the number of columns and their names are identical to those of the VIOLIN table but they are in a different order and have different length attributes.

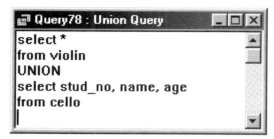

Fig. 7.94 The SQL UNION query for Query 78.

stud_no	name	age
1	Fred	10
3	Sally	11
4	David	10
6	Josey	11

Record: 4 of 4

Fig. 7.95 The output of Query 78.

Notice that the differences in format mentioned above have not caused any problems for SQL. It was simply necessary in line 4 to state the correct order of the columns in the CELLO table so that they would match those in VIOLIN. Even the text and integer versions of AGE matched up. In some SQLs you would have to convert the data type using a function to make them compatible, but Jet, in the case of numbers and text, does this for you.

We got over the problem of different field sequence by just listing the fields in a compatible sequence in the lower SELECT.

7.3.3 Different field names

As we show in the next example, it doesn't matter, in a UNION query, if the field names are different in the two recordsets you want to UNION.

Query 79: List all students who play either violin or flute.

violin : Table

stud_no	name	age
1	Fred	10
3	Sally	11
4	David	10
0		0

Record: 4 of 4

Fig. 7.96 The VIOLIN table.

flute : Table

stud	cname	age
7	Ashfak	12
0		0

Record: 2 of 2

Fig. 7.97 The FLUTE table.

The first two columns in FLUTE have different names from those in VIOLIN. The SQL query for Query 79 is shown in Fig. 7.98.

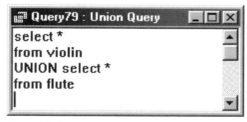

```
select *
from violin
UNION select *
from flute
```

Fig. 7.98 The UNION query for Query 79.

Query79 : Union Query

stud_no	name	age
1	Fred	10
3	Sally	11
4	David	10
7	Ashfak	12

Record: 4 of 4

Fig. 7.99 The output of Query 79.

Notice that different field names cause no problems. SQL simply uses the field names of the first table.

7.3.4 *UNION of recordsets with different numbers of columns*

It is possible to apply the UNION operator to tables where a different number of columns is required from each table. This can be achieved with a combination of projection and *padding*.

Projection is the name given to outputting a subset of the columns of a table. Padding is the name we have given to 'padding out' the fields of a recordset with dummy fields where necessary.

The following example illustrates this process.

Query 80: *Produce a listing of invoices and payments with the following column layout:*

INV_NO DATE INV_AMT PMT_NO PMT_AMT .

The INVOICE and PAYMENT tables are in the **accts.mdb** database, which is described in Appendix 1. Their data is shown in Figs 7.100 and 7.101.

inv_no	c_no	inv_date	amount
940	1	05/12/99	£26.20
1002	4	12/01/00	£149.23
1003	1	12/01/00	£16.26
1004	2	14/01/00	£200.00
1005	3	20/01/00	£510.00
1006	5	21/01/00	£250.10
1017	6	22/01/00	£412.21
0	0		£0.00

Record: 8 of 8

Fig. 7.100 The INVOICE table of the **accts.mdb** database.

inv_no	pmt_no	pmt_date	amount
940	2	12/12/99	£13.00
940	3	19/01/00	£10.00
1005	1	14/01/00	£510.00
1017	1	30/01/00	£100.00
0	0		£0.00

Record: 5 of 5

Fig. 7.101 The PAYMENT table.

Here are two tables that are clearly not column homogeneous as they stand. Referring to the required output report format, certain observations can be made. Firstly, INV_NO is a common column in the two tables. If the query were to be attempted using a more conventional join procedure, INV_NO would constitute the basis of the join criteria, with a WHERE clause of the form:

```
WHERE INVOICE.INV_NO = PAYMENT.PMT_NO
```

However, the following SQL query *will associate invoices and their relevant payments by sorting the output on INV_NO.* (Rather obscure but it works!)

The SQL is shown in Fig. 7.102.

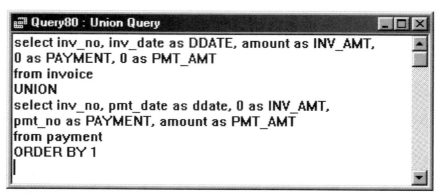

Fig. 7.102 This SQL UNION query 'UNIONs' two very different tables.

inv_no	DDATE	INV_AMT	PAYMENT	PMT_AMT
940	05/12/99	£26.20	0	£0.00
940	12/12/99	£0.00	2	£13.00
940	19/01/00	£0.00	3	£10.00
1002	12/01/00	£149.23	0	£0.00
1003	12/01/00	£16.26	0	£0.00
1004	14/01/00	£200.00	0	£0.00
1005	14/01/00	£0.00	1	£510.00
1005	20/01/00	£510.00	0	£0.00
1006	21/01/00	£250.10	0	£0.00
1017	22/01/00	£412.21	0	£0.00
1017	30/01/00	£0.00	1	£100.00

Record: 1 of 11

Fig. 7.103 The output from the UNION query of Fig. 7.102.

The sort occurs due to the ORDER BY clause in line 8. '1' means that the sort is in ascending order of the *first* column INV_NO. We could have used 'ORDER BY inv_no' instead. The ORDER BY clause in a query using a UNION operator relates to the *whole* query so that there is no need to repeat the ORDER BY clause in each SELECT statement and there is no need for brackets.

The query interpreter will often perform a sort-merge operation where two or more tables are involved (for speed and to detect duplicates) and since INV_NO is the 'most significant' (leftmost) column, the ORDER BY is not always necessary, depending on the DBMS in use.

Data from two tables appear under the same five report columns. For example, the second output column, the transaction date, contains data from INVOICE.IN-V_DATE and PAYMENT.PMT_DATE. This is possible since they both have the same format, that is, they are both DATE-TIME columns.

Under the third column INV_AMT, the value for an invoice is taken from the INV.AMOUNT column and the value for a payment is set to zero since there is no invoice amount column in the PAYMENT table.

This process of 'padding' is necessary to make the projections (subsets of columns) of the two tables column homogeneous, that is, to make them match up. Corresponding columns should be of the same type so that a numeric column in the first table has the corresponding position in the second table 'padded' with some numeric value, here zero.

A similar situation exists with respect to payment number. This column exists in PAYMENT but not in INVOICE, which consequently requires a 'padding' zero in this position in the SELECT line.

There is also the question of what column title will appear in the output. In the two tables INVOICE and PAYMENT, both the invoice amount and the payment amount columns are called AMOUNT. The form of the column aliases used in this SQL query is such as to remove any ambiguity or dependence on query interpreter defaults. All corresponding columns are explicitly given the same alias names. Finally, note that the output date column is called DDATE rather than date because DATE may be a reserved word in some SQLs and might 'confuse' the query interpreter, resulting in an error condition.

In summary, this query demonstrates that it is possible and sometimes meaningful to perform a UNION on tables with considerably different columns. It also demonstrates a way of associating rows from different tables using ORDER BY with UNION.

We stated above that column type compatibility must be maintained. We can use the fact that in Jet a text field is compatible with numeric fields by replacing the zeros with empty strings (''). This leads to a neater output.

Figure 7.104 shows the modified SQL.

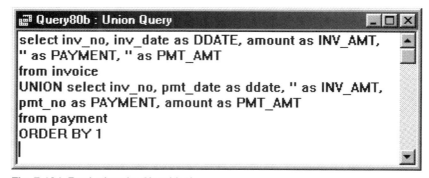

Fig. 7.104 Replacing the 0's with ' '.

Figure 7.105 shows the improved output layout that results.

Query80b : Union Query

inv_no	DDATE	INV_AMT	PAYMENT	PMT_AMT
940	05/12/99	26.2		
940	12/12/99		2	13
940	19/01/00		3	10
1002	12/01/00	149.23		
1003	12/01/00	16.26		
1004	14/01/00	200		
1005	14/01/00		1	510
1005	20/01/00	510		
1006	21/01/00	250.1		
1017	22/01/00	412.21		
1017	30/01/00		1	100

Record: 1 of 11

Fig. 7.105 The output of the SQL UNION query of Fig. 7.104.

7.3.5 *Simulating an INTERSECT*

Just as Jet has the set operation UNION, some other SQLs also have INTERSECT and MINUS set operations. Jet doesn't have these, so we have to simulate them – implement their logic by other means.

Consider the following example, which refers to data in the **musicians.mdb** Jet database.

Query 81: List details of all students who play both violin and piano.

Remembering that the data for violinists and pianists are in two different tables VIOLIN and PIANO and that these tables have the same format, the query in SQLs that have the INTERSECT set operation is simply:

```
select *
from violin
intersect
select *
from piano
```

The set of students selected in lines 1 and 2 is intersected with the set of students in lines 4 and 5 and only those students in *both* sets appear at the output:

STUD_NO	NAME	AGE
4	David	10

Jet SQL doesn't have INTERSECT, so we have to think of some other SQL method of approaching the problem. Remembering the property of the INNER

JOIN whereby only rows of two recordsets that matched were joined and passed to the output, consider the following solution (Fig. 7.106).

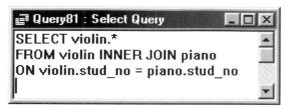

Fig. 7.106 The INNER JOIN way of simulating an INTERSECT.

stud_no	name	age
4	David	10

Fig. 7.107 David is the only musician who plays violin and piano.

We join the two tables VIOLIN and PIANO. Because it's an INNER JOIN, only those records that have a STUD_NO in both tables are output.

Here's another example of INNER JOIN simulating an INTERSECT:

> *Query 82: List the product numbers of all products that have current deliveries.*

What we really want to do here is to take the intersection of the set of product numbers in the PRODUCT table and the set of product numbers in the DELIVERY table.

However, we can simulate this intersect operation, once again, with INNER JOIN. The database in use here is **prod_del.mdb**.

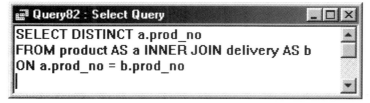

Fig. 7.108 Simulating INTERSECT between data in tables of different structure.

According to the English version of the query, all that is required at the output is the set of product numbers that appear in both the PRODUCT table and the DELIVERY table.

This functionality (essentially an intersection of the set of product numbers in both tables) is easily achieved using INNER JOIN. See Fig. 7.108. The output appears in Fig. 7.109.

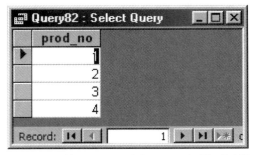

Fig. 7.109 The output of the query in Fig. 7.108.

The DISTINCT in the query is necessary to remove duplicates caused in the situation in which a product has been delivered more than once.

Query 83: List details of students who play violin, piano and cello.

What we would like to do here, were an INTERSECT operation available in Jet SQL, is:

```
select *
from violin
intersect
select *
from piano
intersect
select stud_no, name, age
from cello
```

The second-last line needs to name the columns explicitly because they're in a different order in the CELLO table from the other two tables.

Since INTERSECT is not available in Jet SQL, a three-way INNER JOIN is required.

```
SELECT a.*
FROM (violin AS a INNER JOIN piano AS b
ON a.stud_no = b.stud_no)
INNER JOIN cello AS c
ON b.stud_no = c.stud_no
```

Fig. 7.110 Simulating a three-way intersect with a three-way INNER JOIN.

The SQL for Query 83 is shown in Fig. 7.110 and the output in Fig. 7.111.

Query83 : Select Query

stud_no	name	age
4	David	10

Record: 1 of 1

Fig. 7.111 The output of Query 83.

7.3.6 Combinations of UNION and (simulated) INTERSECT

Query 84: List students who play the piano, or both violin and cello.

Query84 : Union Query

```
select *
from piano
UNION (select a.*
 from violin as a inner join cello as b
 on a.stud_no = b.stud_no)
```

Fig. 7.112 UNION with simulated INTERSECT.

Query84 : Union Query

stud_no	name	age
2	Jane	12
4	David	10
5	Zena	11

Record: 1 of 3

Fig. 7.113 The output of Query 84.

The logic required for Query 84 is PIANO UNION (VIOLIN INTERSECT CELLO). We simulate the INTERSECT with an INNER JOIN in Fig. 7.112. The parentheses are necessary to make it clear that the intersection occurs before the union in this query. The query would in general have different results if the union occurred first. The reason can be found by considering the fact that for three sets A, B and C,

A + (B.C) is not equivalent to (A + B).C

Here, '.' means 'intersection' and '+' means 'union'.

7.3.7 *Simulating a MINUS*

The MINUS operator delivers to the output data from all rows of the table(s) in the first query that do *not* have 'corresponding' rows in the second table. The tables, or at least the subset of columns projected for output, must be column homogeneous, as with UNION and INTERSECT.

While Jet SQL does not have a MINUS operation, it can be simulated in various ways. We illustrate these ways with the following example query.

> *Query 85*: List students who play violin but not piano.

The logic required in this query is:

VIOLIN AND NOT PIANO.

Figure 7.114 gives a NOT IN version.

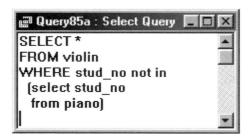

Fig. 7.114 NOT IN version of Query 85.

If a student number appears in the VIOLIN table but not in the PIANO table, it is output.

Figure 7.115 gives a NOT EXISTS version.

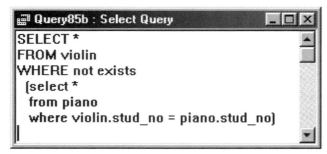

Fig. 7.115 NOT EXISTS version of Query 85.

If there doesn't exist a record in the PIANO table with the same student number as the current record in the VIOLIN table, then output that current VIOLIN record.

Fig. 7.116 gives a LEFT JOIN version of Query 85.

The idea here is that the LEFT JOIN will join a VIOLIN record to NULLs if there is no corresponding PIANO record. We can then test for NULLs.

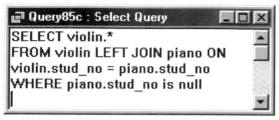

Fig. 7.116 LEFT JOIN version of Query 85.

In each case, the output is as shown in Fig. 7.117.

	stud_no	name	age
▶	1	Fred	10
	3	Sally	11
✳			

Record: |◀| |◀| 1 |▶| |▶I| |▶✳| of 2

Fig. 7.117 The output of Query 85.

Query 86: List the students who play violin but neither piano nor cello.

Calling the sets V, P and C, it is apparent that what is required is:

V.not P.not C

The operation of MINUS on sets A and B, i.e. A MINUS B, is such that:

A MINUS B is equivalent to A.not B

so that the expression for the query can be written:

(V MINUS P) MINUS C but not:

V MINUS (P MINUS C)

which has a different meaning. The difference can be seen by drawing a Venn diagram or by manipulating the expression using the rules of logic. Using De Morgan's law for example,

(V MINUS P) MINUS C can be rewritten as V.not P.not C

whereas

V MINUS (P MINUS C) cannot;

one equivalent is V.(Not P + C).

Given an SQL with a MINUS operator, the SQL for each of these parenthesis placements is given below.

```
(select *
from violin
minus
select *
from piano)
minus
select stud_no, name, age
from cello
```

which produces the output:

STUD_NO	NAME	AGE
1	Fred	10
3	Sally	11

whereas

```
select *
from violin
minus
(select *
from piano
minus
select stud_no, name, age
from cello)
```

produces the output:

STUD_NO	NAME	AGE
1	Fred	10
3	Sally	11
4	David	10

An English interpretation of this latter query might be:

'List all violinists excluding those who also play piano but not cello'

which is not particularly clear; one is tempted to start placing parentheses in such English sentences as an aid to clarity, even though there are many people who will see no problem at all. Clearly it's the former double-minus that we wish to simulate to answer Query 86.

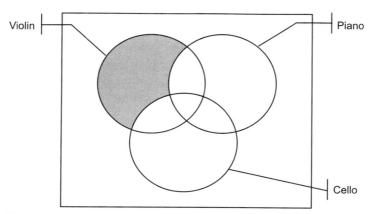

Fig. 7.118 The shaded area is required for Query 86.

In Fig. 7.118 the shaded area represents the set of musicians required to be output.

One SQL formulation that can be used in Jet is shown in Fig. 7.119.

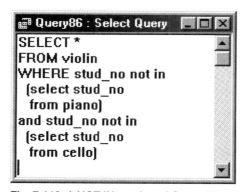

Fig. 7.119 A NOT IN version of Query 86.

This query works on the principle that if a student number exists in the VIOLIN table but in neither the PIANO nor CELLO tables, the corresponding VIOLIN record should be output. Notice that the two subqueries are not nested.

There are several other formulations for this query. Clearly a pair of NOT EXISTS subqueries would also work. A three-way join version could also be tried.

7.4 Queries built on queries – views

In some situations, you may find it useful to query the data from another query, rather than from tables. This is quite possible in the Jet database used in Access and VB. Other SQLs have a mechanism for this. They call the stored queries 'views' and the tables on which they are based 'base tables'. In Jet, you simply query a query. We had an example of this in Query 58b, where one query was joined to another table. One of the advantages of doing this is that a complex query can be broken down into smaller steps, each query in the sequence getting the data in a form more suitable for the final query output. Views can give users sections of the database built up into a format suitable for their particular processing needs. It is also possible to allow users permission to see only a part of a database by giving them permissions to access a query containing a subset of data from base tables.

7.4.1 Simple views

Create a query LONCUS which contains only London customers.

All we need to do with Jet databases to create the required 'view' is to define the query and store it.

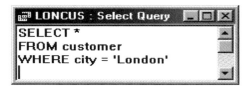

Fig. 7.120 Defining the LONCUS query.

Query 87: List the contents of the LONCUS query.

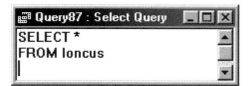

Fig. 7.121 Querying the LONCUS query.

The idea here is that the LONCUS stored query gives a particular 'view' of the underlying base table CUSTOMER. The output from Query 87 is shown in Fig. 7.122. Some people would call LONCUS a 'virtual table' because it acts as if it were a table. You can query it as if it were a table. The view LONCUS can be queried, as we have seen. It can also be used as a part of other queries, just as a table would. For example, LONCUS could be joined to the INVOICE table, or it could even be joined to another query, or used in a subquery.

Fig. 7.122 The output of Query 87.

It is even possible to update the CUSTOMER base table by updating the LONCUS query.

Add a new customer record to the LONCUS stored query.

Fig. 7.123 Adding a new record to the LONCUS stored query.

Fig. 7.124 The CUSTOMER table showing the new record.

Access Help gives a comprehensive description of which stored queries you can use to update the database in this way in the Help item:

When can I update data from a query?

It's possible to update through *any* query based on a single table and *any* query based on a pair of tables sharing a one-to-many relationship. In most other situations, updates through queries are not allowed.

One quick way to see whether a query is updateable is to check the data control at the bottom of the datasheet view. In Fig. 7.122, for example, the asterisked triangle is enabled (not greyed out), and there is an asterisked blank row at the bottom of the datasheet view. This indicates that the stored query *is* updateable.

Note that even though LONCUS is defined as the set of London customers, it is possible to add a non-London customer to the database through this query.

If we run the SQL INSERT INTO command shown in Fig. 7.125 the record is inserted into the CUSTOMER base table.

This occurs even though the new customer is from Leeds.

```
DMLExample33 : Append Query                    _□×
INSERT INTO LONCUS
VALUES (11, 'Mrs', 'Jones', 'A.B.', '1 Low St', 'Leeds', 'LE1 3AB', 1000, 0);
```

Fig. 7.125 Inserting a non-London customer via the LONCUS stored query.

Customer : Table

c_no	title	sname	inits	street	city	postc	cred_lim	balance
1	Mr	Sallaway	G.R.	12 Fax Rd	London	WC1	£1,000.00	£42.56
2	Miss	Lauri	P.	5 Dux St	London	N1	£500.00	£200.00
3	Mr	Jackson	R.	2 Lux Ave	Leeds	LE1 2AB	£500.00	£510.00
4	Mr	Dziduch	M.	31 Low St	Dover	DO2 9CD	£100.00	£149.23
5	Ms	Woods	S.Q.	17 Nax Rd	London	E18 4WW	£1,000.00	£250.10
6	Mrs	Williams	C.	41 Cax St	Dover	DO2 8WD		£412.21
10	Mrs	Carter	S.Q.	1 High Rd	London	E18 3RJ	£1,500.00	£780.11
11	Mrs	Jones	A.B.	1 Low St	Leeds	LE1 3AB	£1,000.00	£0.00
0							£0.00	£0.00

Record: 1 of 8

Fig. 7.126 The CUSTOMER table after the INSERT INTO of Fig. 7.125.

Here's another example of a stored query, again based on a single table, which restricts the columns visible to the user through the query.

> *Create a query SHORTCUS which shows just customer number, credit limit and balance of all customers.*

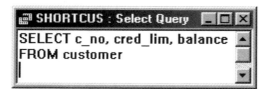

```
SHORTCUS : Select Query   _□×
SELECT c_no, cred_lim, balance
FROM customer
```

Fig. 7.127 The stored query SHORTCUS.

This stored query presents just a subset of the fields of the CUSTOMER table. It illustrates that views can be based on a *projection* of the base table (i.e. a subset of the columns) as well a subset of the rows of a table.

> _Query 88:_ List the contents of the SHORTCUS stored query.

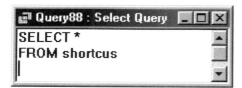

```
Query88 : Select Query
SELECT *
FROM shortcus
```

Fig. 7.128 Querying SHORTCUS.

c_no	cred_lim	balance
1	£1,000.00	£42.56
2	£500.00	£200.00
3	£500.00	£510.00
4	£100.00	£149.23
5	£1,000.00	£250.10
6		£412.21
* 0	£0.00	£0.00

Record: 1

Fig. 7.129 The output of Query 88.

The output here is just the data represented by the SHORTCUS stored query itself. However, we can retrieve subsets of SHORTCUS in the normal way using a WHERE clause, for example.

> _Query 89:_ List all records in SHORTCUS where the balance does not exceed the credit limit.

```
Query89 : Select Query
SELECT *
FROM shortcus
WHERE balance <= cred_lim
```

Fig. 7.130 Retrieving a subset of the rows of LONCUS.

Query89 : Select Query

	c_no	cred_lim	balance
▶	1	£1,000.00	£42.56
	2	£500.00	£200.00
	5	£1,000.00	£250.10
*	0	£0.00	£0.00

Record: ◀◀ ◀ 1 ▶ ▶◀ ▶*

Fig. 7.131 The output of Query 89.

A stored query may also present a subset of rows *and* columns from a table.

> *Create a view (stored query) called MINILONCUS which shows just the customer number, credit limit and balance of London customers.*

MINILONCUS : Select Query

```
SELECT c_no, cred_lim, balance
FROM customer
WHERE city = 'London'
```

Fig. 7.132 Defining the stored query MINILONCUS.

> *Query 90: List the contents of the MINILONCUS stored query.*

Query90 : Select Query

```
SELECT *
FROM miniloncus
```

Fig. 7.133 Query 90.

Query90 : Select Query

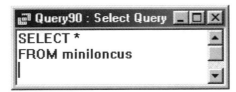

	c_no	cred_lim	balance
▶	1	£1,000.00	£42.56
	2	£500.00	£200.00
	5	£1,000.00	£250.10
*	0	£0.00	£0.00

Record: ◀◀ ◀ 1 ▶ ▶◀ ▶*

Fig. 7.134 This query retrieves the data presented by stored query MINILONCUS.

It is also possible to build one stored query on another and then to query the results from that query. Since stored queries can be thought of as 'views' or 'virtual tables', many users and applications may become more familiar with the views than the actual base tables. One of the ideas behind views is that they present the data to the users in a way more suited to their needs than the base tables do.

In the view (stored query) MINILONCUS shown above, we show three columns from the London rows of the base table CUSTOMER.

We could have achieved the same result by building MINILONCUS on LONCUS. The following stored query LONCUS1 does this.

> *Create a view MINILONCUS1 based on the view LONCUS.*

Here is the definition of LONCUS:

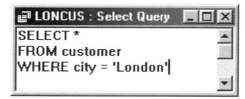

Fig. 7.135 The LONCUS view definition.

We can build another view LONCUS1 based on *this* view:

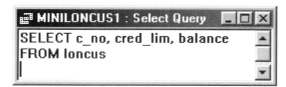

Fig. 7.136 Defining the view MINILONCUS1.

> *Query 91: Query the view MINILONCUS1.*

Fig. 7.137 Retrieving all data from MINILONCUS1.

Query91 : Select Query

c_no	cred_lim	balance
1	£1,000.00	£42.56
2	£500.00	£200.00
5	£1,000.00	£250.10
0	£0.00	£0.00

Record: 1

Fig. 7.138 The output from Query 91.

Note that Fig. 7.138 indicates that this view (stored query) is still updateable, even though it is the output of a view based on a view. If you added a record to the MINILONCUS1 view, it would add just those three fields to the CUSTOMER base table. This would not be an updateable view if the primary key or any other mandatory field were not included in it.

7.4.2 *Summary views*

One common and very useful application of views is in the construction of summary data based on GROUP BY. The data is then always available in this summary form by just calling up the relevant stored query name.

As an example, we may want to create a view called SUMMARY1 containing summary financial data on our customer accounts. The view is to contain, for each city, the total credit limit and the highest balance.

SUMMARY1 : Select Query

```
SELECT city, sum(cred_lim) AS [City risk], sum(balance) AS Debt
FROM customer
GROUP BY city
```

Fig. 7.139 The definition of the view SUMMARY1.

You can of course run this query and obtain the output shown below in Fig. 7.140.

SUMMARY1 : Select Query

city	City risk	Debt
Dover	£100.00	£561.44
Leeds	£500.00	£510.00
London	£2,500.00	£492.66

Record: 1 of 3

Fig. 7.140 The view of the CUSTOMER table presented by SUMMARY1.

You can also query the view SUMMARY1 as if it were a base table, as we do in the following query.

Query 92: From the SUMMARY1 view, list the Leeds data.

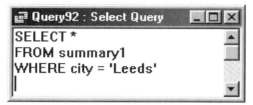

Fig. 7.141 Querying the view SUMMARY1.

The output from Query 92 is shown in Fig. 7.142.

	city	City risk	Debt
▶	Leeds	£500.00	£510.00

Record: ◀◀ ◀ | 1 | ▶ ▶▮ ▶* of 1

Fig. 7.142 The output of Query 92.

Notice here that we have a GROUP BY in a view; the totals are being grouped by city. The column aliases are advisable here to give the view meaningful column names. SUMMARY1 would probably be the basis of a very useful summary report. The means of obtaining the summary (such as the details of the GROUP BY) need not be remembered by end users since the logic is encapsulated in the view. All that is required is to remember the view name. In this way the end user can be insulated from the more involved aspects of the database queries, which can be left to the programmer to develop and test. The view is always up to date because whenever the view is used, its built-in SELECT command is re-run.

Note that the view (stored query) SUMMARY1 is not updateable – you couldn't add or delete or change a record in it. This is shown by the disabled asterisk button on the data control of Fig. 7.142. The reason is that if, for example, you wanted to delete the London record of the view, that would imply the deletion of *all* the London records of the base table CUSTOMER. This is considered an inappropriate action for a view, and views based on GROUP BY are not updateable.

7.4.3 Views based on joins

One of the major uses for views is to give the database user the impression that the database contains tables that are in precisely the format that he or she requires for the application in hand. This makes thinking about the problem and the formulation of SQL queries simpler. Quite often, as we have seen, a query will require more than one database table to be accessed to produce the desired output. In many such cases, associated queries would be easier to write and reports easier to generate if the relevant data appeared to be all in one table.

In Chapter 2 the processes of entity analysis and normalization tended to split data into separate tables, each table corresponding to a 'real world' object type. The major object in doing this was to eliminate data redundancy and the associated insertion, deletion and update anomalies. In creating views of joined tables, we are apparently reversing this process and 'denormalizing'. However, remembering that views do not actually store any data, no data duplication will result, and we will obtain the advantage of having a single 'virtual' table that contains all relevant data items.

One common requirement in accounting systems, in particular the sales ledger subsystem, is to provide customers with a monthly statement of account. The data required in the statement can be broken down into:

- Customer Account data
- Invoice data
- Payment data

Assuming this data is contained in the tables CUSTOMER, INVOICE and PAYMENT, it is possible to create a view, based on a join of corresponding rows in the tables, which will make the writing of a report program to print statements considerably simpler.

The necessary view can be created by storing a query which correctly joins the required tables' rows. Details of this query are given in Section 7.3.

We shall call the view STATEMENT. The stored query defining the STATEMENT view is shown in Fig. 7.143.

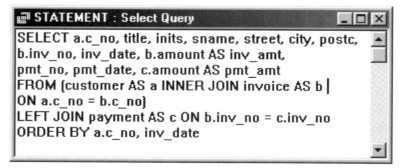

Fig. 7.143 The SQL query defining the view STATEMENT.

The data presented by this view can be seen by simply running it. See Fig. 7.144.

c_no	title	inits	sname	street	city	postc	inv_no	inv_date	inv_amt	pmt_no	pmt_date	pmt_amt
1	Mr	G.R.	Sallaway	12 Fax Rd	London	WC1	940	05/12/99	£26.20	3	19/01/00	£10.00
1	Mr	G.R.	Sallaway	12 Fax Rd	London	WC1	940	05/12/99	£26.20	2	12/12/99	£13.00
1	Mr	G.R.	Sallaway	12 Fax Rd	London	WC1	1003	12/01/00	£16.26			
2	Miss	P.	Lauri	5 Dux St	London	N1	1004	14/01/00	£200.00			
3	Mr	R.	Jackson	2 Lux Ave	Leeds	LE1 2AB	1005	20/01/00	£510.00	1	14/01/00	£510.00
4	Mr	M.	Dziduch	31 Low St	Dover	DO2 9CD	1002	12/01/00	£149.23			
5	Ms	S.Q.	Woods	17 Nax Rd	London	E18 4WW	1006	21/01/00	£250.10			
6	Mrs	C.	Williams	41 Cax St	Dover	DO2 8WD	1017	22/01/00	£412.21	1	30/01/00	£100.00

Record: 9 of 9

Fig. 7.144 The data presented by the view STATEMENT.

Note the use of column aliases to prevent the attempt being made to create a view with two identically named columns AMOUNT. This view could form the basis for an end-of-month statement run in a sales ledger system. The formatting of the output would have to be performed by a report writer of procedural code such as Visual Basic.

Writing the code can be made easier when all the required data is in a single view such as STATEMENT.

Note that this view is updateable, although it would be inadvisable to base updates to the CUSTOMER, INVOICE and PAYMENT tables on this view. It is not in a suitable format for that.

We can also query this view. We may, for example, want to produce a statement for customers in just London and Dover.

> _Query 93_: List all the STATEMENT records for London and Dover.

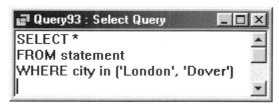

```
Query93 : Select Query
SELECT *
FROM statement
WHERE city in ('London', 'Dover')
```

Fig. 7.145 Querying the STATEMENT view.

c_no	title	inits	sname	street	city	postc	inv_no	inv_date	inv_amt	pmt_no	pmt_date	pmt_amt
1	Mr	G.R.	Sallaway	12 Fax Rd	London	WC1	940	05/12/99	£26.20	3	19/01/00	£10.00
1	Mr	G.R.	Sallaway	12 Fax Rd	London	WC1	940	05/12/99	£26.20	2	12/12/99	£13.00
1	Mr	G.R.	Sallaway	12 Fax Rd	London	WC1	1003	12/01/00	£16.26			
2	Miss	P.	Lauri	5 Dux St	London	N1	1004	14/01/00	£200.00			
4	Mr	M.	Dziduch	31 Low St	Dover	DO2 9CD	1002	12/01/00	£149.23			
5	Ms	S.Q.	Woods	17 Nax Rd	London	E18 4WW	1006	21/01/00	£250.10			
6	Mrs	C.	Williams	41 Cax St	Dover	DO2 8WD	1017	22/01/00	£412.21	1	30/01/00	£100.00

Record: 1 of 7

Fig. 7.146 The output of Query 93.

7.4.4 Joining views

It is possible to join a view to a table or another view. For example, we may wish to join the CUSTOMER table to SUMMARY1 on CITY:

> _Query 94_: Show each customer's balance as a percentage of his or her city's balance.

Figures 7.147, 7.148 and 7.149 give a reminder of the nature of the SUMMARY1 view and the CUSTOMER table.

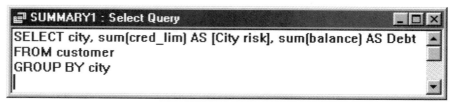

```
SELECT city, sum(cred_lim) AS [City risk], sum(balance) AS Debt
FROM customer
GROUP BY city
```

Fig. 7.147 The SUMMARY1 view.

SUMMARY1 : Select Query

city	City risk	Debt
Dover	£100.00	£561.44
Leeds	£500.00	£510.00
London	£2,500.00	£492.66

Record: 1 of 3

Fig. 7.148 The output of the SUMMARY1 view.

Customer : Table

c_no	title	sname	inits	street	city	postc	cred_lim	balance
1	Mr	Sallaway	G.R.	12 Fax Rd	London	WC1	£1,000.00	£42.56
2	Miss	Lauri	P.	5 Dux St	London	N1	£500.00	£200.00
3	Mr	Jackson	R.	2 Lux Ave	Leeds	LE1 2AB	£500.00	£510.00
4	Mr	Dziduch	M.	31 Low St	Dover	DO2 9CD	£100.00	£149.23
5	Ms	Woods	S.Q.	17 Nax Rd	London	E18 4WW	£1,000.00	£250.10
6	Mrs	Williams	C.	41 Cax St	Dover	DO2 8WD		£412.21
*	0						£0.00	£0.00

Record: 1 of 6

Fig. 7.149 The CUSTOMER table.

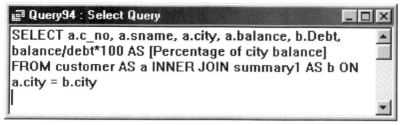

Fig. 7.150 Joining CUSTOMER table to SUMMARY1 view.

c_no	sname	city	balance	Debt	Percentage of city balance
1	Sallaway	London	£42.56	£492.66	8.63881784597897
2	Lauri	London	£200.00	£492.66	40.5959485243373
3	Jackson	Leeds	£510.00	£510.00	100
4	Dziduch	Dover	£149.23	£561.44	26.5798660587062
5	Woods	London	£250.10	£492.66	50.7652336296838
6	Williams	Dover	£412.21	£561.44	73.4201339412938

Record: 1 of 6

Fig. 7.151 The output of Query 94.

The existence of the SUMMARY1 view has made this Query 94 quite straight-forward to write.

7.4.5 *Views may contain duplicates*

Even though views are often thought of as 'virtual tables' and tables in a truly relational database cannot contain duplicate rows, it *is* possible to have duplicate rows in a view. To demonstrate this, consider the stored query in Fig. 7.152, which we are treating as a view.

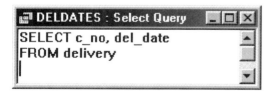

Fig. 7.152 The definition of the view DELDATES.

Query 95: List the data in the view DELDATES.

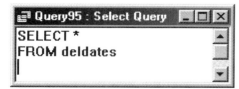

Fig. 7.153 Selecting all the rows from view DELDATES.

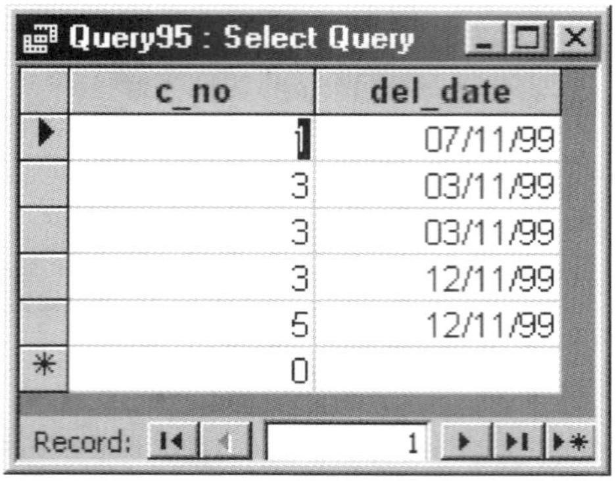

Fig. 7.154 The view DELDATES contains duplicate rows.

It is not surprising that DELDATES contains duplicate rows, because the query on which it is based contains duplicates. These duplicate rows could be removed using DISTINCT if required.

7.4.6 Updating and views

Notice that in Fig. 7.154, there is a blank line at the end which would appear to show that the view was updateable. In fact, this view could not accept a new row being appended because it does not contain the whole of the primary key, which is in this case a composite key consisting of C–NO with PROD–NO with DEL–DATE (see Fig. 7.155).

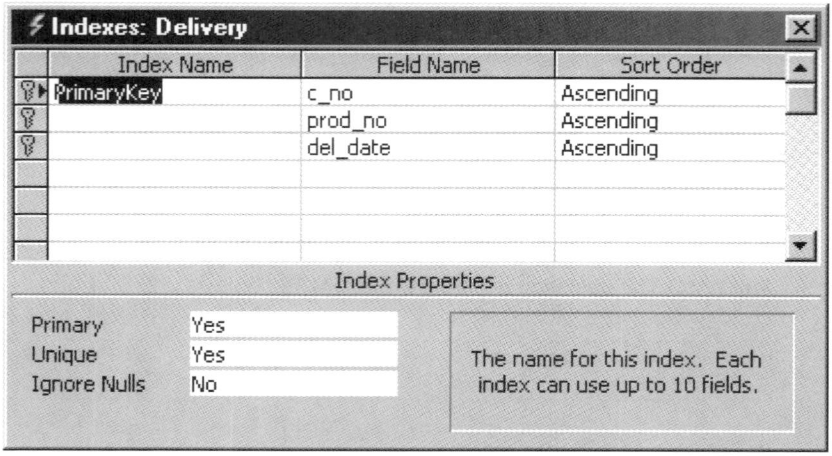

Fig. 7.155 The Primary key of the DELIVERY table.

If you try to add a record to this stored query, there would be no value for PROD–NO, because it's not a field in the view. Since PROD–NO is part of the primary key, it cannot have a NULL value, so the record insert would fail.

Consequently, the DELDATES view is not updateable. The error message actually given by Access 97 Jet Engine 3.5 when you attempt to add a new record to the view is shown in Fig. 7.156.

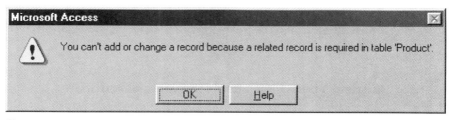

Fig. 7.156 Jet's error message.

The error message is also true; the referential integrity constraint requiring a related record in the PRODUCT table would be violated. There would be a DELIVERY record with no corresponding PRODUCT record. So both the primary key non-NULL constraint and the referential integrity constraint would be violated by the insertion of a record into the DELDATES view of Fig. 7.152.

We saw in Section 7.4.3 that the STATEMENT view (Fig. 7.144), based on three tables, was updateable, although it was unlikely ever to be used for that purpose.

The SUMMARY1 view of Section 7.4.4, Fig. 7.148, was not updateable because it consisted of just summary records. In general, any query containing grouped data is not updateable.

If the stored query just uses a GROUP BY in a subquery associated with a WHERE clause, then it may be updateable. However, if the GROUP BY is in the outer query, the output data will be grouped and therefore not updateable. The rules governing the updating of views vary from one database management system to another. One widely used DBMS only allows views based on single tables to be updated. Jet is a little less restrictive in this respect.

The rules governing which types of stored queries (views) in Jet databases can be updated and in which ways are documented in Access Help under the section:

update queries, data that can be updated.

Here is a simplified list of things likely to prevent you updating a stored query (i.e. a view):

1. Queries containing aggregated data. There should be no GROUP BY in the outer query.
2. Queries that do not contain the whole primary key of the base tables.
3. Queries based on three or more tables in which there is a many-to-one-to-many set of relationships.
4. UNION queries.
5. Queries containing DISTINCT in the outer query.
6. Calculated fields.

7. Crosstab queries (see later for examples of these). These are queries based on a GROUP BY with two variables.

8. SQL pass-through queries. These are queries where the SELECT statement is 'passed through' to be executed on another database.

9. Updates that would violate security permissions of the base tables.

10. Fields in locked records. A record may be locked by another user.

Updating a base table affects the views based on it

All updates to a base table should be immediately reflected in all views that encompass that base table. For example, if the balance of a certain customer in the CUSTOMER table is increased by £100 (Fig. 7.157) then the view LONCUS based on CUSTOMER should show this.

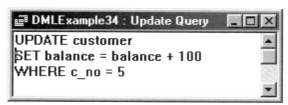

```
DMLExample34 : Update Query

UPDATE customer
SET balance = balance + 100
WHERE c_no = 5
```

Fig. 7.157 An update to one record in the CUSTOMER table.

LONCUS : Select Query

c_no	title	sname	inits	street	city	postc	cred_lim	balance
1	Mr	Sallaway	G.R.	12 Fax Rd	London	WC1	£1,000.00	£42.56
2	Miss	Lauri	P.	5 Dux St	London	N1	£500.00	£200.00
5	Ms	Woods	S.Q.	17 Nax Rd	London	E18 4WW	£1,000.00	£250.10
0							£0.00	£0.00

Record: 1 of 3

Fig. 7.158 The LONCUS view *before* the update of Fig. 7.157.

LONCUS : Select Query

c_no	title	sname	inits	street	city	postc	cred_lim	balance
1	Mr	Sallaway	G.R.	12 Fax Rd	London	WC1	£1,000.00	£42.56
2	Miss	Lauri	P.	5 Dux St	London	N1	£500.00	£200.00
5	Ms	Woods	S.Q.	17 Nax Rd	London	E18 4WW	£1,000.00	£350.10
0							£0.00	£0.00

Record: 1 of 3

Fig. 7.159 The LONCUS view *after* the update of Fig. 7.157.

Figures 7.158 and 7.159 show that updating the CUSTOMER table causes the view LONCUS to be updated. The balance of customer number 5 has been increased by £100.

Updating a view affects the tables it is based on

Similarly, if the *view* is updated, then the base table will reflect the change. Here we update the LONCUS view and show that the update has 'printed through' onto the CUSTOMER base table and the LONCUS view itself.

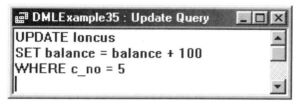

```
DMLExample35 : Update Query
UPDATE loncus
SET balance = balance + 100
WHERE c_no = 5
```

Fig. 7.160 Updating the LONCUS query.

c_no	title	sname	inits	street	city	postc	cred_lim	balance
1	Mr	Sallaway	G.R.	12 Fax Rd	London	WC1	£1,000.00	£42.56
2	Miss	Lauri	P.	5 Dux St	London	N1	£500.00	£200.00
3	Mr	Jackson	R.	2 Lux Ave	Leeds	LE1 2AB	£500.00	£510.00
4	Mr	Dziduch	M.	31 Low St	Dover	DO2 9CD	£100.00	£149.23
5	Ms	Woods	S.Q.	17 Nax Rd	London	E18 4WW	£1,000.00	£250.10
6	Mrs	Williams	C.	41 Cax St	Dover	DO2 8WD		£412.21
0								£0.00

Customer : Table — Record: 7 of 7

Fig. 7.161 The CUSTOMER base table *before* the update of Fig. 7.160.

c_no	title	sname	inits	street	city	postc	cred_lim	balance
1	Mr	Sallaway	G.R.	12 Fax Rd	London	WC1	£1,000.00	£42.56
2	Miss	Lauri	P.	5 Dux St	London	N1	£500.00	£200.00
5	Ms	Woods	S.Q.	17 Nax Rd	London	E18 4WW	£1,000.00	£250.10
0							£0.00	£0.00

LONCUS : Select Query — Record: 1 of 3

Fig. 7.162 The LONCUS view *before* the update.

	c_no	title	sname	inits	street	city	postc	cred_lim	balance
▶	1	Mr	Sallaway	G.R.	12 Fax Rd	London	WC1	£1,000.00	£42.56
	2	Miss	Lauri	P.	5 Dux St	London	N1	£500.00	£200.00
	3	Mr	Jackson	R.	2 Lux Ave	Leeds	LE1 2AB	£500.00	£510.00
	4	Mr	Dziduch	M.	31 Low St	Dover	DO2 9CD	£100.00	£149.23
	5	Ms	Woods	S.Q.	17 Nax Rd	London	E18 4WW	£1,000.00	£350.10
	6	Mrs	Williams	C.	41 Cax St	Dover	DO2 8WD		£412.21
*	0							£0.00	£0.00

Record: 1 of 6

Fig. 7.163 The CUSTOMER base table *after* the update.

	c_no	title	sname	inits	street	city	postc	cred_lim	balance
▶	1	Mr	Sallaway	G.R.	12 Fax Rd	London	WC1	£1,000.00	£42.56
	2	Miss	Lauri	P.	5 Dux St	London	N1	£500.00	£200.00
	5	Ms	Woods	S.Q.	17 Nax Rd	London	E18 4WW	£1,000.00	£350.10
*	0							£0.00	£0.00

Record: 1 of 3

Fig. 7.164 The LONCUS view *after* the update.

To summarize the updating of views:

- See the ten points above regarding the question of when it's possible to update a view.
- Supplement these ten points with the detailed guidelines in Access Help under "update queries, data that can be updated".
- If you update a base table, all the views (stored queries) based on that table will be updated automatically.
- If you update an updateable view (stored query) then all the tables in that view will be updated accordingly.
- When you query a view, the stored query that represents the view is run first. That way, the view always represents the latest data situation.

7.4.7 *Views as programmers' stepping-stones*

Some queries are made much easier to write by breaking them up into separate parts and using a view as a 'stepping stone' between the individual queries. We give here a short example that illustrates this. We take steps towards the final query. Each step is a stored query (a 'view') that presents the original data in a form closer to the final, required, output.

The database in use here is **election.mdb**. This database is described in Appendix 1.

The data in the CANDIDATE table is shown in Fig. 7.165.

cand_no	name	cons_no	party	no_of_votes
1	Fred	1	Labour	100
2	Jim	1	Cons	120
3	Peter	1	Liberal	50
4	John	2	Labour	150
5	Mike	2	SDP	50
6	Jane	2	Cons	100
7	Mary	2	Green	150
8	Keith	1	Ind	150
9	Sue	1	SDP	160
10	U Li	3	Labour	400
11	Ashfak	3	Cons	350
12	Dennis	3	SDP	190
0		0		0

Record: 1 of 12

Fig. 7.165 The CANDIDATE table.

Supposing this was the entire database for a (very small) fictional country, and that we wanted to know which party won the election. In this country, the party with the most won constituencies wins the election. In the election referred to in Fig. 7.165, constituency 1 was won by SDP, constituency 2 by Labour and Green, and constituency 3 by Labour. Having won two out of three constituencies, Labour wins.

Suppose we have the following query:

Query 96: Which party won the election?

This query is quite difficult to implement 'in one go'. It can with advantage be broken down into the following steps:

1. Find the winning party in each constituency.

2. Find the number of constituencies won by each party.

3. Find the party with the highest number of won constituencies.

We shall follow these steps in the following 'stepping stone' queries.

> *Query 96a: List the winning party in each constituency.*

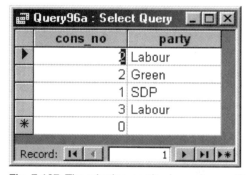

Fig. 7.166 The first stored query Query96a.

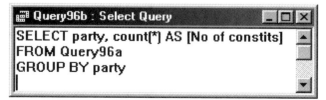

Fig. 7.167 The winning parties in each constituency.

Note that two parties tied for the lead in constituency 2. Note also the use of a correlated subquery. Winning candidates are selected by inspecting all other candidates in the same constituency and checking that none has a higher number of votes.

> *Query 96b: List the number of constituencies won by each party.*

Fig. 7.168 The second stored query Query96b references Query96a.

In this second query, we use the first query Query96a in the WHERE clause. When this query is run, it triggers the prior running of Query96a to provide its input data.

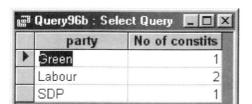

Fig. 7.169 The number of constituencies won by each party.

The next step is to list the party or parties with the highest number of won constituencies. In this case there is just one winner.

Query 96c: Which party won the election?

This takes us back to the original query. We have to find now, from the output of Query96b, the party that won the highest number of constituencies.

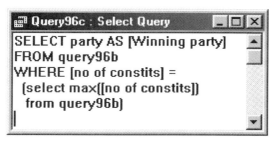

Fig. 7.170 The third stored query Query96c references Query96b.

Fig. 7.171 The winning party.

Note that square brackets had to be used around the field [no of constits] because of its embedded spaces.

The use of views in step-by-step formulation of queries should be the exception rather than the rule. It is wise to look around for a suitable *existing* view to base your query upon.

If your query is going to be stored and reused, make sure that the continued existence of the view (or views – stored queries) is assured. Casual creation of new views can result in their uncontrollable proliferation.

The creation of a view can be justified by:

1. The continued need for a query which needs such a view as a 'stepping stone', as in this example.

2. Convenience. Several tables are frequently used together in queries or reports.

3. Security. Access to data items in the database can be precisely specified.

7.5 SELECT INTO

The normal SELECT statement just displays the output or defines a stored query or recordset. If you want the result of the SELECT statement to be saved into a new table, use SELECT INTO. The syntax for SELECT INTO is:

```
SELECT fields INTO table [IN externaldatabase]
FROM source
```
where
`fields`	is the list of fields being retrieved from source
`table`	is the name of the new table to be created
`externaldatabase`	can be either an ODBC database, or a Paradox, Foxpro, Excel, Access, Lotus 1-2-3, HTML external database, or text

Fig. 7.172 The syntax of the SELECT INTO statement.

The SELECT INTO differs from the INSERT INTO statement in that it creates a new table, whereas INSERT INTO inserts records into an existing table. You can use SELECT INTO to make a temporary copy of all or part of a database for a report, or for archiving.

Query 97: *Create a temporary table containing CUSTOMER and INVOICE details for London customers.*

```
Query97 : Make Table Query
SELECT a.*, inv_no, inv_date, amount INTO temp1
FROM customer AS a INNER JOIN invoice AS b
ON a.c_no = b.c_no
WHERE city = 'London'
```

Fig. 7.173 Creating a new table TEMP1 using SELECT INTO.

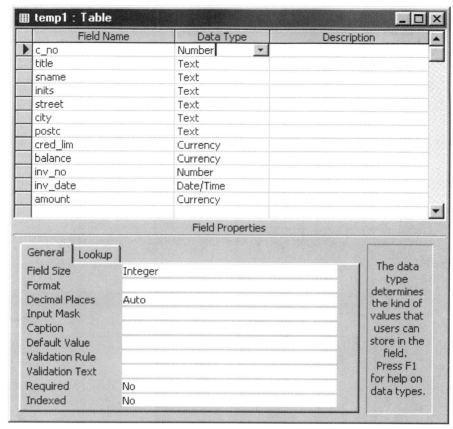

Fig. 7.174 The new table TEMP1 created by the SELECT INTO of Fig. 7.173.

c_no	title	sname	inits	street	city	postc	cred_lim	balance	inv_no	inv_date	amount
1	Mr	Sallaway	G.R.	12 Fax Rd	London	WC1	£1,000.00	£42.56	940	05/12/99	£26.20
1	Mr	Sallaway	G.R.	12 Fax Rd	London	WC1	£1,000.00	£42.56	1003	12/01/00	£16.26
2	Miss	Lauri	P.	5 Dux St	London	N1	£500.00	£200.00	1004	14/01/00	£200.00
5	Ms	Woods	S.Q.	17 Nax Rd	London	E18 4WW	£1,000.00	£350.10	1006	21/01/00	£250.10

Record: 14 ◄ | 1 | ▶ ▶I ▶* of 4

Fig. 7.175 The data contained in TEMP1.

A new table TEMP1 has been created and contains the required records, ready to be processed, archived etc. Note that TABLE1 contains no primary key. If the table were to be required permanently, and was required to be updated, then you would need to create a primary key to prevent data duplication and to have a means of linking it to other tables.

This would be fairly unusual, since the data is a duplication of data available elsewhere on the database (where you just copied it from!). Unlike a stored query (a view), when the original data was updated, the changes would not show through onto the copied table.

The syntax of the IN clause is the same as that discussed in the INSERT INTO command. The `externaldatabase` in Fig. 7.172 can be a database of a different type (e.g. a SQL*Server database) and it can be of the same type. The next example copies a table from one Jet database to another.

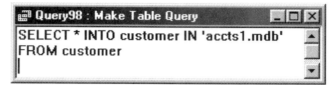

*Query 98: Create a copy of the CUSTOMER table from the **accts.mdb** database into the **accts1.mdb** database.*

Query98 : Make Table Query

```
SELECT * INTO customer IN 'accts1.mdb'
FROM customer
```

Fig. 7.176 Creating a copy of the CUSTOMER table in **accts1.mdb**.

accts1 : Database

Tables | Queries | Forms | Reports | Macros | Modules

cusdetails
customer

Open
Design
New

Fig. 7.177 A new table CUSTOMER has been created in **accts1.mdb**.

customer : Table

c_no	title	sname	inits	street	city	postc	cred_lim	balance
1	Mr	Sallaway	G.R.	12 Fax Rd	London	WC1	£1,000.00	£42.56
2	Miss	Lauri	P.	5 Dux St	London	N1	£500.00	£200.00
3	Mr	Jackson	R.	2 Lux Ave	Leeds	LE1 2AB	£500.00	£510.00
4	Mr	Dziduch	M.	31 Low St	Dover	DO2 9CD	£100.00	£149.23
5	Ms	Woods	S.Q.	17 Nax Rd	London	E18 4WW	£1,000.00	£350.10
6	Mrs	Williams	C.	41 Cax St	Dover	DO2 8WD		£412.21

Record: 1 of 6

Fig. 7.178 The new CUSTOMER table in database **accts1.mdb**.

Copying a database table in this way can also be useful when converting from one version of a database design to another. You might have redesigned parts of your database. It may even be a major redesign. SELECT INTO will not only allow you to save the data from the old database into the new one, it will also allow you to run the two databases in parallel during the changeover period.

7.6 CROSSTAB queries

Where a SELECT query has a GROUP BY, and that GROUP BY is on two columns of the recordset, it is possible to present the aggregated data in the cells of a grid, rather than in straight tabular fashion. This can lead to an easier-to-read presentation of the data.

Suppose we have the database whose schema is shown in Fig. 7.179, and whose data is shown in Figs 7.180, 7.181 and 7.182. This database is **prod_del.mdb**. It is described in Appendix 1.

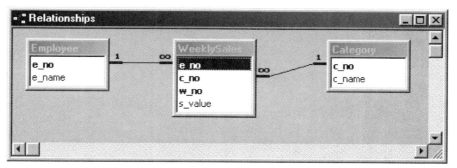

Fig. 7.179 The schema of the **prod_del.mdb** database.

Fig. 7.180 The EMPLOYEE table.

Fig. 7.181 The CATEGORY table.

The CATEGORY table shows the category of products that the employees shown in Fig. 7.180 sell. The WEEKLYSALES table shows how much of each the employees sell week by week.

e_no	c_no	w_no	s_value
1	10	1	£100.00
1	10	2	£150.00
1	20	1	£20.00
1	30	2	£30.00
2	20	2	£60.00
3	10	1	£70.00
3	10	2	£85.00
3	20	1	£160.00
3	30	1	£90.00
3	30	2	£40.00
0	0	0	£0.00

Record: |◀ ◀| 1 |▶ ▶| ▶*| of 10

Fig. 7.182 The WEEKLYSALES table.

The first record in Fig. 7.182 means, for example, that employee number 1 sold goods in category 10 in week 1 to the value of £100.

> *Query 99: For each employee, show his/her total sales in each category.*

One way of presenting this data is by using a conventional double GROUP BY. See Fig. 7.183.

```
SELECT Employee.e_name, Category.c_name,
sum(WeeklySales.s_value) as SumOfs_value
FROM Employee INNER JOIN (Category INNER JOIN WeeklySales
ON Category.c_no = WeeklySales.c_no) ON Employee.e_no =
WeeklySales.e_no
GROUP BY Employee.e_name, Category.c_name
```

Fig. 7.183 A double GROUP BY on the join of the three tables.

The sequence of processing in this query is:

● INNER JOIN the three tables. Smith is eliminated in this process, since he/she has made no sales.

● GROUP BY category within employee.

- Sum the sales for each group.
- List the required fields.

The output is shown in Fig. 7.184.

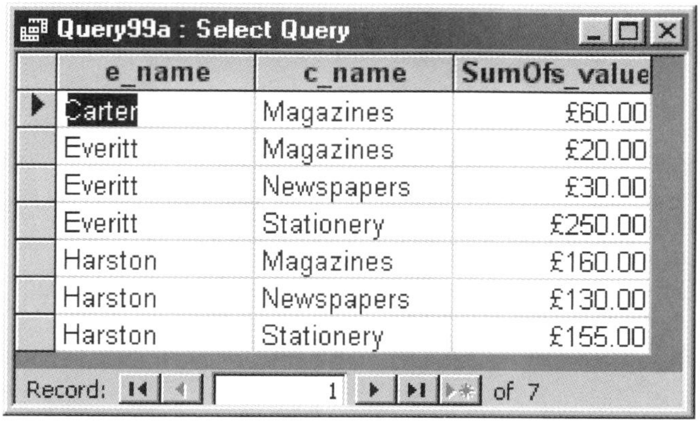

e_name	c_name	SumOfs_value
Carter	Magazines	£60.00
Everitt	Magazines	£20.00
Everitt	Newspapers	£30.00
Everitt	Stationery	£250.00
Harston	Magazines	£160.00
Harston	Newspapers	£130.00
Harston	Stationery	£155.00

Fig. 7.184 The output using a GROUP BY on E_NAME, C_NAME.

While this output is satisfactory, the data can be presented in a more compact form, eliminating the duplication of employee and category names. That is what crosstab queries are for.

The crosstab query version is shown in Figs 7.185 and 7.186.

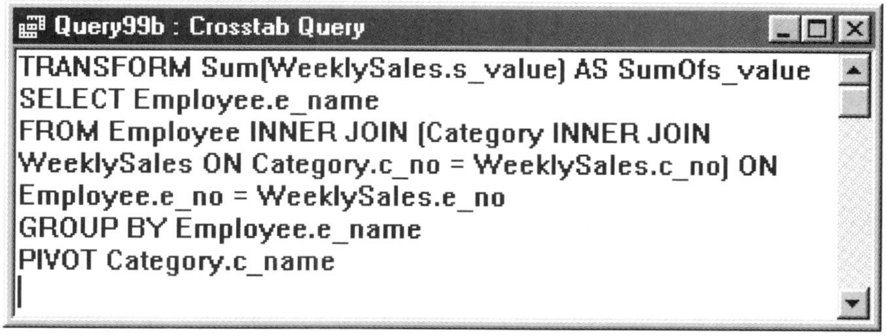


```
TRANSFORM Sum(WeeklySales.s_value) AS SumOfs_value
SELECT Employee.e_name
FROM Employee INNER JOIN (Category INNER JOIN
WeeklySales ON Category.c_no = WeeklySales.c_no) ON
Employee.e_no = WeeklySales.e_no
GROUP BY Employee.e_name
PIVOT Category.c_name
```

Fig. 7.185 The Crosstab query version of Query 99.

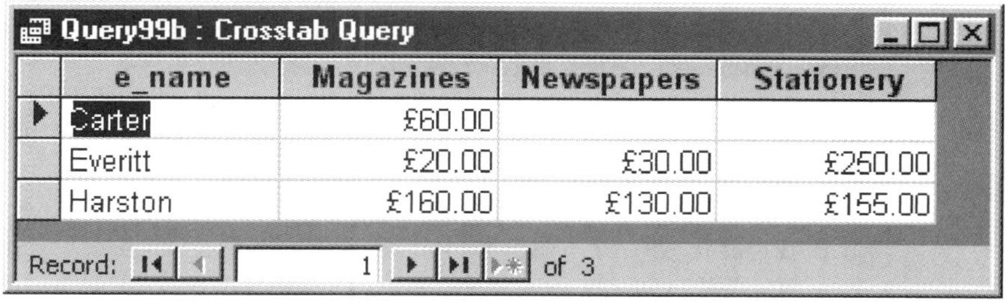

e_name	Magazines	Newspapers	Stationery
Carter	£60.00		
Everitt	£20.00	£30.00	£250.00
Harston	£160.00	£130.00	£155.00

Fig. 7.186 The output of the Crosstab query in Fig. 7.185.

Notice that the 'major group by key' e_name has become the first column and its values are shown in that column, while the values of the 'minor group by key' c_name (category) form the columns.

Clearly, a large number of categories would scroll off to the right. Note also that there is nowhere to put the name of the minor group by key.

To see how to convert a double GROUP BY query into a Crosstab query, let's inspect the SQL for both versions again.

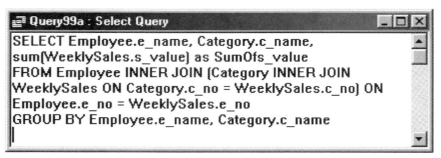

Fig. 7.187 Double GROUP BY version.

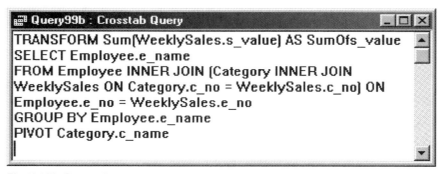

Fig. 7.188 Crosstab query version.

The changes necessary to convert from the double GROUP BY version to the Crosstab version in this query are:

1. The aggregated value to fill the cells of the grid becomes the argument of the TRANSFORM clause.

2. The field whose values are to go in the first column stays in the GROUP BY clause.

3. The field whose values are to go across the rest of the top row of the grid becomes the argument of the PIVOT clause.

It is possible to use WHERE clauses and subqueries in crosstab queries, just as with other SELECT queries. You can also add an IN clause to the PIVOT line to restrict the set of values which will form the columns.

For example, if we were interested only in the sales of magazines and newspapers in the above query, we would modify the PIVOT clause to say:

```
PIVOT Category.c_name IN ('Magazines', 'Newspapers')
```

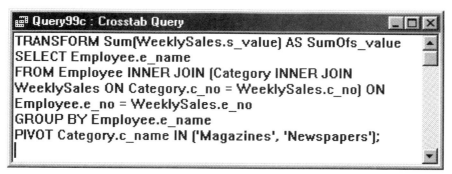

Fig. 7.189 Restricting the columns of the Crosstab query using PIVOT IN.

e_name	Magazines	Newspapers
Carter	£60.00	
Everitt	£20.00	£30.00
Harston	£160.00	£130.00

Fig. 7.190 The output of the query shown in Fig. 7.189.

That concludes our discussion of the SQL SELECT statement.

7.7 Exercises

Write SQL SELECT statements for the following queries. The tables used are from the test databases **accts.mdb** and **musicians.mdb**. Copies of these and all other databases used in this book can be downloaded from:

http://www.databasedesign.co.uk/book

Using the **accts.mdb** database:

1. List, using one query, all customers in the same city as Sallaway. Use a subquery with ' = '.

2. As above. Use a join.

3. List details of all customers who have invoices. Use a subquery with IN.

4. List details of all customers who do *not* have invoices. Use a subquery.

5. List the customer names and invoice numbers for invoices paid in January 2000. Use a join in the outer query and a subquery to check the payment date.

6. List the names of all customers who have made a payment before the invoice was sent. Use a join in the subquery.

7. List details of all customers who have sent a payment over £400. Use two subqueries.

8. List details of all customers who have the highest credit limit. Use a subquery.

9. List details of any customer who has a higher credit limit than every other customer. If two or more customers have the highest credit limit, list no one.

Using the **musicians.mdb** database:

10. List details of children (in the **musicians.mdb** database) who play either violin or cello or both.

11. List details of children who play either violin or cello but not both.

12. List details of children who play both violin and cello.

13. List details of children who play violin but not cello.

Using the **cus_purchase_prod.mdb** database:

14. List details of all customers who have not purchased all products. Use EXISTS and NOT EXISTS.

15. List details of all customers who have not purchased any products.

16. List details of all customers who have purchased at least one product.

17. List details of all customers who have purchased the same product more than once. Show the product and the number of times they have purchased it.

18. List details of any product that has not been purchased.

19. List the total purchases for each product.

20. List in grid form the total purchases of each product by each customer. Use a CROSSTAB QUERY.

Chapter 8

Access forms, macros and reports

In this chapter you will learn:

● how to generate and use Access forms

● how to customize your applications using macros

● how to generate Access reports.

8.1 Introduction

In this chapter, we show how to use the powerful features of Access to design database applications rapidly.

Having carefully designed the database and developed core SQL queries, we are in a position to develop key parts of the user interface to the database.

Access forms with quite sophisticated functionality can be generated very quickly *without programming* and we show several methods of doing this, including the use of Wizards.

The same is true of Access reports. Well-formatted and attractive reports are easy to produce using Access, again without programming. We recommend using Access forms and reports of this kind for standard day-to-day input and output processing wherever possible.

Macros are, in effect, simple programs that you produce by filling in a grid to show sequences of actions. We show how to use Access macros to link Access forms and we show how to use conditions in macros to give additional 'intelligence' to your Access forms.

In Chapter 12, we describe, using several examples, how you can further enhance the intelligence of your database applications by writing VBA program code in Access Modules. These examples range from elementary to quite sophisticated, and include an introduction to transaction processing. The VBA code used in these applications is very similar to that used in the Visual Basic programming Chapters 9, 10 and 11.

We have left the coverage of modules to Chapter 12 because by then you will have acquired the necessary database programming skills.

When you produce forms, reports, macros and modules in Access, all of the code and properties associated with them resides in the database file (the .mdb file) itself.

The version of Access we use for these examples is Access 97, but the applications work equally well in other versions.

8.2 Access forms

Forms are the way your users will perform updates to your database. They will:

- input new records;
- delete records;
- change records.

The forms they use for this should also validate and format the data they enter.

8.2.1 AutoForms

AutoForms are a very quick way of creating useful Access forms.

Creating a Columnar AutoForm for the CUSTOMER table

---

1. Go into Access and open the accts.mdb database. Click the Forms tab and click the New button to create a new form.

2. Choose AutoForm: Columnar, and select the CUSTOMER table from the drop-down list, as shown in Fig. 8.1.

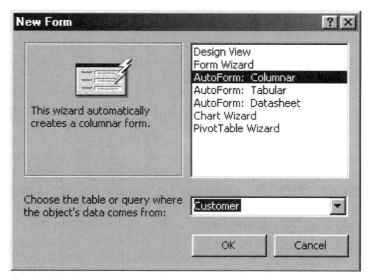

Fig. 8.1 The first step in creating a columnar AutoForm.

3. Click the OK button and Access will generate the form shown in Fig. 8.2 for you.

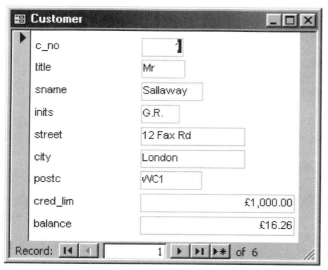

Fig. 8.2 The Columnar AutoForm generated by Access.

Note that the form contains facilities for viewing, adding, deleting and changing the CUSTOMER records.

To Navigate: Click on the following buttons in the data control:

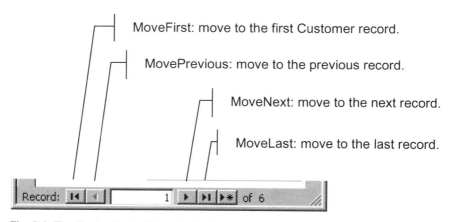

Fig. 8.3 The Navigation buttons in the Access data control.

Note that Access doesn't call this a data control, but that is what it is called in Visual Basic.

Notice that next to the data control you can see the number of records in the recordset. 'Recordset' is a name we give to a set of records stored in memory. A recordset can be derived from a whole table, as here, or from a database query, as in the next example.

To Add a record:

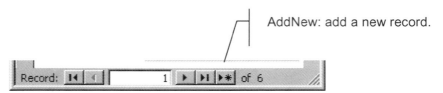

AddNew: add a new record.

Fig. 8.4 The AddNew button in the Access data control.

Clicking the AddNew button on the Access data control adds a new blank record to the recordset and clears the text boxes on the form as shown in Fig. 8.5.

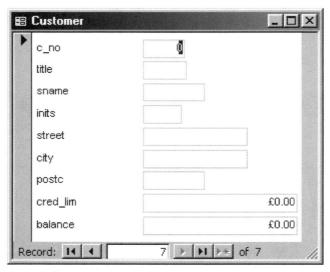

Fig. 8.5 The effect of clicking the AddNew button of the Access data control.

The user can now type the field values of a new record into the form and save the record by moving to a different record.

To Delete a record:

Suppose we had a customer number 7 and we wanted to delete that customer's CUSTOMER record.

At the left of the form is a grey vertical bar which, when writing a new record, shows a pen, and when navigating shows a black triangle. This is known as the record selector bar. The record selector bar is shown in Fig. 8.6.

To delete a record, click the record selector and then press the <Delete> key on the keyboard.

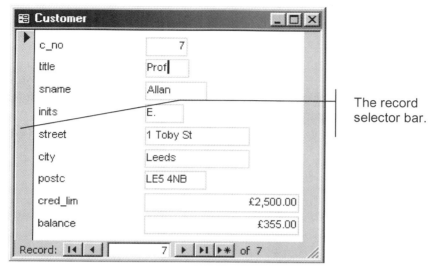

Fig. 8.6 The record selector bar.

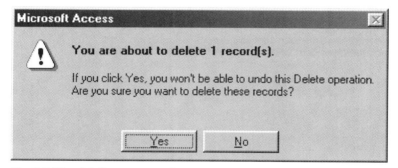

Fig. 8.7 The deletion message box.

Before the deletion actually occurs, you are given a chance to back out of the deletion by a message box (Fig. 8.7).

To Change a record:

To change a record, simply type the required changes into the text boxes. The new data will be saved when you move to a new record.

This simple Access form can be customized in various ways. If you right-click on it, you will obtain the following options:

● *Form Design*: This takes you to the Design view of the form. Here you can change the attributes of the form, add new controls, and add code. We shall show later how to customize forms further in Form Design View by changing the properties of the form and building events.

- *Datasheet View*: This shows you a grid containing all of the records in the record-set, rather than just one, as the Form View (the view shown above) does.

- *Filter by Form*: A filter allows you to restrict the records shown in the form by setting criteria in each text box. This is discussed below.

There are two other kinds of AutoForm available:

- *Autoform Tabular*: This presents the data from the recordset in rows and columns, so that it is possible to see several records on the form at once. This is useful where it is required to pick a record from a selection (e.g. an individual product from a set of products). The Tabular AutoForm is very similar to:

- *AutoForm: Datasheet*: Just presents the data in an unadorned grid.

8.2.2 Filtering, sorting and finding

In the following, we continue with the simple form created above using the Auto-Form technique, although the following applies to any Access form, no matter how it is produced.

> To Filter the recordset:

'Filtering' means restricting the records being displayed in the form to a smaller subset based on some selection criteria.

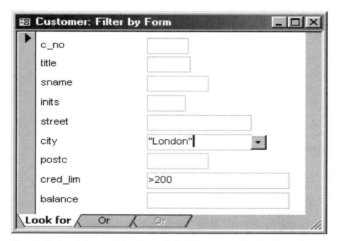

Fig. 8.8 Applying a filter to restrict the records displayed.

In Fig. 8.8 we are restricting the set of customers displayed to those in London who have a credit limit over £200.

Right-click the form and select 'Apply Filter' to apply this filter and 'Remove Filter' to remove it.

Filtering by forms is the same principle as applying criteria in the query grid or conditions in the WHERE clause of an SQL SELECT statement. Notice that you could have used the Or tab to select a *set* of filtering values for a field.

To Sort the recordset:

If you want to sort the records in the recordset, in Form View, select the field you want to sort on by clicking the text box – city for example – and then clicking the sort button in the toolbar at the top of the Access window:

Ascending order  Descending order

To Find a particular record:

Access has a very powerful and easy to use search facility.

This is perhaps not surprising because one of the most basic things you want to do with data is to search it!

To search in Access, you use the binoculars button:

The Find button

To search for a particular record on a particular field, select the field and then click the Find button.

In Fig. 8.9 we are searching for a customer whose Surname begins with 'L'.

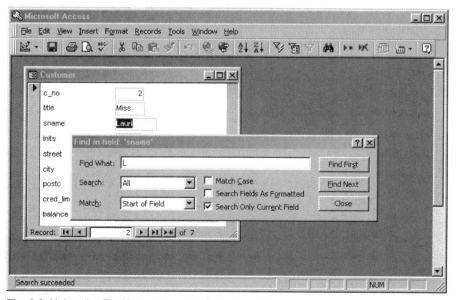

Fig. 8.9 Using the Find button to search on the sname field.

The Find form contains many search options. One of the most powerful is the search for a particular string of data in *any* of the fields in the entire recordset. To do this, just uncheck the Search Only Current Field check box.

The form we have created above is based on data from a single table. It is possible to base the form on data from a stored query. That is one way to display *selected* data from *one or more* database tables. For example, you could display *grouped* data, such as the balance total for each city. Or you could display and update data from the customer and invoice tables.

To do this, all you have to do is choose a query instead of a table in the Auto-Form dialogue box shown in Fig. 8.1.

8.2.3 Form Wizard: Creating a 1:N form

While AutoForms are great for creating a form based on a single table or query, the Form Wizard has the additional power to create 1:N (one to many) forms. These are used when you want to show data from two tables that are linked by a 1:N relationship. If you've created the relationship at database design time, the Form Wizard uses that information to create the form.

Creating a 1:N form linking CUSTOMER and INVOICE

Here we shall create, using the Form Wizard, a 1:N form which displays a single CUSTOMER record in the '1' part of the form and all the associated INVOICE records in the 'N' part of the form. Changing to another customer record will automatically display all of that customer's invoices. The customer details will be shown in text boxes and the invoice details in a grid.

Remember that we created a 1:N relationship between the CUSTOMER and INVOICE tables at database design time. That relationship will be used by the Form Wizard to set up this form. The database schema for accts.mdb is shown in Fig. 8.10.

In Access, the 'N' side of the form is called the 'Subform'.

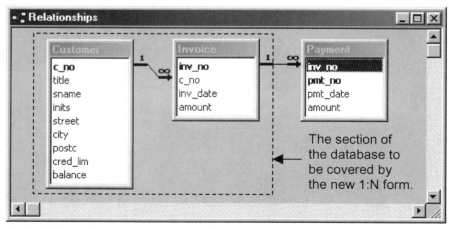

Fig. 8.10 The database schema for accts.mdb.

To create the 1:N form:

1. In the Database window, click the Forms tab and the New command button.

2. Click Form Wizard, leave the recordsource list box blank and click OK.

3. See Fig. 8.11. Click the drop-down list and select the table CUSTOMER. This is the table that our fields for the '1' side of the form are going to come from. Click the >> button to select all the CUSTOMER fields.

4. See Fig. 8.12. Click the drop-down lists again and this time select the table INVOICE. This is the table that the fields for the 'N' side of the form are going to come from. Click the > button to select all fields but c_no for the subform. There is no point in having c_no in the subform because it's shown in the '1' side of the form.

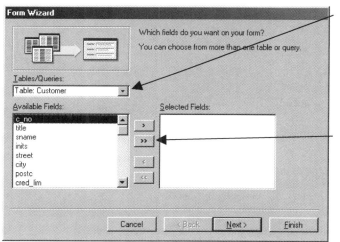

Some of the fields come from the CUSTOMER table.

Click here to select *all* of the CUSTOMER fields for the '1' part of the form.

Fig. 8.11 Selecting the CUSTOMER fields.

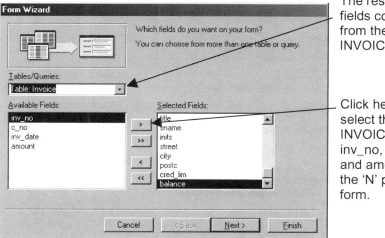

The rest of the fields come from the INVOICE table

Click here to select the INVOICE fields inv_no, inv_date and amount for the 'N' part of the form.

Fig. 8.12 Selecting the INVOICE fields.

5. Click Next and when asked how you want to view your data, select the option Form with Subform. This puts all the data on one form. Click Next. (The Linked Forms option gives you two separate forms – one for the customer data and one for the invoice data – moving to a new customer still gives you the new set of invoices in the other form.)

6. Select Datasheet for the subform layout. 'Tabular' is very similar but takes up a little more space on the form. Click Next.

7. Select a style and click Next. Give the form a title. The 1:N form is now complete and should look like Fig. 8.13.

8. Check the operation of the form and save it. It should be possible to add new

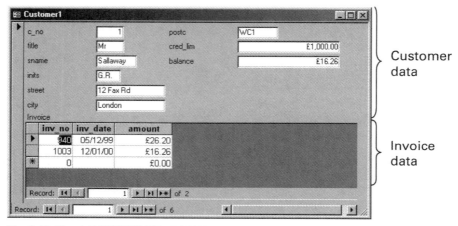

Fig. 8.13 The 1:N CUSTOMER : INVOICE form completed.

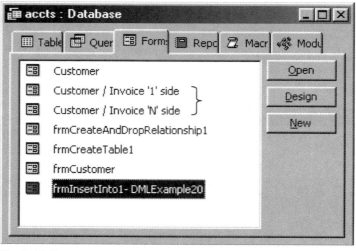

Fig. 8.14 Our new names for the form and subform.

invoices, delete invoices and change invoices for the given customer. Give both the form and the subform a meaningful name. We gave ours the names shown in Fig. 8.14.

Note that if you rename the subform the link between the form and subform is lost! This can be remedied by clicking the Design button for the '1' side form (here, named Customer/Invoice '1' side' in Fig. 8.14). This brings you into Design View for the form (Fig. 8.15). Right-click the white rectangle where the subform should be and change its Source Object property to the new name (here, Customer/ Invoice 'N' side).

For simple forms and subforms we have found the Form Wizard to be ideal. A useful form can be obtained quite quickly.

Given the range of custom options a user might want, it is not surprising that to customize this 1:N form the developer may have to spend quite a bit more time finding the appropriate properties to change.

We take the view that Access Wizards are the best choice for producing simple, standard forms.

8.2.4 Adding a Combo box to an Access form

Suppose we want to have a form for listing, deleting, changing and creating new invoices. When it comes to adding a new invoice, we will always want to add the invoice for an *existing* customer in order to preserve *referential integrity* (every INVOICE record must have a CUSTOMER record with the same customer number). Instead of having to look up the CUSTOMER table to find the correct customer number field to put in the INVOICE.C_NO field, wouldn't it be nice if we could click a list box on the *invoice* form showing all of the customers and select one from there? This is relatively easy to do in Access. Here is one way.

1. Create a columnar AutoForm for the INVOICE table as shown previously (Fig. 8.15).

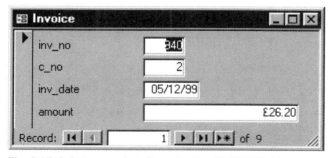

Fig. 8.15 A Columnar AutoForm for the INVOICE table.

2. Right-click in the title bar and go into Form Design view for this form (Fig. 8.16).

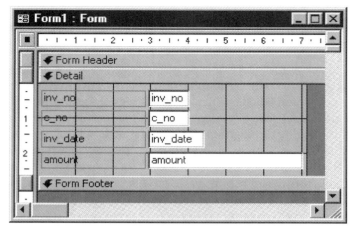

Fig. 8.16 Form Design view for this form.

3. Delete the c_no label and text box from the form and replace it with a Combo box from the Toolbox. To do this, click on the Combo box in the Toolbox and then click on the form where you want the Combo box to go (Fig. 8.17).

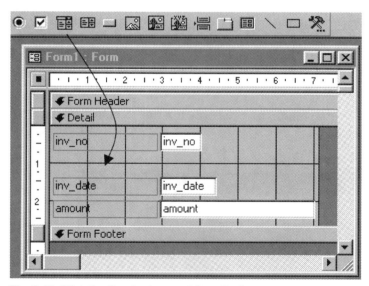

Fig. 8.17 Click the Combo box and then the form.

4. This will bring up the first item in the Combo Box Wizard's dialogue (Fig. 8.18).

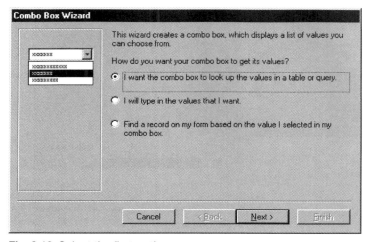

Fig. 8.18 Select the first option.

Select the first option. We will want the data displayed in the Combo box to come from the CUSTOMER table.

5. Click the Next button. Select the CUSTOMER table as the source of the Combo box data (Fig. 8.19).

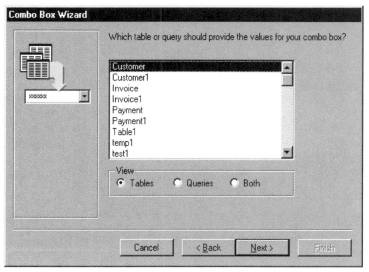

Fig. 8.19 The data displayed in the Combo box will be fields from the CUSTOMER table.

6. Click the Next button. Select the fields to go into the Combo box. The fields we have selected here should be enough for the user to identify the correct customer (Fig. 8.20).

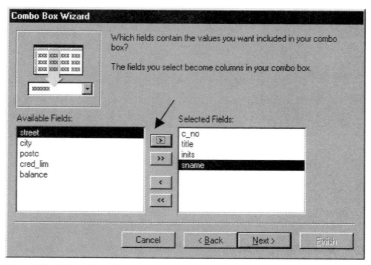

Fig. 8.20 Select the fields to go into the Combo box.

7. Click the Next button. This brings up the next form in the Combo Box Wizard dialogue (Fig. 8.21).

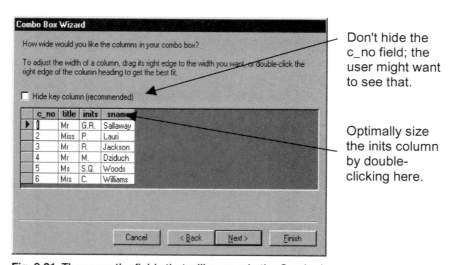

Don't hide the c_no field; the user might want to see that.

Optimally size the inits column by double-clicking here.

Fig. 8.21 These are the fields that will appear in the Combo box.

In this form we decide whether to show the primary key value to the user or not. Here we have chosen to do so because the user might know the customer by its customer number. It's also possible to resize the columns in this form.

8. Click the Next button. We choose the c_no field to identify each customer uniquely (Fig. 8.22).

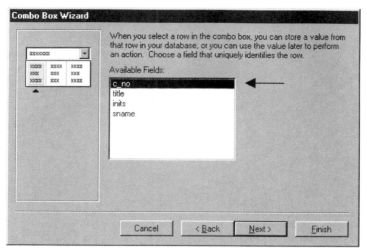

Fig. 8.22 Choose c_no to identify a customer.

9. We are now asked (Fig. 8.23) which field in the INVOICE table we want the c_no value selected from the Combo box to go into. We want it to go into INVOICE.C_NO, so we select that.

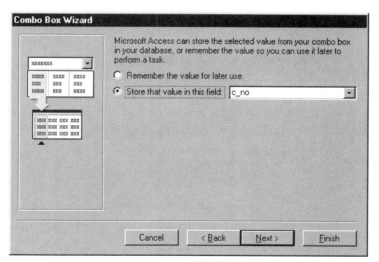

Fig. 8.23 Selecting the INVOICE field that the c_no value from the Combo box will be placed into.

10. Type in the label name you want to appear next to the Combo box. We have chosen 'c_no' (the name of the field). You might want to choose something more meaningful to the user.

Fig. 8.24 Name the label associated with the Combo box.

11. Click the Finish button. This brings up Form Design view (Fig. 8.25). Here you can reposition and resize the Combo box if required.

12. Right-click the form title bar and bring up Form view (Fig. 8.26). When you click the Combo box triangle, a drop-down list containing details all of the customers appears. This is particularly useful when details of a new customer are input.

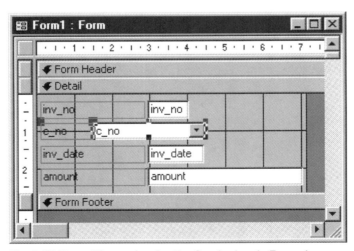

Fig. 8.25 Reposition and resize the Combo box in Form view.

That concludes the description of how to use a Combo box to help to input the foreign key value from the CUSTOMER table into the INVOICE table when inserting a new INVOICE record.

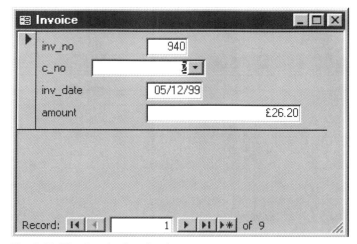

Fig. 8.26 The Combo box in place.

8.2.5 Design view: Creating forms manually

So far we have used AutoForms and the Form Wizard to create forms. Forms can be created manually. While a little more labour intensive, creating forms this way gives you, the application developer, more control over how the form looks and how it performs.

We shall create a simple data entry form for the CUSTOMER table to illustrate this approach.

1. In the Database window, click New. Select Design View and tie the form to the CUSTOMER table in the drop-down Combo box (Fig. 8.27).

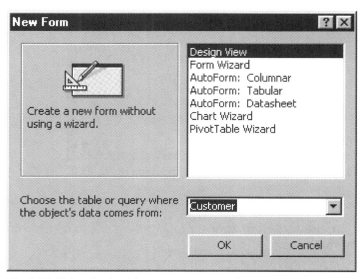

Fig. 8.27 Using Design View to generate an Access form.

2. Click OK. You are then confronted with a blank form (Fig. 8.28).

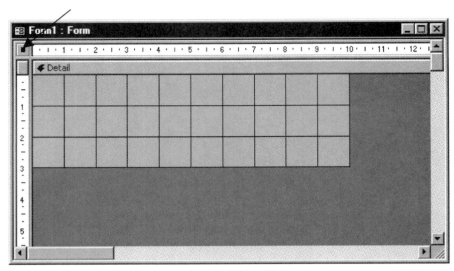

Fig. 8.28 The blank form generated using Design View.

3. Right-click the small button shown in Fig. 8.28. Access will display the Properties of this 'blank' form (Fig. 8.29).

Form				
Format	Data	Event	Other	All

Record Source	Customer
Filter	
Order By	Customer.c_no
Allow Filters	Yes
Caption	
Default View	Single Form
Views Allowed	Both
Allow Edits	Yes
Allow Deletions	Yes
Allow Additions	Yes
Data Entry	No
Recordset Type	Dynaset
Record Locks	No Locks

Fig. 8.29 Some of the properties of the blank form of Fig. 8.28.

Note that many of the properties have already been set, including the important Record Source property. We say that this form is 'tied' to the Customer table.

4. We now want to add some tied text boxes onto the form. Do this as follows (Fig. 8.30).

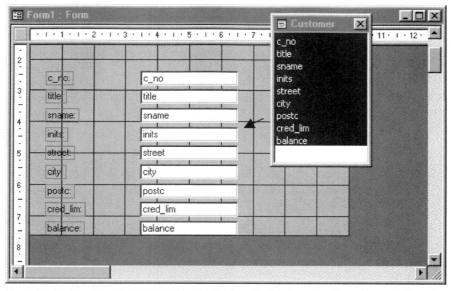

Fig. 8.30 Putting the CUSTOMER table fields onto the form by dragging and dropping.

In the Access menu, click View/Field List.

The field list shows the list of fields associated with the Record Source; in our case, the list of CUSTOMER table fields.

Select all of these fields (by clicking on each field while holding down the <Ctrl> key).

Then drag all these highlighted fields onto the form. Behind the scenes, Access has linked the form to the database table and the text boxes to the fields. Close the field list window.

5. 'Run' the form by going into Form View. You now have an update form, similar to the one that would have been produced using AutoForm or the Form Wizard. Close and save the form.

8.3 Access macros

Access macros are a way of programming sequences of Access actions, such as loading forms and processing code.

A macro is a set of high-level commands that execute sequentially. They are adequate for simple tasks, such as loading forms, and are in general easy to produce, but they lack the flexibility of the lower-level VBA code modules described in Chapter 12.

We demonstrate some simple uses of Access macros in this section.

8.3.1 Linking Access forms via macro code

Our aim here is to have one form Form1 showing data for a single customer, and each time a new customer record is called up, a separate form Form2 is loaded and shows that customer's invoices. The code that links these two events is contained in a macro Macro1.

Creating the CUSTOMER form Form1
1. Using either AutoForm, Form Wizard, or Design view, create a form Form1, whose Record Source is the CUSTOMER table.

Creating the INVOICE form Form2
2. Using either AutoForm, Form Wizard, or Design view, create a form Form2, whose Record Source is the INVOICE table.

3. Note that the forms are entirely independent at this point; the invoices shown in Form2 are not those owned by the customer in Form1 necessarily (Fig. 8.31).

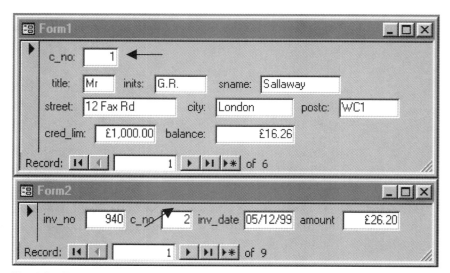

Fig. 8.31 Form1 and Form2 are independent at this point.

Linking Form1 to Form2 using a macro Macro1
What we want to happen is that when Form1 is clicked, Form2 is loaded (if it is not already loaded) and displays the invoices for the customer shown in Form1. We shall put the necessary code in Macro1.

4. Bring up the Properties window for Form1. Do this using either a right-click on the form's title bar, or by clicking the following button on the toolbar.

The Properties button.

Click the Event tab on the Properties window. In the On Click event box, type Macro1 (Fig. 8.32). Now, when Form1 is clicked, Macro1 will run. We now have to write Macro1.

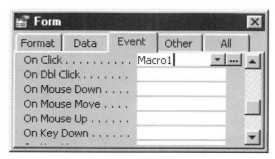

Fig. 8.32 The Properties window for Form1.

Writing Macro1

5. In the Database window, click the Macros tab and then the New button.

6. The Macro design window will open up (Fig. 8.33). The Action column is where one or more actions in our macro will go. You choose an action by clicking the triangle and picking one from the list. Each type of macro action has some associated information ('arguments') that it needs to operate. This information goes into the lower part of the macro design window – the Action Arguments part. Choose the OpenForm action from the list.

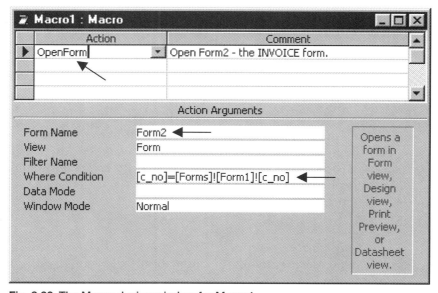

Fig. 8.33 The Macro design window for Macro1.

7. Fill in the Form Name argument to say 'Form2'. This says that the form we want to open is Form2.

8. Fill in the Where Condition argument to:

> [c_no] = [Forms]![Form1]![c_no]

This says that the customer number c_no value of the INVOICE records displayed in Form2 has to be equal to the c_no value displayed in Form1 of the Forms collection. Save Macro1.

9. Go to the Forms tab of the Database window and open Form1. Click the record selector triangle and Form2 will load, showing the first invoice for the customer of Form1. Move to another customer record, click the record selector of Form1, and that customer's records will be shown in Form2.

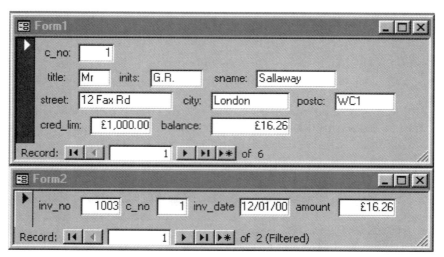

Fig. 8.34 The forms linked by Macro1.

Using the OnCurrent event of Form1 instead of the OnClick event would display the invoices for the new customer *automatically*. Also, changing the Default View of Form2 to Continuous Forms would allow *all* of the invoices for the current customer to be displayed at once. In Exercise 6 at the end of this chapter you make both of these modifications.

Modifying Macro1
We extend Macro1 slightly to automatically tile Form1 and Form2 horizontally. Go into the Macro design window and add the line shown in Fig. 8.35. Note that RunCommand replaces DoMenuItem in earlier versions of Access.

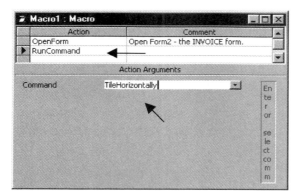

Fig. 8.35 Adding a line to Macro1.

8.3.2 Using conditions in Access macros

An Access macro is a sequence of high-level commands that are executed in sequence. Many of the operations that a user could perform manually using the Access menus and buttons can be automated using macros.

It is even possible to execute certain sections of a macro *conditionally*, using an IF statement. That gives Access macros one of the features you would expect in a programming language.

Another standard feature of programming languages, namely *looping*, is absent, however. In this section, we develop a three-form application, again based on the accts.mdb database.

There is a separate form for each of the three tables.

- *Form1* displays the CUSTOMER table and contains a calculated value Available Credit, which is Credit Limit minus Balance.
- *Form2* displays the INVOICE table. This contains a label that displays a 'No Payments' message if there are no payments; Form2 also contains a command button Command1, which loads Form3 if it is not already loaded.
- *Form3* displays the PAYMENT table. If the current invoice shown on Form2 has no payments, Form3 is minimized.

Linkage between the forms is via macros.

- *Macro1* executes when a move to a new CUSTOMER record occurs in Form1 (the OnCurrent event). It opens Form2 and makes it display the invoices of the customer shown in Form1.
- *Macro2* is called when a move to a new INVOICE record occurs in Form2. It opens Form3 and makes it display the payments of the invoice shown in Form2. If there are *no* payments for the current invoice, Macro2 minimizes Form3.
- *Macro3* is called when the command button Command1 is clicked on Form2. It opens Form3, which might have been minimized by Macro2 because there were no payments.

Creating Form1

1. Go into Form Design view and create a form Form1 with its Record Source set to the CUSTOMER table.

2. Click View/Fieldlist in the Access menu, and select all of the fields and drag them onto the new form. Test the form and save it as Form1.

Adding a calculated field to Form1

3. From the toolbox, add a text box onto Form1. We are going to use this text box to display the available credit for the customer. Change the label caption to 'available credit'.

4. Right-click the new text box to bring up its Properties window. Change the ControlSource property value (Fig. 8.36).

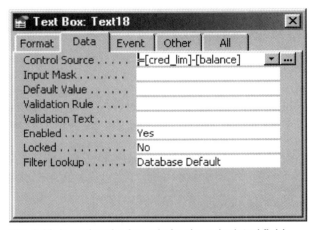

Fig. 8.36 Inserting the formula for the calculated field.

This will show the proper value of available credit. Note formulae must start with an '=' sign.

5. Also set the following properties for the text box:

Format = Currency
Text Align = Right

Form1 is shown in Form Design view in Fig. 8.37.

Creating Form2

6. Figure 8.38 shows Form2, which is used to add, delete and change INVOICE records. Add the label and change its Caption property to 'No Payments'. Change its Font Size to 12. The Properties for any control can be obtained by right-clicking the control.

7. Add a command button to Form2 as shown in Fig. 8.38. Cancel out of the Command Button Wizard if it starts. Change the Caption property of the command button to 'Add Payment'.

Note that there is no connection between Form1 and Form2 yet; they work independently. Macro1 will link them.

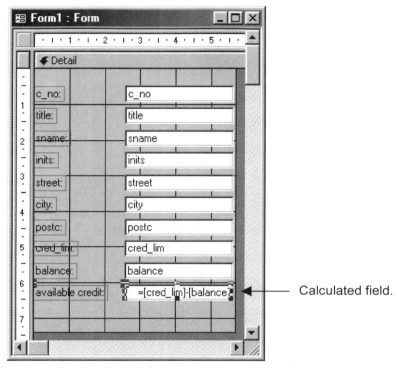

Calculated field.

Fig. 8.37 Form1 – CUSTOMER data (Form Design view).

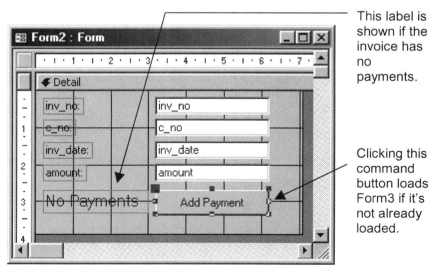

This label is shown if the invoice has no payments.

Clicking this command button loads Form3 if it's not already loaded.

Fig. 8.38 Form2 – INVOICE data (Form Design view).

Creating Form3

8. Create Form3, as in Fig. 8.39. Form3 shows the PAYMENT records for the current INVOICE record. Use the Form Design view to create this form. Set the form's Record Source to the PAYMENT table.

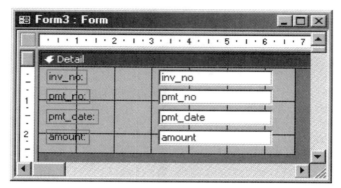

Fig. 8.39 Form3 – PAYMENT data (Form Design view).

Creating Macro1

The purpose of Macro1 is to:

● open Form2 to show invoices for the current customer;
● tile Form1 and Form2 vertically.

This opens Form2.

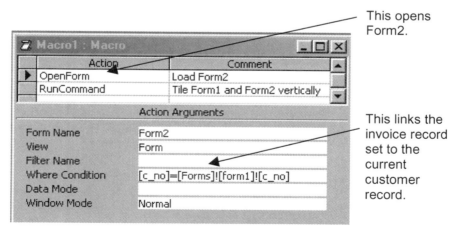

This links the invoice record set to the current customer record.

Fig. 8.40(a) The OpenForm command in Macro1.

The OpenForm command in Macro1 opens Form2, which displays the invoices for the current customer by restricting the recordset using the WHERE condition:

```
[c_no]=[Forms]![form1]!c_no
```

This ensures that only the correct invoices are displayed.

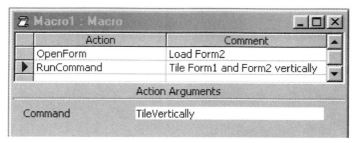

Fig. 8.40(b) The RunCommand command in Macro1.

9. Create the commands for Macro1 as shown in Figs 8.40(a) and (b).

10. Make Macro1 execute whenever a move to a new CUSTOMER record occurs by specifying the On Current event (Fig. 8.41).

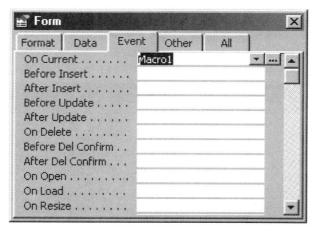

Fig. 8.41 The On Current event for Form1 calls Macro1.

Run Form1 and ensure that Form2 automatically shows the invoices for the customer in Form1. Note that Form2's label and its command button don't do anything as yet.

Creating Macro2
The purpose of Macro2 is to:

- open Form3 to show payments for the current invoice;
- minimize Form3 and make the 'No Payments' label visible if there are no payments; otherwise restore Form3 and make the label invisible;
- tile loaded forms vertically.

11. Create Macro2 as shown in Figs 8.42 and 8.43.

The steps in creating Macro2 are:

- To add the Condition column to the macro, click the button shown below.

The Macro Condition button.

- The ellipsis (. . .) in the Condition column defines the scope of the condition.
- To set the value of a property in a macro, you use the SetValue command.
- Figure 8.43 shows how the Expression Builder can be used to set the value of a property.
- The example it shows is making the 'No Payments' label (Label4) invisible in the last line of the macro.
- Save Macro2.

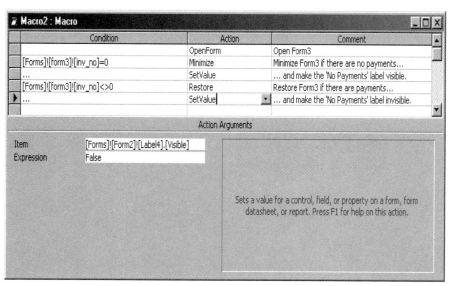

Fig. 8.42 Macro2, with IF conditions.

Macro2 will now work according to the specification above, making the 'No Payments' label visible appropriately.

12. We need Macro2 to run on the OnCurrent event of Form2. Do this in the Properties window Event tab of Form2.

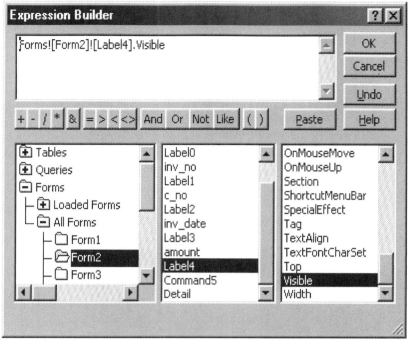

Fig. 8.43 Using the Expression Builder to complete the second SetValue macro command.

Creating Macro3
The purpose of Macro3 is to:

● open Form3 to add a new payment, if Form3 is not already opened.

13. Create Macro3 with the code shown in Fig. 8.44, and save it.

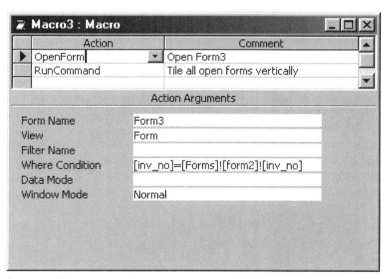

Fig. 8.44 The code for Macro3.

Macro3 first opens Form3 which displays all of the Payment records that match the current invoice.

The condition that links these recordsets is:

```
[inv_no] = [Forms]![form2]![inv_no]
```

[Forms] is the forms collection for the application.

This is similar to an SQL WHERE clause.

Now bring up the Properties window for Form2 and in the On Click event for the command button, insert Macro3. This will cause Macro3 to be run when the user clicks the command button (Fig. 8.45).

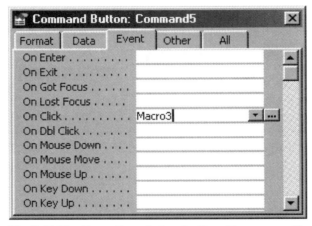

Fig. 8.45 The Properties window for Form2's command button.

This application is now complete. Run Form1 and check that:

- moving to a new customer automatically loads that customer's invoices;
- if an invoice has no payments, the 'No Payments' label becomes visible and Form3 (the payments form) is minimized;
- clicking Form2's 'Add Payment' command button opens Form3 if it is minimized.

Summary
In this section we covered:

- how to link three forms using macros
- how to add a calculated field to a form
- how to use conditions in Macros
- how to use the SetValue command

- how to use the Expression Builder to locate a property of a control
- how to use RunCommand
- how to tile forms automatically
- how to minimize and restore forms.

8.4 Access reports

When your output data is to be presented on paper, use Access reports to give an attractive appearance. Figure 8.47 is probably more appealing than Fig. 8.46.

c_no	title	sname	inits	street	city	postc	cred_lim	balance
1	Mr	Sallaway	G.R.	12 Fax Rd	London	WC1	£1,000.00	£16.26
2	Miss	Lauri	P.	5 Dux St	London	N1	£500.00	£200.00
3	Mr	Jackson	R.	2 Lux Ave	Leeds	LE1 2AB	£500.00	£510.00
4	Mr	Dziduch	M.	31 Low St	Dover	DO2 9CD	£100.00	£149.23
5	Ms	Woods	S.Q.	17 Nax Rd	London	E18 4WW	£1,000.00	£350.10
6	Mrs	Williams	C.	41 Cax St	Dover	DO2 8WD		£412.21
0							£0.00	£0.00

Record: 1 of 6

Fig. 8.46 The CUSTOMER table printed from an Access form.

Customer

c_no	title	sname	inits	street	city	postc	cred_lim	balance
1	Mr	Sallaway	G.R.	12 Fax Rd	London	WC1	£1,000.00	£16.26
2	Miss	Lauri	P.	5 Dux St	London	N1	£500.00	£200.00
3	Mr	Jackson	R.	2 Lux Ave	Leeds	LE1 2AB	£500.00	£510.00
4	Mr	Dziduch	M.	31 Low St	Dover	DO2 9C	£100.00	£149.23
5	Ms	Woods	S.Q.	17 Nax Rd	London	E18 4W	£1,000.00	£350.10
6	Mrs	Williams	C.	41 Cax St	Dover	DO2 8W		£412.21

Fig. 8.47 The CUSTOMER table data presented using an Access report.

The report shown in Fig. 8.47 can be produced very simply using the Report Wizard. We show below some slightly more involved reports – one showing data from linked tables and the other displaying a graph.

8.4.1 Report showing data from two linked forms

In this example, we use the **accts.mdb** database and produce a report showing the invoices for each customer and the total invoice amount. This total is calculated in

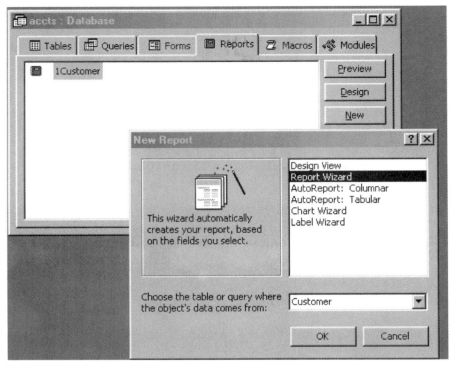

Fig. 8.48 Use the Report Wizard (Step 1).

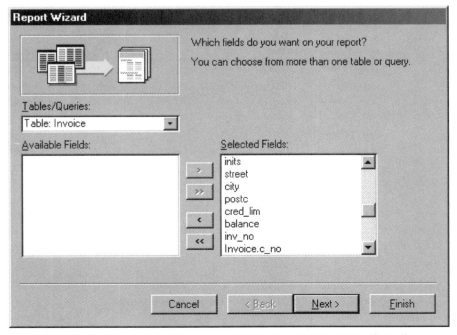

Fig. 8.49 Selecting the CUSTOMER and INVOICE fields for the report (Step 2).

the report writer itself. As the schema diagram for **accts.mdb** in Appendix 1 shows, there is a 1:N relationship between the two tables CUSTOMER and INVOICE in this database.

Steps in producing the 1:N report

1. Use the Report Wizard by going to the Access Database window, clicking the Report tab, then the New button, and selecting the Report Wizard option. Select the CUSTOMER table to be the 'master' table, i.e. the '1' side table, for the report. Click OK (Fig. 8.48).

2. Select all of the CUSTOMER fields and all of the INVOICE fields. Use the Combo box to get to the INVOICE table to select *its* fields. The single-arrow button selects one field at a time and the double-arrow button selects all fields (Fig. 8.49). Click Next.

3. View the data by customer. This means that for each customer, all the invoices will be shown below. Access uses the relationship between the CUSTOMER table and the INVOICE table that we created when we designed the database **accts.mdb** to link the two parts of the report. Click Next (Fig. 8.50).

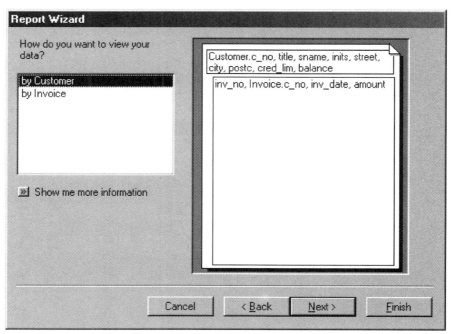

Fig. 8.50 View the data by Customer (Step 3).

4. We want data to be 'grouped' by the whole CUSTOMER record, as it is by default. In this example, grouping prevents the CUSTOMER fields being reproduced alongside each INVOICE line. Click Next.

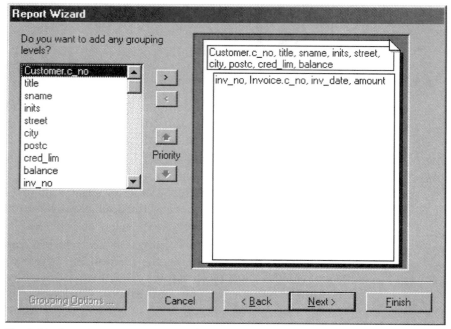

Fig. 8.51 Grouping levels (Step 4).

5. Sort the INVOICE records by INV_NO (Fig. 8.52). Click the Summary Options button.

6. In the Summary Options window (Fig. 8.53), click the Sum check box. Leave

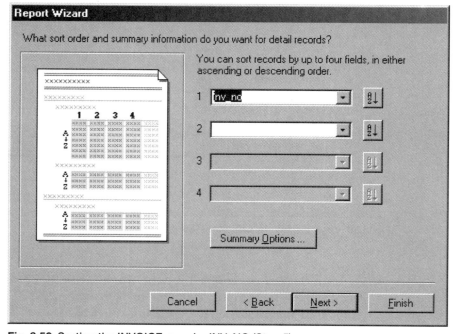

Fig. 8.52 Sorting the INVOICE rows by INV_NO (Step 5).

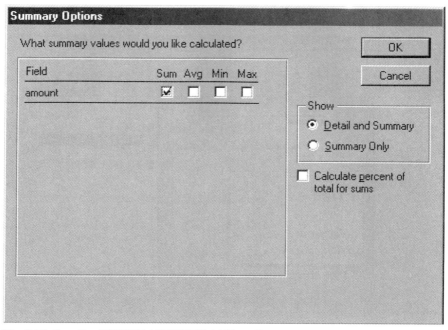

Fig. 8.53 Sum the INVOICE.AMOUNT field (Step 6).

the Show option button on 'Detail and Summary' because we want to see each invoice *and* the amount total. Click OK. Back in the Report Wizard window (Fig. 8.52), click Next.

7. For the Report Layout, choose Align Left 1. Click Next (Fig. 8.54).

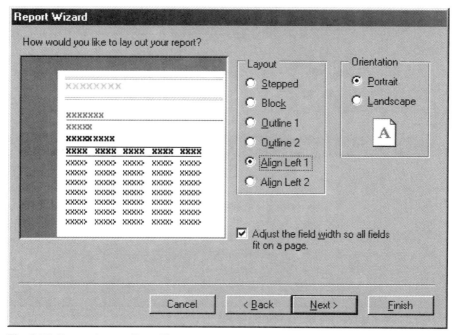

Fig. 8.54 Report layout (Step 7).

8. Choose a style for the report. Click Next (Fig. 8.55).

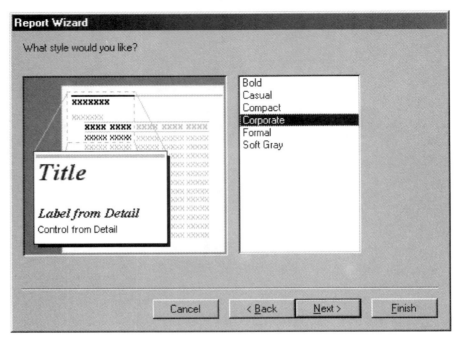

Fig. 8.55 Choose a style (Step 8).

9. Choose a title for the report. Click Finish (Fig. 8.56).

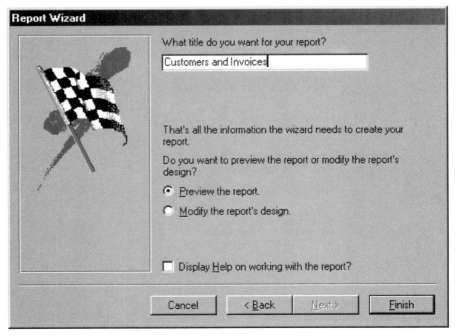

Fig. 8.56 Title the report (Step 9).

10. Figure 8.57 shows part of the report produced by the Report Wizard.

Customers and Invoices

Customer.c_n	1	street	12 Fax Rd	balance	£16.26
title	Mr	city	London		
sname	Sallawa	postc	WC1		
inits	G.R.	cred_lim		£1,000.00	

inv_no	Invoice.c_no	inv_date	amount
940	1	05/12/99	£26.20
1003	1	12/01/00	£16.26

Summary for 'Customer.c_no' = 1 (2 detail records)
Sum £42.46

Customer.c_n	2	street	5 Dux St	balance	£200.00
title	Miss	city	London		
sname	Lauri	postc	N1		
inits	P.	cred_lim		£500.00	

inv_no	Invoice.c_no	inv_date	amount
1004	2	14/01/00	£200.00

Summary for 'Customer.c_no' = 2 (1 detail record)
Sum £200.00

Fig. 8.57 Part of the report.

11. To make minor modifications to the report, click the Design button in the Database window (Fig. 8.58).

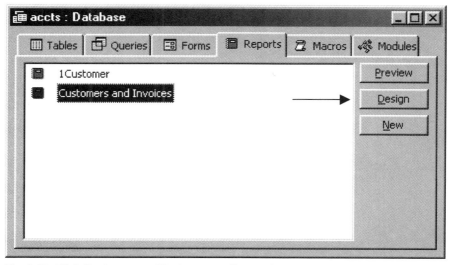

Fig. 8.58 Click Design to modify the report (Step 11).

12. Click on the relevant report item to change it (Fig. 8.59).

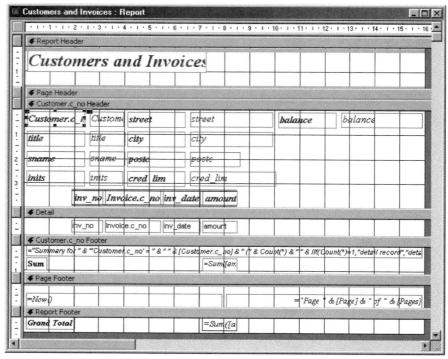

Fig. 8.59 Make minor modifications to the report in Report Design view (Step 12).

8.4.2 Report containing a graph

Graphs can add insight into the nature of the data shown on your reports. They summarize data and show relative values easily. Graphs are easy to produce in Access Reports. You will need the Advanced Wizards installed for what follows.

We shall produce a 'column chart' showing the total outstanding balance for customers in each city.

Steps
   1. We must first create a set of data to base the report on. This is done in this example by creating a stored query based on an SQL SELECT statement using a

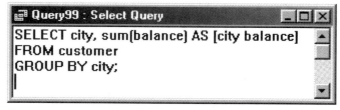

Fig. 8.60 The SQL query that the report will be based on (Step 1).

GROUP BY. How to create SQL queries is discussed in Chapter 6 and the SELECT with GROUP BY is discussed in Section 6.2.8. Create the query shown in Fig. 8.60. Store it as Query99.

2. Run the query and check that the output is correct (Fig. 8.61).

Fig. 8.61 The output of the query (Step 2).

3. Create a new report using the Report Wizard and select Query99 as the data source. Click OK (Fig. 8.62).

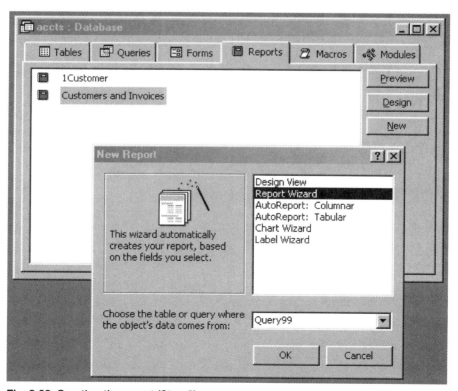

Fig. 8.62 Creating the report (Step 3).

4. Select both fields for the output. Click Next, Next (Fig. 8.63).

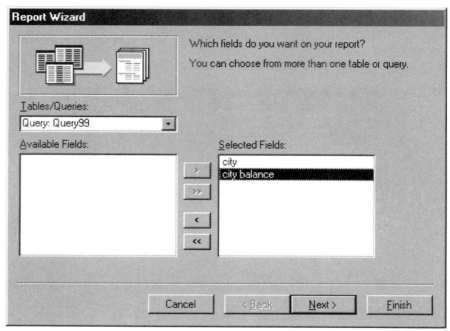

Fig. 8.63 Selecting the output fields (Step 4).

5. Sort the data on the CITY field. Click Next (Fig. 8.64).

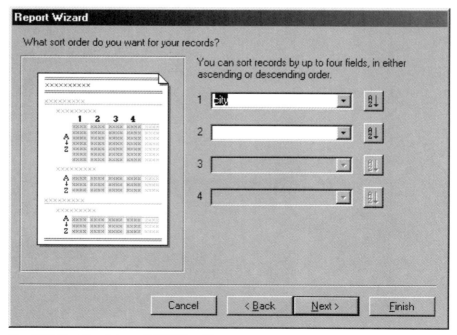

Fig. 8.64 Sort the data on CITY (Step 5).

6. Select a tabular layout for the report. Click Next (Fig. 8.65).

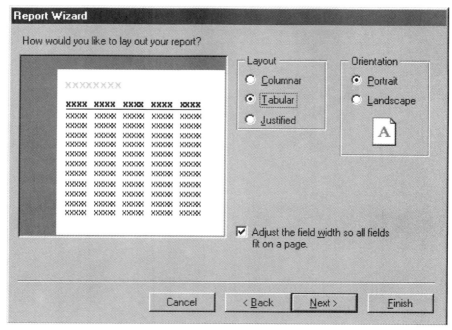

Fig. 8.65 Selecting a report layout (Step 6).

7. Select a report style. Click Next (Fig. 8.66).

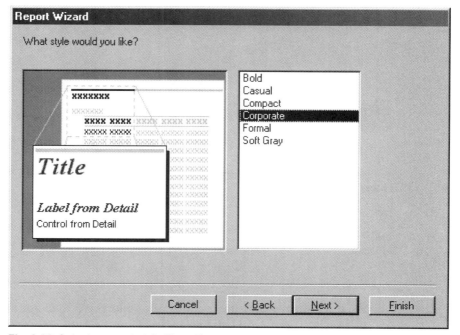

Fig. 8.66 Select a report style (Step 7).

8. Choose a suitable report title. Click Finish (Fig. 8.67).

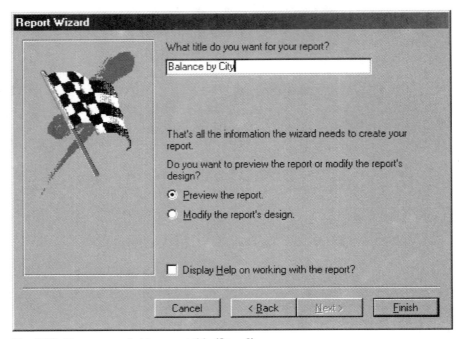

Fig. 8.67 Choose a suitable report title (Step 8).

9. Figure 8.68 shows the report so far.

Balance by City

city	city balance
Dover	£561.44
Leeds	£510.00
London	£566.36

Fig. 8.68 The report so far (Step 9).

10. We now want to add the graph to the report. We shall add it into the Footer section at the bottom of the report. Open the report in Design mode and extend the Footer section (Fig. 8.69).

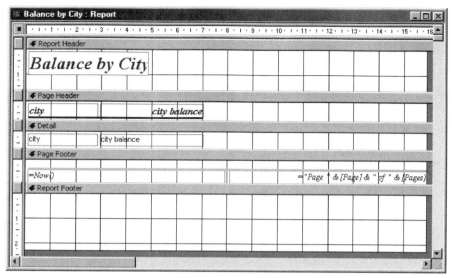

Fig. 8.69 Go into Form Design Mode (Step 10).

11. Click Insert Chart in the Access Menu and drag a chart onto the Footer. This will open the Chart Wizard. Select Query99 as the data source. Click Next (Fig. 8.70).

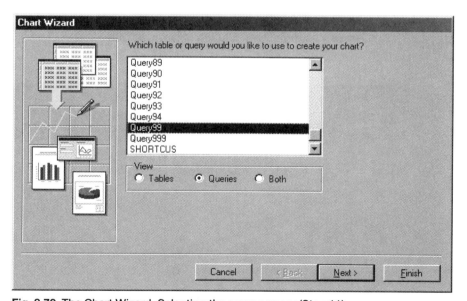

Fig. 8.70 The Chart Wizard. Selecting the source query (Step 11).

12. Select both fields (CITY and CITY BALANCE) for the report. Click Next (Fig. 8.71).

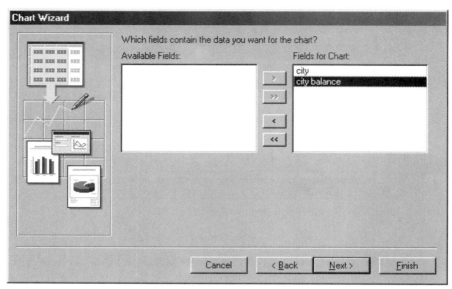

Fig. 8.71 Selecting both query fields for the chart (Step 12).

13. Choose Column chart. Click Next (Fig. 8.72).

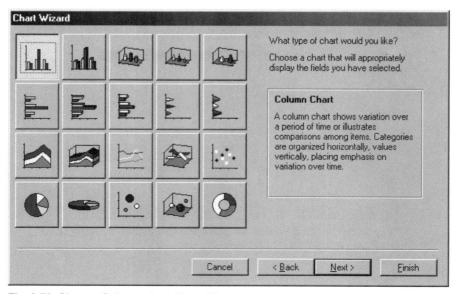

Fig. 8.72 Choose Column chart (Step 13).

14. Check that the wizard has set up the correct axes for the chart. Click Next (Fig. 8.73).

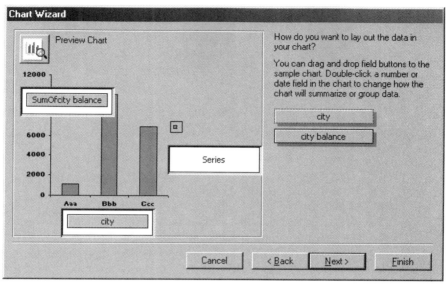

Fig. 8.73 Check the axes are correct for the chart (Step 14).

15. Clear the Report and Chart fields because we want one chart for *all* of the data. Click Next (Fig. 8.74).

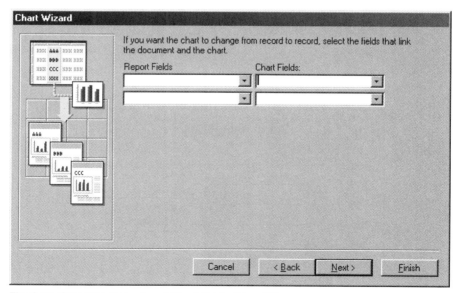

Fig. 8.74 Clear the Report and Chart fields (Step 15).

16. Give the graph a suitable title. Click Finish (Fig. 8.75).

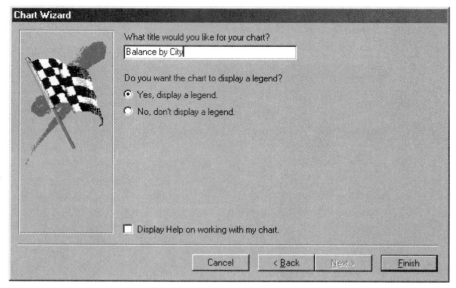

Fig. 8.75 Give the graph a suitable title (Step 16).

17. Preview the report. Go into Design Mode to make any minor changes, then save the report. The report should appear as in Fig. 8.76.

Balance by City

city	*city balance*
Dover	£561.44
Leeds	£510.00
London	£566.36

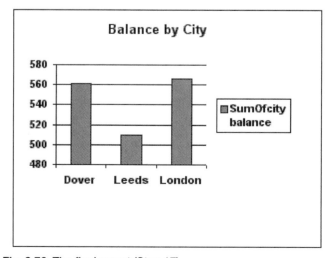

Fig. 8.76 The final report (Step 17).

Conclusion

We have shown how simple reports and graphs can be generated using the Access report writer. The Wizard makes this a fast process.

You might find that in some situations, the report writer is not suitable for your particular application's needs.

We shall see in later chapters that the most flexible method of producing custom reports is using Visual Basic program code. That way you will obtain maximum, programmed control over how the report looks

In the same way, on the input side, producing forms in Access using Wizards is fast, but can lead to complications when you want 'non-standard' functionality.

In later chapters, we see how to use the power of Visual Basic to obtain any degree of customized control you and your users want.

8.5 Exercises

Forms

The schema of the **cus_purchase_prod.mdb** database is reproduced here, from Appendix 1.

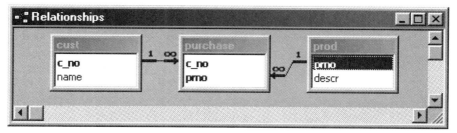

Fig. 8.77 Schema of the **cus_purchase_prod.mdb** database.

1. Produce a 1:N form showing, for each customer, which purchases he or she has made. The '1' side of the form should show the C_NO and NAME fields. The 'N' side of the form (the subform) should show the PRNO and DESCR fields. The subform should be in the form of a grid, showing all the purchases made by that customer.

2. Modify the design to allow entry of new purchases. Use a Combo box in the subform to allow users to click on the product they want to enter.

3. Modify the schema of the database to contain customer address and balance data, purchase quantity and date, and quantity in stock.

4. Add these details to the form.

5. Put a command button on the form that opens a new form which allows the user to see current quantities in stock and to enter new product data and quantities.

Macros

6. In the Macro example of Section 8.3.1, perform the following modifications:

   (a) Modify Form1 so that instead of using the OnClick event to trigger Macro1, use the OnCurrent event. Then Macro1 will change the invoices shown in Form2 to be those for the new customer automatically.

(b) Modify Form2 to show *multiple rows* instead of just one, as in Figs 8.78 and 8.79.

(c) Add a Command button to Form2 which loads a form Form3 which displays all of the PAYMENT records for the current INVOICE record.

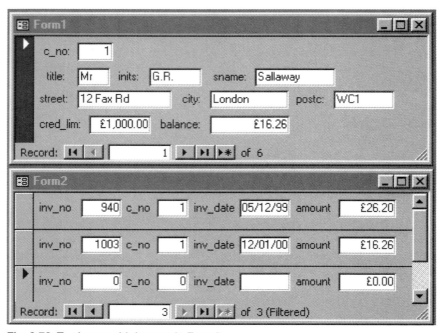

Fig. 8.78 To show multiple rows in Form2 . . .

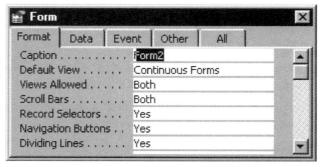

Fig. 8.79 . . . set Default View to Continuous Forms.

Reports

7. Modify the report produced in section 8.4.1 to show all the payments for each invoice.

8. By grouping, show the payment *total* for each invoice.

9

Visual Basic database programming using the Data Control

In this chapter you will learn:

- how to link an Access database to a Visual Basic program using both the DAO and the ADO data controls

- how to write code to update and search the database

- how to use the DAO DBGrid and the ADO Data Grid.

9.1 Introduction

In this chapter we show how to develop Visual Basic programs which link to a Jet database, that is, a database created using Access or VB. We use the Jet database **accts.mdb** in the examples that follow. We start with a brief description of some of the choices the database application developer has when using Microsoft products. There *are* many options and we hope this description helps you to make an informed choice.

Approaches to database application development
Access forms as a method of simple data entry can be produced very quickly using Access Wizards. However, in many cases, you will find that you want your application to do something a bit different from what the wizard-produced forms let you do. You might find that you need a lot of experimentation to get the form to do what you want it to. In many nontrivial applications, procedural code is required to give the required functionality. This can be produced using *Access modules*. Integrating the code you produced in a module with the form and code the wizard produced is then a potential problem. An alternative, again within Access, is to start with a blank form, not tied to the database, and then to program all the functionality yourself.

In the following two chapters, however, we link the industry-standard programming language, *Visual Basic*, to the **accts.mdb** database we created using

Access. This offers a more flexible development environment than module development within Access itself, with more tools available. In this chapter we use a VB control called the *Data Control*. In Chapters 10 and 11 we use an even more flexible approach to database programming – using DAO or ADO statements *without* using a data control. We recommend that the serious database programmer learn to program both with and without the help of a data control. You can use them both in the same project. For the simpler parts of the project where the emphasis is on data entry with relatively simple processing, we recommend the data control. Where you need to perform more complex processing and feel you need to be freed from some of the constraints of the data control, you'd use DAO or ADO programming.

- Access Wizards
- Access Forms tied to a recordsource
- Access Forms not tied to a recordsource and using Access code modules
- Visual Basic Data Control (DAO or ADO)
- Visual Basic DAO or ADO programming, without the data control

Fig. 9.1 Some of the Microsoft methods of developing database applications.

At the top of the list are the methods that allow you to develop simple applications quickly, but whose timesaving features get in the way for more complex or unconventional requirements. They give the application developer the minimum control over the application and can be difficult to update in the light of changing user requirements. They require the minimum knowledge on the part of the developer. They represent Microsoft's various attempts to make database application development simple. What they have actually done is to make simple application development fast.

At the bottom of the list are 'lower-level' methods of database application development that allow developers the maximum control over what the programs will do and how they will do it. The downside is that applications might take longer to develop because more code needs to be written. The developer needs to know more too.

For the experienced non-internet database programmer (database applications on the internet use ADO – see Chapter 15), DAO is usually seen as the starting point for most applications, with the other methods as timesaving conveniences for simple applications.

While it is possible to mix data control and DAO in a single project, it's impracticable to call forms developed in Access from VB. This means you have to make a decision at an early date whether the application is going to use VB code or not – you don't usually want your users to use Access forms for some tasks and VB forms for others. However, if you're in a hurry you might 'prototype' certain key functions in Access so your users can start entering key data and producing key reports at an early date. You can then, in 'version 2', produce the more 'refined' (more functionality, faster, less memory, more natural user interface) VB version.

We summarize in the following list the approach we use most often.

1. Develop the database design (tables, fields, keys, indexes, relationships, constraints) using Access.
2. Develop and test key queries using interactive SQL in Access, and test data.
3. Develop the programs in Visual basic, using Data Controls for simple parts of the project and DAO for the more complex parts. Test all nontrivial embedded SQL statements first using interactive SQL in Access to see that they really do deliver the correct recordset.

Fig. 9.2 A suggested approach to database application development.

9.2 Linking an Access database to Visual Basic using the Data Control

We illustrate this using a simple example. The example below works for all versions of VB, from VB3 upwards.

1. Create a VB form as shown below.

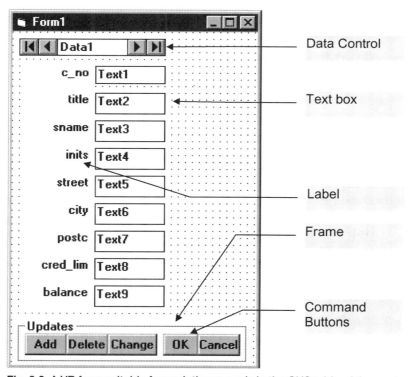

Fig. 9.3 A VB form suitable for updating records in the CUS table of the **accts.mdb** database.

All of the controls on this form (the data control, the text boxes, the labels, the frame and the command buttons) are dragged onto the form from the standard Visual Basic Toolbox. If the Toolbox is not visible, it can be opened from the menu.

The text boxes will be used to display data from the CUSTOMER table in the accts.mdb database. The labels to their left just show what the field name is. In a finished application, the labels would contain more meaningful captions than these. The frame is used here just to improve the form's appearance. The command buttons will be used in the following way.

- *To Add a record*: the user will click the Add button, type the data for the new customer record into the text boxes, and then click the OK button to save the new record or the Cancel button to undo (back out, abort, abandon, cancel) the add.

- *To Delete a record*: the user will click the Delete button, and then click either the OK button to actually delete the record, or the Cancel button to cancel the deletion.

- *To Change a record*: the user will click the Change button, make the changes required in the text boxes, and then click either the OK button to save the changes or the Cancel button to cancel the changes.

This two-step process allows the user to make a conscious decision whether to go ahead with the update or to abandon it. We shall add this functionality to the command buttons later.

2. Link the Data Control to the Database using the Properties window for the Data Control. The two properties you need to set are **Data1.DatabaseName** and **Data1.RecordSource**.

If the Properties window is not visible, it can be opened from the menu. A large part of VB programming concerns changing the *properties* of *controls*. You can set the initial values of some of the properties at design time using the Properties window, and under program control at runtime. The *DatabaseName* property of the *Data1* control is set at design time to link the data control to the database – in our case the **accts.mdb** database. The *RecordSource* property of the data control is set to the name of the source of the data for the data control, that is, the part of the database we want to access using this data control. It can be set to a database table or even a query. Here, we want to link it to the CUSTOMER table.

Linking a data control to a recordsource creates in memory a *recordset*. A recordset is, naturally, a set of records in memory. The data control will point to just one of these records at any one time. That record will be displayed in the text boxes. So that the text boxes 'know' that they have to display this data, we 'tie' them to the data control.

3. Tie the Text boxes to Data1. The properties you need to set are **Text1.DataSource** = Data1, and **Text1.DataField** = c_no etc., for each text box.

Now run the project and you should be able to see each record from the CUSTOMER table, one at a time in the tied text boxes, as you click the data control. The data control contains four buttons. From left to right these are:

- MoveFirst. Clicking this button moves the 'pointer' in the recordset to the first record. That is, it makes the first record in the recordset the 'current' record. The first record's fields are visible in the tied text boxes.

- MovePrevious. Clicking this button moves the 'pointer' in the recordset back one place so that you see the 'previous' record in the text boxes.
- MoveNext. Clicking this button moves the pointer to the next record in the recordset.
- MoveLast. Clicking this button moves the pointer to the last record in the recordset.

So the data control allows you to scroll through the records in the recordset. You can also *change* values in the records (the changes are stored on the database on the disk when you move to another record), but you can't *insert* or *delete* any records. For that you need some VB code.

9.3 Adding, deleting and changing records

4. Set the name property of the first and fourth command buttons to **cmdAdd** and **cmdOK**. Insert the following code for these buttons:

Add Button

```
Sub cmdAdd_Click ()
   current_command = "add"
   Data1.Recordset.AddNew
End Sub
```
Put a blank record at the end of the recordset.

OK Button

```
Sub cmdOK_Click ()
  If current_command = "add" Then
     Data1.Recordset.Update
  End If
End Sub
```
Write the new record to the disk.

In General Declarations declare the variable **current_command**. This needs to be 'visible' to all the Subs (subroutines) on the form, in particular cmdOK_Click, which will act differently for an Add, Change and Delete:

```
Dim current_command
```

Dim stands for 'dimension' and is the way you declare variables in VB. It is possible in the Dim statement to specify what *type* of data item you are declaring. This has an impact on the amount of storage the variable will take and the type of data it can contain. Permitted VB data types include: Byte, Boolean, Integer, Long, Currency, Single, Double, Date, String (for variable-length strings), and String * *length* (for fixed-length strings). If you don't specify any data type, then the default data type is Variant (which can carry numbers or strings). See VB Help for the uses of each of these data types. For example, we could have specified the variable this way:

```
Dim current_command as String
```

You can declare a variable in a subroutine, in which case its 'scope', that is, where it can be 'seen' (accessed from in program code) is just that subroutine.

You can declare a variable in General Declarations in a form, in which case its scope is all subroutines in that form.

You can declare a variable in a code module, in which case the variable can be seen by all the forms in the project. Its value can be changed by one subroutine and its new value will be seen by all subroutines in all forms.

Adding a new CUS record in our program is a two-stage process. First the user clicks the Add button, which executes the cmdAdd_Click subroutine and then, to confirm that he or she wants to save the record, clicks the cmdOK_Click button.

In the subroutine cmdAdd_Click, we set the value of the variable current_command to the string "add" and this value will be seen by the cmdOK_Click subroutine. The next thing that happens in cmdAdd_Click is that the command

```
Data1.Recordset.AddNew
```

is executed. This adds a blank record to the end of the recordset defined by the Data1 data control – in our case, the CUS table recordset. It also clears the tied text boxes on the form, inviting the user to type the field values of the fields in the new record.

When the user has finished typing in the field values, he or she will then click the OK button, so that the code in the cmdOK_Click subroutine will execute. This checks, using the 'if' statement, what the value of the variable current_command is. If it's "add" (as set in the code for the Add button) then the following command is executed:

```
Data1.Recordset.Update
```

This saves the recordset (including the new, added, record), to the database on the disk. It is now possible to add records to the CUS table.

5. Add facilities to the project to allow it to delete the current record.

Delete Button

```
Sub cmdDelete_Click ()
   current_command = "delete"
End Sub
```

Add this code to cmdOK_Click:

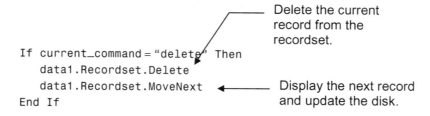

```
If current_command = "delete" Then
   data1.Recordset.Delete
   data1.Recordset.MoveNext
End If
```

Delete the current record from the recordset.

Display the next record and update the disk.

If the user clicks the Delete button, the only thing that happens is that the variable current_command is given the value "delete". The actual deletion of the current record from the recordset does not occur until the user clicks the OK button. Here, the command

```
data1.Recordset.Delete
```

deletes the record from the recordset, and the command

```
data1.Recordset.MoveNext
```

moves the recordset pointer to the next record, so that the user can see some data in the tied textboxes. The MoveNext method also saves the changed recordset to the database on the disk.

6. Add facilities to the project to allow changes to the current record.

Change Button

```
Sub cmdChange_Click ()
   current_command = "change"
   data1.Recordset.Edit  ◄————————  Allow changes to the
End Sub                              current record.
```

The Edit method allows the current record in the recordset to be changed. After clicking this button, the user can change these values by typing into the tied text boxes on the form.

The following code needs to be added to the OK button.

```
If current_command = "change" Then
     data1.Recordset.Update  ◄————
End If                                  Copy the changes onto
                                        the disk database.
```

To save the changes, the Edit must be followed by an Update when the user clicks the OK button.

7. At any point in the proceedings, the user should be able to back out of the update. Here we use a Cancel button, which 'refreshes' the recordset, that is, it retrieves the old data from the disk, overwriting any pending changes.

Cancel Button

```
Sub cmdCancel_Click ()
   Data1.Refresh  ◄————————  Restore the recordset, overwriting
End Sub                       any changes the user has made.
```

Note that in versions of VB from VB5 onwards, the operative line in the Cancel button code should not be a Refresh method but an UpdateControls method. The command should be:

```
Data1.UpdateControls
```

The effect of the command is to overwrite the contents of the recordset in the computer's memory with the data in the disk copy of the database. In the present case, if the user clicks the Cancel button, any changes he or she has made to the CUS recordset will be overwritten from the database CUS table. This is a good way for the user to abort an update.

We now have a very basic project for editing the contents of a single table using a Visual Basic form. Using it we can:

- add new records
- delete records
- change records
- back out of any change using the Cancel button
- save the change using the OK button.

The complete code for this simple project is shown below.

```
Dim current_command
Sub cmdAdd_Click ()
  current_command = "add"
  Data1.Recordset.AddNew
End Sub
Sub cmdChange_Click ()
  current_command = "change"
  Data1.Recordset.Edit
End Sub
Sub cmdDelete_Click ()
  current_command = "delete"
End Sub
Sub cmdOK_Click ()
  If current_command = "add" Then
    Data1.Recordset.Update
  End If
  If current_command = "change" Then
    Data1.Recordset.Update
  End If
  If current_command = "delete" Then
    Data1.Recordset.Delete
    Data1.Recordset.MoveFirst
  End If
End Sub
Sub cmdCancel_Click ()
  Data1.UpdateControls .
  'Use Data1.Refresh for VB4 and VB3
End Sub
```

Fig. 9.4 Complete code for simple DAO data control update of one table.

9.4 Error handling

You might have noticed that various runtime errors can stop the program running; for example, attempting to insert a customer record with a duplicate customer number, or attempting to delete a customer who has INVOICEs. Instead of attempting to write separate program segments for each of these types of error, VB has a mechanism for trapping them wherever they occur. It's called **On Error Goto**. We now add this error-handling code to our project.

1. Make sure the VB form and code you have are as shown in Figs 9.3 and 9.4.

The way we have arranged things, all the runtime errors associated with database navigation should occur in cmdOK_Click. This is where we shall introduce the error-handling code.

2. Modify the cmdOK_Click code as follows.

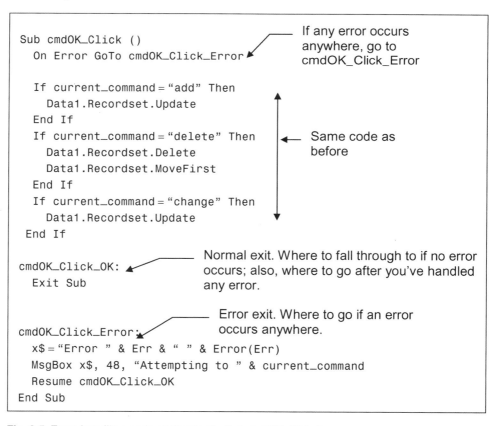

```
Sub cmdOK_Click ()
  On Error GoTo cmdOK_Click_Error          If any error occurs
                                            anywhere, go to
                                            cmdOK_Click_Error

  If current_command = "add" Then
    Data1.Recordset.Update
  End If
  If current_command = "delete" Then        Same code as
    Data1.Recordset.Delete                  before
    Data1.Recordset.MoveFirst
  End If
  If current_command = "change" Then
    Data1.Recordset.Update
  End If

cmdOK_Click_OK:              Normal exit. Where to fall through to if no error
  Exit Sub                   occurs; also, where to go after you've handled
                             any error.

                             Error exit. Where to go if an error
cmdOK_Click_Error:           occurs anywhere.
  x$ = "Error " & Err & " " & Error(Err)
  MsgBox x$, 48, "Attempting to " & current_command
  Resume cmdOK_Click_OK
End Sub
```

Fig. 9.5 Error-handling code added to the Sub cmdOK_Click.

This error-handling code will ensure that a runtime error will not cause the program to crash back to the operating system.

There is a separate section of code to handle the errors. This code is under the *label* cmdOK_Click_Error. A label is a place in VB code where control passes via a

Goto statement. We normally avoid Goto statements and labels when programming since their uncontrolled use can lead to code that is difficult to follow. (A seminal paper by Edgar Dijkstra entitled "Goto's considered dangerous" was pivotal in promoting this idea.) Some programmers call this style of programming 'spaghetti code'. However, for error handling, it's useful, and in VB essential.

The label `cmdOK_Click_Error` also appears at the top of the subroutine in the statement:

```
On Error GoTo cmdOK_Click_Error
```

This statement says, in effect, "if any error occurs *anywhere* in this subroutine, then pass control to the code following the label `cmdOK_Click_Error`". If, for example, a user had attempted to add a new customer record with a customer number that already existed, the resulting 'duplicate value in the primary key' error would cause a transfer of control to this label.

The first line in the error-handling code is:

```
x$ = "Error " & Err & " " & Error(Err)
```

The variable x$ is a string variable. We are going to put into it the error message we want to display in a message box. The string consists of a concatenation of the word "Error ", with the error number delivered by the VB function 'Err', then a space, and then the text error message corresponding to the error code. This text message is delivered by the VB function 'Error'.

The next line is:

```
MsgBox x$, 48, "Attempting to " & current_command
```

This is a call to the VB message box statement MsgBox, which has three parameters (arguments). The first argument is the message that forms the body of the message box – in our case x$. The second argument is a number, which is determined by selecting a combination of buttons and warning symbols in the message box. You can find the possibilities in VB Help. We have chosen a simple exclamation mark and a single OK button. Adding the values for these two gives the value 48. The third argument is the title bar contents. We have included the variable `current_command` in this, to remind the user what he or she was doing when the error occurred.

When the user clicks the OK button on the message box, control is passed back to an Exit Sub statement using the statement:

```
Resume cmdOK_Click_OK
```

Every 'On Error' statement must have a corresponding Resume statement to specify what to do after the error has been 'handled'.

9.5 Error prevention

There are various additional measures we can take to make the application more secure. We have added error trapping to the CUS update VB project. As well as reporting errors the user makes, we can try to prevent some of them by enabling and disabling various parts of the form so that only appropriate sequences of action are possible. For example, it would be inappropriate for the user to click the Add button twice in succession.

Function	Data Control	Add Button	Change Button	Delete Button	OK Button	Cancel Button	Text Boxes
Navigate	x	x	x	x			
Add					x	x	x
Change					x	x	x
Delete					x	x	
OK	x	x	x	x			
Cancel	x	x	x	x			

Fig. 9.6 Table showing which objects on Form1 should be enabled for (after) each function.

Figure 9.6 shows in the first row that if the user is 'navigating', that is, clicking the data control to move between records in the recordset, then the data control itself, the Add button, the Change button and the Delete button should be enabled, but the OK button, the Cancel button and the Text boxes should all be disabled. In the second row, it shows that if the Add button has been clicked, then the data control, the Add button itself, and the Change and Delete buttons should all be disabled.

The other rows show, in a similar way, which controls should be enabled and disabled under various circumstances.

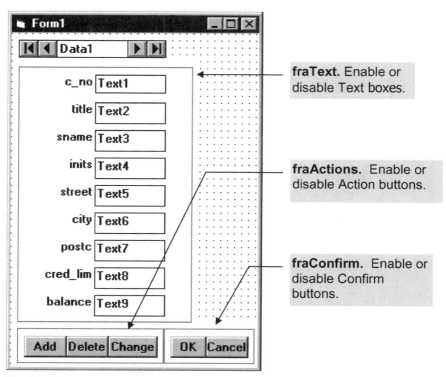

Fig. 9.7 The Frames used to enable and disable form objects in groups.

We can see from this table that the Add, Change and Delete buttons are always enabled or disabled together and so are the OK and Cancel buttons. The text boxes are also all enabled or disabled.

To reduce the code required to enable and disable in all these cases, we group the controls in Frames so they can be enabled or disabled together by disabling the frame.

The frames required are shown in Fig. 9.7 – see previous page. The Data Controls will be enabled and disabled individually.

We now describe the code associated with this project. The complete listing of the code is given below in Fig. 9.8, and the description follows it.

```
Dim current_command 'General Declarations

Sub Form_Load ()
  'Enable Data Control and Action buttons.
  data1.Enabled = True
  fraActions.Enabled = True
  fraConfirm.Enabled = False
  fraText.Enabled = False
  data1.DatabaseName = app.Path &
"\..\database\accts.mdb"
End Sub

Sub cmdAdd_Click ()
  current_command = "add"
  'Enable Confirm (OK & Cancel) buttons and Text boxes
  data1.Enabled = False
  fraActions.Enabled = False
  fraConfirm.Enabled = True
  fraText.Enabled = True
  data1.Recordset.AddNew
End Sub

Sub cmdDelete_Click ()
  current_command = "delete"
  'Enable Confirm (OK & Cancel) buttons
  data1.Enabled = False
  fraActions.Enabled = False
  fraConfirm.Enabled = True
  fraText.Enabled = False
End Sub

Sub cmdChange_Click ()
  current_command = "change"
  'Enable Confirm (OK & Cancel) buttons and Text boxes
  data1.Enabled = False
  fraActions.Enabled = False
  fraConfirm.Enabled = True
```

```
      fraText.Enabled = True
      data1.Recordset.Edit
    End Sub

    Sub cmdOK_Click ()
      On Error GoTo cmdOK_Click_Error
      If current_command = "add" or current_command =
    "change" Then
        data1.Recordset.Update
      End If
      If current_command = "delete" Then
        data1.Recordset.Delete
        data1.Recordset.MoveFirst
      End If
    cmdOK_Click_OK:
      current_command = " "
      'Enable Data control and Action buttons
      data1.Enabled = True
      fraActions.Enabled = True
      fraConfirm.Enabled = False
      fraText.Enabled = False
      Exit Sub
    cmdOK_Click_Error:
      x$ = "Error " & Err & " " & Error(Err)
      MsgBox x$, 48, "Attempting to " & current_command
      Resume cmdOK_Click_OK
    End Sub

    Sub cmdCancel_Click ()
      current_command = " "
      'Enable Data control and Action buttons
      data1.Enabled = True
      fraActions.Enabled = True
      fraConfirm.Enabled = False
      fraText.Enabled = False
      data1.UpdateControls 'data1.refresh for VB3 and VB4
    End Sub
```

Fig. 9.8 Complete code listing for the project associated with the form in Fig. 9.7.

General Declarations

In General Declarations, the variable current_command is declared. This will hold a string that is "add", "change" or "delete". This is set when the user clicks the Add, Change or Delete command button. The value is used to determine what to do when the user clicks the OK button. Each of these operations is a two-step process: for example to delete the current record, the user clicks Delete then either OK to go ahead with the deletion or Cancel to back out of the deletion. Because the value of current_command needs to be accessed by two different subroutines, it is declared in General Declarations.

Form_Load

The Form_Load event occurs first. Here are the first four lines:

```
data1.Enabled = True
fraActions.Enabled = True
fraConfirm.Enabled = False
fraText.Enabled = False
```

The data control is enabled so that the user can move from one record to another. The frame around the Add, Delete and Change buttons – fraActions – is enabled, so that the user can initiate the corresponding actions. The frame around the OK and Cancel buttons – fraConfirm – is *dis*abled, so that the user is *prevented* from clicking either of these buttons at this point. Similarly, the frame around the text boxes – fraText – is disabled to prevent the user changing anything in the text boxes, effectively making the recordset *read-only*. In terms of Fig. 9.6, we are in Navigate mode.

If you have tried to copy your project from one computer to another, you might have noticed that the path for the database needs to be updated. If you keep the database in the same folder as the project, you can use **App.Path**, which is the path to the current application (current project). This can be sorted out at runtime in the Form Load event. Here's how it works.

In the last line,

```
data1.DatabaseName = app.Path & "\..\database\accts.mdb"
```

we are specifying where the database is. In the directory (i.e. folder) hierarchy, the database file accts.mdb is located. App.Path is the path of the current project. Suppose the current project is in the following location:

```
c:\myprojects\project1\Project1.vbp.
```

Then app.path will be:

```
c:\myprojects\project1
```

and app.path & \.. will be:

```
c:\myprojects
```

because \.. means go one level up in the hierarchy. app.Path & \..\database will be:

```
c:\myprojects\database
```

and finally app.Path & \..\database\accts.mdb will be:

```
c:\myprojects\database\accts.mdb.
```

You can see from this that the folder

```
c:\myprojects
```

has two subfolders:

```
c:\myprojects\project1
c:\myprojects\database.
```

The first folder contains the program (i.e. project) code and the second folder contains the database.

Putting the code and the database in the common folder myprojects and using App.Path in this way has the benefit that if you want to copy both to, say, a floppy disk, then copying the common folder to the floppy disk will maintain the relative positions of the program and the database.

Sub cmdAdd_Click ( )

Here we 'remember' that the user has just clicked the Add button in the line:

```
current_command = "add"
```

After the comment, which is signified by the single quote, we include the following four lines:

```
data1.Enabled = False
fraActions.Enabled = False
fraConfirm.Enabled = True
fraText.Enabled = True
```

Here we disable the data control so that, having clicked the Add button, the user is not able to move to another record (which would cause an error).

We disable the Add, Delete and Cancel buttons so that the user cannot click these buttons.

We enable the OK and Cancel buttons so that the user can complete or abandon the Add operation. Finally, we enable the tied text boxes so that the user can type the field values of the new CUS record into the tied text boxes. This corresponds to the Add row of Fig. 9.6.

Finally, we execute the command:

```
data1.Recordset.AddNew
```

which adds a new, blank record to the recordset. As the user types values into the tied text boxes, the values go into the respective fields of this new record.

Sub cmdDelete_Click ( )

Here we specify that the user has clicked the Delete button and enable and disable various parts of the form to prevent the user 'doing anything silly', as described above. This corresponds to the Delete line of Fig. 9.6. The actual deletion of the record does not occur here, because remember we want a two-stage process so that the user has the option to back out using the Cancel button.

Sub cmdChange_Click ( )

After committing to memory the fact that the current command is a Change and enabling and disabling appropriate parts of the form using the frames as before, we execute the command:

```
data1.Recordset.Edit
```

This signals to the Jet Engine that we wish to alter the contents of the current record. The user then makes those changes by typing into the tied text boxes.

Sub cmdOK_Click ( )

The OK button is clicked if the user wants to commit the changes he or she has initiated by clicking the Add, the Delete or the Change button.

The first line in this Sub specifies where to go in case of an error.

The following lines are:

```
If current_command = "add" or current_command =
"change" Then
  data1.Recordset.Update
End If
```

If the previous button clicked had been either an Add or a Change, then to save these results to the database, an Update method is required.

The following lines:

```
If current_command = "delete" Then
  data1.Recordset.Delete
  data1.Recordset.MoveFirst
End If
```

deal with the case of a Delete. The Delete method deletes the record in the recordset and the MoveFirst method moves to the first record in the recordset, so that there is a current record in the recordset, and the record is actually marked as deleted on the database. (It's not possible to access a 'deleted' record in the database. However, the record still occupies space. If you want to remove these 'deleted' records, you can *compact* the database. This is achieved in Access using the following menu option: Tools/Database Utilities/Compact Database. You might want to compact your database after a month or so, if there have been lots of deletions. You might notice a performance improvement and the database would occupy less disk space after the 'compact'.)

The next few lines in the OK button code are:

```
cmdOK_Click_OK:
  current_command = ""
  'Enable Data control and Action buttons
  data1.Enabled = True
```

```
    fraActions.Enabled = True
    fraConfirm.Enabled = False
    fraText.Enabled = False
    Exit Sub
```

This is the 'tidy up' code, which is executed before exiting the OK button sub-routine. It is placed so that it executes whether or not an error has occurred.

What the current command was is 'forgotten' by clearing out the string to a null string (a string with no characters in it). The various parts of the form are then enabled and disabled to take the form back to 'Navigate' mode, as per Fig. 9.6. Execution ceases at the Exit Sub command.

The rest of the OK button Sub is shown below and concerns error handling.

```
cmdOK_Click_Error:
    x$ = "Error " & Err & " " & Error(Err)
    MsgBox x$, 48, "Attempting to " & current_command
    Resume cmdOK_Click_OK
End Sub
```

Processing gets to this point if there has been an error. The On Error command of the first line specifies that. In the first line, a string variable x$ is built up to contain the error number and error message using the Visual Basic functions Err and Error. A message box is then displayed with this error message, a single OK button and warning symbol, and a title bar which reminds the user of what he or she was attempting to do at the time of the error. The second argument is obtained by adding numbers to specify how the message box should look: which buttons and symbol it should have. The programmer can decide upon these using Help.

The Resume command says that processing should resume at the label cmdOK_Click_OK. This executes the 'tidy up' code described above. The End Sub merely signals the physical end of the subroutine, since the exit point is always the Exit Sub statement.

Sub cmdCancel_Click ( )
This button is clicked if the user, having clicked one of the action buttons Add, Delete or Change, decides not to go ahead with the update. After setting the frames to set the form back to 'Navigate' mode, an UpdateControls method is executed against the data control. This restores the recordset to how it was before the aborted changes.

9.6 A FindFirst button

Clearly it would be an advantage for large files to be able to find a given record quickly. Access has an excellent Find facility, which allows searches on all fields for a given string. Here we use the Visual Basic Find command to add a similar but simpler feature to our project. It allows the user to find the first record for a given surname. We create a command button **cmdFind** on the form and give it the code shown in Fig. 9.9.

```
                                        InputBox is an easy way to get
                                        simple user input.
Sub cmdFind_Click ()
  On Error GoTo cmdFind_Error
  x = InputBox("Input first few characters of Customer Surname ", "Find
on Surname")
  data1.Recordset.FindFirst "sname like " & "'" & x & "*" & "'"
cmdFind_OK:
  Exit Sub                   FindFirst finds and displays the first record
cmdFind_Error:                 that matches the selection criteria.
  y = "Error " & Err & " " & Error(Err)
  MsgBox y, 48, "Find on Surname"
  Resume cmdFind_OK
End Sub
```

Fig. 9.9 Code for the Find button.

The error–handling code follows a similar format to that described above. The first thing that happens in this Sub is that the user is prompted to enter the customer's surname:

```
x = InputBox("Input first few characters of Customer Surname ", "Find on
Surname")
```

The VB InputBox function is used here, and after the user enters the surname and clicks the InputBox's OK button, the surname is placed into variable x.

The FindFirst command's argument is similar in syntax to the SQL WHERE clause. The 'selection criteria' are the tests that are performed to locate the desired record.

Note that fuzzy matching can be used by using **like** instead of =. Using like, the search string "?z*", for example, would find customer Dziduch, because '?' stands for any single character and '*' stands for any number of any characters. Here, we just use an asterisk and invite the user to type the first few characters of the surname.

The FindFirst command in this subroutine is:

```
data1.Recordset.FindFirst "sname like" & "'" & x & "*" & "'"
```

Suppose the user had entered 'Dz'. Then we would want the FindFirst command to read:

```
data1.Recordset.FindFirst "sname like 'Dz*'".
```

Note that since the field sname (surname) is a character field, we need quotes around the comparison string 'Dz*'. Each of these single quotes is itself a single-character string and must be concatenated into the search string of the FindFirst command. '&' is the VB string concatenation operator.

Note also that the FindFirst command will start from the *beginning* of the record-set and find only the *first* record that matches. You would need a FindNext operation to find subsequent matches.

The rest of the code should be familiar.

9.7 Adding a menu

Apart from adding a professional appearance, a menu gives a compact way of presenting the user with a hierarchy of options. In the current project it *could* be used as an alternative to the command buttons. We have chosen to give the user both possibilities.

Suppose we want to create the menu shown in Fig. 9.10.

Fig. 9.10 A Menu for the customer update form.

By selecting the Menu Editor from the VB Tools option, we get the form shown in Fig. 9.11 to fill in. Filling in this form builds a menu for the current form Form1.

The items we have chosen for our menu have the following structure:

- Navigate
  - Move Next
  - Move Last
  - Move Previous
  - Move First
- Find
- Actions
  - Add
  - Delete
  - Change
- Confirm
  - OK
  - Cancel

Indenting an item shows that the item is a submenu.

The top half of the menu editor window allows you to fill in the items shown in the lower half. In Fig. 9.11, we are highlighting the second menu item – Move Next (5). In the Caption text box (1), we've typed Move &Next. The '&' means that the 'N' will be underlined, and that the user will be able to opt for that menu item by

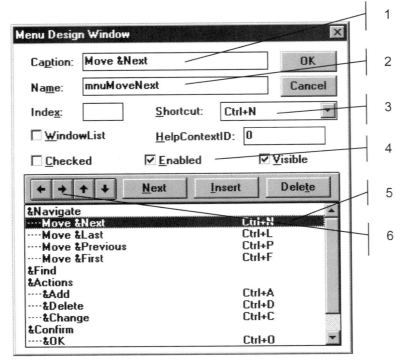

Fig. 9.11 The Menu Editor window.

using the keyboard sequence <Alt> N, as well as accessing it in the normal way using a mouse click.

In the Name text box (2), we have entered mnuMoveNext. That is the name we want to give the Sub that executes when the user clicks this menu item.

Using the Shortcut text box (3), you can select a keyboard sequence. We have opted for <Ctrl> N. This means that if the user clicks <Ctrl> N, a Move Next operation will occur, without having to go through the hierarchical menu sequence Navigate, Move Next. This can speed up processing for experienced users where there is a deep menu hierarchy.

Your program can enable and disable menu options, just as we have done with the command buttons, so that the user is guided into a sensible sequence of operations. The Enabled check box (4) shows this property, but it would normally be set in code. Rather than enabling and disabling the menu options you can make them visible and invisible if you wish, as the next check box shows.

To indent a menu item so that it becomes a submenu, you use the second arrow button (6). The first arrow button will de-indent it, and the up and down arrow buttons can be used to move a menu item up and down in the menu.

Here is the code we have used for the Navigation submenu subroutines.

```
Sub mnuMoveNext_Click ()
  On Error Resume Next
  data1.Recordset.MoveNext
End Sub
```

```
Sub mnuMovePrevious_Click ()
  On Error Resume Next
  data1.Recordset.MovePrevious
End Sub

Sub mnuMoveFirst_Click ()
  data1.Recordset.MoveFirst
End Sub

Sub mnuMoveLast_Click ()
  data1.Recordset.MoveLast
End Sub
```

Each of these subroutines will execute when the corresponding menu item is clicked. If the Move Next menu item is clicked then Sub mnuMoveNext_Click will execute, for example.

If the Move Next menu item is clicked, we execute a MoveNext method on the recordset associated with the data control data1. The On Error Resume Next line is there for error handling. If the user kept clicking this menu item, eventually he or she would get to the end of the recordset. If the user clicked again, an error would occur. On Error Resume Next says that in this event, ignore the error and execute the next instruction, which is the End Sub in this case. So if the user tries to move beyond EOF (end of file) or BOF (beginning of file), a runtime error is avoided. An alternative to this simple strategy would have been to use On Error Goto and tell the user, using a message box, that the end of the recordset had been reached, as we have done in other parts of the program.

The Sub mnuMovePrevious_Click acts in a similar way, preventing the user causing an error by attempting to go beyond the beginning of the recordset.

The mnuMoveFirst and mnuMoveLast subroutines don't need error handling because the first and last records are well defined.

For the Find menu option, it is merely necessary to call the code for the Find command button. They both perform the same function:

```
Sub mnuFind_Click ()
  cmdFind_Click
End Sub
```

All of the remaining menu options also call the code for the corresponding command buttons. However, the menu options need to be enabled and disabled to prevent illogical sequences of user operation, as with the command buttons. Since the menu options call the command button code, we put the code for the enabling and disabling of menu items into the command button subroutines. We show below the example of the Add button code and how it has to be changed.

```
Sub cmdAdd_Click ()
  current_command = "add"
  data1.Enabled = False
  cmdFind.Enabled = False
  fraActions.Enabled = False
  fraConfirm.Enabled = True
```

```
        mnuNavigate.Enabled = False
        mnuFind.Enabled = False
        mnuActions.Enabled = False
        mnuConfirm.Enabled = True
        fraText.Enabled = True
        data1.Recordset.AddNew
End Sub
```

Similar additions are made to the code for all of the other command buttons.

9.8 DBGrid with a single table

Versions 4 and 5 of Visual Basic have a very useful control called the DBGrid. It allows you to inspect, add, delete and update records from a single recordset without using code. Instead of displaying just a single record, which is all you can do with tied text boxes, DBGrid displays *all* of the records in a recordset, using scrollbars. Only one record is the current record at any one time, of course. Version 6 of Visual Basic has an 'improved' version of DBGrid, called the DataGrid. We look at that and its associated new ADO Data Control in Section 9.10.

A DBGrid is 'tied' to a conventional data control, which defines the recordset, just as we have seen in the examples above.

We shall now create a new project using a data control and a DBGrid to display and allow updates of the records in the CUSTOMER table.

1. Create a form as shown:

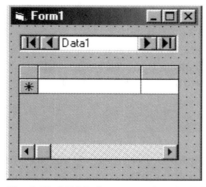

Fig. 9.12 A DAO data control and a DBGrid have been placed on the form.

2. Set the data1.Databasename and data1.recordsource properties.

3. Set DBGrid1.datasource to data1.

4. Right click DBGrid1 and click Retrieve Fields

5. Right click again and set properties, including AllowAddnew and AllowDelete, and column widths (Layout) if required. When you Run, you should now have something like:

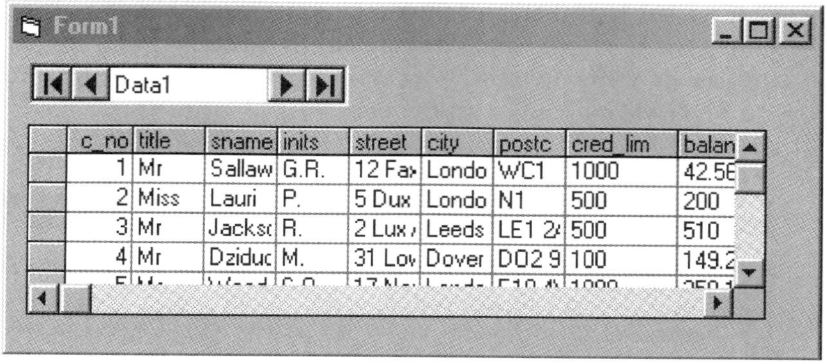

Fig. 9.13 The entire CUSTOMER table displayed in the DBGrid.

6. Check that you can insert, delete and modify records. You add a record in the row marked with an asterisk. To delete a record, click in the greyed first column of the DBGrid to select the record and then press the <Delete> key on the keyboard.

Note that no code is required.

9.9 DBGrid with linked tables in a 1:N form

We now wish to display both customer and invoice data on the same form so that moving to a new customer automatically displays his or her invoices in the second grid.

Create a linked 1:N form using two data controls and DBGrids as shown below. The Databasename property for both data controls should be set to the accts.mdb database. The Recordsource property for Data1 should be the CUSTOMER table, while the Recordsource property for Data2 should be the INVOICE table.

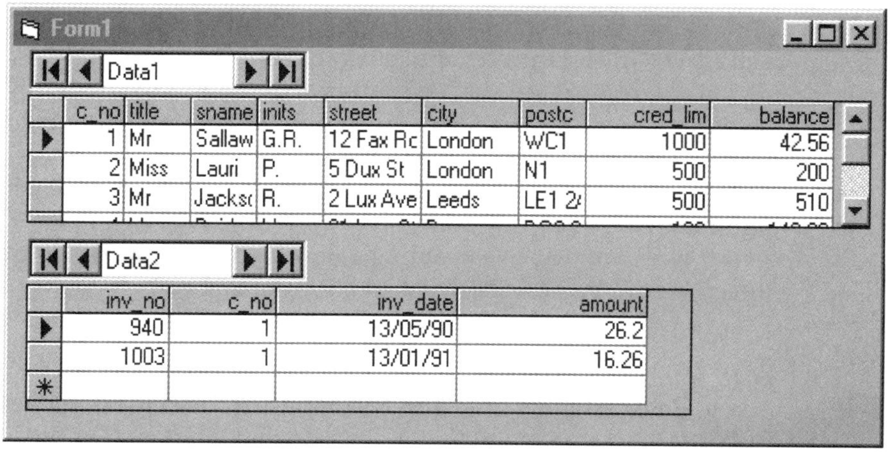

Fig. 9.14 The second grid displays the invoices for the current customer in the first grid (DAO data control).

If we left it at that, customer and invoice data would be displayed independently. The first grid would display all the customers and the second grid would display all of the invoices. If we want to display only the invoices for the *selected* customer, we must add a little code.

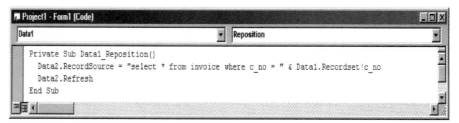

Fig. 9.15 The code necessary to link the DBGrids (DAO data control).

The code necessary to do this is as follows.

```
Data2.RecordSource = "select * from invoice where c_no = " &
Data1.Recordset!c_no
  Data2.Refresh
```

We use the Reposition event for Data1.

This event occurs whenever the user moves to another record. When this happens, we want to display that new customer's invoices in the second grid.

In the first line we build up an SQL statement to create a recordset consisting of all the invoices for the customer whose customer number is the customer number of the current CUSTOMER record.

That recordset becomes the RecordSource for the data control Data2. The Refresh method retrieves the records from the disk database. Since the datasource of DBGrid2 is Data2, it immediately displays the new data.

Inserts, deletes and changes on both tables are possible.

Note that you might want to display only the *current* customer. If so, you would replace DBGrid1 with a set of tied text boxes.

You might also set the Visible property of the data control Data2 to False, because it serves only to define the second recordset; the user can move to another invoice records by clicking the DBGrid.

Note that we have displayed the c_no field in both grids. We have done this to minimize the code.

If it were not displayed, adding a new invoice record would cause a referential integrity error because INVOICE.C_NO would be null.

Getting the Invoice total

Just to demonstrate a little more coding with the DBGrid, let's calculate and display in a label (Label1), the sum of the invoice amounts for the set of invoices for the current customer.

The code will have to implement the following algorithm:

```
initialize total to zero

move to first invoice record

for each invoice
  add invoice amount to total
  move to next invoice
next invoice

display total in label
```

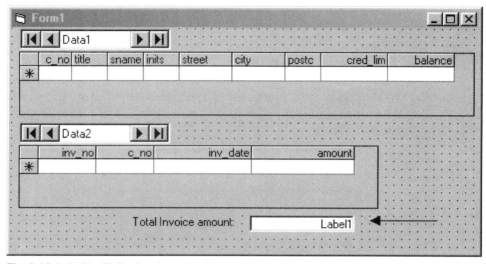

Fig. 9.16 Label1 will display the sum of the invoice amounts (DAO).

The code to do this is shown in Fig. 9.17. We have created a separate Sub called CalculateInvoiceTotal to do this job.

```
Sub CalculateInvoiceTotal()
  Label1 = 0
  If Data2.Recordset.RecordCount > 0 Then
    Data2.Recordset.MoveFirst
    t = 0
    For i = 1 To Data2.Recordset.RecordCount
      t = t + Data2.Recordset!amount
      Data2.Recordset.MoveNext
    Next i
    Label1 = t
  End If
End Sub
Private Sub Data1_Reposition()
  Data2.RecordSource = "select * from invoice where c_no = " & Data1.Recordset!c_no
  Data2.Refresh
  CalculateInvoiceTotal
End Sub
```

Fig. 9.17 The CalculateInvoiceTotal subroutine has been added.

This subroutine is called from the Data1_Reposition event because moving to a new customer will cause a new set of invoices to be displayed.

The subroutine contains a FOR loop. The number of times the loop repeats is the value of the RecordCount property of the recordset. After being initialized to zero, the value of the current invoice amount is added to the variable t each time round the loop. Note that with DBGrids, manipulating data directly from the underlying recordset is usually easier that accessing the data in the grid cells.

Note that it is also possible, with little extra code, to display data from *three or more* linked tables using this DBGrid approach. This would be less easy or perhaps impossible to achieve using Access wizards.

9.10 Using the ADO Data Control – single table updates

As Visual Basic evolves, new methods of accessing data are added. The ADO Data Control (Active-X Data Control) emerged with VB6 and this control makes it easier to connect to remote databases, at the expense of a slightly more involved set-up procedure.

ADO Data Control

ADO DataGrid

Fig. 9.18 Make sure these controls are in your toolbox.

The ADO data control can be used with tied text boxes and with the new Data-Grid (a different grid from the DBGrid of VB4 and VB5).

We now describe a simple application which allows you to update the CUSTOMER table using a DataGrid.

1. Make sure that the ADO Data control and the ADO DataGrid are in your VB toolbox; if not, right-click the toolbox and select Components. Then from the list box, check the check boxes for:

   ● Microsoft ADO Data Control 6.0 (OLEDB)

   ● Microsoft DataGrid Control 6.0 (OLEDB)

2. Create a new project with a form as shown in Fig. 9.19.

3. We now want to connect Adodc1 (ADO data control 1) to the accts.mdb database. This is done by giving a value to the *ConnectionString* property of Adodc1. (This is the equivalent of setting the DatabaseName property of the conventional data control but is a little more involved.) Here are the steps:

   (a) Click on the ConnectionString property of Adodc1 in the Properties window.

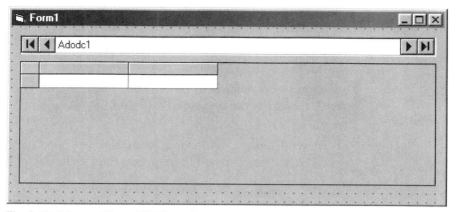

Fig. 9.19 A form with an ADO Data Control and an ADO DataGrid.

(b) Click the ellipsis (three dots) button.

(c) Click the Use Connection String option button.

(d) Click the Build command button.

(e) From the listbox, select Microsoft Jet 3.51 OLE DB Provider (Access 97) or Microsoft Jet 4.0 OLE DB Provider (Access 2000).

(f) Click the Next command button.

(g) Click the ellipsis button to select a database name.

(h) Select the database you want (accts.mdb in this example). This will fill out the text box on the dialogue form, showing the connection string (the path to your database).

(i) Click the Test Connection command button and the OK button when it succeeds. Then click the OK button on the dialogue form.

(j) Now you've built the ConnectionString value, click OK on the final form and the connection string should appear in the ConnectionString property of the Properties window.

4. We now have to set the *RecordSource* property of Adodc1 to say which part of the accts.mdb database we want to access.

(a) Click the ellipsis in the RecordSource property of the Properties window.

(b) By using the drop-down list box, select Command Type to be: 2, which is adCmdTable. Note that we could have used SQL here to retrieve data from several tables if we wanted to.

(c) Click the next drop-down list to select the CUSTOMER table as the record source. Then click the OK button. You will now see the Recordsource property set to Customer in the Properties window.

5. We now want to set the properties of the ADO DataGrid (DataGrid1). Set the properties as follows:

- *DataSource* = Adodc1

  This links DataGrid1 to the recordset defined by Adodc1 – the CUSTOMER table.
- *AllowAddNew* = True

  This allows new records to be entered into the data grid. A row with an asterisk appears at the bottom of the grid.
- *AllowDelete* = True

  This allows deletions. To delete a record the user selects a row by clicking in the greyed first column and then presses the Delete key on the keyboard.
- *AllowUpdate* = True

  This allows the user to make changes to fields by just typing into the grid cells.

6. Run the project. The form should appear as in Fig. 9.20.
7. Check that you can Add, Delete and Change records.

Note that no program code was necessary in this project, although rather a lot of properties had to be set at design time.

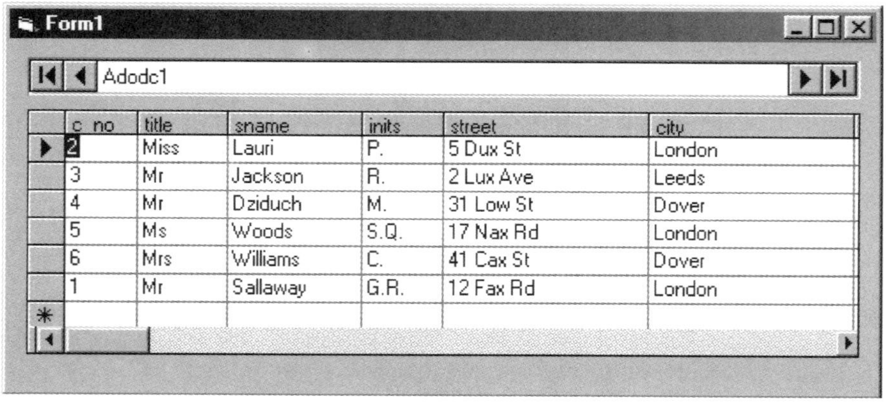

c_no	title	sname	inits	street	city
2	Miss	Lauri	P.	5 Dux St	London
3	Mr	Jackson	R.	2 Lux Ave	Leeds
4	Mr	Dziduch	M.	31 Low St	Dover
5	Ms	Woods	S.Q.	17 Nax Rd	London
6	Mrs	Williams	C.	41 Cax St	Dover
1	Mr	Sallaway	G.R.	12 Fax Rd	London

Fig. 9.20 An ADO Data Control and a tied ADO DataGrid.

We wanted the customer records to appear in order of customer number, so we clicked the ellipsis for the RecordSource property of Adodc1 and changed Command Type to 1 – adCmdText and Command Text to the SQL statement:

```
select * from customer order by c_no
```

This sorted the output into the desired order.

9.11 Using the ADO Data Control – linked tables in a 1:N form

This project is very similar to Section 9.9, where we used a VB4–5 style DBGrid. Here we use the new ADO DataGrid. The user will be able to see both the CUSTOMER and INVOICE tables in two DataGrids on the same form. Clicking on a particular customer record in the first DataGrid will automatically populate the second DataGrid with that customer's invoices. Unlike the DBGrid, the DataGrid does not have a Reposition event. It has instead a MoveComplete event, which behaves in a similar way.

1. Set the required properties for the four controls. The properties are set in a similar way to the previous project.

   Adodc1

   ConnectionString
   Connect to accts.mdb as above.

   RecordSource
   In the dialogue forms, set Command Type to 1 – adCmdText, and Command Text to:

   ```
   select * from customer order by c_no
   ```

   DataGrid1
   DataSource = Adodc1
   AllowAddNew = True
   AllowDelete = True
   AllowUpdate = True

   Note: these last three properties can be set to False if you don't want the user to be able to update customer information on this form.

   There are various reasons why you might want to make a Data Grid (or a DBGrid or even tied Text boxes) *read only*.

   ● Security: users can *see* the data but are not permitted to update it. Employees should probably not be able to update their own salary field, for example.
   ● Routine error prevention: if it's not necessary for a user to update a field, then making the control read-only can help prevent accidental errors.

   Adodc2

   ConnectionString
   Connect to accts.mdb as above.

   RecordSource
   In the dialogue forms, set Command Type to 1 – adCmdText, and Command Text to:

   ```
   select * from invoice
   ```

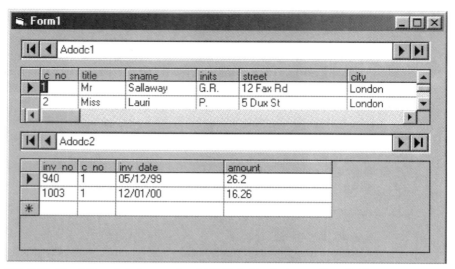

Fig. 9.21 The 1:N update form using ADO Data Controls and DataGrids.

2. Link the two grids using the MoveComplete event for the recordset associated with Adodc1. This event occurs when the user moves to a different CUSTOMER record in DataGrid1. The code redefines the recordset associated with dataGrid2.

(a) Display the Code window for Adodc1 and type in the code shown in Fig. 9.22.

(b) Run the program and check that moving from one customer to another displays the corresponding invoice records in the second grid.

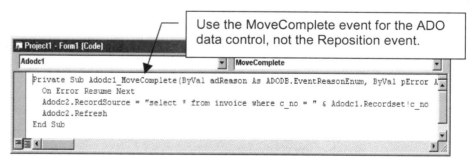

Fig. 9.22 The Code window for the Adodc1_MoveComplete event.

The required code for the MoveComplete event of the ADO data control Adodc1 is:

```
On Error Resume Next
Adodc2.RecordSource = "select * from invoice where c_no = " &
Adodc1.Recordset!c_no
Adodc2.Refresh
```

The first line says that if an error occurs, ignore it and go on to the next statement. The only errors likely here are that the user will click the data control to move beyond BOF (beginning of file) or EOF (end of file) for the customer recordset.

The second line sets the recordsource for the recordset of Adodc2 to be all the invoices for the current customer.

Finally, the Refresh method goes ahead and retrieves the recordset from the INVOICE table on the disk database. This data is automatically displayed in DataGrid2.

9.12 Exercises

Data Control and tied text boxes

1. Create a new project containing a form with a conventional data control and a set of tied text boxes and command buttons that can be used to add, delete and change records in the PRODUCT table of the prod_del.mdb database.

2. Further develop the project to include error-handling code.

3. By using frames to 'fence off' parts of the form, include appropriate error prevention techniques that will prevent the user from executing inappropriate command button sequences.

4. Provide a FindFirst button and enable and disable it appropriately. For example, the user should not be able to click one of the action buttons and then click the Find button.

5. Provide a FindNext button. Use the NoMatch property of the recordset to display a message box when there are no (more) records which match the search string.

Menu and Data Grids

6. Using the **accts.mdb** database, create a new project containing:

   - Three forms frmCustomer, frmInvoice and frmPayment, each of which contains a data control and tied DBGrid, or ADO data control and ADO DataGrid (depending on which version of VB you have – use ADO for VB6, DBGrid for any other version). These forms should contain facilities for adding, deleting and changing records in each of the tables. Include error-handling code to trap errors. Inserting duplicate records, leaving out mandatory fields, and breaking referential integrity should all be 'handled'.

   - A form frmMenu containing a menu only. The first menu item should contain a submenu that enables the user to update the Customer, Invoice and Payment tables by loading (displaying) one of the forms created above. You can load and display a form using, for example, **frmCustomer.Show**. You can 'hide' a form using, for example, **frmCustomer.Hide**. This keeps it in memory. A subsequent Show will not cause a Form_Load event. You can still refer to its controls from another form using, for example, **frmCustomer.Adodc1.Recordset!c_no**. You can unload a form (hide it *and* remove it from memory) using Unload, for example **Unload frmCustomer**. Make frmMenu the startup form.

Check the following:

(a) It is possible to update each table separately.

(b) It is not possible to insert records with duplicate primary key values, for example two customers with the same customer number.

(c) It is not possible to break referential integrity. For example, it should not be possible to delete a customer with outstanding invoices, and it should not be possible to insert an invoice for a customer who does not exist.

(d) It is not possible to insert a record with a null in a mandatory field.

(e) It is not possible to crash the program.

7. Link the forms so that moving to a new customer record in frmCustomer causes the set of invoices displayed in the form frmInvoice (if it is loaded) automatically to change to the current customer's invoices and the set of payments displayed in the form frmPayment to automatically change to the payments for the current invoice. For the conventional data control and DBGrid (VB4 and VB5) use the reposition event and for the ADO data control and ADO DataGrid use the MoveComplete event of the respective data control.

8. Add FindFirst and FindNext functionality to each of the forms. The search should be on c_no (surname) for frmCustomer, and inv_no for frmInvoice and frmPayment. Note: Only FindFirst functionality will then be necessary on frmCustomer. Why?

9. Add a generalized Find form, called from a separate Find menu item, which will search all three tables for a given number or string. The functionality should be similar to Access's Find facility. This will require a separate form frmFind.

10. On frmInvoice and frmPayment, automatically display the invoice and payment totals respectively. The totals should immediately reflect any changes to these amount fields in the data grids.

10

Visual Basic database programming using Data Access Objects (DAO)

In this chapter you will learn:

- the DAO database programming commands
- about DAO recordsets
- how to program using DAO properties and methods
- how to embed SQL commands in Visual basic code.

10.1 Introduction

In the previous chapter, we took advantage of the ability of the data control to help in developing fast database applications. That approach of tying a data control to a database and recordset and a set of text boxes has its limitations, however. If you want to have more control over the way the program interacts with the database, then the most popular way to do this at present is the DAO (Data Access Objects) approach. In the next chapter, we describe Microsoft's latest database programming approach, ADO. However, most of the Visual Basic code you will see for some time to come will be DAO code. It is of course possible to use all three approaches in the same application, but we recommend that you separate their use into clearly different parts of the application. Many applications use just DAO.

Using DAO, you, the application developer, will be responsible for writing explicit code for connecting to a database (or databases), defining recordsets, manipulating field values and so on. Fortunately, you can use embedded SQL commands to retrieve the right data from the database or even to update it. Using SQL to define the recordsets you need, containing no more data than necessary from the disk database, and then manipulating the rows individually using DAO commands is 'the way to go' if you want efficient database processing. In many ways, DAO frees you to use your knowledge of the database and your algorithm-writing skills to produce fast code that uses minimal memory.

We follow now with a summary of the main DAO commands you will need. These commands will cover most of the database manipulation you will ever require. Fine details of each of these commands can be found in Help. We cover here the DAO commands used with Jet 2.5/3.0 upwards. These will work with VB4 upwards. Equivalent commands for earlier versions of the Jet Engine are given in Appendix 2.

10.2 DAO commands (Jet 2.5/3.0 and above)

Opening a database
```
Set MyDb = OpenDatabase("accts.mdb")
```

Opening a table
```
Dim MyTable as Recordset
Set MyTable = MyDb.OpenRecordset("Customer", dbOpenTable)
```

Opening a Dynaset
```
Dim MyDynaset as Recordset
Set MyDynaset = MyDb.OpenRecordset("Customer", dbOpenDynaset)
```
or, using an SQL query to retrieve data:
```
Dim MyDynaset as Recordset
Set MyDynaset = MyDb.OpenRecordset("select c_no, sname from customer
where city = 'London'", dbOpenDynaset)
```

Opening a Snapshot
```
Dim MySnapshot as Recordset
Set MySnapshot = MyDb.OpenRecordset("Customer", dbOpenSnapshot)
```

Referring to a field
```
MyDynaset!sname = "Lauri"
```
or
```
MyDynaset!fields(2) = "Lauri"
```

Closing a Recordset
```
MyDynaset.Close
```

Closing a database
```
MyDb.Close
```

Navigating
```
MyDynaset.MoveFirst
MyDynaset.MoveLast
MyDynaset.MoveNext
MyDynaset.MovePrevious
MyDynaset.FindFirst
MyDynaset.FindNext
```

Inserting a record

```
MyDynaset.AddNew

Insert field values for the new record here

MyDynaset.Update
```

Deleting a record

```
MyDynaset.Delete
MyDynaset.MoveFirst (or MoveLast, MovePrevious, MoveNext)
```

Changing a record

```
MyDynaset.Edit

Make changes to the current record's field values here

MyDynaset.Update
```

- A *recordset* is a set of rows of data that have been extracted into memory from the disk database.
- A table type recordset is a copy of the whole table.
- A *dynaset* is a recordset that can be updated. The recordset can be based on an SQL query.
- A *snapshot* is a recordset that cannot be updated. The recordset can be based on an SQL query.

You specify which type of recordset you want in the second parameter of the OpenRecordset command.

Table recordsets and snapshots are said to be faster to process than dynasets, but we have found that for small to medium recordsets, there is little noticeable difference. We have also found that in general the greatest determinant of speed for processing large numbers of records is the algorithm you use and whether you use indexes appropriately. Table recordsets allow fast searches on an index, using the *Seek* command. There is an example of Seek below.

It's a good idea to close recordsets and databases when you have finished with them. This frees up system recources.

The navigation and update commands are the same as with the data control.

We continue this chapter with programming examples using these DAO commands.

10.3 Displaying data in a VB Grid

We illustrate some of the principles involved in procedural database programming in VB by filling a VB Grid with data from the CUS table. Grids are a useful device for displaying more than one record of a database at once.

The VB form as shown in Fig. 10.1 contains a command button and a Grid. **Grid1.Cols** = **10** has been specified in the properties window. This is because we

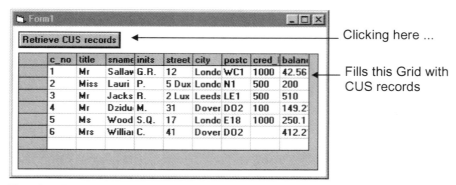

Fig. 10.1 Form with Grid used to display whole CUS table.

want to display the CUS table, which has nine columns (fields). We need one column for each of the nine CUS fields and one fixed column, which will allow the user to change the heights of the grid rows. Here is the VB code.

```
Dim db1 As database  ◄─────────── Declare the database variables in
Dim ta1 As table                  General Declarations

Sub Form_Load ()
  Show                         ─── Link up to the database
  'Link up to database ◄
  Set db1 = OpenDatabase(app.Path & "\..\..\database\accts.mdb")
  Set ta1 = db1.OpenTable("cus") ◄─── Open the CUS table
  'Put headings into Grid
  grid1.Row = 0                    ◄──── You have to set the
  grid1.Col = 1: grid1.Text = "c_no"     row and column
  grid1.Col = 2: grid1.Text = "title"    number of the grid
  grid1.Col = 3: grid1.Text = "sname2"   to define the current
  grid1.Col = 4: grid1.Text = "inits"    cell before you can
  grid1.Col = 5: grid1.Text = "street"   insert text into it.
  grid1.Col = 6: grid1.Text = "city"
  grid1.Col = 7: grid1.Text = "postc"
  grid1.Col = 8: grid1.Text = "cred_lim"
  grid1.Col = 9: grid1.Text = "balance"
  grid1.HighLight = False
  grid1.Rows = 2               ─── A loop is used to access one CUS
  grid1.Row = 1                    record at a time. A MoveNext
End Sub                            operation goes to the next record.

Sub Command1_Click ()
  Row = 1 'used by AddItem to show position in Grid1 where record
should go
  Do While Not ta1.EOF
    grid1.AddItem Chr(9) & ta1!c_no & Chr(9) &
```

```
ta1!title & Chr(9) & ta1!sname & Chr(9) &
ta1!inits & Chr(9) & ta1!street & Chr(9) &
ta1!city & Chr(9) & ta1!postc & Chr(9) &
ta1!cred_lim & Chr(9) & ta1!balance, Row
    Row = Row + 1
    ta1.MoveNext
  Loop
End Sub
```

This long line inserts a CUS record into Grid1 at row Row. The fields to be inserted must be separated by a Tab chr(9).

In General Declarations, we define db1 as a database object and ta1 as a table object. You can of course call these objects anything you want. They will be referred to by these names throughout the form. If they were required to be accessed more globally, say in other forms, then they would be Dim'ed in a module.

The initialization is performed in Form_Load. Show makes the form visible immediately. This is sometimes useful when debugging: you can see the effects on the form of various instructions when single-stepping through the code. The db1 database object is set to the acctd.mdb database. This 'setting' is simply a naming operation; accts.mdb will, in this program, be known as 'db1'. The means of doing this is the OpenDatabase method. app.path is the path of the current application. and the \..\..\ indicate that the folder 'database', in which the accts.mdb database is to be found, is two levels of folder up from the current path. Normally, app.path and the '..' device would not be necessary; you would just put the whole absolute pathname in the OpenDatabase argument. The '..' device is useful where you are moving a project and its database at the same time, say from a floppy disk to a hard disk, and the database is in a fixed position with respect to the code.

In the next line, the table object ta1 is set to be the table CUS in the database object db1. In the object-oriented language that Visual Basic uses, the OpenTable *method* is applied to the db1 database *object* to produce the ta1 table object. What is actually happening is that VB looks in the db1 database and finds the CUS table. It then reads that table into memory and calls the resulting *recordset* ta1. Note that we had to Dim (declare) db1 and ta1 in General Declarations so that these object names, the db1 database and the ta1 recordset, would be accessible to the other Sub (subroutine) in the project, Command1_Click.

As you can see from the figure, this program simply reads data from the CUS table and displays it in a Grid. There are various forms of grid in the various versions of Visual Basic. Be prepared, when moving between versions, to have to tell VB where the relevant .vbx or .ocx file is to be found. There are essentially two types of grid – the simple grid, and the data-aware grid. The data-aware grid is linked to a data control and cuts out a lot of the coding, and is suitable for simple applications. It has a large number of properties and a large number of methods. Here we are using the simple grid. It offers more flexibility at the expense of more coding (the usual situation in database programming).

Here are some of the main properties of grids:

Rows   the number of rows in the grid
Cols   the number of columns in the grid
FixedRows   the number of fixed (greyed) rows at the top
FixedCols   the number of fixed (greyed) columns at the left
Row   the current row number, starting at 0
Col   the current column number, starting at 0
Text   the data in a cell

It's often a good idea to have a fixed row and a fixed column because then your user can change the column widths and row heights by clicking and dragging in the lines between the cells. In the current project, the following settings were made at design time in the properties window:

```
grid1.fixedrows = 0
grid1.fixedcols = 0
```

If I wanted to put the string "hello" into the fourth row of the third column of a grid called grid1, I would have to use the following code:

```
grid1.row = 3          'set the row
grid1.col = 2          'set the column
grid1.text = "hello"   'put the data in
```

Remember that the numbering of rows and columns starts from zero.

If I wanted to read data from the twelfth row and nineteenth column into a text box text1, I would use the code:

```
grid1.row = 11              'set the row
grid1.col = 18              'set the column
text1.text = grid1.text     'get the data
```

Back in Form_Load of the current project, the first line that accesses the grid is grid1.Row = 0. This sets the current row to the top row.

In the next nine lines of code, the column number is progressively set to 1, 2 . . . 9 and at each step, the column heading is put into the cell. These column headings correspond to the field names of the CUS table. In a real application, names that were more user-friendly would be used. The colon (:) allows two or more VB statements to be put on the same line.

The line grid1.HighLight = False is a way of removing the default grid behaviour of making the currently 'selected' cells blue. The next two lines may appear a bit odd. We set the current number of rows to two and the current row to that second row. This is so that we can use the AddItem method in the Command1_Click routine. AddItem adds a whole row to the grid at once.

We now describe the Command1_Click code. The first argument of the AddItem method is the row of data you want to add to the grid, and the second argument is the position you want to add it. If you leave the second argument as it is, and don't increment it, you might find that the data as added to the grid comes out upside-down, i.e. last database row first. We get round this by always having a blank row at the end of the grid and incrementing the value of the second parameter each time. We have called the variable we have used to do this Row. The first argument of the AddItem method is the actual row of data we want to add to the grid. This has to be a single string with the data items separated by Tab characters. The ASCII code for Tab is 9 and the VB Chr function produces this value. '&' is the string concatenation character in VB. Note that the first column, a fixed column in our grid, is skipped by starting the string with a Tab.

When we enter the Command1_Click code, the recordset has already been opened by Form_Load and the recordset is now resident in memory. The current record is the first record in the recordset ta1. We refer to individual fields in this record using the recordset name (ta1) followed by an exclamation mark (!) and then the field name. There are three common ways to refer to a database field in VB. For example, we can refer to the c_no field as any one of:

```
ta1!c_no
ta1.fields("c_no")
ta1.fields(0)
```

'Fields' refers to the fields *collection*, as VB calls it, associated with the recordset. The last method gives the ordinal position of the field in the database table and the corresponding recordset. It's only useful if you are not sure of the field name or if you want to process each field in a loop, a FOR loop for example. Here we are using the first form.

We use a Do While loop (rather than a FOR loop) because we don't know how many records are in the recordset. 'ta1.EOF' becomes true when the end of the recordset is reached, that is, when we attempt to move past the last record in the recordset. At the end of the Do While loop the statement Row = Row + 1 puts the AddItem pointer at the bottom (blank) row of the grid and ta1.MoveNext moves the pointer to the next record in the recordset. There *is* a property of the recordset called Recordcount. We could have used it in a FOR loop instead of the Do While. However, RecordCount may not (according to VB Help) always be correct unless you precede it with a MoveLast (and then a MoveFirst to get you back to the beginning of the recordset). That's extra code, so the current Do While format seems to us preferable.

10.4 Editing data in a VB Grid

To illustrate some more points in DAO programming, we now show how to use the KeyDown event in a VB grid to edit cells and then show how to save the affected record using SelChange.

The strategy we shall adopt is that when the user changes row in the grid, two things happen:

(a) the field values in the current row are put into the current record, and

(b) the change is saved by performing an Update operation.

This is similar to the operation of an Access grid.

This is a conventional Grid. Data from the CUS table has been copied into it using VB code. In addition, users can type into a grid cell to change the corresponding record field value. Any change is saved when the current row number of the grid is changed and when the form is unloaded.

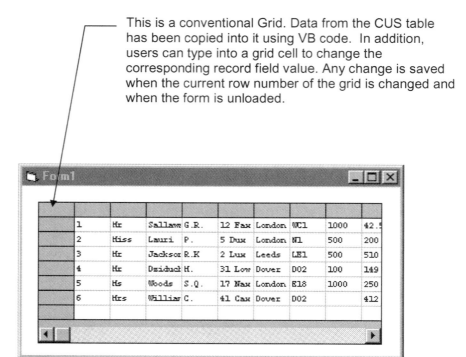

Fig. 10.2 Simple VB form allowing changes to be made.

The code for this project is shown below. A description of the code follows.

```
Dim db1 As database
Dim ta1 As table
Dim Grid1CurrentRow
Dim Grid1Changes

Sub Form_Load ()
  Set db1 = OpenDatabase(app.Path & "\accts.mdb")
  Set ta1 = db1.OpenTable("cus")
  grid1.HighLight = False
  n = 0
  GetCusRecords
  grid1.Row = 1
  Grid1CurrentRow = grid1.Row
  Grid1Changes = False
End Sub

Sub GetCusRecords ()
  grid1.Rows = 2
  ta1.MoveFirst
  grid1.Row = 0
  Do While Not ta1.EOF
```

```
      grid1.Row = grid1.Row + 1
      grid1.AddItem Chr(9) & ta1!c_no & Chr(9) & ta1!title & Chr(9)
& ta1!sname & Chr(9) & ta1!inits & Chr(9) & ta1!street & Chr(9) &
ta1!city & Chr(9) & ta1!postc & Chr(9) & ta1!cred_lim & Chr(9) &
ta1!balance, grid1.Row
      ta1.MoveNext
  Loop
End Sub

Sub Grid1_KeyPress (keyascii As Integer)
  'The KeyPress event occurs when user types in a grid cell
  Grid1Changes = True
  If keyascii = 8 Then 'backspace
    x = Len(grid1.Text)
    If x > 0 Then
      grid1.Text = Left(grid1.Text, x - 1)
    End If
  Else
    grid1.Text = grid1.Text & Chr(keyascii)
  End If
End Sub

Sub Grid1_SelChange ()
  'The SelChange event occurs when the user changes to another cell.
  'When it's a new row and changes have been made (KeyDown event), save
record.
  x = grid1.Row: y = grid1.Col
'Save the new row number
  If grid1.Row <> Grid1CurrentRow Then
'User has moved to a new row
    SaveAnyChanges
  End If
  grid1.Row = x: grid1.Col = y
'Restore new row number
  Grid1CurrentRow = x
  Grid1Changes = False
End Sub

Sub SaveAnyChanges ()
    If Grid1Changes = True Then
'User may have made changes, detected by Grid1_KeyPress event
      grid1.Row = Grid1CurrentRow
'Go back to the old row and save the values into the database.
      grid1.Col = 1
'Make the corresponding database record current . . .
      ta1.Index = "PrimaryKey"
'You can't FindFirst in a Table; you have to Seek . . .
```

```
        ta1.Seek " = ", Val(grid1.Text)
        ta1.Edit
    'Edit it . . .
        grid1.Col = 1: ta1!c_no = grid1.Text
    'Put the new values into the current record . . .
        grid1.Col = 2: ta1!title = grid1.Text
        grid1.Col = 3: ta1!sname = grid1.Text
        grid1.Col = 4: ta1!inits = grid1.Text
        grid1.Col = 5: ta1!street = grid1.Text
        grid1.Col = 6: ta1!city = grid1.Text
        grid1.Col = 7: ta1!postc = grid1.Text
        grid1.Col = 8: ta1!cred_lim = grid1.Text
        grid1.Col = 9: ta1!balance = grid1.Text
        ta1.Update
    'Write the changed record to disk.
      End If
    End Sub


    Sub Form_Unload (Cancel As Integer)
      SaveAnyChanges
    End Sub
```

Description of the code

In the `General Declaration` section, we first declare `db1` as the database object and `ta1` as the table object that will be used in the project. We declare them here, as we do the following two items, in `General Declarations` rather than individual `Sub` procedures, so that they are 'visible' from all the `Sub`s in the project. We say they are 'global' to the form. If there were several forms and we wanted the database and recordset to be common across them all, we would have declared them in a separate code module. `Grid1CurrentRow` and `Grid1Changes` are declared here for the same reason.

In `Form_load` for this form, we define the database and table objects as in the previous project. Notice that this time, the database is in the same folder as the project (the 'App' – application). We are again accessing the whole `CUS` table. The syntax here is for VB3 and VB4, and would be different in VB5 and VB6:

Instead of:

```
Set ta1 = db1.OpenTable("cus")
```

we would have

```
Set ta1 = db1.OpenRecordset("cus",dbOpenTable)
```

These minor differences in syntax are discussed in Appendix 2.

`GetCusRecords` is a call to a subroutine to populate the grid with the current set of records in the CUS table. Having retrieved the records, the current grid row is set to 1 and the flag `Grid1Changes` is set to False.

We now describe the `GetCusRecords` subroutine. Its purpose is to populate the grid `grid1` with the current set of CUS records. The code is almost identical to that used in the previous project. The first line sets the number of grid rows to 2. Next, we ensure that the current record is the first in the recordset, just in case the pointer had been moved by previous processes. Remember that this routine can be called from several different places in the project, some of which may alter the current record position.

A slightly different approach to giving a value to the second parameter of the `AddItem` grid method is taken here. It's initialized to zero and incremented first thing in the loop. The effect is the same. As before, the first parameter of the `AddItem` method, the string containing the data field values of the current row of the recordset, separated by `Tab` characters, is formed. `AddItem` adds this recordset row to the grid. This is followed by a `MoveNext`, which moves the pointer to the next record in the recordset.

The next Sub we shall look at is the `Grid1_KeyPress` routine. Its purpose is to respond to any key presses the user makes in the grid. Any character other than backspace (ASCII code 8) is simply appended to the contents of the current grid cell. Pressing backspace results in the rightmost character in the current grid cell being deleted. This is how the code does that: First the flag `Grid-1Changes` ('flag' is programmer jargon for a variable with two values – true and false; flags are often used to show whether something has happened or not) is set to True. In this program this flag is used in the `SaveAnyChanges` subroutine to decide whether it's necessary to update the database table CUS or not (see later).

In the `IF` statement that follows, we check the value of the `keyascii` argument that is native to the `KeyPress` event. This contains the ASCII code for the last keyboard key pressed. If it's backspace (code 8), we first get the length of the text in the current grid cell. Clearly we don't want to attempt to chop off the last character if the string is empty – that would lead to a runtime error, so we check to see if the length of the current grid cell's content is zero. We use the `Len` function to do this. The actual truncation of the last character is performed using the `Left` function. The first argument of the `Left` function is the text under consideration; the second argument is the number of characters (starting from the left) you want to retain. (VB contains other similar string manipulation functions `Right` and `Mid`, which you could check out in Help.)

For any keystroke other than `Backspace`, the `Else` part of the `If` statement applies. This simply concatenates `keyascii`, the character just pressed, to the end of the data in the current cell.

The question arises, having made a change to the data in the grid, when should we save that change into the actual recordset and the database table CUS? In the extreme case, you could save the changes after every keystroke. At the other extreme, you could have a command button that saves the changes when the user requests it.

Another alternative is that after a fixed interval, controlled by a timer, changes are automatically saved. If you adopted that approach, you'd also have to ensure that changes were saved when the user closed the form. When we use VB to code the database processing, we have the *choice* of which approach to use. The approach used here is that the change is saved when the user clicks on another row in the grid. This is the approach used in Access – changing to a new row saves any changes to the current row. The code that does this is contained in the Sub `Grid1_SelChange`.

Consequently, we now move to the subroutine `Grid1_SelChange`, which, like `GetCusRecords`, is a routine we have created ourselves, as distinct from being a standard event routine. After the two comments at the beginning of `Grid1_Sel-Change`, we save the new row and column number. The previous row number is stored in the global variable `Grid1CurrentRow`. The `If` statement that follows checks whether the change of cell is actually a change of row. If it is, our subroutine `SaveAnyChanges` is called. We shall look at this Sub shortly. Since `SaveAny-Changes` may have (and probably *has*) changed the current row and column, we restore these to their previous values in the next line of `Grid1_SelChange`.

We now turn our attention to the subroutine `SaveAnyChanges`. In this routine we first test the variable `Grid1Changes`. That was set to True by any changes being made in the `Grid1_KeyPress` event's code. If it's false, we exit this Sub. Otherwise the following happens.

First we return to the row that has just been changed. Remember that the changes are saved to the database only when the user clicks on another row. This could be *any* row. However, the statement `grid1.Row = Grid1CurrentRow` goes back to the current row, which is where the data the user has just changed in the grid is located. Having moved to the right grid row, it's now necessary to make the corresponding record in the recordset the current record. We have to do this so that we can copy the new data from the grid row into it and then save it to the database.

Since the `ta1` recordset was opened as a table object, the record can only be sought using a Seek method. Seek uses an index to locate the desired record. Here the field we are searching on is the primary key field `c_no`, whose value is located in column 1 of the grid. We make the correct cell in the grid current with `grid1.Col = 1` and then select the current index to be the primary key index `PrimaryKey`. We do this with the instruction:

```
ta1.Index = "PrimaryKey".
```

We then use the command

```
ta1.Seek " = ", Val(grid1.Text)
```

to locate the right record in the recordset.

The next step is to edit the recordset record using `ta1.Edit`. You must do this before making changes to any record in the recordset. In the following nine lines, the values in the current row of the grid are transferred to the fields in the current record in the recordset.

After the values have been transferred from the grid to the current record, we then save the changes to the database on disk by using the Update method. The command `ta1.Update` means 'update the data on the database, i.e. on the disk, to make it identical with the data in the recordset in memory'.

Note that in the `Form_Unload` routine, the `SaveAnyChanges` subroutine is called. This is necessary to cover the case where the user closes the current form without moving to a new row to save the changes.

10.5 Editing data in a VB Grid: two forms

In this project, full Add, Change and Delete facilities are achieved and a Grid is used to select the desired record (Click event) and a separate form is used to add new records into the grid and the recordset and make changes.

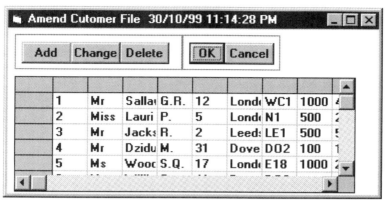

Fig. 10.3 The main form.

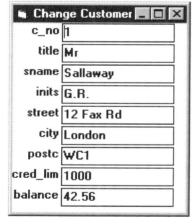

Fig. 10.4 The Edit form.

Navigation
To find the desired record, the user scrolls through the records displayed on the grid. To select a record, the user just clicks the grid anywhere in that record. The grid click event code ensures that the corresponding record in the recordset in memory is selected.

Add
To add a new record, the user clicks the Add button. This loads Form2 with blank text boxes and the cursor in the first text box. The user types in the new customer record and then clicks the OK button. The user can back out, i.e. cancel the Add at any time by clicking the Cancel button. There is full error handling, so that if, for

example, the user tries to enter a duplicate customer number (which is not allowed because c_no is the primary key), a message box is displayed and the Add operation is cancelled.

Change

To change a record, the user clicks the record image on the grid to select it and then clicks the Change button. This loads the Edit form, where the user can make the changes required. The user can cancel the change at any time with the Cancel button or save the changes with the OK button.

Delete

This simply involves selecting the record by clicking the grid and then either backing out with the Cancel button, or confirming the deletion with the OK button.

The code

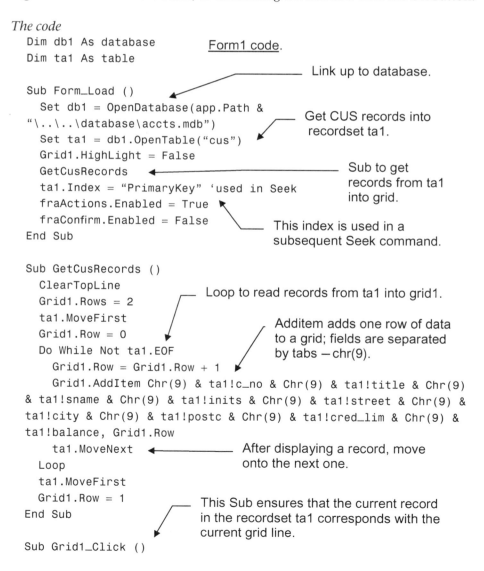

```
Dim db1 As database          Form1 code.
Dim ta1 As table
                                        Link up to database.

Sub Form_Load ()
  Set db1 = OpenDatabase(app.Path &
"\..\..\database\accts.mdb")              Get CUS records into
  Set ta1 = db1.OpenTable("cus")          recordset ta1.
  Grid1.HighLight = False
  GetCusRecords                           Sub to get
  ta1.Index = "PrimaryKey" 'used in Seek  records from ta1
  fraActions.Enabled = True               into grid.
  fraConfirm.Enabled = False
End Sub                                   This index is used in a
                                          subsequent Seek command.

Sub GetCusRecords ()
  ClearTopLine
  Grid1.Rows = 2              Loop to read records from ta1 into grid1.
  ta1.MoveFirst
  Grid1.Row = 0                          Additem adds one row of data
  Do While Not ta1.EOF                   to a grid; fields are separated
    Grid1.Row = Grid1.Row + 1            by tabs — chr(9).
    Grid1.AddItem Chr(9) & ta1!c_no & Chr(9) & ta1!title & Chr(9)
& ta1!sname & Chr(9) & ta1!inits & Chr(9) & ta1!street & Chr(9) &
ta1!city & Chr(9) & ta1!postc & Chr(9) & ta1!cred_lim & Chr(9) &
ta1!balance, Grid1.Row
    ta1.MoveNext               After displaying a record, move
  Loop                         onto the next one.
  ta1.MoveFirst
  Grid1.Row = 1               This Sub ensures that the current record
End Sub                        in the recordset ta1 corresponds with the
                               current grid line.

Sub Grid1_Click ()
```

```
     On Error GoTo grid1_click_error
     'Make correct record current
     x = Grid1.Col 'save current col position
     Grid1.Col = 1 'move to col 1 to key c_no
     ta1.Seek " = ", Val(Grid1.Text) 'make correct CUS record
current
     Grid1.Col = x 'go back to col
     If ta1.NoMatch Then
        MsgBox "Record not found", 48, "Attempting to reposition"
        ta1.MoveFirst
        Grid1.Row = 1: Grid1.Col = 1
     End If
grid1_Click_OK:
     Exit Sub
grid1_click_error:
     x = "Error " & Err & " " & Error(Err)
     y = "Attempting to reposition"
     MsgBox x, 48, y
     Resume grid1_Click_OK
End Sub

Sub cmdAdd_Click ()
     current_command = "Add"
     form2.Show
     ClearForm2Fields
     fraActions.Enabled = False
     fraConfirm.Enabled = True
End Sub

Sub cmdChange_Click ()
     current_command = "Change"
     fraActions.Enabled = False
     fraConfirm.Enabled = True
     Grid1.Enabled = False
     form2.Show
     move_grid_row_to_form2
End Sub

Sub cmdDelete_Click ()
     current_command = "Delete"
     fraActions.Enabled = False
     fraConfirm.Enabled = True
End Sub

Sub cmdOK_Click ()
     On Error GoTo cmdOK_Click_Error
     If current_command = "Change" Or current_command = "Add" Then
        If current_command = "Change" Then ta1.Edit
```

A Seek locates the CUS record using the current index PrimaryKey.

Standard error handling.

Allow a new CUS record to be added using Form2.

Call a Sub (see below) to clear the text boxes in Form2.

Allow changes to occur to the current CUS record.

Move data from current grid row to Form2.

Allow deletion of the current CUS record.

A change to a record must be preceded by Edit.

AddNew adds a new
blank record.

```
    If current_command = "Add" Then ta1.AddNew
    move_data_to_current_record
    ta1.Update
  End If
```

Save the changes to
disk.

```
  If current_command = "Delete" Then
      ta1.Delete
```

Delete the current
record.

```
      ta1.MoveFirst
  End If
cmdOK_Click_OK:
```

After a Delete, there is no
current record, so MoveFirst.

```
  GetCusRecords
  Grid1.Enabled = True
  form2.Hide
```

Read the records from the
updated recordset back into
the grid.

```
  fraActions.Enabled = True
  fraConfirm.Enabled = False
  current_command = ""
  Exit Sub
cmdOK_Click_Error:
```

Standard error handling.

```
  x = "Error " & Err & " " & Error(Err)
  y = "Attempting to " & current_command
  MsgBox x, 48, y
  Resume cmdOK_Click_OK
End Sub

Sub cmdCancel_Click ()
  form2.Hide
```

Cancelling changes to the
database simply involves
hiding Form2 and enabling the
grid and the action buttons.

```
  fraActions.Enabled = True
  fraConfirm.Enabled = False
  Grid1.Enabled = True
  current_command = ""
End Sub

Sub move_grid_row_to_form2 ()
  For i = 9 To 1 Step - 1
    Grid1.Col = i: form2.Text1(i) = Grid1.Text
  Next i
End Sub

Sub ClearForm2Fields ()
  For i = 1 To 9
    form2.Text1(i).Text = ""
  Next i
  form2.Text1(1).SetFocus
End Sub
```

```
Sub ClearTopLine ()
  Grid1.Row = 1
  For i = 1 To 9
    form1.Grid1.Col = i: form1.Grid1.Text = ""
  Next i
  form1.Grid1.Row = 1: form1.Grid1.Col = 1
End Sub
```

Move the field values from Form2 to the current record.

```
Sub move_data_to_current_record ()
  For i = 1 To 9
    ta1.Fields(i − 1) = form2.Text1(i).Text
  Next i
End Sub
```

Move the field values from Form2 to the current row in the grid.

```
Sub move_data_to_grid ()
  For i = 1 To 9
    form1.Grid1.Col = i: form1.Grid1.Text = form2.Text1(i).Text
  Next i
  form1.Grid1.Col = 1
End Sub
```

This Sub makes the grid expand when the user expands Form1, the grid columns expand, and Form2 stays 'attached' to the right-hand side of Form1.

```
Sub Form_Resize ()
  Grid1.Width = .9 * Me.Width
  Grid1.Height = .6 * Me.Height
  For i = 1 To 9
    Grid1.ColWidth(i) = (Grid1.Width − Grid1.ColWidth(0)) / 9
  Next i
  form2.Left = form1.Left + form1.Width
  form2.Top = form1.Top
End Sub
```

Timer1.Interval is 1000. Every 1000mS, Now puts the date and time into Form1.Caption.

```
Sub Timer1_Timer ()
  Me.Caption = "Amend Customer File " & Now
  'Beep
End Sub
```

Form2 Code. Form2 sites itself next to Form1 and displays relevant caption.

```
Sub Form_Activate ()
  Me.Left = form1.Left + form1.Width
  Me.Top = form1.Top
  Me.Caption = current_command & " Customer"
End Sub
```

Module1 code. The variable current_command has to be accessible to both Form1 and Form2. It must therefore be declared in a Module.

```
Global current_command
```

Code description

In General Declarations, db1 is declared as a database object and ta1 is declared as a table object. This project was developed using VB3. For later versions of VB, minor changes have to be made. These are described. In later versions of VB, ta1 would be declared as follows:

```
Dim ta1 As Recordset
```

We now describe the code in Form_Load for Form1. First, the database is opened using the OpenDatabase method. This gives the path to the Jet database file accts.mdb. Then the table recordset ta1 is opened. This creates the recordset ta1 in memory by copying the data from the CUS table of the database. The OpenTable method is used. In later versions of VB the DAO code is:

```
Set ta1 = db1.OpenRecordset("cus", dbOpenTable)
```

The statement Grid1.HighLight = False removes the blue coloration from the currently selected cell in the grid, which can be a bit of a distraction when it is not needed.

Next, our subroutine GetCusRecords is called. This copies the records from the CUS recordset ta1 into the grid, so that when the program first starts, the user can see the CUS table data. The code for GetCusRecords is described below. Next, in Form_Load for Form1, the current index for the ta1 recordset is set. You have to do this if you want to use the Seek command because Seek retrieves a record using an index. In our case we shall want to retrieve a given customer record via its c_no (customer number) field. This happens to be the primary key of the CUS table, so we set the index to 'PrimaryKey'. As we have discussed before, when you create a Jet database table and specify a field or fields as the primary key, Jet creates an *index* called PrimaryKey.

We have placed two VB Frames on Form1. We use these as an easy way of enabling the two groups of Command buttons on the form. When the user clicks on a button in the Add, Change, Delete group, that group is disabled until the user completes that operation by subsequently clicking either the OK or the Cancel button. This prevents the user from carrying out inappropriate sequences of operations. In Form_Load for Form1, we enable the frame around the Add, Change, Delete button group (called 'fraActions'), and disable the frame around the OK and Cancel buttons (called 'fraConfirm'), because it wouldn't be appropriate to click either the OK button or the Cancel button before having clicked one of the buttons in the first group.

We now describe the subroutine GetCusRecords. This first calls our subroutine ClearTopLine which sets all the cells in the top row of the grid to empty string ("") to remove any data currently there, and sets the current cell to row 1, column 1. It's not necessary to clear *all* of the grid rows, since the next line sets the number of rows to 2, the first row – row 0 is the fixed row at the top, which perhaps ought to contain the column titles, and the second row – row 1.

There follows a Do While loop, which loops while there are more rows in the recordset ta1. The Additem method applied to grid1 adds a complete row of data to the grid. The individual fields have to be separated by the ASCII tab character. Its code is 9, so the (unprintable) tab character is represented using the VB function Chr.

We have found that it's wise to leave the last row of a grid blank and to increment the second argument of the AddItem method as shown. The last command in the loop is ta1.MoveNext, which moves to the next record on the ta1 recordset, ready for it to be copied (the next time round the loop) into the next row of the grid.

When the MoveNext eventually moves past the last record in the recordset ta1, it encounters the end-of-file marker and the EOF property of the recordset becomes true, ending the loop. After the loop is completed, we move the record pointer to the first record in the recordset, and the grid row is set at row 1, just to ensure that the grid and the recordset are 'in line'. After Form_Load, nothing happens until there is a user-initiated event, such as a click on the grid or on one of the buttons.

We now describe the Sub Grid1_Click. While it seems unlikely that a runtime error could be caused by the user clicking the grid, this subroutine includes error handling. The line:

```
On Error GoTo grid1_click_error
```

'says' that, should any error occur during the execution of *any* instruction within the current Sub, go to the code following the label grid1_click_error. This is a useful approach to error handling because it

- prevents us having to create lots of input validation code;
- prevents us having to write individual segments of code for each possible error;
- after corrective action, allows processing to proceed.

The 'corrective action' is more critical where an attempt at an update to a database has gone wrong in some way, because we don't want to leave the database in an 'inconsistent state'. The error-handling code (in our case after the label grid1_click_error), would have to take corrective action depending on the nature of the error, as determined by the error code returned by the Jet Engine and/ or the operating system Windows.

The next line in the Grid1_Click subroutine saves the current column position in the row. Then we move to column 1 to pick up the value of the field c_no. This is used in the Seek operation to locate in the recordset ta1 the record whose customer number *is* that value. The current grid column can then be restored. After the seek, we include some explicit error-handling code which tells the user that the required record could not be found. The NoMatch property of the recordset becomes true only after a failed Seek. The code displays a message box and goes back to the first record in the recordset.

We now pass to a consideration of the update operations that can occur in this program.

If the user clicks the Add button, the subroutine cmdAdd_Click executes. The variable current_command, declared in a separate code module Module1 to make it visible to both forms in this project (see below), is given the value "Add". This is used in the cmdOK_Click subroutine to decide what sort of follow-up action to carry out. Form2 is then loaded and the routine ClearForm2Fields executed so that the text boxes on Form2 are blank. Then the frame containing the command buttons Add, Change and Delete is disabled, and that containing the OK and Cancel buttons enabled. This is to ensure a logical sequence of button clicks.

After the Add button is clicked, the user will type values for the fields into Form2. If the OK button is then clicked to save the new record, subroutine cmdOK_Click will execute.

This is described below.

If the Change button is clicked, cmdChange_Click executes and it sets current_command to "Change". The command buttons are then enabled and disabled as above, the Grid is disabled to prevent the user clicking to another record, Form2 is loaded, and the routine move_grid_row_to_form2 is executed. This moves the data in the current grid row to the text boxes in Form2 ready for editing.

If the Delete button is clicked, current_command is set to "Delete" and the command buttons enabled and disabled as above.

We now describe the code in the cmdOK_Click subroutine.

If any error occurs anywhere in this subroutine, control is passed to label cmdOK_Click_Error. The current command variable shows which button was previously clicked.

If it was the Add button then an AddNew method is run against the recordset ta1. This puts a blank record at the end of the recordset.

If the previous command button clicked was Change, then an Edit method is executed, allowing the current record in the recordset to be edited. In either case, the subroutine move_data_to_current_record is executed and this moves the data from Form2, field by field, to the current record. The Update method is then executed to save the changes to the database on disk.

If it was the Delete button that was clicked, then a Delete method deletes the current record from the recordset and the MoveFirst method ensures there is a current record after this delete operation. MoveNext (or MovePrevious) could have been used, but that would cause an error if it was the last (or first) record that had just been deleted. MoveLast is an alternative.

If no error has occurred, execution drops through past the label cmdOK-_Click_OK and the updated data from the recordset is then displayed in the grid by a call to the previously described subroutine GetCusRecords. The grid is enabled so the user can click in it again to specify the current record, and the Edit form Form2 is hidden. Hiding a form makes it invisible but leaves it in memory. If it subsequently has a Show method applied to it, it becomes visible more quickly because no Form_Load event occurs for it. Unloading a form, using for example the command:

```
Unload Form2
```

will remove it from memory and when it is in future either loaded or shown, a Form_Load event will occur.

The next step in the cmdOK_Click_OK section of code is to enable the Action buttons and disable the Confirm buttons (see above). The variable current_command is then cleared and the subroutine exited.

If any error occurs, control is passed to the label `cmdOK_Click_Error`. Here, the variable `x` is built up. This will contain the message in the message box. A typical error message in this message box is shown below.

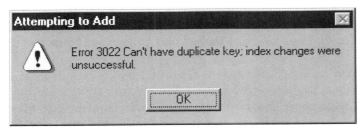

Fig. 10.5 Typical error message box from this program.

The variable `x` consists of the string "`Error `" followed by a call to the subroutine `Err`, which in this case (an attempt was made to add a record with a customer number that already exists) evaluated to 3022. Then a space " " is concatenated to the string and finally the error message in its string version is obtained by feeding the error code into the `Error` function. This is then concatenated to the string `x`.

The variable `y` consists of the string "`Attempting to `", concatenated onto the value of the variable `current_command`.

In the message box call, `x` is used as the first argument, which is the message in the message box. The variable `y` is used in the third argument, the value of the title bar of the message box. This is useful as it reminds the user what was being attempted when the error occurred.

Having displayed the error, execution is resumed at the label `cmdOK_Click_OK`, where tidy-up operations that are wanted whether or not an error has occurred are carried out.

If the user wants to back out of a partially completed Add, Change or Delete operation, he or she can click the Cancel button. The effect of this is a call to the subroutine `cmdCancel_Click`.

First the Edit form, no longer needed, is hidden. Then the relevant command buttons are enabled and disabled, as described above, the grid is enabled, and the variable `current_command` is cleared. Note that there is no necessity to perform any database recovery commands, such as Refresh etc., as in this program, all the database update commands are contained in the `cmdOK_Click` subroutine.

We now point out some coding features of the various utility subroutines this project contains.

In `move_grid_row_to_form2` and `ClearForm2Fields` it can be seen that the input text boxes are a control array Text1(1) . . . Text1(9). This makes operations like clearing the text boxes more compact because a For loop can be used. Similarly, in `move_data_to_current_record`, we wish to access all of the fields in the recordset one by one. Instead of having to name each field, we use instead the index of the *fields collection* to refer to each field in turn using its subscript (i.e. its 'index' as VB calls it).

The subroutine `Form_Resize` is useful in that it allows the user to see more of the data in the grid by increasing the size of the form. The code even increases the width of each of the columns in the grid. When the user resizes the form, the Form_Resize event routine executes. The width of the grid is made to be 0.9 of the width of the form, and the grid height 0.6. These figures were obtained through experiment.

The For loop sets the width of each grid column to be a ninth of the grid width minus the width of column zero, which we don't want to expand. Finally, Form2's Top and Left properties are adjusted so that it remains attached to the top right of Form1.

Finally, in Sub Timer1_Timer, Form1, which can, as here, be referred to as 'Me', has its caption set each second, under the control of Timer1, to the string "Amend Customer File " with the current time appended to the end. The current time can be obtained from the system clock using the function call Now.

The only code associated with Form2 is the Form Activate routine. This executes whenever Form2 is either loaded or shown (unlike Form_Load, which executes only when the form is loaded). The code positions Form2 at the top right of Form1.

Note that in many places in this project, Form2 objects' properties are referred to in Form1 code by the simple device of prefixing the object name with 'Form2'. For example, in the subroutine ClearForm2Fields, we find the line:

```
form2.Text1(i).Text = " "
```

This code is in Form1 and is referring to a Form2 object Text1(i) by prefixing it with 'Form2'.

Finally, the single line in Module1, a separate code module independent of any form. The line:

```
Global current_command
```

is used to declare the variable current_command. When a variable or Sub is defined as Global in a code module, it is 'visible' to the code in all forms and other modules. This is necessary here, because we want current_command to be visible to both Form1 and Form2.

10.6 Displaying data from a 1:N relationship using a VB Grid

Using the CUS_INVOICE_PAYMENT database tables (Fig. 10.6), we wish to display the data in the form shown in Fig. 10.7.

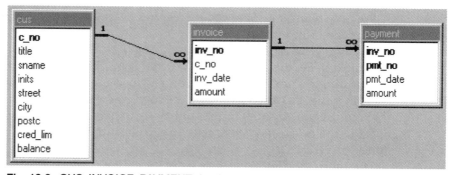

Fig. 10.6 CUS_INVOICE_PAYMENT database tables.

This project brings out a few more DAO database programming techniques. At the top-left of the form is a picture box containing the customer's account code, name and address. At the top-right of the form are two labels displaying invoice details of the current invoice for that customer.

In the grid below, details of all the payments the customer has made are shown in a grid. Clicking the 'Next Invoice' command button moves to the next invoice for that customer and displays any payments the customer has made towards that invoice.

If there are no more invoices for that customer, the next customer and his first invoice and associated payments are shown, and so on.

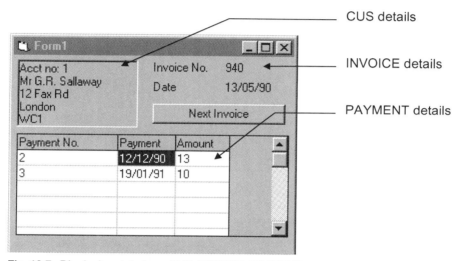

CUS details

INVOICE details

PAYMENT details

Fig. 10.7 Displaying data from CUS_INVOICE_PAYMENT using a Grid for the PAYMENT data.

General strategy for this project
1. Join the entire CUS and INVOICE tables once in Form_Load to create recordset rs1.

2. Display the CUS details in a Picture box using Picture1.Print.

3. Display the INVOICE details in two labels.

4. Retrieve all PAYMENT records for the current invoice to create recordset rs2. This recordset is retrieved each time a new invoice is accessed. The payments are displayed in the Grid.

An alternative strategy would have been to work with a single recordset consisting of a join of all CUS, INVOICE and PAYMENT records. The program code would of course be different and the major weakness of this approach would be that the recordset would be unnecessarily large, containing all the data from the three tables, some of it duplicated because of the effects of the joins.

Another strategy would have been to go for a minimum storage approach. Recordset rs1 in the strategy adopted contains more data than is actually displayed on the form at any one time. It contains a join of all CUS records with *all* of those customers' INVOICE records, even though only one invoice is displayed at a time. If a customer had, say, 30 invoices, the recordset containing the join will have 30 copies of the CUS record, each joined to a different invoice – that's the nature of a join operation, as we have seen in the SQL chapters. A minimum storage strategy would have in memory three recordsets. The first recordset would contain just *one* CUS record, the second recordset would contain that customer's INVOICE records, and the third recordset would contain just the PAYMENT records for the current INVOICE record.

The strategy we have adopted (see steps above) seems a reasonable compromise and is perhaps conceptually simpler and has simpler code than the third approach. For large databases, strategy three would be better.

Program code

```
Dim db1 As Database                          ◄─────── General Declarations
Dim rs1 As Recordset 'cus-invoice
Dim rs2 As Recordset 'payment

Private Sub Form_Load()
  Show
  'set up the grid
  Grid1.Row = 0
  Grid1.ColWidth(0) = 1500
  Grid1.ColWidth(1) = 850
  Grid1.ColWidth(2) = 800
  Grid1.Col = 0                ◄─────── Initialize Grid headings
  Grid1.Text = "Payment No."             and column widths.
  Grid1.Col = 1
  Grid1.Text = "Payment Date"
  Grid1.Col = 2
  Grid1.Text = "Amount"
  'Open the database
  Set db1 = OpenDatabase(App.Path & "\accts32_stud.mdb")
  'Database is in same folder as this application.   Create the
   'create cus-invoice recordset rs1      ◄──         CUS-
  x$ = "select cus.*,inv_no,inv_date,amount"          INVOICE
  x$ = x$ & "from cus, invoice"                       recordset
  x$ = x$ & "where cus.c_no = invoice.c_no"           rs1.
  x$ = x$ & "order by cus.c_no, inv_date"
  Set rs1 = db1.OpenRecordset(x$, dbOpenSnapshot)
  display_cus_inv_pmts 'call the subroutine
End Sub


Private Sub display_cus_inv_pmts()
  'This subroutine is called from Form_Load
```

```
    'and Command1_Click
    Picture1.Cls
    Picture1.Print "Acct no: " & rs1!c_no
    Picture1.Print rs1!Title & " " & rs1!inits & " " & rs1!sname
    Picture1.Print rs1!street
    Picture1.Print rs1!city
    Picture1.Print rs1!postc
    Label2.Caption = rs1!inv_no
    Label4.Caption = rs1!inv_date
    'Clear the grid
    For i = 1 To 10
      Grid1.Row = i
      For j = 0 To 2
        Grid1.Col = j
        Grid1.Text = ""
      Next j
    Next i
    'Retrieve set of payments for current inv_no
    x$ = "select pmt_no, pmt_date, amount"
    x$ = x$ & "from payment"
    x$ = x$ & "where inv_no = "
    x$ = x$ & rs1!inv_no
    Set rs2 = db1.OpenRecordset(x$, dbOpenSnapshot)
    'Display payments
    If rs2.RecordCount > 0 Then
      Grid1.Row = 0
      Do While Not rs2.EOF
        Grid1.Row = Grid1.Row + 1
        Grid1.Col = 0
        Grid1.Text = rs2!pmt_no
        Grid1.Col = 1
        Grid1.Text = rs2!pmt_date
        Grid1.Col = 2
        Grid1.Text = rs2!amount
        rs2.MoveNext
      Loop
    End If
End Sub

Private Sub Command1_Click()
  If rs1.EOF Then Exit Sub
  rs1.MoveNext
  If rs1.EOF Then Exit Sub
  'Display current cus-invoice details
  display_cus_inv_pmts 'call this subroutine
  End Sub
```

Display the CUS details.

Display the INVOICE details.

Clear the Grid of old payments.

Retrieve set of PAYMENTs for INVOICE.

Display the PAYMENTs in the Grid.

When Command1 is clicked, move to next **rs1** row and call subroutine to display new data.

Explanation

In General Declarations, the database object db1 and the two recordset objects rs1 and rs2 are declared. The recordset rs1 will contain a join of all CUS and INVOICE records. Recordset rs2 will contain just the set of PAYMENT records for the current INVOICE record.

Program execution starts with Form_Load. The Show statement loads the form immediately. This is useful for debugging when single-stepping through the Form_Load code to see the effects on the form. Otherwise, the form is not visible until *after* Form_Load has exited.

The first section of VB code sets some of the grid attributes. It is possible to set individual column widths at runtime using the method shown. This can't be done at design time. The headings are then placed in row 0 of the grid. In this project, there is one fixed row and no fixed columns.

The next thing that happens in Form_Load is the opening of the database. App.Path is the path to the current application (i.e. this project) and you can see from the OpenDatabase statement that the database accts32_stud.mdb is in the same folder.

The next step is to create a string variable (called x$ in this example) to contain the SQL statement that will be used to create recordset rs1. Rather than put the SQL statement all on one line, we have built up the string in pieces, which then are concatenated together. This simply gives a more readable look to the code. The SQL statement is:

```
SELECT cus.*, inv_no, inv_date, amount
FROM cus, invoice
WHERE cus.c_no = invoice.c_no
ORDER BY cus.c_no, inv_date
```

If you've read the SQL chapters, this SQL code will seem straightforward. In the top line, we select from the two tables the fields we want to display in the picture box and the labels. The FROM clause specifies where the data is to come from – the two tables CUS and INVOICE. The WHERE clause specifies the *join criteria*, i.e. the criteria for deciding which CUS records are joined to which INVOICE records. Finally the ORDER BY clause specifies that we want the resulting recordset to be sorted on invoice date within customer number. That way, as the user flicks through the customers' invoices, they will appear in a sensible order, not the order they are stored on the database, necessarily.

Notice that we are using the 'old' ANSI-86 SQL syntax here. An *inner join* is implicit in this old syntax. An inner join is appropriate here, since we don't want to display customers who have no invoices. The ANSI-92 syntax for this query would of course have been:

```
SELECT cus.*, inv_no, inv_date, amount
FROM cus INNER JOIN invoice
ON cus.c_no = invoice.c_no
ORDER BY cus.c_no, inv_date
```

The Jet database engine will accept both versions of the SQL syntax.

Having formed the string x$ containing the SQL query, it is now time to execute it and retrieve the data from the database and put it in a recordset in memory. This is performed by the line:

```
Set rs1 = db1.OpenRecordset(x$, dbOpenSnapshot)
```

Here the VB5/6 syntax (Jet 3.5) for opening a recordset is used. In previous Jet versions you would have had to write:

```
Set rs1 = db1.OpenSnapshot(x$)
```

The second parameter of our OpenRecordset method specifies that the recordset is to be a *snapshot* recordset. This means that it's read-only and so we can't change the data in it by using, for example, AddNew, Edit, Delete and Update methods. Snapshots recordsets are reputed to be faster to process than *dynasets*, which are updateable recordsets. Snapshots and dynasets allow you to retrieve data from more than one table, whereas table recordsets restrict you to retrieving and updating data from a single table. Having executed this command, we now have in memory (in recordset rs1) all the CUS records joined to all their INVOICE records.

Form_Load then calls our subroutine display_cus_inv_pmts. This subroutine call is necessary here because the user will expect to see the data for the first customer when the form first loads.

We now describe the code for the Sub display_cus_inv_pmts. The purpose of this routine is to display the current CUS and INVOICE data, and to generate SQL that will retrieve all the PAYMENT records for the current invoice and display them in the grid. First the picture box Picture1 is cleared using the Cls method and then the Print method is used to display in the picture box the data from the customer part of the current record in the recordset rs1. The title, initials and surname of the customer are concatenated in the second Print statement. Next the invoice number and invoice date from the same record in recordset rs1 are displayed in Label2 and Label4.

Now it is time to retrieve and display any PAYMENT records for the current invoice into the grid.

First, the grid is cleared in a nested FOR loop. Then it is necessary to build up an SQL SELECT statement to retrieve the PAYMENT records. The required PAYMENT records will have the same invoice number as the current record in recordset rs1. The value of the current invoice number in recordset rs1 is rs1!inv_no and this is concatenated onto the end of the string x$. Suppose the current invoice number is 940. Then the SQL SELECT statement we want to execute would be as shown in the first figure below. We simply select payment records with an inv_no value of 940. The fields we want to display in the grid are pmt_no, pmt_date and amount so they appear in the SELECT line.

```
SELECT pmt_no, pmt_date, amount
FROM payment
WHERE inv_no = 940
```

However, we can't hard-code the invoice number 940 into the string x$, so we first generate the 'constant' part of in x$ the code:

```
x$ = "select pmt_no, pmt_date, amount"
x$ = x$ & "from payment"
x$ = x$ & "where inv_no = "
```

We then concatenate on the value of the current invoice number using the code:

```
x$ = x$ & rs1!inv_no
```

Having generated this dynamic (i.e. formed at runtime) SQL statement, we execute it using the OpenRecordset method against the database object db1. The first parameter of the OpenRecordset method is x$, the SQL statement we have just formed, and the second parameter is the type of recordset we require – in this case a snapshot. When this line is executed, a recordset rs2 will appear in memory and it will contain the three fields requested from all the PAYMENT records for the current invoice number.

The RecordCount property of the recordset rs2 is checked. If there are any records in the recordset, the Do While loop progresses through the recordset row by row, inserting the field values from each row into the corresponding row of the grid.

Finally, we describe the code in the subroutine Command1_Click.

Clicking this button has the effect of moving to the next record in the recordset rs1. Remember this contains a join of all the customer and corresponding invoice records. If the recordset is empty, the Sub is exited. This means of course that in this program there is no means of going back to a previous invoice or customer. Otherwise we execute a MoveNext command to move to the next rs1 record. Notice that there are *two* tests for end-of-file (EOF), that is, the end of the recordset. The first one executes if you were previously already at EOF, i.e. one step beyond the last record. The second executes if you were previously on the last record and have just moved to EOF. If there is a record to display, the subroutine display_cus_inv_pmts is called and, as we have seen, it displays the current customer and invoice details and the payments for the current invoice (if any) in the grid.

10.7 Producing reports

There are several possibilities for producing reports from databases using Visual Basic. Here are some of the options available:

- High-level methods
  - Access Reports
  - Crystal Reports
  - VB6 Data Report
- Low-level methods
  - The PrintForm method
  - Print #
  - The Printer Object

If you are producing reports of a simple hierarchical format that reflect the relationships between tables in your database, then Report Writers of various types are available. We call these high-level methods because they don't require much effort on the part of the programmer. We look at Access Reports (previously covered in Chapter 8), Crystal Reports (a separate general-purpose report writer) and the VB6 Data Report tool.

If the simple report-writers mentioned above do not give you the functionality you need for your particular report, or make it difficult to achieve, you will need to program the report yourself using Visual Basic. We call these low-level methods because they require varying degrees of detailed programming in VB.

We may sometimes use `PrintForm`, which simply prints an impression of a report printed on a form. Another option is `Print #`, which prints text-only reports to a file which can later be printed from an editor. We also include printing reports using the `Printer` object, which allows full control over the printers available and the same quality of output as the report writers. This approach offers the greatest flexibility.

Of these options, we give most prominence in this section to `Print #` and the Printer object.

High-level methods of producing reports

Access reports

Part of the Access package, the Access Report Writer is a popular method of producing conventional reports. It is normally used separately from the VB programs and the report definitions are normally stored in the **.mdb** file along with the forms, macros, queries, tables etc. These reports can then be produced by going into Access separately for those reports. In a system of any size, some reports will be produced directly from the VB program, some from Access etc. Access reports are covered in Chapter 8.

Crystal reports

For a long time, Crystal Reports has been the standard way of producing a database report from a Visual basic program. Crystal Reports is bundled with versions of Visual Basic up to VB6. It is not, however, installed by default in VB6. While having the ability to be used independently of VB (it is really a separate package) and to access various database formats apart from Jet, it was not really designed for Jet databases and its terminology and usage pattern are different from what you would expect from a normal Windows package.

VB6 data reports

Used with a VB6 data environment, a VB6 data report is relatively simple to produce just using drag and drop. Reports are limited to those where the format of the report follows pretty closely the underlying structure of the database.

Low-level methods of producing reports

You will find high-level report writing methods very useful for producing quick reports where those reports are conceptually simple and have an orthodox structure (even though the SQL commands on which they are based may be fairly complex). By 'orthodox structure', we mean a structure following pretty closely the structure of the database. However, for more complex reports, or reports where the report structure differs considerably from the database structure, programming using VB code will be necessary. As an example of the limitations of the high-level reporting approach, consider the following report request:

> **Print the sum of all sales values from the SALES table and subtract from it the sum of all purchase values from the PURCHASES table.**

It is quite possible that the SALES table and PURCHASES tables are unrelated by database relationships. This would make it impossible to use a VB6 Data Reports approach, even though this is conceptually simple and relatively easy to program.

Print

If you are producing a report that is purely text-based and that you would like to allow your users to edit later, then printing the report to a file using the VB `Print #` command is an option.

Since it produces a simple ASCII text file, you can use Notepad to view the results before printing.

Printing a simple report

```
Private Sub Command1_Click()
  x$ = App.Path
  x$ = x$ & "\" & "TESTFILE"
  Open x$ For Output As #1 Len = 80
  Print #1, Tab(35); "HEADING"
  Print #1,
  Print #1, Tab(30); "Quantity"; Tab(40); "Discount%"
  Print #1,
  Print #1, Tab(35); "10"; Tab(45); "0"
  Print #1, Tab(35); "20"; Tab(45); "5"
  Print #1, Tab(35); "30"; Tab(45); "8"
  Print #1, Tab(35); "40"; Tab(45); "10"
  Close #1
End Sub
```

This code prints the report, shown in Fig. 10.8 in a Notepad window.

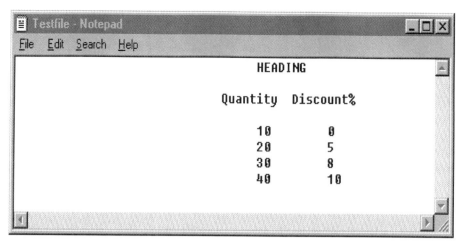

Fig. 10.8 The output from the program.

In the first two lines, `App.Path` is the path (the position on the disk) of the current application. The string variable `x$` is built up to put the output file TESTFILE in the same folder as the VB application itself.

The `Open` command opens a text file for output and the next three lines print the headings. To print to a text file, the `Print #` statement is used. `#1` is file number 1 and corresponds to the file number in the `Open` statement. The rest of the program produces a simple report. Note the use of the `Tab` function to produce a columnar effect. As you can see, this program just prints a simple constant report; it does not access the database.

Since the report is printed to a file (TESTFILE in this example), the user of the report has the opportunity to edit it before printing it. In fact, to print it at all, an editor is required. Here we are using Notepad. Apart from giving the user the opportunity to edit the report, it also converts the text file to a printer file in the format of the printer the system has set as the default printer. Compare this to printing to the printer object (next section), where the print file is produced by the program itself.

10.8 Printing a report (using Print #) displaying data from one table

```
Private Sub Command1_Click()
  x$ = App.Path
  x$ = x$ & "\" & "CUS_REP"
  Open x$ For Output As #1 Len = 80
  Print #1, Tab(32); "CUSTOMER REPORT"
  Print #1,
  Print #1, Tab(20); "Customer Number"; Tab(40); "Name"
  Print #1,
  Set db1 = OpenDatabase("c:\Access 7 Advanced\Database\students
accts database\accts32_stud.mdb")
  Set ta1 = db1.OpenRecordset("cus", dbOpenTable)
```

```
   ta1.MoveFirst
   Do While Not ta1.EOF
     Print #1, Tab(28); ta1!c_no; Tab(40); ta1!Title & " " &
ta1!inits & " " & ta1!sname
     ta1.MoveNext
   Loop
   ta1.Close
   db1.Close
   Close #1
   End
End Sub
```

This produces the following output file contents:

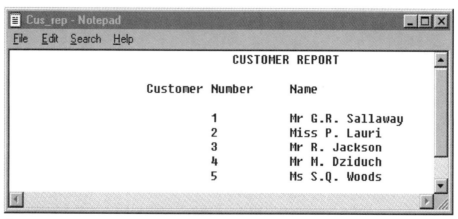

Fig. 10.9 The output from the program above.

The Set db1 = line uses the OpenDatabase method to open the database. This finds the position on the disk of the database. The Set ta1 = line opens a recordset. A recordset is a set of records in the computer's memory (RAM). A recordset can be a whole table, as here – the table CUS. In this case, the second parameter of the OpenRecordset method is dbOpenTable, a VB system constant. The command, ta1.MoveFirst, moves the record pointer to the first record.

In the Do While loop, the customer number and name of each record in the recordset are printed out. Field values are referred to by naming the recordset and the field name, separated by the exclamation mark '!'. In the Print # line, Tab and the concatenation operator & are used to lay out the report lines. After each line is printed, a Movenext method is applied to the recordset object ta1. Finally, outside the loop, the table object and database objects are both closed, and the print file itself is closed.

10.9 Printing a report (using Print #) displaying data from three related tables

We extend the simple report from one database table CUS to show how data from three related tables CUS, INVOICE and PAYMENT can be output. The report lists all customers, and their associated invoices and payments.

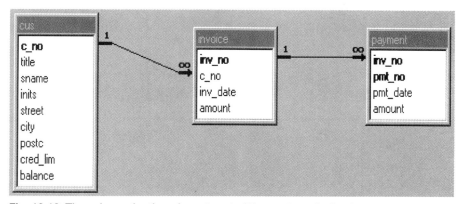

Fig. 10.10 The schema for the relevant part of the accts.mdb database.

```
                                    CUSTOMER REPORT
                                     19 August 1998
                                        09:16:16

Customer Number   Name              Inv.No    Date        Amount

    1             Mr G.R. Sallaway
                                      940      13/05/90    £26.20
                                      Pmt      12/12/90    £13.00
                                      Pmt      19/01/91    £10.00
                                      1003     13/01/91    £16.26

    2             Miss P. Lauri
                                      1004     01/01/90    £0.00

    3             Mr R. Jackson
                                      1005     20/01/91    £510.00
                                      Pmt      14/01/91    £510.00
```

Fig. 10.11 A section of the report involving data from three tables.

The forms in this partially completed project

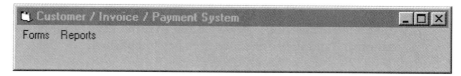

frmStartup.frm

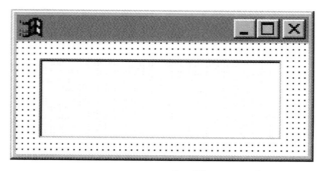

frmMessage.frm

The code for frmStartup

```
Private Sub mnuCusInvPmtList_Click()
    'Print a simple report showing for each customer his invoices and
payments.
    'Author: J.R. Carter 14—8—98.
    'The database is assumed to be in the current folder (i.e. same folder
as this application).
    'Put the report in the current folder too.

    frmMessage.Show
    frmMessage.label1.Caption = "Please wait while report is being
produced."
    frmMessage.Refresh
    x$ = App.Path
    x$ = x$ & "\" & "CUS_REP" 'Report name is 'CUS_REP'.
    Open x$ For Output As #1 Len = 80
    Print #1, Tab(33); "CUSTOMER REPORT"
    Print #1, Tab(33); Format(Now, "long date")
    Print #1, Tab(36); Format(Now, "long time")
    Print #1,
    Print #1, Tab(20); "Customer Number"; Tab(40); "Name"; Tab(50);
"Inv.No"; Tab(57); "Date"; Tab(68); "Amount"
    Set db1 = OpenDatabase(App.Path & "\accts32_stud.mdb") 'Database is
in same folder as this application.
```

```
        Set ta1 = db1.OpenRecordset("cus", dbOpenTable)
        Do While Not ta1.EOF '*** For each CUS record
          Print #1,
          Print #1, Tab(28); ta1!c_no; Tab(40); ta1!Title & " " & ta1!inits &
      " " & ta1!sname
          z$ = "select * from invoice where c_no = " & ta1!c_no
          Set ss1 = db1.OpenRecordset(z$, dbOpenSnapshot)
          Do While Not ss1.EOF '*** For each INVOICE record
            Print #1, Tab(50); Trim(ss1!inv_no); Tab(57); ss1!inv_date;
      Tab(68); Format(ss1!amount, "currency")
              y$ = "select * from payment where inv_no = " & ss1!inv_no
              Set ss2 = db1.OpenRecordset(y$, dbOpenSnapshot)
              Do While Not ss2.EOF '*** For each PAYMENT record
                Print #1, Tab(50); " Pmt"; Tab(57); ss2!pmt_date; Tab(68);
      Format(ss2!amount, "currency")
                ss2.MoveNext
            Loop
            ss1.MoveNext
          Loop
          ta1.MoveNext
        Loop
        ta1.Close
        ss1.Close
        ss2.Close
        db1.Close
        Close #1
        frmMessage.Hide
      End Sub
```

When the program is run, the first thing that happens is that the startup form frmStartup loads. When the user clicks the relevant menu item, mnuCusInv-PmtList_Click() runs.

The program starts by showing a form to tell the user that the program is running and producing the report. It then establishes the path for the report file and opens the file for output. The report headings are then written. Db1 is then set to be the database object using the OpenDatabase method. Ta1 is set to be the recordset object using the OpenRecordset method against the database object db1. The recordset is the table CUS. Note that an SQL statement could be placed here to retrieve fields from one or more tables. In this case, the second parameter of the OpenRecordset method would be 'dbOpenDynaset' if the recordset were to be updateable, or 'dbOpenSnapshot' if read-only.

A Do While loop is then set up to process, one by one, the records of the CUS table. Ta1.EOF becomes true when End Of File is reached on the ta1 recordset. The second Print # statement in this loop formats and prints data from the current CUS record.

It is then necessary to retrieve all the INVOICE records for that customer. This is done by dynamically generating an SQL statement with the current customer concatenated onto the end of the SQL SELECT statement's WHERE clause. Assuming the first customer number is 1, `ta1!c_no` will be 1. The string variable `z$` will consequently contain the string

```
"select * from invoice where c_no = 1".
```

Remember that & is the VB string concatenation character. The object `ss1` is set to be a snapshot recordset that results from executing this SQL SELECT statement using the `OpenRecordset` method. The next `Do While` loop (inside the outer loop processing the CUS table recordset `ta1`) processes each of the INVOICE records retrieved.

The processing is simply to print out the invoice fields. The `Print #` statement contains a couple of useful VB formatting functions. `Trim` removes any leading or trailing spaces. `Format` formats the amount field in currency format, with leading currency sign and two decimal places.

Within the INVOICE loop it is necessary to form a loop to process all the payments for the current invoice.

This is done, as before, by first generating an SQL string containing a SELECT statement with the current invoice number tacked on the end and using this string to retrieve the recordset using the `OpenRecordset` method against the database object `db1`. The loop itself sequentially processes each retrieved PAYMENT record and prints it to the printer file.

At the end of each loop, there is a `MoveNext` command to move to the next record in the recordset so that it can be printed.

At the end of all of the loop statements, the program closes all the recordsets and the database. The form displaying the message to the user is then hidden.

The printer object

The Visual Basic printer object is considered by some to be difficult to use. This is probably because producing a report using the printer object requires programming.

However, we have found Printer object programming the method of choice for database reports. The programmer is more in control of what the report looks like, and is also in control of the database navigation that retrieves the required data. This also gives the programmer greater flexibility in selecting efficient methods of database navigation.

The printer object comes with a large number of properties and methods. Many of these will already be familiar to Visual Basic users because other objects have the same properties.

Unlike the sequential file approach of `Print #`, your program can move up and down and left and right on the printer object using the `CurrentX` and `CurrentY` properties.

You may worry whether your print program will work on the variety of printers that your clients will use. This is not a problem because the printer object attributes are geared towards the printer your user has set as the default printer. In other words, Windows looks after it. When users install printers, they install printer *drivers*. This piece of system software sits between your program and the printer and presents the printer's properties to your program. All relevant properties of the printer are accessible by your program too. Where the user has several printers installed, your program can detect them all and it can (under user control if you wish) select the required printer. Without any user intervention, the report will be sent to the default printer. You can see which of the printers is the default using the Windows Control Panel.

The idea then is that you send the printer output to the printer via this printer object. If you divert the printer output to a file instead, it will produce a .prn file. If you look at this file using an editor, it will look nothing like your report is supposed to look. The printer object contains a set of commands for controlling the printer's microprocessor. This is what gives modern laser printers their flexibility – they are programmable. The printer driver converts your VB printer requests into this printer language. Two popular printer languages are PCL and PostScript.

One disadvantage of using the printer object stems from this fact. You can't see what the output is going to look like before you print it! This is not a problem for those of your report writing programs that have been up and running for some time and have consequently been thoroughly tested. However, it is possible to waste quite a lot of paper developing and testing programs that write directly to the printer object. We include below a program that attempts to ameliorate this situation by allowing the user to see a page of the report in a *picture box* before committing to a print. This can be extended to viewing *any* page, or a *set* of pages before printing.

We now consider some VB report-writing programs using this low-level but flexible programming approach. We shall use DAO database commands for the database access and the Printer object to print the report on.

10.10 Printing a report (using the printer object) displaying data from three related tables

The form shown in Fig. 10.12 is used with the code described below to print a formatted report to the Picture box contained on it, or to the default Printer object for the PC, depending on which option button is selected. As explained above, in the latter case, the installed printer driver will take care of the issue of placing the text and graphics on the correct place on the printer stationery. However, it's useful for the user to see what the output looks like before committing to a print. Let's assume the user has opted to display part of the report to the picture box.

With the option button set to 'Picture Box' and the command button clicked, the form appears as follows.

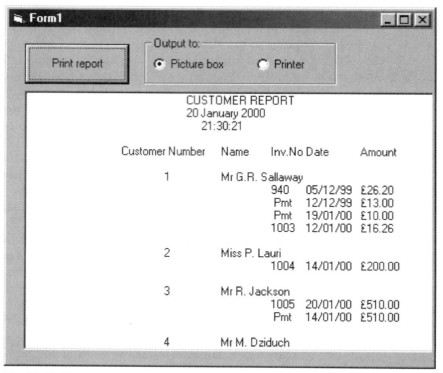

Fig. 10.12 The form used to print to a Picture box and/or the Printer object.

The VB code that achieves this report is shown below.

```
Private Sub Command1_Click()
  Dim ob1 As Object
  Picture1.Width = Printer.ScaleWidth
  Me.Refresh
  If Option1.Value = True Then
    Set ob1 = Picture1
  Else
    Set ob1 = Printer
  End If
  With ob1
  ob1.Print Tab(33); "CUSTOMER REPORT"
  ob1.Print Tab(33); Format(Now, "long date")
  ob1.Print Tab(36); Format(Now, "long time")
  ob1.Print
    ob1.Print Tab(20); "Customer Number"; Tab(40); "Name"; Tab(50);
"Inv.No"; Tab(57); "Date"; Tab(68); "Amount"
    Set db1 = OpenDatabase("C:\My
Documents\NewBook\Databases\Access97Jet3_5\accts.mdb")
    Set ta1 = db1.OpenRecordset("customer", dbOpenTable)
    Do While Not ta1.EOF
```

```
        ob1.Print
        'PRINT CUSTOMER LINE
        ob1.Print Tab(28); ta1!c_no; Tab(40); ta1!Title & " " & ta1!inits
& " " & ta1!sname
        z$ = "select * from invoice where c_no = " & ta1!c_no
        Set ss1 = db1.OpenRecordset(z$, dbOpenSnapshot)
        Do While Not ss1.EOF
          'PRINT INVOICE LINE
          ob1.Print Tab(50); Trim(ss1!inv_no); Tab(57); ss1!inv_date;
Tab(68); Format(ss1!amount, "currency")
          Y$ = "select * from payment where inv_no = " & ss1!inv_no
          Set ss2 = db1.OpenRecordset(Y$, dbOpenSnapshot)
          Do While Not ss2.EOF
            'PRINT PAYMENT LINE
            ob1.Print Tab(50); " Pmt"; Tab(57); ss2!pmt_date; Tab(68);
Format(ss2!amount, "currency")
            ss2.MoveNext
        Loop
        ss1.MoveNext
      Loop
      ta1.MoveNext
    Loop
    ta1.Close
    db1.Close
    End With
    Printer.EndDoc
End Sub
```

All of the code for this project is contained in the command button1 Click event.

Since we want to use the same code for printing to the picture box and the printer object, we take advantage of the fact that we can define a general object and later assign it to either a picture box or a printer.

A general object ob1 is defined in the first line. Depending on which option button is set, object ob1 is set to either Picture1 or the Printer. For the rest of the program, print output is sent to ob1. The With command facilitates this. The rest of the code is identical to the previous example, except that to actually send data accumulated in the printer buffer to the printer, the command Printer.EndDoc is used.

10.11 Listing the printers available

It is possible to list all the printer devices available on your system and to allow the user then to select the one required. The following form shows a list of available printers and their drivers.

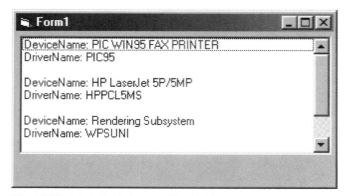

Fig. 10.13 A list of printers and their drivers.

The VB code necessary to produce this list is shown below.

```
Private Sub Form_Load()
  Dim X As Printer
  For Each X In Printers
    List1.AddItem "DeviceName: " & X.DeviceName
    List1.AddItem "DriverName: " & X.DriverName
    List1.AddItem ""
  Next
End Sub
```

Each printer in the Printers collection has a number of properties which can be accessed and reset if required at runtime. By setting an object to the required device name, the user can select the required printer and its settings at runtime.

10.12 Exercises

1. Change the 'Editing CUS data in a VB Grid' project of section 10.4 to allow record insertions and deletions.

2. Change the 'Displaying data from a 1:N relationship in a VB grid' project of Section 10.6 to allow bi-directional navigation through the recordsets.

3. Change the 'Displaying data from a 1:N relationship in a VB Grid' project of Section 10.6 to allow changes, insertions and deletions. Error handling code and input validation should be included.

4. Extend the 'Printing a report' project of Section 10.10 to give the user the option of selecting a printer from those available.

11

Visual Basic database programming using Active X Data Objects (ADO)

In this chapter you will learn:

- the new terminology associated with ADO

- how to convert from DAO to ADO

- how to connect to a database using ADO

- how to write database programs using ADO

- how to share data on a LAN-based database.

11.1 The ADO approach

ADO (Active X Data Objects) is Microsoft's latest approach to database programming. Its biggest difference from DAO, from a programming point of view, is that the OpenDatabase method of DAO is replaced by a Connection string. This approach gives ADO a uniform method of connecting to a variety of data sources via OLE DB, which is a set of interfaces to various types of data source that provides ODBC – Open Database Connectivity. VB6 introduced ADO, which acts as a simple consistent API (Application Programming Interface). ADO is thus a 'bridge between application and OLE DB', as VB6 Help puts it.

In this chapter, we first compare the commands used in ADO with their DAO equivalents and illustrate the new commands with simple examples. We then show further examples using ADO, including examples to update databases.

In Chapter 15, we show how ADO can be used with VBScript in ASP (Active Server Pages) to access and update databases on the internet.

Note that to run examples using ADO code in VB, you need to have the ADO library available. This is achieved in VB6 by:

- clicking Project / References

- selecting Microsoft ActiveX Data Objects 2.1 (or 2.5) Library.

A summary of the differences between ADO and DAO database commands is given in Appendix 2.

11.2 Displaying data in a List Box: ADO and DAO compared

The aim here is to highlight the differences between ADO code and DAO code. We produce two similar projects, one using ADO, and one using DAO, and compare the code. The functionality of both projects is identical.

Figure 11.1 shows the output of both projects.

The code for the DAO version is shown in Fig. 11.2 and the code for the new ADO version in Fig. 11.3.

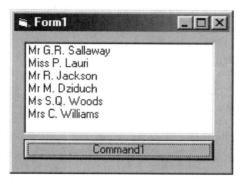

Fig. 11.1 Both programs list customer data.

```
Private Sub Command1_Click()
  '--- Make a DAO connection to the database ---
  x = "D:\My Documents\NewBook\Databases\Access97Jet3_5\accts.mdb"
  Set db1 = OpenDatabase(x)
  '--- Open a recordset using DAO ---
  Set Rs1 = db1.OpenRecordset("customer", dbopensnapshot)
  '--- List the customers using DAO ---
  Do While Not Rs1.EOF
    List1.AddItem Rs1!Title & " " & Rs1!inits & " " & Rs1!sname
    Rs1.MoveNext
  Loop
End Sub
```

Fig. 11.2 The DAO version.

```
                                        ┌─────────────────────┐
                                        │ Use 4.0 for Access  │
                                        │ 2000 databases      │
                                        └─────────────────────┘
Private Sub Command1_Click()
  '--- Make an ADO connection to the database ---
  Set Conn1 = New ADODB.Connection
  x = "Provider = Microsoft.Jet.OLEDB.3.51;"
```

```
    x = x & "Data Source = D:\My
Documents\NewBook\Databases\Access97Jet3_5\accts.mdb"
    Conn1.Open x
    '--- Open a recordset using ADO ---
    Set Rs1 = New ADODB.Recordset
    Rs1.Open "Customer", Conn1
    '--- List the customers using ADO ---
    Do While Not Rs1.EOF
        List1.AddItem Rs1!Title & " " & Rs1!inits & " " & Rs1!sname
        Rs1.MoveNext
    Loop
End Sub
```

Fig. 11.3 The ADO version.

Differences between the DAO and ADO versions of the program

1. **Making a connection to the database**: The DAO *OpenDatabase* method is replaced by the ADO *Connection.Open* method. Let's compare the relevant lines of code for opening a database.

```
    '--- Make a DAO connection to the database ---
    x = "D:\My Documents\NewBook\Databases\Access97Jet3_5\accts.mdb"
    Set db1 = OpenDatabase(x)
```

Fig. 11.4 Opening a database in DAO.

```
                                                    ┌─────────────────────┐
                                                    │ Use 4.0 for Access  │
                                                    │ 2000 databases      │
                                                    └─────────────────────┘
    '--- Make a ADO connection to the database ---
    Set Conn1 = New ADODB.Connection
    x = "Provider = Microsoft.Jet.OLEDB.3.51;"
    x = x & "Data Source=D:\My
Documents\NewBook\Databases\Access97Jet3_5\accts.mdb"
    Conn1.Open x
```

Fig. 11.5 Making a connection to a database in ADO.

Both examples open the same Jet database.

In the DAO version, the OpenDatabase method is used. We establish the path to the database, open it using OpenDatabase, and give the database the name db1.

In the ADO version, instead of 'opening a database', we 'establish a connection' to it. All of the steps shown are necessary. Here are the steps:

(a) In the first line, we specify Conn1 as a new ADO database connection.

(b) In the second and third lines we build up a *connection string* containing:

- *Provider*.   This specifies the *type* of database
- *Data Source*.   This specifies the *path* to the database.

(c) In the fourth line, we use the connection string to Open the connection Conn1.

There are various Providers, and ADO wants you to name them explicitly, even if you're connecting to a Jet database. Naming a Provider calls up an interface program that converts your VB commands into the language of the type of database you want to connect to.

2. **Opening a recordset**: The DAO *OpenRecordset* method is replaced by the ADO *Recordset.Open* method. Again, let's compare the relevant lines of code.

```
'--- Open a recordset using DAO ---
Set Rs1 = db1.OpenRecordset("customer", dbopensnapshot)
```

Fig. 11.6 Opening a recordset using DAO.

```
'--- Open a recordset using ADO ---
Set Rs1 = New ADODB.Recordset
Rs1.Open "Customer", Conn1
```

Fig. 11.7 Opening a recordset using ADO.

In the DAO example, we apply the OpenRecordset method to the database object db1 to create a recordset Rs1 based on the Customer table.

In the ADO version, we specify Rs1 as a new ADO database recordset. We then Open the recordset and say that it's to contain the Customer table.

3. **Referring to fields:** The way this is done is the same in both DAO and ADO. The code in both programs follows.

```
'--- List the customers using ADO ---
  Do While Not Rs1.EOF
    List1.AddItem Rs1!Title & " " & Rs1!inits & " " & Rs1!sname
    Rs1.MoveNext
  Loop
```

Fig. 11.8 Referring to fields in both DAO and DAO.

```
Private Sub Command1_Click()
  '--- Make a connection ---
  Set Conn1 = New ADODB.Connection
  Conn1.Provider = "Microsoft.Jet.OLEDB.3.51;"
  Conn1.ConnectionString = "D:\My
Documents\NewBook\Databases\Access97Jet3_5\accts.mdb"
  Conn1.Open
  '--- Open a recordset ---
  Set Rs1 = New ADODB.Recordset
```

```
    Rs1.Open "Customer", Conn1
    '--- List the customers ---
    Do While Not Rs1.EOF
      List1.AddItem Rs1!Title & " " & Rs1!inits & " " & Rs1!sname
      Rs1.MoveNext
    Loop
  End Sub
```

Fig. 11.9 An alternative ADO version using 'neater' connection syntax.

Figure 11.9 shows ADO which is entirely equivalent to the ADO code in Fig. 11.3. However, instead of using a string x containing the connection data, it uses two properties of the connection object, the Provider and ConnectionString properties.

11.3 Creating and using a Data Source Name (DSN)

In the previous example, to connect up to the database, we specified the *connection string* explicitly in the lines:

```
  '--- Make an ADO connection to the database ---
    Set Conn1 = New ADODB.Connection
    x = "Provider = Microsoft.Jet.OLEDB.3.51;"
    x = x & "Data Source = D:\My
Documents\NewBook\Databases\Access97Jet3_5\accts.mdb"
    Conn1.Open x
```

Fig. 11.10 Making a connection to a database in ADO using a *connection string*.

The data necessary to make the connection is in the connection string inserted into the variable x as follows:

```
    x = "Provider = Microsoft.Jet.OLEDB.3.51;"
    x = x & "Data Source = D:\My
Documents\NewBook\Databases\Access97Jet3_5\accts.mdb"
```

As mentioned above, the connection string contains the following information:

- Provider   the type of data and the name of the software that links your program up to it (Microsoft call these OLE DB providers)
- Data Source   where the data is (Microsoft call these ODBC data sources).

This is called a DSN-less connection, because it gives this information explicitly in the connection string and doesn't use a *DSN*.

So what *is* a DSN? It's a Data Source Name. If you create a DSN you store the connection information there and in your program you just need to mention the DSN when you want to connect up to the database.

Using a DSN

Using a DSN instead of an explicit connection string in your ADO database program further simplifies the look of the program. In Fig. 11.11, we show the latest version of our simple program to list CUSTOMER details in a list box, this time using a DSN. After discussing the code, we show how we created that DSN.

```
Private Sub Command1_Click()
  '--- Make a connection ---
  Set Conn1 = New ADODB.Connection
  Conn1.Open "My 1st ADO Example DSN"
  '--- Open a recordset ---
  Set Rs1 = New ADODB.Recordset
  Rs1.Open "Customer", Conn1
  '--- List the customers ---
  Do While Not Rs1.EOF
    List1.AddItem Rs1!Title & " " & Rs1!inits & " " & Rs1!sname
    Rs1.MoveNext
  Loop
End Sub
```

Fig. 11.11 Using a DSN called "My 1st ADO Example DSN".

You can see that in Fig. 11.11 the connection code looks even simpler when we use a previously created DSN. In the line:

```
Conn1.Open "My 1st ADO Example DSN"
```

we open the connection using the DSN "My 1st ADO Example DSN". This DSN contains all the connection information required, including the values for the Provider and ConnectionString properties. We only have to create this DSN once, and then it can be used by any program that needs it. Now let's see how we create this DSN. It has to be created before we can use it in a program, of course.

Creating the DSN "My 1st ADO Example DSN"

We shall create the DSN independently of Visual Basic. We'll do it using the ODBC Data source Administrator. ODBC stands for Open DataBase Connectivity, which is basically a philosophy that says that you should be able to move data between different locations even if they're in different formats (different DBMSs, spreadsheet formats, raw text etc.)

Having created the DSN, we'll use it instead of the long connection string shown in Fig. 11.10. Here are the steps in creating the DSN.

ODBC Data
Sources (32bit)

1. Starting from the Windows Start button, click Start, Settings, Control Panel, ODBC Data Sources (32 bit). This will bring up the ODBC Data Source Administrator dialogue box (Fig. 11.12).

2. Click the Add button. We are going to add a new DSN.

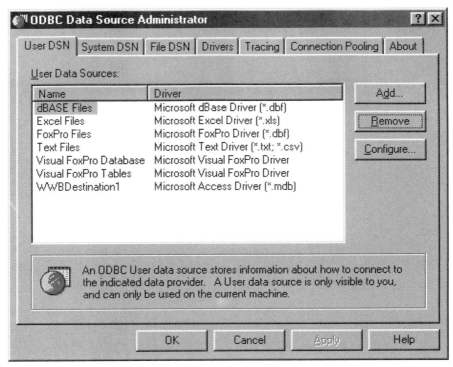

Fig. 11.12 The ODBC Data Source Administrator dialogue box (Step 1).

3. Specify that you want to use the Microsoft Access Driver, because we want to connect to an Access database accts.mdb (Fig. 11.13).

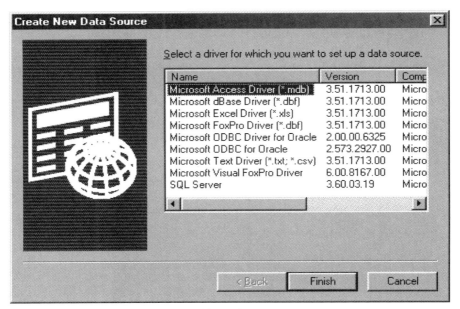

Fig. 11.13 Specify the Access Driver (Step 3).

4. Specify the name for the new DSN. You can also enter a brief description of what the DSN is for (Fig. 11.14).

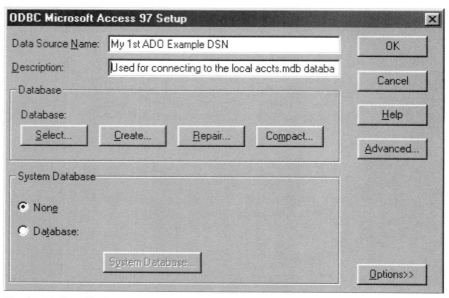

Fig. 11.14 Specify the name for the new DSN (Step 4).

5. Click the Select button, and locate the database you want the DSN to connect to (Fig. 11.15).

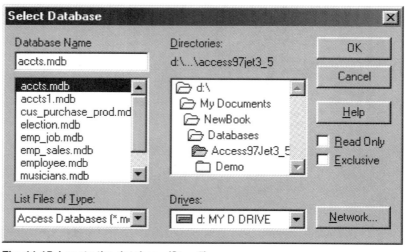

Fig. 11.15 Locate the database (Step 5).

6. Click OK, and you will see that the new DSN has been added to the collection on your machine (Fig. 11.16).

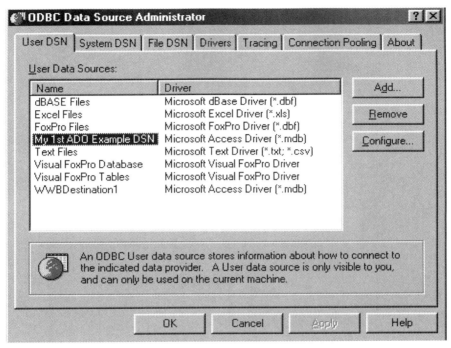

Fig. 11.16 The new DSN has been added (Step 6).

That completes the setting up of this DSN. It can now be used in your Visual Basic ADO programs to connect to the accts.mdb database, as shown in the program listing of Fig. 11.11.

11.4 Updating a single table using ADO

We now show how ADO commands are used in single table updates. Figure 11.17 shows a simple data update form for displaying, adding, changing and deleting CUSTOMER records from the accts.mdb database. We have kept the program as simple as possible, and used the two-step method of update used in a previous chapter because it gives the user an opportunity to back out of an update. Moving to another record will not save any changes either. The user has to click OK. We have also kept with the idea of using frames to enable and disable appropriate parts of the form to prevent inappropriate keystroke sequences (e.g. clicking Add and then clicking Next). The code is shown in Fig. 11.18 and this is discussed below.

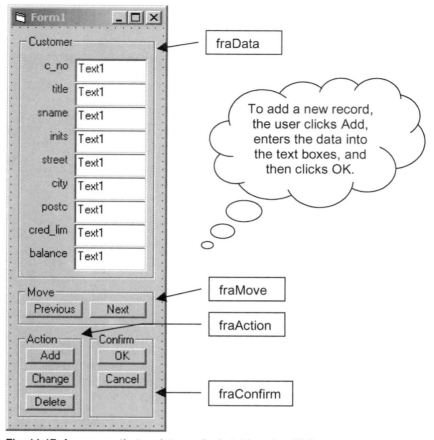

Fig. 11.17 A program that updates a single table using ADO.

```
Dim conn1
Dim rs1
Dim CurrentCommand
Private Sub Form_Load()
  fraData.Enabled = False
  fraMove.Enabled = True
  fraAction.Enabled = True
  fraConfirm.Enabled = False
  CurrentCommand = ""
  'Make connection to database
  Set conn1 = New ADODB.Connection
  conn1.Provider = "microsoft.jet.oledb.4.0;"
  conn1.ConnectionString = App.Path & "\accts.mdb"
  conn1.Open
  'Create the recordset
  Set rs1 = New ADODB.Recordset
```

```
    rs1.Open "customer", conn1, adOpenDynamic, adLockOptimistic
    Show
    Call DisplayTheCurrentRecord
End Sub

Sub DisplayTheCurrentRecord()
  For i = 0 To rs1.Fields.Count - 1
    If Not IsNull(rs1.Fields(i)) Then
      Text1(i) = rs1.Fields(i)
    Else
      Text1(i) = ""
    End If
  Next i
End Sub

Private Sub cmdNext_Click()
  rs1.MoveNext
  If rs1.EOF Then rs1.MoveLast
  Call DisplayTheCurrentRecord
End Sub

Private Sub cmdPrevious_Click()
  rs1.MovePrevious
  If rs1.BOF Then rs1.MoveFirst
  Call DisplayTheCurrentRecord
End Sub

Private Sub cmdAdd_Click()
  fraData.Enabled = True
  fraMove.Enabled = False
  fraAction.Enabled = False
  fraConfirm.Enabled = True
  CurrentCommand = "Add"
  For i = 0 To 8
    Text1(i) = ""
  Next i
  Text1(0).SetFocus
End Sub

Private Sub cmdChange_Click()
  fraData.Enabled = True
  fraMove.Enabled = False
  fraAction.Enabled = False
  fraConfirm.Enabled = True
  CurrentCommand = "Change"
End Sub
```

```
Private Sub cmdDelete_Click()
  fraData.Enabled = False
  fraMove.Enabled = False
  fraAction.Enabled = False
  fraConfirm.Enabled = True
  CurrentCommand = "Delete"
End Sub

Private Sub cmdOK_Click()
  On Error GoTo cmdOKError
  If CurrentCommand = "Add" Then
    rs1.AddNew
    For i = 0 To 8
      rs1.Fields(i) = Text1(i)
    Next i
    rs1.Update
  End If
  If CurrentCommand = "Change" Then
    For i = 0 To 8
      rs1.Fields(i) = Text1(i)
    Next i
    rs1.Update
  End If
  If CurrentCommand = "Delete" Then
    rs1.Delete
    rs1.MoveFirst
    Call DisplayTheCurrentRecord
  End If
cmdOKEnd:
  fraData.Enabled = False
  fraMove.Enabled = True
  fraAction.Enabled = True
  fraConfirm.Enabled = False
  Exit Sub
cmdOKError:
  X = "Error " & Err & " " & Error(Err)
  MsgBox X, vbCritical + vbOKOnly, CurrentCommand
  rs1.CancelUpdate
  Resume cmdOKEnd
End Sub

Private Sub cmdCancel_Click()
  fraData.Enabled = False
  fraMove.Enabled = True
  fraAction.Enabled = True
  fraConfirm.Enabled = False
End Sub
```

Fig. 11.18 The VB ADO code for the single table update program.

We now discuss each Sub in this application.

Form_Load

```
Private Sub Form_Load()
  fraData.Enabled = False
  fraMove.Enabled = True
  fraAction.Enabled = True
  fraConfirm.Enabled = False
  CurrentCommand = " "
  'Make connection to database
  Set conn1 = New ADODB.Connection
  conn1.Provider = "microsoft.jet.oledb.4.0;"
  conn1.ConnectionString = App.Path & "\accts.mdb"
  conn1.Open
  'Create the recordset
  Set rs1 = New ADODB.Recordset
  rs1.Open "customer", conn1, adOpenDynamic, adLockOptimistic
  Show
  Call DisplayTheCurrentRecord
End Sub
```

> Use oledb.3.51 for Access 97 databases

Referring to the code listing above, we start with Form_Load, which in VB is the Sub that executes first when a form is loaded. In our example, this form is Form1, the form shown in Fig. 11.17.

First the frames are appropriately enabled and disabled. We disable fraData to prevent accidental changes while viewing. fraMove is enabled to enable the cmd-Next and cmdPrevious buttons so the user can move from record to record. fraction is enabled so the user can Add, Change and Delete records. fraConfirm is disabled until one of the action buttons is clicked, at which time fraAction is disabled and fraConfirm is enabled. The variable CurrentCommand is used so that the OK button 'knows' which of the action buttons was previously pressed. Here it is initialized.

Then in Form_Load we open a new ADO connection. This involves naming a new connection (here conn1), specifying the type of data by naming the driver (here microsoft.jet.oledb.4.0), saying where the database is (here, in the same folder as the program), what its name is (here accts.mdb), and opening it.

Next, in Form_Load we open the recordset rs1. Note the parameters in the line:

```
rs1.Open "customer", conn1, adOpenDynamic, adLockOptimistic
```

Here we are opening the CUSTOMER table in the database conn1 is connected to. This creates a recordset rs1 in memory that contains all of the CUSTOMER records. We could have replaced the `"customer"` parameter with an SQL statement that filtered, grouped, sorted and joined data from several tables.

We have chosen the *cursor type* adOpenDynamic. There are four possibilities here and their functionality depends on the server. VB Help attempts to explain these complex dependencies. At the end of this section we discuss the Cursor Type parameter more fully. We use adOpenDynamic here because it allows simultaneous updates and allows you to move both forwards and backwards. This is what you will want to do in most cases.

The Show command forces VB to 'paint' the form (i.e. display it), and then we call the subroutine `DisplayTheCurrentRecord` to display the current record, which will be the record for the first customer.

DisplayTheCurrentRecord
```
Sub DisplayTheCurrentRecord()
  For i = 0 To rs1.Fields.Count − 1
    If Not IsNull(rs1.Fields(i)) Then
      Text1(i) = rs1.Fields(i)
    Else
      Text1(i) = " "
    End If
  Next i
End Sub
```

We have used a control array for the text boxes (i.e. we have used an array of text boxes), numbered text1(0) to text1(8). There are nine database fields to be displayed (c_no to balance). Since we don't have to refer to each text box by a separate name, we can use a For loop to access the fields. This is a standard advantage of an array compared with differently named variables, of course. `rs1.Fields.Count` is the number of fields in recordset rs1. The subroutine just moves the data from the fields of the current record into the text boxes. There is one minor snag. Text boxes can't cope with null values (!), which are of course standard in relational databases, so we have to put in a test and put an empty string where the Null field value would go.

cmdNext_Click
```
Private Sub cmdNext_Click()
  rs1.MoveNext
  If rs1.EOF Then rs1.MoveLast
  Call DisplayTheCurrentRecord
End Sub
```

The Next button and the Previous button are used in this program to navigate in the simplest possible way: move to the next record or move to the previous record in the recordset rs1.

Here we use the MoveNext command to move to the next record in the recordset, i.e. move the cursor to the next record – make it the 'current' record. Note that if the user keeps clicking, the cursor will first fall off the end of the recordset onto EOF (the End Of File marker) and if the user continues to click the Next button, an error would result. We cure this by moving to the last record whenever EOF is detected. After the move has occurred, we display the current record using our subroutine `DisplayTheCurrentRecord`.

What we are doing here is of course copying the functionality of VB's built-in Data Control, which we described in Chapter 9. To complete the simulation of the

Data Control, we really need First (MoveFirst) and Last (MoveLast) buttons. Another useful feature would be 'Fast forward' and 'Fast back' buttons, which could move, say, 10 records ahead or back.

cmdPrevious_Click

```
Private Sub cmdPrevious_Click()
  rs1.MovePrevious
  If rs1.BOF Then rs1.MoveFirst
  Call DisplayTheCurrentRecord
End Sub
```

Similar code here, except we are using MovePrevious and looking for BOF (Beginning of File), whence we MoveFirst.

cmdAdd_Click

As in previous programs, we use our tried-and-tested two-step approach to database updates. This two-step strategy works well and avoids the kind of problem you can get into with the Data Control, or Access, which goes something like this:

(a) Let's add a record.

(b) Woops, I made a mistake – I didn't really want to add that record.

(c) Let's delete it and start again.

(d) It's telling me I made a mistake again.

(e) (After some confusion) . . . Let's put a fictitious valid record in and then delete it.

(f) Now what have I added? Have I accidentally added a new customer somewhere in the hundred thousand existing ones?

The confusion in this situation can be exacerbated by the fact that the Data Control and Access automatically save any changes to the existing record if you move to a new record. So trying to run away from the problem doesn't work either.

There is no reason why we have to do things this way. If we write our own update code (instead of using the Data Control or Access Forms), we can use better methods. Here is our two-step approach:

- *Step 1* The user decides whether he/she wants to:
  - ○ Add a record (Add button, Sub amdAdd_Click),
  - ○ Change the current record (Change button, Sub cmdChange_Click), or
  - ○ Delete the current record (Delete button, Sub cmdDelete_Click)
- *Step 2* The user decides whether he/she wants to:
  - ○ Click OK to confirm the Add, Change or Delete (OK button, Sub cmdOK_Click), or
  - ○ Click Cancel to cancel the update (Cancel button, Sub cmdCancel_Click)

No update to either the recordset or the database occurs until the user clicks the OK button. We also enable and disable frames to allow the user to do only those things appropriate in a given situation. One of the ideas behind event-driven programming is that events can occur in any order – the initiative is with the user. Here, we are ensuring events occur only in the sequences that make sense. The initiative is with the program. For routine work like data entry, this makes sense and can reduce errors caused by casual users, at the expense perhaps of more keystrokes. Now to the code for cmdAdd_Click.

```
Private Sub cmdAdd_Click()
  fraData.Enabled = True
  fraMove.Enabled = False
  fraAction.Enabled = False
  fraConfirm.Enabled = True
  CurrentCommand = "Add"
  For i = 0 To 8
    Text1(i) = ""
  Next i
  Text1(0).SetFocus
End Sub
```

After enabling the text boxes (fraData) and the OK and Cancel buttons (fraConfirm) and disabling everything else, we set the value of the form-global variable CurrentCommand to "Add". This is so that the OK button will 'know' that it was an Add that it must now implement, not a Change or Delete. We then clear the text boxes and put the cursor in the first one.

cmdChange_Click

```
Private Sub cmdChange_Click()
  fraData.Enabled = True
  fraMove.Enabled = False
  fraAction.Enabled = False
  fraConfirm.Enabled = True
  CurrentCommand = "Change"
End Sub
```

The code and the logic are very similar here, except that we don't want to clear the text boxes. The user will want to see what he or she is going to be making changes to.

cmdDelete_Click

```
Private Sub cmdDelete_Click()
  fraData.Enabled = False
  fraMove.Enabled = False
  fraAction.Enabled = False
  fraConfirm.Enabled = True
  CurrentCommand = "Delete"
End Sub
```

Very similar code here too. But there's no need to enable the text boxes. The user will either delete the record or leave it as it is.

cmdOK_Click

All of the updating, to both the recordset, and, if nothing bad happens, to the database itself, occurs here. By clicking this button, the user has signalled that he/she is willing to let the update (Add, Change or Delete) go ahead.

```
Private Sub cmdOK_Click()
  On Error GoTo cmdOKError
  If CurrentCommand = "Add" Then
    rs1.AddNew
    For i = 0 To 8
      rs1.Fields(i) = Text1(i)
    Next i
    rs1.Update
  End If
  If CurrentCommand = "Change" Then
    For i = 0 To 8
      rs1.Fields(i) = Text1(i)
    Next i
    rs1.Update
  End If
  If CurrentCommand = "Delete" Then
    rs1.Delete
    rs1.MoveFirst
    Call DisplayTheCurrentRecord
  End If
cmdOKEnd:
  fraData.Enabled = False
  fraMove.Enabled = True
  fraAction.Enabled = True
  fraConfirm.Enabled = False
  Exit Sub
cmdOKError:
  X = "Error " & Err & " " & Error(Err)
  MsgBox X, vbCritical + vbOKOnly, CurrentCommand
  rs1.CancelUpdate
  Resume cmdOKEnd
End Sub
```

First, the error handling. This has been described earlier, but we give the basics again here.

```
On Error GoTo cmdOKError
```

says that if VB or Windows or the database server detects any error, control will pass to label cmdOKError. Here, a message box displays the error details and the update is cancelled with the (new to ADO – not in DAO) command

```
rs1.CancelUpdate
```

which cancels the update. VB, Windows and the server software will (hopefully) do the right things here. There is a bit of tidying up to do, which, in this program, needs to be done whether or not an error occurs, so we use the line

```
Resume cmdOKEnd
```

which passes control back to

```
cmdOKEnd:
  fraData.Enabled = False
  fraMove.Enabled = True
  fraAction.Enabled = True
  fraConfirm.Enabled = False
  Exit Sub
```

which enables and disables the right frames on the form and then exits.

For an **Add**, the code executed is:

```
If CurrentCommand = "Add" Then
  rs1.AddNew
  For i = 0 To 8
    rs1.Fields(i) = Text1(i)
  Next i
  rs1.Update
End If
```

In this code,

```
rs1.AddNew
```

adds a new blank record at the end of the recordset. Then a For loop is used to move the data from the text boxes into the fields of this new record. Finally, the line

```
rs1.Update
```

attempts to add the new record to the database. If any errors occur, for example the database doesn't like a blank address or a duplicate primary key has been detected or the database server is down, the error will be handled by the

```
On Error GoTo cmdOKError
```

and the code under the cmdOKError: line as already described.

For a **Change**, the code executed is:

```
If CurrentCommand = "Change" Then
  For i = 0 To 8
    rs1.Fields(i) = Text1(i)
  Next i
  rs1.Update
End If
```

Here there is no need to add a blank record. Note also that here the ADO code is different from what would be required for DAO. DAO would require a line

```
rs1.Edit
```

to precede the For loop.

Then the change made in the recordset is made to the database using the command

```
rs1.Update
```

For a **Delete**, the code executed is:

```
If CurrentCommand = "Delete" Then
  rs1.Delete
  rs1.MoveFirst
  Call DisplayTheCurrentRecord
End If
```

This deletes the record from the recordset *and* the database. No Update command is used. How curious.

So that the user has something to look at on the form (something that still exists, that is) we do a MoveFirst and display the record.

cmdCancel_Click
```
Private Sub cmdCancel_Click()
  fraData.Enabled = False
  fraMove.Enabled = True
  fraAction.Enabled = True
  fraConfirm.Enabled = False
End Sub
```

Here we have no cleaning up to do. No partial updates. Since all the update code is in the OK button (none anywhere else), all the Cancel button has to do is to reset the frames to enable an appropriate set of objects on the form.

That concludes the description of the (nice, simple) ADO code for updating a single table.

Similar examples appear in ASP form in Chapter 15. ASP uses ADO commands for databases. In the ASP case, both the database and the update program are on the *server* on the internet, not on a local hard disk or LAN as here. In ASP the code is actually in VBScript, a language similar to VB. Instead of being interpreted locally by a local copy of VB, in the ASP situation, the VBScript is interpreted on the server by a program called IIS. And instead of being able to read and write from/to a VB form, the VBScript has to generate HTML code for the user's browser (IE or Netscape) to interpret. So the Input / Output is different, and the program runs on the server to generate HTML code that runs on the client – that's different, but the basic language is the same, and the database commands (ADO) are very similar. The ideas about recordsets (moving, updating, searching) and the database commands you use are identical in VB and ASP.

11.5 The ADO Recordset Open command – cursors and locking

Earlier, in Form_Load, we had the following ADO Open command, which opens a recordset.

```
rs1.Open "customer", conn1, adOpenDynamic, adLockOptimistic
```

Let's now look at the syntax of this command in more detail.

The full syntax of the Open command is:

recordset.Open Source, ActiveConnection, CursorType, LockType, Options

Source

This is the source of the data and can be either a table name or an SQL query such as "select customer.c_no, sname, sum(amount) as invoicetotal from customer inner join invoice on customer.c_no = invoice.c_no group by c_no, sname" . You can use any SQL select statement here, involving any number of tables, giving remarkable flexibility and delivering to your recordset just the data you want, making your program use less memory and making the program easier to write. We have mentioned elsewhere that SQL is the heart of database access.

ActiveConnection

In our example, we used the following code to give a value to this parameter:

```
Set conn1 = New ADODB.Connection
conn1.Provider = "microsoft.jet.oledb.4.0;"
conn1.ConnectionString = App.Path & "\accts.mdb"
conn1.Open
```

This specifies the type and location of the data.

Cursor type

Here is a simplified description of the four cursor types. (A 'cursor' by the way is the name some people give to a recordset; they also use the same word for the pointer to the current record in a recordset. What a 'cursor type' is in the present context is nothing other than a recordset. So what we are looking at here is the four types of recordset available in ADO.) In this book we prefer to use the term *recordset* for a recordset and *current record* for the current record – the record currently being 'pointed at'.

Cursor Type

adOpenDynamic

Allows all types of movement (MoveNext, MovePrevious, MoveFirst, Move-Last, jumps using Find (see next section) etc.). You can add, change, and delete, and if you're sharing the database concurrently with other users, all the updates they make (adds, changes and deletions) to parts of the database that your recordset uses will appear in your recordset.

adOpenKeyset

Allows all types of movement (MoveNext, MovePrevious, MoveFirst, Move-Last, jumps using Find (see next section) etc.). You can add, change, and delete, and if you're sharing the database concurrently with other users, the changes and deletions to parts of the database that your recordset uses will appear in your recordset. *But other users' Adds won't appear in your recordset.* Not until you re-create the recordset by closing it and open ing it again.

adOpenStatic

Allows all types of movement (MoveNext, MovePrevious, MoveFirst, Move-Last, jumps using Find (see next section) etc.). You can add, change, and delete records. *But other users' Adds, Changes and Deletes won't appear in your recordset.* Not until you re-create the recordset – close it and open it again.

adOpenForwardOnly

Allows only MoveNext. You can add, change, and delete records. *But other users' Adds, Changes and Deletes won't appear in your recordset.* Not until you re-create the recordset – close it and open it again.

Fig. 11.19 ADO Cursor Type.

We have found that in practice, for a single user accessing a local Jet database, *all* values of this parameter allow *all* types of movement and *all* types of update. The only way to get a 'forward only' is to leave the cursor type parameter out, as in:

```
rs1.Open "customer", conn1
```

LockType
Record locking is used by a 'provider' (usually a DBMS such as Jet or SQL*Server or Oracle) to ensure against update anomalies caused when more than one process is accessing the same record. Here are a couple of examples:

The 'Lost Update' problem
In this type of concurrency problem, two or more processes ('transactions') are attempting to update the same record at the same time and the effects of the first update are overwritten by the second update. Here's an example. Transaction A wants to add £100 to customer 2's balance of £200, and Transaction B wants to add £50 to it.

1. Transaction A fetches the CUSTOMER record for customer 2.

2. Transaction B fetches the same record.

3. Transaction A adds £100 to the BALANCE field.

4. Transaction B adds £50 to the BALANCE field.

5. Transaction A writes the customer 2 record back to the database with a BALANCE of £300.

6. Transaction B writes the Customer 2 record back to the database with a BALANCE of £250.

CUSTOMER.BALANCE is now £250 but it should be £350. Transaction A has been lost.

Clearly, Transaction A (which 'got there first') should lock the record for customer 2 until it has written its result back to the database.

The 'Inconsistent Analysis' problem

In this type of concurrency problem, a value such as a count, sum or average is being calculated from one or more database tables, and while this is happening, the records concerned are being updated. Here's an example. Transaction A is calculating the total balance of all customers. At the same time, Transaction B is transferring £100 from customer 2's BALANCE field to customer 2000's BALANCE field. If the transfer interleaves in an unfortunate way with the sum, an incorrect sum will result. Here's the unfortunate sequence:

1. Transaction A starts summing CUSTOMER.BALANCE.

2. After Transaction A has added customer 2's balance to its running total but before it gets to customer 2000, Transaction B deducts £100 from customer 2's balance and adds it to customer 2000's balance.

3. Transaction A now gets to customer 2000's record and adds in the extra £100 to its running total, having missed the reduction in customer 2's balance.

4. The result is that Transaction A reports an incorrect total.

Clearly, Transaction A (which 'got there first') should lock the whole CUSTOMER table until it's finished its entire scan of the table.

Locking should ideally lock only those records that need to be locked and for the minimum time necessary to avoid the types of error above. What should be avoided is the over-zealous use of locking, because this could delay transactions and even cause 'deadlock' – a situation in which a group of transactions each locks records which one or more of the others needs. ADO has four lock types (Fig. 11.20), and you specify them when opening the recordset.

Lock Type

adLockOptimistic

The DBMS leaves the locking of the record until the transaction calls the Update method. So if you are about to change the BALANCE field of a CUSTOMER record, such as customer 2, you will open a recordset and apply the Edit method, then go away to another part of the database, for example totalling INVOICE and PAYMENT amounts, and by the time you get back to the recordset to apply the Update method, another process has changed the balance of customer 2. You apply the ADO Update method and the effects of the other update process are lost – the lost update problem as above. You have to be optimistic to use this type of locking, hoping that this unfortunate interleaving of transactions doesn't happen too often. The good side of it is that the records involved will be locked for the minimum period. And you could program the update such that the recordset is not created until the invoice and payment calculations are complete. That way the Edit and Update methods are close together in time and the risk of a lost update is minimized.

adLockPessimistic

The records involved in the recordset are locked immediately upon editing.

adLockReadOnly

This is the default, meaning that if you give no value to the LockType parameter, you get this. No updates are allowed.

adLockBatchOptimistic

This is the locking method you must use if you are doing batch updates. With batch updates, you store up changes to records and then apply them all in one 'run'. You use the UpdateBatch method to do this. Any individual updates from other users' transactions are halted until your batch update has completed.

Fig. 11.20 ADO Lock Type.

In an experiment to test the concurrency properties of the **adOpenDynamic** cursor type (we use the term concurrency here to mean several users simultaneously accessing the same database), we set up the situation shown in Fig. 11.21, overleaf.

We created security permissions on the folder so that the students had update rights on the shared database. Each student was given a copy of the CUSTOMER table update program of Figs 11.17 and 11.18 to run on his/her PC. The Connection-String property was altered as shown in Fig. 11.22 to access this shared database. Then all 18 students started their update programs, connecting to the shared database.

In practice, we found that for cursor type adOpenDynamic and locking type adLockOptimistic, the following behaviour occurred. To see records *added* by other users, you had to stop the program and start it again, re-creating the recordset. *Changes* that other users made were immediately visible in each user's recordset. If

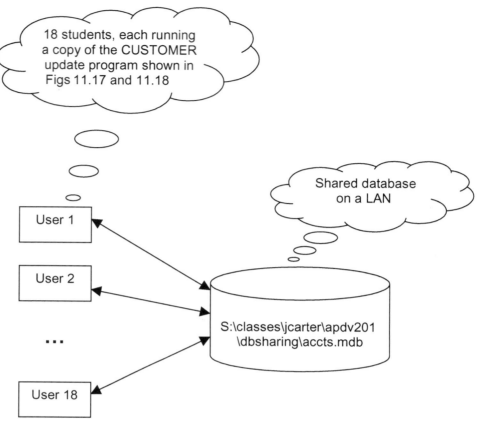

Fig. 11.21 Concurrent update of shared accts.mdb Access 2000 database on LAN.

```
'Make connection to database
  Set conn1 = New ADODB.Connection
  conn1.Provider = "microsoft.jet.oledb.4.0;"
  conn1.ConnectionString =
"S:\classes\jcarter\apdv201\dbsharing\accts.mdb"
  conn1.Open
  'Create the recordset
  Set rs1 = New ADODB.Recordset
  rs1.Open "customer", conn1, adOpenDynamic, adLockOptimistic
```

Fig. 11.22 Modification to Form_Load to make program link up to LAN database.

another user had *deleted* a record, attempting to access that record would result in a
runtime error, but restarting your program (re-creating the recordset) would clear
the error.

More details of these concurrency experiments can be found on:

http://www.databasedesign.co.uk

It is clear that adequate error handling in a program that is intended for concurrent database access needs to consider errors caused by the activities of *other users*. In our program (Fig. 11.17, Fig. 11.18), this can be effected quite simply by adding standard On Error Goto code in Sub cmdDelete_Click and Sub cmdPrevious_Click.

11.6 Find buttons

We now extend our simple one-table ADO example by adding Find first and Find next buttons. The ADO syntax is different (and simpler) from that used in DAO. DAO used FindFirst and FindNext, whereas ADO just used Find.

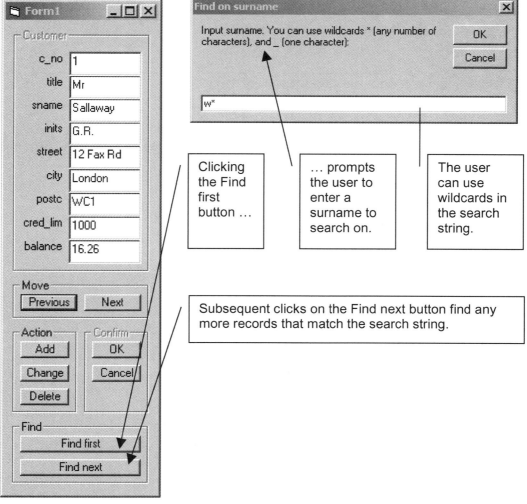

Fig. 11.23 Adding Find buttons.

```
Private Sub cmdFindFirst_Click()
  cmdFindNext.Enabled = False
  x = InputBox("Input surname. You can use wildcards * (any number of
characters), and _ (one character):", "Find on surname")
  rs1.MoveFirst
  rs1.Find "sname like " & "'" & x & "'"
  If rs1.EOF Then
    MsgBox "No such customer", vbInformation + vbOKOnly, "Find on
surname"
    rs1.MoveFirst
  Else
    Call DisplayTheCurrentRecord
    cmdFindNext.Enabled = True
  End If
End Sub
```

Fig. 11.24 The code for the Find first button.

```
Private Sub cmdFindNext_Click()
  rs1.MoveNext
  rs1.Find "sname like " & "'" & x & "'"
  If rs1.EOF Then
    MsgBox "Reached end of file.", vbInformation + vbOKOnly, "Find on
surname"
    rs1.MoveFirst
  Else
    Call DisplayTheCurrentRecord
  End If
End Sub
```

Fig. 11.25 The code for the Find next button.

We can see that exactly the same Find command is used for finding the first
record matching some criterion as for finding subsequent records that match the
criterion:

```
rs1.Find "sname like " & "'" & x & "'"
```

Here we have the search string in a variable x which gets a value from the user,
including wildcards, in Sub cmdFindFirst_Click(). This variable x must be
declared in General Declarations so that it's global to both Subs. Fuzzy matching is
used here by employing the SQL 'like' syntax. Because the sname field is text, the
value of x we're searching for must be enclosed in single quotes. These are concatenated onto the front and back of the value of x. The single quote characters are
themselves string data, so they have to be enclosed in double quotes.

cmdFindFirst

First, we disable the FindNext button so that it is disabled until a successful find. We then use an InputBox to obtain the value of the search string. The user can use * to signify any number of characters and _ for a single character, __ for two characters etc. We then move to the beginning of the recordset rs1, which contains the customer records, and apply the Find method. If no such record exists, rs1.EOF will evaluate to True, and we can display a message box to that effect and move back to the start of the recordset. If there is a successful find, we display the record and the FindNext button is enabled. It remains enabled until the user clicks the Find first button again, signifying he/she wants to begin a new search.

cmdFindNext

We move off the first match and using the same search string, execute another Find command. If it's unsuccessful, we display the fact in a message box, and move to the first record. The variable x still retains its value and the user can look at the hits again by clicking Find next. If successful, the record is displayed.

11.7 Exercises

Note: if you have not already created your own copy of the database *accts.mdb* used in these exercises, you can download it from the website **http://www.databasedesign.co.uk**.

1. Define the following terms:

   (a) ADO

   (b) DAO

   (c) OLE DB

   (d) ODBC

   (e) Provider

   (f) Data Source

   (g) Connection String

   (h) Connection.Open method

   (i) DSN

   (j) Cursor and CursorType

   (k) Concurrency

   (l) Lost Update problem

   (m) Inconsistent Analysis problem

   (n) Locking and LockType

2. Convert the project of Section 10.6 to ADO.

3. Convert the project of Section 10.10 to ADO.

4. *Navigation* In the ADO project of Figs 11.17 and 11.18, we really need First (MoveFirst) and Last (MoveLast) buttons (Access has these), and possibly Fast forward

and Fast back buttons (Access doesn't have these), which could move, say, 10 records ahead or back. Implement these.

5. *Error handling*   In the ADO project of Figs 11.17 and 11.18, update the Sub cmd-Next_Click and cmdPrevious_Click so that they contain suitable error-handling code. This was found necessary, remember (end of section 11.5), to cope with errors that could be caused by other concurrent users of the database.

6. *Search*   In the ADO project of Figs 11.17 and 11.18, enhance the Find facility so that

 (a) the user gets to choose a field to search on;

 (b) the user gets to choose a *combination* of fields to search on (you could use the approach used in Fig. 12.8, which also lets the user choose the *selection criteria*, e.g. > 500; <> 'Leeds' etc.).

7. *Sort*   In the ADO project of Figs 11.17 and 11.18, add a Sort button and, optionally, give the user these extra facilities:

 (a) choosing the sort field(s);

 (b) choosing the sort sequence: ascending or descending, on each field.

8. The ADO update program of Figs 11.17 and 11.18 updates just a single table CUS-TOMER in the *accts.mdb* database. Create a project that has forms to update the CUSTOMER, INVOICE and PAYMENT tables. It should have the following capabilities:

 (a) Add new CUSTOMER records.

 (b) Add new INVOICE records.

 (c) Add new PAYMENT records.

   Note: If, as we suggested, you have enforced *referential integrity* (see section 3.6) on the relationships between the CUSTOMER and INVOICE tables, and the relationship between the INVOICE and PAYMENT tables, it won't be possible to add an invoice for a customer who doesn't exist, and it won't be possible to add a payment for an invoice that doesn't exist. That is what we want. Make sure your program contains error-handling code to handle any attempt to break the referential integrity rule. A simple warning that a record for the customer must be set up before allocating him/her an invoice should suffice. Handling an error (using On Error Goto in VB) is sometimes called error trapping. The error is a 'trappable error' because it is 'trapped' before it can cause a crash.

 (d) Change existing CUSTOMER records.

 (e) Change existing INVOICE records.

 (f) Change existing PAYMENT records.

   Note: If, as we suggested, you have enforced *cascade update* in the relationships between these three tables in the *accts.mdb* database (see section 3.6), changing the primary key value of either the CUSTOMER or INVOICE tables (CUSTOMER.C_NO and INVOICE.INV_NO) shouldn't create an error. The changed c_no will just 'cascade' down to all of that customer's invoices. It's the same for inv_no in the INVOICE and PAYMENT tables. Changing INVOICE.INV_NO for an invoice should automatically change all the corresponding invoice numbers in the PAYMENT table.

(g) Delete existing CUSTOMER records.

(h) Delete existing INVOICE records.

(i) Delete existing PAYMENT records.

Note: If, as we have suggested, you have *not* enforced *cascade delete* in the relationships between these three tables in the *accts.mdb* database, the deleting a CUSTOMER record for a customer who has INVOICE records will create an error. Make sure you trap the error (by using On Error Goto, for example). A suitable strategy might be to ask the user to delete the invoices and payments first – give them a list, perhaps. That will make them ask the relevant questions about the proposed deletion. Alternatively, provide a button to delete the customer record and all its invoices and payments, but make them say they are sure they want to do it. Then your program can do this chore itself.

9. **Enhance the program of 8. by adding the following features:**

(a) A form to show, for a given customer, all his/her invoices and associated payments.

(b) A facility for updating the customer's current balance (CUSTOMER.BALANCE) based on the following formula:

new balance = old balance + Σ invoice amounts – Σ payment amounts

(c) A form to print a statement of account on paper, similar to that in section 10.10.

(d) Find facility – see 6. above. Think about which fields in which tables the user is most likely to want to search on.

10. **Enhance the program of 8. (or 9.) to have a security feature in which no password is required to view data from *accts.mdb*, a password is required to add and delete invoices and payments and to make changes to customer addresses, and a different password is required to add and delete customer records and to change any field other than the address fields.**

Chapter 12

Visual Basic database programming using Access modules

In this chapter you will learn:

- how to program Access modules in VBA
- how to permit code to be shared between different applications
- how to use DAO commands within Access modules
- how to program transactions.

12.1 Introduction

We continue our coverage of Visual Basic database programming, but this time within the context of Access modules. In Chapters 3 to 8 we covered the issues of database design, queries, forms, macros and reports in Access. We continue by covering Access modules.

12.2 Access modules

Modules are where you write VB code to do the detailed database manipulation that can't be done using Access forms (AutoForms and wizards) and macros. Having seen Visual Basic database programming in the three previous chapters, we are now in a good position to return to Access modules and give some examples of programming in this environment. In previous chapters we have developed the VB database code in separate VB project and form files. When you write Access modules, the code is usually stored in the .mdb file along with the tables, queries, forms and macros. The principles are the same, however, and the language is virtually identical.

Advantages of Access modules over Access macros
While macros allow us to string together a number of commands which we could have done manually, and even allow us to execute commands conditionally,

modules give us the full power of a programming language, including looping (iteration). As we have said, the language used in modules is Visual Basic, but in the context of Access modules it is sometimes called VBA – Visual Basic for Applications. The core of VBA is identical to the Visual Basic we have used in previous chapters, and is also used in other packages, such as Excel.

Whether you should use modules or macros in an Access application, or a mixture of the two, depends on the application.

Advantages of modules

In general, the characteristics of modules (compared with macros) include the following:

1. Modules are algorithmic, allowing all the programming structures associated with programming languages, such as sequence, selection and iteration.

2. Modules give the programmer more control over *how* a process is to be carried out. The programmer can define the precise steps he or she wants.

3. In the hands of a good programmer, the VBA database code in modules can result in faster processing and/or more efficient use of memory.

4. Modules can give the application greater control over error handling than the default error handling of Access.

Event-driven programming

When you program in VBA you write *procedures*. Many VBA procedures in Windows applications are *event driven*: they are written to respond to an event such as a user clicking a command button or a different record becoming current or a certain date/time occurring. Other (non-event-driven) procedures on the other hand can be called directly from your code. In Visual Basic all procedures are coded as Subs (subroutines).

Form modules

Each Access form has a *module* associated with it; it's called its *form module*. This is where the procedures for the objects on that form go. Each object has a set of properties and events. Each event has a procedure – a Sub. The code in the Sub executes when the event occurs.

You can either tie an Access form to a database using the form's recordsource property, as we did in Chapter 8, or you can leave the recordsource blank and then be in a development environment similar to the Visual Basic environment.

Standard modules

It is also possible to create modules that are independent of forms, by clicking the Modules tab in the main database window. This is where you would store general-purpose procedures callable from anywhere. These are Standard modules. You have to name them yourself.

12.3 Form modules and Standard modules

We use here a very simple example to illustrate the difference between Form modules and Standard modules.

Creating a Form module

1. Create, using Design view, a new form. Don't tie it to a Record Source.

2. Put a command button onto the form. Cancel out of the Command Button Wizard. Our command button is called Command0.

3. In the Properties window, change the command button's Caption property to 'Click here'. You can change the Name property in the Properties window too if you want to.

4. Put a label onto the form. In the label, click the spacebar to clear the caption.

5. You should now have a form that looks something like Fig. 12.1.

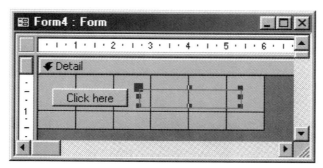

Fig. 12.1 A simple form to demonstrate event-driven programming.

6. Run the form and you will see that absolutely nothing happens when you click the command button. That's because we have not included any code to respond to this event – the Command0_Click event. Notice also that since this form is not to be used to display data, we can remove the Record Selectors and set the Navigation Buttons' properties to No.

7. To include code into the command button, right-click it and select Build Event, then Code Builder. This should open up the Code window and show the Click

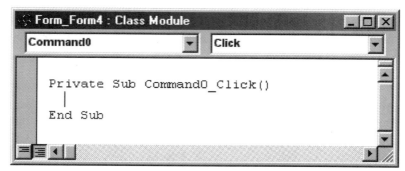

Fig. 12.2 The Code window.

Event Sub for the command button Command0 (Fig. 12.2). This is very similar to the Visual Basic development environment we have seen in previous chapters.

8. Find the name Access has given to the label using the Properties window. Our label is called Label5. Add code to set the value of its Caption property to "Hello" when the command button is clicked (Fig. 12.3).

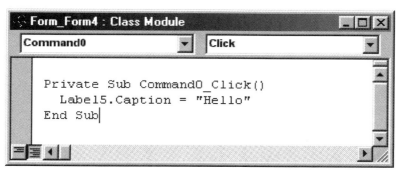

Fig. 12.3 Code has been added.

9. Run the form and click the command button. "Hello" should appear in the label.

10. Modify the code as shown in Fig. 12.4. Clicking the command button will now cause a beep. DoCmd is a useful 'object' to execute Access 'actions'. An action is a command that could appear in a macro.

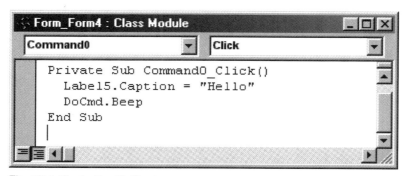

Fig. 12.4 Illustrating DoCmd.

Each control you add to the form can have code added to respond to the various events that 'happen' to the control.

We have seen in this example one difference between programming in 'raw' Visual Basic, and VB in Access. The DoCmd ('Do Command') object is a special Access extension to Visual Basic. You can use DoCmd to run Microsoft Access actions from Visual Basic. An action performs tasks such as opening forms and setting the property values of controls. For example, you can use the OpenForm method of the DoCmd object to open a form as follows:

```
DoCmd.OpenForm "Form1"
```

Note that from Access 97 onward, the syntax for DoCmd has altered slightly from previous versions:

The DoCmd object replaces the DoCmd statement from versions 1.x and 2.0 of Microsoft Access. The actions that were used as arguments for the DoCmd statement are now methods of the DoCmd object. For example, in Microsoft Access 2.0, you could have used the code DoCmd OpenForm "Orders" to open a form from Access Basic [Access Help].

Creating a Standard module

As we mentioned above, Access Standard modules are independent of forms. Standard modules are where you would store general-purpose procedures (Subs) callable from anywhere. If you create a standard module you have to name it yourself. We give a very simple example here that nevertheless illustrates how to create a standard module.

1. Create a new blank form: Database Window, Forms tab, New button, Design View, and leave recordsource combo blank. Insert a text box and a command button onto the form (Fig. 12.5). We are going to arrange things so that clicking the command button calls a subroutine SayHello in a module. This subroutine will simply put the word "Hello" into the textbox.

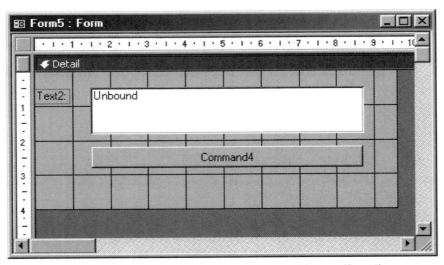

Fig. 12.5 An unbound form and a text box and command button (Step 1).

2. In the Database Window, click the Modules tab, click New, and create the subroutine shown in Fig. 12.6.

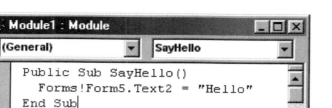

Fig. 12.6 A simple Sub in the module Module1.

3. In Form5, right-click the command button, select Build Event, and type the call to the subroutine (Fig. 12.7).

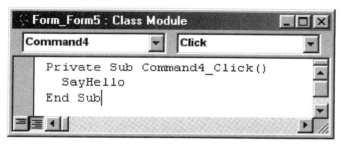

Fig. 12.7 Calling the Sub from Form5's command button's click event.

4. Save the Module1 and Form5.

5. Run Form5 (right-click its title bar and select Form View). Click the command button and you should see "Hello" appear in the text box. The subroutine SayHello in the 'Standard' module Module1 has been called from Form5.

This section has illustrated the differences between modules bound to forms, and standard modules.

12.4 Example: Database filtering on more than one criterion

We use this as a small case study to further develop our understanding of programming in Access VBA. We use an entirely DAO (Data Access Objects) approach, which means that we do not tie a Form to a recordset, but instead use OpenRecordset, MoveFirst, MoveNext etc.

Note that when developing VBA program code in Access, it is wise to compile the module before running it, so that the specific line causing the problem is revealed. To do this, highlight the Code window and from the Menu, select Run, Compile Loaded Modules.

In many situations, it is useful to be able to search through a large database to retrieve all records that obey one or more criteria. Access itself allows you to search for simple criteria on one field. By writing SQL queries, or using the Access query grid, various combinations of criteria can be used. However, each combination requires a different query.

In this application, we allow users to set combinations of conditions in an *ad hoc* fashion. We use the CUSTOMER table to demonstrate this. This table has nine fields. The application builds up a dynamic SQL SELECT command at runtime with a WHERE clause for each non-blank condition.

The form used is shown in Fig. 12.8.

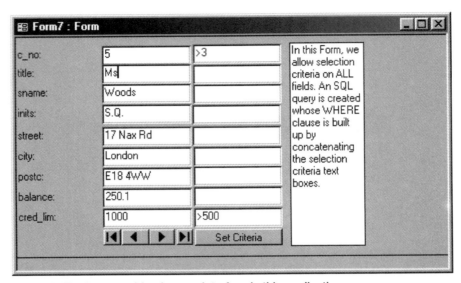

Fig. 12.8 The form used for the user interface in this application.

Typing criteria in the second column of text boxes and then clicking the 'Set Criteria' command button retrieves all the CUSTOMER records that satisfy the combination of criteria into a recordset. Navigating through the resulting recordset is achieved by clicking the custom navigation command buttons shown under the first column of text boxes. Each of these four command buttons has had its Picture property set to a suitable bitmap.

The names of the relevant controls on this form are as follows:

- The nine text boxes in the first column are named according to the corresponding CUSTOMER table field: txtc_no, txttitle, . . . , txtbalance.
- The nine 'criteria' text boxes are named as txtC_noCriteria, txtTitleCriteria, . . . , txtCred_limCriteria.
- The four 'navigation' command buttons are named as cmdMoveFirst, cmdMoveLast, cmdMoveNext, and cmdMovePrevious.
- The 'Set Criteria' command button is named cmdSetCriteria.

Since the code needed to make this form work is not needed by any other form, we have located it in the form itself. Most of the code is in General Declarations in custom subroutines. Each of the five command buttons calls one of these Subs. Form_Load also calls subroutines in General Declarations.

Notice that we are providing all of the code ourselves and thus have total control over how this form works.

The program code

```
Dim db1 As Database 'These three lines in General Decs
Dim ta1 As Recordset
Dim x$

Private Sub Form_Load() 'Event procedure
  Set db1 = CurrentDb
  procSetCriteria
  procDisplayCusRecord
End Sub

Private Sub procSetCriteria() 'in General Decs
  On Error GoTo L2
  Dim FirstCriterion As Integer 'Used to decide on WHERE or AND
in the WHERE clause
  Dim x$ 'Contains the final built-up SQL string used for the
recordsource
  FirstCriterion = True
  x$ = "select * from cus"
  If Not IsNull(txtC_noCriteria) Then
    x$ = x$ & " where c_no " & txtC_noCriteria
    FirstCriterion = False
  End If
  If Not IsNull(txtTitleCriteria) Then
    If FirstCriterion Then
      x$ = x$ & " where title " & txtTitleCriteria
      FirstCriterion = False
    Else
      x$ = x$ & " and title " & txtTitleCriteria
    End If
  End If
  If Not IsNull(txtSnameCriteria) Then
    If FirstCriterion Then
      x$ = x$ & " where sname " & txtSnameCriteria
      FirstCriterion = False
    Else
      x$ = x$ & " and sname " & txtSnameCriteria
    End If
  End If
  If Not IsNull(txtInitsCriteria) Then
    If FirstCriterion Then
      x$ = x$ & " where inits " & txtInitsCriteria
      FirstCriterion = False
```

```
          Else
            x$ = x$ & " and inits " & txtInitsCriteria
          End If
        End If
        If Not IsNull(txtStreetCriteria) Then
          If FirstCriterion Then
            x$ = x$ & " where street " & txtStreetCriteria
            FirstCriterion = False
          Else
            x$ = x$ & " and street " & txtStreetCriteria
          End If
        End If
        If Not IsNull(txtCityCriteria) Then
          If FirstCriterion Then
            x$ = x$ & " where city " & txtCityCriteria
            FirstCriterion = False
          Else
            x$ = x$ & " and city " & txtCityCriteria
          End If
        End If
        If Not IsNull(txtPostcCriteria) Then
          If FirstCriterion Then
            x$ = x$ & " where postc " & txtPostcCriteria
            FirstCriterion = False
          Else
            x$ = x$ & " and postc " & txtPostcCriteria
          End If
        End If
        If Not IsNull(txtBalanceCriteria) Then
          If FirstCriterion Then
            x$ = x$ & " where balance " & txtBalanceCriteria
            FirstCriterion = False
          Else
            x$ = x$ & " and balance " & txtBalanceCriteria
          End If
        End If
        If Not IsNull(txtCred_limCriteria) Then
          If FirstCriterion Then
            x$ = x$ & " where cred_lim " & txtCred_limCriteria
            FirstCriterion = False
          Else
            x$ = x$ & " and cred_lim " & txtCred_limCriteria
          End If
        End If
        Set ta1 = db1.OpenRecordset(x$, dbOpenDynaset)
        procDisplayCusRecord
    L1:
```

```
      Exit Sub
    L2:
      e$ = "Error " & Err & " " & Error(Err)
      MsgBox e$, 48, "Error opening recordset"
      Resume L1
    End Sub


    Private Sub procDisplayCusRecord() 'in General Decs
      On Error GoTo L4
      txtc_no = ta1!c_no
      txttitle = ta1!title
      txtsname = ta1!sname
      txtinits = ta1!inits
      txtstreet = ta1!street
      txtcity = ta1!city
      txtpostc = ta1!postc
      txtbalance = ta1!balance
      txtcred_lim = ta1!cred_lim
    L3:
      Exit Sub
    L4:
      e$ = "Error " & Err & " " & Error(Err)
      If Err = 3021 Then
        e$ = e$ & " There are no customer records like this."
      End If
      MsgBox e$, 48, "Error opening recordset"
      Resume L3
    End Sub


    Private Sub cmdMoveFirst_Click()   'Event procedure
      ta1.MoveFirst
      procDisplayCusRecord
    End Sub


    Private Sub cmdMoveLast_Click()    'Event procedure
      ta1.MoveLast
      procDisplayCusRecord
    End Sub


    Private Sub cmdMoveNext_Click()    'Event procedure
      ta1.MoveNext
      If ta1.EOF Then ta1.MovePrevious
      procDisplayCusRecord
    End Sub


    Private Sub cmdMovePrevious_Click()   'Event procedure
      ta1.MovePrevious
```

```
      If ta1.BOF Then ta1.MoveFirst
      procDisplayCusRecord
   End Sub


   Private Sub cmdSetCriteria_Click()   'Event procedure
      procSetCriteria
   End Sub
```

Explanation of program code
We now describe the function of each of the parts of this program. First, consider the three Dim statements in General Declarations.

```
Dim db1 As Database   'These three lines in General Decs
Dim ta1 As Table
Dim x$
```

We first define db1 as a database object type. This is the name we shall give to the current database (accts.mdb) in this program. We are accessing only one table in the database – the CUSTOMER table. We shall refer to the recordset as ta1. We also use a variable x$ in this form. We declare it here in General Declarations because it is referred to in several different subroutines.

The first event that occurs when the form runs is Form_Load.

Form_Load
```
   Private Sub Form_Load()
      Set db1 = CurrentDb
      procSetCriteria
      procDisplayCusRecord
   End Sub
```

The first line sets the name of the current database (accts.mdb) into the object variable db1. The database will subsequently, in the following code, be referred to as db1. CurrentDb is a function call which delivers the name of the current database. Remember that with Access, all the code is contained in the .mdb file.

Form_Load calls the two subroutines procSetCriteria and procDisplayCusRecord. The Sub procSetCriteria is used to form the SQL SELECT statement which retrieves the required set of records from the CUSTOMER database table. The set of records it retrieves is governed by the contents of the second column of text boxes, which of course on Form_Load, are all blank. When we describe the procSetCriteria subroutine, we shall see that this results in the whole of the CUSTOMER table being retrieved. The subroutine procDisplayCusRecord displays the current CUSTOMER record by copying the relevant field values into the first column of text boxes.

procSetCriteria
This subroutine is used to form an embedded SQL SELECT statement that will retrieve the records the user wants from the CUSTOMER table, governed by the selection criteria he or she puts in the second column of text boxes. For the selection criteria shown in Fig. 12.8, for example, the required SQL command is:

```
SELECT *
FROM CUSTOMER
WHERE C_NO > 3
AND CRED_LIM > 500
```

Notice that what the procedure must do is produce a WHERE clause for the first selection criterion, and an AND clause for each of the other criteria.

There might of course be *no* criteria, and the first criterion could be any of the nine fields c_no to cred_lim.

The string variable x$ is used to contain the SQL SELECT statement.

The error handling in this procedure is standard:

```
On Error GoTo L2

Bulk of code goes here.

L1:
  Exit Sub
L2:
  e$ = "Error " & Err & " " & Error(Err)
  MsgBox e$, 48, "Error opening recordset"
  Resume L1
```

Any error transfers control to label L2:, where a message box displays the error message.

```
Dim FirstCriterion As Integer
```

The variable FirstCriterion is declared. It will be set to True when the first non-blank criterion text box is encountered, and then set to False. This is part of the mechanism for putting WHERE in the first condition clause of the SQL SELECT, and AND in the rest.

```
Dim x$
```

x$ will contain the SELECT statement.

```
FirstCriterion = True
x$ = "select * from cus"
If Not IsNull(txtC_noCriteria) Then
  x$ = x$ & " where c_no " & txtC_noCriteria
  FirstCriterion = False
End If
```

This section of code covers the txtC_noCriteria text box. If it's not null (empty), x$ will contain a WHERE clause. The first part of the string x$ will contain "select * from cus" and the second part "where c_no = *value*", where *value* is the value in the text box. If none of the criteria text boxes contains anything, x$ will end up containing just "select * from cus", which is what we want. If this criteria text box does contain something, then the flag variable FirstCriterion will be set to False. This is used in subsequent code to switch from WHERE to AND in the SELECT statement.

The next sections of code each deal with a remaining criterion text box:

```
If Not IsNull(txtTitleCriteria) Then
    If FirstCriterion Then
      x$ = x$ & " where title " & txtTitleCriteria
      FirstCriterion = False
    Else
      x$ = x$ & " and title " & txtTitleCriteria
    End If
  End If
```

If the text box is not null then if it's the *first* non-null one, a WHERE clause is added to the SQL SELECT string; otherwise an AND clause is added.

This is repeated for each of the remaining criteria text boxes.

Finally in this procedure, the SQL SELECT string x$ is used to retrieve the desired CUSTOMER records:

```
Set ta1 = db1.OpenRecordset(x$, dbOpenDynaset)
```

Here a dynaset type recordset is created, although since this version of the program has no update facility, a snapshot recordset would be satisfactory.

The subroutine ends with a call to the subroutine procDisplayCusRecord to display the current record in the recordset in the first column of text boxes.

Note that error handling is important in this Sub, because the users could type 'any old rubbish' in the criteria text boxes. On Error Goto handles all such errors.

procDisplayCusRecord
```
  Private Sub procDisplayCusRecord() 'in General Decs
    On Error GoTo L4
    txtc_no = ta1!c_no
    txttitle = ta1!title
    txtsname = ta1!sname
    txtinits = ta1!inits
    txtstreet = ta1!street
    txtcity = ta1!city
    txtpostc = ta1!postc
    txtbalance = ta1!balance
    txtcred_lim = ta1!cred_lim
  L3:
    Exit Sub
  L4:
    e$ = "Error " & Err & " " & Error(Err)
    If Err = 3021 Then
      e$ = e$ & " There are no customer records like this."
    End If
    MsgBox e$, 48, "Error opening recordset"
    Resume L3
  End Sub
```

The purpose of this procedure is simply to transfer the data from the current CUSTOMER record in the recordset retrieved by the procSetCriteria subroutine to the first column of text boxes on the form.

Notice that the error handling displays a special message for an error 3021, which, we found by experiment, is the message you get when an empty recordset results from the SQL SELECT statement. Any other type of error results in the general-purpose message "Error opening recordset".

The event procedures

```
Private Sub cmdMoveFirst_Click() 'Event procedure
  ta1.MoveFirst
  procDisplayCusRecord
End Sub


Private Sub cmdMoveLast_Click() 'Event procedure
  ta1.MoveLast
  procDisplayCusRecord
End Sub


Private Sub cmdMoveNext_Click() 'Event procedure
  ta1.MoveNext
  If ta1.EOF Then ta1.MovePrevious
  procDisplayCusRecord
End Sub


Private Sub cmdMovePrevious_Click() 'Event procedure
  ta1.MovePrevious
  If ta1.BOF Then ta1.MoveFirst
  procDisplayCusRecord
End Sub


Private Sub cmdSetCriteria_Click() 'Event procedure
  procSetCriteria
End Sub
```

These procedures respond to the clicks the user makes on the five command buttons.

cmdMoveFirst_Click and cmdMoveLast_Click simply set the current record in the ta1 recordset to be either the first or last record, and then display that record in the text boxes.

The cmdMoveNext_Click and cmdMovePrevious_Click Subs are a little different. We must guard against attempting to 'fall off' either end of the recordset. If the user has performed a move next and we are now beyond the end of the recordset (EOF), then the code moves back to the previous record. A similar thing happens at the beginning of the recordset, using the BOF condition.

12.5 Example: Transaction processing

A transaction is a set of related updates to a database where *all* of the updates have to occur and in which, if *only some* of the updates were to occur for some reason (e.g. the system crashed or the computer was switched off), the database would be left in an inconsistent state.

The Jet database engine define transactions by using the following statements:

- BeginTrans begin the transaction
- CommitTrans commit the changes
- Rollback undo the changes.

In the following example, we illustrate the effects of these commands in the implementation of changes to the surname of customers. We make a change and then inspect the database and note that the change has been made. We then roll back the change and note that it has been undone.

The form we use is shown in Fig. 12.9. As in the previous examples in this chapter, the form is unbound.

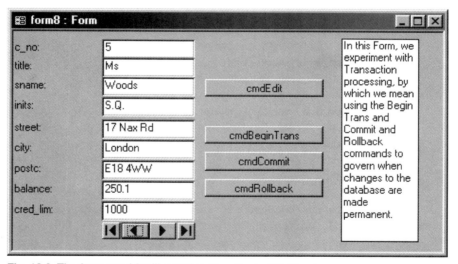

Fig. 12.9 The form used for illustrating the effect of Rollback.

As we can see, the surname of customer number 5 is currently Woods. If we change the name in the sname textbox and click the cmdEdit button, the record is edited (using the Edit method), and the change is saved (using the Update method). That was doing the update *without transaction processing*.

If before changing the name in the text box and editing, we click the cmdBegin-Trans command button (which begins a transaction), and after editing and updating, we click the cmdRollback command button, then the change is *not* saved. Similarly, we could perform a whole batch of changes to the customer table after the BeginTrans, and if we followed those changes with a Rollback, all the changes would be reversed.

The Jet database keeps track of all the uncommitted changes using a *transaction log*.

If you *rollback*, none of those changes occur on the disk, although they will have been made in the recordset and you will see them in the text boxes.

If you *commit*, the changes will be saved on disk.

The code for this program follows:

```
Dim db1 As Database
Dim ta1 As Table
Dim x$
Private Sub procDisplayCusRecord()
  On Error GoTo L4
  txtc_no = ta1!c_no
  txttitle = ta1!title
  txtsname = ta1!sname
  txtinits = ta1!inits
  txtstreet = ta1!street
  txtcity = ta1!city
  txtpostc = ta1!postc
  txtbalance = ta1!balance
  txtcred_lim = ta1!cred_lim
L3:
  Exit Sub
L4:
  e$ = "Error " & Err & " " & Error(Err)
  If Err = 3021 Then
    e$ = e$ & " There are no customer records like this."
  End If
  MsgBox e$, 48, "Error opening recordset"
  Resume L3
End Sub

Private Sub cmdBeginTrans_Click()
  BeginTrans
End Sub

Private Sub cmdCommit_Click()
  CommitTrans
End Sub

Private Sub cmdEdit_Click()
  txtsname.SetFocus
  ta1.Edit
  ta1!sname = txtsname.Text
```

```
      ta1.Update
   End Sub
   Private Sub cmdMoveFirst_Click()
     ta1.MoveFirst
     procDisplayCusRecord
   End Sub

   Private Sub cmdMoveLast_Click()
     ta1.MoveLast
     procDisplayCusRecord
   End Sub
   Private Sub cmdMoveNext_Click()
     ta1.MoveNext
     If ta1.EOF Then ta1.MovePrevious
     procDisplayCusRecord
   End Sub

   Private Sub cmdMovePrevious_Click()
     ta1.MovePrevious
     If ta1.BOF Then ta1.MoveFirst
     procDisplayCusRecord
   End Sub

   Private Sub cmdRollback_Click()
     Rollback
   End Sub

   Private Sub Form_Load()
     Set db1 = CurrentDb
     Set ta1 = db1.OpenRecordset("cus", dbOpenDynaset)
     procDisplayCusRecord
   End Sub
```

The code for retrieving the recordset and displaying it is very similar to that of
the program of Section 12.4. Here we concentrate on the editing and transaction
processing subroutines, which are shown below:

```
   Private Sub cmdEdit_Click()
     txtsname.SetFocus
     ta1.Edit
     ta1!sname = txtsname.Text
     ta1.Update
   End Sub

   Private Sub cmdBeginTrans_Click()
     BeginTrans
   End Sub
```

```
Private Sub cmdCommit_Click()
  CommitTrans
End Sub


Private Sub cmdRollback_Click()
  Rollback
End Sub
```

In Sub cmdEdit_Click, the current record is first edited, the data is transferred from the surname text box to the sname field in the recordset, and an update is performed. If no transaction has been defined (i.e. the BeginTrans button had not been clicked), then this change would be saved to disk immediately. If a transaction has been defined, the changes would be made to the recordset in memory but not yet to the disk, and the changes would be registered in the transaction log. Then if a Rollback is requested, the changes are not saved and the recordset is restored to its original condition. If a CommitTrans is executed, the disk database is updated and the changes made permanent.

12.6 Exercises

1. In Section 12.4, the procedure procSetCriteria contains many repetitions of similarly structured code. Find ways of reducing this duplication of code.

2. Modify the program to display the number of records retrieved.

3. Modify the program to display multiple records in a grid that the user can scroll through.

Transaction processing

4. Suppose a transfer of funds has to be made between two bank accounts. The basic steps are:

   (a) Find the 'giver' account record.

   (b) Decrement the balance by X, where X is the transfer amount.

   (c) Find the 'taker' account record.

   (d) Increment its balance by X.

   If the system were to crash after step (b) and before the end of (d), the 'giver' balance would have gone down by X, but the 'taker' account balance would still be the same. The answer to this problem is to define a *transaction* that begins before step (a) and ends after step (d).

   1. In a new Jet database, create a table tblBankAccount with the fields shown in Fig. 12.10.

   2. Insert into the table the records shown in Fig. 12.11. You are going to write a program to allow a fund transfer of £50 from Sallaway to Carter.

3. Create a simple unbound form for this program, as shown in Fig. 12.12.

4. Including all necessary error-handling code, code cmdTransfer so that it:

   (a) finds the bank account record whose number is shown in txtGiver (use FindFirst);

   (b) subtracts £50 from tblBankAccount!balance and updates the record;

   (c) finds the record whose acct_no is shown in txtTaker;

   (d) adds £50 to that account and updates it.

Check that both updates have occurred by inspecting the records.

5. Using the code in section 12.5 as inspiration, incorporate BeginTrans, CommitTrans and Rollback commands into your code and test their effectiveness. You might try to simulate a crash using a VBA checkpoint.

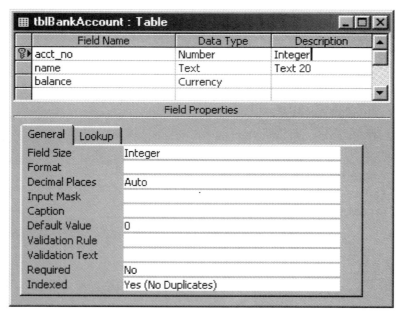

Fig. 12.10 The tblBankAccount table.

Fig. 12.11 Test data in tblBankAccount.

Fig. 12.12 frmBankAccountFundTransfer.

5. Another use for Rollback is in implementing an Undo button. Implement this so that the user can undo even after having clicked a Save button which performs an update. Can you make it work with a Delete (i.e. can you restore a 'deleted' record?).

Chapter

13

The internet, WWW, and ASP

In this chapter you will:

- learn when it's appropriate to put a database on the internet
- learn the basics of web database technology
- learn about clients and web servers
- learn about browsers and scripting
- learn how ASP works
- see examples of client-side and server-side scripting
- learn about alternatives to ASP
- see and use examples of ASP applications accessing read-only and updateable web-based Access databases.

13.1 Introduction

We now turn to the question of how to put your database onto the internet. There are many new terms associated with this and lots of alternative approaches. Here are some of the keywords we'll cover: ISP, browser, Internet Explorer, Netscape, HTML, client-side scripting, server-side scripting, JavaScript, VBScript, CGI, Perl, Java, PWS, IIS, ASP, FrontPage, FTP. In this chapter we consider some of the available approaches to putting a database on the internet. In Chapter 14 we'll give details of how to write HTML code to give full and efficient control of your web pages; and in Chapter 15 how to develop database-ed websites using ASP, offering full custom control of your websites. We even give you free webspace on our server to upload and test your ASP web applications. First, though, we need to get you up to speed on internet terminology. In this chapter we assume no prior knowledge of web page development.

13.2 Why put your database on the web?

If you put ('upload') your database onto a web database server, and make it possible for users to see the database contents via web pages, the database then becomes truly sharable. Users from anywhere in the world will be able to see its content. And you can also allow selected users to *update* the database from anywhere in the world. You can determine which users can update the database using passwords. Examples of this are given in Chapter 15. If you want to see an example of a database on the internet, log in now to **http://www.databasedesign.co.uk/ chatline** and leave a comment on our chatline database. Figure 13.1 shows what you will see there.

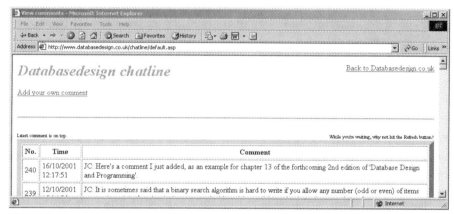

Fig. 13.1 The comments for this chatline are stored on an Access database on the internet. The program code for this and other ASP applications is given in Chapter 15.

The database for the chatline application is held on a web server in a simple Access database. Previous chapters have shown how to design Access databases. The database was *uploaded* (moved) onto the web server using a program called FTP (File Transfer Protocol). We describe how to use FTP to upload your web application later.

If you want to use e-commerce, then buying, selling and publicizing products and services via the internet is what you'll want to do. An online database that is accessible from the web and can be readily and easily updated without re-creating web pages is very likely to be necessary for this.

As a simple example, a hardware company might like to sell its products over the internet. As the product lines are constantly changing, and prices and quantities in stock will be constantly changing too, it will be necessary to hold records of products in an online (on the web) database so that customers can see what's available and at what price, without phoning or consulting paper catalogues and (probably out-of-date) stock lists. It would also be an advantage if customers could place their orders online, so customer account records, order and order line records, invoices, and payments would need to be included in the database, so that the hardware company and the customer can see up-to-date product, order and account details at any time and from any internet connection. This is a considerable advantage.

Putting a database on the internet is not *always* appropriate. Let's now consider possible disadvantages arising from putting your database on the internet.

If a database will only ever be used on a single PC then it's not necessary to put it on the internet. The data can be made mobile by putting it on a zip drive (if there's enough space) or by using a portable PC. If it will be shared but only within the confines of a LAN, then it's not necessary to put it on the internet either.

There are costs associated with putting a database on the internet. There is the cost of the webspace. If you're an individual or a small business, you will need to acquire space on an Internet Service Provider (ISP) who is capable of running ASP applications. Costs depend on the amount of space you use, and how much of the responsibility for your web database development you leave to the ISP. ASP webspace costs are, however, likely to be a very small proportion of an IT department's overall costs. Larger organizations may consider installing their own web server and arranging for its connection to, and registration on, the internet. This is considerably more costly, not just in the expenditure associated with hardware and software, but also systems, development and operational staff needed to ensure continuity and integrity of the installation and its connection to the internet.

The development staff will need technical skills in ASP database application development and the software they use to achieve it. In this chapter and Chapters 14 and 15, we give a straightforward and economical way of developing ASP applications. However, if one of the many web development environments is to be used, there will be a cost in training or acquiring staff who'll be able to use these multi-function, complex, continually evolving, expensive and sometimes error-prone software packages.

Security is another consideration. The data on an internet-based database, particularly if an ISP rather than an in-house installation is used, is not necessarily physically located anywhere near its owner. Control over the data by its owner could consequently be lessened. The ISP will be responsible for holding what may be valuable and perhaps confidential data. Today, many organizations would find it hard to continue without access to the data contained on their databases. Backup, archiving and recovery will be in the hands of the ISP. One argument in favour of this is that a good ISP specializes in just this sort of activity and can therefore usually be relied on to perform these duties as well or better than perhaps overstretched in-house operational staff.

When you develop your ASP applications, you will have to ensure, by using passwords for example, that only the people you want to read and/or update certain parts of your web-based database, and run certain applications, can do so. This is also true of stand-alone and LAN applications, but remember that when the database is placed on the internet, the security features you build in must resist the attempts to bypass them by a much larger audience. You will have to ensure they can't download the whole database! This is largely in the hands of the ISP, who must provide secure access to the section of the disk on which your database resides. Organizations who own their own web server may feel more secure in this area, but remember that the database and its programs are still connected to the internet, even though they may be physically located on the organization's own premises. Some organizations encrypt sensitive data.

Finally, consider the question of speed. If a database is located on your hard drive, the data on the hard disk is only inches from the screen on which the results of a query or update will be displayed. The bandwidth (number of data bits sent per second) of the PC's data buses is measured in tens, hundreds or even thousands of megabits per second. The limiting speed factor is likely to be the efficiency of the search method your program uses, how well the database has been designed and maintained, the speed of the hard disk (how densely the data has been stored, its speed of rotation and the efficiency of caching), and to a lesser extent the processor speed. With a LAN, data has to move further, along channels of considerably less bandwidth, and it has to share those channels with other data traffic. With the internet, bandwidth is considerably further degraded. An indication of the sorts of speed you can expect is that the *fastest* modem you can buy will, under ideal conditions, send data at 33,600 kilobaud (33,600 bits per second) and receive it at 56KB (56,000 kilobaud). This limitation is brought about by the bandwidth of telephone lines. The internet is made up of many different links of many different bandwidths and allows alternative routes for your data according to instantaneous data traffic conditions. A significant determinant of the speed of response of your internet-located database to a user enquiry will very often be the internet's inherent maximum bandwidth and traffic bottlenecks. Just as with road networks, the internet is constantly being improved, sections having their bandwidth increased, bypasses introduced etc. Some measures the developer can take in improving internet application speed include:

- produce an efficient database design;
- design SQL queries carefully so that minimum-sized recordsets are retrieved – only retrieve the data you need;
- don't clutter up the application with needless graphics;
- regularly archive data that's rarely used.

On the plus side, placing your database on the internet affords worldwide database access and using a professional ISP with ASP capability can offload much of the responsibility for DBMS purchase and usage, backup, and efficient and reliable internet connectivity to a company that specializes in just those skills. And provided server-side (rather than client-side) scripting for the important parts of database activity is used, you can expect the database activity to be faster because the ISP will have powerful, regularly updated DBMS facilities and servers. Your customers will just need a browser/PC of modest specification because all the hard work is being done on the server.

Let's now introduce some of the essential internet buzzwords and how we use them in this book.

13.3 Browsers

A web *browser* is the software you use to view (browse through) web pages. When you develop your website, your 'users' (the visitors to your website) will look at the

web pages from your website using a browser. Two popular browsers are Microsoft Internet Explorer (IE) and Netscape.

In Fig. 13.2 we show part of the home page of our website **http://www.databasedesign.co.uk**. The *home page* is simply the page the user will usually be directed to first. Most websites consist of a number of web pages connected together with *hyperlinks*. Note that the web 'pages' need not all be of the same length.

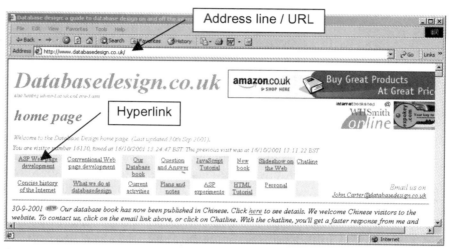

Fig. 13.2 Microsoft Internet Explorer rendering databasedesign's home page.

When using a browser, you specify the website you want to see by entering its *web address* in the Address line. The web address is also known as the *URL* – Universal Resource Locator or Uniform Resource Locator. Figure 13.3 shows a close-up of the Address line of Fig. 13.2.

Fig. 13.3 Close-up of Address line from Fig. 13.2.

Each web page has its own address. You usually move between pages by clicking on a *hyperlink* on an existing page rather than typing in the URL each time. The hyperlink will take you to another web page. In Fig. 13.2 you can see various hyperlinks on our home page, including one to the chatline, which in our website has the address **http://www.databasedesign.co.uk/chatline**. You can also save on URL typing by saving your favourite URLs in the browser. Click on Favourites.

13.4 Creating web pages

You can't *create* web pages with a browser – you just look at them with it. You create web pages either by using a package like Microsoft FrontPage or by typing in HTML (Hypertext Markup Language) commands to make up the web page. In fact that is what a web page *is* – a file of HTML commands. The browser interprets (obeys) these HTML commands, which tell it what to put on the user's screen. We say the browser *interprets* or *renders* the HTML commands into text and pictures on the user's screen. The HTML tells it what text and pictures to put there. If you use FrontPage to produce your web pages, you enter the text and pictures into FrontPage and it generates the HTML file for you. Figure 13.4 gives an impression of how HTML looks. Your browser will show you the HTML for any page. In Internet Explorer you can use the menu – click on View / Source.

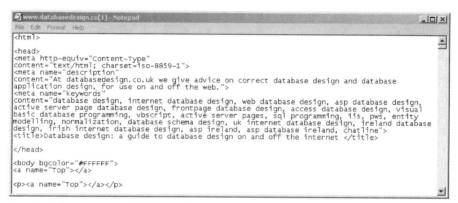

Fig. 13.4 An example of HTML – the first few lines of HTML for the web page of Fig. 13.2.

In Chapter 14, we take you through the process of producing web pages using HTML. Learning the HTML language is virtually essential for 'proper' ASP programming. Fortunately, it's pretty simple and easy to learn and use. HTML generators like FrontPage are advantageous if you want to get a simple website up and running quickly and don't want to learn HTML.

13.5 Organizing web pages into a website

A website is a collection of related web pages. It's best to be aware of the structure of your website – where all the pages are. We like to keep all of the pages in any one of our websites in a single folder. Then we can put different parts of our website into different folders within the main folder if required. For simple websites consisting of closely related pages, use just one folder for the whole website. FrontPage calls the top-level folder a 'web'. If you organize your website this way – all in one folder, it's simple to make a copy of it for development work at more than one site, and it's easy to move the website if you want. For example, you may want to move your website from one web server to another.

Typically, you might do some of the development work at work or college, and do some of it at home or at a client's site. Then having the whole website in a single folder on, say, a Zip drive or even a floppy disk for smaller sites, will allow you this mobility. You must remember to keep all copies of the folder up to date though. Our rule is that the Zip drive copy is always the most up to date. Any changes we make we put onto the Zip drive copy. You may have other schemes. When this system fails, and we're not sure where the latest versions of our files are, the method we use is to have two copies of Windows Explorer open on the screen, show one version of the website in each, sort ascending on filename, and check the dates and times of the last update on each file. To make this work, you must have the clock set correctly on all of the computers you use.

13.6 Your development environment

By 'development environment', we mean the essentials you must have to develop and use ASP web pages. There are various approaches to developing ASP

Development approach	Resources required	Purpose
Microsoft FrontPage	Microsoft FrontPage	To develop complete websites the FrontPage way
	ASP platform (ASP web server) such as PWS or IIS	To test your ASP pages on
	Modem connection to ISP (if dialling up from home or office to internet-based ASP platform)	The ISP connects you to the internet so you can access the ASP platform
	Web browser such as Internet Explorer or Netscape	To view the uploaded web pages with
HTML + VBScript	Microsoft Access	To create the database(s) with
	Text editor such as Microsoft NotePad	To create and edit the ASP files
	Knowledge of HTML	To create basic web pages
	Knowledge of VBScript	To write the ADO code for controlling the database accesses, and code for processing HTML form input and producing HTML output
	ASP platform (ASP web server) such as PWS or IIS	To test your ASP pages on
	Modem connection to ISP (if dialling up from home or office to internet based ASP platform)	The ISP connects you to the internet so you can access the ASP platform
	FTP package such as the DOS ftp command or a Windows-based package such as Terrapin FTP. Alternatively, in Windows 2000, you can simply copy to a folder in My Network Places.	To copy ('upload') your ASP pages to the web server and to (occasionally) copy ('download') them back to your development location
	Web browser such as Internet Explorer or Netscape	To view the uploaded web pages with

Fig. 13.5 Two development approaches compared.

websites that use server-located databases, many of them distinguished by the use of different development packages. Two methods – using FrontPage and using HTML + VBScript and the resources you'll require for each (apart from a normal PC) – are shown in Fig. 13.5.

All the terms used in Fig. 13.5 are explained in Fig. 13.6. Note that in both cases (FrontPage and HTML + VBScript) you need to have access to an ASP server to test and ultimately use ('publish') your pages on. In the past, with Windows 95 and 98, you could install a local ASP called PWS – Personal Web Server on your hard drive. With Windows 2000 and beyond, you download a copy of IIS instead. We have found that, in practice, you don't need to test your pages offline in this way – it's viable to instead test your ASP pages by uploading them immediately to the ASP server.

You can see from Fig. 13.5 that the second, more 'low-level' approach requires simpler software but has more steps in it. Note that the Microsoft Visual Basic package is not required. You use VBScript, which has a very similar syntax to the VB you've been using in the previous chapters of this book. There are lots of examples of VBScript in Chapter 15. The VBScript you write is executed by the ASP software (e.g. IIS) that resides on the web server. All your web pages, including the plain HTML pages and ASP (HTML + VBScript) pages, and your database(s) are also 'up' there on the web server so everyone can access them via the internet.

Before we describe how the 'client' (the user's PC) interacts with the 'server' (the web server containing your website's web pages and your database(s) and IIS to process the VBScript in your web pages), let's define more fully all the terms used in Fig. 13.5. Figure 13.6 does this. You might want to scan Fig. 13.6 now, and come back to it as the terms are used in later text. These terms also appear (in alphabetical order) in the Glossary.

Term	Meaning
Microsoft FrontPage	A package for developing web pages. FrontPage 2000 can develop ASP web pages.
Web page	A collection of HTML commands and text, and related graphics and (sometimes) sounds, held in files on a web server. The commands and text for a web page are held in one file and each graphic and sound is held in a separate file. Your browser interprets these files as text, pictures and sounds on your PC. You tell the browser which web pages you want to see by specifying the web address of the page. The web address is also known as the URL. A website will usually contain many web pages, linked together by hyperlinks. The HTML and text for a page are held in a .htm or .html or .asp file, the graphics are held in .bmp or .gif or .jpg or .png or various formats of video files. Sound files can be .wav or .mid (typically).
URL	Universal Resource Locator, or Uniform Resource Locator. A web address. The address of a web page on the internet. Here's an example URL: **http://www.databasedesign.co.uk**
Web site	A website will usually contain a collection of related web pages, linked together by hyperlinks.

Home page	The page on a website that viewers will normally view first.
Web browser or 'browser'	The program you run on your PC to view web pages with. The main browsers in common use are Microsoft Internet Explorer and Netscape.
Hyperlink	When you click on a hyperlink on one web page, it 'takes you' to another web page. To put it another way, when you click on a hyperlink, the browser fetches ('downloads') the page the hyperlink cites and displays that new page.
HTML	Hypertext Markup Language. Most web pages consist entirely of HTML commands and text. ASP pages also contain scripts. The browser converts the HTML code you get from a website into the text, pictures and sound you receive on your PC.
ASP	Active Server Pages. Web pages with the extension .asp ('normal' web pages have the extension .htm or .html). Active Server Pages contain HTML commands like normal web pages, but also contain 'server side' VBScript scripts.
Script	A piece of VBScript in an ASP page. There may be several scripts in one page. A script can be a server-side script or a client-side script.
Server-side script	A script that is intended to be executed (run) on the server. We use VBScript in this book, but JavaScript can also be used.
Server	A computer that 'serves' a network (LAN or Internet) with programs or data. An ASP server serves data in the form of HTML web pages, which the web browser on the 'client' (user PC) converts to the web page the user sees.
Client-side script	A script that is intended to be executed on the user's (client's) PC. Can be VBScript or JavaScript, but is normally JavaScript because Netscape can't handle VBScript. Internet Explorer, the other main browser, can handle both. Because both browsers are used, it's more usual for client-side scripts to be written in JavaScript.
ASP web server	A server that can process ASP pages. It has to have the appropriate software (e.g. IIS) installed.
IIS	Microsoft Internet Information Server. This is the software that runs on the ASP server to process your ASP pages. It executes the VBScript parts of your ASP page. This determines what HTML is sent over the internet to the browser on the client's (user's) computer. Often, the VBScript will ask IIS to get some data from a database and put it into HTML format.
PWS	Microsoft Personal Web Server. Similar to IIS. Designed to run on the developer's PC so he/she can test his/her ASP pages before uploading to the web server. Designed to work with Windows 95 and 98. Not really needed now, as IIS is now available on the Windows 2000 (and above) installation CD, and downloadable from **www.microsoft.com**. Alternatively, you can just upload your pages to the server each time to test them.

VBScript	The VB-like program code you put into your web pages. It can be client-side VBScript or server-side VBScript. The language is the same but the client-side VBScript is surrounded with <script> and </script>, whereas server side VBScript is surrounded with <% and %>.
ISP	Internet Service Provider. An ISP is used to connect your PC to the internet when you're dialling up from home. Software on your PC dials the ISP's telephone number.
Modem	You need a modem to connect your home PC to an ISP via a telephone line. It converts the digital data transmitted from your PC into analogue form for the telephone line and from analogue to digital when receiving. Converting from digital to analogue is called 'modulation' and converting from analogue to digital is called 'demodulation'. 'Modem' is an amalgamation of these two words. The speed of the modem is a limiting factor in dial-up connections. An ordinary telephone line will give up to 56KBPS (56,000 bits per second) and an ISDN line two to three times as fast as that.
Upload	To copy web pages, graphics and sound files, databases etc. 'up' onto a web server so they can be accessed via the internet. FTP is one approach used for uploading.
Download	To copy web pages, graphics and sound files, databases etc. 'down' onto files on your PC so you can edit them etc. You could use FTP to do this. The term can also mean reading web pages from the internet using a browser.
ADO	Active-X Data Objects. Database-oriented VBScript commands. You write ADO commands into your server-side scripts to access server-side databases.
Server side database	A database situated on a server. A database held on a server has the advantage that it can be shared via a local area network ('LAN') if it's held on a server there, or the internet if it's on a server on the internet.
FTP	File Transfer Protocol. One method of copying files from one place on the internet to another. For example, you could use FTP to upload your web pages onto a web server. There are various alternative methods of FTP-ing: 1. Go into DOS and call up the FTP command. 2. Use a Windows-based FTP utility such as Terrapin FTP. 3. Create a folder in My Network Places in Windows 2000. 4. Use special-purpose software provided by the ISP.

Fig. 13.6 Some web-database terminology.

13.7 The web client/server dialogue – non-ASP

In Fig. 13.7 we illustrate the dialogue that occurs between a client PC seeking a web page and the server machine holding that web page. As you can see, it is very simple in principle. Roughly speaking, the client requests a page, the server finds it and sends it back to the client so the user can see it. Here are the steps in a little more detail:

1. The user at the client PC types the URL (Universal Resource Locator) into the Address box in the browser. In this example the URL is http://www.abc.com/page1.htm. The URL is unique across the whole web. This request is sent via the internet through a system of *routers*, which are computers on the internet that look up the web address in a list and convert it to an IP (Internet Protocol) address, passing the request on to a router nearer the destination and so on, until the web server is found. If a page name is not specified (e.g. user just enters http://www.abc.com), most (but not all) web servers will look for index.htm or index.html and display that. ASP servers will look for default.htm.

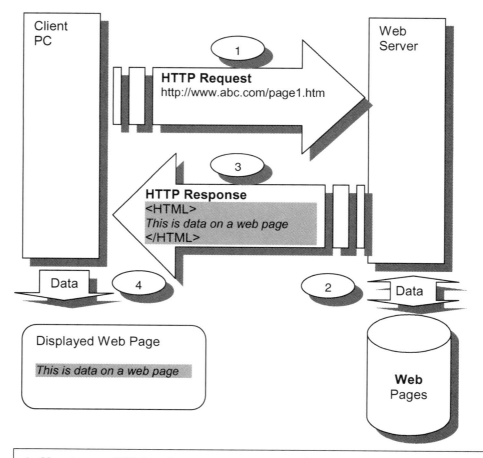

1. User types a URL into browser to request a web page.
2. Web server gets the HTML page.
3. Web server sends HTML page to browser.
4. Browser 'renders' the web page and displays the graphical result on the client screen.

Fig. 13.7 The dialogue between the client PC and the web server (non-ASP).

2. The web server finds the relevant file, here page1.htm, which is located on the file space associated with that website. A web server may contain many websites, and within each website, many files. Page1.htm may contain references to graphics (and possibly sound) files, and these are also located and sent to the client ('downloaded') along with the web page. Large graphics and sound files may take some time to download.

3. The web server sends the web page HTML, and any graphics and sound files used, to the client via the internet. Routers on the internet use the IP address of the client, which was sent with the original request.

4. The client's browser converts the HTML to text, pictures, and sound on the client's PC.

13.8 The web client/server dialogue – ASP

When an ASP page is requested the dialogue between client and server has an extra step, as is shown in Fig. 13.8. The server knows it's an ASP request rather than an ordinary HTML request because the page the client requests has a .asp extension. Ordinary HTML pages have a .htm or .html extension. The web server has to have IIS (Internet Information Server) installed so it can interpret the server-side scripts embedded in the .asp page that has been requested. Roughly speaking, the dialogue goes like this: the user requests an ASP page, the server finds it, *runs the server-side script*, and sends the resulting HTML back to the user. The server-side script (VBScript) generates the HTML 'live'. This means the HTML can include, say, the current time, or a table containing up-to-date data (e.g. latest stock prices) retrieved from a database. Here are the steps in a little more detail:

1. As before, the user at the client PC types the URL http://www.abc.com/page1.asp into the Address box in the browser. Note the asp extension. On an ASP server, if no page name is specified by the user, for example if just http://www.abc.com is entered, the web server will look for index.htm or index.html or default.asp. It's best that all folders in your website contain just one, if any, of these, so that the server knows what to take as the default page.

2. As before, the ASP web server IIS finds the requested file, here page1.asp. If the file has a .htm or .html extension, IIS knows it contains just HTML code and it can pass the file straight back to the client. If it has a .asp extension, IIS knows that it has to check for server-side ASP code, which is included within <% and %>.

3. If there are server-side scripts, IIS interprets and executes them. A typical server-side ASP script might contain VBScript code to open a database that's on the server, extract some data from it, and convert it to HTML format to download to the user. The rest of the file will be outside the <% and %> brackets and be conventional HTML, used for layout, formatting, graphics and fixed data. To make this clearer, we reproduce a typical ASP file ('page') in Fig. 13.9, just to show how the ASP scripts and standard HTML code look. We explain the details of HTML and ASP later.

4. As before, the web server sends the web page HTML and any graphics and sound files used, to the client via the internet. Routers on the internet use the IP address of the client, which was sent with the original request.

5. As before, the client's browser converts the HTML to text, pictures, and sound on the client's PC.

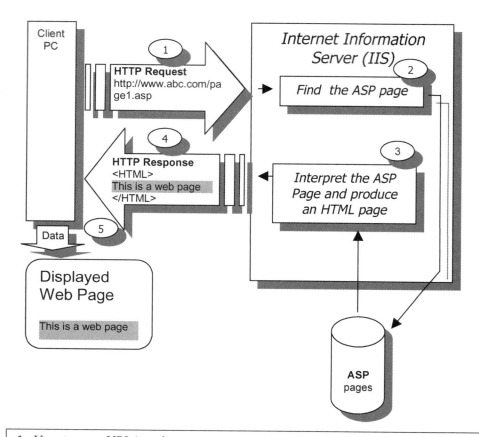

1. User types a URL into browser to request an ASP page.
2. Web server (IIS or PWS) finds the ASP page.
3. Web server interprets the ASP page and produces an HTML page.
4. Web server sends HTML page to browser.
5. Browser 'renders' the web page and displays the graphical result on the client screen.

Fig. 13.8 The dialogue between the client PC and the web server – for an ASP page.

Here, as promised (Fig. 13.9), is an example of an ASP page – that is, a file with the .asp extension that contains server-side scripts. The scripts are contained in <%

Fig. 13.9 (opposite) An ASP page can contain HTML and server-side scripts. This ASP page contains a single VBScript server-side script that extracts data from a database called comments.mdb and generates some extra HTML statements to display this data.

```
<html>
<head>
<title>View comments</title>
<!-- #INCLUDE FILE = "adovbs.inc" - ->
</head>
<body>
<table border = 0 width = 100% cellspacing = 0 cellpadding = 0>
<tr valign = top>
<td align = left width = 60%>
<a href = ".\getcomment.htm">Add your own comment</a>
</td>
<td align = right width = 4%>
<a href = ".\deletecomment.htm"><font color = white>Delete a
comment</font></a>
</td>
```
⟵ HTML

```
<%
'-- Connect to the comments.mdb database - -
set conn1 = server.createobject("ADODB.connection")
conn1.open "Provider = Microsoft.Jet.OLEDB.4.0;Data
Source = d:\websites\databa\www\chatline\comments.mdb"
'-- Open the comments table - -
set rs1 = server.createobject("ADODB.Recordset")
rs1.open "select * from comments order by TimeOfComment desc",
conn1
'-- Show the comments on the form - -
rs1.movefirst
'-- List the comments in an HTML table - -
'-- Create the table headings - -
x = "<table border = 10 cellpadding = 4><tr><th>No.</th><th>Time</
th><th>Comment</th></tr>"
response.write x
while not rs1.eof
  x = "<tr><td>" & rs1("CommentNumber") & "<td>" &
rs1("TimeOfComment") & "<td>" & rs1("Comment") & "</tr>"
  response.write x
  rs1.movenext
wend
response.write "</table>"
rs1.close
conn1.close
set rs1 = nothing
%>
```
⟵ VBScript

```
<hr>
<p>
<a href = "http://www.databasedesign.co.uk"><font
size = 1>Databasedesign.co.uk</font></a>
</body>
</html>
```
⟵ HTML

and %>. The intention here is just to let you see how the HTML statements and the VBScript are mixed.

You can see from the above that ASP is a viable approach to developing database applications where the database is on the internet and can thus be shared and accessed from anywhere.

When you develop your ASP application using FrontPage, all of the HTML and VBScript is generated for you. If instead you develop your web database application 'by hand', you will write both the HTML and VBScript yourself. Chapter 14 describes how to write HTML and Chapter 15 describes how to embed VBScript scripts into the HTML to create ASP pages. Even if you use FrontPage, you will find it an advantage to be able to 'tweak' the HTML and VBScript.

13.9 Client-side and server-side scripting

Note that the above discussion refers to *server-side* scripts. There can also be *client-side* scripts in the web page. They are not processed at all at the server – they are intended to be processed at the client PC and are often there just to make the display more dynamic. Client-side scripts can also be used to perform other functions, such as accessing a local database or performing advanced graphics.

Apart from the fact that client-side scripts cannot be used to access server-side resources such as shared databases on the web, server-side scripting also has two other advantages over client-side scripting.

First, the processing is being done on a powerful server rather than the client's PC, whose possibly modest specification can be allocated to other, more local tasks. The term *thin client* is sometimes used. This is a client computer that can have a quite limited hardware and software specification because most of the processing (such as data retrieval and/or updates on a web-based database) is being performed on the server.

Second, the client's browser can be of low specification, possibly an early version of IE (Microsoft Internet Explorer) or Netscape Navigator, since it is not required to run scripts locally. There is another complication related to this. Netscape Navigator cannot run client-side VBScript without special software (a 'plug-in') having to be downloaded to give it that capability. It can only run JavaScript scripts. IE can run both. JavaScript is a language that can be used for both client-side and server-side scripts, embedded, as VBScript is, in the HTML page.

As you can see, client-side and server-side scripts perform functions at different ends of the internet connection. Many web applications will have both.

13.10 Alternative web application development approaches

There are several approaches and corresponding development software systems currently used in developing websites capable of accessing databases. We briefly review some of these here. The aim is to give you an idea of what the aims of each of these are, and to be able to compare them to the VBScript/ASP approach adopted in Chapters 14 and 15 of this book, and decide if they're a feasible alternative.

13.11 Java

Java is emerging as a popular object-oriented *general-purpose* programming language. Like VB, it's interpreted rather than compiled. Learning Java is useful because increasing numbers of applications are being developed in this language, and it fits in well with internet applications. In complexity it sits somewhere between C, C++ and Perl at one end, and VB at the other. More and more people are coming into contact with Java through its adoption as a first programming language in computer and engineering courses. Like VB, Java is probably here to stay for some time. The language JavaScript, which, like VBScript, can be embedded in HTML code, has some similarity with Java. It is probably fair to say that many non-internet applications can be developed faster by most programmers in VB than in Java, because of VB's simpler syntax.

13.12 VBScript and JavaScript

VBScript and JavaScript are in effect competitors in the same marketplace. They perform the same function and are used in the same way in the same places. They can both be used for client-side scripting and server-side scripting in ASP. They are both embedded in HTML and are both interpreted – by IIS in ASP at the server side, and by the browser at the client side. Each has an advantage over the other. JavaScript can be interpreted by both Netscape and Internet Explorer, while Netscape requires a plug-in to be able to handle client-side VBScript. VBScript has the simpler syntax and is thus likely to offer more developer productivity. The developer only has to learn one language – VBScript – very similar to VB. We now briefly compare JavaScript with VBScript. In Figs 13.10 to 13.13 we give a simple example which shows their similarities. The program gets data from an HTML form (covered in Chapter 14) and performs some simple maths on it. Note that the

```
01JavaScriptEx01Pythagoras.htm - Notepad

File   Edit   Format   Help

<head><title>JavaScriptEx01.htm</title></head>
<body>
<form name=form1>
<b>Enter details of right-angled triangle:</b><p>
base: <input type=text name=x><p>
height: <input type=text name=y><p>
<input type=button value=Compute onclick=calculate()><p>
<b>Calculated hypotenuse:</b><p>
Hypotenuse: <input type=text name=z><p>
</form>
<script language=javascript>
function calculate()
{ xx=form1.x.value
  yy=form1.y.value
  form1.z.value = Math.pow(xx*xx + yy*yy, 0.5)
}
</script>
</body>
</html>
```

Fig. 13.10 HTML page containing simple JavaScript client-side script.

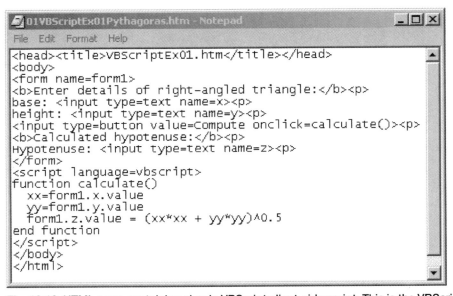

Fig. 13.11 The page of Fig. 13.10 run in Internet Explorer.

```
<head><title>VBScriptEx01.htm</title></head>
<body>
<form name=form1>
<b>Enter details of right-angled triangle:</b><p>
base: <input type=text name=x><p>
height: <input type=text name=y><p>
<input type=button value=Compute onclick=calculate()><p>
<b>Calculated hypotenuse:</b><p>
Hypotenuse: <input type=text name=z><p>
</form>
<script language=vbscript>
function calculate()
  xx=form1.x.value
  yy=form1.y.value
  form1.z.value = (xx*xx + yy*yy)^0.5
end function
</script>
</body>
</html>
```

Fig. 13.12 HTML page containing simple VBScript client-side script. This is the VBScript equivalent of Fig. 13.10.

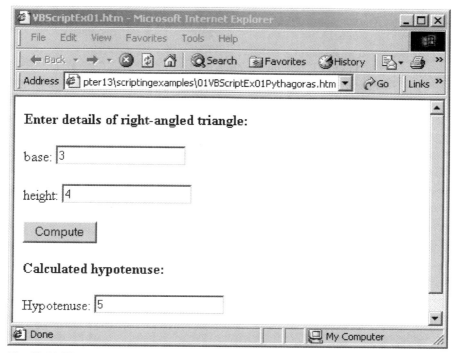

Fig. 13.13 The page of Fig. 13.12 run in Internet Explorer.

JavaScript and VBScript versions are similar. We have made an effort here to make the JavaScript version as tidy as possible by removing optional statement separators and other formatting.

The above pages were both run on Internet Explorer. On trying to run them on Netscape, however, the situation alters. Neither page runs. Both produce errors:

- In the JavaScript version, Netscape requires the line

  ```
  xx = form1.x.value
  ```

  to be replaced by

  ```
  xx = document.form1.x.value
  ```

- Netscape can't run the VBScript version without a plug-in that you have to download.

In Figs 13.14 and 13.15 we show how JavaScript code can appear more cluttered than VBScript. The example does some simple input validation on an input field submitted in a form. VBScript is more readable and less error-prone, but the examples illustrate the overall similarity of JavaScript to VBScript. We use VBScript in this book, but you can see that converting to JavaScript is not too problematic, even for a VB programmer who doesn't use C, C++ or Java.

```
<head><title>VBScriptEx02.htm</title></head>
<body>
<form name = form1>
<b>Enter a number from 5 to 10:</b><p>
number: <input type = text name = n><p>
<input type = button value = "Check the number"
onclick = CheckTheNumber()><p>
</form>
<script language = vbscript>
function CheckTheNumber()
  xx = form1.n.value
  if not isnumeric(xx) then
    msgbox "Should be numeric."
    form1.n.value = ""
  else
    if xx < 5 or xx > 10 then
      msgbox "Out of range."
      form1.n.value = ""
    end if
  end if
end function
</script>
</body>
</html>
```

Fig. 13.14 HTML/VBScript page to perform simple validation of an input field.

```
<head><title>VBScriptEx02.htm</title></head>
<body>
<form name = form1>
<b>Enter a number from 5 to 10:</b><p>
number: <input type = text name = n><p>
<input type = button value = "Check the number"
onclick = CheckTheNumber()><p>
</form>
<script language = javascript>
function CheckTheNumber()
{
  xx = form1.n.value
  if (parseFloat(xx) != xx)
  {
    alert('Should be numeric.')
    form1.n.value = ""
  }
  else
  {
```

```
        if ((xx >5) || (xx < 10))
        {
          alert('Out of range.')
          form1.n.value = ""
        }
      }
    }
  </script>
  </body>
  </html>
```

Fig. 13.15 HTML/JavaScript version of Fig. 13.14. Note the roundabout way of checking a field is numeric using *parsefloat* and performing a logical *or* in an If statement. VBScript seems neater.

13.13 CGI

Here we briefly consider the older CGI (Common Gateway Interface) approach to server-side scripting. CGI scripts can potentially do everything ASP pages can do. With the CGI approach, the developer writes separate programs or 'scripts' in a language such as C, C++, Perl or Tcl, and then compiles them and uploads them to the server. The CGI scripts can perform all the functions that programs normally perform, including accessing server-side databases. ISAPI (Internet Server Application Programming Interface) is a similar Microsoft approach where the script runs as a DLL (Dynamic Link Library) on the server. CGI scripts have to be called up each time they are required whereas ISAPI DLLs stay resident in server memory. Apart from handling database processing, a typical application for a CGI or ISAPI script would be to process the data from an HTML form. As we shall see in Chapters 14 and 15, there are facilities in HTML forms for passing form data to a script or to send it via email. As a CGI script programmer, you have to write the script and test it separately before loading it into a special folder on the website called \scripts.

The main differences between the CGI / ISAPI approach and ASP are that:

- With CGI and ISAPI, the script is held in a file separate from the HTML page, whereas ASP code is usually embedded in the HTML page.

- ASP code is interpreted – translated and executed as required. Since translation takes finite time, CGI scripts, which are already compiled, may run marginally faster.

- ASP scripts use the familiar VB syntax (familiar if you've read the previous chapters of this book!). You don't have to use the lower-level languages such as C, C++, Java or Perl.

13.14 ISAPI and Java Servlets

These are further, emerging alternatives to ASP, which have their own advantages and disadvantages in database-driven web development.

13.15 Exercises

1. There are several internet-based ASP database applications on our website **http://www.databasedesign.co.uk**. The website tells you how to use them. Some are updateable. Some require a password, which is given. Here's a brief description of each application:

   (a) Our home page: **http://www.databasedesign.co.uk**

   General chat about database development on and off the internet, with several links. The hit counter showing your visitor number uses a database called visitors.mdb, which is on our web server.

Fig. 13.16 Our home page.

   (b) Our chatline: **http://www.databasedesign.co.uk/chatline**

   Add your own comment. Ask questions about the book and several people will answer. You might be able to answer other people's questions and comments too. All

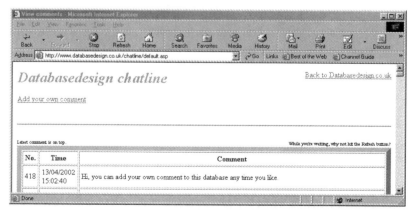

Fig. 13.17 Our Chatline ASP application. How to develop ASP applications is described in Chapters 14 and 15.

the comments are held on an Access database on the internet which we called comments.mdb.

(c) Updating a product list: **http://www.databasedesign.co.uk/cws/01prodlist/ update**

Again, the database for this application is on an ASP server in Heathrow, near London. Several users can update and read it simultaneously. Try this. The application will ask you for a password. The password is 'knucklebones'. Please leave the database as you would expect to find it. :-)

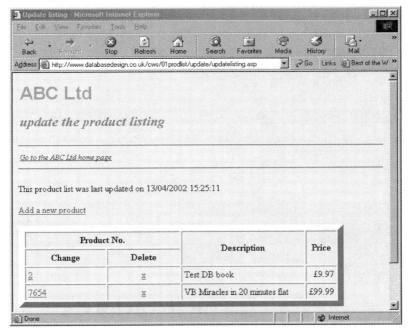

Fig. 13.18 You can add, change and delete products in this application. Have a go.

(d) Items for Sale: **http://www.databasedesign.co.uk/itemsforsale**

A similar application to the above. The home page is shown (Fig. 13.19). You have the facility to list items, and add your own. Some humorous entries. Please keep it clean. Remember, this database, being on the internet, can be viewed from anywhere in the world.

(e) Travel advice: **http://www.databasedesign.co.uk/traveladvisoryservice/**

A non-updateable application. Uses frames (see Chapter 14). You select a destination from a series of list boxes (Fig. 13.20), and it searches an Access database located on our web server to give you details of travel agents who can sell you tickets to get there.

2. **Discuss the situations in which you consider it appropriate and inappropriate to place a database on the internet, giving the advantages and disadvantages in each case. You may find it convenient to present your account in a tabular format.**

Fig. 13.19 Items for Sale application. Add one. You might even sell something!

Fig. 13.20 In this application you select a destination and are given a list of travel agents who will take you there.

3. Produce a list of company types that you think would benefit from e-commerce, in particular, having online databases, and say what you think the benefits would be.

4. Explain why you think Active Server Pages are called that.

5. What is the software element that an ASP server contains and a conventional web server doesn't? Explain its purpose.

6. Discuss the advantages and disadvantages of ASP compared to other database server approaches.

7. Discuss the advantages and disadvantages of using 'raw' HTML and VBScript for developing database-driven websites, compared to using a package like FrontPage.

8. Discuss the advantages and disadvantages of client-side and server-side scripting.

9. Discuss the relative advantages and disadvantages of VBScript and JavaScript as scripting languages.

10. Do a survey of current web development packages and list the facilities of each. Form an opinion as to how complex or otherwise each application appears to be.

14

Creating web pages using HTML

In this chapter you will learn:

- how a browser interprets HTML to produce a web page on screen
- how to develop a website using HTML
- how to upload your website to the internet.

14.1 Introduction

Our aim is to show you how to put your database on the internet so that lots of users can access it. As we have seen in Chapter 13, the way this is done is to upload the database to a server on the internet. The server then generates HTML web pages with the data contained in them and sends them to the browser of the user who requested them. Not all servers can do this. In this book we concentrate on ASP servers. They have a program running called IIS that handles the database requests. This is shown in Fig. 13.8.

What the programmer has to do to get his/her database application on the internet is:

1. Create the database.

2. Upload the database onto the server by using FTP.

3. Create ASP web pages that tell IIS what to get from the database and how to present it on the web page (or, in an update situation, how to gather update data from the user, how to update the database and how to show the results on the web page).

4. Upload the ASP web pages by using FTP.

The web pages are written in HTML (Hypertext Markup Language) mixed with scripts. For accessing the data from the database, we will be using VBScript (see Chapter 15). But first we need to know HTML – the language of web pages.

In this chapter we give a brief introduction to HTML – enough to get pretty sophisticated web pages developed. We describe all the main *tags* and give examples of their use. You won't need very sophisticated software to develop your website – just Notepad (or any other simple text editor) and a browser (Internet Explorer or Netscape) to look at the web pages the HTML you write generates.

14.2 How to develop web pages using HTML

Later in this chapter, we show how to develop a multi-page website. The pages will be linked together using hyperlinks. First though, we develop a website consisting of just a single page. This is done in section 14.4.

A website will normally consist of a whole set of web page files (all ending in .htm or .html or .asp) and a set of graphics files, all ending (usually) in .jpg or .gif or .bmp. The pictures (images, graphics) that will appear on the web page are held in these separate files.

For non-ASP applications, the web page files will normally end in (i.e. have the 'extension') .htm. You, the developer, will type the HTML into NotePad. The HTML consists of raw text and a series of *tags* enclosed in angle brackets < and >.

All web pages contain HTML tags. Appendix 3 gives a list of these tags. When you develop your web page, you could use special web page editors such as MS FrontPage, or you could type in the HTML yourself, which is what we'll do. We'll first develop our web page(s) offline, i.e. locally on our hard disk, and when we're happy with them, upload them to a web server, using FTP. FTP stands for File Transfer Protocol. At that stage, we (and everyone else on the internet) will be able to see our website. Figures 14.1 and 14.2 show our initial set-up, where we're developing our web page offline.

The steps are:

1. In one window on his/her PC, the developer types in the contents of the web page using text and HTML tags.

2. The developer saves the text in a file called index.htm. It's best to call the home page (the normal opening page of your website) index.htm, because most browsers will look for this file first on a website by default, so your users will not have to type it into the URL. On an ASP page, the default name is default.htm, so for an ASP site you'd call your home page that.

3. In another window on his/her PC, the developer checks how the web page now looks in the browser. He/she must remember to click the browser's Refresh button to retrieve the latest saved version of the web page.

This process is repeated until the web pages are finished. In Figs 14.1 and 14.2, we have shown just one web page. Each web page in a multi-page website is in a separate file and the pages would be linked using hyperlinks. You would also expect to see one or more graphics files (e.g. .jpg's and .gif's) in the same folder. The whole website is kept together in one folder so that uploading (copying to a web server on the internet) is made simple – you just upload the whole folder. Keeping the folder and file names the same on your hard drive and on the server helps keep things organized. When you subsequently make a change to a file on your hard drive, you will just upload that. We talk about uploading to a web server below.

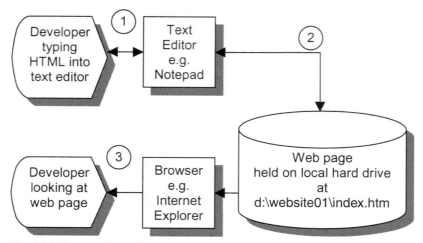

Fig. 14.1 Developing web pages offline using just a text editor and a browser.

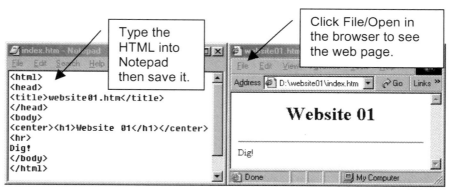

Fig. 14.2 The editor window and the browser window. Make your change in the editor window, save, and click Refresh in the browser to see the effect.

This approach to web page development does have its limitations. You have to know HTML (see below, and Appendix 3), and it's slower than using FrontPage. But it gives you more control, and we have found it much simpler in the long run. You can have a separate copy of Notepad for each page you're developing. And it's a great way of learning HTML! As we've mentioned before, if you want to be a 'real' web developer, you should know HTML, particularly since ASP pages consist of an intimate mixture of VBScript and HTML, and ASP pages are our goal (see Chapter 15).

14.3 How to upload your web pages onto the internet

We now cover the uploading of the website onto a web server on the internet. We'll use the simple one-page website above to show how. We are going to upload to our own web server itsjc.biz, located at Heathrow, England, but your own ISP (Internet Service Provider) will probably give you webspace for your own websites and this will be satisfactory for the non-database websites of this chapter. In Chapter 15 we discuss various ways of obtaining ASP webspace so you can have websites with database connections.

Figure 14.3 shows the uploading and viewing of the website and Fig. 14.4. shows the web page viewed by a user using a browser on the internet, in the normal fashion. You might like to try it yourself. It's at **http://www.itsjc.biz/website01/ index.htm**. You usually won't have to type in the index.htm bit, because the browser will automatically look for a file of that name.

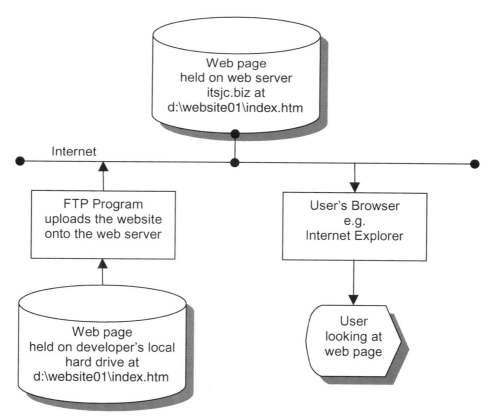

Fig. 14.3 You can upload your website to a web server by using FTP. Then everyone can see it on the internet.

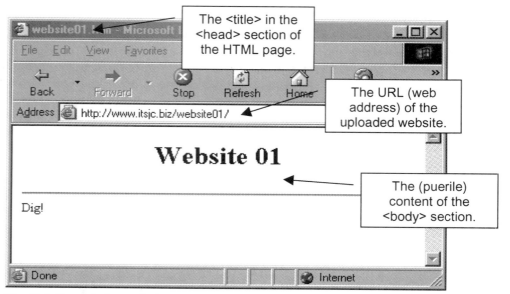

Fig. 14.4 The website on the internet. Note the URL.

FTP options

Some webspace providers provide special purpose programs for uploading your web pages to their webspace. In Windows, depending on the version you are using, it's possible to create Web Folders that are associated with your web server space. We found the Windows 2000 version works quite well.

We now describe two of the FTP methods available for uploading your web pages, that are independent of operating system version – Terrapin FTP and DOS FTP. You need a User Name and a Password to be able to upload to a web server. See **hyttp://www.itsjc.biz** for details of how you can use our web server for experimental uploads, including uploads of ASP pages.

14.3.1 Windows-based FTP packages

Terrapin FTP

Here we describe the FTP package we use most often – a windows-based package called Terrapin FTP, available from **http://www.tpin.com**. Figure 14.5 shows Terrapin FTP. You can see both the file structure of the web server and your local hard drive. You upload by just dragging your local folder to the web server. This process of making your web pages public is sometimes called 'publishing' your web pages. Another bit of terminology: the place on the web server you copy to is sometimes called an 'FTP site'.

Other Windows-based FTP packages

Other windows-based FTP packages exist, and can be found, for example, using **www.yahoo.com** and navigating to:

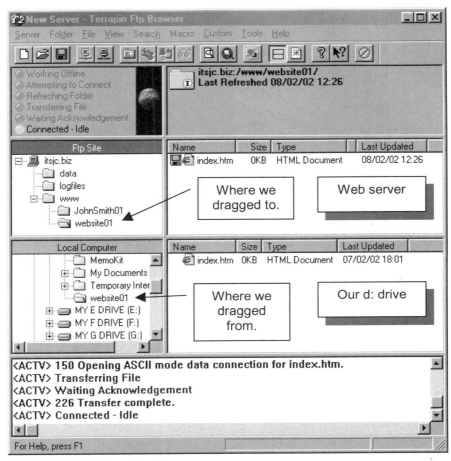

Fig. 14.5 An example of a windows-based FTP package.

Home > Computers and Internet > Software > Shareware > **FTP**

CuteFTP and FTPExplorer are two such packages that seem popular.

14.3.2 DOS FTP

To use Terrapin FTP to upload, it has to be installed on your local machine. When we're uploading from other sites, where Terrapin FTP is not available, we use FTP in a DOS window. This is always available, but is a little less user-friendly than Terrapin FTP and other windows FTP packages. You have to know the FTP commands.

Figure 14.6 shows the sequence of DOS FTP commands we used to upload the website01 website from our D: drive to our **www.itsjc.biz** web server.

These are the steps we used:

1. Open a DOS window: Start / Programs / MS-DOS Prompt.
2. Make sure we're *in* the directory website01. Do cd website01 if necessary.
3. Type ftp to get into the FTP program.

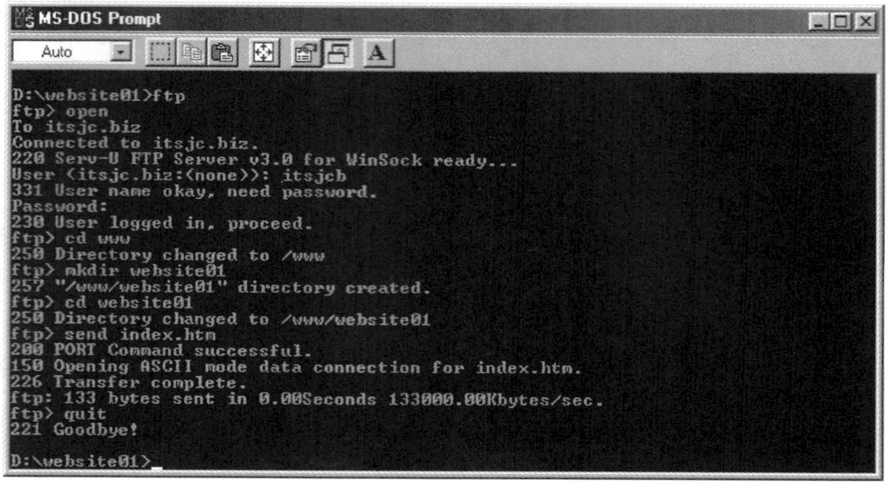

Fig. 14.6 Uploading website01 to www.itsjc.biz using DOS FTP.

4. Type open to say you want to open an ftp connection.

5. Type the name of the 'ftp server', which in our case is itsjc.biz.

6. Type your user name.

7. Type the password.

8. Type cd www. This changes directory (puts us in) to the directory www.

9. Type mkdir website01. This makes a directory (folder) called website01.

10. Type cd website01. This puts us in the directory website01.

11. Now we are 'in' d:\website01 at the sending end (our PC's hard disk) and 'in' the folder www\website01 at the receiving end (the web server). Type send index.htm. This will send index.htm from our hard disk via the internet to the server.

12. Type quit to leave FTP.

The organization that provides your webspace will tell you which folder to put your web pages (and databases if it's an ASP site) into and it will also give you a user name and password.

If you want to upload experimentally to our ASP website, the **http://www.itsjc.biz** homepage will give you the latest instructions on how to do it.

14.4 A single page website showing many of HTML's features

We now turn to the HTML language itself. The single web page shown in Figs 14.7 and 14.8 contains many of the tags you need to know to create web pages in HTML. We've put it into a folder called website02 on the itsjc.biz server, so you can see it at **http://www.itsjc.biz/website02**.

```
<html>
<head>
<title>website02.htm — single page website illustration some
common HTML tags </title>
<meta name = description content = website02.htm — single page
website illustration some common HTML tags>
<mets name = keywords content = html, tag>
</head>

<body bgcolor = yellow>
<center>
<h1>Website 02</h1>
<h2>A simple one-page website illustrating many common HTML
tags</h2>
</center>
<hr height = 2 color = red>

<!--------------- TEXT --------------->
<h3>Text</h3>
This is text in default font.<br>
<b>This text is in bold.</b><br>
<i>This text is in italics.</i><br>
<b><i>This text is in bold and italics.</i></b><br>
<u>This text is underlined.</u> We avoid underlining text because it
looks like it's a hyperlink.<br>
<font size = 1 color = red>This is font size 1 colour red.</font>
<br>
<font size = 7 color = blue>This is font size 7 colour blue.</font>
<br>
<font size = 3 color = #884400>This is font size 3 with colour
#884400.</font><br>
<font face = "comic sans ms">This is type face Comic Sans MS</font>
<p>
<!--------------- LISTS — --------------->
<h3>Lists</h3>
<h4>Unordered list</h4>
<ul><li>Bacon<li>Eggs</ul>
<h4>Ordered list</h4>
<ol><li>Gin<li>Tonic</ol>
<h4>Lists within a list</h4>
<ul>
<li>Things to do
<ul>
<li>Eat
<li>Sleep
</ul>
<li>Things to say
```

```
<ul>
<li>Yeah
<li>Whatever
</ul>
</ul>
<p>
<!--------------- IMAGES --------------->
<h3>Images</h3>
<img align = bottom height = 100 width = 70 border = 3 src =
77SunsetStrip.jpg> TV show  
<img align = bottom height = 100 width = 70 border = 3 src =
EfremZimbalist1.jpg> TV Star
<p>
<!--------------- TABLES — --------------->
<h3>Tables</h3>
<table border = 10 bordercolor = #557799 bordercolorlight =
#7799bb
cellpadding = 5 cellspacing = 5 cols = 2 valign = top width = 50%>
<tr>
<th align = left bgcolor = pink>Artist</th>
<th align = left bgcolor = pink>Track</th>
</tr>
<tr><td>John Lennon<td>No. 9 Dream</tr>
<tr><td>Lynyrd Skynyrd<td>Freebird</tr>
<tr><td>Marc Bolan<td>Get It On</tr>
</table>
</body>
</html>
```

Fig. 14.7 The HTML for the single web page shown in Fig. 14.8, showing many basic HTML commands in use.

We now discuss the tags used in the simple web page of website02 shown above. There are more options available in most of the tags than we have shown in either this example or Appendix 3. For more details of HTML tags, visit **http://www.htmlgoodies.com**. What we show here and in Appendix 3 is sufficient for all the examples in this book.

14.4.1 Structure of the web page

Referring to Fig. 14.7, observe the following tags:

```
<html>
<head>
. . .
</head>
```

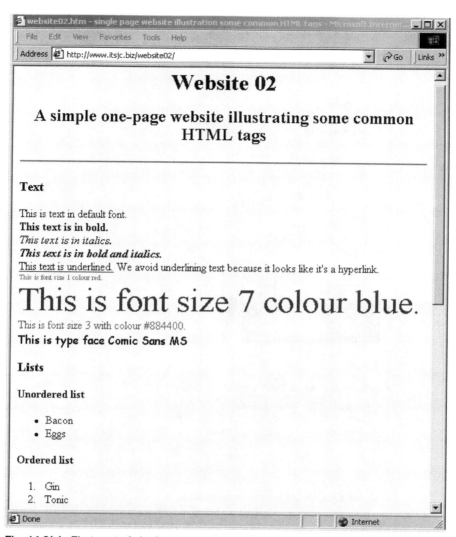

Fig. 14.8(a) First part of single-page website whose HTML is shown in Fig. 14.7.

```
<body bgcolor = yellow>
. . .
</body>
</html>
```

Tags are surrounded in angle brackets < and >. Tags often come in pairs. The 'slash' / shows that the scope of the tag has ended.

The whole web page is surrounded with <html> and </html>. Within this, most web pages, i.e. those without frames, contain just two sections, the head and the body. (See Appendix 3 for the structure of frames.) The head is delineated by <head> and </head>, and the body by <body> and </body>.

The purpose of the head section is to give the web page a title and help in saying what its content is all about. The body section contains the tags that determine

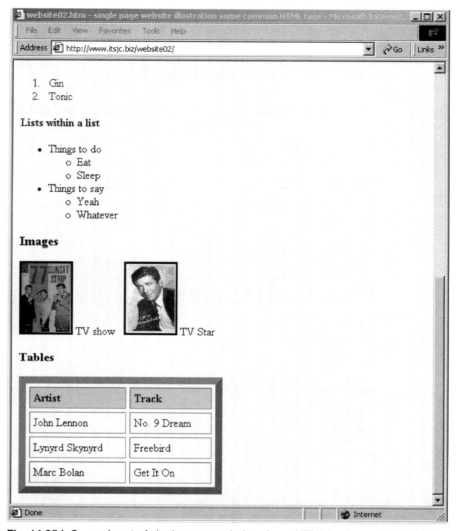

Fig. 14.8(b) Second part of single-page website whose HTML is shown in Fig. 14.7.

what the actual content of the page is, i.e. what will appear in the browser window – the text, pictures, hyperlinks etc.

14.4.2 Head tags

Using our example (Fig. 14.7), let's have a look at some of the main tags you are likely to find in the <head> section of web pages. Head tags are surrounded by <head> and </head>.

<title>

In our example we find the tag:

```
<title>website02.htm — single page website illustration some
common HTML tags </title>
```

The purpose of the <title> tag is to contain the text that will be displayed in the browser's title bar (in Internet Explorer it's the blue stripe at the top). It will also be displayed when a user moves his/her mouse over a minimized web page. It's useful here to put something that identifies the page. Here, we have put the name of the file and a brief indication of what the web page is all about.

If you want people using *search engines* such as Yahoo, MSN, Hotbot, Alta Vista etc. to find your page, you will want these search engines to know about your page. The search engines use the contents of the <title> tag and the <meta> tags to decide how to index your site. Some also use the contents of all or part of your home page. Some search engines go searching for new websites themselves, and will index your pages, sometimes in incredible detail (the programs that do this are sometimes called *web crawlers* or *agents*). Other search engines require you to register your website with them. How to do this is shown on their own home pages, e.g. **http://www.yahoo.com**. How high up on the list of websites you come when someone uses a search engine depends on various factors. Some web developers have tried to get higher up on the search engine lists by repeating key words multiple times in their home page (in invisible letters) and <meta> tags (see below). This, apparently, no longer works.

The point to note here is that if you want to publicize your website it's worthwhile to use <head> tags and to make your home page content as to-the-point as possible.

<meta name = description >

```
<meta name = description content = website02.htm — single page
website illustration some common HTML tags>
```

This is used to give a brief description of the web page. If it's the home page, you'll probably want to give a description of the whole website (all your linked pages – see below) here. The search engine will display this description so that users searching the web using the search engine will know whether to look at your page or not.

<meta name = keywords >

```
<mets name = keywords content = html, tag>
```

The keywords meta tag is used to give the search engine some key words to index your site on. In our example, if the user using the search engine types html as a key word then if the search engine has indexed your site, there's a fair chance that your website will be listed. You may want to add more keywords in the hope that a) users doing a very focused search with several key words are more likely to be led to your site and b) more users doing less focused searches with just one or two key words will 'hit' your site. Here's another example of a keywords meta tag. It comes from our website **http://www.databasedesign.co.uk**. We might have overdone it a bit. Note our attempt to include combinations of key words and their abbreviations. How best to get good hits is a whole separate subject.

```
<meta name = "keywords" content = "database design, internet
database design, web database design, asp database design, active
server page database design, frontpage database design, access
database design, visual basic database programming, vbscript,
active server pages, sql programming, iis, pws, entity modelling,
normalization, database schema design, uk internet database
design, ireland database design, irish internet database design,
asp ireland, asp database ireland, chatline">
```

Just to summarize head tags, remember:

● They're used to name and describe your website and enable search engines to index your website; they don't produce any visible effect on the web page body.

● Search engines have different indexing policies.

● Search engines will use the <title> tag, the <meta> tag and home (and possibly other) page content to try to deduce what your website's all about.

● To further publicize your website, you might go to the search engine's own site and fill in its form to help it index your site.

14.4.3 Comments

Just as the <head> tags don't produce a visible effect in the body of the user's browser, neither do comments. As we say in Appendix 3, comments are there just to help any developer reading your HTML to understand what you are doing, just as comments in other programming languages do. (We consider HTML to be a programming language interpreted by browsers.)

Comments are enclosed in <!-- and -->. Here's an example of a comment from our page of Fig. 14.7:

```
<!--------------- TEXT --------------->
```

Here's another example:

```
<!-- The following lines were amended 19–2–02 by J. Smith -->
```

You can 'comment out' multiple lines of HTML using <!-- before them and --> after them.

14.4.4 Body tags

The <body> section of the page contains all of the tags that will produce visible effects in the user's browser window. There are various options in the <body> tag itself. We have used one to set the background colour of the page:

```
<body bgcolor = yellow>
```

The body section ends with </body>.

14.4.5 Text

If you just want plain, unadorned, unformatted text to appear on your web page, just type it into the <body> part of the page. When you look at the page in the browser though, you will notice that it removes most of the spaces you put in. It will remove any blank lines and any tabs. To format the text you have to use text formatting tags.

<h> Header

The <h> tag is used for headings. It's quite a simple tag. Heading sizes go from <h1> (largest) to <h6> (smallest). Figure 14.9 shows the relative sizes of the header tags <h1> to <h6>. The <font> tag can be used instead (see below) and it gives more control over the appearance of the text, but the header tag is simpler. It automatically produces a space line under it. It can be used to show the natural hierarchical structure of a subject without using numbering. As with many HTML tags, the end of the scope of an h tag is shown with a slash, e.g. <h2> . . . </h2>.

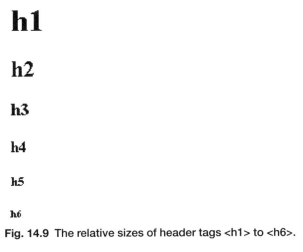

Fig. 14.9 The relative sizes of header tags <h1> to <h6>.

In our example (Fig. 14.7), we use header tags quite frequently, the following being an example that provides a maximum sized heading for the whole page:

```
<h1>Website 02</h1>
```

<p> Paragragh

The <p> tag gives a space line. It's used to separate paragraphs.

 Break

The <br> tag gives a line feed without a space line.

< > Space

This is used to insert spaces.

The effects of these three tags can be seen in Fig. 14.10. Note that the first and second sentences are on the same line because neither <br> nor <p> was used to separate them. The fourth and fifth sentences are separated by four spaces.

```
<p>
Here is a sentence.
Here is a second sentence.<br>
Here is a third sentence.<p>
Here is a fourth sentence.    
Here is a fifth sentence.
```

Fig. 14.10(a) HTML example using
 (break) and <p> (paragraph) tags.

Here is a sentence. Here is a second sentence.
Here is a third sentence.

Here is a fourth sentence.   Here is a fifth sentence.

Fig. 14.10(b) How the HTML of Fig. 14.10(a) is rendered in the browser window.

Note that you can 'stack up'
 tags but not <p> tags.

 will give three linefeeds, but <p><p><p> will give only one blank line.

<b> Bold, <i> Italics, <u> Underline

The effects of these tags can be seen in this extract from the sample web page of Fig. 14.7:

```
<b>This text is in bold.</b><br>
<i>This text is in italics.</i><br>
<b><i>This text is in bold and italics.</i></b><br>
<u>This text is underlined.</u>
```

Fig. 14.11(a) HTML example using <b> Bold, <i> Italics, and <u> Underline tags.

This text is in bold.
This text is in italics.
This text is in bold and italics.
This text is underlined.

Fig. 14.11(b) How the HTML of Fig. 14.11(a) is rendered in the browser window.

Note that you can nest these tags to get their combined effects.

<font> Font

This tag is used to determine the appearance of the current font. You can vary the size, colour and typeface (the shape) of the font. The following extract from the example of Fig. 14.7 shows some of the main things you can do with <font>:

```
<font size = 1 color = red>This is font size 1 colour red.</font><br>
<font size = 7 color = blue>This is font size 7 colour blue.</font><br>
<font size = 3 color = #884400>This is font size 3 with colour
#884400.</font><br>
<font face = "comic sans ms">This is type face Comic Sans MS</font>
```

Fig. 14.12(a) HTML example using the <font> tag.

This is font size 1 colour red.

This is font size 7 colour blue.

This is font size 3 with colour #884400.

This is type face Comic Sans MS

Fig. 14.12(b) How the browser renders the HTML of Fig. 14.12(a).

Note that with the color = parameter of the <font> tag, there are certain standard colours, but the third example shows how to produce a custom colour.

```
color = #884400
```

The first two digits are the amount of red in a scale of 0 to 255, expressed in hexadecimal (00 to FF), the middle two digits are the amount of green (00 to FF) and the last two are the amount of blue (00 to FF). The values shown give a kind of brown. The total number of colours you can get using this method is clearly $255 \times 255 \times 255 = 16,581,376$.

The type face mentioned in the face = parameter will be used in the user's rendered web page (i.e. what they see in the browser window) if their browser has that font available. Otherwise the browser will display a 'standard' font.

Regarding font sizes, Fig. 14.13 shows the relative sizes of the seven sizes available.

font size 1 font size 2 font size 3 font size 4 font size 5

font size 6 font size 7

Fig. 14.13 The seven font sizes available.

14.4.6 Positioning

The default positioning on web page content is left justified, with automatic wrapping on the right. To get precise control over where things appear on the rendered web page we often use tables (see below). However, the <center>, <div align = >, Indent, and <pre> tags can help with basic positioning.

<center> Centre

All text and other content between the <center> and </center> tags is centred (left-to-right) on the user's browser window. Here's an example from the web page of Fig. 14.7:

```
<center>
<h1>Website 02</h1>
<h2>A simple one-page website illustrating many common HTML
tags</h2>
</center>
```

This centres the headings.

<div align = > Align

Aligns a 'division' of content. An example is shown in Fig. 14.14.

Indents – using <dl> and <dd>

We have found that indents to any level can be implemented. You use <dl><dd> to indent, and </dl> to de-indent. An example is shown in Fig. 14.14.

<pre> Preserve

This 'preserves' the spacing you put in your web pages. Within the scope of <pre> . . . </pre>, all spacing is preserved. An example is shown in Fig. 14.14.

```
<p>
<div align = right>Hi there. Glad you could make
it.<br>Nice to see you.</div>To see you — nice.
<p>
Things<dl><dd>Books<br>Pens<dl><dd>Red<br>Blue</dl>Ru
ler</dl>Notions<dl><dd>Peace<br>Truth</dl>
<p>
<pre>
    Name     Hobby
    Pauline Pets
    Robert  Machines
</pre>
    More text.
```

Fig. 14.14(a) HTML containing <div align = >, <dl><dd>, and <pre> tags.

The <div> tag defines a division and here we are using its align = parameter to align some text to the right of the window. Next we use <dl> and <dd> tags to perform simple indentation. Finally, we use <pre> to preserve the spaces in our HTML document onto the rendered web page.

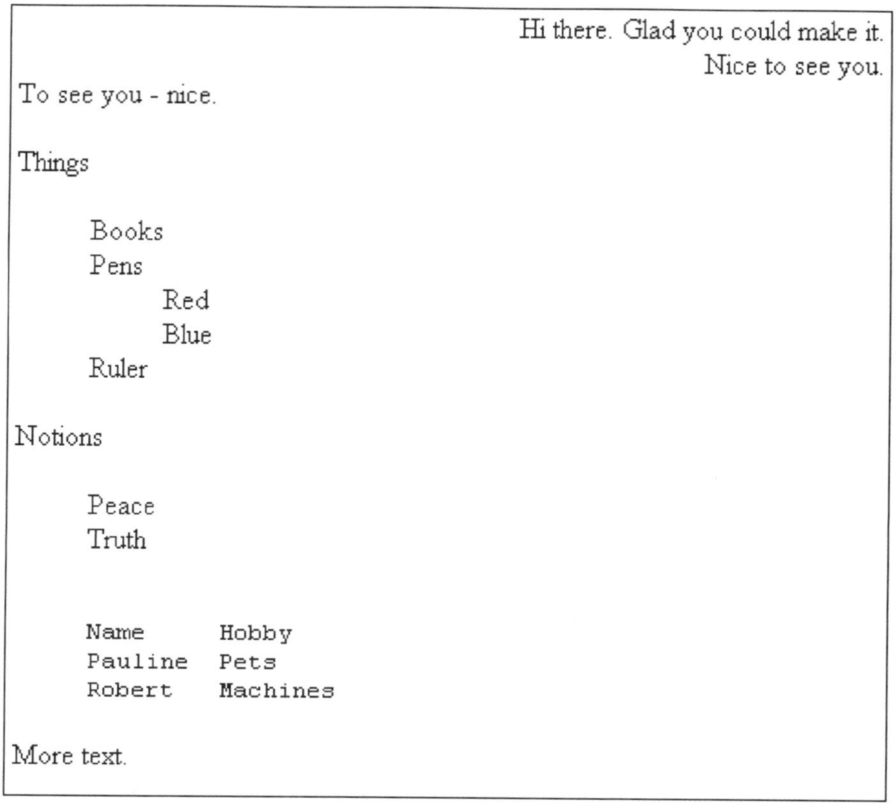

```
                                                   Hi there. Glad you could make it.
                                                            Nice to see you.
        To see you - nice.

        Things

                Books
                Pens
                        Red
                        Blue
                Ruler

        Notions

                Peace
                Truth


                Name      Hobby
                Pauline   Pets
                Robert    Machines

        More text.
```

Fig. 14.14(b) How the browser renders the HTML of Fig. 14.14(a).

14.4.7 Lists

'Lists' are the HTML name for bullet points – numbered <ol> (ordered lists) and un-numbered <ul> (unordered lists). We revert again to our example of Fig. 14.7 to show how these work.

<ul> Unordered List

These are sometimes called 'bullet points'. As an example,

```
<p>Breakfast<ul><li>Bacon<li>Eggs</ul>
```

will produce the effect:

Breakfast
● Bacon
● Eggs

<li> stands for 'list item'.

You can have lists within lists, as in this example:

```
<p>
Style guide
<ul>
<li>Things to do
<ul>
<li>Eat
<li>Sleep
</ul>
<li>Things to say
<ul>
<li>Yeah
<li>Whatever
</ul>
</ul>
```

which produces in the browser window:

Style guide
- Things to do
  - Eat
  - Sleep
- Things to say
  - Yeah
  - Whatever

As you can see from the HTML, the lists of 'things to do' and 'things to say' are lists in their own right, embedded within the main list.

<ol> Ordered lists

These differ from <ol> only in that the list items are numbered.

```
<ol><li>Gin<li>Tonic</ol>
```

produces the effect:

1. Gin
2. Tonic

14.4.8   Lines

<hr> Horizontal Rule

This is simply a horizontal line that automatically resizes itself as the user resizes the browser window.

<hr> looks like this:

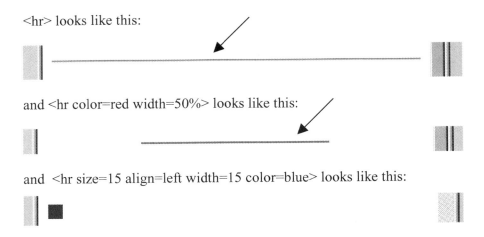

and <hr color=red width=50%> looks like this:

and <hr size=15 align=left width=15 color=blue> looks like this:

14.4.9 *Images*

Images (pictures) can be placed into your web page using the <img> tag.

<img> Image

We illustrate this tag using the simple web page of Fig. 14.7. It is also worth noting that the <img> tag can be placed inside table cells and hyperlinks (see both below). In order not to get the dreaded

symbol on your web page (it means "I can't find the picture." – that's the web browser talking), you must make sure you say correctly where the image file *is*. We always keep copies of our image files in the same folder as the web page that uses them. Then when we move or copy our website, all the picture files go with it. It might surprise you to know that pictures are held in separate files. They aren't in Word, for example – they're embedded in the Word document. In a website then, you can expect to see a number of .htm files, one for each page, and a number of .jpg and .gif files (and possibly some other graphics/image/picture formats) – one for each picture.

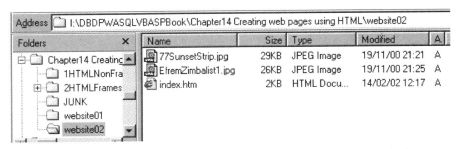

Fig. 14.15(a) The files in the simple website website02 of Fig. 14.7. Note the home page index.htm and the two graphics files.

```
<img align = bottom height = 100 width = 70 border = 3 src =
77SunsetStrip.jpg> TV show  
<img align = bottom height = 100 width = 70 border = 3 src =
EfremZimbalist1.jpg> TV Star
```

Fig. 14.15(b) The HTML used to include the two images (graphics files) into the index.htm page.

Fig. 14.15(c) What the HTML of (b) causes to appear in the browser window.

Note that in Fig. 14.5(a), each picture in a web page is stored separately in its own file. Graphics files like .jpg and .gif files are compressed to reduce download time. They can be viewed and edited in packages like Paint Shop Pro, available from JASC Software.

src =
The src = parameter in the <img> tag says what the 'source' of the picture is i.e. where it is.

height =, width =
The height and width parameters (measured in pixels) specify the number of pixels the image will take. The browser will stretch the image to this size. A pixel is the size of the smallest dot your screen can reproduce and so it depends on the type of screen and the screen resolution in use. The screen resolution can be found (in MS Windows) by right-clicking an empty part of the screen and selecting Properties. Some common screen resolutions ('screen areas') are 1024 × 768, 800 × 600 and 640 × 480. The graphics in our example are of width 70 pixels. So for a screen width of 1024, the image will take up 70 / 1024 = 6.8% (about a fifteenth) of the screen width. If the screen width is 640, the image will take up 70 / 640 = 10.9% (about a ninth) of the screen width.

align =
The alignment parameter, align = , determines the alignment of nearby text with respect to the picture. For align = bottom, the text will align with the bottom of the picture. Figure 14.16 illustrates the effects of this parameter of the <img> tag.

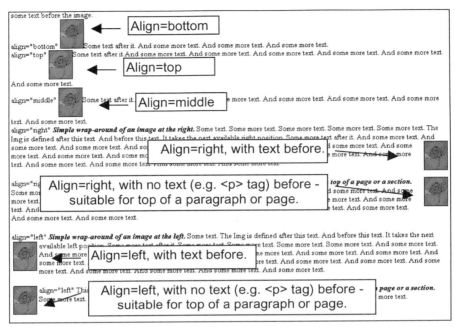

Fig. 14.16 Some of our experiments with the align = parameter of the HTML <img> tag. You can see this page 'live' at **http://www.databasedesign.co.uk/html/index.htm.**

14.4.10 Tables

HTML tables consist of a set of rows and columns. They are very useful in positioning text and graphics on the web page. In Chapter 15, we make extensive use of them in displaying database records retrieved from a web located database, using ASP. Here's a simple example:

```
<table border = 1 cols = 3>
<tr><th>Customer No.<th>Name<th>Balance</tr>
<tr><td>1<td>Sallaway<td align = right>£42.56</tr>
<tr><td>2<td>Lauri<td align = right>£200.00</tr>
<tr><td>3<td>Jackson<td align = right>£510.00</tr>
</table>
```

Fig. 14.17(a) HTML <table> tag in use to display simple rows of text.

Customer No.	Name	Balance
1	Sallaway	£42.56
2	Lauri	£200.00
3	Jackson	£510.00

Fig. 14.17(b) How it looks in the browser window.

Tables begin with <table> and end with </table>. Each row begins with <tr> and ends with </tr>. Each cell in the row begins with <td> (table data) and ends with </td>, although you can leave out the </td> and the browser will understand. If you want to have the text in bold, as for a heading, you use <th> (table header) instead of <td>. You say how many columns there are using cols = in the <table> tag, but the browser may not require this.

We test all our web pages on both the Internet Explorer and Netscape browsers and if neither of them needs a tag, we leave it out. If you want to be sure your page will be rendered properly in all versions of all browsers, however, put in 'optional' parameters and tags like cols = and </td>.

We used border = 1. If you put border = 0 or leave the parameter out, no borders are shown and just the cell content is shown, without any lines between. However, increasing the border size only affects the perimeter of the whole table, leaving the lines between the cells as they are. Figure 14.7(c) shows the effect of setting border = 10 in the HTML of Fig. 14.17(a).

Customer No.	Name	Balance
1	Sallaway	£42.56
2	Lauri	£200.00
3	Jackson	£510.00

Fig. 14.17(c) The effect of setting border = 10.

We've used align = right in the cells of the second column to get the decimal points underneath each other.

Now let's look at the table from the simple web page of Fig. 14.7, which shows a few more <table> features (Fig. 14.18).

```
<table border = 10 bordercolor = #557799 bordercolorlight =
#7799bb
cellpadding = 5 cellspacing = 5 cols = 2 valign = top width = 50%>
<tr>
<th align = left bgcolor = pink>Artist</th>
<th align = left bgcolor = pink>Track</th>
</tr>
<tr><td>John Lennon<td>No. 9 Dream</tr>
<tr><td>Lynyrd Skynyrd<td>Freebird</tr>
<tr><td>Marc Bolan<td>Get It On</tr>
</table>
```

Fig. 14.18(a) Another <table> example.

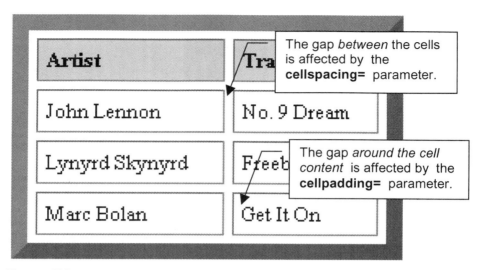

Fig. 14.18(b) How the browser renders the HTML of Fig. 14.18(a).

Note the effect of the cellspacing and cellpadding parameters. The units are pixels. If cellspacing is put to zero, there is still a narrow line separating the cells. bordercolor and bordercolorlight affect the colours of the top and left, and bottom and right parts of the border respectively. The width = 50% parameter says that the table should be expanded or contracted by the browser so that it occupies half the width of the browser window.

It is possible to put images in tables cells. Fig. 14.19 gives an example.

```
<table border = 1>
<tr><td><img src = WavesOnShore02.jpg width = 200 height =
141><td><img src = ForestAndPond02.jpg width = 200 height =
141></tr>
<tr><td><img src = Waterfall02.jpg width = 200 height =
141><td><img src = WavesOnShore01.jpg width = 200 height =
141></tr>
<tr><td colspan = 2 align = center><i>Sylvia's Pictures
www.eire-1.com/sylvia</i></tr>
</table>
```

Fig. 14.19(a) A <table> containing pictures.

In

```
<td><img src = WavesOnShore02.jpg width = 200 height = 141>
```

note the use of the <img> (image) embedded in the <td> (table data). Note also the use of the width = and height = parameters to set the image sizes.

Fig. 14.19(b) The result shown in the browser window.

Note also the use of the column spanning (row spanning also exists) to get the cell at the bottom to span two columns:

```
<tr><td colspan = 2 align = center><i>Sylvia's Pictures
www.eire-1.com/sylvia</i></tr>
```

It is even possible to embed a table within the cell of another table (Fig. 14.20).

```
<table border = 1>
<tr><td>o<td> <td>o</tr>
<tr><td> <td>
<table border = 1>
<tr><td>x<td> <td>x</tr>
<tr><td> <td>o<td> </tr>
<tr><td>x<td> <td>o</tr>
</table>
<td> </tr>
<tr><td>o<td> <td>x</tr>
</table>
```

Fig. 14.20(a) This example embeds one table inside another . . .

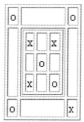

Fig. 14.20(b) . . . with this result.

Note in Fig. 14.20 the gratuitous use of   (space). If you leave a cell empty, the browser will remove its border. We use   just to put something in the cell to keep its border. Figure 14.20(c) shows how the table looks without the 's.

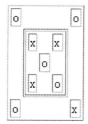

Fig. 14.20(c) Empty cells (e.g. <td><td>) lose their cell borders, as here.

14.5 Multi-page websites and hyperlinks

Most websites contain a number of linked pages. The pages are linked using *hyperlinks*. You click on a hyperlinked piece of text or a hyperlinked image and the browser takes you to another web page. The browser underlines hyperlinked text so you can see it's hyperlinked. HTML uses just one tag, the <a> tag, for hyperlinks. You can also use the <a> tag to jump to a particular position in a page (you use two <a> tags there, one to jump from – the hyperlink, and one to show where to jump to – the label – see below) and to open the user's email package so he/she can send an email to someone. The <a> tag is indeed a useful tag. When you hyperlink to another page, that page can be in your own website, or in someone else's. If the web page you're hyperlinking to is in your own website, you just use its filename; if it's in another website, you use the URL. So we now cover:

- hyperlinking to other pages in your own website
- hyperlinking to a page on someone else's website
- hyperlinking to a specific location on a page
- hyperlinking to an email address
- hyperlinking using images rather than underlined text

14.5.1 *Hyperlinking to another page in your own website*

You can create each HTML page using Notepad and the same tags described in section 14.4. In the following example, we have the very simple case of a website containing just three pages:

- index.htm – the home page for ABC Ltd;
- aboutus.htm – a page containing address and telephone data for ABC Ltd;
- pricelist.htm – a page containing a price list.

When you design and develop a website, it's a good idea to document its structure. Figure 14.21 shows the structure of this simple website.

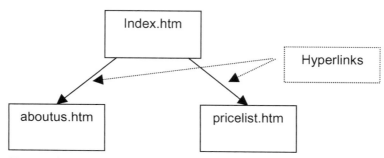

Fig. 14.21 Structure of a simple website – website03.

The three web pages in this example are shown below. They have been kept as simple as possible to highlight the hyperlink aspect only.

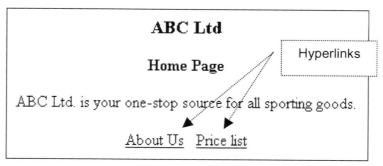

Fig. 14.22(a) index.htm.

```
<head><title>website03 index.htm hyperlinks example</title>
</head>
<body>
<center><h3>ABC Ltd</h3><h4>Home Page</h4>
```

```
ABC Ltd. is your one-stop source for all sporting goods.<p>
<a href = aboutus.htm>About Us</a>
  
<a href = pricelist.htm> Price list</a>
</body>
</html>
```

Hyperlinks

Fig. 14.22(b) HTML for index.htm. Note the two hyperlinks.

ABC Ltd

About Us

Tel. 071 12345
Fax. 071 12346

Fig. 14.23(a) aboutus.htm.

```
<head><title>website03 aboutus.htm</title>
</head>
<body>
<center><h3>ABC Ltd</h3><h4>Home Page</h4>
<p>Tel. 071 12345<br>Fax. 071 12346
</body>
</html>
```

Fig. 14.23(b) HTML for aboutus.htm.

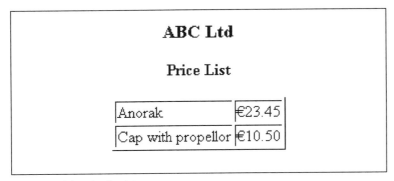

ABC Ltd

Price List

| Anorak | €23.45 |
| Cap with propellor | €10.50 |

Fig. 14.24(a) pricelist.htm.

```
<head><title>website03 pricelist.htm</title>
</head>
<body>
<center><h3>ABC Ltd</h3><h4>Price List</h4>
<table border = 1>
<tr><td>Anorak<td>23.45</tr>
<tr><td>Cap with propellor<td>10.50</tr>
</table>
</body>
</html>
```

Fig. 14.24(b) HTML for pricelist.htm.

Clicking on either of the hyperlinks of Fig. 14.22(a), the home page, will retrieve the respective file – either aboutus.htm or pricelist.htm, and display it in the browser window. These three files are held in the website's folder website03, as shown in Fig. 14.25. It's a good idea, as we have remarked before, to keep all the files for a website in one folder if possible. You can use subfolders to further categorize files if you want to.

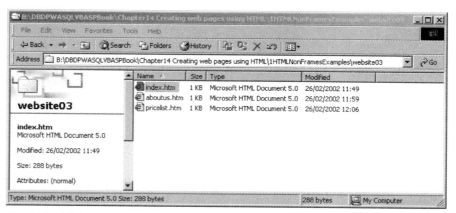

Fig. 14.25 We've kept the three web pages in the same folder. Note we haven't uploaded them yet. See section 14.3 on how to upload.

The pages aboutus.htm and pricelist.htm are unremarkable. The home page index.htm, however, contains two hyperlinks, one to each of the other pages. Let's consider the first hyperlink:

```
<a href = aboutus.htm>About Us</a>
```

It uses the hyperlink tag – the <a> tag. The href = parameter ('hyperlink reference') shows where you want to hyperlink to, in this case the file aboutus.htm. Because aboutus.htm is in the same folder as the page calling it, there is no need to show any path name. Putting an absolute path (e.g. href = d:\mywebsites\website03\aboutus.htm) would cause a problem when uploading because the server will put your files at some other absolute address. So we name the file *relative* to the calling file. If you leave out the pathname as we have done here, the server will look in the same folder for the file. When you put the full ('absolute') path in (as you might do on a LAN or intranet – where you're sharing someone else's pages) we call this *absolute* addressing; when you don't, we call it *relative* addressing because the location of the hyperlinked file is to be found in a fixed position relative to the current location. The next example gives another example of relative addressing. Getting the href = parameter right is important if you want to avoid the dreaded error 404 (Fig. 14.26).

Fig. 14.26 Your users will see this if you get the <a> tag href = wrong.

Still considering the first hyperlink in index.htm (see below) the only other part, the part between the start and end of the hyperlink, i.e. the text 'About Us', is the text you want to appear on the page for the user to click.

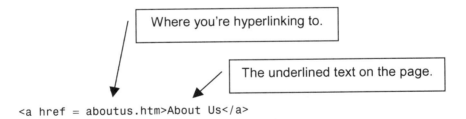

```
<a href = aboutus.htm>About Us</a>
```

If you want a hyperlinked page to come up in a new window, use target = new in the <a> tag. For example, we could make the About Us page appear in a new window (instead of going over the top of the home page) by doing this:

```
<a href = aboutus.htm target = new>About Us</a>
```

Suppose for some reason your About Us page was in a subfolder called CompanyData (see Fig. 14.27).

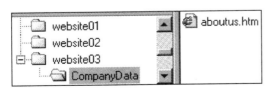

Fig. 14.27 Here, the aboutus.htm page has been placed in a subfolder for some reason.

Then the <a> tag would need to be:

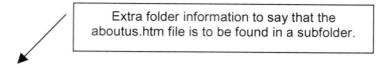

Extra folder information to say that the aboutus.htm file is to be found in a subfolder.

```
<a href = companydata\aboutus.htm>About Us</a>
```

Note that this is still 'relative addressing' because there is no absolute path given. If the main folder is moved, the subfolder will be moved with it, and the hyperlink will still work.

If you need to refer to a web page that is up a level in a folder hierarchy, you use a ..\. Suppose the arrangement is as in Fig. 14.27 (aboutus.htm in a subfolder CompanyData) and you wanted to put a link from aboutus.htm back to the home page, which is a level up. This is what your aboutus.htm page would look like:

ABC Ltd

About Us

Tel. 071 12345
Fax. 071 12346

Home

Fig. 14.28(a) A 'Home' link added to aboutus.htm.

```
<html>
<head><title>website03 aboutus.htm</title>
</head>
<body>
<center><h3>ABC Ltd</h3><h4>About Us</h4>
<p>Tel. 071 12345<br>Fax. 071 12346
<p>
<a href = ..\index.htm>Home</a>
</body>
</html>
```

A link back to the home page.

Fig. 14.28(b) Note the ..\ device to say 'go up a level' in the <a> tag.

You can go up two levels using ..\..\, and so on. Of course if aboutus.htm and index.htm were in the same folder, the <a> tag of Fig. 14.28(b) would be simply:

```
<a href = index.htm>Home</a>
```

If necessary, you could use an absolute address to name the source of a page on your PC or on your LAN that you want to hyperlink to.

Here is an example in which we are using absolute addressing (unnecessarily) to hyperlink from the home page above (Fig. 14.22) to the aboutus.htm page:

```
<a href = "B:\DBDPWASQLVBASPBook\Chapter14 Creating web pages using
HTML\1HTMLNonFramesExamples\website03\Comp
anyData\aboutus.htm">About Us</a>
```

Fig. 14.29 <a> tag: using a full path name for a page on a local drive.

Note the long path name. Also note the fact that we *need* the quotes around the pathname in this example because one of the folder names (`Chapter14 Creating web pages using HTML`) contains embedded spaces. One problem with this absolute address is that if the file is moved (for example, if we upload the website to another server), the hyperlink will no longer work. Using relative addressing and keeping our linked pages in a fixed relation to the calling page (preferably in the same folder or a subfolder) remedies this.

14.5.2 *Hyperlinking to a page on a LAN*

If you are hyperlinking to a web page on a LAN, it's usual to have the general area you want to access *mapped* to a drive number. In Windows, you can do this using My Computer or Windows Explorer. In the following example, we have mapped a certain section of the LAN (another server in fact) to the drive letter S:

```
<a href = S:\eb2\Notes\01Website01\page2.htm>page2</a>
```

Fig. 14.30 <a> tag: hyperlinking to a web page on a LAN, using a mapped drive letter.

Note that the 'S:' mapping is only meaningful to your LAN account. If another LAN user with a different account code (user name) were to try to use your web page containing this <a> tag, it wouldn't work, because 'S:' may have no meaning for them, or be the name they've given to an entirely different LAN location.

One way to get round this (Fig. 14.31) is to use the whole LAN pathname instead – all LAN users will agree on this, and provided the other user has the required security privileges (access rights determined by the page owner and network administrator), he/she will be able to access the page.

```
<a href =
\\Rosses\Shared\Classes\JCarter\eb2\Notes\01Website01\
page2.htm>page2</a>
```

Fig. 14.31 <a> tag: hyperlinking to a web page on a LAN, using the full LAN path name.

14.5.3 *Hyperlinking to a page on the internet*

If you want to hyperlink to a page on the internet, you use its URL. For example, suppose we want to extend our website (website03 – Fig. 14.21) by adding, on our home page, a link to http://www.databasedesign.co.uk, which is the home page of another website. We would simply put this URL (web address) into an <a> tag as follows:

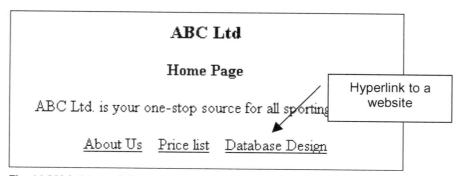

Fig. 14.32(a) A hyperlink to an internet website has been added.

```
</html>
<head><title>website03 index.htm hyperlinks example</title>
</head>
<body>
<center><h3>ABC Ltd</h3><h4>Home Page</h4>
ABC Ltd. is your one-stop source for all
sporting goods.<p>
<a href = aboutus.htm>About Us</a>
  
<a href = pricelist.htm>Price list</a>
  
<a href = http://www.databasedesign.co.uk>Database
Design</a>
</body>
</html>
```

The <a> tag that produces the hyperlink.

Fig. 14.32(b) The HTML now includes a new <a> tag hyperlinking the page to the Database Design website's home page.

When you hyperlink to a website, the server will usually look, by default, for a file called index.htm or index.html, and if it's an ASP server, default.asp. These are possible names for the home page. If the website has some other name for its home page (e.g. homepage.htm), you'll have to include that in the href = parameter, as in:

```
<a href = http://www.xyz.com/homepage.htm>xyz</a>
```

If you want to access a particular page in a web-based page then just name it in the <a> tag. If the page you want is in a folder of the website, then you put the folder name in the <a> tag (Fig. 14.33).

```
<a href = http://www.xyz.com/salespromotions>xyz's sales
promotions</a>
```

Fig. 14.33(a) Hyperlinking to the default page in the /salespromotions folder of xyz.com.

```
<a href = http://www.xyz.com/salespromotions/armchairs.htm>xyz's
armchair sale</a>
```

Fig. 14.33(b) Hyperlinking to a particular page in the /salespromotions folder of xyz.com.

Note that if the URL contains an embedded space, you'll have to surround it with double quotes, as in:

```
<a href = "http://www.xyz.com/sales promotions">xyz's sales
promotions</a>
```

14.5.4 *Hyperlinking to a specific location on a page*

By default, when a page is loaded the first time, the browser will display the top of the page. Sometimes you will want to hyperlink to a position further down the new page. On other occasions, you may want to have a hyperlink on a page that allows a jump to another position on that page. There is a simple mechanism for this. You use *two* <a> tags, one to jump *from* and one to jump *to*. We call the one you jump to the 'label', by analogy with labels in Visual Basic and other programming languages, where a label is a location in the program you jump to using a goto statement. Two examples should suffice.

In the first example (Fig. 14.34), the hyperlink jumps to a position within the existing page:

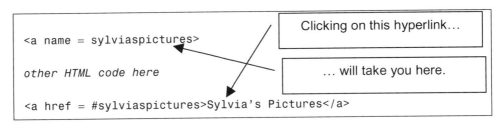

Fig. 14.34 Hyperlinking within a page.

Note the use of the name = parameter in the label, and the # (hash) sign in the hyperlink. One common example of hyperlinking within a page is to have links to the top of a page. This is particularly useful in a long page:

```
<body>
<a name = top>

other HTML code here

<a href = #top>Top</a>

other HTML code here

<a href = #top>Top</a>
```

Fig. 14.35 Hyperlinking to the top of a long page.

It's also possible to hyperlink to a named position (a label) in a different page. In Fig. 14.36, we link to a label in a page on the internet.

```
<a href = http://www.databasedesign.co.uk/#HTML Tutorial>Go to John's
old HTML tutorial</a>
```

Fig. 14.36 Hyperlinking to a specific position in a web page on the internet.

14.5.5 *Hyperlinking to an email address*

It's useful to be able to have hyperlinks to email addresses on web pages. What actually happens is that when a user clicks on an email hyperlink, it opens up their email package and puts the email address in the To: box of the email package window. Here's an example:

```
<a href = mailto:John.Carter@databasedesign.co.uk>Email us</a >
```

Fig. 14.37(a) An email hyperlink.

Email us

Fig. 14.37(b) How the email hyperlink appears in the browser window.

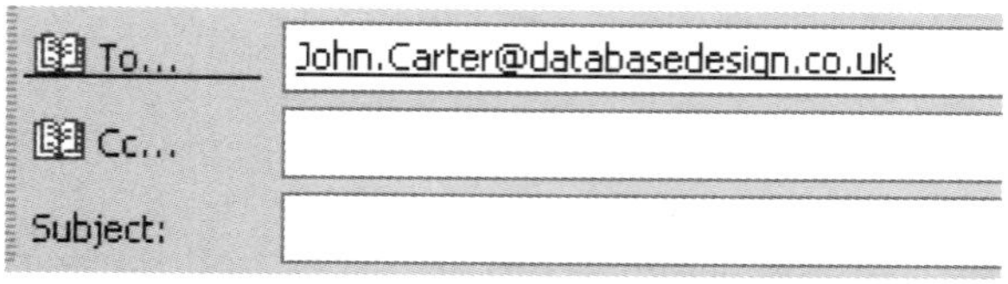

Fig. 14.37(c) The email hyperlink opens up the user's email package and inserts the To: address.

14.5.6 *Hyperlinking a graphic*

You can hyperlink a graphic so that when the user clicks the graphic (image) it takes the user to another page just as hyperlinked text (all the examples above) does. All you do is place an <img> tag inside the <a> tag as in the example below.

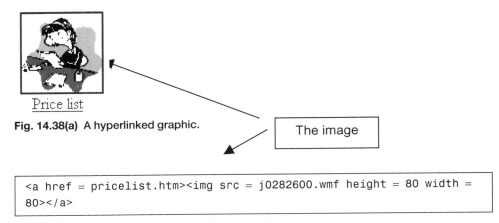

The image

Fig. 14.38(a) A hyperlinked graphic.

```
<a href = pricelist.htm><img src = j0282600.wmf height = 80 width =
80></a>
```

Fig. 14.38(b) The HTML that produced the hyperlinked graphic.

In this example we have used a simple clip art image, but any graphic of any size can be used. When the user clicks the graphic, it will take him/her to pricelist.htm. Remember to copy the graphic into the folder the web page is in (for convenience, as discussed previously). Graphics can be of any type, including .bmp, .jpg, .gif, .wmf etc. We obtained this clip art from Microsoft.com, and have retained its original file name.

Notice we have also added a text version of the hyperlink. This makes it clearer what the hyperlink is about. We could have left it as just text, but we've hyperlinked it too. Why not? So the effect shown in Fig. 14.38(a) was *really* produced by:

```
<a href = pricelist.htm><img src = j0282600.wmf height = 80 width =
80></a><br>  
<a href = pricelist.htm>Price list<a>
```

Fig. 14.38(c) The HTML for the hyperlinked graphic and 'title'.

14.6 Frames

Frames are a means of dividing up the browser window. Each frame contains a separate web page so using frames you can see several web pages in a single browser window at the same time. We use this in our first example to keep one frame on the screen all the time. It contains just hyperlinks and allows you to navigate between several pages and still be able to see the hyperlinks.

14.6.1 Frames example 1: simple contents example

This example contains two frames, and the user chooses which page to load into the right-hand frame by clicking a hyperlink in the left frame. We have called the left frame 'leftframe' and the right one 'rightframe'.

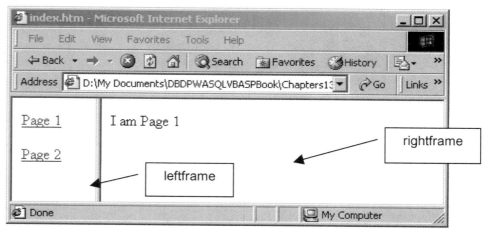

Fig. 14.39 This example uses two frames – leftframe and rightframe. contents.htm is currently loaded into leftframe, and page01.htm into rightframe.

The *structure* of the frames, the place where you set them up, is in a separate file which is not itself visible. In our example, that file is index.htm, our home page. As you can see in Fig. 14.40, index.htm 'consists' of two frames, leftframe and rightframe. They are gathered together into a frameset. The pages that are initially loaded into these two frames are to be contents.htm and page01.htm respectively. These two pages are quite conventional and are shown in Figs 14.41 and 14.42.

```
<html>
<head><title>index.htm</title></head>
<frameset cols = 20%,80%>
<!-- frames and their initial pages - ->
<frame name = leftframe src = contents.htm>
<frame name = rightframe src = page01.htm>
</frameset>
<noframes>
<body>
Your browser doesn't support frames.
</body>
</noframes>
</html>
```

Fig. 14.40 index.htm – not visible but gives the structure of the frames.

```
<html>
<head><title>contents.htm</title></head>
<body>
<a href = page01.htm target = rightframe>Page 1</a><p>
<a href = page02.htm target = rightframe>Page 2</a>
</body>
</html>
```

Fig. 14.41 contents.htm – carries the hyperlinks to the pages to be displayed in rightframe.

```
<html>
<head><title>page01.htm</title></head>
<body>
I am Page 1
</body>
</html>
```

Fig. 14.42 page01.htm – one of the pages called up to appear in rightframe.

index.htm

Let's look in detail at the contents of our frame-defining page – index.htm (Fig. 14.40). The frames that will appear in the browser window are specified using the <frameset> tag and each individual frame is specified using a <frame> tag:

```
<frameset cols = 20%,80%>
<!-- frames and their initial pages – ->
<frame name = leftframe src = contents.htm>
<frame name = rightframe src = page01.htm>
</frameset>
```

In

```
<frameset cols = 20%,80%>
```

we have specified that the browser window is to be divided up into two columns, the first of which is to take up 20% of the browser window width, and the second the other 80%. The parameter rows = would instead divide the browser window up into rows.

In

```
<frame name = leftframe src = contents.htm>
```

we are saying that the name of the left frame is leftframe and its (initial) source is to be the page contents.htm.

And in

```
<frame name = rightframe src = page01.htm>
```

we are saying that the name of the right frame is rightframe and its (initial) source is to be the page page01.htm.

The name = parameter of the <frame> tag is important, because we will need a name for it so that we can (elsewhere in the website pages) say which frame we want to load pages into.

In Fig. 14.40, the rest of the HTML code is:

```
<noframes>
<body>
Your browser doesn't support frames.
</body>
</noframes>
```

This <noframes> section is only executed if the user's browser doesn't allow frames. Up-to-date browsers do. In this section you could direct the user to a non-frames version of your website. But you might consider maintaining two versions of your website too much work. An alternative is to insert a hyperlink inviting the user to download a browser that does support frames.

contents.htm
Now let's look at the page we loaded into leftframe – contents.htm.

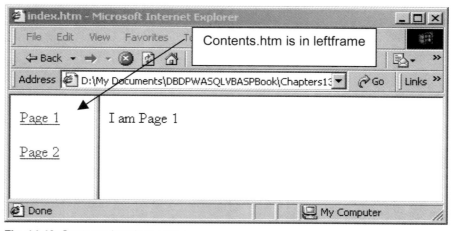

Fig. 14.43 Contents.htm is in leftframe.

```
<html>
<head><title>contents.htm></title></head>
<body>
<a href = page01.htm target = rightframe>Page 1</a><p>
<a href = page02.htm target = rightframe>Page 2</a>
</body>
</html>
```

Fig. 14.44 contents.htm – carries the hyperlinks to the pages to be displayed in rightframe.

When the user clicks either of the hyperlinks, the href = parameter says which file to get (e.g. page01.htm) *and* which frame to display it in (e.g. target = rightframe):

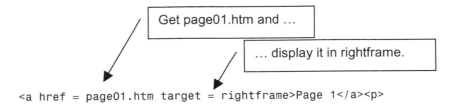

```
<a href = page01.htm target = rightframe>Page 1</a><p>
```

This simple example has shown the basics of how frames work. The next two examples show a few variations.

14.6.2 Frames example 2: simple contents with banner

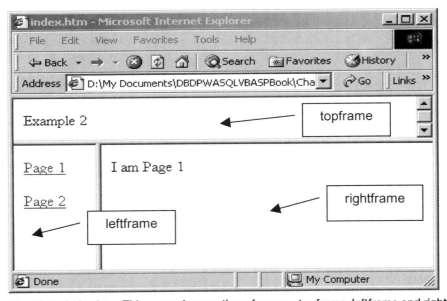

Fig. 14.45 index.htm. This example uses three frames – topframe, leftframe and rightframe.

```
<html>
<head><title>index.htm</title></head>
<frameset rows = 20%,80%>
<frame name = topframe src = banner.htm>
<frameset cols = 20%,80%>
<!-- frames and their initial pages - ->
<frame name = leftframe src = contents.htm>
<frame name = rightframe src = page01.htm>
</frameset>
```

A frameset *within* a frameset

```
</frameset>
<noframes>
<body>
Your browser doesn't support frames.
</body>
</noframes>
</html>
```

Fig. 14.46 index.htm – not visible but gives the structure of the frames.

```
<html>
<head><title>contents.htm</title></head>
<body>
<a href = page01.htm target = rightframe>Page 1</a><p>
<a href = page02.htm target = rightframe>Page 2</a>
</body>
</html>
```

Fig. 14.47 contents.htm – carries the hyperlinks to the pages to be displayed in rightframe.

```
<html>
<head><title>page01.htm</title></head>
<body>
I am Page 1
</body>
</html>
```

Fig. 14.48 page01.htm – one of the pages called up to be displayed in rightframe.

```
<html>
<head><title>contents.htm</title></head>
<body>Example 2</body>
</html>
```

Fig. 14.49 banner.htm – shows in topframe.

14.6.3 Frames example 3: right frame contains two subframes

Simple book – the chapter number is shown <u>here</u> and the chapter itself is shown <u>here</u>. The contents are shown <u>here</u>.

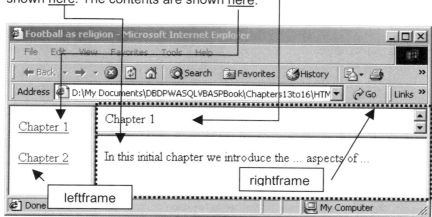

Fig. 14.50 Our third frames example. Rightframe contains two subframes.

```
<html>
<head><title>Football as religion</title></head>
<!-- frames and their initial pages -->
<frameset cols = 20%,80%>
<frame name = leftframe src = contents.htm>
<frame name = rightframe src = chapter01frames.htm>
</frameset>
<noframes>
<body>
Your browser doesn't support frames.
</body>
</noframes>
</html>
```

> The source for rightframe is *another* frameset.

Fig. 14.51 index.htm – not visible but gives the structure of the frames.

> When the user clicks <u>Chapter 1</u>, a frameset (containing the chapter heading and the chapter contents - see Fig. 14.53) is copied into rightframe.

```
<html>
<head><title>contents.htm></title></head>
<body>
<a href = chapter01frames.htm target = rightframe>Chapter 1</a><p>
<a href = chapter02frames.htm target = rightframe>Chapter 2</a>
```

```
</body>
</html>
```

Fig. 14.52 contents.htm – carries the hyperlinks to the pages to be displayed in rightframe.

```
<html>
<head><title>chapter01frames.htm</title></head>
<frameset rows = 20%,80%>
<frame name = topframe src = chapter01heading.htm>
<frame name = bottomframe src = chapter01.htm>
</frameset>
</html>
```

Fig. 14.53 chapter01frames.htm – contains the frames for the chapter heading and the chapter itself – one such frame file for each chapter.

```
<html>
<head><title>chapter01heading.htm</title></head>
<body>Chapter 1</body>
</html>
```

Fig. 14.54 chapter01heading.htm – shows in topframe.

```
<html>
<head><title>chapter01.htm</title></head>
<body>
In this initial chapter we introduce the . . . aspects of . . .
</body>
</html>
```

Fig. 14.55 chapter01.htm.

Note that in this example, each chapter needs *three* files – the file containing the frameset (here, chapter01frames.htm), the file containing the heading (here, chapter01heading.htm), and the file containing the chapter itself (here, chapter01.htm).

14.7 Forms

All of the tags and examples above were concerned with how web pages are displayed. If you want to gather information from your users, you will have to use HTML forms. We will need forms in Chapter 15 where our web pages will be interacting with the user – gathering passwords, gathering input data for database queries, updates etc. The data gathered from the user can be processed in two basic ways. It can be sent via email to someone, or it can be processed by a server-side script. In both cases the set of tags used for data entry is the same. We conclude this chapter with an example covering all major form tags.

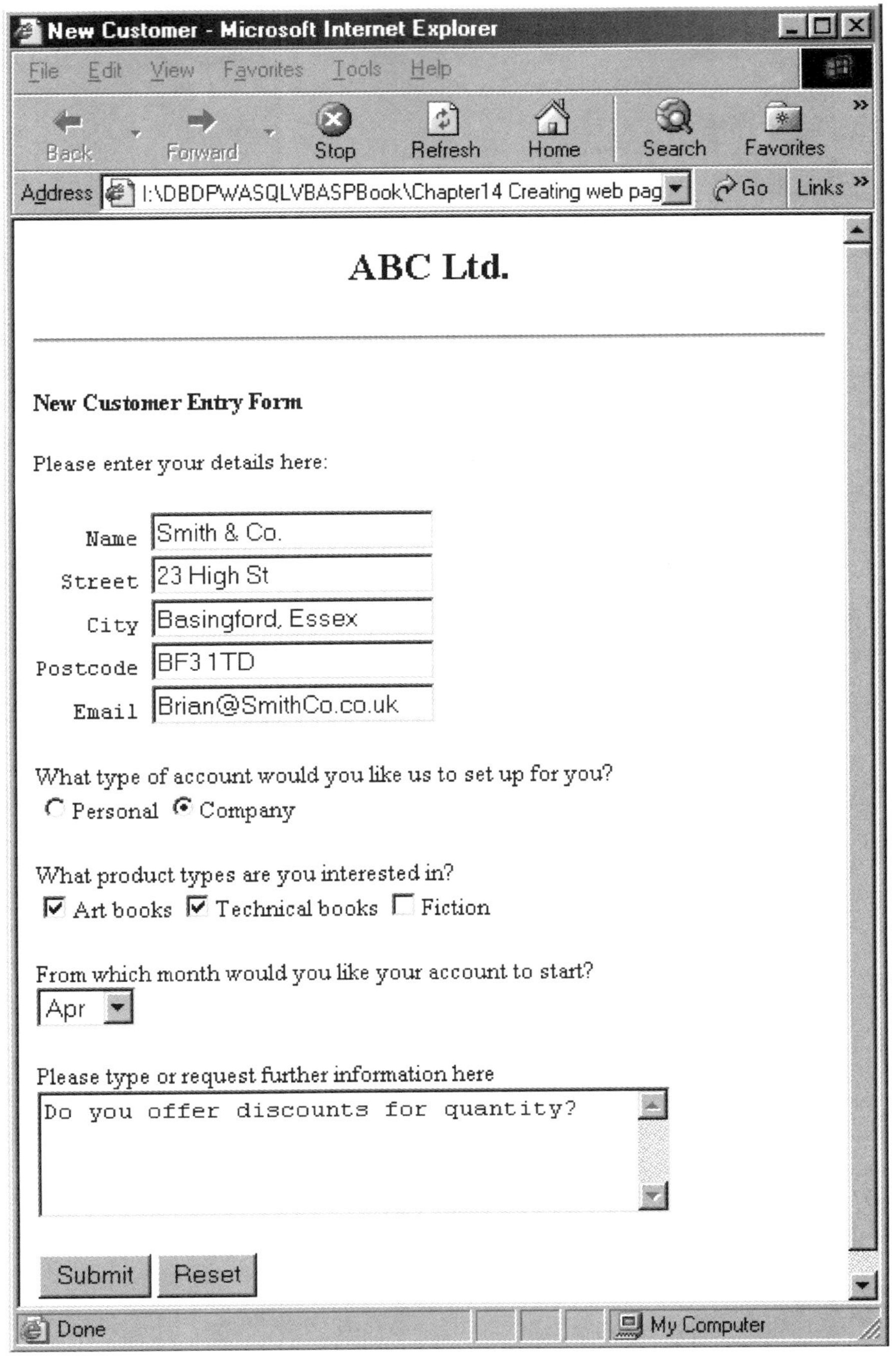

Fig. 14.56(a) The HTML to produce this data entry form is shown in Fig. 14.56(b).

```
<html>
<head><title>New Customer</title></head>
<body>
<center><h2>ABC Ltd.</h2>
</center>
<hr>
<h4>New Customer Entry Form</h4>
<p>
Please enter your details here:
<p>
<form method = post action = mailto:accounts@abcltd.biz>
<input type = hidden name = ourformtype value = newcustomer>
<pre>
    Name <input type = text name = cusname size = 20>
  Street <input type = text name = street size = 20>
    City <input type = text name = city size = 20>
Postcode <input type = text name = postc size = 20>
   Email <input type = text name = email size = 20>
</pre>
<p>
What type of account would you like us to set up for you?
<br>
<input type = radio name = accounttype value = p>Personal
<input type = radio name = accounttype value = c>Company
<p>
What product types are you interested in?
<br>
<input type = checkbox name = intinartbks>Art books
<input type = checkbox name = intintechbks>Technical books
<input type = checkbox name = intinfiction>Fiction
<p>
From which month would you like your account to start?
<br>
<select name = acctstartmonth size = 1>
<option
selected>Jan<option>Feb<option>Mar<option>Apr<option>May<option>
Jun<option>Jul<option>Aug<option>Sept<option>Oct<option>
Nov<option>Dec</select>
<p>
Please type or request further information here
<textarea name = furtherinfo rows = 4 cols = 40></textarea>
<p>
<input type = submit value = Submit>
<input type = reset value = Reset>
</form>
</body>
</html>
```

Fig. 14.56(b) The HTML for the form shown in Fig. 14.56(a).

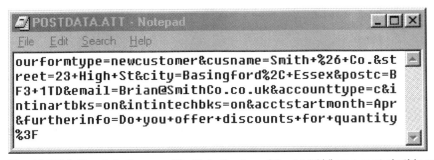

Fig. 14.56(c) The data the user filled into the form (Fig. 14.56(d) was sent via this email attachment.

```
ourformtype = newcustomer
&cusname = Smith + %26 + Co.
&street = 23 + High + St
&city = Basingford%2C + Essex
&postc = BF3 + 1TD
&email = Brian@SmithCo.co.uk
&accounttype = c
&intinartbks = on
&intintechbks = on
&acctstartmonth = Apr
&furtherinfo = Do + you + offer + discounts + for + quantity%3F
```

Fig. 14.56(d) The email attachment separated into lines.

Figure 14.56(a) is a form used to send basic customer details to a company called ABC Ltd. The HTML file used to produce this form is shown in Fig. 14.56(b). We consider this in detail shortly.

When the user clicks the Submit button, the data he/she typed into the form is sent via an email attachment, shown in Fig. 14.56(c). In Fig. 14.56(d) we have separated this string of data into lines for greater legibility. In this example, the data was sent to ABC Ltd using an email attachment. An alternative is to pre-process the data at the server side using an ASP script. We show how to do this in Chapter 15. If, as here, an email attachment is used to get form data to the website owner, the data will have to be unpacked from the email attachment. This can be done quite simply in a VB (or other) program on the website owner's local PC, which could also write the data into a local Access (or other) customer database. As you can see from Figs 14.56(c) and 14.56(d), lines are separated with the & character and spaces are represented by the + character. Some characters are represented by their hexadecimal ascii code, preceded by % (e.g. a comma is represented by %2C).

We now discuss the <form> tags used in this page and contained in Fig. 14.56(b) in detail.

14.7.1 *The Form tag*

<form>

The whole of the form section is enclosed in <form> and </form>. You are allowed to have more than one form on a page if you want to, but usually you will have just one, as here.

In the <form> tag there are two parameters, method = and action = . When the user clicks the Submit button, the form data he or she has typed in is sent via the internet to the server to be processed. The method = and action = parameters of the <form> tag specify how that processing is to be done. The action = parameter says which server program will process the form data, and the method = parameter says how the server program will expect to receive it. Let's consider the action = parameter first.

action =

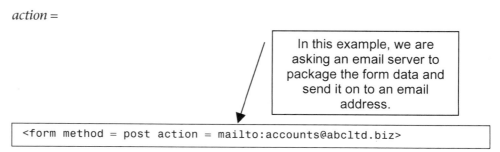

In this example, we are asking an email server to package the form data and send it on to an email address.

```
<form method = post action = mailto:accounts@abcltd.biz>
```

Fig. 14.57 Sending the form data to an email server.

The action = parameter specifies which program on the server we want to process the form data the user has typed in. In our example (Fig. 14.57), we specify that the form data will be processed by the server's email program. The email server knows that all it has to do is send an email to the address specified after the : and attach the form data to it. It will then be up to the recipient (ABC Ltd in our example) to process the data locally.

If we had wanted to send the form data to a server-side ASP script called, for example, processanewcustomer.asp, we would have named the script in the action parameter, e.g.:

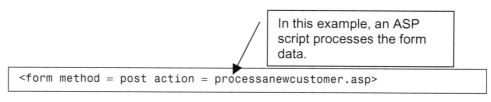

In this example, an ASP script processes the form data.

```
<form method = post action = processanewcustomer.asp>
```

Fig. 14.58 Sending the form data to an ASP script.

Being able to use a server-side script like this offers us great flexibility in the range of ways we can process the form data. Here are some things we could ask the ASP script processanewcustomer.asp to do:

- validate the form data;
- insert a new customer record in a server-side database;
- send a page to the customer confirming that the data has been processed.

We show how to write ASP scripts in Chapter 15.

method =
There are two methods of sending: post and get. When the user clicks the Submit button, a message is sent to the server program mentioned in the action = parameter. The message starts with the URL of the website, so that it gets to the right server. The 'get' method attaches the form data to this, separated by a question mark. The 'post' method sends it separately.

Some form-processing programs on servers, such as search engines, where only a small amount of data is to be sent to them (a few key words), will use method = post. Here is an example of a search using the google.com search engine:

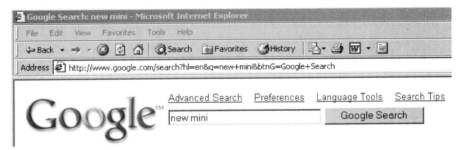

Fig. 14.59(a) A search using the Google search engine.

```
A program called search on the
google.com website is being fed
two keywords, using method=get
```

```
http://www.google.com/search?hl = en&q = new + mini&btnG = Google +
Search
```

Fig. 14.59(b) A close-up of the URL of Fig. 14.59(a).

```
<form name = gs method = GET action = /search>
<INPUT TYPE = hidden name = hl value = en>
<input type = text name = q size = 31>
<input type = submit name = btnG value = "Google Search">
</form>
```

Fig. 14.59(c) A simplified version of the <form> tag used in the web page of Fig. 14.59(a).

Figure 14.59(a) shows part of the web page that Google uses to gather key words for its search. Figure 14.59(b) shows the URL for a search on the two key words 'new' and 'mini'. These are fed to the program called 'search' by attaching them to the URL. Figure 14.59(c) shows the HTML <form> tag used in this search. You can see in the top line that the form data is to be sent using method = get and that it's to be sent to a program called search, using the action = parameter of the form tag.

Other form-processing programs, such as email servers (SMTP servers), where a larger amount of data is to be sent to them (the contents of an email message), require post as the method, because it would be impracticable to attach all the email text to the URL. We discuss the post and get methods further in Chapter 15, and give examples of their use in ASP programs.

14.7.2 Hidden input

Sometimes it's desirable to send 'hidden' data from the form to the program that processes the data. In Fig. 14.56(b), we find the following line in the form:

```
<input type = hidden name = ourformtype value = newcustomer>
```

Fig. 14.60(a) A hidden field called ourformtype.

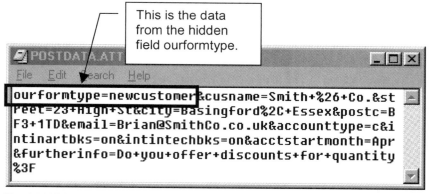

Fig. 14.60(b) How the data from the hidden field ourformtype appears in the data sent from the form when the user clicks the Submit button.

You don't *have* to send hidden data, but in this example, you can see how useful it can be. This data (ourformtype = newcustomer in our example) could be used to decide which program will be used to process the rest of the form data. Examples of other data you might want to send with the form are given in some of the examples in Chapter 15.

14.7.3 Text

The simplest way to capture data from the user in an HTML form is to use a text box. We give each form object a name so that the data can be identified. The following example from the form of Fig. 14.56 explains this.

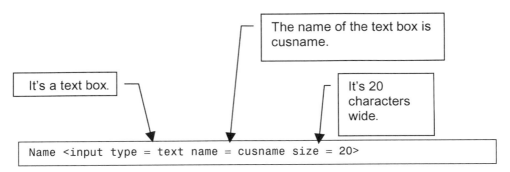

Fig. 14.61(a) An HTML <form> text box.

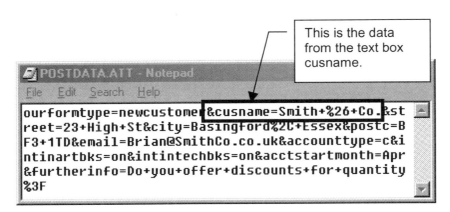

Fig. 14.61(b) How the text box looks on the form.

Fig. 14.61(c) How the data from the cusname text box appears in the data sent from the form when the user clicks the Submit button (assuming they'd typed Smith & Co. in the text box).

If for any reason you want to give the text box an initial value, you could do this:

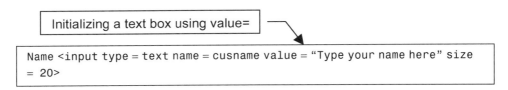

Fig. 14.62(a) Initializing a text box value.

Name `Type your name here`

Fig. 14.62(b) How the initial value appears in the text box.

Note the use of <pre> and </pre> to help plan ('preserve') the layout and alignment of the text boxes:

```
<pre>
     Name <input type = text name = cusname size = 20>
   Street <input type = text name = street size = 20>
     City <input type = text name = city size = 20>
 Postcode <input type = text name = postc size = 20>
    Email  <input type = text name = email size = 20>
</pre>
```

14.7.4   Text area

This is a larger and scrollable version of the text box. It's useful for allowing the user to input larger amounts of unstructured data, or for you to display it (using value = , as above). An example from the form of Fig. 14.56 is:

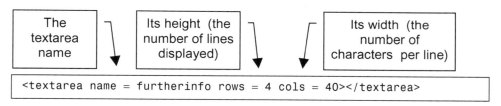

Fig. 14.63(a) An example of a text area called furtherinfo.

Fig. 14.63(b) How the text area appears in the user's browser window.

Fig. 14.64 Text can be displayed by inserting it between the <textarea> and </textarea> tags.

14.7.5 Radio buttons

Radio buttons are used in forms when there is just *one* choice to be made from several (rather than a *number* of choices from several, for which we would use check boxes – see below). A simple example of this is shown in our example of Fig. 14.56:

```
<input type = radio name = accounttype value = p>Personal
<input type = radio name = accounttype value = c>Company
```

Fig. 14.65(a) Radio buttons in use. Note the same name is used for each option – because only one will be selected.

```
 C Personal  C Company
```

Fig. 14.65(b) How the radio buttons of Fig. 14.65(a) appear in the browser window. The user clicks one.

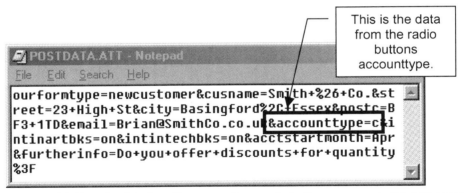

This is the data from the radio buttons accounttype.

```
ourformtype=newcustomer&cusname=Smith+%26+Co.&st
reet=23+High+St&city=Basingford%2C+Essex&postc=B
F3+1TD&email=Brian@SmithCo.co.uk&accounttype=c&i
ntinartbks=on&intintechbks=on&acctstartmonth=Apr
&furtherinfo=Do+you+offer+discounts+for+quantity
%3F
```

Fig. 14.65(c) How the data from the accounttype radio buttons appears in the data sent from the form when the user clicks the Submit button (assuming they'd chosen 'Customer').

14.7.6 Check boxes

Check boxes are used in forms when there are a *number* of choices to be made from several (rather than *one* choice from several, for which we would use radio buttons – see above). A simple example of this is shown in our example of Fig. 14.56:

```
<input type = checkbox name = intinartbks>Art books
<input type = checkbox name = intintechbks>Technical books
<input type = checkbox name = intinfiction>Fiction
```

Fig. 14.66(a) Check boxes in use. Note that (unlike radio buttons) a different name is used for each check box – because the user can select more than one.

☑ Art books ☑ Technical books ☐ Fiction

Fig. 14.66(b) How the check boxes of Fig. 14.65(a) appear in the browser window. The user clicks any combination of them.

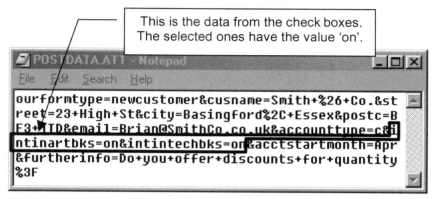

This is the data from the check boxes. The selected ones have the value 'on'.

```
ourformtype=newcustomer&cusname=Smith+%26+Co.&st
reet=23+High+St&city=Basingford%2C+Essex&postc=B
F3+MTD&email=Brian@SmithCo.co.uk&accounttype=c&i
ntinartbks=on&intintechbks=on&acctstartmonth=Apr
&furtherinfo=Do+you+offer+discounts+for+quantity
%3F
```

Fig. 14.66(c) How the data from the check boxes appears in the data sent from the form when the user clicks the Submit button (assuming they'd chosen 'Art books' and 'Technical books').

14.7.7 Select dropdown

This is the <select> tag. It's used where you want the user to select from one of a large or variable number of options. To get a variable number of options from a database and put them in a <select>, you'd need an ASP script – see Chapter 15. In our present example, there is a fixed number of options – the twelve months of the year.

```
<select name = acctstartmonth size = 1>
<option
selected>Jan<option>Feb<option>Mar<option>Apr<option>May
<option>Jun<option>Jul<option>Aug<option>Sept<option>Oct
<option>Nov<option>Dec</select>
```

Fig. 14.67 The <select> tag of the <form> shown in Fig. 14.56.

If you set its size = parameter to 1, just the initially selected option (usually the first one) will appear, as in Fig. 14.68.

Fig. 14.68(a) Select of Fig. 14.67 (with size = 1, as shown in Fig. 14.67), *before* clicking.

Jan is highlighted (before the user makes a selection) because it has <option selected> – rather than just <option> – in the <select> tag. If the user doesn't click the select dropdown, Jan will be the default.

Fig. 14.68(b) Select of Fig. 14.67 (with size = 1, as shown in Fig. 14.67), *after* clicking. Note that the item with <option selected> appears highlighted and will be the default. The user can subsequently select any option, though.

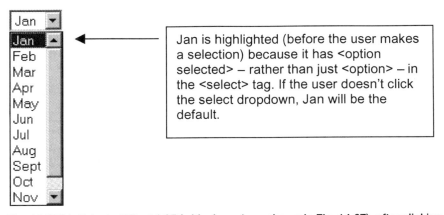

Fig. 14.69(a) This is how the <select> dropdown appears with size = 5 (before the user clicks it), as in Fig. 14.69(b).

```
<select name = acctstartmonth size = 5>
<option
selected>Jan<option>Feb<option>Mar<option>Apr<option>May
<option>Jun<option>Jul<option>Aug<option>Sept<option>Oct
<option>Nov<option>Dec
</select>
```

Fig. 14.69(b) The same <select> tag, but with size altered to 5.

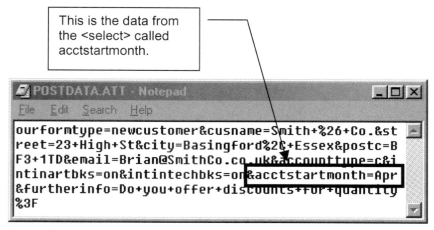

Fig. 14.70 How the data from the <select> startmonth appears in the data sent from the form when the user clicks the Submit button (assuming they'd chosen 'Apr').

14.7.8 Submit and Reset buttons

Fig. 14.71(a) The Submit and Reset buttons.

```
<input type = submit value = Submit> <input type = reset value = Reset>
```

Fig. 14.71(b) The HTML code for the Submit and Reset buttons.

Finally, the Submit button (Fig. 14.71) is used to send the form data to the destination shown in the action = parameter. The user can clear all of data he/she entered by using the Reset button.

14.8 Exercises

1. Explain the following terms:

   (a) Web page

   (b) Home page

   (c) index.htm

   (d) default.asp

   (e) HTML

   (f) HTML tag

   (g) hyperlink

   (h) absolute and relative addressing

   (i) http://www.abcltd.co.uk/springsale/kitchens.htm

   (j) upload and download

   (k) FTP

   (l) client and server

   (m) browser

(n) ISP

(o) head tags

(p) body tags

(q) search engine

(r) meta tags

(s) .jpg, .bmp, .gif, .wmf

(t) Error 404

(u) frame

(v) target frame

(w) form

(This question should help you become more familiar with web page development terms.)

2. Most institutions have rules governing what you can and cannot put on a web page that can be associated with them. Describe and evaluate the 'acceptable use policy' at your institution.

(This question should help you develop your own ideas on what should be allowed on web pages.)

3. Using your browser, view the source HTML from a selection of online web pages. See how many tags you can recognize.

(Doing this could help you see how other web developers write their HTML. Set your browser up so that it opens Notepad (rather than a complex 'development environment') when you view a page's source code).

4. Produce a single web page similar to the one shown in Fig. 14.8(b).

(This question should help you become familiar with HTML tags and also help you get practice in using the simple Notepad–Browser 'development environment': edit the HTML in Notepad and look at it in the browser; for each change in Notepad, do File/Save and click Refresh in the browser.)

5. Produce a personal home page.

(This will give you more practice in developing a single page website.)

6. Add two hyperlinked pages to your home page.

(This will give you practice in creating hyperlinks using the <a> tag. Remember to use relative addressing where possible. Make one of the hyperlinks an image rather than underlined text.)

7. Create a folder called websites and within it another folder ws01. This will contain the set of three related web pages and a graphic that make up the simple website shown in Fig. 14.72. Create this website.

(This question is suitable for an assignment or 1–2-hour practical test. It develops a small three-page website containing a form.)

ABC Ltd
Home Page

ABC Ltd. can supply all your sporting goods.

Call in to one of our high street stores or click the link below for details of our mail order service.

High St. stores   Mail Order   Email us

Fig. 14.72(a) ABC Ltd. Home Page index.htm.

ABC Ltd
High Street Stores

Address	Phone
42 High St, Ildon	0208 123 4567
19 The Links, Croyford	0208 765 4321
61 Mandela Place, Dubway	071 1234

Home

Fig. 14.72(b) ABC Ltd. High Street Stores page highstreetstores.htm.

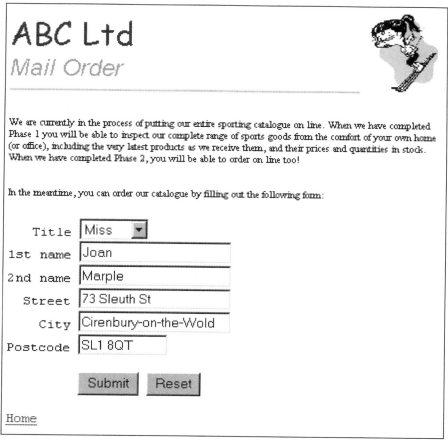

Fig. 14.72(c) ABC Ltd. Mail Order page mailorder.htm.

Check that the output from the form is correct. The attachment to the email you should get for the data entered in Fig. 14.72(c) is shown in Fig. 14.72(d).

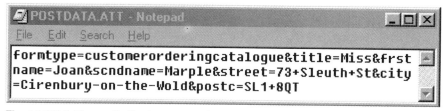

Fig. 14.72(d) The mail attachment received at abcltd.co.uk when Submit was clicked in Fig. 14.72(c).

Note: In this exercise, the order for the catalogue is sent to ABC Ltd. via an email attachment. There is no online catalogue and ABC's customers will have to send in their orders manually by email or by post. We show how to display and order online in Chapter 15. Because of the large number of stock items and the users' need to search for the product types they want, and ABC's need to add, change and delete products quickly, the data will be held on an online database.

8. Upload your website to an ASP server using FTP and check that all the links and the transmission of the form data by email still work.

(This question is to give you practice in using FTP for uploading your web pages. Use DOS FTP or a Windows-based FTP program.)

9. ABC Ltd (see question 7) has a two-phase development plan for selling its sports goods online:

Phase 1

ABC Ltd will put its product catalogue online so that customers will be able to inspect the complete range of ABC's sports goods, including new product lines as they become available, and the latest prices and quantities in stock.

Phase 2

Customers will be able to order online.
(a) Discuss the advantages and disadvantages of implementing each of these phases of ABC's development plan.

(b) Draw diagrams of possible configurations for each phase, showing where (client or server) each element (software, hardware, database(s)) will reside. Discuss the advantages and disadvantages of each configuration. Hint: there are three locations involved:

    (i) the customer client site

    (ii) ABC's server site

    (iii) ABC's client site.

(c) Investigate the possibilities of ABC Ltd avoiding databases completely and discuss the advantages and disadvantages of this approach, and the conditions under which it would be appropriate. Hints: Some of the factors you might consider could be simplicity, cost, development time, software requirements, expertise required, susceptibility to errors, number of product lines, speed of update when things change, and server costs.

(This question could be adapted to become suitable as an exam question or assignment. It helps you to consider the design possibilities for a typical online catalogue/order processing system.)

15

Creating ASP web pages using HTML and VBScript

In this chapter you will learn:

- how to put a database on the internet
- how to develop ASP database applications

15.1 Introduction

In Chapter 13 we introduced the scenario in which ASP web page development occurs and many of the definitions relating to ASP and web page development. We said that ASP web pages contain, in addition to the normal HTML, scripts written (in this book) in VBScript that run on the server to generate extra HTML statements 'in real time'. These 'server side' scripts (scripts that are executed on the web server) can be used to retrieve data from a database that is loaded on the web server and that is therefore accessible via the internet and can be shared and possibly updated by multiple users.

In Chapter 14 we described, with lots of examples, how HTML can be used to develop conventional web pages, and showed how the web pages can be uploaded to a web server on the internet using FTP.

In this chapter we shall be uploading Access databases to the internet and then developing ASP scripts (HTML + VBScript) to read and update them.

Here is a summary (see Chapter 13 for a fuller description) of the steps involved in ASP web page development (by you, the developer, who develops the ASP pages) and in ASP web page usage (by your users/customers/lecturers, who look at your ASP web pages):

Steps involved in ASP web page development (Developer)
1. Specify aims and basic layout of your website.

2. If a database is involved, design and develop the database tables and relationships using the techniques described in Chapters 1 to 3, namely entity

modelling, normalization and database implementation using Access (or any other DBMS), and design and develop key queries using the techniques described in Chapters 4 to 7.

3. Upload the database to the server, using FTP. FTP usage is described in Chapter 14.

4. Develop the non-ASP pages as described in Chapter 14. Much of this can be performed offline with the web pages held on the developer's local PC, and using a text editor such as FrontPage and a browser such as Internet Explorer (IE) on the developer's local PC.

5. Develop the ASP pages, as shown in this chapter.

6. Upload the web pages using FTP.

7. Test and debug all web pages and database. This time the web pages must be held on an ASP server running IIS, which will run your ASP page scripts to generate HTML which is then sent to the user's browser via the internet. After each change to a web page (done locally on the developer's PC), the web page has to be uploaded to the ASP server again, using FTP.

Steps in looking at an ASP web page (User)

1. Type the URL (e.g. http://www.abc.com) of the web page into a browser such as IE.

2. The internet finds the server holding the abc.com website and retrieves the website's default web page. The default web page will be index.htm or index.html or default.asp. Alternatively, the user could bypass the default web page by naming the page he/she wants to retrieve explicitly, for example http://www.abc.com/productlist.asp.

3. For conventional HTML pages (.htm, .html), the server simply sends the pages, as they are, to the client's PC via the internet. For ASP pages (.asp), the server first processes the page, which consists of VBScript (or JavaScript, but this book covers only VBSCript) commands ('scripts') and HTML commands, using its IIS program. IIS runs the scripts, which generates further HTML commands, and then the 'compiled' HTML page is sent to the client's PC via the internet.

15.2 ASP example 1: a password page

This example doesn't use a database, but is useful, and demonstrates how ASP works. ASP scripts run on the server and generate HTML that is then downloaded to the user's browser. The user never gets to see the VBScript source code that's contained in the page. If he/she views the source using his/her browser, all that will be seen is the HTML that was generated, not the VBScript. We use this fact in this example.

In this example, the user types a password into page1.htm (Fig. 15.2), which is a conventional HTML page containing a form with a text box and a submit button. The form tag sends the output of the form to page2.asp. VBScript code in page2.asp checks the password and only shows the page2.asp content if the password is correct. Note the extension .asp. IIS will only interpret the VBScript if the page has an .asp extension.

The correct password 'abc' is contained in a VBScript 'If' statement (Fig. 15.5), but the user never sees it because it's in the VBScript, not in the generated HTML. As you will see, the syntax of VBScript is virtually identical to Visual Basic.

Figure 15.1 shows the structure of the website. (We use the term website here to mean any collection of related web pages, usually stored in a common folder.)

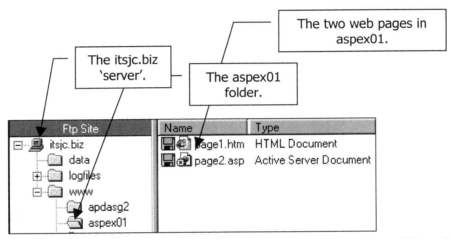

Fig. 15.1 Example 1 is held in folder aspex01 and contains two pages: page1.htm gets a password from the user and page2.asp checks the password and displays content if the password is correct.

Figure 15.2 shows the web page page1.htm and Fig. 15.3 shows the HTML code that it contains.

The form in page1.htm contains a text box of a special type – 'password'. This is different from an ordinary text box in that data entered is shown as asterisks. In the form tag, action = page2.asp means that when the submit button is clicked, the contents of the password box will be passed to page2.asp. The method = post part means the form data will be sent to page2.asp using a request object rather than being sent in the header (as with method = get), which would make the password visible in the browser address box. The 'request' object is ASP's name for a notional object that is sent *from* the user's browser. The 'response' object is ASP's name for a notional object that is sent *to* the user's browser.

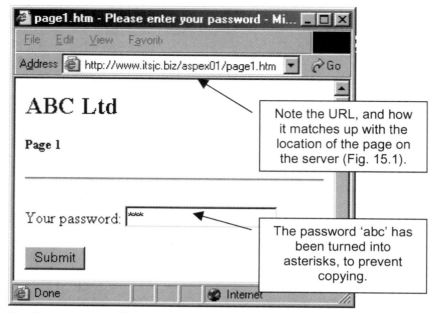

Fig. 15.2 page1.htm. If the user types the correct password, page2.asp content will be displayed.

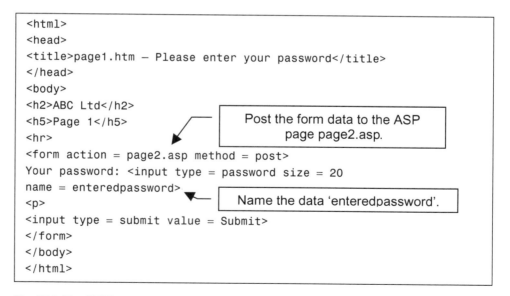

Fig. 15.3 The HTML for page1.htm. Note the form.

Figure 15.4 shows the page2.asp content that is displayed if the password is correct.

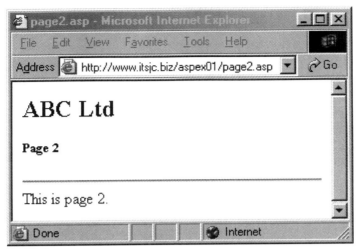

Fig. 15.4 The page2.asp content displayed in the user's browser if the password entered into page1.htm is correct.

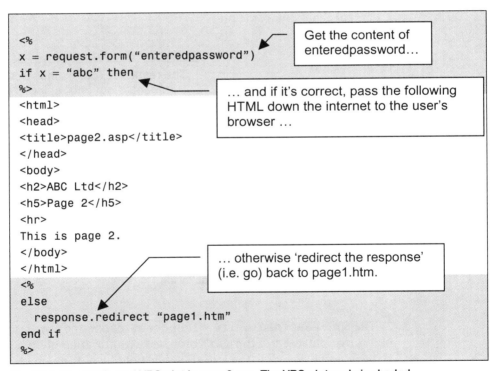

Fig. 15.5 The HTML and VBScript in page2.asp. The VBScript code is shaded.

This first ASP page shows how VBScript is in control of what HTML is sent to the user. That's what an ASP page is: server-side VBScript controlling the generation of the HTML code that's sent to the user's browser. If the user had typed the correct password ('abc') in, then the HTML shown unshaded in Fig. 15.5 would be sent to them. Note that the VBScript *isn't* sent. This means a user couldn't discover a password by viewing the source code of the web page. The VBScript is surrounded by <% and %>. You can think of these VBScript 'scripts' as telling IIS what HTML to generate.

In this example, if the user types in an incorrect password, the line

```
response.redirect "page1.htm"
```

just takes them back to the password page page1.htm. Let's modify page2.asp slightly so that the user gets an error message instead.

```
<%
x = request.form("enteredpassword")
if x = "abc" then
%>
<html>
<head>
<title>page2.asp</title>
</head>
<body>
<h2>ABC Ltd</h2>
<h5>Page 2</h5>
<hr>
This is page 2.
</body>
</html>
<%
else
   'response.redirect "page1.htm"
   response.write "Incorrect password"
end if
%>
```

> The response.redirect has been commented out and replaced with response.write.

Fig. 15.6 A small modification to page2.asp.

The line `response.write "Incorrect password"` writes to the response object (the data sent to the user's browser) with the effect shown in Fig. 15.7.

We could have made the error message bold by putting <b> HTML tags around the text, like this:

```
response.write "<b>Incorrect password</b>"
```

Response.write writes HTML content to the response object; that is, it sends HTML content to the user's browser.

Fig. 15.7 The error message produced by the new code in Fig. 15.6.

Here's a diagram that gives the basic idea of the request object and the response object:

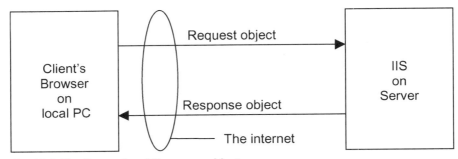

Fig. 15.8 The Request and Response objects.

15.3 ASP example 2: a hit counter

As our first example of ASP being used with a database, let's take a simple but useful application in which a web page displays how many times it has been seen. A simple Access database visitors.mdb is held on the server and every time the web page default.asp is retrieved from the server, a new record is written to the database. The record contains the date and time of the web page access. The web page announces the hit number and the date and time, and the date and time of the previous hit. An example of this can be seen on the home page of **http:// www.databasedesign.co.uk**.

Website structure
Figure 15.9 shows the structure of the website. It has been uploaded to our itsjc.biz ASP server, but you can of course upload it to an ASP web server of your choice.

There is just one web page – default.asp. We only need one page to illustrate how the hit counter works. You can see default.asp in Fig. 15.12. You'll notice in Fig. 15.12 that there is no need for the user to name the page in the browser's Address

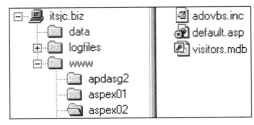

Fig. 15.9 Location and structure of website aspex02.

box. This is because IIS automatically looks for a page called default.asp to start with.

The file adovbs.inc in Fig. 15.9 is an *include* file. It contains code necessary in ASP pages that use ADO database commands, and our web page does. You can download a copy of adovbs.inc from:

http://www.databasedesign.co.uk/bookdbdpvbawebpages/root.htm

under the heading 'Other downloads'.

Database design
The database has just two fields, VisitNo and VisitTime, as shown in Fig. 15.10.

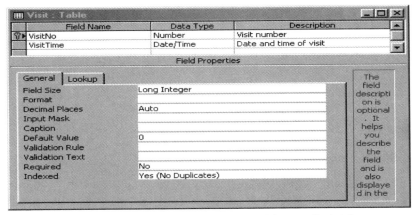

Fig. 15.10 The structure of the VISIT table in the visitors.mdb database.

Fig. 15.11 The VISIT table of Access database visits.mdb.

Web page

Fig. 15.12 Default.asp, showing the hit counter output.

Web page code

```
<html>
<head>
<title>default.asp - a hit counter</title>
<!-- #INCLUDE FILE = "adovbs.inc" -->
</head>
<body>
<%


'-- Connect to the visitors.mdb database --
set conn1 = server.createobject("ADODB.Connection")
x = "Provider = Microsoft.Jet.OLEDB.4.0;"
x = x & "Data
Source = d:\websites\itsjcb\www\aspex02\visitors.mdb"
conn1.open x


'-- Get the VISIT recordset --
set rs1 = server.createobject("ADODB.Recordset")
rs1.open "select * from visit", conn1, adOpenDynamic,
adLockOptimistic, adCmdText


'-- Get the last VISIT number and time --
rs1.movelast
varLastVisitNo = rs1("visitno")
varLastVisitTime = rs1("visittime")


'-- Calculate this VISIT number and time --
varThisVisitNo = varLastVisitNo + 1
```

adovbs.inc contains ADO command info and must be included.

This is the path to your database on the server.

Retrieve the data from the VISIT table in the visitors.mdb database.

```
varThisVisitTime = dateadd("h", + 0, now) 'for BST

'-- Add the new VISIT record --
rs1.addnew                          ┌──────────────────────────────┐
rs1("visitno") = varThisVisitNo     │ Add a VISIT record to the    │
rs1("visittime") = varThisVisitTime │ database for the current visit.│
rs1.update                          └──────────────────────────────┘

'-- Close recordset and database connection --
rs1.close
set rs1 = nothing      ┌──────────────────────────────┐
conn1.close            │ Close connection to database. │
set conn1 = nothing    └──────────────────────────────┘
%>
<center>
<h2>ABC Ltd</h2>          ┌────────────────────────────────────────────┐
<h5>Home Page</h5>        │ Include VBScript data in HTML. This is shorthand for: │
</center>                 │ <% response.write varThisVisitNo %>          │
<p>                       └────────────────────────────────────────────┘
<font size = 2>You are visitor number
<% = varThisVisitNo%>, timed at <% = varThisVisitTime%>
BST. The previous visit was at <% = varLastVisitTime%> BST</font>
<hr>

</body>
</html>
```

Fig. 15.13 HTML and VBScript code in ASP page default.asp.

Description of code (Fig. 15.13)
The VBScript code is between <% and %>.

```
<!-- #INCLUDE FILE = "adovbs.inc" -->
```

is placed in the <head> section. It includes lines like:

```
Const adOpenDynamic = 2
```

which simply give the numerical value of constants used in ADO commands.

```
'-- Connect to the visitors.mdb database --
set conn1 = server.createobject("ADODB.Connection")
x = "Provider = Microsoft.Jet.OLEDB.4.0;"
x = x & "Data Source = d:\websites\itsjcb\www\aspex02\visitors.mdb"
conn1.open x
```

Fig. 15.14 Connecting to the uploaded database visitors.mdb.

Connecting to the database follows the methods described in Chapter 11. A couple of points are worth noting:

1. Jet Engine driver version.

```
Provider = Microsoft.Jet.OLEDB.4.0
```

is for Access 2000 databases. For older databases, use:

```
Provider = Microsoft.Jet.OLEDB.3.51
```

Note that the version depends on the driver they're using on the *server*, which is not necessarily the version you or your clients use on your PCs.

2. Path to the database.

```
d:\websites\itsjcb\www\aspex02\visitors.mdb
```

is the location of the database on our server itsjc.biz. Replace this with the correct path for your database. Information on how to upload to our server for experimental purposes can be found on **http://www.itsjc.biz**.

```
'-- Get the VISIT recordset --
set rs1 = server.createobject("ADODB.Recordset")
rs1.open "select * from visit", conn1, adOpenDynamic,
adLockOptimistic, adCmdText
```

Fig. 15.15 Creating a recordset rs1 containing the VISIT table.

This code retrieves *all* the records from the VISIT table, using the simple SQL statement shown. Later we will want to add a new record so adOpenDynamic is used because it allows updates. We chose adLockOptimistic for locking, since there is no chance of other updates interleaving with this simple one-record insertion. We had to choose adCmdText for the last parameter, because we are using an SQL statement to retrieve the recordset. Details of these parameter options are discussed in Chapter 11.

```
'-- Get the last VISIT number and time --
rs1.movelast
varLastVisitNo = rs1("visitno")
varLastVisitTime = rs1("visittime")
```

Fig. 15.16 Getting details of the most recent previous visit to the website from the VISIT table.

We move to the last record in the recordset since that contains details of the most recent visit. The field visitno is the primary key of the VISIT table, and Access indexes and sorts ascending on the primary key – we just happen to know that. With some (non-Access) databases it may be necessary to change the SQL in the open statement from

```
select * from visit
```

to:

```
select * from visit order by visitno
```

to guarantee the recordset is sorted on visitno. An alternative would be to just retrieve the latest record, using:

```
select top 1 * from visit order by visitno desc
```

In

```
varLastVisitNo = rs1("visitno")
varLastVisitTime = rs1("visittime")
```

we put the values of the visitno and visittime fields into a couple of local variables. We have prefixed the variable names with 'var' so we don't mix them up with field names. These two variables are used later in the program. Their values are embedded in HTML statements to put in the user's browser window.

```
'-- Calculate this VISIT number and time --
varThisVisitNo = varLastVisitNo + 1
varThisVisitTime = dateadd("h", + 0, now) 'for BST
```

Fig. 15.17 Calculating the current visit number and time – to add to the VISIT table.

We add one to the previous highest visit number. The time is quite interesting. In

```
varThisVisitTime = dateadd("h", + 0, now) 'for BST
```

now is a function evaluating to the time now. dateadd is a VBScript function that allows you to add a given number of hours ("h") to a given time. You can consult VB help for details. Look under 'DateAdd function'. This line allows you to compensate for the difference in time that the server thinks it is and the time you want to display. At one time, we used an ASP server in New York and wanted to display UK time. UK time is five hours ahead of US time, so we had this in our web page:

```
varThisVisitTime = dateadd("h", + 5, now) 'for BST
```

Now our server is in the UK, and we still want to display UK time, so we have changed the value to + 0.

```
'-- Add the new VISIT record --
rs1.addnew
rs1("visitno") = varThisVisitNo
rs1("visittime") = varThisVisitTime
rs1.update
```

Fig. 15.18 Adding the new VISIT record to the VISIT table.

Conventional ADO commands are used here. Note the syntax for referring to fields. A blank record is appended to recordset rs1, the values of the two fields are filled in, and the update command saves the new record into the VISIT table on the visitors.mdb database.

```
'-- Close recordset and database connection --
rs1.close
set rs1 = nothing
conn1.close
set conn1 = nothing
```

Fig. 15.19 Closing down the recordset and the connection to the visitors.mdb database.

It is normal practice on web-based databases to open and close them for single transactions, so that you don't tie up server and database resources unnecessarily.

```
<center>
<h2>ABC Ltd</h2>
<h5>Home Page</h5>
</center>
<p>
<font size = 2>You are visitor number <% = varThisVisitNo%>, timed at <%
= varThisVisitTime%> BST. The previous visit was at <% =
varLastVisitTime%> BST</font>
<hr>
```

Fig. 15.20 HTML with embedded VBScript values.

You can embed VBScript (as here in Fig. 15.20) or have it control the generation of HTML commands directly by doing things like:

```
response.write "<h1>ABC Ltd</h1>"
```

You'll often want to embed values that have been calculated in the VBScript parts of your page into the HTML parts. VBScript gives you a compact (if strange-looking) way of doing this. You just precede the variable name with = and surround the result with <% and %>. An alternative would have been for us to do it this way:

```
<font size = 2>You are visitor number <% response.write
varThisVisitNo %>, timed at <% response.write varThisVisitTime
%> BST. The previous visit was at <% response.write
varLastVisitTime %> BST</font>
<hr>
```

which is clearer but less compact. It means the same thing.

Summary of example 2

We've shown how to read and update a database located on the internet and display data from the database onto a web page.

In the next example, we display a whole database table on a web page.

15.4 ASP example 3: displaying an internet database table

In some ways this example is simpler than the previous one, because in the previous example there was a database update, and here, we are just going to display the contents of the CUSTOMER table from the accts.mdb database onto a web page. We'll display each CUSTOMER record in a separate row of an HTML <table>. What this example has going for it is that this is exactly the sort of thing you will want to do in many of your ASP database applications.

Web page

<table>
<tr><td colspan="3" align="center">Customer Listing</td></tr>
<tr><td colspan="3" align="center">London Region</td></tr>
<tr><td>Cus.No.</td><td>Name</td><td>Address</td></tr>
<tr><td>1</td><td>Mr G.R. Sallaway</td><td>12 Fax Rd London WC1</td></tr>
<tr><td>2</td><td>Miss P. Lauri</td><td>5 Dux St London N1</td></tr>
<tr><td>5</td><td>Ms S.Q. Woods</td><td>17 Nax Rd London E18 4WW</td></tr>
</table>

Fig. 15.21 Exercise 3 default.asp web page.

Web page code

```
<html>
<head>
<title>Display CUSTOMER table</title>
<!-- #include file = adovbs.inc -->
</head>
<body>
<center>
<h2>Customer Listing</h2>
<h4>London Region</h4>
<hr><p>
<%
'-- connect to accts.mdb database --
set conn1 = server.createobject("adodb.connection")
```

```
conn1.open "provider = microsoft.jet.oledb.4.0;data source =
d:\websites\itsjcb\www\aspex03\accts.mdb"
'-- get CUSTOMER recordset ---
set rs1 = server.createobject("ADODB.Recordset")
rs1.open "select c_no, title, inits, sname, street, city, postc from
customer where city = 'London'", conn1
'-- show the customers in an HTML table --
'--- create the table headings ---
x = "<table border = 1><tr><th>Cus.No.<th>Name<th>Address</tr>"
response.write x
'--- list each customer ---
rs1.movefirst
while not rs1.eof
   x = "<tr><td>" & rs1("c_no") & "<td>" & rs1("title") & " " &
rs1("inits") & " " & rs1("sname") & "<td>" & rs1("street") & " " &
rs1("city") & " " & rs1("postc") & "</tr>"
   response.write x
   rs1.movenext
wend
response.write "</table>"
'-- close the database --
rs1.close
conn1.close
set rs1 = nothing
%>
</center>
</body>
</html>
```

Fig. 15.22 Exercise 3 default.asp code.

Description of code (Fig. 15.22)

```
'-- connect to accts.mdb database --
set conn1 = server.createobject("adodb.connection")
conn1.open "provider = microsoft.jet.oledb.4.0;data source =
d:\websites\itsjcb\www\aspex03\accts.mdb"
```

Fig. 15.23 Connecting to the accts.mdb database.

This is similar to the ADO code in Chapter 11 and the previous example in this chapter.

```
'-- get CUSTOMER recordset ---
set rs1 = server.createobject("ADODB.Recordset")
rs1.open "select c_no, title, inits, sname, street, city, postc from
customer where city = 'London'", conn1
```

Fig. 15.24 Creating recordset rs1 – a subset of the accts.mdb CUSTOMER table.

Here we are retrieving only the data we require – naming the columns required for the report, and retrieving only rows for the London customers. For large databases and databases on the internet (both of which factors tend to reduce speed) it is advisable to retrieve only the data you need.

Notice also that since this is a read-only application, we have opted for the default parameters (which are read-only) in the open command.

```
'--- create the table headings ---
x = "<table border = 1> <tr><th>Cus.No.<th>Name<th>Address</tr>"
response.write x
```

Fig. 15.25 Creating the table headings.

Here we are creating a string containing the HTML code for the headings and then writing that HTML straight to the response object – i.e. to the user's browser window.

```
'--- list each customer ---
rs1.movefirst
while not rs1.eof
  x = "<tr><td>" & rs1("c_no") & "<td>" & rs1("title") & " " &
rs1("inits") & " " & rs1("sname") & "<td>" & rs1("street") & " " &
rs1("city") & " " & rs1("postc") & "</tr>"
  response.write x
  rs1.movenext
wend
response.write "</table>"
```

Fig. 15.26 Creating the table rows containing the CUSTOMER data.

Each row in the table starts with <tr> and contains three cells, each starting with <td>. The first cell contains the customer number c_no; the second contains a concatenation of title, initials and surname, separated by spaces; the third contains a concatenation of street, city and postcode, again separated by spaces. Each row is constructed into a variable x, then written out to the response object. Then the tag signifying the end of the table is output.

```
'-- close the database --
rs1.close
conn1.close
set rs1 = nothing
%>
</center>
</body>
</html>
```

Fig. 15.27 Closing the database and the HTML page.

Finally, the recordset is closed, the connection to the database is closed, and the web page is closed. Since this database application is on the internet, it can be viewed from anywhere in the world by many people at once. You can see it now at **http://www.itsjc.biz/aspex03**.

15.5 ASP example 4: updating an internet database table

The previous example just *displays* the CUSTOMER table in the database accts.mdb (located on the server itsjc.biz) in a web page. The user can *see* the internet database table on his/her browser (no matter where he/she is, so long as there's an internet connection). We now show how to *update* the CUSTOMER table, again using a browser, the server-side database accts.mdb, and a set of ASP programs.

Structure of website
First, let's look at the structure of the website. See Fig. 15.28.

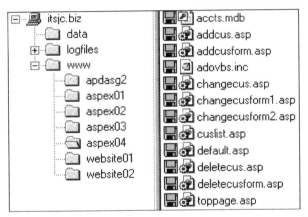

Fig. 15.28 The structure of website **www.itsjc.biz/aspex04**.

Figure 15.29 below explains what each file is for:

default.asp	Home page. This website uses frames. Default.asp just describes the frame structure and says what initial pages to load into these frames. There are two frames: topframe and bottomframe. Figure 15.31.
toppage.asp	This goes (and stays) in topframe. It contains the heading and three hyperlinks: **Add**, **Change** and **Delete**. Figure 15.31.
cuslist.asp	This goes into bottomframe. It's a list of the entire customer table. bottomframe is also used for gathering update data, but after each update, cuslist.asp

	is displayed again to show the (now updated) customer table. Figure 15.31.
addcusform.asp	**Add** calls this. It contains a form for adding a new customer. Figure 15.36.
addcus.asp	addcusform.asp calls this. It gets the new customer data from addcusform.asp and adds a new customer record.
changecusform1.asp	**Change** calls this. It contains a form asking for the customer number (c_no) of the customer the user wants to change.
changecusform2.asp	changecusform1.asp calls this. It contains a form for changing an existing customer record (everything but the primary key c_no, that is). It gets the c_no from changecusform1.asp and creates a form with that customer's data in it, ready for the user to change.
changecus.asp	changecusform2.asp calls this. It gets the data from changecusform2.asp and changes the customer record.
deletecusform.asp	**Delete** calls this. It contains a form asking for the customer number (c_no) of the customer the user wants to delete.
deletecus.asp	deletecusform.asp calls this. It gets the c_no from deletecusform.asp and deletes the customer record.
accts.mdb	The database.
adovbs.inc	An include file containing ADO constants.

Fig. 15.29 The purpose of each file in example 4 – www.itsjc.biz/aspex04.

Note that in every example, we use a separate copy of the database. This is just for compactness and modularity in the examples. In the 'real world' of course, there would be just one copy of the database and all the various applications would read and update that. Here we find it convenient to have everything needed for an example in one folder. Figure 15.30 shows which ASP pages are activated for Add, Change and Delete.

You could log onto **http://www.itsjc.biz/aspex04** and try this example out. If you do, please add, change and delete your own records. Leave ours there. Appendix 1, Fig. A1.2 (and Fig. 15.31) show how the CUSTOMER table should look.

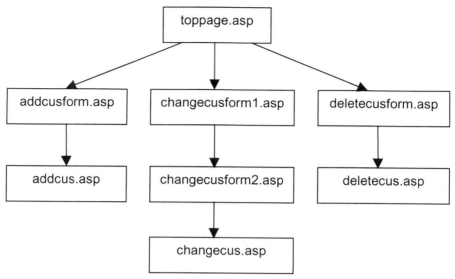

Fig. 15.30 How one page calls another in this application (example 4).

default.asp

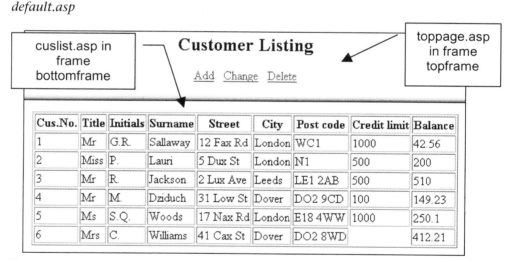

Fig. 15.31 The 'home' page of itsjc.biz/aspex04 – default.asp.

```
<html>
<head>
<title>default.asp</title>
</head>
<frameset rows = 100,*>
<frame name = topframe src = toppage.asp>
```

```
<frame name = bottomframe src = cuslist.asp>
</frameset>
</html>
```

Fig. 15.32 Code for default.asp.

As you can see in Fig. 15.32, we have used frames for this application, just to make it look neater and so that we can keep toppage.asp visible all the time. We keep toppage.asp in the top frame 'topframe' all the time. We could include company logo etc. in toppage.asp. Toppage.asp also contains hyperlinks to the Add, Change and Delete update pages. Bottomframe has cuslist.asp initially loaded into it.

toppage.asp

```
<html>
<head></head>
<body>
<center>
<h2>Customer Listing</h2>
<a href = addcusform.asp target = bottomframe>Add</a>  
<a href = changecusform1.asp target = bottomframe>Change</
a>  
<a href = deletecusform.asp target = bottomframe>Delete</a>
</body>
</html>
```

Fig. 15.33 Code for toppage.asp.

All that needs to be noted here is the way we ensure the page we hyperlink to goes into the correct frame using target = . You can see the correspondence between these hyperlinks (the <a> tags) and the top set of arrows in Fig. 15.30.

cuslist.asp

```
<html>
<head>
<title>Display CUSTOMER table</title>
<!-- #include file = adovbs.inc -->
</head>
<body>
<center>
<%
'-- connect to accts.mdb database --
set conn1 = server.createobject("adodb.connection")
conn1.open "provider = microsoft.jet.oledb.4.0;data source =
d:\websites\itsjcb\www\aspex04\accts.mdb"
```

```
'-- get CUSTOMER recordset ---
set rs1 = server.createobject("ADODB.Recordset")
rs1.open "select * from customer", conn1
'-- show the customers in an HTML table --
'--- create the table headings ---
x = "<table border =
1><tr><th>Cus.No.<th>Title<th>Initials<th>Surname<th>
Street<th>City<th>Post code<th>Credit limit<th>Balance</tr>"
response.write x
'--- list each customer ---
rs1.movefirst
while not rs1.eof
   x = "<tr><td>" & rs1("c_no") & "<td>" & rs1("title") & "<td>" &
rs1("inits") & "<td> " & rs1("sname") & "<td>" & rs1("street") & "<td> " &
rs1("city") & "<td> " & rs1("postc") & "<td>" & rs1("cred_lim") & "<td>"
& rs1("balance") & "</tr>"
   response.write x
   rs1.movenext
wend
response.write "</table>"
'-- close the database --
rs1.close
conn1.close
set rs1 = nothing
%>
</center>
</body>
</html>
```

Fig. 15.34 Code for cuslist.asp.

This code is very similar to that for example 3, so for an explanation of this code, see the description of the code for Fig. 15.22. The only real difference is that here we are displaying *all* the fields of the CUSTOMER table. Here's that monster line again:

```
x = "<tr><td>" & rs1("c_no") & "<td>" & rs1("title") & "<td>" &
rs1("inits") & "<td> " & rs1("sname") & "<td>" & rs1("street") & "<td> " &
rs1("city") & "<td> " & rs1("postc") & "<td>" & rs1("cred_lim") & "<td>"
& rs1("balance") & "</tr>"
```

Fig. 15.35 Whew! Keep this all on one line. This is to construct one row of the HTML table, which displays one record of the CUSTOMER table.

addcusform.asp

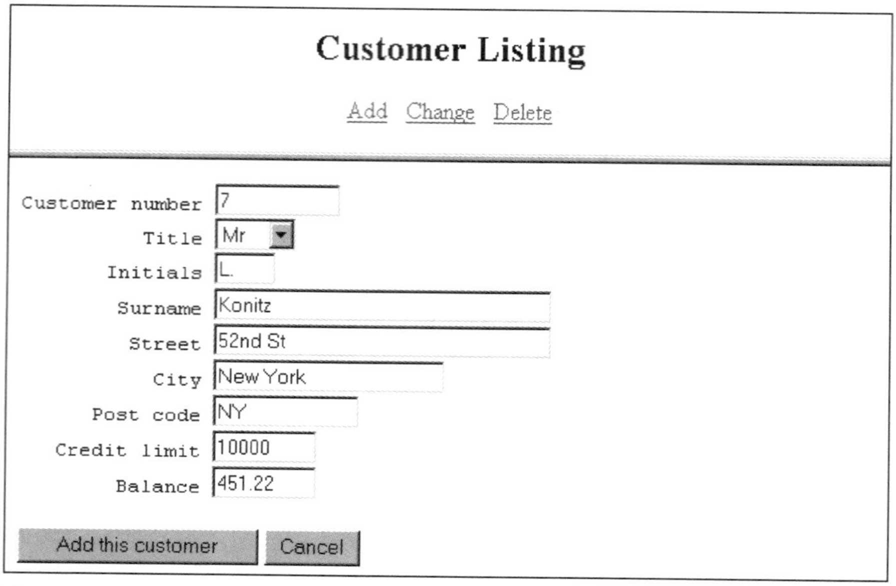

Fig. 15.36 The lower frame contains addcusform.asp.

```
<html>
<head>
<title>Add a new customer</title>
</head>
<body>
<form method = post action = addcus.asp>
<pre>
Customer number <input type = text name = frmc_no size = 10>
            Title <select name = frmtitle size =
1><option>Mr<option>Mrs<option>Miss<option>Ms<option>Dr
            </select>
        Initials <input type = text name = frminits size = 4>
         Surname <input type = text name = frmsname size = 30>
          Street <input type = text name = frmstreet size = 30>
            City <input type = text name = frmcity size = 20>
       Post code <input type = text name = frmpostc size = 12>
    Credit limit <input type = text name = frmcred_lim size = 8
value = 0>
         Balance <input type = text name = frmbalance size = 8
value = 0>
</pre>
<input type = submit value = "Add this customer">
<input type = reset value = "Cancel">
</form>
```

```
    </body>
    </html>
```

Fig. 15.37 Code for addcusform.asp.

This is a conventional form. There is no VBScript here, so we *could* have called this page addform.htm. Note the careful naming of all the form elements. These names are used by the page addcus.asp. We tell the form that it should send the values for these form elements to addcus.asp in the line:

```
    <form method = post action = addcus.asp>
```

Forms are covered in detail in Chapter 14.

addcus.asp

```
<html>
<head>
<!-- #INCLUDE FILE = "adovbs.inc" -->
</head>
<body>
<%
'-- connect to accts.mdb database --
set conn1 = server.createobject("adodb.connection")
conn1.open "provider = microsoft.jet.oledb.4.0;data source =
d:\websites\itsjcb\www\aspex04\accts.mdb"


'-- get CUSTOMER recordset ---
set rs1 = server.createobject("ADODB.Recordset")
rs1.open "select * from customer", conn1,            ◄─────  Retrieve an
adopendynamic, adlockoptimistic, adcmdtext                   updateable
                                                             CUSTOMER
'-- add new record --                                        recordset rs1.
rs1.addnew
x = request.form("frmc_no")
y = replace(x, " ", "") 'remove any spaces in primary key
rs1("c_no") = y
x = request.form("frmtitle")
rs1("title") = x & " " 'Access doesn't like empty strings in text
fields
x = request.form("frminits")
rs1("inits") = x & ""
x = request.form("frmsname")
rs1("sname") = x & ""
x = request.form("frmstreet")                       ◄─────  Add a blank record
rs1("street") = x & ""                                      to rs1, get the data
x = request.form("frmcity")                                 the user filled into
rs1("city") = x & ""                                        addcusform.asp,
x = request.form("frmpostc")                                and put it into the
```

```
rs1("postc") = x & " "
x = request.form("frmcred_lim")
rs1("cred_lim") = x
x = request.form("frmbalance")
rs1("balance") = x
rs1.update
rs1.close
set rs1 = nothing
conn1.close
set conn1 = nothing
response.redirect "cuslist.asp"
%>
</body>
</html>
```

fields of the new record. Then save the new record and close the database connection.

Then go back and display the updated customer list in this frame.

Fig. 15.38 Code for addcus.asp.

Request.form is how data is retrieved from the Request object. 'form' is the default sub-object in the request object (to use/interpret the OO jargon) so you can leave it out if you like, as in:

```
x = request("frmc_no")
```

In

```
y = replace(x, " ", "")
```

we are using the VBScript replace function to remove any spaces that the user might have inadvertently put into the c_no field. Note that there is no input validation or error handling in this program. We cover these points in section 15.6. Validation and error handling can easily overwhelm the code in an update program. We have left them out here, so as not to obscure the basic update commands used in ASP database programs.

In the second line of:

```
x = request.form("frmtitle")
rs1("title") = x & " "
```

we are appending a space onto the title field. We do this with all of the text fields because the user might leave a form text box blank and this would result in an empty string being sent to the Access database accts.mdb. Access databases may produce an error if you attempt to do this, so we have ensured that there's at least one space in the field. A better procedure would be to do this:

```
if x = "" then
   x = " "
end if
rs1("title") = x
```

This code checks if the text box is empty and puts a space there if it is. An even better alternative, if you have designed the database yourself, would be to allow empty strings in text fields in the Access database table. This can be done in the Access design window by selecting 'allow zero length', as in Fig. 15.39.

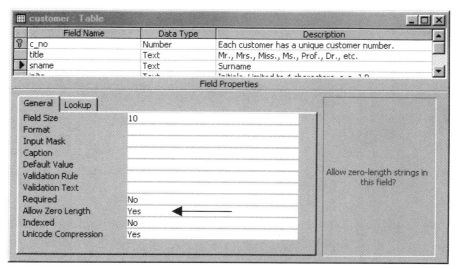

Fig. 15.39 You might want to allow zero-length strings in some of your database fields.

Unfortunately, you might not have designed the database yourself, or some other constraint requires there to be a value in the field. This is really a validation and error-handling issue, which we cover in section 15.6.

Finally, the line:

```
response.redirect "cuslist.asp"
```

ensures that when the update is complete, the new, updated customer list appears in the same place the addcusform.asp did, namely the frame bottomframe of default.asp.

changecusform1.asp

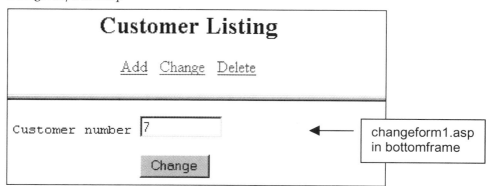

Fig. 15.40 changeform1.asp gets the number of the customer the user wants to change.

```
<html>
<head>
```

```
<title>Change a customer's details</title>
</head>
<body>
<form method = post action = changecusform2.asp>
<pre>
Customer number <input type = text name = frmc_no1 size = 10>
<p>
                    <input type = submit value = "Change">
</pre>
</form>
</body>
</html>
```

Fig. 15.41 Code for changeform1.asp.

This is just a conventional HTML page containing a form to collect the customer number of the customer record the user wants to change and pass it on to changeform2.asp.

changeform2.asp

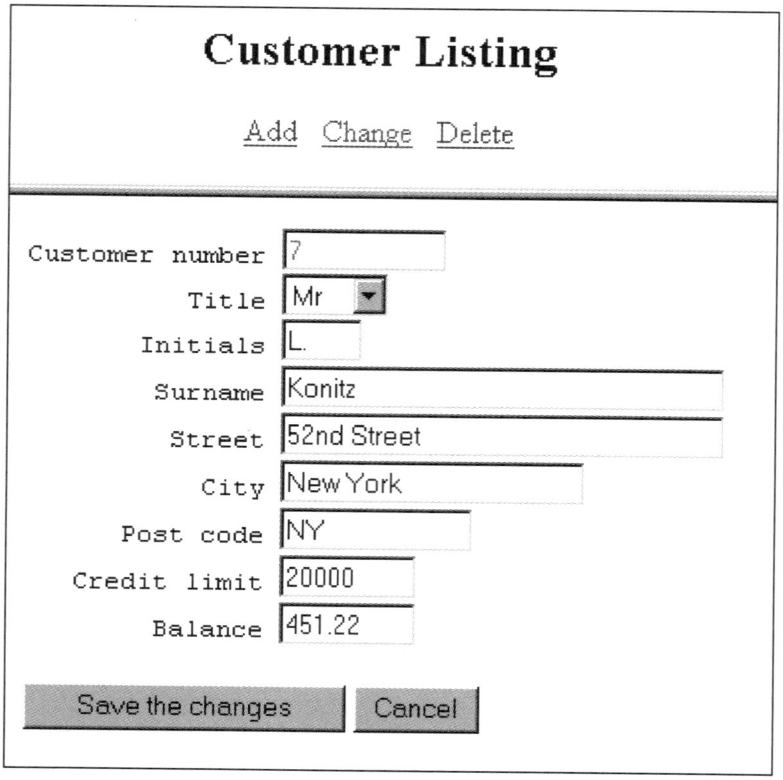

Fig. 15.42 changeform2.asp displays the record for the selected customer and allows the user to make changes.

Code for changeform2.asp

```
<html>
<head>
<!-- #INCLUDE FILE = "adovbs.inc" -->
<title>Change an existing customer's details</title>
</head>
<body>
<%
'-- get the CUSTOMER record the user wants to update --
set conn1 = server.createobject("adodb.connection")
conn1.open "provider = microsoft.jet.oledb.4.0;data
source = d:\websites\itsjcb\www\aspex04\accts.mdb"
set rs1 = server.createobject("ADODB.Recordset")
rs1.open "select * from customer where c_no = " &
request.form("frmc_no1"), conn1
%>
<!-- display the CUSTOMER values in a form so the user can make
changes -->
<form method = post action = changecus.asp>
<input type = hidden name = frmc_no value = <% = rs1("c_no")%>>
<pre>
Customer number <input type = text disabled = true value = <% =
rs1("c_no")%> size = 10>
          Title <select name = frmtitle size = 1><option
selected><% = rs1("title")%>
<option>Mr<option>Mrs<option>Miss<option>Ms<option>Dr</select>
        Initials <input type = text name = frminits value =
"<% = rs1("inits")%>" size = 4>
         Surname <input type = text name = frmsname value =
"<% = rs1("sname")%>" size = 30>
          Street <input type = text name = frmstreet value =
"<% = rs1("street")%>" size = 30>
            City <input type = text name = frmcity value =
"<% = rs1("city")%>" size = 20>
       Post code <input type = text name = frmpostc value =
"<% = rs1("postc")%>" size = 12>
    Credit limit <input type = text name = frmcred_lim value =
<% = rs1("cred_lim")%> size = 8>
         Balance <input type = text name = frmbalance value =
<% = rs1("balance")%> size = 8>
</pre>
<input type = submit value = "Save the changes">
<input type = reset value = Cancel>
</form>
<%
'-- close database connection --
```

← Connect to the database and get the CUSTOMER record the user wants to change.

Display the record's data in a form and allow the user to make changes.

```
rs1.close
set rs1 = nothing
conn1.close
set conn1 = nothing
%>
</body>
</html>
```

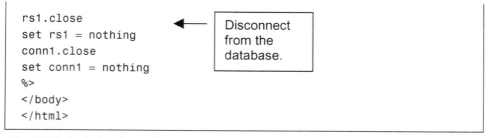
Disconnect from the database.

Fig. 15.43 Code for changeform2.asp.

Explanation of code for changeform2.asp
This page displays the fields of the CUSTOMER record the user selected into a form. In the form the user can make any changes required, except for changes to the primary key c_no. The form data is then passed on to changecus.asp in the form's top line:

```
<form method = post action = changecus.asp>
```

The user is prevented from changing the customer number in the line:

```
Customer number <input type = text disabled = true value = <% =
rs1("c_no")%> size = 10>
```

Fig. 15.44 Displaying the customer number in the form.

'Disabled = true' prevents the user typing in this text box. If a form object is disabled, its data, unfortunately, can't be passed on to the action = script, so we have had to use this line:

```
<input type = hidden name = frmc_no value = <% = rs1("c_no")%>>
```

Fig. 15.45 Using a hidden form field.

to pass the data on to changecus.asp. Hidden fields don't appear on the form but you can use them to pass data on to the next script.

Notice in these commands that we are embedding short pieces of VBScript in conventional HTML. We just surround the scripts in <% and %>. We are also reducing the size of the scripts where just the value of a variable is needed, by replacing, for example:

```
<%response.write rs1("c_no")%>
```

with

```
<% = rs1("c_no")%>
```

When selecting the title, we use a drop-down list (a <select> with size = 1) and want to allow the user to change the title (e.g. Ms to Dr) but default to what it already is. We do this using the <option selected> clause in:

```
Title <select name = frmtitle size = 1><option selected><% =
rs1("title")%>
<option>Mr<option>Mrs<option>Miss<option>Ms<option>Dr</select>
```

Fig. 15.46 Using option selected to default to the current value in a <select> box.

Unfortunately, this has the effect of repeating the current title. This is put up with in the cause of simpler code. The reader is invited to remove this 'bug'.

Note that in:

```
Initials <input type = text name = frminits
value = "<% = rs1("inits")%>" size = 4>
```

the quotes shown are necessary wherever the data could have embedded spaces. This is true of HTML generally, as we have noted in Chapter 14. If you leave them out, the data 'New York' displayed in the city text box would appear as 'New', for example.

changecus.asp

```
<html>
<head>
<!-- #INCLUDE FILE = "adovbs.inc" -->
</head>
<body>
<%
'-- connect to accts.mdb database --
set conn1 = server.createobject("adodb.connection")
conn1.open "provider = microsoft.jet.oledb.4.0;data source =
d:\websites\itsjcb\www\aspex04\accts.mdb"

'-- get CUSTOMER record the user wants to update ---
set rs1 = server.createobject("ADODB.Recordset")
rs1.open "select * from customer where c_no = " &
request.form("frmc_no"), conn1, adopendynamic, adlockoptimistic,
adcmdtext

'-- change the record --
rs1("title") = trim(request("frmtitle")) & ""
```

```
rs1("inits") = trim(request("frminits")) & ""
rs1("sname") = trim(request("frmsname")) & ""
rs1("street") = trim(request("frmstreet")) & ""
rs1("city") = trim(request("frmcity")) & ""
rs1("postc") = trim(request("frmpostc")) & ""
rs1("cred_lim") = request("frmcred_lim")
rs1("balance") = request("frmbalance")
rs1.update

'-- disconnect from the database --
rs1.close
set rs1 = nothing
conn1.close
set conn1 = nothing
response.redirect "cuslist.asp"
%>
</body>
</html>
```

Fig. 15.47 The code for changecus.asp. This program saves onto the database the changes the user entered in changecusform2.asp.

Explanation of changecus.asp code
There should be no real surprises here. The code follows pretty well that for addcus.asp. We connect to the database, get the record for the customer in question, update the values of all but the primary key field c_no, close the database, and redirect to the script cuslist.asp, which lists the updated CUSTOMER table.
    In:

```
rs1("title") = trim(request("frmtitle")) & ""
```

we are trimming any leading and trailing spaces from the field frmtitle, then adding one, just in case the database field won't accept a zero-length string and the user has left the field blank. Notice also that we have contracted 'request.form' to just 'request'.

deletecusform.asp
Deletecusform.asp (Fig. 15.48) gets the customer number (c_no) of a customer record the user wants to delete and passes it, using the post method, to delete-cus.asp. Note the use of <pre> for alignment of objects on the form, and the fact that there's no Reset button. All an <input type = reset> button does is clear the form objects. Since there's only one text box here, it doesn't seem necessary to have a reset button. If the user wants to back out of the delete, he/she just hits the browser's back button.

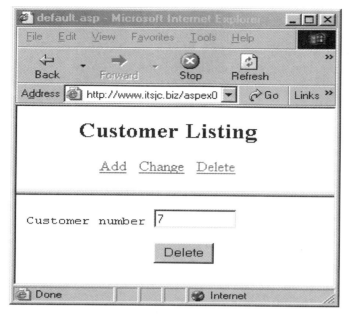

Fig. 15.48(a) deletecusform.asp is used to get the number of a customer record to delete.

Code for deletecusform.asp

```
<html>
<head>
<title>Delete a customer</title>
</head>
<body>
<form method = post action = deletecus.asp>
<pre>
Customer number <input type = text name = frmc_no size = 10>
<p>
                <input type = submit value = "Delete">
</pre>
</form>
</body>
</html>
```

Fig. 15.48(b) Code for deletecusform.asp, which calls deletecus.asp.

Code for deletecus.asp

```
<html>
<head>
<!-- #INCLUDE FILE = "adovbs.inc" -->
</head>
<body>
<%
'-- connect to accts.mdb database --
set conn1 = server.createobject("adodb.connection")
conn1.open "provider = microsoft.jet.oledb.4.0;data source =
d:\websites\itsjcb\www\aspex04\accts.mdb"

'-- get CUSTOMER record ---
set rs1 = server.createobject("ADODB.Recordset")
x = request.form("frmc_no")
rs1.open "select * from customer where c_no = " & x, conn1,
adopendynamic, adlockoptimistic, adcmdtext

'-- delete CUSTOMER record --
rs1.delete
rs1.update
rs1.close
set rs1 = nothing
conn1.close
set conn1 = nothing
response.redirect "cuslist.asp"
%>
</body>
</html>
```

Fig. 15.49 The code for the ASP page deletecus.asp.

Description of code for deletecus.asp
By now this code should look quite familiar. The five steps of:

- connecting to the database
- retrieving a recordset containing the data to be updated
- updating the data
- disconnecting from the database
- redirecting to another page

follow the pattern described for the Add and Change functions of this application.

15.6 ASP example 5: error handling

The application in example 4 shows how to add, change and delete records in a database, but omits error handling. We now show how to add error handling, using the program addcus.asp from example 4. The method used is similar, but not identical to the method used in Visual Basic programs, since there we used On Error Goto, and VBScript doesn't have On Error Goto. We use On Error Resume Next instead.

On Error Resume Next means that if an error is detected by IIS in the current statement then it will just go on to the next statement, rather than reporting the error. What we are then obliged to do is to put error-handling code immediately after every VBScript statement we think could incur an error. IIS, remember, is Internet Information Server – the program on the server that analyses and executes the VBScript statements you have embedded in your ASP pages. If there are any errors, it will report them in its own way, usually on the user's browser window, with no suggestion as to how to recover. Our custom error-handling code will handle the error more sensibly, including passing a readable message to the user, that reports the error and tell them what to do about it.

Now you won't want to place error-handling code after *every* statement. The beauty of On Error Goto was that it was saying: If an error occurs *anywhere* below, then jump to a certain label. Now we only have On Error Resume Next, you might think that we would need error-handling code after *every* VBScript statement. However, most VBScript statements are unlikely to cause errors. The statements most likely to cause errors should be identified by the programmer and error-handling code placed under *them*. Before we add error handling to addcus.asp, here are some general points about error handling in ASP scripts:

---

1. VBScript doesn't have On Error Goto, it only has On Error Resume Next.

2. VBScript doesn't support labels (e.g. L1) so we can't jump down to an error handler.

3. If you don't use On Error Resume Next, IIS will abandon the rest of the page when it finds an error.

4. If you do use On Error Resume Next, IIS will ignore any errors, so that if an error occurs near the top of a script (e.g. you fail to delete an invoice record) then IIS will plough on and try to perform all the rest of the code (e.g. it will try to delete a related customer record, which you would have wanted to avoid, given the previous error). Continually checking err.number = 0 before executing further code is one way to handle this. Jumping past it using On Error Goto, as in VB, would have been neater but VBScript doesn't have On Error Goto.

5. If you attempt to use a message box to display error information, it will be displayed on the *server*, which is of no use. You *could* start writing embedded client-side VBScript to get round this. We have chosen to use response.write instead, which is simpler.

Fig. 15.50 General points about error handling in VBScript.

In the example below, we add error handling to the addcus.asp program from example 4. We could add it just after the rs1.update statement, which is where the record is added to the database, and where an error is most likely to happen. The error could be due, for example, to the Jet database engine objecting to an invalid data type or length for a field in the accts.mdb database, or a duplicate primary key value. However, just to illustrate the general point made in 4 of Fig. 15.50, we'll cater for errors occurring in these *three* places:

1. connecting to the database – maybe someone's moved it;

2. creating the recordset rs1 – maybe someone's renamed the table;

3. adding the new customer record – maybe this customer number already exists, or some field value is invalid.

We think you'll agree that if we fail in step 1, we won't want to attempt steps 2 or 3, and if we fail in step 2, we won't want to attempt step 3. Since we can't GoTo an error handler at the end of the code, jumping further statements following the error, we're forced to use the nested if approach given below.

Sample output from addcus.asp modified to include error handling
In Fig. 15.51 we can see the message that results if the user creates an error by attempting to add a new customer record with a customer number that already

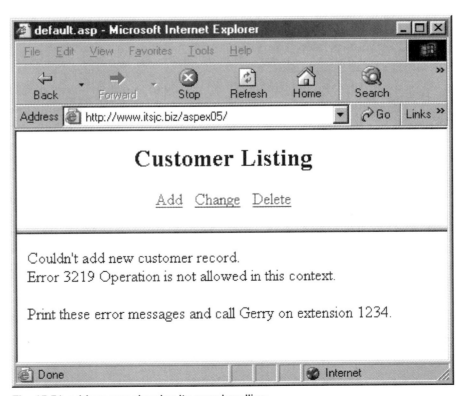

Fig. 15.51 addcus.asp showing its error handling.

exists in the table. The second (not very helpful) line would be all IIS would report. Here Gerry (presumably the database guru) will be able to trace what went wrong more easily. By looking at the code for addcus.asp, he'll be able to locate the exact instruction that caused the error. More could be done, for example printing the program name and the time of the error and perhaps even the programmer's name (assuming he/she's not in Eilat soaking up the sun).

Code for addcus.asp modified to include error handling

```
<html>
<head>
<!-- #INCLUDE FILE = "adovbs.inc" -->
</head>
<body>
<%
```

> The on error resume next statement. This is the best VBScript has for error handling.

```
on error resume next
'-- connect to accts.mdb database --
set conn1 = server.createobject("adodb.connection")
conn1.open "provider = microsoft.jet.oledb.4.0;data source =
d:\websites\itsjcb\www\aspex04\accts.mdb"
if err.number <> 0 then
  response.write "<p>Couldn't connect to database.<br>"
  x = "Error " & err.number & " " & err.description & "<br>"
  response.write x
else
```

> You put error-handling code after every statement likely to cause an error.

```
  '-- get CUSTOMER recordset --
  set rs1 = server.createobject("ADODB.Recordset")
  rs1.open "select * from customer", conn1, adopendynamic,
adlockoptimistic, adcmdtext
  if err.number <> 0 then
    response.write "<p>Couldn't create customer recordset.<br>"
    x = "Error " & err.number & " " & err.description & "<br>"
    response.write x
  else
```

> You use response.write for error reporting. Don't use msgbox (see text)

```
    '-- add new record --
    rs1.addnew
    x = request.form("frmc_no")
    y = replace(x, " ", "") 'remove any spaces in primary key
    rs1("c_no") = y
    x = request.form("frmtitle")
    rs1("title") = x & " " 'Access doesn't like empty strings in
text fields
    x = request.form("frminits")
    rs1("inits") = x & ""
    x = request.form("frmsname")
    'rs1("sname") = x & ""
    rs1("sname") = x
```

```
            x = request.form("frmstreet")
            rs1("street") = x & ""
            'rs1("street") = x
            x = request.form("frmcity")
            rs1("city") = x & ""
            x = request.form("frmpostc")
            rs1("postc") = x & ""
            x = request.form("frmcred_lim")
            rs1("cred_lim") = x
            x = request.form("frmbalance")
            rs1("balance") = x
            rs1.update
            rs1.close
            set rs1 = nothing
            conn1.close
            set conn1 = nothing
            if err.number <> 0 then
              response.write "Couldn't add new customer record.<br>"
              x = "Error " & err.number & " " & err.description & "<br>"
              response.write x
            else
              response.redirect "cuslist.asp"
            end if
          end if
          response.write "<p>Print these error messages and call
        Gerry on extension 1234."
        end if
        %>
        </body>
        </html>
```

> You use if statements to prevent IIS 'ploughing on' after an error.

> You tell the user what to do if any errors have occurred. Adding the program name and the time of the error would be good too.

Fig. 15.52 ASP script addcus.asp with error-handling code (highlighted darker).

15.7 ASP example 6: validation

Error-handling code, covered in the previous section, is used to handle errors that have already occurred. Some errors can be prevented – errors caused by incorrect input data filled into a form, for example. You can either wait for the database engine to report that it doesn't like you putting letters into a numeric field, for example (error handling), or you can *validate* the input data first. The advantages of validation of this sort over error handling include:

1. Speed: it takes time for the Jet engine (or SQLServer, Oracle etc.) database engine to discover and report the error.

2. The error message, if written by you, the programmer, can be made more human-readable (more meaningful – easier to understand by the users who are likely to need to act on it (see Fig. 15.51 for example)) than standard error messages produced by Jet or IIS. It will of course be a waste of everyone's time if *your* error messages can't be understood either!

3. The error message can be specific to a particular field and a particular error.

4. Decoding error messages from IIS or Jet can be as time-consuming as writing your own validation code.

Writing input validation can be quite a long task, since, as we have intimated in the third point above, the potential number of validation checks your code could perform could be large (something like the number of fields multiplied by the number of ways the value in each field could be wrong). However, some validation is usually worth while. We give an example of input validation below, again using addcus.asp.

addcus detecting input validation errors

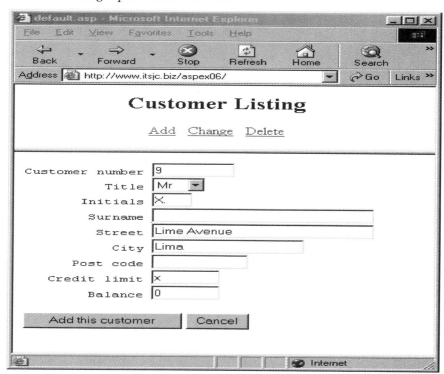

Fig. 15.53 Surname is blank and credit limit is non-numeric . . .

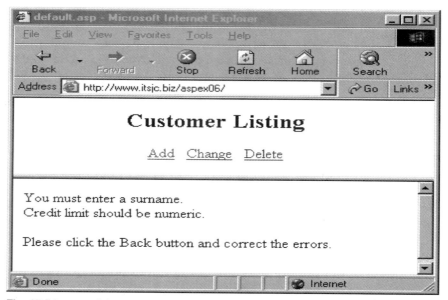

Fig. 15.54 . . . and these errors are reported by the validation code shown in Fig. 15.55.

code for addcus.asp with examples of validation code highlighted

```
<html>
<head>
<!-- #INCLUDE FILE = "adovbs.inc" -->
</head>
<body>
<%
on error resume next
'-- connect to accts.mdb database --
set conn1 = server.createobject("adodb.connection")
conn1.open "provider = microsoft.jet.oledb.4.0;data source =
d:\websites\itsjcb\www\aspex04\accts.mdb"
if err.number <> 0 then
  response.write "<p>Couldn't connect to database.<br>"
  x = "Error " & err.number & " " & err.description & "<br>"
  response.write x
else
  '-- get CUSTOMER recordset ---
  set rs1 = server.createobject("ADODB.Recordset")
  rs1.open "select * from customer", conn1, adopendynamic,
adlockoptimistic, adcmdtext
  if err.number <> 0 then
    response.write "<p>Couldn't create customer recordset.<br>"
    x = "Error " & err.number & " " & err.description & "<br>"
    response.write x
  else
```

Clear the validation error flag.

```
'-- add new record --
ve = 0 'validation error flag — stays 0 for no errors
rs1.addnew
x = request.form("frmc_no")
y = replace(x, " ", "") 'remove any spaces in primary key
rs1("c_no") = y
x = request.form("frmtitle")
rs1("title") = x & " " 'Access doesn't like empty strings in
text fields
x = request.form("frminits")
rs1("inits") = x & ""
x = request.form("frmsname")
if len(trim(x)) = 0 then
  response.write "You must enter a surname.<br>"
  ve = 1
else
  rs1("sname") = x
end if
x = request.form("frmstreet")
rs1("street") = x & ""
x = request.form("frmcity")
rs1("city") = x & ""
x = request.form("frmpostc")
rs1("postc") = x & ""
x = request.form("frmcred_lim")
if not isnumeric(x) then
  response.write "Credit limit should be numeric.<br>"
  ve = 1
else
  rs1("cred_lim") = x
end if
x = request.form("frmbalance")
rs1("balance") = x
if ve = 1 then
  response.write "<p>Please click the Back button and correct
the errors.<p>"
  rs1.cancelupdate
else
  rs1.update
end if
rs1.close
set rs1 = nothing
conn1.close
set conn1 = nothing
```

Set the validation error flag if surname is empty.

Set the validation error flag if the credit limit is non-numeric.

If there have been any validation errors, don't do the update.

```
      if err.number <> 0 then
        response.write "Couldn't add new customer record.<br>"
        x = "Error " & err.number & " " & err.description & "<br>"
        response.write x
      end if
      if err.number = 0 then
        if ve = 0 then
          response.redirect "cuslist.asp"
        end if
      else
        response.write "<p>Print these error messages and call
Gerry on extension 1234."
      end if
    end if
  end if
%>
</body>
</html>
```

> If there have been no validation errors and no database errors, list the updated customer table..

Fig. 15.55 addcus.asp with samples of validation code (highlighted darker).

It would be possible of course to perform the field validation using client-side scripting (provided the user's browser can do VBScript or you feel like breaking into a bit of client-side JavaScript). One advantage of that would be a reduction in internet traffic for your application – you wouldn't have to send the form to the server if a validation error were detected. However, we consider this marginal benefit not worth the added complexity.

15.8 Exercises

1. Modify Fig. 15.5 in the simple password system of example 1 so that instead of just going back to the password page, an error message is displayed in

   (a) the browser window

   (b) a separate browser window.

2. Modify Fig. 15.5 in the simple password system of example 1 so that instead of going back to the password page, an error message is displayed after three failed attempts, i.e. three incorrect passwords.

3. Modify example 2 so that instead of retrieving *all* records from the VISIT table, the code retrieves only the last (latest) record.

4. Modify Example 2 so that the dates and times of the previous *three* visits are displayed. If there are fewer than three previous visits just display those.

5. Modify example 3 so that the user can select which city's customers to list. Hint: use an HTML form with a drop-down list.

6. Modify example 3 so that customer *and* invoice data is displayed. Hint: change the SQL in the ADO open statement.

7. Modify example 3 so that the user can find a customer based on surname, i.e. add a Find button.

8. Modify example 4 so that when adding a new customer, the program calculates the next highest customer number and inserts it into the text box frmcusno of addcusform.

9. Modify example 4 so that appropriate input validation and error handling are used when entering and updating customer data.

10. Modify example 4 so that anyone can see the customer list but a password is needed for any update.

11. Modify example 4 so that a 'log' is kept of all updates – who made an update, what they did, when.

12. Modify example 5 so that error handling is added to all database updates in all web pages.

13. With regard to example 5, discuss the advantages and disadvantages of VBScript error handling compared with VB error handling. Hint: consider the notions of 'structured' programming and 'goto-less' programming.

14. Modify example 6 so that input validation is performed using client-side rather than server-side VBScript. Discuss the advantages and disadvantages of client-side and server-side input data validation.

15. Modify example 6 so that passwords are required for updates. Note that it shouldn't be possible to bypass the password page.

16. Design an online multi-choice exam system. You will first have to design the database and then the ASP pages. Here are some ideas:

   - forms
   - questions
   - four possible answers (one correct) for each question
   - correct answer identified
   - candidates' answers stored
   - marking process
   - candidates' test scores stored
   - security.

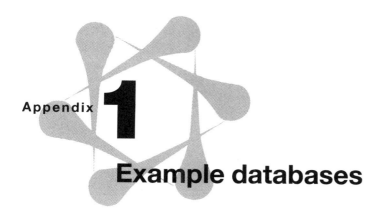

Example databases

In this appendix, we include descriptions of all of the databases used in the examples in this book.

These small databases are in no way intended to represent realistic, usable databases. They have been included to illustrate various SQL and programming principles in the simplest possible way. Consequently, the number of tables in each database is less than you are likely to find in practice.

Similarly, the number of records in each table has been kept to a minimum so that the results displayed from queries don't take up too much space on the page. The aim has been to provide 'test data' only.

In some examples throughout the book, minor changes may be made to illustrate individual points.

Throughout the book, the relationship diagram has also often been referred to rather loosely as the *schema*. A full schema would include details of *all* structural aspects of the database. The Access Relationship diagram is a convenient way to represent the entity-relationship aspects and the attributes of the database schema.

All the *primary keys* are shown in bold in the Relationship diagrams. You can tell what the *foreign keys* are because the relationship lines point to them on the Relationship diagrams.

All of these databases can be downloaded via the website

http://www.databasedesign.co.uk/book

Full details of individual field types, indexes etc. can be obtained by downloading these databases as required and in the Database window of Access, clicking the Tables tab and the Design button.

accts.mdb

This database shows, for each customer, which invoices are currently outstanding and for each invoice, what payments they have made. It may form part of a very simple Sales Ledger system. In practice, you would probably want to associate customers with their invoices via their orders and order-lines.

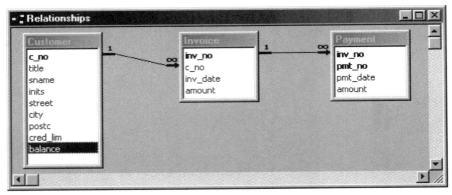

Fig. A1.1 The Relationship diagram of the **accts.mdb** database.

Customer : Table

	c_no	title	sname	inits	street	city	postc	cred_lim	balance
▶	1	Mr	Sallaway	G.R.	12 Fax Rd	London	WC1	£1,000.00	£42.56
	2	Miss	Lauri	P.	5 Dux St	London	N1	£500.00	£200.00
	3	Mr	Jackson	R.	2 Lux Ave	Leeds	LE1 2AB	£500.00	£510.00
	4	Mr	Dziduch	M.	31 Low St	Dover	DO2 9CD	£100.00	£149.23
	5	Ms	Woods	S.Q.	17 Nax Rd	London	E18 4WW	£1,000.00	£250.10
	6	Mrs	Williams	C.	41 Cax St	Dover	DO2 8WD		£412.21
*	0							£0.00	£0.00

Record: ⏮ ◀ [1] ▶ ⏭ ▶* of 6

Fig. A1.2 The CUSTOMER table of **accts.mdb**.

Invoice : Table

inv_no	c_no	inv_date	amount
940	1	05/12/99	£26.20
1002	4	12/01/00	£149.23
1003	1	12/01/00	£16.26
1004	2	14/01/00	£200.00
1005	3	20/01/00	£510.00
1006	5	21/01/00	£250.10
1017	6	22/01/00	£412.21
0	0		£0.00

Record: ⏮ ◀ [1] ▶ ⏭ ▶* of 7

Fig. A1.3 The INVOICE table of **accts.mdb**.

inv_no	pmt_no	pmt_date	amount
940	2	12/12/99	£13.00
940	3	19/01/00	£10.00
1005	1	14/01/00	£510.00
1017	1	30/01/00	£100.00
0	0		£0.00

Record: 1 of 4

Fig. A1.4 The PAYMENT table of **accts.mdb**.

Notes

1. Customer number 1 (Sallaway) has two invoices. Everyone else has one. There are consequently *no* customers without invoices – a limitation of this test database perhaps.

2. Invoice number 940 (one of Sallaway's) has two payments – payment numbers 2 and 3. What happened to payment 1? Assume it has been deleted.

3. There *are* some invoices that have, as yet, received no payments (e.g. invoice 1002).

4. There are two customers who have exceeded their credit limits. The field CRED_LIM shows the customer's credit limit – the maximum he or she is allowed to owe 'us' – the clients – the owners of the database. The BALANCE field shows how much they actually owe us.

5. One customer (Williams) has a Null credit limit.

cus_purchase_prod.mdb

This database shows, for each customer, what purchases he has made, and for each product, what purchases have been made.

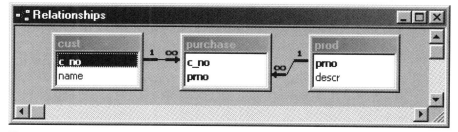

Fig. A1.5 The Relationship diagram of the **cus_purchase_prod.mdb** database.

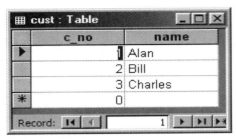

Fig. A1.6 The CUST table of **cus_purchase_prod.mdb**.

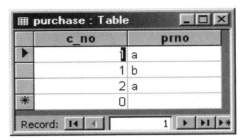

Fig. A1.7 The PURCHASE table of **cus_purchase_prod.mdb**.

Fig. A1.8 The PROD table of **cus_purchase_prod.mdb**.

Notes

1. Notice the compound key in the PURCHASE table. It happens to consist of the concatenation of the foreign keys from the CUST and PROD tables.

2. An interesting query on this table, discussed in Chapter 7, is "Who has purchased all products?".

3. It can be seen that with this test data, Alan has purchased all products, Bill has purchased just one, and Charles has purchased none.

4. To be in any way realistic in a commercial sense, the database would have to be able to distinguish between different purchases of the same product at different times, and record the quantities purchased, unit prices, and quantities in stock. Customer details also need to be extended. The fields shown are sufficient to illustrate the programming points in the text.

Exercise

Modify the database schema to include the features mentioned in Note 4.

election.mdb

This database shows all the candidates participating in an election and the number of votes they received.

Fig. A1.9 The schema of the **election.mdb** database.

cand_no	name	cons_no	party	no_of_votes
1	Fred	1	Labour	100
2	Jim	1	Cons	120
3	Peter	1	Liberal	50
4	John	2	Labour	150
5	Mike	2	SDP	50
6	Jane	2	Cons	100
7	Mary	2	Green	150
8	Keith	1	Ind	150
9	Sue	1	SDP	160
10	U Li	3	Labour	400
11	Ashfak	3	Cons	350
12	Dennis	3	SDP	190
0		0		0

Record: 1 of 12

Fig. A1.10 The CANDIDATE table of the **election.mdb** database.

Notes

1. Cand_no is the candidate number, and is the primary key.

2. Cons_no is the constituency number.

3. There is only one table in this database but it contains a surprising amount of data.

4. A very interesting query in this database is "Who won the election?". The winner is the party (or parties) with the greatest number of won constituencies. A party wins a constituency if its candidate receives more votes than any other candidate does in the constituency. This query *can* be written as a single SQL

statement, but that is a real challenge. It is better to build up to the final answer with a series of stored queries, each query built upon the one before. The first query might be "Which party won in each constituency?".

5. Another interesting query is "Which party received the most votes?". This might give you a different answer from Note 4!

emp_job.mdb

This database shows two separate things: employee details and job details.

Fig. A1.11 The schema for **emp_job.mdb**.

e_no	name	salary
1	Alan	£10,000.00
2	Bill	£20,000.00
3	Carol	£30,000.00
0		£0.00

Record: 1 of 3

Fig. A1.12 The EMPLOYEE table of **emp_job.mdb**.

Descr	Std_salary
Accountant	£18,000.00
Clerk	£9,000.00
Manager	£25,000.00
	£0.00

Record: 1

Fig. A1.13 The JOB table of **emp_job.mdb**.

Notes

1. This database is unusual in that there is no relationship between the tables. It has been contrived to illustrate some SQL points in Queries 47 and 48.

2. One interesting query is "What jobs should each employee do to increase his salary?".

emp_sales.mdb

This database shows, for each employee, the sales of each category of goods he or she achieved in each week.

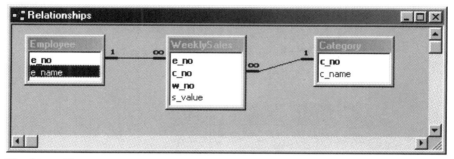

Fig. A1.14 The schema of the **emp_sales.mdb** database.

Fig. A1.15 The EMPLOYEE table of **emp_sales.mdb**.

Notes

1. Note the three-field compound key of the WEEKLYSALES table. Three fields are needed to distinguish between sales by the same person of products in the same category over different weeks.

2. The WEEKLYSALES table is a very good candidate for a *crosstab query*, because it would be 'natural' to want to know sales by, say, employee and category. To do this in a crosstab query, you would use GROUP BY on two of the fields in the compound key.

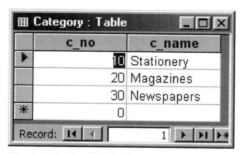

Fig. A1.16 The WEEKLYSALES table of emp‗sales.mdb.

Fig. A1.17 The CATEGORY table of emp‗sales.mdb.

employee.mdb

This database consists of a single table EMPLOYEE. It shows, for each employee, his or her name, salary and manager.

Fig. A1.18 The schema of the employee.mdb database.

emp_no	name	salary	mgr_no
1	Audrey	£10,000.00	3
2	Betty	£20,000.00	4
3	Carol	£15,000.00	2
4	Denise	£15,000.00	7
5	Erica	£20,000.00	
6	Fabi	£22,000.00	5
0		£0.00	0

Record: 1 of 6

Fig. A1.19 The EMPLOYEE table of the **employee.mdb** database.

Notes

1. What's interesting about this database is that there is an implicit *unary relationship* in it. For each employee, we can find out who his or her manager is (mgr_no is a foreign key from emp_no), and in turn who his or her manager is, and so on. The table represents a tree structure because managers are themselves employees. For example, we can see that Audrey's manager is Carol, and *her* manager is Betty etc.

2. Interesting queries here are:

    (a) "Who is Audrey's manager?"

    (b) "Whom does Erica manage?"

    (c) "Who's managed by nobody?"

    (d) "Who manages nobody?"

musicians.mdb

This database contains four tables, one for each type of musician.

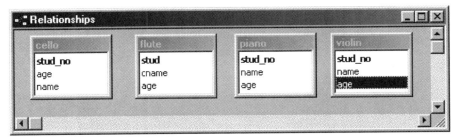

Fig. A1.20 The schema of the **musicians.mdb** database.

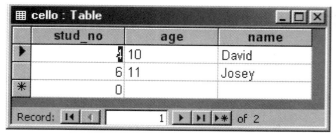

Fig. A1.21 The CELLO table of **musicians.mdb**.

stud_no	age	name
4	10	David
6	11	Josey
0		

Fig. A1.22 The FLUTE table of **musicians.mdb**.

stud	cname	age
7	Ashfak	12
0		0

Fig. A1.23 The PIANO table of **musicians.mdb**.

stud_no	name	age
2	Jane	12
4	David	10
5	Zena	11
0		0

Fig. A1.24 The VIOLIN table of **musicians.mdb**.

stud_no	name	age
1	Fred	10
3	Sally	11
4	David	10
0		0

Notes

1. There are no relationships between any of the tables.

2. This is rather an unrealistic database design, because in practice it is highly likely that all of this data would be contained in three tables: Student, Instrument, and StudentInstrument or 'Ability'.

3. The reason for the present design is its usefulness in illustrating UNION, INTERSECT and MINUS functionality in SQL.

Exercise

1. Redesign this database in a more rational way, as described in Note 2 above.

prod_del.mdb

This database shows all the deliveries for each product.

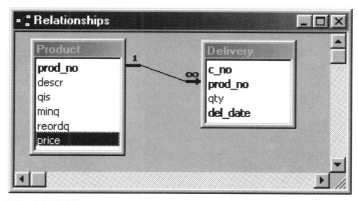

Fig. A1.25 The schema of the **prod_del.mdb** database.

	prod_no	descr	qis	minq	reordq	price
►	1	Bat	10	5	10	£12.00
	2	Ball	5	5	20	£2.00
	3	Hoop	3	5	10	£3.00
	4	Net	2	5	10	£20.00
	5	Rope	1	10	10	£6.00
*	0		0	0	0	£0.00

Record: I◄ ◄ 1 ► ►I ►* of 5

Fig. A1.26 The PRODUCT table of **prod_del.mdb**.

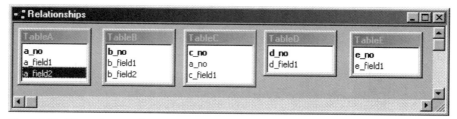

c_no	prod_no	qty	del_date
3	1	3	03/11/99
3	2	2	03/11/99
1	4	6	07/11/99
3	3	1	12/11/99
5	3	4	12/11/99
0	0	0	

Record: |◄ ◄ | 1 | ► ►| ►* | of 5

Fig. A1.27 The DELIVERY table of **prod_del.mdb**.

Notes

1. The way 'delivery' is defined here, each delivery is of one product, so that if several product types were delivered at the same time to the same customer, each product type would be called a separate delivery.

2. c_no is customer number, qis is quantity in stock, minq is the minimum quantity, reordq is the reorder quantity. If qis goes below minq, then we order reordq of the product from our suppliers. In a stock control application it's important to name these fields unambiguously.

3. The adequacy of the compound primary key in the DELIVERY table depends on the assumption that a customer won't receive more than one delivery of the same product on the same day.

4. Every product has had a delivery except product 5.

5. Product 3 has had two deliveries.

tablea_tableb.mdb

This database is used in this text for a completely theoretical purpose – illustrating aspects of inner join, left join and right join.

Relationships

TableA	TableB	TableC	TableD	TableE
a_no	**b_no**	**c_no**	**d_no**	**e_no**
a_field1	b_field1	a_no	d_field1	e_field1
a_field2	b_field2	c_field1		

Fig. A1.28 The schema of the **tablea_tableb.mdb** database.

TableA : Table

a_no	a_field1	a_field2
1	a11	a12
2	a21	a22
0		

Record: 1 of 2

Fig. A1.29 TABLEA of tablea–tableb.mdb.

TableB : Table

b_no	b_field1	b_field2
1	b11	b12
3	b31	b32
0		

Record: 1 of 2

Fig. A1.30 TABLEB of tablea–tableb.mdb.

TableC : Table

c_no	a_no	c_field1
1	1	c11
2	1	c21
3		c31
0	0	

Record: 1 of 3

Fig. A1.31 TABLEC of tablea–tableb.mdb.

TableD : Table

d_no	d_field1
1	d1
2	
0	

Record: 1 of 2

Fig. A1.32 TABLED of tablea–tableb.mdb.

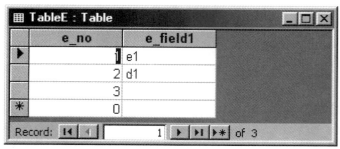

Fig. A1.33 TABLEE of tablea_tableb.mdb.

Notes

1. TABLED and TABLEE contain some records with null field values.

2. The queries in the text that use these tables are Queries 50 to 53 of Chapter 6.

Appendix 2

Differences in database programming commands in VB versions

The variations we cover below are:

- *Jet1*: Jet version 1 as used in VB3 and Access2.
- *DAO*: Jet 2.5/3.0, 3.5, 3.51, 4.0 in VB4 and above, and Access95 and above.
- *ADO*: Jet 3.51, 4.0 in VB6 and above and Access 2000 and above.
- *ASP*: As ADO.

The examples we show are 'minimalist'. However, they are sufficient for many purposes. Consult Access or VB Help for full details of all parameters of each property or method.

Opening a database

```
Jet 1:  Set db1 = OpenDatabase("accts.mdb")
DAO:   Set db1 = OpenDatabase("accts.mdb")
ADO:   Set db1 = New ADODB.Connection
       db1.Provider = "Microsoft.Jet.OLEDB.3.51;"
       db1.ConnectionString =
       "D:\MyDocuments\Access97Jet3_5\accts.mdb"
       db1.Open
ASP:   set conn1 = server.createobject("adodb.connection")
       conn1.open "provider = microsoft.jet.oledb.4.0;data
       source = d:\websites\itsjcb\www\aspex04\accts.mdb"
```

Note: the full pathname is *required* in ADO.

Opening a table

```
Jet 1:  Set rs1 = db1.OpenTable("Customer")
DAO:  Dim rs1 as Recordset
      Set rs1 = db1.OpenRecordset("Customer", dbOpenTable)
```

```
ADO:  Set rs1 = New ADODB.Recordset
      rs1.Open "Customer", db1, adOpenDynamic, adLockOptimistic
```

Opening a 'Dynaset' (updateable recordset)
```
Jet 1:  Set rs1 = db1.CreateDynaset("Customer")
DAO:  Dim rs1 as Recordset
      Set rs1 = db1.OpenRecordset("Customer".dbOpenDynaset)
ADO:  Set rs1 = New ADODB.Recordset
      rs1.Open "Customer", db1 adOpenDynamic, adLockOptimistic
```

or, using an SQL query to retrieve data:

```
Jet 1:  Set rs1 = db1.CreateDynaset("select c_no, sname from
        customer where city = 'London'")
DAO:  Dim rs1 as Recordset
      Set rs1 = db1.OpenRecordset("select c_no, sname from
      customer where city = 'London'".dbOpenDynaset)
ADO:  Set rs1 = New ADODB.Recordset
      rs1.Open "select c_no, sname from customer where city =
      'London'", db1, adOpenDynamic, adLockOptimistic
ASP:  rs1.open "select * from customer", conn1, adopendynamic,
      adlockoptimistic, adcmdtext
```

Opening a 'Snapshot' (non-updateable recordset)
```
Jet 1:  Set rs1 = db1.CreateSnapshot("Customer")
DAO:  Dim rs1 as Recordset
      Set rs1 = db1.OpenRecordset("Customer", dbOpenSnapshot)
ADO:  Set rs1 = New ADODB.Recordset
      rs1.Open "Customer", db1
```
or
```
      Set rs1 = New ADODB.Recordset
      rs1.Open "Customer", db1, adOpenStatic, adLockReadOnly
ASP:  rs1.open "select * from customer", conn1
```

See Chapter 11 for the meaning of the Open method's parameters.

Referring to a field
Jet 1, DAO, and ADO:

```
  rs1!sname = "Lauri"
```

or

```
  rs1!fields(2) = "Lauri"
```

ASP

```
  rs1("sname") = "Lauri"
```

Note: The first field in a recordset is called fields(0).

Closing a Recordset
Jet 1, DAO, ADO and ASP:

```
rs1.Close
set rs1 = Nothing
```

Closing a database
Jet 1, DAO, ADO and ASP:

```
db1.Close
set db1 = Nothing
```

Navigating
Jet 1, DAO, ADO and ASP:

```
rs1.MoveFirst
rs1.MoveLast
rs1.MoveNext
rs1.MovePrevious
rs1.FindFirst
rs1.FindNext
rs1.index = "PrimaryKey"
rs1.seek " = " x
```

Inserting a record
Jet 1, DAO, ADO and ASP:

```
rs1.AddNew
Insert field values for the new record here
rs1.Update
```

Deleting a record
Jet 1, DAO, ADO and ASP:

```
rs1.Delete
rs1.MoveFirst (or MoveLast, MovePrevious, MoveNext)
```

Changing a record
Jet 1, DAO, ADO and ASP:

```
rs1.Edit (In Jet 3.51 but not in Jet 4.0)
Make changes to the current record's field values here
rs1.Update
```

Cancelling an update
Jet1 and DAO: `rs1.refresh`
ADO & ASP: `rs1.cancelupdate`

HTML tag examples

The following table gives examples of the main tags used in putting *comments* into your HTML web pages, defining the *structure* of a web page, and specifying the contents of the *head* and *body* sections of the web page.

Function	Example
comment	`<!-- This is a comment. You can put comments in both the head and body sections of web pages. – ->`

structure of web page without frames	`<html>`
	`<head>`
	`. . .`
	`</head>`
	`<body>`
	`. . .`
	`</body>`
	`</html>`
	
	Head tags go in here. They document (i.e. describe) the web page. Search engines such as Google use these tags to index the web page.
	
	Body tags go in here. They tell the browser what to put on the web page (text and graphics) and how to format it.

structure of web page with frames	`<html>`
	`<head>`
	`. . .`
	`</head>`
	`<frameset cols = 20%,80%>`
	`<frame name = leftframe src = contents.htm>`
	`<frame name = rightframe src = page01.htm>`
	`</frameset>`
	`<noframes>`
	`<body>`
	`. . .`
	`</body>`
	`</noframes>`
	`</html>`

Head tags

title	<title>This appears in the browser title bar</title>
meta	<meta name = description content = "HTML tutorial"> <meta name = keywords content = "html,tag,web,page">

Body tags

text	This is some text without any tags.
paragraph	<p>This text is preceded by a blank line. <p align = center>This is centred</p>
break	 This text starts on a new line.
space	There are two spaces between this and this.
header	<h1>Largest</h1><h6>Smallest</h6>
horizontal rule	<hr>
bold	This is bold. This isn't.
italics	<i>This is in italics</i>
underline	<u>This is underlined</u>
font	<font color = red size = 1>This is smallest red text.</font> <font color = #ffff00 size = 7>This is largest yellow text</font> <font face = "Comic Sans MS">Gee, Batperson</font>
centre	<center>This text is middle justified.</center>
division	<div align = right>This text is right justified.</div>
indent	Things<dl><dd>books pens</dl>

preserve	<pre>
	   Name Hobby
	   Pauline Pets
	   Robert Machines
	</pre>

image	<img align = bottom height = 50 width = 40 border = 1 src = rose1.jpg>
unordered list	<ul><li>item1<li>item2</ul>
ordered list	<ol><li>item1<li>item2</ol>
table	<table border = 10 cols = 2> <tr><th>Artist</th><th>Track</th></tr> <tr><td>Skynyrd</td><td>Freebird</td></tr> </table>
hyperlink	<a href = page1.htm>Go to page 1</a> <a href = .\folder1\page1.htm>Go to page 1</a> <a href = \\Rosses\Shared\Classes\JCarter\page1.htm>page 1</a> <!-- LAN --> <a href = http://www.abc.com/folder1/page1.htm> Go to page 1</a> <a href = "../folder1/page 1.htm">Go to page 1</a> <a href = page1.htm><img src = rose1.jpg></a> <a href = page1.htm target = new>Go to page 1</a>

	<a href = page1.htm target = rightframe>Go to page 1</a> <a href = page1.asp?data = 6>Send 6 to page1.asp</a> <a name = Section 1></a> <a href = #Section 1>Go to Section 1</a> <a href = http://www.databasedesign.co.uk#History of Internet>A concise history of the internet</a> <a href = mailto:john.carter@databasedesign.co.uk> Send an email to John Carter</a>
form	<form method = post action = mailto:accounts@abcltd.biz> <form method = post action = processanewcustomer.asp> <form name = gs method = get action = /search> <form enctype = "multipart/form-data" method = post action = processthisfile.asp>
	<input type = hidden name = ourformtype value = newcustomer>
	<input type = text name = cusname size = 20>
	<input type = password name = enteredpassword size = 10>
	<input type = radio name = accounttype value = p>Personal
	<input type = checkbox name = intinartbks>Art books
	<input type = file size = 20 name = file1>
	<select name = acctstartmonth size = 1> <option selected>Jan<option>Feb</select>
	<textarea name = furtherinfo rows = 4 cols = 40></textarea>
	<input type = submit value = Submit> <input type = reset value = Reset>
	</form>

Appendix 4

SQL SELECT statement – short summary

The following table gives examples of the main clauses used in the SQL SELECT statement. The SELECT statement is used for retrieving data from relational databases.

Function	Example
select from	select * from customer select c_no, sname from customer
distinct	select distinct c_no from invoice
order by	select * from customer order by sname select * from customer order by city, balance desc
where	select * from customer where city = 'London' and balance < = cred_lim
between	select * from invoice where inv_date between #10-dec-99# and #14-1-00#
like	select * from customer where sname like 'Dz*'
in	select * from customer where city in ('London', 'Leeds')
avg,count,max, min,sum,var, stddev	select sum(balance) from customer select count(*) from customer select sum(balance) as TotalBalance from customer select sum(balance), max(cred_lim) from customer
group by	select city, sum(balance) from customer group by city select city, max(balance) as [Highest balance for this city] from customer group by city
having	select city, sum(balance) group by city having sum(balance) > 500
top	select top 2 * from customer order by balance desc select top 1 city, sum(balance) from customer group by city order by sum(balance) desc select top 20 percent * from customer order by balance desc
inner join	select a.c_no, sname, inv_no, amount from customer as a inner join invoice as b on a.c_no = b.c_no where city = 'London' and balance > 100

left join	select a.c_no, sname, inv_no, amount from customer as a left join invoice as b on a.c_no = b.c_no where city = 'London' and balance > 100
subquery	select * from customer where city = (select city from customer where sname = 'Sallaway') select * from customer where c_no not in (select c_no from invoice)
any, all	select * from employee where salary < any (select salary from employee) select * from employee where salary > = all (select salary from employee)
exists, not exists	select * from customer where not exists (select * from invoice where customer.c_no = invoice.c_no)
union	select * from violinplayers union select * from pianoplayers
from a query	select * from query1 where city = 'London'
select into	select * into temp1 from customer where city = 'London' select * into customer in 'accts1.mdb' from customer
crosstab query	transform sum(weeklysales.s_value) as sumofs_value select employee.e_name from employee inner join (category inner join weeklysales on category.c_no = weeklysales.c_no) on employee.e_no = weeklysales.e_no group by employee.e_name pivot category.c_name

Glossary

ActiveX   controls that are broadly associated with the internet.

ADO   ActiveX Data Objects. The latest Microsoft approach to linking applications to database, with an orientation towards the internet. In the context of ASP pages, ADO commands are database-oriented VBScript commands. You write ADO commands into your server-side scripts to access server-side databases.

ANSI   American National Standards Institute.

ASP   Active Server Pages. Web pages with the extension .asp ('normal' web pages have the extension .htm or .html). Active Server Pages contain HTML commands like normal web pages, but also contain 'server side' VBScript or other scripting language scripts.

ASP web server   a server that can process ASP pages. It has to have the appropriate software (e.g. IIS) installed. An ordinary web server, such as an ISP might provide, will probably not be an ASP web server.

Atomic primary key   a primary key with just one attribute.

Attribute   a quality of an entity type whose value we want to store.

Autoform   a form that is generated automatically by Access to allow the user to view and update a table or query.

BOF   Beginning Of File.

Browser   the program you run on your PC to view web pages with. The main browsers in common use are Microsoft Internet Explorer and Netscape.

Candidate key   a possible choice for primary key.

Cardinality   whether a relationship is one:many, many:one, one:one, or many:many.

Client-side script   a script that is intended to be executed on the user's (client's) PC. Can be VBScript or JavaScript, but is normally JavaScript because Netscape can't handle VBScript. Internet Explorer, the other main browser, can handle both. Because both browsers are in use, it's more usual for client-side scripts to be written in JavaScript.

Collection   a set of objects. For example the fields collection, or the printers collection.

Column   another name for a field.

Composite primary key   or 'composite key'. A primary key containing more than one attribute.

Compound primary key   another name (usually) for composite key.

Control   items such as text boxes, labels, control buttons etc. that the user uses to interact with the program.

Crosstab query   a query in which the results are presented with one variable determining the rows and one variable determining the columns.

DAO   Data Access Objects. The standard, established approach to Microsoft database programming.

Data Control   a VB control that allows you to develop simple database applications with minimal programming. There are two types – the convention data control and the ActiveX data control.

Database   an ordered collection of data.

DBMS   Database Management System. Access is a DBMS.

Dim   a VB statement used to declare a variable and its type.

Domain   a notional set of legal values that fields in a database table can take.

Download   to copy web pages, graphics and sound files, databases etc. 'down' onto files on your PC so you can edit them etc. You could use FTP to do this. The term can also mean reading web pages from the internet using a browser.

DSN   Data Source Name. A file you create that contains connection details for a source of data you often use.

DCL   Data Control Language. The commands in a query language that allow you to allocate access privileges to the database to other users.

DDL   Data Definition Language. The commands in a query language that allow you to define new tables and indexes, and remove and alter existing tables and indexes.

DML Data Manipulation Language. The commands in a query language that allow you to retrieve and update records in a database.

Dynaset an updateable recordset.

Embedded SQL an SQL command that is contained within a program.

Entity modelling a technique for identifying the entity types and relationships that will be used in a database.

Entity type a type of object we want to store data about. A collection of entities all of the same type.

EOF End Of File.

Field space for one data item in a record. A field holds an attribute value.

Filter in Access, a way of retrieving a subset of records by defining constraints.

Folder a container for a set of related files.

Foreign key a minimal set of attributes (usually one) in a table, which is used to form a link to another table. The value of the foreign key in the table will be the value of the primary key in another table.

Form a rectangular window. The basic method of interaction with the user.

FTP File Transfer Protocol. One method of copying files from one place on the internet to another. For example, you could use FTP to upload your web pages onto a web server. There are various alternative methods of FTP-ing in a Microsoft environment:

1. Go into DOS and call up the FTP command.
2. Use a Windows-based FTP utility such as Terrapin FTP.
3. Create a folder in My Network Places in Windows 2000.
4. Use special-purpose software provided by the ISP.

Fuzzy matching a way of retrieving a subset of records based on matching text fields on just *some* of their characters.

General Declarations an area in a form's code where you declare variables that must be shared among several subroutines.

Grid a control that allows you to display data in rows and columns.

Home page the page on a website that viewers will normally view first.

HTML Hypertext Markup Language. Most web pages consist entirely of HTML commands and text. ASP pages also contain scripts. The browser converts the HTML code you get from a website into the text, pictures and sound you receive on your PC. The basis – the underlying language – of the World Wide Web.

Hyperlink When you click on a hyperlink on one web page, it 'takes you' to another web page. To put it another way, when you click on a hyperlink, the browser fetches ('downloads') the page the hyperlink cites and displays that new page.

IIS Microsoft Internet Information Server. This is the software that runs on the ASP server to process your ASP pages. It executes the VBScript parts of your ASP page. This determines what HTML is sent over the internet to the browser on the client's (user's) computer. Often, the VBScript will ask IIS to get some data from a database and put it into HTML format.

ISP Internet Service Provider. An ISP is used to connect your PC to the internet when you're dialling up from home. Software on your PC dials the ISP's telephone number.

Index a subsidiary table, used to speed up access to records.

IP address Internet Protocol address. A typical address would be 128.145.16.5. Every computer on the internet has an IP address. Routers use IP addresses to deliver packets of data to the right destination.

Join a technique used in queries to join records from (usually) different tables.

Macro in Access, a collection of commands.

Method a command applied to an object.

Microsoft FrontPage a package for developing web pages. FrontPage 2000 can develop ASP web pages.

Modem You need a modem to connect your home PC to an ISP via a telephone line. It converts the digital data transmitted from your PC into analogue form for the telephone line and from analogue to digital when receiving. Converting from digital to analogue is called 'modulation' and converting from analogue to digital is called 'demodulation'. 'Modem' is an amalgamation of these two words. The speed of the modem is a limiting factor in dial-up connections. An ordinary telephone line will give up to 56KBPS (56,000 bits per second) and an ISDN line two to three times as fast as that.

Module   a collection of subroutines.

Navigation   moving around in a database.

Normalization   a technique for checking the design of tables.

Null   a special value that a field can take. Often used to denote either 'missing' or 'inapplicable'.

ODBC   Open Database Connectivity. An approach to application development that allows exchange of data between data sources that are in different locations and different formats.

OLE DB   Object Linking and Embedding for Databases. Similar to ODBC, but allows access to more types of data than ODBC does.

Optionality   whether a relationship between entities is necessary or not.

Primary key   a minimal set of attributes (usually one) in a table that is used to uniquely identify each record. No two records in a table should have the same value for the primary key.

Publish   in the internet context, uploading web pages onto a web server so they can be viewed via the web using a browser.

Project   a VB application. A project consists of one project file (.vbp), one or more form files (.frm) and zero or more code module files (.bas).

PWS   Microsoft Personal Web Server. Similar to IIS. Designed to run on the developer's PC so he/she can test his/her ASP pages before uploading to the web server. Designed to work with Windows 95 and 98. Not really needed now, as IIS is now available on the Windows 2000 (and above) installation CD, and downloadable from **www.microsoft.com**.

Query   a way of retrieving data from a database.

Record   a collection of fields and their values. In a relational database, a table consists of a collection of records.

Recordset   a set of records or parts of records stored in memory. Your program interacts with the database on the disk via a recordset. You define the recordset by naming a table or using a query.

Relation   another name for a table.

Relational database   a database in which data on entity types is held in tables and relationships are represented by primary key – foreign key links.

Relationship   an association between entities.

Report   a printed document produced by an Access or VB application.

Router   a computer on the internet which routes an internet request to a router nearer the destination. Routers do this dynamically, passing different packets of information along different routes, depending on the traffic at a particular instant.

Row   another name for a record.

Server   a computer that 'serves' a network (LAN or Internet) with programs or data. An ASP server serves data in the form of HTML web pages, which the web browser on the 'client' (user PC) converts to the web page the user sees.

Server-side database   a database situated on a server. A database held on a server has the advantage that it can be shared via a local area network ('LAN') or the internet.

Server-side script   a script that is intended to be executed (run) on the server. We use VBScript in this book, but JavaScript can also be used for server-side scripting.

Script   in the context of web pages, a script is a piece of VBScript in an ASP page. There may be several scripts in one page. A script can be a server-side script or a client-side script.

Snapshot   a non-updateable recordset.

SQL   Structured Query Language. A widely used database language. It allows you to retrieve and manipulate data on a relational database.

Sub   subroutine.

Subform   the lower part of a form, where the main (upper) part is associated with the 'one' side of a relationship, and the subform is associated with the 'many' side of the relationship.

Subroutine   This is where program code is written. Start with **Sub** and end with **End Sub**.

Table   a collection of records. Each record stores data on a particular entity within an entity type. The data items are stored in fields. Each record has the same fields.

Transaction   a collection of database updates that must all succeed, otherwise the database would be left in an inconsistent state.

Tuple   another name for a record.

Upload   to copy web pages, graphics and sound files, databases etc. 'up' onto a web server so they can be accessed via the internet. FTP is one approach used for uploading.

URL   Universal Resource Locator, or Uniform Resource Locator. A web address. The address of a web page on the internet. Here's an example URL: **http://www.databasedesign.co.uk**.

VB   Visual Basic.

VBA   Visual Basic for Applications. The name Microsoft gives for VB when it is embedded in applications other than purely VB applications, such as Access and Excel applications.

VBScript   the VB-like program code you put into your web pages. It can be client-side VBScript or server-side VBScript. The language is the same but the client-side VBScript is surrounded with <script> and </script>, whereas server-side VBScript is surrounded with <% and %>.

View   a subset of database data, often based on a query, which is presented to the user. Usually called a stored query in Microsoft applications.

Web browser or **'browser'**   the program you run on your PC to view web pages with. The main browsers in common use are Microsoft Internet Explorer and Netscape.

Web page   a collection of HTML commands and text, and related graphics and (sometimes) sounds, held in files on a web server. The commands and text for a web page are held in one file and each graphic and sound is held in a separate file. Your browser interprets these files as the text, pictures and sounds you see on your PC. You tell the browser which web pages you want to see by specifying the web address of the page. The web address is also known as the URL. A website will usually contain many web pages, linked together by hyperlinks. The HTML and text for a page are held in a .htm or .html or .asp file, the graphics are held in .bmp or .gif or .jpg or .png or various formats of video files. Sound files can be .wav or .mid (typically).

Website   A website will usually contain a collection of related web pages, linked together by hyperlinks.

Wizard   a utility in Access that lets you develop a simple application without programming.

References

Books

1. Atzeni, Ceri, Parabosche, Torlone. (1999) *Database Systems, Concepts, Languages and Architecture*, McGraw-Hill. ISBN 007–709500–6.
2. Carter, J.R. (1995) *The Relational Database*, International Thomson Computer Press. ISBN 1–85032–255–4.
3. Date, C.J. (1995) *An Introduction to Database Systems*, 6th edn, Addison-Wesley. ISBN 0–201–82458–2.

Websites

1. http://www.mcgraw-hill.co.uk
2. http://www.databasedesign.co.uk
3. http://www.databasedesign.co.uk/chatline
4. http://www.databasedesign.co.uk/book
5. http://www.itsjc.biz
6. http://www.vb-web-directory.com/
7. http://searchvb.techtarget.com/
8. http://msdn.microsoft.com/vbasic/

News groups

1. comp.databases.ms-access
2. microsoft.public.vb
3. microsoft.public.vb.controls
4. microsoft.public.vb.database
5. microsoft.public.vb.database.ado
6. microsoft.public.database.dao

Help files

1. Access Help
2. Visual Basic Help

Index